Communications
in Computer and Information Science   **1355**

More information about this series at http://www.springer.com/series/7899

Emmanouel Garoufallou ·
María-Antonia Ovalle-Perandones (Eds.)

Metadata and Semantic Research

14th International Conference, MTSR 2020
Madrid, Spain, December 2–4, 2020
Revised Selected Papers

 Springer

Editors
Emmanouel Garoufallou (iD)
International Hellenic University
Thessaloniki, Greece

María-Antonia Ovalle-Perandones (iD)
Complutense University of Madrid
Madrid, Spain

ISSN 1865-0929   ISSN 1865-0937   (electronic)
Communications in Computer and Information Science
ISBN 978-3-030-71902-9   ISBN 978-3-030-71903-6   (eBook)
https://doi.org/10.1007/978-3-030-71903-6

This Springer imprint is published by the registered company Springer Nature Switzerland AG
The registered company address is: Gewerbestrasse 11, 6330 Cham, Switzerland

Preface

Metadata and semantics are integral to any information system and important to the sphere of Web data. Research and development addressing metadata and semantics is crucial to advancing how we effectively discover, use, archive, and repurpose information. In response to this need, researchers are actively examining methods for generating, reusing, and interchanging metadata. Integrated with these developments is research on the application of computational methods, linked data, and data analytics. A growing body of literature also targets conceptual and theoretical designs providing foundational frameworks for metadata and semantic applications. There is no doubt that metadata weaves its way through nearly every aspect of our information ecosystem, and there is great motivation for advancing the current state of understanding in the fields of metadata and semantics. To this end, it is vital that scholars and practitioners convene and share their work.

Since 2005, the International Metadata and Semantics Research Conference (MTSR) has served as a significant venue for dissemination and sharing of metadata and semantic-driven research and practices. 2020 marked the 14th MTSR, drawing scholars, researchers, and practitioners who are investigating and advancing our knowledge on a wide range of metadata and semantic-driven topics. The 14th International Conference on Metadata and Semantics Research (MTSR 2020) was organized by the Complutense University of Madrid, Spain, between 2 and 4 December, 2020. Due to the COVID-19 pandemic and taking into account all the available information and ongoing uncertainties and our concerns about the health and wellbeing of our community, the MTSR 2020 Organizing Committees decided to organize MTSR 2020 as an Online Conference. The MTSR 2020 Chairs, Organizing Committees, and Steering Committee worked together to change step by step the organizational structure of the conference.

MTSR conferences have grown in number of participants and paper submission rates over the past decade, marking it as a leading international research conference. Continuing the successful legacy of previous MTSR conferences (MTSR 2005, MTSR 2007, MTSR 2009, MTSR 2010, MTSR 2011, MTSR 2012, MTSR 2013, MTSR 2014, MTSR 2015, MTSR 2016, MTSR 2017, MTSR 2018, and MTSR 2019), MTSR 2020 brought together scholars and practitioners who share a common interest in the interdisciplinary field of metadata, linked data, and ontologies. 386 professionals registered for the MTSR 2020 online conference, from 43 countries.

The MTSR 2020 program and the proceedings show a rich diversity of research and practices from metadata and semantically focused tools and technologies, linked data, cross-language semantics, ontologies, metadata models, semantic systems, and metadata standards. The general session of the conference included 14 papers covering a broad spectrum of topics, proving the interdisciplinary view of metadata. Metadata as a research topic is maturing, and the conference supported the following eight tracks: Digital Libraries, Information Retrieval, Big, Linked, Social, and Open Data;

Agriculture, Food, and Environment; Open Repositories, Research Information Systems, and Data Infrastructures; Digital Humanities and Digital Curation; Cultural Collections and Applications; European and National Projects; Knowledge IT Artifacts in Professional Communities and Aggregations; and Metadata, Identifiers, and Semantics in Decentralized Applications, Blockchains, and P2P Systems.

Each of these tracks had a rich selection of short and full research papers, in total 23, giving broader diversity to MTSR, and enabling deeper exploration of significant topics. MTSR 2020 also co-hosted the DOAbLE International inter-disciplinary conference, which brought together researchers, scholars, practitioners, educators, and information professionals coming from libraries, archives, museums, cultural heritage institutions, and organizations from the educational sector.

All the papers underwent a thorough and rigorous peer-review process by two to seven reviewers. The review and selection for this year was highly competitive and only papers containing significant research results, innovative methods, or novel and best practices were accepted for publication. From the general session, only seven submissions were accepted as full research papers, representing 24.1% of the total number of submissions, and seven as short papers. An additional 17 contributions from tracks covering noteworthy and important results were accepted as full research papers, representing 42.5% of the total number of submissions, and six as short papers, bringing the total of MTSR 2020 accepted contributions to 37. The acceptance rate of full research papers for both the general session and tracks was 34.7% of the total number of submissions.

The Complutense University of Madrid was founded by Cardinal Cisneros as a result of the "Inter cetera" Papal Bull granted by Pope Alexander VI on 13 April 1499. Nowadays the Complutense University of Madrid has three main objectives: to educate professionals who will be useful for society, to foster scientific research, and to disseminate knowledge and the intrinsic values of the University. A wide range of degrees are offered to meet the expectations of intellectual, economic, and scientific demands. The Department of Library and Information Science at the Faculty of Documentation Sciences, which was the School of Library and Information Science before 2006, has the following research lines: Society and library; Information policies, Information and Communication Technologies (ICT), and scientific communication; Management, assessment, and administration in information science units; and Photo documentation.

MTSR 2020 was pleased to host a remarkable keynote presentation by Ricardo Baeza-Yates, Professor in the Khoury College of Computer Sciences, Northeastern University at Silicon Valley, USA. In his presentation "Bias on the Web: A Content Accessibility Point of View", Professor Baeza-Yates aimed to make people aware of the different biases that affect all of us on the Web. "The Web is the most powerful communication medium and the largest public data repository that humankind has created. Its content ranges from great reference sources such as Wikipedia to fake news. Indeed, social (digital) media is just an amplifying mirror of ourselves. Hence, the main challenge of search engines and other websites that rely on web data is to assess the quality of such data. However, as all people have their own biases, web content as well as our web interactions are tainted with many biases. Data bias includes redundancy and spam, while interaction bias includes activity and presentation bias. Awareness is the first step to be able to fight and reduce the vicious cycle of web bias."

MTSR 2020 hosted a workshop on "Metadata enriching and filtering through FRBR and RDA" organized and presented by Dr. Getaneh Alemu, Cataloguing and Metadata Librarian, Solent University, UK.

We conclude this preface by thanking the many people who contributed their time and efforts to MTSR 2020 and made this year's conference possible despite the unforeseen obstacles caused by COVID-19. We also thank all the organizations that supported this conference. We thank all the institutions and universities that co-organized MTSR 2020. We extend our sincere gratitude to the members of the Program Committees both main and special tracks, the Steering Committee, and the Organizing Committees (both general and local), to all the special track chairs, and to the conference reviewers who invested their time generously to ensure the timely review of the submitted manuscripts. A special thanks to keynote speaker Professor Ricardo Baeza-Yates, and to workshop organizer Dr. Getaneh Alemu. Also a special thank you to María-Antonia Ovalle-Perandones, Miguel-Angel Sicilia, Anxhela Dani, Ilias Nitsos, Vasiliki Georgiadi, Chrysanthi Chatzopoulou, Chrysanthi Theodoridou, and Iro Sotiriadou for supporting us throughout this event, and to Anxhela Dani and Chrysanthi Chatzopoulou who assisted us with the preparation of proceedings; and to Vasiliki, Nikoleta, and Stavroula for their endless support and patience. Our thanks go to our gold sponsor Elsevier, and our best paper and best student paper sponsor euroCRIS. Finally, our deepest thank you goes to all the authors and participants of MTSR 2020 for making the event a great success.

December 2020   Emmanouel Garoufallou
                                          María-Antonia Ovalle-Perandones

Organization

General Chair

Emmanouel Garoufallou   International Hellenic University, Greece

Chair for MTSR 2020

María-Antonia   Complutense University of Madrid, Spain
Ovalle-Perandones

Special Track Chairs

Miguel-Ángel Sicilia	University of Alcalá, Spain
Francesca Fallucchi	Guglielmo Marconi University, Italy
Riem Spielhaus	Georg Eckert Institute – Leibniz Institute for International Textbook Research, Germany
Ernesto William De Luca	Georg Eckert Institute – Leibniz Institute for International Textbook Research, Germany
Armando Stellato	University of Rome Tor Vergata, Italy
Nikos Houssos	Sentio Solutions, Greece
Michalis Sfakakis	Ionian University, Greece
Lina Bountouri	EU Publications Office, Luxembourg
Emmanouel Garoufallou	International Hellenic University, Greece
Jane Greenberg	Drexel University, USA
Richard J. Hartley	Manchester Metropolitan University, UK
Stavroula Antonopoulou	Perrotis College, American Farm School, Greece
Rob Davies	Cyprus University of Technology, Cyprus
Fabio Sartori	University of Milano-Bicocca, Italy
Angela Locoro	Università Carlo Cattaneo - LIUC, Italy
Arlindo Flávio da Conceição	Federal University of São Paulo (UNIFESP), Brazil

Steering Committee

Juan Manuel Dodero	University of Cádiz, Spain
Emmanouel Garoufallou	International Hellenic University, Greece
Nikos Manouselis	AgroKnow, Greece
Fabio Sartori	Università degli Studi di Milano-Bicocca, Italy
Miguel-Ángel Sicilia	University of Alcalá, Spain

Local Organizing Committee

Michela Montesi   Complutense University of Madrid, Spain
Isabel Villaseñor Rodríguez   Complutense University of Madrid, Spain

Organizing Committee

Chrysanthi Chatzopoulou   European Publishing, Greece
Anxhela Dani   Hellenic Foundation for Culture, Greece
Vassiliki Georgiadi   International Hellenic University, Greece
Iro Sotiriadou   American Farm School, Greece
Chrysanthi Theodoridou   International Hellenic University, Greece

Technical Support Staff

Ilias Nitsos   International Hellenic University, Greece

Program Committee Members (TBC)

Trond Aalberg   Norwegian University of Science and Technology
                             (NTNU), Norway
Rajendra Akerkar   Western Norway Research Institute, Norway
Getaneh Alemu   Solent University, UK
Arif Altun   Hacettepe University, Turkey
Stavroula Antonopoulou   Perrotis College, American Farm School, Greece
Ioannis N. Athanasiadis   Wageningen University, The Netherlands
Sophie Aubin   INRAE, France
Thomas Baker   Sungkyunkwan University, Korea
Panos Balatsoukas   King's College London, UK
Wolf-Tilo Balke   TU Braunschweig, Germany
Tomaž Bartol   University of Ljubljana, Slovenia
José Alberto Benítez   University of León, Spain
Hugo Besemer   Wageningen UR Library, The Netherlands
Ina Bluemel   German National Library of Science
                             and Technology TIB, Germany
Lina Bountouri   EU Publications Office, Luxembourg
Derek Bousfield   Manchester Metropolitan University, UK
Karin Bredenberg   The National Archives of Sweden, Sweden
Patrice Buche   INRAE, France
Gerhard Budin   University of Vienna, Austria
Federico Cabitza   University of Milano-Bicocca, Italy
Özgü Can   Ege University, Turkey
Caterina Caracciolo   Food and Agriculture Organization (FAO)
                             of the United Nations, Italy
Christian Cechinel   Federal University of Santa Catarina, Brazil
Artem Chebotko   DataStax, USA

Philipp Cimiano	Bielefeld University, Germany
Sissi Closs	Karlsruhe University of Applied Sciences, Germany
Ricardo Colomo-Palacios	Universidad Carlos III de Madrid, Spain
Mike Conway	University of North Carolina at Chapel Hill, USA
Constantina Costopoulou	Agricultural University of Athens, Greece
Phil Couch	The University of Manchester, UK
Sally Jo Cunningham	University of Waikato, New Zealand
Ernesto William De Luca	Georg Eckert Institute – Leibniz Institute for International Textbook Research, Germany
Milena Dobreva	UCL, Qatar
Juan Manuel Dodero	University of Cádiz, Spain
Erdogan Dogdu	Çankaya University, Turkey
Manuel Palomo-Duarte	Universidad de Cádiz, Spain
Gordon Dunsire	University of Strathclyde, UK
Biswanath Dutta	Documentation Research and Training Centre (DRTC), Indian Statistical Institute, India
Jan Dvořák	Charles University of Prague, Czech Republic
Ali Emrouznejad	Aston University, UK
Juan José Escribano Otero	Universidad Europea de Madrid, Spain
Francesca Fallucchi	Guglielmo Marconi University, Italy
María-Teresa Fernández Bajón	Complutense University of Madrid, Spain
Arlindo Flavio da Conceição	Federal University of São Paulo (UNIFESP), Brazil
Muriel Foulonneau	Knowledge Engineer at Amazon, UK
Enrico Francesconi	EU Publications Office, Luxembourg
Panorea Gaitanou	Ministry of Justice, Transparency and Human Rights, Greece
Ana García-Serrano	ETSI Informática - UNED, Spain
María Teresa García	University of León, Spain
Emmanouel Garoufallou	International Hellenic University, Greece
Manolis Gergatsoulis	Ionian University, Greece
Elena González-Blanco	Universidad Nacional de Educación a Distancia, Spain
Jorge Gracia	University of Zaragoza, Spain
Jane Greenberg	Drexel University, USA
Jill Griffiths	Manchester Metropolitan University, UK
Siddeswara Guru	The University of Queensland, Australia
Richard J. Hartley	Manchester Metropolitan University, UK
Steffen Hennicke	Georg Eckert Institute – Leibniz Institute for International Textbook Research, Germany
Nikos Houssos	Sentio Solutions, Greece
Carlos A. Iglesias	Universidad Politécnica de Madrid, Spain
Antoine Isaac	Vrije Universiteit Amsterdam, The Netherlands
Keith Jeffery	Keith G Jeffery Consultants, UK
Frances Johnson	Manchester Metropolitan University, UK
Dimitris Kanellopoulos	University of Patras, Greece

Thomas Zschocke   World Agroforestry Centre (ICRAF), Kenya
Maja Žumer   University of Ljubljana, Slovenia

Track on Metadata and Semantics for Digital Libraries, Information Retrieval, Big, Linked, Social and Open Data

Track Chairs

Emmanouel Garoufallou   International Hellenic University, Greece
Jane Greenberg   Drexel University, USA

Program Committee

Panos Balatsoukas   King's College London, UK
Özgü Can   Ege University, Turkey
Sissi Closs   Karlsruhe University of Applied Sciences, Germany
Mike Conway   University of North Carolina at Chapel Hill, USA
Phil Couch   The University of Manchester, UK
Milena Dobreva   UCL, Qatar
Ali Emrouznejad   Aston University, UK
Panorea Gaitanou   Ministry of Justice, Transparency and Human Rights, Greece
Stamatios Giannoulakis   Cyprus University of Technology, Cyprus
Jane Greenberg   Drexel University, USA
Richard J. Hartley   Manchester Metropolitan University, UK
Nikos Korfiatis   University of East Anglia, UK
Rebecca Koskela   University of New Mexico, USA
Dimitris Rousidis   International Hellenic University, Greece
Athena Salaba   Kent State University, USA
Miguel-Ángel Sicilia   University of Alcalá, Spain
Christine Urquhart   Aberystwyth University, UK
Evgenia Vassilakaki   National Library of Greece, Greece
Sirje Virkus   Tallinn University, Estonia
Georgia Zafeiriou   University of Macedonia, Greece
Marios Zervas   Cyprus University of Technology, Cyprus

Track on Metadata and Semantics for Agriculture, Food and Environment (AgroSEM'20)

Track Chair

Miguel-Ángel Sicilia   University of Alcalá, Spain

Program Committee

Ioannis Athanasiadis   Wageningen University, The Netherlands
Patrice Buche   INRAE, France

Caterina Caracciolo	Food and Agriculture Organization (FAO) of the United Nations, Italy
Stasinos Konstantopoulos	NCSR Demokritos, Greece
Claire Nédellec	INRAE, France
Ivo Pierozzi	Embrapa Agricultural Informatics, Brazil
Armando Stellato	University of Rome Tor Vergata, Italy
Maguelonne Teisseire	Irstea Montpellier, France
Jan Top	Wageningen Food and Biobased Research, The Netherlands
Robert Trypuz	John Paul II Catholic University of Lublin, Poland

Track on Metadata and Semantics for Open Repositories, Research Information Systems & Data Infrastructures

Track Chairs

Nikos Houssos	Sentio Solutions, Greece
Armando Stellato	University of Rome Tor Vergata, Italy

Honorary Track Chair

Imma Subirats	Food and Agriculture Organization (FAO) of the United Nations, Italy

Program Committee

Sophie Aubin	INRAE, France
Thomas Baker	Sungkyunkwan University, South Korea
Hugo Besemer	Wageningen UR Library, The Netherlands
Gordon Dunsire	University of Strathclyde, UK
Jan Dvořák	Charles University of Prague, Czech Republic
Jane Greenberg	Drexel University, USA
Siddeswara Guru	The University of Queensland, Australia
Keith Jeffery	Keith G Jeffery Consultants, UK
Nikolaos Konstantinou	The University of Manchester, UK
Rebecca Koskela	University of New Mexico, USA
Jessica Lindholm	Chalmers University of Technology, Sweden
Paolo Manghi	Institute of Information Science and Technologies-Italian National Research Council (ISTI-CNR), Italy
Brian Matthews	Science and Technology Facilities Council, UK
Eva Méndez Rodríguez	University Carlos III of Madrid, Spain
Joachim Schöpfel	University of Lille, France
Kathleen Shearer	Confederation of Open Access Repositories (COAR), Germany
Jochen Schirrwagen	University of Bielefeld, Germany
Birgit Schmidt	University of Göttingen, Germany
Chrisa Tsinaraki	European Commission, Joint Research Centre, Italy

Yannis Tzitzikas	University of Crete and ICS-FORTH, Greece
Zhong Wang	Sun Yat-sen University, China
Marcia Zeng	Kent State University, USA

Track on Metadata and Semantics for Digital Humanities and Digital Curation (DHC2020)

Track Chairs

Ernesto William De Luca	Georg Eckert Institute – Leibniz-Institute for international Textbook Research, Germany
Francesca Fallucchi	Guglielmo Marconi University, Italy
Riem Spielhaus	Georg Eckert Institute – Leibniz-Institute for international Textbook Research, Germany

Program Committee

Maret Nieländer	Georg Eckert Institute – Leibniz Institute for International Textbook Research, Germany
Elena González-Blanco	Universidad Nacional de Educación a Distancia, Spain
Steffen Hennicke	Georg-Eckert Institute – Leibniz-Institute for International Textbook Research, Germany
Ana García-Serrano	ETSI Informática - UNED, Spain
Philipp Mayr	GESIS, Germany
Noemi Scarpato	San Raffaele Roma Open University, Italy
Andrea Turbati	University of Rome Tor Vergata, Italy
Christian Scheel	Georg-Eckert Institute – Leibniz-Institute for International Textbook Research, Germany
Armando Stellato	University of Rome Tor Vergata, Italy
Wolf-Tilo Balke	TU Braunschweig, Germany
Andreas Lommatzsch	TU Berlin, Germany
Ivo Keller	TH Brandenburg, Germany
Gabriela Ossenbach	UNED, Spain
Francesca Fallucchi	Guglielmo Marconi University, Italy

Track on Metadata and Semantics for Cultural Collections and Applications

Special Track Chairs

| Michalis Sfakakis | Ionian University, Greece |
| Lina Bountouri | EU Publications Office, Luxembourg |

Program Committee

| Trond Aalberg | Oslo Metropolitan University, Norway |
| Enrico Francesconi | EU Publications Office, Luxembourg, and Consiglio Nazionale delle Recerche, Italy |

Track on Metadata and Semantics for European and National Projects

Track Chairs

Program Committee

Track on Knowledge IT Artifacts (KITA) in Professional Communities and Aggregations (KITA 2020)

Track Chairs

Program Committee

Federico Cabitza	University of Milano-Bicocca, Italy
Riccardo Melen	University of Milano-Bicocca, Italy
Aurelio Ravarini	Università Carlo Cattaneo - LIUC, Italy
Carla Simone	University of Siegen, Germany
Flávio Soares Corrêa da Silva	University of São Paulo, Brazil
Cecilia Zanni-Merk	INSA Rouen Normandie, France

Track on Metadata and Semantics for Metadata, Identifiers and Semantics in Decentralized Applications, Blockchains and P2P Systems

Special Track Chair

Miguel-Ángel Sicilia	University of Alcalá, Spain

Program Committee

Sissi Closs	Karlsruhe University of Applied Sciences, Germany
Ernesto William De Luca	Georg Eckert Institute – Leibniz Institute for International Textbook Research, Germany
Juan Manuel Dodero	University of Cádiz, Spain
Francesca Fallucchi	Guglielmo Marconi University, Italy
Jane Greenberg	Drexel University, USA
Nikos Houssos	Sentio Solutions, Greece
Nikos Korfiatis	University of East Anglia, UK
Dimitris Rousidis	International Hellenic University, Greece
Salvador Sánchez-Alonso	University of Alcalá, Spain
Michalis Sfakakis	Ionian University, Greece
Rania Siatri	International Hellenic University, Greece
Armando Stellato	University of Rome Tor Vergata, Italy
Robert Trypuz	John Paul II Catholic University of Lublin, Poland
Sirje Virkus	Tallinn University, Estonia

MTSR 2020 Conference Co-organized by

GEOЯG ECKERT
INSTITUTE
for International Textbook Research

Department of Informatics, Systems and Communication
University of Milano-Bicocca, Italy

School of Information

International Hellenic University, Greece

Department of Library Science
Archives and Information Systems

UNIVERSIDAD
COMPLUTENSE
MADRID

Cyprus
University of
Technology

Sponsors Supporting MTSR 2020 Conference

Gold

Awards Sponsored by

Contents

**Track on Metadata and Semantics for Agriculture, Food
and Environment (AgroSEM'20)**

**Track on Metadata and Semantics for Open Repositories,
Research Information Systems and Data Infrastructures**

**Track on Metadata and Semantics for Digital Humanities
and Digital Curation (DHC2020)**

Track on Metadata and Semantics for Cultural Collections and Applications

Track on European and National Projects

Track on Knowledge IT Artifacts (KITA) in Professional Communities and Aggregations (KITA 2020)

Metadata, Linked Data, Semantics and Ontologies - General Session

Biodiversity Image Quality Metadata Augments Convolutional Neural Network Classification of Fish Species

Jeremy Leipzig[1]([✉]) [iD], Yasin Bakis[2] [iD], Xiaojun Wang[2] [iD], Mohannad Elhamod[3] [iD], Kelly Diamond[4,5] [iD], Wasila Dahdul[6] [iD], Anuj Karpatne[3] [iD], Murat Maga[4,5] [iD], Paula Mabee[7] [iD], Henry L. Bart Jr.[2] [iD], and Jane Greenberg[1] [iD]

[1] College of Computing and Informatics, Metadata Research Center, Drexel University, Philadelphia, PA 19104, USA
jnl47@drexel.edu

[2] Tulane University Biodiversity Research Institute, 3705 Main St., Building A3, Belle Chasse, LA 70037, USA

[3] Department of Computer Science, Virginia Tech, Rice Hall Information Technology Engineering Building, 22904, 85 Engineer's Way, Charlottesville, VA 22903, USA

[4] Division of Craniofacial Medicine, Department of Pediatrics, University of Washington, Seattle, WA, USA

[5] Center for Development Biology and Regenerative Medicine, Seattle Children's Hospital, Seattle, WA, USA

[6] Department of Digital Services, UC Irvine Libraries, Irvine, USA

[7] National Ecological Observatory Network Program, Battelle, Boulder, CO, USA

Abstract. Biodiversity image repositories are crucial sources for training machine learning approaches to support biological research. Metadata about object (e.g. image) quality is a putatively important prerequisite to selecting samples for these experiments. This paper reports on a study demonstrating the importance of *image quality metadata* for a species classification experiment involving a corpus of 1935 fish specimen images which were annotated with 22 metadata quality properties. A small subset of high quality images produced an F1 accuracy of 0.41 compared to 0.35 for a taxonomically matched subset low quality images when used by a convolutional neural network approach to species identification. Using the full corpus of images revealed that image quality differed between correctly classified and misclassified images. We found anatomical feature visibility was the most important quality feature for classification accuracy. We suggest biodiversity image repositories consider adopting a minimal set of image quality metadata to support machine learning.

Keywords: Image classification · Convolutional neural networks · Image metadata · Quality metadata

© Springer Nature Switzerland AG 2021
E. Garoufallou and M.-A. Ovalle-Perandones (Eds.): MTSR 2020, CCIS 1355, pp. 3–12, 2021.
https://doi.org/10.1007/978-3-030-71903-6_1

1 Introduction

1.1 Quality Metadata for Species Image Repositories

The extensive growth in open science repositories, and, in particular, the underlying application of rich metadata has potential value for data mining, machine learning and deep learning (ML/DL). Research confirms value of metadata for machine learning, automatic document classification [1], and reproducible research pipelines [2, 3]. Less common, but of paramount importance is metadata that denotes the quality of the object being represented. Metadata addressing quality control characteristics of data can support the data cleaning steps common to virtually all ML/DL analyses. Computer vision offers proof with quality-specific metadata that's important for selecting, training, and validation and test image sets. For example, Ellen et. al found the use of context metadata, consisting of hydrographic, geotemporal, and geometric data, representing plankton images improved the accuracy of a convolutional neural network (CNN) classifier [4]. Tang found a 7% gain in mean average precision after including GPS coordinates in a general image classification task [5]. These studies shed light on an important area of metadata research that has broad implications for leveraging collections of digital images across nearly every scientific discipline.

Of particular interest is biological specimen image collections, given their value as a data source for species identification and morphological study [6, 7]. The research presented in this paper addresses this topic in the context of an NSF supported Harnessing the Data Revolution (HDR) project, Biology-Guided Neural Networks for Discovering Phenotypic Traits (BGNN). A team of information and computer scientists, biologists, and image experts are collaborating to develop a novel set of artificial neural networks (ANNs) for classifying fish species and extracting data on fish external morphological features from images of fish specimens. Unlike genomic data, specimen trait data is largely unstructured and not machine readable. The paucity of usable trait data for many groups of organisms has led to efforts to apply neural network-based classification and morphological analysis to the extensive store of existing species photographic images to automatically extract trait data in an unsupervised manner. The product of these efforts, the focus of BGNN, should improve our ability to derive phenotype data from digital analogs of specimens. Image quality metadata is recognized as an important factor in the selection of images for ML/DL.

1.2 Image Metadata Content Description and Quality

Over the last few decades a number of metadata schemes have been developed that describe specimens found in large scale digital specimen repositories. These metadata standards focus chiefly on description, with limited attention to image quality. The MODAL framework [8, 9] provides a mechanism for understanding the range and diversity of these metadata standards with their domain foci (general to specific) and limited number of image quality properties. Metadata for analog images, our immediate focus, falls into two classes: *descriptive metadata*, generated by a curator; and *technical metadata*, automatically generated by technology capturing the image.

The Dublin Core, Darwin Core, and the Audubon Core offer properties that accommodate quality at a high level. The more technically oriented metadata standards identified in Table 1 provide a richer set of image quality properties, although they need to be measured against parameters defining quality.

Table 1. Example technical and biomedical metadata standards

Metadata standard	Primary focus	Metadata quality property
PREMIS	Long term preservation	Fixity
EXIF	Image formats	X/Y dimensions, compression, color space
DICOM [10]	Medical imaging	imageQuality (1–100)

Semantic ontologies and controlled vocabularies can also be used to indicate value. Table 2 identifies two ontologies, and example semantics describing image quality.

Table 2. Selected ontologies

Ontology	Primary focus	Semantics/metadata values
Biomedical Image Ontology (BIM) [11]	Biomedical images	Image filters, ImagePreProcessing, ImagePostProcessing
OntoNeuroBase [12]	Neuro imaging	Structure of interest, orientation, segmentation result

Overall, the schemes identified here vary in their coverage of content description for discovery, provenance tracking, and technical aspects that can help determine aspects of quality. Our assessment finds there does not yet exist a targeted metadata standard that captures the specimen image quality. This limitation motivates our research purpose and goals.

1.3 Purpose and Goals

The overall aim of our research was to examine the importance of image quality metadata for species classification. Our goals were the following: 1) Determine if the annotated image quality affected classification accuracy. 2) Determine which specific quality annotations were most important for classification accuracy. 3) Make recommendations for future image quality metadata in large image repositories.

2 Methods

To address the above goals, we conducted an empirical analysis as described below.

2.1 Sample

A sample of 23,807 digital images of fish specimens was obtained from the Illinois Natural History Survey (INHS) Fish Collection,from the Great Lakes Invasives Network (GLIN) Project [13]. Duplicate images were removed, and file formats, institution code, catalog numbers and suffixes to file names, the images were transferred to a BGNN file server for analysis. Specimen collection information (occurrence records) for the images were gathered from FishNet2 [14] and the scientific names were updated using Eschmeyer's Catalog of Fishes [15].

Next, we established a set of metadata properties to record image quality for the digitized fish specimens (Suppl. Table 1). The set of properties is based on the expertise of informaticians, fish experts, and data entry technicians at Tulane University's Biodiversity Research Institute, with feedback from members of the Metadata Research Center, Drexel University. The scheme includes 22 metadata properties, requiring the content-value of a categorical concept, free text, a Boolean operator, or a score. A web-based form, and an underlying SQL-based database help to expedite capturing the metadata content (Fig. 1).

2.2 Descriptive Statistical Analysis of Quality

A basic exploratory data analysis was performed on quality metrics. Quality averages by taxonomic groups (genus and species) were examined in order to understand potential biases.

2.3 Implementation of a CNN-Based Classification Pipeline

A convolutional neural network image classification pipeline was developed using PyTorch [16] with Torchvision [17] extensions. Genera (genus groups) and species (genus + specific epithet combinations) were trained and inferred simultaneously using a novel multi-classifier model, called a Hierarchy-Guided Neural Network (in submission). Several hyperparameters, including learning rate, regularization lambda, early stopping patience were tuned prior to this quality analysis.

2.4 Classification Accuracy Using High vs Low Quality Subsets

Using the composite median image_quality score of 8, we divided the data set into low-quality and high-quality subsets. Some species are inherently more visually similar to others, so in a classification scenario, an unbalanced distribution of taxa would confound our aim of measuring the isolated effect of image quality. To address this we sampled images based on equal distributions of individuals by species (See Suppl. Methods) totaling 221 individuals among high and low quality subsets.

2.5 Quality Features Distinguishing Correctly and Incorrectly Identified Species

Using a dataset of 1703 quality annotated images with 20 or more individuals per species (in order to achieve enough training and test data), the holdout test set of 341 images (17 species over 8 Genera) was then divided into correctly classified and misclassi-fied images. Quality features between these two subsets were compared, and pairs of correct/incorrect within species were examined closely.

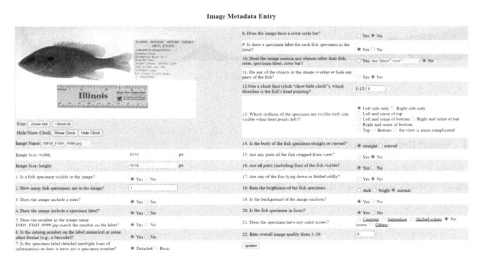

Fig. 1. Web form for quality metadata entry

At the time of this publication, metadata annotations indicating quality have been created for a total of 1935 images. In order to prepare images for classification, Advanced Normalization Tools in R (ANTsR) [18] was used to subtract background shading, rulers, and labels using a supervised segmentation with a training set developed in 3D Slicer [19]. Our analysis focused on comparing low and high-quality images that were roughly balanced by genus and species composition, in order to control for the effect of inherent differences in identification difficulty that vary among taxa. We noted that image quality varied non-randomly between species, perhaps due to batch effects as well as anatomic differences between fish taxa that affect photographic fidelity (Fig. 2).

Fig. 2. Examples of very low (1) and very high (10) quality images of *Esox americanus*

3   Results

3.1   Low/High Subset Comparison

A t-test of F1 scores generated by several runs on the small balanced high and low quality subsets showed a small but significant difference in accuracy (0.41 vs 0.35, pval = 0.031) (Fig. 3).

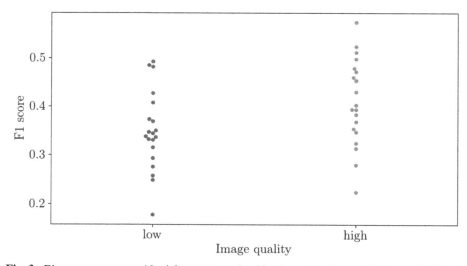

Fig. 3. F1 test score across 19 trials on genus classification using low quality (mean 0.35) and high quality (mean 0.41). Using high quality images produced better F_1 scores (0.41 vs 0.35, pval = 0.031).

3.2 Quality by Classification Outcome

Here we compared correctly classified vs misclassified images using a test set of 341 images (278 correctly classified and 63 misclassified). A confusion matrix (Suppl. Fig. 3) shows that most misclassifications occur between species within the same genus, although these misclassifications are not symmetric.

Comparing the means of quality scores between correctly classified images reveals five quality features correlated with classification accuracy: *if_curved*, *if_parts_visible*, *if_overlapping*, and *image_quality*, and two negatively correlated:*if_background_uniform*, and *if_fins_folded*. While image_quality is the strongest variable, a logistic regression which includes all features except image_quality (to avoid collinearity), reveals if_parts_visible (p-val = 0.0001) as the sole significant covariate. (Suppl. Table 2).

4 Discussion

In this paper we show that image quality measures impact classification accuracy. This was demonstrated using two approaches - a dichotomous split of the image corpus using the manually-annotated image_quality metric (Suppl. Fig. 2), and a comparison of correctly and incorrectly classified images from the entire quality-annotated data set. Our abilities to discern the importance of quality are hampered by three factors: 1) a relative paucity of low-quality images in our dataset, 2) the nature of classification - some fish are simply more similar to their brethren (Suppl. Fig. 3) - but we have attempted to control for this where possible, and 3) some taxa are inherently more difficult to position or illuminate for photography. Although image quality was high overall within this collection, it varied substantially, and perhaps more importantly, unevenly with respect to taxa within image repositories, which may belie both individual variation in photography and batch effects associated with submitters (Fig. 4). Our results lead to a number of recommendations for assessing quality of images from biodiversity image repositories to support machine learning analyses.

The *quality_score* assigned by curators, while based on a rubric, does lend itself to some inter-rater error. We surmised that a composite metric of the binary quality items (e.g. if_curved, if_fins_folded, etc..) could represent a more objective score, and explored this, but it ultimately did not prove substantially better than "image_quality".

The quality scores generated by our curators included some that are strictly technical (blur, color issues), those that would apply to any biodiversity catalog (*if_parts_visible*) and those that are specific to fish (e.g. *if_fins_folded*). We contend that all three types of quality (technical, biospecimen, taxon-specific) are important to include for biorepositories. The automated measurement of technical image quality, and possible higher-level judgments, can help accelerate the collection of this metadata. Local features [20, 21] such as fin-level textures that would indicate lepidotrichia and global features such as large segmented areas and basic image characteristics of color and shape are logically distinct from semantic quality judgments made by the curators in this project ("folded fins"/"label obstruction"), though automated semantic quality annotations are within the capabilities of neural networks.

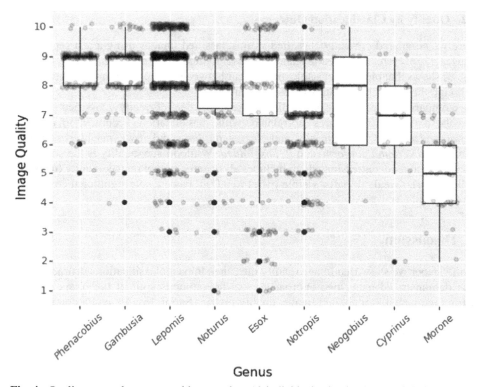

Fig. 4. Quality scores by genera with more than 10 individuals clearly show variability within and between genera.

We suggest repositories enforce provenance tracking metadata to assist in identifying batch effects or other confounds introduced by disparate labs photographing specimens with different settings and equipment.

We observed that the classification task is hampered by its dependence on accuracy instead of more direct intermediate measures, for example, the number of features detected. Certain types of low-quality images may serve to augment robustness to classify real-world specimens - a technique called "noise injection". These uses suggest annotating for quality, rather than simply culling, is a preferable strategy. Quality metadata to aid robustness and generalizability in machine learning, rather than a narrow focus on pristine specimens, is an open area for future work.

5   Conclusion

The main objective of this research was to determine if annotated image quality metadata impacted generic and species-level classification accuracy of a convolutional neural network. We conducted an empirical analysis to examine which specific quality annotations, based on 22 metadata properties, were important for classification accuracy.

Our key finding was that images with high-quality metadata metrics had significantly higher classification accuracy in convolutional neural network analysis than images with low-quality metadata metrics.

We offer a number of recommendations for assessing the quality of images from biodiversity image repositories to support machine learning analyses. This investigation serves as a baseline study of useful metadata for assessing image quality. The methodology, our approach, and the base-level scheme of 22 metadata properties, serves to inform other research that seek to record image quality; and, further study the impact on classification for other fishes, other specimens, and even other disciplines where the image is a central object. Overall the research conducted serves the needs of the BGNN project, and biologically-focused, machine-learning projects generally, for determining whether images for biodiversity specimen image repositories are useful for higher-level analysis.

6 Supplemental Materials

Supplementary materials are available at https://doi.org/10.6084/m9.figshare.13096199.
Raw data is available at https://bgnn.org/INHS. Reproducible code is available at https://github.com/hdr-bgnn/iqm.

Acknowledgements. Research supported by NSF OAC #1940233 and #1940322.

We acknowledge Tulane University Technology Services for server set-up and access supporting this research; Justin Mann, Aaron Kern, Jake Blancher for curation work; and Chris Taylor, Curator of Fishes and Crustaceans, INHS, for providing the fish specimen images and metadata (INHS support: NSF Award #1400769).

Competing Interests. The authors have declared that no competing interests exist.

References

1. Han, H., Giles, C.L., Manavoglu, E., et al.: Automatic document metadata extraction using support vector machines. In: 2003 Joint Conference on Digital Libraries, 2003. Proceedings, pp. 37–48 (2003)
2. Schelter, S., Boese, J.-H., Kirschnick, J., et al.: Automatically tracking metadata and provenance of machine learning experiments. In: Machine Learning Systems workshop at NIPS (2017)
3. Leipzig, J., Nüst, D., Hoyt, C.T., et al.: The role of metadata in reproducible computational research. arXiv [cs.DL] (2020)
4. Ellen, J.S., Graff, C.A., Ohman, M.D.: Improving plankton image classification using context metadata. Limnol. Oceanogr. Methods **2**, 17 (2019)
5. Tang, K., Paluri, M., Fei-Fei, L., et al.: Improving image classification with location context. In: Proceedings of the IEEE International Conference on Computer Vision, pp. 1008–1016 (2015)
6. Borges, L.M., Reis, V.C., Izbicki, R.: Schrödinger's phenotypes: herbarium specimens show two-dimensional images are both good and (not so) bad sources of morphological data. Methods Ecol. Evol. (2020). https://doi.org/10.1111/2041-210X.13450

7. Hernández-Serna, A., Jiménez-Segura, L.F.: Automatic identification of species with neural networks. PeerJ **2**, e563 (2014)
8. Willis, C., Greenberg, J., White, H.: Analysis and synthesis of metadata goals for scientific data. J Am Soc Inf Sci Technol **63**, 1505–1520 (2012)
9. Greenberg, J.: Understanding metadata and metadata schemes. Cataloging Classif. Q. **40**, 17–36 (2005)
10. Bidgood, W.D., Jr., Horii, S.C.: Introduction to the ACR-NEMA DICOM standard. Radiographics **12**, 345–355 (1992)
11. Bukhari, A.C., Nagy, M.L., Krauthammer, M., et al.: BIM: an open ontology for the annotation of biomedical images. In: ICBO (2015)
12. Temal, L., Lando, P., Gibaud, B., et al.: OntoNeuroBase: a multi-layered application ontology in neuroimaging. In: Second Workshop: Formal Ontologies Meet Industry (FOMI 2006) (2006)
13. Great Lakes Invasives Network Home. https://greatlakesinvasives.org/portal/index.php. Accessed 2 Aug 2020
14. FishNet2. https://www.fishnet2.net/. Accessed 2 Aug 2020
15. Eschmeyer's Catalog of Fishes. https://www.calacademy.org/scientists/projects/eschmeyers-catalog-of-fishes. Accessed 2 Aug 2020
16. Paszke, A., Gross, S., Massa, F., et al.: PyTorch: an imperative style, high-performance deep learning library. In: Wallach, H., Larochelle, H., Beygelzimer, A., et al. (eds.) Advances in Neural Information Processing Systems, vol. 32, pp 8026–8037. Curran Associates, Inc. (2019)
17. Marcel, S., Rodriguez, Y.: Torchvision the machine-vision package of torch. In: In: Proceedings of the 18th ACM international conference on Multimedia, pp. 1485–1488. Association for Computing Machinery, New York (2010)
18. Avants, B.B., Kandel, B.M., Duda, J.T., et al.: ANTsR: ANTs in R: quantification tools for biomedical images. R package version 0542 (2019)
19. Kikinis, R., Pieper, S.D., Vosburgh, K.G.: 3D slicer: a platform for subject-specific image analysis, visualization, and clinical support. In: Jolesz, F.A. (ed.) Intraoperative Imaging and Image-Guided Therapy, pp. 277–289. Springer, New York (2014). https://doi.org/10.1007/978-1-4614-7657-3_19
20. Shyu, C.R., Brodley, C.E., Kak, A.C., et al.: Local versus global features for content-based image retrieval. In: Proceedings, IEEE Workshop on Content-Based Access of Image and Video Libraries (Cat. No.98EX173), pp 30–34 (1998)
21. Vogel, J., Schwaninger, A., Wallraven, C.: Categorization of natural scenes: local vs. global information. In: Proceedings of Conference Army Physicians Cent Mediterr Forces (2006)

Class and Instance Equivalences in the Web of Linked Data: Distribution and Graph Structure

Salvador Sanchez-Alonso[1]([✉]), Miguel A. Sicilia[1], Enayat Rajabi[2], Marçal Mora-Cantallops[1], and Elena Garcia-Barriocanal[1]

[1] University of Alcalá, Alcalá de Henares, Spain
{salvador.sanchez,msicilia,marcal.mora,elena.garciab}@uah.es
[2] Cape Breton University, Sydney, Canada
enayat_rajabi@cbu.ca

Abstract. The Web of Linked Open Data (LOD) is a decentralized effort in publishing datasets using a set of conventions to make them accessible, notably thought RDF and SPARQL. Links across nodes in published datasets are thus critical in getting value for the LOD cloud as a collective effort. Connectivity among the datasets can occur through these links. Equivalence relationship is one of the fundamental links that connects different schemas or datasets, and is used to assert either class or instance equivalence. In this article, we report an empirical study on the equivalences found in over 59 million triples from datasets accessible via SPARQL endpoints in open source data portals. Metrics from graph analysis have been used to examine the relationships between repositories and determine their relative importance as well as their ability to facilitate knowledge discovery.

Keywords: Linked Open Data · Equivalence · RDF · SPARQL

1 Introduction

The cloud of Linked Open Data (LOD) is the result of the effort of different institutions or individuals in publishing schemas and data openly based upon a set of conventions including RDF as the fundamental information sharing model and following the philosophy of lack of centralized storage or control of the World Wide Web. Similar to the Web, the value of LOD depends critically on links across nodes which support aggregating or contrasting information at different levels. Among all the possible semantics that links may bear, `equivalence` is of special importance, as it provides a basis for merging either schemas or concrete data, depending on the resources being asserted as equivalent.

Class equivalence axioms entail *replaceability* of two classes (or in general, of class expressions), which in practical terms when considering graphs of linked data results in the possibility of merging graphs that may reside at different

E. Garoufallou and M.-A. Ovalle-Perandones (Eds.): MTSR 2020, CCIS 1355, pp. 13–21, 2021.
https://doi.org/10.1007/978-3-030-71903-6_2

nodes. Further, this provides an extension for all the asserted instances of the classes. Thus, those equivalences are extremely important in interoperability and schema reuse of data in the LOD cloud, so they deserve special attention. Instance equivalence assertions have a scope limited to pairs of individuals, and complement class assertions with the important benefit of theoretically allowing for aggregating data on particular entities. We have left other declarative expressions as property equivalences or declaring that two individuals are different for further work.

In spite of the practical importance of equivalence relationships, existing studies suggest that they are not in widespread use in the LOD cloud, and are not consistently used to frame the semantics of the data exposed by nodes in an attempt to maximize opportunities for merging or fusing with other nodes. In this paper, we report preliminary results for a systematic study of equivalences across the Web of Data, as a first step towards a more complete account of the topic. Results show that general purpose repositories such as DBpedia or Geonames play a central role in the LOD cloud, acting as a bridge for other repositories to be linked to the other datsets, which in turn provides better possibilities for knowledge discovery to data consumers.

The rest of this paper is structured as follows. Section 2 provides an overview of the axioms that enable interlinking in the LOD repositories and briefly surveys previous studies. Section 3 details the procedure carried out to collect the data that is later analyzed in Sect. 4. Finally, conclusions are provided in Sect. 5.

2   Background

Links across datasets are a key element in the LOD cloud. Arguably, one of the most valuable types of relationships between entities in the LOD datasets is equivalence. We take here the notions of equivalence that appear in the OWL2 language.

An equivalent classes axiom `EquivalentClasses(CE1 ... CEn)` states that all of the class expressions `CEi`, $1 \leq i \leq n$, are semantically equivalent to each other. This axiom allows one to use each class as a synonym for one other. In other words, in any expression in the ontology containing such an axiom, any `CEi` can be replaced with `CEj` without affecting the meaning of the ontology. This has strong implications. In the case of asserting the equivalence of two primitive classes in different datasets, this entails that the graphs can be merged and taken together.

Similarly, an individual equality axiom `SameIndividual(a1 ... an)` states that all of the individuals `ai`, $1 \leq i \leq n$, are equal to each other. In consequence, their names should in theory be used interchangeably.

The `owl:sameAs` axiom has been subject to different studies starting from those of Halpin et al. [1]. The problems identified with the use of `sameAs`, and the different uses have been known for more than a decade now, but they appear to persist [2,3]. [4] also identified several issues involving the `owl:sameAs` property in a linked data context including merging assertions from sources with different contexts, and the need to explore an operational semantic distinct from the strict logical meaning provided by OWL. The `sameas.cc` dataset [5] is a large collection of identity assertions extracted from the Web of Data. However, we are more interested in the graph structure of equivalences in this article, as it happens when traversing linked data.

3 Data Collection

The point of departure for data collection was checking the SPARQL endpoints available in CKAN that are used to generate LOD cloud diagrams.

Concretely, we systematically checked each of the nodes appearing in datahub[1] to discover the existing live SPARQL endpoints of datasets. Out of 711 Linked Open Data datasets with SPARQL endpoints, 93 endpoints were responding to queries. The examination of availability of each endpoint was performed by writing a simple Python script using the SPARQLWrapper[2].

It should be noted that this procedures may have two important limitations. On one hand, not necessarily every published dataset in the LOD cloud is registered and curated at that repository. On the other hand, the availability of SPARQL endpoints may vary over time [6], therefore, the obtained sample cannot be guaranteed to be comprehensive, but at least it represents a snapshot in time of collecting datasets from the LOD cloud.

Equivalences were obtained by using a simple SPARQL query as follows:

```
PREFIX owl: <http://www.w3.org/2002/07/owl#>
SELECT ?s ?p ?o
WHERE  { ?s  ?p ?o.
    FILTER (?p IN ( owl:equivalentClass , owl:sameAs ) ) }
```

It was observed that some endpoints returning high round figures of results, which might be attributed to some constraints on the query engine for large result sets. In order to check that possible behaviour, SPARQL queries aggregating the number of results with `COUNT(*)` were used.

4 Results and Discussion

4.1 About Node IDs

According to the W3C definition[3], a blank node ID, also known as "blank node" or "bNode", is a local identifier used in some concrete RDF syntaxes or RDF store implementations. A node ID is not, therefore, any special type of data record but instead a way to refer to a certain node within the confines of a given

---

[1] https://old.datahub.io.

[2] https://pypi.org/project/SPARQLWrapper/.

[3] https://www.w3.org/TR/rdf11-concepts/.

file or knowledge-base: outside of the file where the node ID appears, the node is unnamed and thus cannot be linked or referred.

In our study, a total of 329 triples containing node IDs (0.3% of the total of 123,387 equivalent class axioms) were found in 11 repositories. The Brazilian Politicians dataset, for instance, includes triples like the following:

http://purl.org/ontology/mo/Arranger,equivalentClass,nodeID://b19867

This triple states that an equivalence between the class `Arranger` and an unnamed resource `b19867` exists. The use of node IDs is handy to identify things via e.g. an inverse functional property in a knowledge-base when we do not want to give a reasoner on the file excess work. At the same time, unnamed nodes are heavily used in `rdf:List` structures. Given that the Brazilian politicians repository, in our example, includes seven blank nodes declared to be equivalent to the class http://purl.org/ontology/mo/Arranger, we assume that a list of seven resources, whose names are unknown to the outside knowledge-bases, are "`Arrangers`". In the same way, seven `Listeners` and seven `Conductors` are listed among others. We also understand that all such resources have a value for an inverse functional property, which can be used to refer to the nodes from outside the knowledge-base.

The complete distribution of triples including node IDs per repository is shown in Table 1:

Table 1. NodeIDs per repository.

Repository	# nodeIDs
AEMET metereological dataset	9
Allie Abbreviation and Long Form Database in Life Science	18
Brazilian politicians	44
DBpedia in Japanese	11
DBpedia in Portuguese	44
Library of the Chilean national congress	3
GeoLinkedData	6
Open Data from the Italian National Research Council	6
Dbnary (Wiktionary as Linguistic Linked Open Data)	148
UniProt RDF schema ontology	7
Environment data UK	1

4.2 Equivalent Classes

A total of 123,387 equivalent class axioms were found in the data collected from the responsive datasets (see Sect. 3). Out of a total of 59,383,718, this number represents only the 0.2% of the collected triples.

Inspecting the subjects of the predicates, the most frequent one was FOAF 0.1 `Person` with 96 occurrences. Th other highly referenced FOAF classes are `Agent`, `Image` and `Document`. Other frequent objects above 20 occurrences include a number of classes in the DBPedia ontology among others such as `Person`, `Organization`, `Event`, `Work`, `Place`, `Language`, `City` or `Country`. Two highly ranked classes in the http://www.openlinksw.com/schemas/ namespace were `Tweet` and `User`.

Looking at the objects, the most frequent concept is Schema.org, including `CreativeWork` and `Person` with 61 and 60 occurrences respectively. Other Shema.org classes above 25 occurrences are `ImageObject` and `Product`. Occurrences above 25 among others are `Person` in DBPedia and FOAF, `Agent` in Dublin Core, `UserAccount` and `Post` in SIOC, and `Person` in PIM datasets.

Looking at the endpoints, a number of DBPedia instances had between 400 and 1,500 equivalences (pt, ja, de, fr) and the global http://dbpedia.org/sparql amounted for 10,000 (maybe capped by the SPARQL query). The URI Burner[4] data service was the most frequent amounting to 100,000 records. Given that this endpoint is an aggregation service, it can be considered as a special case.

Although other perspectives were possible, the analysis of relationships between different repositories was prioritized as the most interesting possible study. Therefore, we proceeded to extract the relationships between repositories to further analyse the data. The procedure implied the creation of a file with relationships between the repositories: for all triples including the `equivalent class` axiom, source and target repositories were recorded. The extraction was carried out in the following steps:

- In step 1, a Python script extracted the URLs of the two repositories, removed the name of the resources, and obtained the rest of the URL.
- In step 2, human experts cleaned the data by removing duplicates and fixing errors to later identify the repository to which each URL belonged.

With this file as an input, we built a weighted directed graph where the weight assigned to a given relationship between repository A and repository B depended on the number of classes in A related by equivalent class axioms to the other classes in B, duplicates excluded. A first version of the graph was created including 96 nodes and 214 relationships. This graph was later revised to transform `node IDs` (see previous section) to self links, remove the isolated nodes and small graphs. We finally obtained the "giant component" (which is a finite connected fraction of the entire graph's vertices), shown in Fig. 1, and consisted of only 41 nodes and 125 relationships. Knowledge-bases like AEMET metereological dataset, Datos.bcn.cl, Environment Agency Bathing Water Quality, Geo Vocab, Semantic Sensor Network Ontology, Lotico or MindsWap, which had no links to the other repositories, were filtered out.

In Fig. 1, the node size has been adapted according to the in-degree value – i.e. the number of incoming relations from other repositories– of each repository. Not surprisingly, general purpose knowledge-bases such as DBPedia or common

---

[4] http://linkeddata.uriburner.com/.

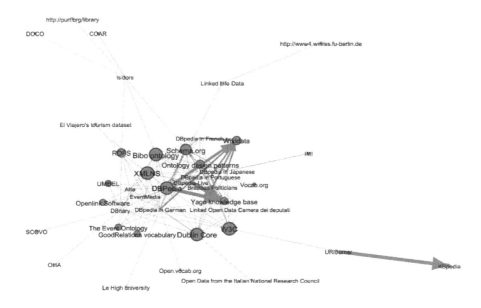

Fig. 1. Equivalent class axioms graph.

use ontologies and schemes such as W3C, Dublin Core, the BIBO ontology or Schema.org are among the most referenced nodes. In the same Figure, 4 communities were identified and coloured in green, purple, orange and blue. According to the algorithm used [7], two repositories belong to the same cluster (community) if they are more densely connected together than to the rest of the network, so this was the criterion to cluster nodes together in a community.

4.3 Same-as Relationships

In the data collected from the responsive datasets, a total of 59,260,331 `sameAs` axioms were found out of a total of 59,383,718 (this represents a 99.8% of all triples collected). The endpoints with larger number of axioms are the British National Library ($\sim$2M), the Isidore scientific collection[5] ($\sim$1M), the OpenLink Virtuoso public endpoint and the Portuguese DBPedia ($\sim$200K each) and the Allie Database of abbreviations in science and the French DBPedia ($\sim$100K each).

The distribution of the subjects and objects is relatively flat, with only elements from the *Last.fm* endpoint having more than 300 occurrences, in which appears to be a specificity of the internals in that node.

Following a similar procedure to the one described for equivalent classes, a weighted directed graph including 275 nodes and 491 relations was built. The giant component (again, removing disconnected nodes and sub-graphs) was 269

---

[5] https://isidore.science/.

nodes and 485 relationships. The most referenced repositories were DBPedia, Geonames, the Library of Congress, and other repositories that are either general purpose or a reputed source of information for a given field. Although one could expect the fact that DBPedia has a higher in-degree value due to incoming links from external knowledge-bases, it is not so clear how DBPedias in minority languages such as Sanskrit, Yoruba, Yiddish, Zhōngwén, Wallon or Volapük –to name just a few– can attract large number of links from the other repositories.

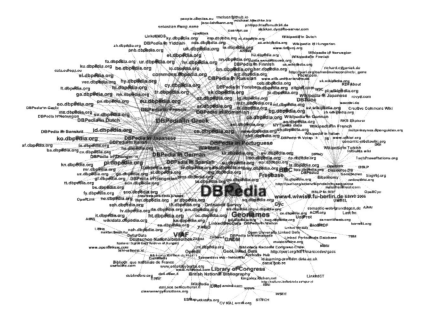

Fig. 2. Same as axioms graph.

Figure 2 shows how the repositories in the full graph can be classified into five communities. The biggest one –including most DBpedias in many different languages– contains 72% of the nodes, while the rest contain 15% (ontologies and semantic Web institutions), 5% (libraries), 4.73% and 2.55%. In the Figure, node size is proportional to the in-degree value of each repository.

If only those nodes with relations with four or more repositories are chosen –the 4-core graph– we have what is shown in Fig. 3. This graph, where the node size is proportional to the repository in-degree value –i.e. the number of references from external repositories–, shows the more referenced repositories according to the number of relationships. As one would expect, general purpose knowledge-bases such as DBpedia, Geonames, and Freebase are among the most central ones.

According to the Linked Open Data model, it is important for a repository to be linked to as many other repositories as possible, as this promotes new

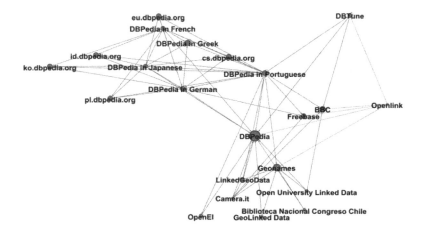

Fig. 3. 4-core subgraph.

knowledge discovery. Betweenness centrality, which is a Social Network Analysis property that measures the extent to which a node lies on the paths between other nodes, is the most representative metric from our perspective to evaluate discoverability. Figure 4 shows the subset of repositories with a higher betweenness value, which in some way represents the datasets that provide better discovery pathways to their knowledge-base users. Perhaps not surprisingly, the repositories with higher betweenness centrality are also those with a higher number of outgoing links –out-degree metric in Social Network Analysis–. These are therefore the repositories whose resources distribute better their outgoing links, i.e. reference resources in a higher number of other repositories.

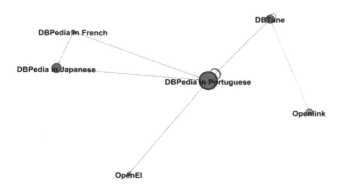

Fig. 4. Repositories with higher betweenness value.

5   Conclusions and Outlook

This paper has described insights about class and instance equivalences from a sample of SPARQL endpoints in the cloud of Linked Open Data. Class equivalences show sparse connection patterns, with most frequent equivalences unsurprisingly from and to "upper concepts" as *person*, together with some technology specific concepts as *user* or *tweet*. Instance equivalences appear evenly distributed in terms of subjects and objects, suggesting a sparse distribution, but showing a more imbalance distribution considering endpoints.

General purpose repositories such as DBpedia, Geonames or Freebase are more central than the rest of repositories, as expected. This fact highlights that linking a dataset to these repositories opens better possibilities for knowledge discovery and it is highly beneficial for both dataset publishers and dataset consumers.

Properties like out-degree and betweennes centrality seem to be quite connected. This can lead us to the conclusion that the more varied datasets with high centrality we (as data creators) link our datasets, the more likely we are to be a connected to the other repositories on the Web. Also, betweenness centrality can be used as a metric in knowledge discovery to determine the flow of information in a knowledge graph.

References

1. Halpin, H., Hayes, P.J., McCusker, J.P., McGuinness, D.L., Thompson, H.S.: When owl:sameAs isn't the same: an analysis of identity in linked data. In: Patel-Schneider, P.F., et al. (eds.) ISWC 2010. LNCS, vol. 6496, pp. 305–320. Springer, Berlin, Heidelberg (2010). https://doi.org/10.1007/978-3-642-17746-0_20
2. Halpin, H., Hayes, P.J., Thompson, H.S.: When owl:sameas isn't the same redux: towards a theory of identity, context, and inference on the semantic web. In: Christiansen, H., Stojanovic, I., Papadopoulos, G. (eds.) CONTEXT 2015. LNCS, vol. 9405, pp. 47–60. Springer, Cham (2015). https://doi.org/10.1007/978-3-319-25591-0_4
3. Raad, J., Pernelle, N., Saïs, F., Beek, W., van Harmelen, F.: The sameas problem: a survey on identity management in the Web of data. ArXiv preprint arXiv:1907.10528 (2019)
4. Ding, L., Shinavier, J., Finin, T., McGuinness, D. L.: owl:sameAs and linked data: an empirical study. In: Proceedings of the 2nd Web Science Conference, April 2010 (2010)
5. Beek, W., Raad, J., Wielemaker, J., Van Harmelen, F.: sameAs.cc: the closure of 500M owl:sameAs statements. ESWC 2018. LNCS, vol. 10843, pp. 65–80. Springer, Cham (2018). https://doi.org/10.1007/978-3-319-93417-4_5
6. Rajabi, E., Sanchez-Alonso, S., Sicilia, M.A.: Analyzing broken links on the web of data: an experiment with DBpedia. J. Assoc. Inf. Sci. Technol. **65**(8), 1721–1727 (2014)
7. Blondel, V., Guillaume, J., Lambiotte, R., Lefebvre, E.: Fast unfolding of communities in large networks. J. Stat. Mech: Theory Exp. **2008**, 10008 (2008)

Predicting the Basic Level in a Hierarchy of Concepts

Laura Hollink$^{(\boxtimes)}$ ⓘ, Aysenur Bilgin ⓘ, and Jacco van Ossenbruggen ⓘ

Centrum Wiskunde & Informatica, Amsterdam, The Netherlands
{laura.hollink,aysenur.bilgin,jacco.van.ossenbruggen}@cwi.nl

Abstract. The "basic level", according to experiments in cognitive psychology, is the level of abstraction in a hierarchy of concepts at which humans perform tasks quicker and with greater accuracy than at other levels. We argue that applications that use concept hierarchies could improve their user interfaces if they 'knew' which concepts are the basic level concepts. This paper examines to what extent the basic level can be learned from data. We test the utility of three types of concept features, that were inspired by the basic level theory: lexical features, structural features and frequency features. We evaluate our approach on WordNet, and create a training set of manually labelled examples from different part of WordNet. Our findings include that the basic level concepts can be accurately identified within one domain. Concepts that are difficult to label for humans are also harder to classify automatically. Our experiments provide insight into how classification performance across different parts of the hierarchy could be improved, which is necessary for identification of basic level concepts on a larger scale.

1 Introduction

Applications that use metadata rely on knowledge organization systems – taxonomies, thesauri, ontologies and more recently knowledge graphs – to provide controlled vocabularies and explicit semantic relationships among concepts [27]. While these various knowledge organization systems (KOSs) may use different formal languages, they all share similar underlying data representations. They typically contain instances and classes, or concepts, and they use subsumption hierarchies to organize concepts from specific to generic.

In this paper, we aim to enrich the concept hierarchy of a widely used KOS, WordNet, by predicting which level of abstraction is the 'basic level.' This is a notion from the seminal paper by Rosch et al. [22] in which they present the theory of "basic level categories"[1]. The core idea is that in a hierarchy of concepts there is one level of abstraction that has special significance for humans. At this level, humans perform tasks quicker and with greater accuracy than at

---

[1] Note that vocabulary varies per research community and throughout time. Rosch's "categories" would be called "classes" or "concepts" in recent Knowledge Representation literature.

© Springer Nature Switzerland AG 2021
E. Garoufallou and M.-A. Ovalle-Perandones (Eds.): MTSR 2020, CCIS 1355, pp. 22–34, 2021.
https://doi.org/10.1007/978-3-030-71903-6_3

superordinate or subordinate levels. In a hierarchy of edible fruits, this so called 'basic level' is at the level of *apple* and not at the levels of *granny smith* or *fruit*; in a hierarchy of tools it is at the level of *hammer* rather than *tool* or *maul*; and in a hierarchy of clothing it is at the level of *pants*. In a series of experiments, Rosch demonstrated that humans consistently display 'basic level effects' – such as quicker and more accurate responses – across a large variety of tasks.

In contrast, in current knowledge graphs (and other KOSs) each level in the hierarchy is treated equally. To illustrate why this may be problematic, consider the following example. Using a taxonomy of fruits combined with a metadata record saying that an image displays a granny smith, we can infer new facts: that it displays an apple and that it displays a fruit. However, that doesn't tell us which is the best answer to the question "What is depicted?"– a granny smith, an apple or a fruit? In cases where the concept hierarchy is deep, there might be dozens of concepts to choose from, all equally logically correct descriptions of the image. KOSs generally have no mechanism for giving priority to one level of abstraction over another.

We argue that applications that use knowledge graphs could significantly improve their user interfaces if they were able to explicitly use basic level concepts when appropriate. In other words, if they were able to predict for which concepts in the graph users can be expected to display basic level effects. In the example above, we illustrated how computer vision systems could be designed to describe the objects they detect at the basic level rather than at subordinate or superordinate levels, so that users can react as quickly as possible. Another example is an online store, that could cluster products at the basic level to give users a quick overview of what is sold, rather than choosing more specific or more general clusters. Automatic summarization systems could describe the contents of an article at the basic level, etc. It is important to note that we do not argue that the basic level should *always* be the preferred level of abstraction. For example, in indexing as it is done in digital libraries, it is often advisable to select concepts as specific as possible. Also, in application-to-application situations where there is no interaction with a human user, basic level effects are obviously irrelevant.

Motivated by these example scenarios, our goal is to predict which concepts in a given concept hierarchy are at the basic level. We do this in a data-driven manner, in contrast to the laboratory experiments with human users that have been conducted in cognitive psychology.

We train a classifier using three types of features. Firstly, we elicit lexical features like word-length and the number of senses of a word, since it has commonly been claimed that basic level concepts are denoted by shorter and more polysemous words [8, 18, 25]. Secondly, we extract structural features, such as the number of subordinates of a concept and the length of its description. This is motivated by a definition of the basic level being "the level at which categories carry the most information" [22]. Finally, we obtain features related to the frequency of use of a word, since basic level concepts are thought to be used often by humans.

To test our approach, we apply it to the concept hierarchy of WordNet, a widely used lexical resource, and classify WordNet concepts as basic level or not-basic level. For training and testing, we create a gold standard of 518 manually labelled concepts spread over three different branches of the WordNet hierarchy.

Frequency features are extracted from Google Ngram data. Lexical and structural features are extracted from the concept hierarchy itself, i.e. from WordNet. In a series of experiments, we aim to answer three research questions: 1) to what extent can we predict basic level concepts within and across branches of the hierarchy, 2) how can we predict the basic level in new, previously unseen parts of the hierarchy, and 3) how does machine classification compare to human classification, i.e. what is the meaning of disagreement between human annotators? We believe the answer to these three questions will bring us one step closer to the overall aim of being able to predict the basic level on a large scale in all kinds of concept hierarchies, helping applications built on top of them to interact with users more effectively.

All data is publicly available[2]: the gold standard of manually labelled concepts, the annotation protocol, code used for feature extraction, as well as an RDF dataset of all predicted basic level concepts in WordNet.

2   Background: The Basic Level

Rosch et al. [22] demonstrated basic level effects across a large variety of tasks. For example, they found that people, when asked to verify if an object belonged to a category, reacted faster when it was a basic level category ("Is this a chair" is answered quicker than "Is this furniture?"); when asked to name a pictured object, people chose names of basic level concepts (They said "It is an apple" rather than "It is a golden delicious"); and when asked to write down properties of a concept, people came up with longer lists if the concept was at the basic level (many additional properties were named for "car" compared to the properties of it's superordinate "vehicle", while few additional properties were mentioned for "sports car"). In the present paper, we aim to derive 'basic levelness' in a data driven manner, rather than by performing psychological experiments, to allow for enrichment of concept hierarchies at a large scale.

Rosch's initial experiments were done on a relatively small set of nine hierarchies of ten concepts each. She chose common, tangible concepts, such as fruits, furniture and musical instruments. Later, basic level effects were also demonstrated in other types of concepts, such as events [21], geographical features [15], sounds [14] and categories with artificially created names [18]. These results show that basic level effects exist on a much wider scale than Rosch's relatively clearcut examples, strengthening our claim that there is a need to automatically derive the basic level in large concept hierarchies.

The basic level is relatively universal since it is tightly coupled with universal physiological features such as what humans can perceive and what movements

---

[2] http://cwi.nl/~hollink/basiclevelmtsr2020/.

they are capable of [13]. That being said, it should be acknowledged that there are also individual factors that affect to what extent basic level effects occur. One of those factors is expertise. Domain experts may process subordinate levels with equal performance in the context of their domain of expertise [11,25]. Similarly, the familiarity of a person with an object plays a role, where familiarity increases basic level effects [24]. Finally, the prototypicality of an object is a factor; if someone perceives an object as a prototypical example of its class, basic level effects may increase [23]. These individual factors are outside the scope of the present paper, where we focus on the universal nature of basic level effects.

3   Related Work

The idea of a 'basic level' has been used in various applications that use conceptual hierarchies. In the context of the semantic web, it has been used in ontology creation [9,26], automatic ontology generation [3,4,7], ontology matching [8] and entity summarization [20].

Ordonez et al. [19] stress the importance of the basic level in computer vision. They propose a mapping between basic level concepts and the thesaurus of concept names that is used by existing visual recognition systems. Mathews et al. [16] use collaborative tags to predict basic level names of recognized objects in an automatic image captioning task.

For all these applications there is a need to identify which concepts are at the basic level. In the papers mentioned above this was done either manually [9,26], using heuristics [8,20], by looking at the frequency and order of occurrence of user generated tags [7,16,19], or using a measure called category utility [3,4].

The category utility [6] of a concept c is a measure of how well the knowledge that item i is a member of c increases the ability to predict features of i. For example, knowledge that i is a bird allows one to predict that i can fly, has wings, lays eggs, etc. Belohlavek and Trneck [1] compared the category utility measure for basic level prediction to two similar measures that were proposed earlier, such as cue validity [22] and Jones' category-feature collocation measure [12], and found that they lead to similar predictions.

In contrast to category utility, cue validity and the category-feature collocation measure, our approach does not rely on the availability of explicit information about all features of a concept. In our experience, features such as "can fly" and "has wings" are seldom encoded in a concept hierarchy. Our approach builds on the idea of using tag frequency by including the frequency of occurrence of a concept in a natural language text corpus as a feature. Finally, our approach is inspired by some of the heuristics proposed before, e.g. with respect to the use of depth in the hierarchy [20] and lexical properties [8].

4   A Method for Basic Level Prediction

We cast the task of basic-level prediction as a binary classification problem: a concept in a hierarchy either is or is not at the basic level. In future work, we intend to look into a multi-class classification task, distinguishing basic level, more specific and more generic concepts. Figure 1 shows an example hierarchy in which the basic level concepts have been identified. The figure illustrates that the basic level concepts can be at different levels in the hierarchy for different branches, and some branches may not include any basic level concepts.

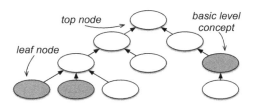

Fig. 1. Example hierarchy, basic level concepts in grey.

4.1   Extracting Three Types of Features

As input to the classifier, we extract structural, lexical and frequency features. We use the conceptual hierarchy to extract structural features about a concept. Rosch et al. [22] showed that at the basic level people tend to give longer descriptions when asked to describe a concept and were able to list most new attributes at this level. They concluded that the basic level is "the level at which categories carry the most information." Based on this, we hypothesize that the amount of explicit information about a concept in a KOS can be used as a signal for basic level prediction. Accordingly, we collect the number of relations that the concept has in the KOS. Depending on the conceptual hierarchy, these can be is-a relations such as `rdfs:subClassof`, `skos:broader` or `wordnet:hyponym`. If other types of relations are present in the KOS, such as part-of relations, we count these as well. If the conceptual hierarchy contains natural language descriptions of the concepts, we include the length of the description as a feature. We also store the depth of the concept in the hierarchy, measured as the shortest path of is-a relations from the concept to the top node.

The use of lexical features is motivated by the fact that the basic level can be recognized in natural language. Many have claimed that basic level concepts are generally denoted by shorter and more polysemous words [8,18,25]. They are also the first words acquired by children [2]. The extraction of lexical features requires a mapping from concepts to words. In knowledge representation languages commonly used for KOSs, this mapping is for example given by `rdfs:label` or `skos:preferredLabel`. We extract the following lexical features for each concept: the length of the word(s) (measured in characters), the number of senses of the word(s) (i.e. polysemy) and the number of synonyms of the word.

Finally, we include the frequency of occurrence of a concept as a feature. Rosch's initial experiments [22] demonstrated that people often choose basic level concepts when asked to describe an object, rather than subordinate or superordinate concepts. Therefore, we hypothesize that the frequency of occur-rence of a word in a natural language corpus is a signal for basic level prediction.

Both lexical and frequency features are based on words. In many KOSs, one concept can be denoted by multiple words. Examples are the synonymous words *piano* and *pianoforte*, or *contrabass* and *double bass* (we treat multi-word phrases the same as single words). If this is the case, we need to aggregate multiple word-level feature values into one concept-level feature value. We use mean and minimum or maximum values for this purpose, depending on the feature.

4.2   Creating Manual Concept Labels for Training and Testing

We ask human annotators to manually label concepts as being basic level or not. An annotation protocol was provided that includes a short description of what the basic level is, as well as the results from Rosch's initial experiments. For each concept, we provide the annotators with the synonyms that denote the concept, the position in the hierarchy, and a natural language description of the concept. The protocol lists additional sources that the annotator may consult: Wikipedia, Google web search and/or Google image search, all with a standardized query consisting of a word that denotes the concept and optionally a word of a superordinate concept. Finally, the protocol provides some hints that may help the annotator to decide on the correct label in case of doubt. For example, "at the basic level an item can often easily be identified even when seen from afar", "at the basic level there is often a recognisable movement associated with the concept," and "at the basic level images of the item often all look alike."

5   Experiments and Evaluation on WordNet

We apply our basic level prediction method to WordNet, a lexical database of English [17]. It contains 155k words, organized into 117K synsets[3]. A synset can be seen as a set of words that denote the same concept. Synsets are connected to each other through the `hyponym` relation, which is an is-a relation. Each synset has a natural language description called a `gloss`. We train and test our approach on a subset of WordNet consisting of 518 manually labelled noun synsets.

WordNet presents a particularly interesting test ground considering (1) the depth of its hierarchy, making the identification of the basic level challenging and valuable, (2) its wide scope that includes all concepts that Rosch used in her orig-inal experiments, and (3) its widespread use: basic level predictions in WordNet are valuable for all knowledge graphs that have been linked to WordNet.

We extract lexical and frequency features from WordNet. For frequency fea-tures, we use Google Ngrams[4], which provides data about how often a phrase – or "ngram" – appears in the Google Books corpus. This is expressed as the num-ber of times a given ngram appears in a given year, divided by the total number

---

[3] https://wordnet.princeton.edu/documentation/wnstats7wn.
[4] https://books.google.com/ngrams.

of ngrams in that year. In the present study, the two most recent years of the Google Books corpus 'English 2012' were used, which comprises of 3.5K books in the English language. Table 1 details how each feature was operationalized. For feature selection details we refer to our preliminary work in [10].

Table 1. Operationalization of structural, lexical and frequency features

Type	Feature name and operationalization
Struct.	**nr_of_hyponyms** Hyponym, the main is-a relation in WordNet, is transitive. We count the nr. of synsets in the complete hyponym-tree under the synset
Struct.	**nr_of_direct_hypernyms** Hypernym is the inverse relation of hyponym. As WordNet allows for multiple classification, some synsets have multiple hypernyms. We count the number of hypernyms directly above the synset
Struct.	**nr_of_partOfs** The number of holonym plus meronym relations of the synset
Struct.	**depth_in_hierarchy** The number of hyponyms in the shortest path from the synset to WordNet's root noun *entity.n.01*
Struct.	**gloss_length** The number of characters in the synset gloss
Lex.	**word_length_min** The n.r of characters of the shortest word in the synset
Lex.	**polysemy_max** The number of synsets in which the most polysemous word of the synset appears
Lex.	**nr_of_synonyms** The number of words in the synset
Freq.	**G.Ngrams_score_mean** the mean ngram score of the words in the synset

5.1 Training and Test Set

The training and test set consists of synsets from three branches of WordNet: the complete hierarchies under the synsets *hand_tool.n.01*, *edible_fruit.n.01* and *musical_instrument.n.01*. In this paper, we will refer to these three hierarchies as "domains." They correspond to three of the six non-biological hierarchies that Rosch reported in her seminal paper on basic level effects [22]. The WordNet hierarchies used in the present paper, however, are larger than Rosch's experimental data; they consist of 150+ concepts per domain, whereas Rosch's hierarchies consisted of 10 concepts each. What we call "domains" should not be confused with the topic-, usage- and geographical domain classification that WordNet provides for a small subset of synsets. All synsets in the training and test set were labelled by three annotators (the authors), with substantial inter-rater agreement (Krippendorf's $\alpha = 0.72$). They labelled 518 synsets, of which 161 as basic level.

6 Results

6.1 Comparing Algorithms, Baselines and Annotators

We measure classification performance using a 10-fold cross-validation setup. In cases there the three annotators disagreed on the label, we use the majority vote. Table 2 lists (median) performance for five classifiers, which we implemented using an off-the-shelve toolkit[5]. We report Accuracy and Cohen's Kappa (κ) – two measures commonly used for classification tasks – as well as Precision and Recall - two Information Retrieval measures, for which we consider basic level as the positive class. The best performing algorithm on all measures is the Random Forest, which we ran with the SMOTE algorithm to deal with class imbalance. Differences between algorithms are small and not in all cases significant.

Table 2. Classification performance on entire training- and test set.

		Accuracy	Kappa	Precision	Recall
Classifiers: (median values)	LDA	0.81	0.59	0.73	0.74
	Decision tree	0.77	0.49	0.68	0.61
	K-nearest neighbors	0.70	0.37	0.59	0.63
	SVM	0.81	0.59	0.74	0.74
	Random Forest	0.82	0.61	0.75	0.76
Manual:	Basic level at fixed depth	0.64	0.17	0.50	0.36
Randomly guessing:	All as basic level	0.36	0.00	0.36	1.00
	None as basic level	0.64	0.00	NaN	0.00
	50% as basic level	0.49	−0.02	0.35	0.49
	36% as basic level	0.54	0.01	0.37	0.37
Random Forest using labels: (median values)	Of annotator 1	0.83	0.60	0.75	0.75
	Of annotator 2	0.83	0.63	0.79	0.73
	Of annotator 3	0.81	0.58	0.72	0.76
	On which all agreed	0.88	0.73	0.78	0.85
	Majority vote	0.82	0.61	0.75	0.76

There are, to the best of our knowledge, no existing baseline algorithms that we can compare our results to. Instead, to place our results in context, we do two things. First, we compare the performance of the classifiers to an intuitive manual method that is based on the most important feature in the classification (as will be discussed in Sect. 6.2): depth in the hierarchy. We pick the level in the hierarchy with the highest number of basic level synsets (by looking at the training- and test set) and label all synsets at that level as basic level. This leads to a relatively high accuracy of .64 but a low κ of 0.17 (Table 2), both lower

---

[5] The CARET Library in R http://topepo.github.io/caret/index.html.

than any of the classifiers ($p <= 0.01$). Second, we examine how far we would get with randomly assigning a percentage of the synsets to the basic level class: 100%, 0%, 50% or 36% (where the latter is the true percentage of basic level synsets in the data set). As expected, when we label all synsets as basic level, we achieve perfect recall; when we assign none of them to basic level, we achieve a high accuracy, which is on par with the accuracy of the manual method. All random guessing scenarios lead to a κ value of around zero (Table 2).

Next, we compare the three annotators, by looking at prediction performance when training and testing on manual labels given by annotator 1, 2 or 3. We find no significant differences here, which is good: it should not matter which annotator was chosen. Finally, we compare performance when training and testing is done on the majority vote of the annotators versus performance on only those synsets where all three annotators agree on the label (417 out of 518 synsets). We observe that performance is higher on the agreed labels, with median κ increasing from 0.61 to 0.73 (although this is not significant, $p = 0.06$).

To gain insights into what causes the observed difference between performance on agreed versus all synsets, we train a model on the agreed synsets (417 synsets), and test it on the synsets for which there was disagreement (101 synsets). When we evaluate this using the majority vote labels, κ drops to 0.06, an almost random classification. We hypothesize that concepts on which humans disagree are inherently difficult to classify because maybe there are no clear basic level effects in these cases. Concepts on which the annotators disagreed were, for example, rarely seen (by our annotators) fruits like the sweetsop, and the sibling concepts raisin, prune and dried apricot. The concept of berry was also a cause for disagreement, where one annotator labelled berry as basic level, while the other two labelled its hyponyms strawberry and blackberry as basic level. Future work will have to clarify whether basic level effects exist in these cases.

For brevity, in further experiments we only report κ, as this measure takes into account chance agreement [5], of the Random Forest and the manual method, trained and tested on majority vote labels. Other measures and the full results of the 10-fold cross validation will be part of the online supplementary data.

6.2   Basic Level Prediction Within and Across Domains

In Table 3a, we compare prediction performance of local models trained and tested on a single domain (Tools, Fruit, or Music) to performance of a global model on the entire data set (All). Results in Tools and Fruit are good (median $\kappa = 0.84$ and 0.79 resp.), while Music is more challenging (median $\kappa = 0.50$). The global model, with a median κ of 0.61, performs lower than most of the single domain models, suggesting that (some) features may not transfer well from one domain to another. This makes sense, as the distributions of feature values differ a lot over the three domains. For example, the mean gloss length is 20% longer in the Music hierarchy of WordNet. And, in our data set, part-of relations are rare except in the Fruit hierarchy. Table 3b lists feature importance in the global model and the single domain models, where the feature with the highest weight is ranked 1. The lists are relatively stable, with some marked differences, such as the importance of the gloss length and the number of partOf relations.

The manual method performs well on single domains (κ between 0.36 and 0.78, Table 3a) but badly when domains are pooled ($\kappa = 0.17$). Apparently, within a domain, basic level synsets reside largely at the same level; what this level is, varies per domain.

Finally, we examine what we consider the most realistic scenario: to predict basic level synsets in a new domain, for which we don't have manually labelled examples in the training set. To simulate this situation, we train on two domains, and test on a third. For example, we train on tools+fruit and test on music. Table 4 shows that performance of the Random Forest drops dramatically to κ values between -0.10 and 0.37 depending on which domain is considered as new. The manual method is even worse (κ between 0.02 and -0.42) because it relies on the level with the most basic level concepts, which is different in each domain.

To improve transfer learning, we include a per-domain normalization step: we divide the feature value by the mean feature value within the domain. Table 4 shows that normalization of structural features leads to a substantial performance gain (κ increases to $0.32 - 0.62$ depending on the domain). Normalization of lexical or frequency features is not beneficial or even harmful to the results.

Table 3. Comparing local models (Tools, Fruit, Music) to a global model.

(a) Classification performance

Random Forest (median (κ))	
All	0.61
Tools	0.84
Fruit	0.79
Music	0.50
Manual method (κ)	
All	0.17
Tools	0.78
Fruit	0.72
Music	0.36

(b) Features ranked in order of importance

Feature	All	Tool	Fruit	Music
depth_in_hierarchy	1	1	1	2
G.Ngram_score	2	2	3	3
gloss_length	3	4	4	1
word_length_min	4	5	6	4
polysemy_max	5	3	5	7
nr_of_partOfs	6	8	2	8
nr_of_hyponyms	7	6	8	5
nr_of_synonyms	8	7	7	6
nr_of_direct_hypern.	9	9	9	9

Table 4. Performance (κ) in a new domain, with and without normalization.

Tested on:	Trained on:	RF	Manual	RF with normalization of features:		
				Structural	Lexical	Frequency
Tools	Fruit+Music	0.37	0.02	0.62	0.43	0.34
Fruit	Tools+Music	-0.10	-0.42	0.41	0.06	-0.13
Music	Tools+Fruit	0.35	-0.01	0.32	0.21	0.34

6.3   Towards a Data Set of Basic Level Synsets in WordNet

We provide an RDF dataset of basic level concepts identified in the entire noun hierarchy of WordNet, using our approach with the best performing settings, i.e. a Random Forest trained on manually labelled synsets on which all annotators agreed, with per-domain normalization of structural features. With this data set, we aim to enable research into the use of basic level concepts in applications.

Per-domain normalization in a large knowledge graph like WordNet is non-trivial, as it requires a decision on what constitutes a domain. In our training and test set, this decision was intuitively easy: it consists of three disjoint branches, that correspond to three of Rosch' high level categories. To split the 82K nouns in WordNet into domains is especially complicated due to many cases of multiple inheritance and its irregular structure with leave nodes at every level of the hierarchy. We have implemented an ad hoc algorithm to split up WordNet into domains. It consists of 3 rules: (1) subbranches with between 50 and 300 nodes are treated as a single domain, (2) concepts with multiple parents from different domains are assigned to the smallest of those domains and (3) subbranches with less than 50 nodes are grouped together in a domain with their parent node.

To make the training set more representative, we manually labelled an additional 18 synsets; those synsets in the WordNet hierarchy that are between the three domains and WordNet's top noun *entity.n.01*. Inter-rater agreement on this set was perfect, as all of them are by definition above the basic level.

The above results in an RDF data set of 10K basic level synsets.

7   Discussion, Future Work and Conclusion

We present a method to classify concepts from a conceptual hierarchy into basic level and not-basic level. We extract three types of concept features: lexical features, structural features and frequency features.

We show that, based on these features, a classifier can accurately predict the basic level within a single domain. The performance of a global model across multiple domains is slightly lower. Predictions in a new, previously unseen domain are meaningful only after a normalization step. Normalization can be straightforward, but does require a modularisation of the knowledge graph into domains.

A simple manual method – choosing a fixed depth in the hierarchy as basic level – gives reasonable results when applied to a single domain. When applied to a data set including multiple domains, or to a new domain, it doesn't produce meaningful results. We conclude that, also for the manual method, modularisation is a key aspect of basic level prediction. For small to medium size knowledge graphs, it may be feasible to do the modularization manually.

All three types of features proved important for the prediction. We believe that further improvements are possible from inclusion of additional frequency features. The Google Ngram scores that we used as frequency features gave a strong signal, and they did not need per-domain normalization. Other frequency features could include: the frequency of occurrence of words in specific corpora such as children's books or language-learning resources, and the frequency of occurrence of concepts in other conceptual hierarchies. WordNet contains also sense frequency counts, but they are available for less than 10% of our concepts.

A post-hoc discussion among the human annotators learned that for most concepts labelling was straightforward. A few cases were hard and annotators would have preferred to not make a choice between basic level or not. If it is true that there are concepts to which the basic level theory does not apply, it would be worthwhile to classify them a such, which would result in a classification into basic-level, not-basic-level and not-applicable. Concepts that are difficult to label for human annotators seem to be more challenging for the classifier as well. Applications will gain most from a correct classification of the straightforward cases, for which basic level effects can be expected to be strongest. In future work we intend to measure basic level effects for a larger set of concepts in a crowd-sourcing environment.

We ran our method with best performing settings on all noun concepts in WordNet and provide this as an RDF data set for reuse and further research.

References

1. Belohlavek, R., Trnecka, M.: Basic level in formal concept analysis: interesting concepts and psychological ramifications. In: Proceedings of IJCAI, pp. 1233–1239 (2013)
2. Brown, R.: How shall a thing be called? Psychol. Rev. **65**(1), 14 (1958)
3. Cai, Y., et al.: Context-aware ontologies generation with basic level concepts from collaborative tags. Neurocomputing **208**, 25–38 (2016)
4. Clerkin, P., Cunningham, P., Hayes, C.: Ontology discovery for the semantic web using hierarchical clustering. In: Semantic Web Mining, vol. 27 (2001)
5. Cohen, J.: A coefficient of agreement for nominal scales. Educ. Psychol. Measur. **20**(1), 37–46 (1960)
6. Corter, J.E., Gluck, M.A.: Explaining basic categories: feature predictability and information. Psychol. Bull. **111**(2), 291 (1992)
7. Golder, S.A., Huberman, B.: The structure of collaborative tagging systems. J. Inf. Sci. **32** (2005)
8. Green, R.: Vocabulary alignment via basic level concepts. Final Report 2003 OCLC / ALISE Library and Information Science Research Grant Project (2006)
9. Hoekstra, R., Breuker, J., Di Bello, M., Boer, A.: The LKIF core ontology of basic legal concepts. In: CEUR Workshop Proceedings, vol. 321, pp. 43–63 (2007)
10. Hollink, L., Bilgin, A., van Ossenbruggen, J.: Is it a fruit, an apple or a granny smith? predicting the basic level in a concept hierarchy. arXiv:1910.12619 (2019)
11. Johnson, K.E., Mervis, C.B.: Effects of varying levels of expertise on the basic level of categorization. J. Exp. Psychol. **126**(3), 248–277 (1997)
12. Jones, G.V.: Identifying basic categories. Psychol. Bull. **94**(3), 423–428 (1983)
13. Lakoff, G.: Women, Fire, and Dangerous Things. University of Chicago Press, Chicago (2008)
14. Lemaitre, G., Heller, L.M.: Evidence for a basic level in a taxonomy of everyday action sounds. Exp. Brain Res. **226**, 253–264 (2013)
15. Mark, D.M., Smith, B., Tversky, B.: Ontology and geographic objects: an empirical study of cognitive categorization. In: International Conference on Spatial Information Theory, pp. 283–298 (1999)

16. Mathews, A., Xie, L., He, X.: Choosing basic-level concept names using visual and language context. In: 2015 IEEE Winter Conference on Applications of Computer Vision, pp. 595–602. IEEE (2015)
17. Miller, G.A.: WordNet: a lexical database for English. Commun. ACM **38**(11), 39–41 (1995)
18. Murphy, G.L., Smith, E.E.: Basic-level superiority in picture categorization. J. Verbal Learn. Verbal Behav. **21**(1), 1–20 (1982)
19. Ordonez, V., Deng, J., Choi, Y., Berg, A.C., Berg, T.L.: From large scale image categorization to entry-level categories. In: Proceedings of ICCV, pp. 2768–2775 (2013)
20. Peroni, S., Motta, E., d'Aquin, M.: Identifying key concepts in an ontology, through the integration of cognitive principles with statistical and topological measures. In: Proceedings of the 3rd Asian Semantic Web Conference, ASWC, pp. 242–256 (2008)
21. Rifkin, A.: Evidence for a basic level in event taxonomies. Mem. Cogn. **13**(6), 538–556 (1985). https://doi.org/10.3758/BF03198325
22. Rosch, E., Mervis, C.B., Gray, W.D., Johnson, D.M., Boyes-Braem, P.: Basic objects in natural categories. Cogn. Psychol. **8**(3), 382–439 (1976)
23. Rosch, E., Simpson, C., Miller, R.S.: Structural bases of typicality effects. J. Exp. Psychol. Hum. Percept. Perform. **2**(4), 491–502 (1976)
24. Smith, E.: Effects of familiarity on stimulus recognition and categorization. J. Exp. Psychol. **74**(3), 324–332 (1967)
25. Tanaka, J.W., Taylor, M.: Object categories and expertise: is the basic level in the eye of the beholder? Cogn. Psychol. **23**(3), 457–482 (1991)
26. Uschold, M., King, M.: Towards a methodology for building ontologies. In: Proceedings of the Workshop on Basic Ontological Issues in Knowledge Sharing, held in conjunction with IJCAI (1995)
27. Zeng, M.: Knowledge organization systems (KOS). Knowl. Organ. **35**, 160–182 (2008). https://doi.org/10.5771/0943-7444-2008-2-3-160

Validating SAREF in a Smart Home Environment

Roderick van der Weerdt[1]([envelope]) [iD], Victor de Boer[1] [iD], Laura Daniele[2] [iD],
and Barry Nouwt[2] [iD]

[1] Vrije Universiteit Amsterdam, Amsterdam, The Netherlands
{r.p.vander.weerdt,v.de.boer}@vu.nl
[2] TNO - Netherlands Organization for Applied Scientific Research,
The Hague, The Netherlands
{laura.daniele,barry.nouwt}@tno.nl

Abstract. SAREF is an ontology created to enable interoperability between smart devices. While the IoT community has shown interest and understanding of SAREF as a means for interoperability, there is a lack in the literature of practical examples to implement SAREF in real applications. In order to validate the practical implementation of SAREF we perform two experiments. First we map IoT data available in a smart home into RDF using SAREF. In the second part of the paper an IoT environment is created by using the Knowledge Engine, a framework created to allow communication between smart devices, operating on Raspberry Pi's emulating IoT devices, where the communication of the IoT devices is performed by sharing knowledge represented with SAREF. These experiments demonstrate that SAREF is an ontology that is successfully applicable in different situations, with data-mapping showing that SAREF is able to represent the information of different smart devices and by using the Knowledge Engine showing that SAREF can enable interoperability between smart devices.

Keywords: IoT · Ontology · Data mapping · Smart home.

1 Introduction

Over the last years more and more companies have started making smart devices that can be connected to the Internet of Things (IoT). Connecting multiple devices brings the promise that all those devices are now able to interact with each other in meaningful ways. Unfortunately the reality is that devices are not nearly as interconnected as one would want [1], often devices can only be accessed from specific (vendor-based) apps, other times the devices are not able to communicate because they do not speak the same language. In order to make the interoperability between smart devices within IoT possible the Smart Applications REFerence ontology (SAREF) has been created [2], an ontology specifically designed to encompass the information that smart devices need to exchange in order to have meaningful interactions.

© Springer Nature Switzerland AG 2021
E. Garoufallou and M.-A. Ovalle-Perandones (Eds.): MTSR 2020, CCIS 1355, pp. 35–46, 2021.
https://doi.org/10.1007/978-3-030-71903-6_4

SAREF has been validated before [3,4] to determine the quality of the ontology. But until now there has not been a practical implementation of the SAREF ontology, to validate if it satisfies requirements needed to map real data from real devices. The goal of this paper is to create an example of said implementation, validating the ontology in two ways, its ability to express all the information available from multiple smart devices in a home and its ability to enable interoperability by representing messages in a meaningful manner allowing for communication between smart devices.

To achieve the first goal we map data collected in a smart home (Sect. 3) into RDF using SAREF. For the second goal the Knowledge Engine is proposed to validate the effectiveness of using SAREF for communication (Sect. 4). The paper will start with describing the SAREF ontology and related research.

2   Related Work

To provide a background to our experiments we will first present an in depth examination of the SAREF ontology, followed by three related ontologies and lastly other validation studies using competency questions to validate ontologies.

2.1   SAREF

The Smart Applications REFerence ontology (SAREF) is a reference ontology for IoT applications (https://saref.etsi.org/) [5]. Its development started in 2013, when the European Commission, in collaboration with the European Telecommunication Standardization Institute (ETSI), launched an initiative to build a common ontology in close collaboration with the smart appliances industry[1] [2]. In a fragmented landscape of IoT standards, platforms and technologies across different vertical domains [6,7], SAREF was created as a shared model of consensus that could enable the communication among various IoT devices from different manufacturers that use different protocols and standards [8]. The first proof-of-concept solution based on SAREF was demonstrated and implemented in 2017 on existing commercial products in the energy domain[2] [4]. SAREF is published as a series of ETSI technical specifications, consisting of a modular framework that comprises a generic core ontology for IoT [5] and 10 domain-specific extensions (ETSI TS 103 410, parts 1–10), such as SAREF for Energy, Buildings and Cities, amongst others. The SAREF framework is maintained and evolved by ETSI and experts from several European organizations that successfully collaborate with each other[3]. One of the latest supported initiatives is the

---

[1] https://ec.europa.eu/digital-single-market/en/blog/new-standard-smart-appliances-smart-home.

[2] https://ec.europa.eu/digital-single-market/en/news/digitalising-energy-sector-common-language-consumer-centric-world.

[3] See, for example, https://portal.etsi.org/STF/STFs/STF-HomePages/STF534, https://portal.etsi.org/STF/STFs/STF-HomePages/STF566 and https://portal.etsi.org/STF/STFs/STF-HomePages/STF578.

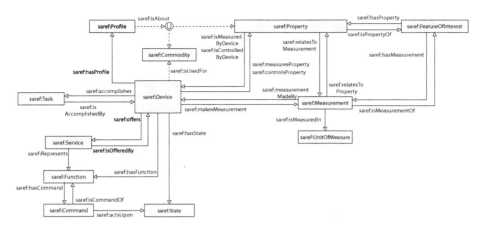

Fig. 1. Overview of the SAREF ontology (Image taken from: https://saref.etsi.org/core/v3.1.1/#Figure_1).

development of an open portal for the SAREF community and industry stake-holders, so that they can contribute directly to the SAREF evolution (https://forge.etsi.org/rep/SAREF).

Figure 1 shows an overview of the main classes and relationships in SAREF. In total SAREF contains 81 classes, 35 object properties and 5 data properties. The starting point is the concept of *Device*, which is defined as a tangible object designed to accomplish a particular *Task*. In order to accomplish this task, the device performs a *Function*. For example, a temperature sensor is a device of type saref:Sensor, is designed for tasks such as saref:Comfort, saref:WellBeing or saref:EnergyEfficiency, and performs a saref:SensingFunction. Functions have commands. A *Command* is a directive that a device needs to support to perform a certain function. Depending on the function(s) it performs, a device can be found in a corresponding *State*. A device that wants (a certain set of) its function(s) to be discoverable, registerable, and remotely controllable by other devices in the network can expose these functions as a *Service*. A device can also have a *Profile*, which is a specification to collect information about a certain *Property* or *Commodity* (e.g. Energy or Water) for optimizing their usage in the home/building in which the device is located. A *Property* is defined as anything that can be sensed, measured or controlled by a device, and is associated to measurements. For example, a temperature sensor measures a property of type saref:Temperature. A *Measurement* is the measured value made over a property and must be associated to an unit of measure and a timestamp. The *Feature of Interest* concept further allows to represent the context of a measurement, i.e., any real world entity from which a property is measured. For example, whether the measured temperature is that of a room or of a person. A more detailed description of the SAREF classes and properties can be found in [5].

2.2 Related Ontologies

The Semantic Sensor Network (SSN) ontology, was specifically created for the modeling of sensors and their observations[9]. This strict focus on sensors allows for a modular use of the ontology with other ontologies. A sensor is defined as "anything that observes", which means it does not include all the different kinds of smart devices that a smart home offers. The Sensor, Observation, Sample, and Actuator (SOSA) ontology is an extension and partial replacement of SSN created to model "the interaction between the entities involved in the acts of observation, actuation, and sampling"[10]. Because SSN was considered to rigid SOSA was created to be more flexible, having 13 concepts and 21 properties compared to the 41 concepts and 39 object properties of SSN.

The Web of Things Thing Description (TD) is a newer ontology that was also created by W3C [11]. This ontology models the metadata of the devices instead of the measurements. The creators envision that every smart device will its own TD to serve as identification and as a starting point for interaction with the device, similar to a index page of a website. But it lacks the representation of the measurements made by the devices that is needed for our experiments.

2.3 Competency Questions for Validation

Validation of an ontology can be done by creating a scenario and formulating a set of competency questions. Competency questions are proposed as a way to informally define requirements for an ontology, the resulting ontology should be able to answer all of the competency questions to prove it is the correct ontology to use in this scenario [12].

Competency questions have been used to validate SAREF before, as demonstrated in the research by Moreira et al. [4]. In their work they created a model that maps a knowledge graph using the SSN ontology into a knowledge graph using the SAREF ontology. Using an example situation of a wind sensor represented using the SSN ontology they were able to map the data to a knowledge graph, but were not able to keep all of the information that was available in the original representation. Competency questions were used to define the requirements that the ontologies required and showed that the new knowledge graph did not retain enough information from the original. The experiment they performed used an example specifically created for SSN, in this paper we will use data that comes from smart devices in a home setting, which is what SAREF was developed for and should therefore allow a better evaluation of SAREF.

Another example of competency questions being used as a tool to select different ontologies can be found in [3]. Bajaj et al. use the competency questions they define to determine which classes an ontology requires to fit to their requirements. For example SAREF was rejected by the authors as a suitable ontology because it lacked a class to define the concept of location. Since then a new addition to the SAREF ontology has been the Feature of Interest class, which allows for exactly such a definition.

Sagar et al. [13] extend the SOSA/SSN ontology in order to allow for smart sensors, sensors that are able to select and run different algorithms resulting in different data, to be modelled accurately. They create 13 competency questions and based on those reject existing ontologies, including SAREF. The S3N ontology that they propose was able to resolve all the competency questions. Instead of trying to model the algorithms behind "smarter" observations the decision was made to only look at the output of the devices for our experiment since this is the relevant information that we have available. Similarly we only look at the output of a thermometer and not at the intricate ways the device measures the temperature of the room.

3   Mapping Data Sources

The main purpose of SAREF is to enable interoperability between different devices and services [5]. In order to validate SAREF this experiment will focus on whether SAREF is capable of expressing all of the information from a smart home by mapping the smart devices to a knowledge graph using SAREF.

3.1   Method

This experiment will take data from 33 smart devices in a smart home and transforms it into a knowledge graph using the SAREF ontology. The smart home is part of a pilot from a large construction company experimenting with adding smart devices to the houses they build. We started with removing duplicate smart devices that were used multiple times in the house such as the thermometer in the living room and in the bedroom. This resulted in nine data sources that will be used for this experiment:

- *current temperature*, measurement of the room temperature in degrees Celsius.
- *CO2 levels*, measurement of the ppm CO2 in a room.
- *last time movement detected*, marks the most recent moment (timestamp) that movement was detected in a room. Used to determine when residents are at home.
- *first time movement detected*, marks the beginning (timestamp) of new movement detected in a room. Used to determine when residents are at home.
- *motion detected*, returns a yes or no state based on whether the sensor detected motion.
- *presence detected*, returns a yes or no state based on whether the sensor detected presence, based on the CO2 levels in a room.
- *humidity*, measurement of the percentage of humidity in a room.
- *smart switch actuator*, an actuator that can be turned on or off by sending it an on/off command.
- *target temperature*, the desired temperature of a room in degrees Celsius, controlled by the thermostat.

All the sensors send updated information every five seconds, which is recorded with a timestamp. The complexity of the data from the sensors differs from the "simpler" *thermometer* to the more elaborate *last time movement detected*. As was discussed in Sect. 2.3 we only focus on the output of the device and not the internal calculations.

The combination of these data sources can be used in multiple scenarios, a possible scenario would be to adjust the room temperature when there are no people present. Using a combination of the *first time movement detected* data and the *last time movement detected* data, which in turn is based on the *motion detected* and *presence detected* data, we can determine whether a home is occupied. When there are no people present the target temperature could be set to a lower setting, meaning lower as opposed to the target temperature when there are people present. When the current temperature is below the target temperature a command can be send to the heating system of the home (in the case that one of the smart switch actuators is connected to a heating system) shutting it down, this would allow a home to only be heated when it is needed.

3.2   Implementation

Not all classes shown in Fig. 1 are used in the mapping for a data source. For example a command that is sent to a smart actuator will not be using the `saref:Measurement` class. The Technical Specification [5] describing the SAREF ontology is used to make a selection of relevant classes for each smart device. The relevant classes for each device can be seen in Table 1. Most mappings are easily performed by selecting the straightforward SAREF class, for example for the `saref:Property` class in the mapping of the thermometer we can use its subclass `saref:Temperature` to mean that the measurement in this graph pattern relates to temperature.

For the sake of clarity this paper only contains mappings for two data sources and a summary of the special cases where the decisions made need an explanation. The complete mapping of all the data sources can be found online[4] where all the mappings are represented as triples.

In Depth Mapping Explanations. The two examples that are chosen to be clarified are the data from the thermometer and the data from the CO2 sensor. The thermometer mapping is an example of a mapping where all the relevant classes are already available. For the CO2 sensor two new subclasses have to be added. The OM1.8: Units of Measure ontology [14] was chosen to use to represent the units of measure, as suggested in [5].

Thermometer. The thermometer makes a measurement of the temperature in a room. The mapping requires the:

– `saref:Measurement` class for the value of the temperature and timestamp.

---

[4] https://github.com/RoderickvanderWeerdt/IoT_data_SAREF_mappings.

Table 1. Overview of the classes used to model each data source.

	ct	Cl	ftmd	ltmd	md	pd	h	ssa	tt
saref:Measurement	x	x					x		x
saref:UnitOfMeasure	x	x					x		
saref:Property	x	x	x	x	x	x	x	x	x
saref:FeatureOfInterest	x	x	x	x	x	x	x	x	x
saref:Device	x	x	x	x	x	x	x	x	x
saref:Commodity									
saref:Profile									
saref:Task	x	x	x	x	x	x	x	x	x
saref:Service								x	
saref:Function	x	x	x	x	x	x	x	x	x
saref:Command								x	
saref:State			x	x	x	x	x		

legend ct: *current temperature*, Cl: *CO2 levels*, ftmd: *first time movement detected*, ltmd: *last time movement detected*, md: *motion detected*, pd: *presence detected*, h: *humidity*, ssa: *smart switch actuator*, tt: *target temperature*.

- saref:UnitOfMeasure class for the unit of the measurement, we can use the subclass saref:TemperatureUnit and om:degree_Celcius as its instance.
- saref:Property class to map what the measurement is measuring, in this case temperature, so we can use its subclass saref:Temperature.
- saref:FeatureOfInterest class represents the feature of interest, in this case the room of which the measurements are made. The URI would represent the name of the room.
- saref:Device class to represent the device itself that is making the measurements, we can use the subclass saref:Sensor.
- saref:Task class to represent the goal of saref:Comfort for the user.
- saref:Function class to define the function as a saref:SensingFunction.

CO2 sensor. The CO2 sensor makes a measurement of the CO2 levels in a room. The mapping requires the:

- saref:Measurement class for the CO2 levels and the timestamp.
- saref:UnitOfMeasure, SAREF does not have a unit of measure subclass for CO2, a new subclass of UnitOfMeasure is created to represent CO2 measurements and the parts per million unit of OM1.8 was used as unit instance, resulting in the additional triple:
  om:parts_per_million rdf:type ex:CO2Unit
- saref:Property, in this case CO2 levels, for which a class in not available in SAREF, but can be easily added:
  <PROPERTY_URI> rdf:type ex:CO2
- saref:FeatureOfInterest, similar to the thermometer mapping.

- `saref:Device`, similar to the thermometer mapping.
- `saref:Task` class to represent the goal of the `saref:WellBeing` of the user.
- `saref:Function`, similar to the thermometer mapping.

Aside from the two cases described above there was one other case where extra work was required. Just like with the CO2 levels measurements the humidity measurements requires a new subclass for `saref:UnitOfMeasure` to express that it is a humidity measure. It uses the OM1.8 instance for percentage: `om:percent rdf:type ex:HumidityUnit`

4   Sharing Data with SAREF

This part of the paper is designed to test the capability of SAREF to enable interoperability between different devices. First the scenario will be detailed and the competency questions will be formulated accordingly. To achieve interoperability, multiple separate devices should be setup that 1) do not have direct or hard links between them and 2) communicate exclusively using SAREF. To the best of our knowledge no other ontology-based interoperability framework in smart homes allows for the data to remain at the source where it is produced. Our findings should generalize to other interoperability frameworks.

The Knowledge Engine will be shortly described in Sect. 4.2, followed by the implementation and its results.

4.1   Competency Questions

For the sake of simplicity, the paper uses an simple scenario of a temperature controlled room, meaning we will need: information about what room the information is about, information about the temperature of the room, information about the desired temperature and the possibility to control the temperature of the room. Although more competency questions can be defined based on this scenario, we define here the following three competency questions as an example:

1. What is the temperature of a specific room?
2. Is this higher or lower than the threshold temperature?
3. Should the heater be turned on or off?

4.2   Knowledge Engine

The Knowledge Engine is a framework that allows multiple IoT devices to exchange knowledge in an interoperable way within a network. It is used by adding a smart connector to each device and registering this smart connector in the service directory, a visualization can be found in Fig. 2. The smart connector provides two functions to achieve interoperability: translation and discovery. It *translates* between a common ontology and the specific language of the device it is connected to, allowing devices from different vendors to understand each

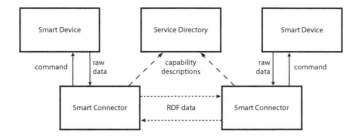

Fig. 2. Visualization of the data flow in the Knowledge Engine.

other. It also dynamically *discovers* other smart connectors that can supply relevant data, which prevents hard links between devices. These two functions of the smart connector allow connections between devices in a network to be solely based on concepts and relations from a common ontology. This means that any device in the network can potentially be replaced by a similar one from a different vendor without loss of function i.e. they are interoperable with each other.

Both the translation and the discovery functions of the smart connector require configuration. Regarding the translation, this configuration consists of custom code provided by a developer that maps the specific device language to the common ontology. For discovery, the smart connector needs to be configured with the capabilities of the device (i.e. the *knowledge demand* and *knowledge supply*). The demand describes (in terms of the common ontology) the data that the device requires to function, while the supply describes the data that the device can provide to other devices. These capability descriptions use a SPARQL-like syntax to describe graph patterns, see Fig. 3. Apart from this configuration, the discovery function also requires a component called "Service Directory" to which all smart connectors in the network register themselves and from which they can retrieve the other smart connectors currently available.

A single smart connector is an extended version of the Apache Jena Fuseki triple store that is not used for actually storing the triples, but for its reasoner to orchestrate the knowledge exchange process. This reasoner uses rules that are based on the configuration (i.e. capabilities) of all available smart connectors in the network about which every smart connector regularly retrieves updates from the service directory. Whenever a device publishes or requests data, the smart connectors make sure that it is received by or from the correct device. Mutually, the smart connectors use a combination of SPARQL and a publish/subscribe mechanism to communicate.

For example, a thermometer device would have a supply capability description, like the one shown in Fig. 3b. The thermostat requesting this information uses a demand capability description that looks identical, because both supply and demand capability descriptions follow the same SPARQL-like structure, multiple triples with variables for the data that it either demands or supplies.

The Knowledge Engine can use any ontology to structure the knowledge that it shares (both capability descriptions and RDF data). For this experiment

```
@prefix rdf: <http://www.w3.org/1999/02/22-rdf-syntax-ns#>
@prefix rdfs: <http://www.w3.org/2000/01/rdf-schema#>
@prefix sosa: <http://www.w3.org/ns/sosa/>
@prefix saref: <https://saref.etsi.org/core/>
@prefix ex: <http://example.org/>
```

```
?id rdf:type ex:Room .
ex:Room rdfs:subClassOf saref:FeatureOfInt...
?id ex:hasName "Room1" .
?act saref:hasFeatureOfInterest ?id .
?act saref:actsUpon saref:OnOffState .
?act rdf:type ?command .
```

```
?id rdf:type ex:Room .
ex:Room rdfs:subClassOf saref:FeatureOfInterest .
?id ex:hasName "Room1" .
?obs rdf:type saref:Measurement .
?obs saref:isMeasurementOf ?id .
?obs saref:isMeasuredIn saref:TemperatureUnit .
?obs saref:hasValue ?temp .
```

(a)   (b)

Fig. 3. Two capability descriptions that can be used with the Knowledge Engine.

SAREF was used, but it could also work with different ontologies like SOSA/SSN [10]. By using the Knowledge Engine we can validate SAREF by implementing it for the knowledge that is exchanged within its communications.

4.3   Implementation

The smart connectors run on Raspberry Pi 4B's, allowing easy configuration relevant to the device it is connected to with a config file[5]. The configuration requires a name and short description of the device and allows for inclusion of their capability descriptions. For this experiment, the smart device and smart connector are on one device with the devices being controlled with a python script that "makes" the devices smart allowing for communication with the Apache Fuseki server. A separate laptop runs the service directory and lastly, a WiFi router allows the smart connectors to connect to each other and to the service directory, as represented by the dashed lines in Fig. 2.

The first Raspberry Pi functions as a thermometer. It has one knowledge supply containing the temperature measurements made by the connected thermometer and the room it is located in. This knowledge supply can be found in Fig. 3b, ?room is the name of the room and ?temp is the latest measurement of the temperature.

The second Raspberry Pi functions as a thermostat, it has an internal desired state for the temperature of this room which can be adjusted with the connected buttons. It demands the temperature of this room (knowledge demand in Fig. 3b) and supplies a command based on that current temperature (knowledge supply in Fig. 3a), if the current temperature is below the desired state the smart connector will send saref:OnCommand for ?command, if it is higher it will send saref:OffCommand.

The last Raspberry Pi represents a heating device, demanding a command for this room (knowledge demand in Fig. 3a). When the smart connector receives a saref:OnCommand it will turn on the heater (in this case the led light will turn on) and when it receives a saref:OffCommand it will turn it off.

---

[5] https://jena.apache.org/documentation/fuseki2/fuseki-configuration.html.

```
:Room1 rdf:type ex:Room .              :Room1 rdf:type ex:Room .
ex:Room rdfs:subClassOf saref:FeatureOfInt..  ex:Room rdfs:subClassOf saref:FeatureOfInterest .
:Room1 ex:hasName "Room1" .            :Room1 ex:hasName "Room1" .
:act1 saref:hasFeatureOfInterest :Room1 .  :obs1 rdf:type saref:Measurement .
:act1 saref:actsUpon saref:OnOffState .  :obs1 saref:isMeasurementOf :Room1 .
:act1 rdf:type saref:OnCommand .        :obs1 saref:isMeasuredIn saref:TemperatureUnit .
                                        :obs1 saref:hasValue "17.0" .
```

(a)   (b)

Fig. 4. Example of a graph pattern from the thermostat smart connector (a) and the thermometer smart connector (b) answering the competency questions.

When all three of these smart connectors communicate correctly they will be able to control the temperature in a room. Smart connector b will receive the temperature of the room from smart connector a, compare it with the desired temperature (which can be adjusted with its buttons) and based on that send either an on or off command towards smart connector c.

4.4 Answering the Competency Questions

In order to make all of the knowledge exchanges between the smart connectors possible two different capability descriptions are required, shown in Fig. 3.

Using the information from these devices we are able to answer all three of the competency questions. The graph patterns that are sent by the smart connector connected to the thermometer (Fig. 4b) answers the first question, the temperature of the room. The second competency question is answered internally in the smart connector connected to the thermostat and the third competency question is solved by the thermostat smart connector sending its graph pattern that is received by the third smart connector that interprets and either turns the heater off or, in the case of Fig. 4a, on.

5   Conclusion

In the first part of the paper we validated how data sources of a smart home scenario could be mapped to SAREF. We demonstrated that this can be done in a straightforward way. In the two cases were there were exceptions, as shown in Sect. 3.2 they were simple to add given the flexibility by design of SAREF. On the other hand, this could potentially lead to incompatibility issues if different people create their own extensions for similar situations. To that end, ETSI has recently created a open community portal (saref.etsi.org) where SAREF users can submit their contributions that will then be considered in the official standardization process to become part of new SAREF releases.

The second part of the paper showed a simple, practical implementation of SAREF using the Knowledge Engine, which is a promising framework that allows multiple IoT devices to exchange knowledge in an interoperable way within a network. The example used a scenario in which three devices shared knowledge to control the temperature of a room.

We acknowledge that the scenario presented in the paper is rather simple and more work in the immediate future is aimed at increasing the number and type of sensors in a more complex scenario than only heating the room, also considering more than one household. More future work could recreate the scenario we presented with other interoperability frameworks or using different ontologies.

Acknowledgements. This work is part of the Interconnect project (interconnect-project.eu/) which has received funding from the European Union's Horizon 2020 research and innovation program under grant agreement No 857237.

References

1. Hsu, C.L., Lin, J.C.C.: An empirical examination of consumer adoption of internet of things services: network externalities and concern for information privacy perspectives. Comput. Human Behav. **62**, 516–527 (2016)
2. Daniele, L., den Hartog, F., Roes, J.: Created in close interaction with the industry: the Smart Appliances REFerence (SAREF) ontology. In: Cuel, R., Young, R. (eds.) FOMI 2015. LNBIP, vol. 225, pp. 100–112. Springer, Cham (2015). https://doi.org/10.1007/978-3-319-21545-7_9
3. Bajaj, G., Agarwal, R., Singh, P., Georgantas, N., Issarny, V.: A Study of Existing Ontologies in the IoT-Domain (2017). arXiv preprint: arXiv:1707.00112
4. Moreira, J., et al.: Towards IoT Platforms' Integration Semantic Translations between W3C SSN and ETSI SAREF. In: SEMANTICS Workshops (2017)
5. ETSI TS: 103 264 V3.1.1, SartM2M; Smart Applications; Reference Ontology and oneM2M Mapping (2020)
6. ETSI TS: 103 375: SmartM2M; IoT Standards Landscape and Future Evolutions (2016)
7. ETSI TS: 103 376: SmartM2M; IoT LSP Use Cases and Standards Gaps (2016)
8. Daniele, L., Strabbing, W., Roelofsen, B., Aalberts, A., Stapersma, P.: Study on Ensuring Interoperability for Demand Side Flexibility. Technical report, European Commission (2018). https://doi.org/10.2759/26799
9. Compton, M., et al.: The SSN ontology of the W3C semantic sensor network incubator group. J. Web Semant. **17**, 25–32 (2012)
10. Janowicz, K., Haller, A., Cox, S.J., Le Phuoc, D., Lefrançois, M.: SOSA: a lightweight ontology for sensors, observations, samples, and actuators. J. Web Semant. **56**, 1–10 (2019)
11. W3C: Web of Things (WoT) Thing Description (2020). https://www.w3.org/TR/2020/REC-wot-thing-description-20200409/
12. Gruninger, M., Fox, M.: Methodology for the design and evaluation of ontologies. In: IJCAI 1995, Workshop on Basic Ontological Issues in Knowledge Sharing (1995)
13. Sagar, S., et al.: Modeling smart sensors on Top of SOSA/SSN and WoT TD with the semantic smart sensor network (S3N) modular ontology. In: 9th International Semantic Sensor Networks Workshop (2018)
14. Rijgersberg, H., van Assem, M., Top, J.: Ontology of units of measure and related concepts. Semant. Web **4**(1), 3–13 (2013)

An Approach for Representing and Storing RDF Data in Multi-model Databases

Simen Dyve Samuelsen, Nikolay Nikolov, Ahmet Soylu,
and Dumitru Roman$^{(\boxtimes)}$

SINTEF AS, Oslo, Norway
{simendyve.samuelsen,nikolay.nikolov,ahmet.soylu,dumitru.roman}@sintef.no

Abstract. The emergence of NoSQL multi-model databases, natively supporting scalable and unified storage and querying of various data models, presents new opportunities for storing and managing RDF data. In this paper, we propose an approach to store RDF data in multi-model databases. We identify various aspects of representing the RDF data structure into a multi-model data structure and discuss their advantages and disadvantages. Furthermore, we implement and evaluate the proposed approach in a prototype using ArangoDB—a popular multi-model database.

Keywords: RDF · Multi-modal databases · Storage

1 Introduction

The adoption of the linked data paradigm and the RDF format has grown significantly over the past decade. Even though RDF is getting a wider acceptance, there are two major challenges: systems' scalability and generality [9]. Working with RDF graphs, which are typically highly connected and distributed, results in matching and querying large volumes of data, thus making the issue with scalability more pressing. In this respect, NoSQL databases can handle larger volumes of data without restricting value types and data structures; however, most NoSQL databases support a single data model – either document, key-value storage or graph. Therefore, they either cannot handle relations between data very well (in the case of key-value and document stores), or they don't perform as good when it comes to querying large amounts of homogeneous data stored on a node (in the case of graph stores).

Over the past recent years, new types of NoSQL solutions have emerged (referred to as *multi-model databases*) that attempt to combine the benefits of multiple storage methods from traditional NoSQL databases [4] and could offer a better alternative to earlier approaches aiming to store RDF on relational databases (e.g., [3,5]). In this paper, we describe a practical approach to model, represent and store RDF graph data in a multi-model database. This approach takes advantage of the flexible data modelling offered by graph-model-based databases and the schema-less design of NoSQL. The contributions of this paper

© Springer Nature Switzerland AG 2021
E. Garoufallou and M.-A. Ovalle-Perandones (Eds.): MTSR 2020, CCIS 1355, pp. 47–52, 2021.
https://doi.org/10.1007/978-3-030-71903-6_5

include: (i) an approach for mapping RDF data to a multi-model database representation; (ii) an implementation of the proposed approach using ArangoDB; and (iii) an evaluation of query performance for different types of NoSQL, multi-model, and RDF stores.

The rest of this paper is organised as follows. Section 2 introduces multi-model databases and discusses their benefits. Section 3 describes three different ways of defining the mapping between the RDF and multi-model database storage formats. Section 4 describes a prototype implementation of the proposed approach, while Sect. 5 provides an evaluation of the implementation. Section 6 summarises our contributions and provides suggested directions for future work.

2   Multi-model Databases

Multi-model databases (e.g., ArangoDB, OrientDB, and Redis) are not a new concept and have existed in different forms for a long time [6]. Initially, multi-model databases served as systems to process complex data models. With the emergence of NoSQL databases, the term "multi-model database" has been expanded to support multiple connected storage models – typically document, key-value, and graph. Thereby, such databases are able to offer the benefits of different data models simultaneously, such as scalability and query performance of document and key-value databases and the flexibility and extensibility of graph databases.

The main difference between triple stores and multi-model databases (and even traditional graph databases) is in how they model graphs. In RDF, the nodes of the graph tend to store fine-grained attributes of entities, i.e., attribute values. In the multi-model database context, the units of disclosure are richer entity objects (i.e., they include object attributes) and cross-entity relationships. Multi-model database implementation of the graph model allows for flexible modelling of data within one domain or namespace, rather than multiple domains as in RDF. Furthermore, the fact that entity collections in multi-model databases can be treated as simple key-value or document stores allows performing queries over large volumes of data without the performance penalty of graph traversal/matching. Thus, this class of databases trades off multi-domain standardisation and universal usage with better support within a single domain (scalability, flexibility of data model). An appropriate approach to store self-describing, semantically enriched multi-domain RDF data in a multi-model database can be used to overcome the shortcomings of both representations.

3   Representing RDF Data in ArangoDB

We chose ArangoDB for our study, since it is currently among the best performers for multi-model storage solutions[1] and offers ease of use and non-functional support for different deployments. ArangoDB organizes data using two types of

---

[1] https://www.arangodb.com/performance.

entities - documents (i.e., nodes) and edges, which are saved in separate stores, referred to as collections[2]. We identified three mapping strategies: (i) direct representation with respect to the RDF data model – each node in the RDF mapping corresponds to a node in the document collection; (ii) direct representation storing the predicate data in edge documents, connecting the subject and object; and (iii) RDF flattening – using a set of heuristics for mapping RDF nodes and literals to the multi-model structure.

3.1   Direct Representation

This approach uses a direct representation that maps each node in an RDF triple to a node in the multi-model database connected through entries in the edge collections. As any RDF triple is built up by a subject, predicate and object, the direct representation would contain one node for each of these values and two edges connecting these nodes. Within each node, we define an attribute "rdf" to store the fully qualified name (URI), which allows to retain the semantics of the RDF node. This approach offers the most expressive representation in terms of querying and matching data within the generated graph. However, multi-model databases (and also graph databases) are not optimised to work with very large numbers of small objects (containing one attribute/value apart from the key), which makes this approach the least suitable for storage out of the three.

3.2   Direct Representation with Edge Values

The direct approach with edge values is similar to the direct approach, but instead of mapping each value of the RDF triple to one node each, the predicate value is stored directly on the edge connecting nodes. The result is then two nodes (the subject and object) connected with one edge (containing the predicate value), the expressiveness of the direct approach is kept while gaining a reduction in data size. This second approach handles larger datasets comparatively better than the direct mapping, but is still rather verbose.

3.3   RDF Flattening

When using normal graph databases, the challenge is to balance between having too large or too small objects when representing data. Using small objects results in extremely large graphs and thus a large number of traversals when querying data. Using too large objects increases query time when matching values, because of the need to go through all values within each node. Document databases, on the other hand, do handle large objects very well and store entries in attribute-value pairs allowing for high-performance querying. This approach to storing and handling RDF data within a multi-model database is, therefore, based on taking advantage of the data model of multi-model databases to store properties as object attributes within a document. This approach allows to store RDF in the most natural way with respect to graph/multi-model databases.

---

[2] https://www.arangodb.com/docs/stable/data-modeling-concepts.html.

4   Implementation

The implementation of RDF flattening was done using ArangoDB through the following rules:

- URI nodes are mapped JSON objects, which serve as nodes in the representation.
- URIs, which in RDF uniquely identify nodes, are used to generate unique numeric keys for the JSON object (numeric keys enable more efficient storage and lookup). This is done using a standard hash function and the keys themselves are stored in a special attribute called _key.
- Edges between nodes are generated based on the predicates between URI nodes in the RDF mapping template. An exception to this rule applies to *rdf:type* mappings – in RDF, these are used to specify type mappings for RDF entities. Types in RDF are URI nodes, which point to the semantic classes in an ontology or vocabulary, similarly to classes in object-oriented programming. The classes specified are instead stored in a 'type' JSON attribute, which contains an array of all entity types.
- RDF literals are mapped to JSON attributes for the URI node objects. An exception to this rule applies to *rdfs:label* – in RDF, these mappings are used to denote textual labels of entities. In the multi-model mapping, these values are stored in a 'label' attribute.
- Prefixes and fully qualified RDF URIs are also stored in the resulting JSON object. The specified prefixes in the mapping are additionally kept in separate JSON objects in the document collection to avoid overlaps with other prefixes and for enabling namespace-based lookups (based on the RDF namespaces defined in the mapping).

The implementation of RDF flattening was done using the Grafterizer data transformation tool [8] (available in the DataGraft platform [7]) and published on GitHub[3]. Two experimental instances of the ArangoDB database were deployed. They have two different configurations. The first configuration uses a three-node in-memory cluster. It was used for initial experimentation for lower-volume data, which was sharded over the three different instances. The second configuration uses a single-node deployment with the persistent storage engine of ArangoDB. The latter configuration has lower memory requirements (as it stores data persistently rather than in memory), which is more appropriate when dealing with Big Data. Both instances of the database were deployed using the Docker-based deployment option of ArangoDB.

5   Evaluation

To make a comparison of how the flattened RDF representation proposed in this paper performs compared to a triple store, we generated RDF data from the

---

[3] https://github.com/samuelsen/RDF---NoSQL-test.

data dump [2] used in the NoSQL benchmark test from ArangoDB [1]. We also deployed instances of Neo4j[4] and OrientDB[5] (with default configuration) as was done in the benchmark. Each query from the test was re-written for both RDF and the flattened representation in ArangoDB. The RDF values were uploaded to a Jena Fuseki SPARQL server[6], which was deployed on the test server where we validated the benchmark results. The test server uses the following configuration: Ubuntu 17.10 (4.13.13), 16x3 GHz AMD Ryzen 7 1700 Eight-Core Processor, 62.9GiB of memory and a SSD of 457GiB. Each test was ran five times averaging the results of these five runs. The tests performed were as follows:

- *Shortest-path* – For 1000 sets of IDs, the time taken to find the shortest path between all sets of IDs;
- *Neighbors* – For 1000 IDs find all neighbors of these IDs;
- *Neighbors 2* – For 1000 IDs find all neighbors of these and all neighbors of the retrieved neighbors;
- *Single read* – Average read time for (100.000 reads);
- *Aggregate* – For all entries count the number of occurrences of different edges.

Database	Shortest Path	Neighbors	Neighbors 2	Single read	Aggregate
ArangoDB (file system)	1.28	1.04	4.71	3.84	0.15
ArangoDB (in-memory)	2.49	0.96	4.75	9.08	0.19
OrientDB	125.32	1.24	29.03	9.31	0.56
Neo4j	1.47	0.28	3.76	1.81	0.25
Jena Fuseki	n/a	11.73	9.81	d.n.f	1.60

* all results given in milliseconds

Fig. 1. Benchmarking results (with default configurations of the databases)

As can be seen in the Fig. 1, Neo4j performs best in the graph traversal benchmark due to its being specifically designed to support the graph model. However, Neo4j does not support document-key-value storage and respective querying capabilities, and was thus not our chosen solution, but is given as baseline. In terms of multi-model storage, we tested ArangoDB with the in-memory and file-system based storage, as well as OrientDB. Out of the tested multi-model databases, ArangoDB outperforms OrientDB in all benchmarks and comes closest to Neo4j in terms of graph traversal capabilities in multi-model stores. With respect to triple store, the tested solution – Jena Fuseki – has much worse performance. We were not able to perform the shortest path experiment due to a memory exception. Furthermore, Fuseki did not finish the test for single reads, which attempted to perform 100 000 reads to get the average response time.

---

[4] https://neo4j.com.
[5] https://www.orientdb.org.
[6] https://jena.apache.org/documentation/fuseki2.

This is due to the lack of scalability of the SPARQL endpoint API in comparison to the proprietary APIs of the other storage solutions, which can support multiple simultaneous connections and larger load. In the other tests, Fuseki was up to an order of magnitude slower than ArangoDB. A notable limiation of this experiment is that all databases were configured using the default configuration.

6   Conclusions

In this paper, we presented an approach to model and store RDF data in a multi-model database. Using our proposed RDF flattening approach, it is possible to retrieve results when looking for specific values without needing graph traversals, which significantly improves query performance. Additionally, due to the use of the document structure to store predicate and literal values directly within an entity object (representing the RDF node), the data size is reduced. A possible direction for future work is to expand the comparison by using different benchmarks, especially ones that are traditionally used to evaluate RDF stores. Furthermore, the evaluation can be extended to implement a more extensive exploration of the currently available triple stores by including a larger number of them. Another possible direction for future work would be to set up procedures for producing RDF triples out of the graph database representation presented in this work.

Acknowledgements. The work in this paper was partly funded by the EC H2020 projects euBusinessGraph (732003), EW-Shopp (732590), and TheyBuyForYou (780247).

References

1. ArangoDB NoSQL Performance Benchmark. https://www.arangodb.com/2018/02/nosql-performance-benchmark-2018-mongodb-postgresql-orientdb-neo4j-arangodb
2. Pokec social network - data set dump. https://snap.stanford.edu/data/soc-pokec.html
3. Bornea, M., et al.: Building an efficient RDF store over a relational database. Proc. SIGMOD **2013**, 121–132 (2013)
4. Lu, J., Holubová, I.: Multi-model databases: a new journey to handle the variety of data. ACM Comput. Surv. **52**(3), 1–38 (2019)
5. Pan, Z., Heflin, J.: DLDB: Extending relational databases to support semantic web queries. In: Proceedings of PSSS1 2003, pp. 109–113 (2003)
6. Płuciennik, E., Zgorzałek, K.: The multi-model databases - a review. Proc. BDAS **2017**, 141–152 (2017)
7. Roman, D., et al.: Datagraft: one-stop-shop for open data management. Semant. Web **9**(4), 393–411 (2018)
8. Sukhobok, D., et al.: Tabular data cleaning and linked data generation with Grafterizer. In: Sack, H., Rizzo, G., Steinmetz, N., Mladenić, D., Auer, S., Lange, C. (eds.) ESWC 2016. LNCS, vol. 9989, pp. 134–139. Springer, Cham (2016). https://doi.org/10.1007/978-3-319-47602-5_27
9. Zeng, K., et al.: A distributed graph engine for web scale rdf data. Proceedings of the VLDB Endowment **6**(4), 265–276 (2013)

Knowledge-Based Named Entity Recognition of Archaeological Concepts in Dutch

Andreas Vlachidis[1]($\boxtimes$) (iD), Douglas Tudhope[2] (iD), and Milco Wansleeben[3]

[1] Department of Information Studies, UCL, Gower Street, London WC1E 6BT, UK
a.vlachidis@ucl.ac.uk
[2] School of Computing and Mathematics, University of South Wales, Newport CF37 1DL, UK
douglas.tudhope@southwales.ac.uk
[3] Faculty of Archaeology, Leiden University, Einsteinweg 2, 2333 CC Leiden, The Netherlands
m.wansleeben@arch.leidenuniv.nl

Abstract. The advancement of Natural Language Processing (NLP) allows the process of deriving information from large volumes of text to be automated, making text-based resources more discoverable and useful. The attention is turned to one of the most important, but traditionally difficult to access resources in archaeology; the largely unpublished reports generated by commercial or "rescue" archaeology, commonly known as "grey literature". The paper presents the development and evaluation of a Named Entity Recognition system of Dutch archaeological grey literature targeted at extracting mentions of artefacts, archaeological features, materials, places and time entities. The role of domain vocabulary is discussed for the development of a KOS-driven NLP pipeline which is evaluated against a Gold Standard, human-annotated corpus.

Keywords: Named Entity Recognition · Archaeology · Grey literature · CIDOC-CRM · Knowledge Organization Systems

1 Introduction

Across Europe, the archaeological domain generates vast quantities of text in form of unpublished fieldwork and specialist reports often referred to as "grey literature" [1]. In the Netherlands, it is estimated that just under 60,000 of such reports have been produced over the last 20 years with a current estimated growth rate of 4,000 reports per year [2]. Access to the valuable information contained in such reports is a known problem. The detrimental effect on archaeological knowledge, as a result of the inaccessibility and difficulty of discovery of these texts, has in recent years, begun to be increasingly recognised as a significant problem within the domain. The role of the Natural Language Processing (NLP) has been recognised as vital for the automatic indexing, metadata generation, retrieval and dissemination from integrated online catalogues [3]. The results of Brandsen's [4] study on the uses of Named Entity Recognition (NER) for the development of effective search experiences, agree with earlier findings that NER applications can enable semantic indexing of archaeological grey literature for the purposes of retrieval and cross searching [5].

E. Garoufallou and M.-A. Ovalle-Perandones (Eds.): MTSR 2020, CCIS 1355, pp. 53–64, 2021.
https://doi.org/10.1007/978-3-030-71903-6_6

The paper discusses the development and evaluation of a NER system of Dutch archaeological grey literature targeted at extracting mentions of artefacts, archaeological features, materials, places and time entities. The system uses a rule-based information extraction technique supported by domain vocabulary, utilising the GATE (General Architecture for Text Engineering) framework [6] and contributing to NLP aims of the European FP7 project ARIADNE [7]. The main motivation of the work is to enable the semantic annotation of archaeological reports with a core set of entities of interest for automating metadata generation. The extracted output of entities is delivered in a structured and interoperable XML format, constituting a document index which can be further analysed and used to identify patterns, trends, and "important" words or terms within text by subsequent applications. Such semantic annotation interoperable outputs have been delivered by previous studies in English to facilitate archaeological information discovery, retrieval, comparison, analysis, and link texts to other types of data [8]. The current study expands the method of automatic metadata generation using NER, previously available in English, in the context of Dutch archaeological reports.

2   Background

The field of Named Entity Recognition has been consistently growing over the past two decades. The early rule-based (handcrafted) systems which provided good performance at a relatively high system engineering cost were succeeded by the machine learning (supervised) systems which allowed for greater scalability and domain adaptation but required human-annotated data for system training [9]. The latest developments in NER explore semi-supervised and unsupervised learning techniques which promise to overcome some of the limitations of supervised ML methods and to provide information extraction results without the prerequisite of an annotated corpus [10]. Our decision to employ a rule-based approach for the development of the Dutch system was based on the absence of an annotated corpus and on the availability of the Rijksdienst vor het Cultureel Erfgoed (RCE) Thesauri which supported the rule matching approach with a breadth of domain vocabulary.

Information Extraction (IE) aims to identify instances of a particular prespecified class of entities, relationships and events in natural language texts, and the extraction of the relevant properties (arguments) of the identified entities, relationships or events. NER is specified as a subtask of IE and the term was first used during the Sixth Message Understanding Conference (MUC-6) [11] to describe the task of extracting instances of people, organizations, geographic location, currency, and percentage expressions from text. Similarly, the task of NER was defined by the 2002 Conference on Computational Natural Language Learning as the extraction of 'phrases that contain the names of persons, organizations, locations, times, and quantities' [12]. However, there is no single definition of NER as the task has kept on expanding and diversifying through the years to include additional entities of interest such as products, events, diseases, to name but a few [13]. In the context of archaeological fieldwork reports the entities that have extracted the most interest relate to physical object, material, spatial and temporal information [5].

A number of projects have employed IE and NER techniques on archaeological literature. An early pilot application was carried out by Amrani, Abajian and Kodratoff

[14] which used string matching to extract information from archaeological literature. The OpenBoek project experimented with memory based learning to extract chronological and geographical terms from Dutch archaeological texts [15]. Byrne and Klein [16] also investigated the extraction of information from archaeological literature primarily focusing on extraction of events from unstructured text. The Archaeotools project adopted a machine learning approach to enable access to archaeological grey literature via a faceted classification scheme of What (what subject does the record refer to), Where (where, location, region of interest), When (archaeological date of interest) and Media (form of the record) which combined databases with information extracted from reports in an interesting faceted browser interface [17]. The OPTIMA system applied a rule-based, Knowledge Organization System (KOS) driven approach to semantic indexing of archaeological grey literature [18]. It used named entity recognition, relation extraction, negation detection and word sense disambiguation for associating contextual abstractions with classes of the standard ontology (ISO 21127:2006) CIDOC Conceptual Reference Model (CRM) for cultural heritage together with concepts from English Heritage thesauri and glossaries.

Indexing and metadata creation can be time consuming and may lack consistency when done by hand, and when created it is rarely integrated with the wider archaeological domain data. Moreover, the traditional model of manual cataloguing and indexing practices has been receiving less attention and priority. For example, prominent European research projects such as the eContentplus explicitly did not fund the development of metadata schemas and the creation of metadata itself [13]. Natural language processing techniques can support automatic generation of rich metadata, providing methods for disclosing information in large text collections whilst enabling semantic search of grey literature across disparate collections and datasets [3, 8]. Such approaches compensate full text indexing techniques, enabling retrieval on multiple meanings and allowing researchers to search on concepts taking account for synonymy and polysemy [4].

A significant amount of research effort has been spent on information extraction in English, covering NER as well as higher-level IE tasks such as relation and event extraction. Comparatively less attention has been spent on non-English languages. The performance of non-English IE systems is usually lower and linguistic phenomena impose challenges [19]. Such challenges include lack of whitespace, which complicates word boundary disambiguation; productive compounding, which complicates morphological analysis in German and Dutch; and proper name declension forms in Greek and Slavic languages which complicate named entity recognition [20].

The Dutch NER pipeline discussed in the paper, is challenged by language related issues that directly affected recognition of compound noun forms, place names and time entities. The following sections discuss the methods and techniques used in an attempt to address some of these challenges and to deliver a customised application for the extraction of entities of interest from Dutch archaeological grey literature.

3 Method

This section discusses the stages of developing an NLP pipeline which employed rule-based information extraction techniques and integrated a range of domain vocabulary resources for supporting the task of entity recognition. The final pipeline is the result of an iterative process which involved the definition and evaluation of an earlier pipeline version. The earlier version adapted the domain vocabulary to the NLP task by utilising the SKOSified[1] version of the RCE thesauri[2], designed and developed the IE rules and evaluated the performance of the NER pipeline. The updated version of the Dutch NER pipeline, improved a range of vocabulary issues in connection to coverage, spelling variations and synonyms, refined the gold standard and modified the entity matching rules for better performance.

The employment of rule-based IE and domain vocabulary resources distinguishes our approach from supervised machine learning methods, which heavily relies on the existence and quality of training data. The absence of a training corpus coupled with the availability of a significant volume of high quality domain-specific knowledge organization resources, such as a conceptual model, thesauri and glossaries were contributing factors to the adoption of the rule-based techniques. Hand-crafted rules invoke input from ontologies and thesauri that provide to the entity recognition rules specific terms of predefined groups, such as person names, organisation names, week days, months etc. In addition, the rules exploit a range of lexical, part of speech and syntactical attributes that describe word level features, such as word case, morphological features and grammar elements that support definition of rich extraction rules, which are employed by the NER process.

3.1 Vocabulary GATEfication

The NER pipeline is designed to extract core concepts (entities) of research interest in the context of Dutch archaeological grey literature, such as artefacts (finds or physical objects), features (archaeological context e.g. posthole), materials, monuments types, places (focus on place names such as districts) and time entities (periods and time appellations including numerical appellations e.g. 480 BC). The following RCE thesauri have been selected to support extraction of the above entities; archaeological artifact types, materials, archaeological complex (features) types, locations, archaeological periods and landscape elements of object types thesaurus.

The process of importing the RCE thesauri resources into the GATE framework involved retrieval of the thesauri resources and their serialisation (transformation) to the Ontology Web Language (OWL-Lite) format using automated methods (i.e. XSL templates). The original serialisation of the thesauri can be only partially parsed from the framework, causing the rich thesaurus structure to flatten and in turn restricting the definition of rules that can exploit the broader/narrower semantic relationships. Hence, the transformation of the original resources was necessary for exploiting the hierarchical relationships of the resources, enabling matching on alternative labels and synonyms, and enhancing matches with useful interoperable attributes already available in the original

---

[1] Simple Knowledge Organization System (SKOS) is a Semantic Web format and aW3C recommendation designed for representation of thesauri, classification schemes, taxonomies, subject heading systems, or any other type of structured controlled vocabulary https://www.w3.org/2004/02/skos/.

[2] http://openskos.org/api/collections/rce:EGT.html.

resources, such as SKOS unique identifier. In addition, the transformation process created new human-readable uniform resource identifiers (URIs) while maintaining the original references for individual entries (i.e. *rna:contentItem* and *skos:Concept* and *rdf:about*). The necessity to provide new human-readable URIs for classes is dictated by GATE's behaviour towards exposing class URI to JAPE rules.

GATE enables Ontology Based Information Extraction (OBIE) techniques using OWL-Lite that purely support the aims of information extraction and are not stand alone formal ontologies for logic based purposes. Such ontological structures in GATE provide the necessary conceptual framework for driving the NER task and contribute the glossary input to the matching mechanism. Their main benefit is that they allow the definition of matching rules (JAPE) that exploit the transitive relationships of an ontological structure. As a result, matching rules become flexible and capable of exploiting only those parts of the ontological resource that fall within the scope of an entity definition. For example, a single line rule can exploit and consequently provide matches from a Monument Type resource, only for those entries that are described as "Defensive Structures", including "castles", "tower" and their sub types. In addition, individual ontological classes or instances benefit from the use of parameters holding spelling variations, synonyms, SKOS identifiers and any other sort of bespoke parameters useful to the NER task. Thus, matches derived from an ontological resource enjoy dimensions that could be useful for further information retrieval and interoperability purposes.

Transformation of the RCE thesauri to OWL-Lite was performed with XSL templates which produced human-readable URIs based on a combination of a temporary base URI with the preferred label of individual entries. In order to comply with canonical URI definitions, the preferred labels were cleaned from illegal characters, such as ampersand, slash, etc., while spaces were replaced with underscores. The *dcterms:identifier*, due to its general purpose scope seemed an appropriate choice for holding the unique SKOS reference for individual entries instead of the original *skos:Concept* property, which is specific to thesauri not to ontology Parent/Child structures. The *rdfs:seeAlso* annotation property is used for holding the unique reference of the RCE node element while the *rdfs:subClassOf* structure was used to implement the broader-narrower terms as Parent/Child relationships.

The NER pipeline is composed by several general purpose, domain independent NLP modules and a series of bespoke JAPE transducers which contain the hand-crafted rules that exploit contextual evidence and domain vocabulary. In detail, the pipeline integrates the modules in the following order; Apache Open NLP[3] (Tokenizer, Sentence Splitter, Dutch part-of-speech tagger), the Snowball stemmer[4], the GATE OntoRoot Gazetteer[5] and finally a range of JAPE transducers responsible for extracting entities of interest from text. The pipeline runs in a cascading order where each module adds a layer of semantics to the output, hence, the order of the modules is important. The stemmer output is critical for the operation of the OntoRoot gazetteer module which produces lookup annotations that link to the specific concepts or relations from the ontology. The output of the OntoRoot module is then exploited by the NER matching rules which combine

---

[3] https://opennlp.apache.org/.

[4] https://snowballstem.org/.

[5] https://gate.ac.uk/sale/tao/splitch13.html#x18-33400013.8.

lookup and token input, for example the following rules matches in text transitively all instances of the ontology class artefact which are tagged by the part-of-speech tagger as nouns.

```
{Token.category ==N, Lookup.class ==Artefact}
```

In addition, a flat gazetteer containing period related suffixes, such as A.D, B.C, voor Christus was built and used in the definition of JAPE rules targeted at matching numerical dates e.g. *1200 AD, 800 v.Chr.* Similarly, a set of JAPE rules was defined for matching grid references and geographic coordinates (numerical places), such as 216.518/568.889.

3.2 The NER Pipeline

The updated version of the Dutch NER pipeline addressed shortcomings following the review of the earlier NER pipeline. Such imperfections concerned the coverage and suitability of the RCE Thesauri to support the NER task and under performance of JAPE rules in connection to vocabulary and pattern matching. The updated version did not address issues of compound noun extraction and negation detection which were also revealed during the review.

The main effort of vocabulary improvement was focused on resolving overloaded vocabulary entries into individual term components. The RCE thesauri were not necessarily developed with Natural Language Processing in mind and as a result contain entries that are not suitable for automatic and algorithmic term matching due to their multiterm, sometimes descriptive and verbose punctuation structure. For example, the vocabulary entries amulet/talisman and its child entry *amulet/talisman – kruisvormig* (cruciform) do not correspond to the way in which such terms are used in natural language text.

Most likely either amulet or talisman will be found as individual entries and if an adjective is used, such as *kruisvormig* this will follow a grammatically correct syntax form (i.e. *kruisvormig amulet* instead of *amulet kruisvormig*). Vocabulary entries like the above should be enhanced with labels that are closer to what is likely to appear in text rather than containing descriptive and non-natural language descriptions.

A set of XSL templates was developed which addressed label patterns that joined synonyms and specialisations together under a single label. For example, the forward slash (/) character joins synonyms as in the case amulet/talisman, the hyphen (−) character adds specialisation as in the case *amulet/talisman – kruisvormig* and the comma (,) character adds a form of periphrastic description which can be treated as an alternative label. The XSL templates incorporated the above patterns to generate the new vocabulary labels where for example amulet/talisman delivers two separate labels (amulet, talisman) and *amulet/talisman – kruisvormig* delivers the labels *kruisvormig* amulet and *kruisvormig talisman*. In most cases, special characters for joining synonyms and expressing specialisations or generalisations are standard across the thesauri and the transformation delivered useful alternative labels. However, there are cases that do not follow the standard use of special characters or are very verbose (e.g. *huisplattegrond:4-schepig - type St.Oedenrode*). Such cases due to their complexity were not matched by the transformation templates and were ignored.

The updated NER pipeline incorporated improvements to the JAPE matching rules which addressed vocabulary use and matching coverage. A new set of rules was introduced for matching grid references of places and new rules were also included for exploiting input from the Landscape elements of the Objecttypen thesaurus. Rules were also improved for matching the gazetteer lists in connection to dates enabling matching of date range such as *tussen 1600 en 1900* (between 1600 and 1900). In addition, the restriction that any match of a Place entity must commence with an upper-case letter has been lifted, to include matching for place names commencing with s', such as *'s-Heerenberg, and 's-Graveland* which is quite common in Dutch.

The Dutch NER pipeline has been deployed into the GATE Cloud[6] where it is freely available for accessing through a web interface and a dedicated API. Example semantic annotations of archaeological entities of interest include, Time Appellation, Physical Object and Place (see Fig. 1) such as, *Swifterbant* which a town in province of Flevoland, the object *Trechterbeker* (Funnel beaker), the time appellation *Steentijd* (Stone Age) and the materials *Houtskool* (charcoal), *Vuursteen* (flint), *Zandsteen* (sandstone). In addition, a range of attributes are assigned on each individual annotation that carry pieces of information about the origin of a term (contributing thesaurus), unique reference (URI) and a corresponding terminological reference to the RCE thesaurus which is uniquely identified by URI.

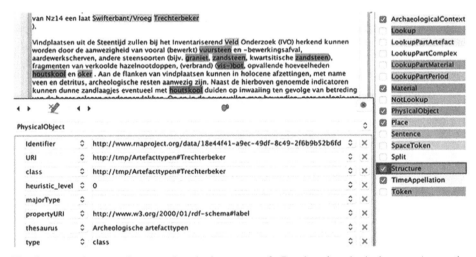

Fig. 1. Example semantic annotations in the context of a Dutch archaeological report. Annotation types are highlighted and annotation attributes are shown in respective fields.

4 Evaluation

The system performance was benchmarked via a Gold Standard (GS) set of manual annotations defined for the purposes of the ARIADNE project by a group of Dutch

---

[6] https://cloud.gate.ac.uk/shopfront/displayItem/archaeology-ner-nl.

archaeologists (Leiden University). The Gold Standard refers to a set of human annotated documents which represents the desirable result and is used for comparison with system produced automatic annotations. Results are reported on the measurement of Precision and Recall and their weighted average F-measure, established as standard measurement units for measuring the performance of IE by the second Machine Understanding Conference, MUC 2. The Gold Standard consisted of 7 long (some are up to 300 pages) grey literature reports containing approximately 10,000 annotated instances of several entity types, including Archaeological Context (Feature), Artefact, Event, Material, Method, Monument, Place, Period and Person. The entities Event, Method, and Person were not in the scope of the NER pipeline and are not included in the evaluation.

The manually annotated GS was very helpful for the purposes of an early evaluation task, revealing several issues with regards to vocabulary coverage and suggesting potential rule matching strategies for a range of different entities. However, it was regarded to be a bit long and quite repetitive for the evaluation of a rule-based system and more appropriate for training a Machine Learning system. In the case of rule-based evaluation, since training is not required, we need a representative manually annotated corpus that covers as many as possible different cases of annotation without repeating the same annotation cases again and again. For example, a place name ("Veemarktterrein") which was not initially included in the rule-based system vocabular is frequently found in text, affecting recall over long documents. This is rather straight forward to rectify the system by including the missing term in the vocabulary.

The early NER pipeline was evaluated against the GS delivering the performance figures as seen on Table 1. The overall score of Precision and Recall were encouraging, reaching 57% and 61% respectively and delivering an F-Measure score of 59%.

Table 1. System performance of the Early NER system for a range of entities

Entity	Recall	Precision	F-Measure
Arch.Context	0.87	0.63	0.73
Artefact	0.36	0.50	0.42
Material	0.50	0.62	0.55
Monument	0.36	0.45	0.40
Place	0.60	0.65	0.63
Time Period	0.72	0.70	0.71
All (Total)	**0.57**	**0.61**	**0.59**

The least performing entity is the Monument both in terms of Precision (36%) and Recall (45%), followed closely by the Artefact entity which shares the same Precision score and slightly better (50%) Recall. The pipeline delivers slightly better scores for the Material and Place Entities with Precision scores between 50%–60% with Recall scores between 62%–65% respectively. The best performing entity is Archaeological Context which enjoys a Precision score of 87% and Recall 63%, followed by the Period entity which scores 72% Precision and 71% Recall. The contribution of vocabularies is critical to the performance of the pipeline with respect to the discussed entities. Clearly, Precision can be harmed by using too many terms from the available vocabulary which do not fail within the scope of the targeted entity. At the same time, Recall is affected by using too few terms from the vocabulary, hence, matching rules should be also improved for allowing an optimum use of the available vocabulary.

The updated version of the NER pipeline utilised an extended and NLP friendlier vocabulary resource, which has addressed various labelling pattern issues as discussed in Sect. 3. In addition, the pipeline incorporated new improved hand-crafted rules aimed at improving performance and strengthening the matching accuracy. For example, a rule aimed at matching instances of the artefact class, which previously included two conditions, it was strengthen to include five separate conditions as seen below.

```
{!NotLookup, !Context, !Physical_Thing, Token.category ==
N, Lookup.class == [rceArtefact n=ArcheoArtefactTypes]}
```

The rule matches all instances of the RCE Artefact Types class, excluding from matching; certain areas of the resource previously annotated as NotLookup, Archaeological Context, and Monuments (Physical Thing) whilst requiring each match to conform to Noun token-category. The updated version delivers improved results (Table 2).

Table 2. System Performance of the Early NER system for a range of entities

Entity	Recall	Precision	F-Measure
Arch.Context	0.90	0.63	0.74
Artefact	0.53	0.60	0.56
Material	0.55	0.62	0.58
Monument	0.64	0.65	0.65
Place	0.61	0.72	0.66
Time Period	0.80	0.76	0.77
All (Total)	**0.67**	**0.68**	**0.67**

The Precision of the NER pipeline is improved by 10% whereas Recall also is also improved by 7%, reaching overall 67% Precision and 68% Recall. Most significantly, the performance of the pipeline has been considerably improved for the Artefact and Monument entities types, with Precision score nearly doubling and increasing from 36% to 54% and 64% respectively. The performance of the pipeline is comparable with the results of the AGNES system [4] which employed a supervised ML approach for the recognition of Artefact, Time Period and Material entities in Dutch archaeological grey literature. In particular, both systems have reported similar scores in respect to recognition of Artefact entity types which presents certain domain challenges. Overall, the ML system delivered a higher Precision 71% score but a lower Recall 48% score, resulting to an F-Measure 56% compared to 66% delivered by the rule-based, KOS-driven system. The above comparison is only indicative and highlights the challenges imposed by the archaeological domain in NER. A full-scale comparative study across the rule-based, ML (supervised and unsupervised) methods of NER would be appropriate for delivering safer conclusions as each method has its own merits and limitations. It is evident that the RCE Thesauri proved a valuable resource to drive the NER effort, providing a significant vocabulary breadth which benefited the Recall rates of the system. At the same time, the hand-crafted rules as improved during the iterative process allowed for a maximum use of the available vocabulary whilst imposing conditions which protected the overall Precision rates of the system.

5   Conclusion and Future Work

A major development of the NER rule-based and KOS-driven approach has been the generalisation of the previous rule based techniques [18] to Dutch archaeological grey literature. The work faced challenges in connection to a different set of vocabularies available via the RCE Thesaurus and also in connection to differences in language characteristics. The NER techniques were focused on the general archaeological entities of Archaeological Context, Artefact, Material, Monument, Place, and Time Period and the method proved capable of extracting entities of interest with relative success. The RCE Thesauri proved to be a valuable resource in support of the NER task, however, archaeological vocabularies do pose a challenge. Unlike highly specialised domains, which have vocabularies unique to that domain, archaeological terminology consists of common everyday words, for example "wall", and "ditch". In addition, such domain vocabulary resources in many cases have been defined with Information Science principles in mind, and not to support NLP operations. The Gold Standard (GS) evaluation revealed performance drawbacks influenced by structural, labelling and coverage issues of the vocabulary. The results of the evaluation phase lead to resolving the overloaded vocabulary entries into individual term components. Therefore, labelling adjustment and enrichment techniques are necessary for making the vocabulary resources "friendlier" to the NER as discussed in Sect. 3.

The updated version of the NER pipeline improved many cases of underspecified rules that were identified during evaluation of the earlier and also identified some new cases of underperformance. Future improvements include extraction of compound noun forms which appear in Dutch regularly, joining period terms with objects, object terms with material, material terms with archaeological contexts etc. A way forward of tackling such cases could be is to employ partial matching over words instead of the whole word matching currently performed by the NER system. Partial matching is possible but should be planned and executed carefully due to the significant amount of noise that might be generated. A future system should also be able to address negated entities (e.g. *geen vondsten/finds*) which provide facts of no evidence, i.e. a comment in the report that no evidence has been found for a potential finding and thus should not be annotated. Last but not least, the current NER pipeline imposes a noun-validation restriction which excluded adjectives from matching. However, the Gold Standard revealed many material entities of adjectival form, such as *bronzen* (bronze), *stenen* (stone), etc. The restriction can be lifted but careful planning is required in order to conclude whether such cases are annotated as individual material entities or as moderators of object or monument entities.

Acknowledgments. This work was supported by the European Commission under the Community's Seventh Framework Programme, contract no. FP7-INFRASTRUCTURES-2012-1-313193 (the ARIADNE project). Thanks, are due to ARIADNE project partners from Leiden University who helped with the definition of the Gold standard

References

1. Evans, T.N.: A reassessment of archaeological grey literature: semantics and paradoxes. Internet Archaeol. **40** (2015)
2. Rijksdienst vvor het Cultureel Erfgoed. Archis Invoer. https://archis.cultureelerfgoed.nl. Accessed 05 May 2019 (2019)
3. Richards, J., Tudhope, D., Vlachidis, A.: Text mining in archaeology: extracting information from archaeological reports. In: Barcelo, J.A., Bogdanovic, I. (eds.) Mathematics and Archaeology, pp. 240–254. CRC Press, Boca Raton (2015)
4. Brandsen, A., Lambers, K., Verberne, S., Wansleeben, M.: User requirement solicitation for an information retrieval system applied to Dutch grey literature in the archaeology domain. J. Comput. Appl. Archaeol. **2**(1), 21–30 (2019)
5. Vlachidis, A., Tudhope, D.: A knowledge- based approach to Information Extraction for semantic interoperability in the archaeology domain. J. Assoc. Inf. Sci. Technol. **67**(5), 1138–1152 (2016)
6. Cunningham, H., Tablan, V., Roberts, A., Bontcheva, K.: Getting more out of biomedical documents with GATE's full lifecycle open source text analytics. PLoS Comput. Biol. **9**(2), e1002854 (2013)
7. Meghini, C., et al.: ARIADNE: a research infrastructure for archaeology. J. Comput. Cult. Heritage (JOCCH) **10**(3), 18 (2017)
8. Tudhope, D., May, K., Binding, C., Vlachidis. A.: Connecting archaeological data and grey literature via semantic cross search. Internet Archaeol. **30** (2011)
9. Nadeau, D., Sekine, S.: A survey of named entity recognition and classification. Lingvisticae Investigationes **30**(1), 3–26 (2007)
10. Toledo, J.I., Carbonell, M., Fornés, A., Lladós, A.J.: Information extraction from historical handwritten document images with a context-aware neural model. Pattern Recogn. **86**, 27–36 (2019)
11. Grishman, R., Sundheim, B.: Message understanding conference-6: a brief history. In: 16th International Conference on Computational Linguisitics, pp. 466–471 (1996)
12. Tjong Kim Sang, E.F.: Introduction to the CoNLL-2002 shared task: language-independent named entity recognition. In: Proceedings of CoNLL-2002, pp. 155–158 (2002)
13. Hooland, S., De Wilde, M., Verborgh, R., Steiner, T., Van de Walle, R.: Exploring entity recognition and disambiguation for cultural heritage collections. Digit. Sch. Hum. **30**(2), 262–279 (2013)
14. Amrani, A., Abajian, V., Kodratoff, Y.: A chain of text-mining to extract information in archaeology. In: Annual IEEE Computer Conference, International Conference on Information and Communication Technologies: From Theory to Applications, and ICTTA, 3rd International Conference on Information and Communication Technologies: From Theory to Applications, 7–11 April (2008)
15. Paijmans, H., Wubben, S.: Preparing archaeological reports for intelligent retrieval. In: Posluschny, A., Lambers, K., Herzog, I. (eds.) Layers of Perception. Proceedings of the 35th International Conference on Computer Applications and Quantitative Methods in Archaeology (CAA) Berlin, Germany, April 2–6, pp. 212–217 (2007)

16. Byrne, K.F., Klein, E.: Automatic extraction of archaeological events from text. In: Frischer, B., Crawford, J.W., Koller, D. (eds.) Making History Interactive. Proceedings of the 37th Computer Application in Archaeology Conference, pp. 48–56 (2009)
17. Jeffrey, S., Richards, J., Ciravegna, F., Waller, S., Chapman, S., Zhang, Z.: The archaeotools project: faceted classification and natural language processing in an archaeological context. Philosoph. Trans. Ser. A. Math. Phys. Eng. Sci. **367**(1897), 2507–2519 (2009)
18. Vlachidis, A.: Semantic indexing via knowledge organization systems: applying the CIDOC-CRM to archaeological grey literature. Doctoral dissertation, University of Glamorgan (2012)
19. Piskorski, J., Yangarber, J.R.: Information extraction: past, present and future. In: Poibeau, T., Saggion, H., Piskorski, J., Yangarber, R. (eds.) Multi-source, Multilingual Information Extraction and Summarization, pp. 23–49. Springer, Berlin, Heidelberg (2013). https://doi.org/10.1007/978-3-642-28569-1_2
20. Piskorski, J., Wieloch, K., Sydow, M.: On knowledge-poor methods for person name matching and lemmatization for highly inflectional languages. Inf. Retr. **12**(3), 275–299 (2009)

FAIRising Pedagogical Documentation for the Research Lifecycle

Deborah A. Garwood$^{(\boxtimes)}$ (ID) and Alex H. Poole (ID)

Metadata Research Center, Drexel University, Philadelphia, PA 19104, USA
dgarwood@drexel.edu

Abstract. How can pedagogical research complement academic research and vice versa? This case study revisits two research projects on curricular resources: the first, in 2019, analyzes partially structured syllabi data in digital humanities, and the second, in 2021, focuses on unstructured course titles and descriptions in LIS course catalogs. Findings reexamine data collection and analysis processes in which the lack of linked semantic metadata and persistent digital objects in curricular resources impedes fruitful research on how (inter)disciplinary topics are taught and future researchers trained. Consequently, the case study locates a gap: the role of pedagogical documentation in the research lifecycle has not been considered. As suggested by the emergence of FAIR principles, metadata expertise is a foundation for establishing the findability, accessibility, interoperability, and reuse of persistent digital objects in research outputs. FAIRising pedagogical documentation for the research lifecycle holds potential to link curricular resources with other research outputs. Information professionals have a leadership role in assisting faculty to create FAIRised pedagogical documentation, and curricular resources so prepared address the gap for integrating pedagogical documentation with the research lifecycle. Benefits include recognition of curricular resources as vital research outputs and facilitating longitudinal research on (inter)disciplinary pedagogical practices in the FAIR ecosystem.

Keywords: Metadata · Linked semantic metadata · Pedagogical research · (Inter)disciplinary research · Persistent digital objects · FAIR digital objects · FAIR ecosystem

1 Introduction

How can pedagogical research complement academic research and vice versa? To explore the research question, this case study first considers literature on the research lifecycle and the role of metadata expertise. Second, background on metadata's increasing utility for measures of integrity in scholarly publications adumbrates the FAIR principles' inclusive approach to research outputs well beyond scholarly publications [1, 2]. The literature leaves a gap for exploring how curricular resources contribute to the research lifecycle, and how "FAIRised" [2, p. 8] pedagogical documentation aids scholarly analysis of (inter)disciplinary pedagogy practices.

© Springer Nature Switzerland AG 2021
E. Garoufallou and M.-A. Ovalle-Perandones (Eds.): MTSR 2020, CCIS 1355, pp. 65–72, 2021.
https://doi.org/10.1007/978-3-030-71903-6_7

The third section presents the case study's reexamination of semi-automatic and manual data collection and analysis techniques for two pedagogical research projects, one investigating open source digital humanities syllabi, the other analyzing unstructured course titles and descriptions in Library & Information Science (LIS) course catalogs at American Library Association accredited US LIS programs. Fourth, a discussion section outlines the implications of findings. Fifth, the conclusion summarizes key points and recommends future research directions.

2   The Research Lifecycle, Metadata's Role, and the FAIR Ecosystem

Information professionals whose metadata expertise assists faculty to prepare scholarly research for publication and data deposit perform a crucial step in the research lifecycle [3–5]. Teams of faculty and students launch academic research projects and often consult with information professionals to deploy metadata and build skills [3, 4, 6]. Information professionals – librarians, archivists, and data curators who often have overlapping technical and soft skills – are well-positioned to participate in research initiatives and guide the process of metadata creation throughout projects [7–9].

In short, pedagogy, research outputs, and metadata expertise are intertwined, yet the role of curricular resources in the research lifecycle has not been considered. Rather, metadata's capacity to structure research outputs historically is associated with scholarly publications. The FAIR principles (Findability, Accessibility, Interoperability, and Reusability) reach far beyond scholarly publications to include such research outputs as software, workflows, algorithms – all components of the research lifecycle [1, 2]. Curricular resources are not yet recognized as research outputs, however.

Ensuring that all research outputs are reliable and persistent, machine actionable digital objects is the primary objective of the FAIR principles [2]. The holistic research culture FAIR envisions relies on networks of policies, data management plans, persistent identifiers, standards, and repositories, and the FAIR ecosystem is representative of stakeholders' investment in the integrity of global open science [2].

Metadata has a key role in implementing major changes to entrenched tenets of the predominant research culture, notably that of scholarly publications as the sine qua non for research integrity and professional recognition [1, 2, 10, 11].

2.1   Metadata's Role in Research Integrity as a Precursor to the FAIR Principles

Prior to FAIR's emergence, measures of research integrity and professional recognition centered on scholarly publications. In the 2000s, scholars in the scientific community proposed to structure abstracts with metadata as part of the peer review process [12, 13]. The tool at hand was text mining software, and the structuring technique involved fitting abstracts with "electronically annotated information," or EAI [12, p. 1178].

Proponents viewed publishers as arbiters of research integrity due to the connection between publications and their deposit in electronic databases. Proponents held that if EAI necessarily began with researchers, peer review during the publication process mitigated bias and ensured research integrity [12, 13]. Conversely, proponents assigned a secondary role to a curator "versed in the particular content descriptors for a given species or subject of research" [13, p. 1]. In sum, the scientific scholars considered metadata expertise ancillary to peer review.

By the 2010s, publishers based accountability for research integrity on reproducible data sets [14, 15]. The unreliability of researcher data sets, however, posed obstacles to—even a crisis in—reproducibility [5, 7, 14, 16, 17]. Greater integration of journals and data repositories, along with the involvement of researchers in data management, now supports research integrity whether data is discrete or aggregated [6, 16, 18, 19]. Persistent digital objects are key to this integrated process but do not, in themselves, ensure the success of (re)using resource content. Persistent digital objects must be reliable to sustain the integrity of resource content [1, 2, 11]. By the middle of 2016, FAIR crystallized these concerns and provided a way forward [1].

Scholars increasingly view FAIR as an assist for (inter)disciplinary research and knowledge creation. The FAIR principles highlight far-reaching opportunities for data (re)use to enrich scholarship, substantiate incentives for scholars, and promote a broader FAIR research ecosystem[1, 2, 20, 21]. Yet even as scholars embrace the FAIR principles' importance for research outputs, they have not considered these principles' application in pedagogy. This case study explores how pedagogical research can complement academic research and contribute to the research lifecycle via "FAIRised" [2, p. 8] pedagogical documentation.

3 Pedagogical Research on Digital Humanities Syllabi and LIS Curricular Resources

Given the absence of digital objects in syllabi and LIS curricula more generally, two studies relied on semi-automated and manual data collection techniques to analyze curricular resources in two areas: digital humanities syllabi and health-related LIS courses [22, 23].

3.1 Digital Humanities Syllabi Research

The first study, completed in 2019, represents combined semi-automatic and manual content analysis techniques as a means for exploring the relationship between formal digital humanities training and skills needed to conduct public-funded (inter)disciplinary research [22]. Digital humanities syllabi links, uploaded to an open access Zotero group, provided a means to analyze digital humanities training [24]. Zotero is a software platform for citing bibliographic data and permits subscribers to create "groups" for sharing resources. Spiro's (2012) Zotero groups upload digital humanities syllabi links for this purpose.[1]

Revisiting the "DHSyllabi" subfolder on August 20, 2020 for the present case study indicates that syllabi link uploads stopped in 2014 with the exception of one entry added

---

[1] https://www.zotero.org/groups/25016/digital_humanities_education/items/collectionKey/MXXEMX7P.

in 2015 and one in 2017.[2] Use of syllabi links in the 2019 study found that most are inoperable, but exporting syllabi links from Zotero reuses semi-structured data in the links. All Zotero metadata fields were selected for export into a spreadsheet. Analysis of 236 syllabi links spanning a 17-year period from 1998–2014 appears in Table 1.

Table 1. Analysis of data in syllabi links exported from Zotero group "DHSyllabi".

Zotero field with syllabi data	Syllabi data description	Total cells with data	Percent of sample
Item Type	Webpage	236	100%
Title	Course title	236	100%
URL	Syllabi hyperlink	236	100%
Date Added	Month-day-year	236	100%
Date Modified	Month-day-year	236	100%
Access Date	Month-day-year	236	100%
Date	Syllabi dated by URL	95	40.25%
Author	Instructor name	56	23.73%
Publication Year	Year (i.e. 2014)	34	14.41%
Publication Title	Course title	30	12.71%
Abstract Note	Course description	22	9.32%
Short Title	Course title	13	5.51%
Type	Syllabus	10	4.24%
Manual tags	Instructor keywords	9	3.81%

Zotero automatically parses syllabi data into the 14 Zotero-labeled fields in column 1, "Zotero field with syllabi data".[3] Column 2, "Syllabi data description" corresponds to fields in syllabi. For example, Zotero's "Item Type" identifies each syllabus as a webpage, "Title" fills with the course title if provided, random data or a blank cell if not; and "URL" fills with the syllabi's hyperlink. These three fields apply to all 236 records (100%). Three other fields at 100%, "Date Added", "Date Modified", and "Access Date" refer to the link's Zotero upload date and activities.

Although more than half of the Zotero fields are sparsely populated, six ("Date", "Author", "Publication Title", "Abstract note", "Type", and "Manual Tags") suggest crosswalks to basic syllabi elements. Unfortunately, essential syllabi elements, namely student assessments and course readings, drop out completely on export. More robust options for syllabi metadata are imperative for digital object properties.

[2] https://www.zotero.org/groups/25016/digital_humanities_education/collections/MXX EMX7P/items/R5WVPCUP/collection.

[3] A few fields inapplicable to the syllabi, such as "Interviewer" and "Cosponsor", populated sparsely with random data and are not included in Table 1. The "Cosponsor field sparsely filled with "English", suggesting that "Language" could be a useful field in structured syllabi.

3.2 LIS Course Catalog Research

The second pedagogical research project, completed in 2021, utilizes American Library Association (ALA) links to accredited LIS programs in the US to gather health-related course titles and descriptions from institutions' course catalogs [23]. Course descriptions' unstructured format necessitates laborious preprocessing to generate a coding system. Of 118 course titles and descriptions collected manually from 40 LIS programs, subsequent manual analysis techniques winnowed this data set to 35 (29.66%) having relevance for the project [23].

Conversely, curricular resources as digital objects could permit seamless extraction from course catalogs on institutions' websites. Health and other (inter)disciplinary topics represent especially promising areas in which FAIR principles undergird topic genealogies and how they change over time. Data may be accessed and directed to problems devised by humans, or even by machines [11]. The tremendous potential for "FAIR-ised" [2, p. 8] curricular resources to enhance the research lifecycle and augment the global FAIR ecosystem lies as yet untapped.

4 Discussion

FAIR principles are a key step toward machine actionability, defined as a "continuum of possible states wherein a digital object provides increasingly more detailed information to an autonomously-acting, computational data explorer" [1, p. 3]. In order to apply FAIR principles and reap their benefits, digital objects must first have unique and persistent identifiers [1, 2]. The persistent identifier, part of a metadata application profile, wraps a digital object core, includes a license, and provides for long-term access on the Semantic Web [2, 25].

Structuring curricular resources with metadata proper to their status as persistent digital objects is a first step toward making them FAIR for the classroom as well as for research. As suggested in the 2019 and 2021 projects, "FAIRised" [2, p. 8] pedagogical documentation is needed to facilitate efficient and reliable pedagogical research on how (inter)disciplinary topics are taught and students trained. An added benefit is the capability to link curricular resources to publications and data sets in academic libraries, archives, and data repositories [7, 18, 26]. The (re)use of research outputs, inclusive of curricular resources, allows for more complete comprehension of interdependencies within the research lifecycle [27]. Consequently, "FAIRised" [2, p. 8] pedagogical documentation can function as an access point to entire networks of related (inter)disciplinary research outputs in the (inter)disciplinary research lifecycle [8, 28].

This case represents a starting point for "FAIRising" [2, p. 8] syllabi digital object properties. Much as syllabi are sources for investigation, course titles and descriptions undergird LIS pedagogical research in the 2021 project [23]. As exemplified in Table 2, Zotero metadata and syllabi metadata may help prototype digital object metadata for curricular resources.

"FAIRised" [2, p. 8] curricular resources including syllabi, course titles and descriptions, and course content such as student assessments and readings could be reliably implemented with future reuse in mind. Future research on "FAIRising" [2, p. 8] pedagogical documentation may advance pedagogical research along three lines. First, digital

Table 2. Zotero metadata, syllabi metadata, and digital object metadata for curricular resources

Zotero metadata	Syllabi metadata	Digital object metadata for curricular resources
Item type	Webpage	Webpage(s)
Title	Course title	Course title
URL	Syllabus hyperlink	Syllabus hyperlink
Publication year	Year (syllabus date)	Syllabus date, semester
Author	Instructor name	Institution, department
Abstract note	Course description	Course description
Type	Syllabus	Syllabus
Manual tags	Instructor keywords	(inter)disciplinary topics
Manual tags	Student assessments	Projects, tools, course outputs
Manual tags	Course readings	Links to external research outputs

object properties and metadata are to be determined, as suggested by case study research. Second, metadata for curricular resources should be linked to journal publications and data sets, fostering data (re)use. Third, because metadata both constitutes and contains documentation for curricular resources over time, "FAIRising" [2, p. 8] concerns both longitudinal and cross-institutional investigations. Based on these three recommendations, pedagogical research on "FAIRised" [2, p. 8] pedagogical documentation can complement academic research, enhance the research lifecycle, and advance the FAIR ecosystem long term.

5 Conclusion

Pedagogical research has potential to complement academic research, but the role of curricular resources in the research lifecycle has not been considered. This potential is circumscribed while pedagogical documentation remains unstructured text. "FAIRised" [2, p. 8] curricular resources are imperative for conducting pedagogical research on how (inter)disciplinary topics are taught and students trained. As part of the research lifecycle, such curricular resources augment research outputs. "FAIRising" [2, p. 8] pedagogical documentation for the research lifecycle is as much an opportunity for individual researchers and institutions as it is a necessary step in advancing scholarship holistically throughout the global FAIR ecosystem.

References

1. Wilkinson, M.D., et al.: The FAIR Guiding Principles for scientific data management and stewardship. Sci. Data **3**, 1–9 (2016)
2. Collins, S., et al.: Turning FAIR into reality: final report and action plan from the European Commission expert group on FAIR data. Publications Office of the European Union, LU (2018)

3. Tenopir, C., et al.: Research data services in academic libraries: data intensive roles for the future? J. eSci. Libr. **4**(2), e1085 (2015)
4. Vitale, C.R.H., Marshall, B., Nurnberger, A.: You're in good company: unifying campus research data services. Bull. Am. Soc. Inf. Sci. Technol. (Online) **41**(6), 26–28 (2015)
5. Stodden, V., et al.: Setting the default to reproducible: reproducibility in computational and experimental mathematics. In: Stodden, et al. (eds.): ICERM Workshop on Reproducibility In Computational and Experimental Mathematics, ICERM, pp. 1–19. Brown University, Providence, RI (2013)
6. MacMillan, D.: Data sharing and discovery: what librarians need to know. J. Acad. Libr. **40**(5), 541–549 (2014)
7. Akmon, D., et al.: Building tools to support active curation: lessons learned from SEAD. Int. J. Digit. Curation **12**(2), 76–85 (2018)
8. Mayernik, M.S., et al.: Enriching education with exemplars in practice: iterative development of data curation internships. Int. J. Digit. Curation **10**(1), 123–134 (2015)
9. Hirsch, B.D.: Digital Humanities Pedagogy: Practices, Principles and Politics. Open Book Publishers, Cambridge, MA (2014)
10. Harrower, N., et al.: Sustainable and FAIR Data Sharing in the Humanities: Recommendations of the ALLEA Working Group E-Humanities. In: Harrower, N. et al. (eds.) ALLEA Report February 2020, pp. 1–42. All European Academies, Berlin (2020)
11. Thompson, M., et al.: Making FAIR easy with FAIR tools: from creolization to convergence. Data Intell. **2**(1–2), 87–95 (2020)
12. Leitner, F., Valencia, A.: A text-mining perspective on the requirements for electronically annotated abstracts. FEBS Lett. **582**(8), 1178–1181 (2008)
13. Seringhaus, M., Gerstein, M.: Manually structured digital abstracts: a scaffold for automatic text mining. FEBS Lett. **582**(8), 1170 (2008)
14. Christian, T.-M., et al.: Operationalizing the replication standard. Int. J. Digit. Curation **13**(1), 114–124 (2018)
15. Dafoe, A.: Science deserves better: the imperative to share complete replication files. PS: Polit. Sci. Polit. **47**(01), 60–66 (2014)
16. International Society for Biocuration: Biocuration: distilling data into knowledge. PLOS Biol. **16**(4), e2002846 (2018)
17. Marwick, B.: Computational reproducibility in archaeological research: basic principles and a case study of their implementation. J. Archaeol. Method Theor. **24**(2), 424–450 (2017)
18. Niu, J.: Archival intellectual control in the digital age. J. Arch. Organ. **12**(3–4), 186–197 (2015)
19. Marshall, B., et al.: Organizing, contextualizing, and storing legacy research data: a case study of data management for librarians. Issues Sci. Technol. Libr. https://explore.openaire.eu/sea rch/publication?articleId=datacite____::5c55fcc1fbbcb531a1f7a378ae4d9845. Accessed on 02 Mar 2017
20. Dunning, A., De Smaele, M., Böhmer, J.: Are the FAIR principles fair? Int. J. Digit. Curation **12**(2), 177–195 (2017)
21. Hank, C., Bishop, B.W.: Measuring FAIR principles to inform fitness for use. Int. J. Digit. Curation **13**(1), 35–46 (2018)
22. Garwood, D.A., Poole, A.H.: Pedagogy and public-funded research: an exploratory study of skills in digital humanities projects. J. Doc. **75**(3), 550–576 (2019)
23. Garwood, D.A., Poole, A.H.: Vital signs: health literacy and library and information science pedagogy in the United States. J. Educ. Libr. Inf. Sci. **62**(1), n–n (2021)
24. Spiro, L.: Opening up digital humanities education. In: Hirsch, B.D. (ed.) Digital Humanities Pedagogy: Practices, Principles and Politics, pp. 331–363. Open Book Publishers, Cambridge, England (2012)

25. Greenberg, J., et al.: A metadata best practice for a scientific data repository. J. Libr. Metadata **9**(3–4), 194–212 (2009)
26. Ramírez, M.L.: Whose role is it anyway? A library practitioner's appraisal of the digital data Deluge. Bull. Am. Soc. Inf. Sci. Technol. (Online). Silver Spring, **37**(5), 21–23 (2011). Accessed 02 Mar 2017
27. Borgman, C.L., Wallis, J.C., Mayernik, M.S.: Who's got the data? Interdependencies in science and technology collaborations. Comput. Support. Coop. Work (CSCW) **21**(6), 485–523 (2012)
28. Giles, C.L.: Scholarly big data: information extraction and data mining. In: Proceedings of the 22nd ACM International Conference on Conference on Information & Knowledge Management 2013, pp. 1–2. CIKM, San Francisco, California, USA (2013)

LigADOS: Interlinking Datasets in Open Data Portal Platforms on the Semantic Web

Glaucia Botelho de Figueiredo[1]([✉]), Kelli de Faria Cordeiro[2]([✉]),
and Maria Luiza Machado Campos[1]([✉])

[1] Federal University of Rio de Janeiro (UFRJ), Rio de Janeiro, RJ 21941-916, Brazil
glaucia.botelho@ufrj.br, mluiza@ppgi.ufrj.br
[2] Center of Naval System Analysis of Brazilian Navy, Rio de Janeiro, RJ 20091-000, Brazil
kelli@marinha.mil.br

Abstract. The fostering of data opening has been largely motivated by sets of laws on access to information, which establish the need to make data related to governmental activities available to citizens and society in general, as well as results from business processes or scientific research, also for accountability and transparency. There are several ways of making data available to the public, from a simple website to sophisticated applications for accessing the data. In this context, one of the options is the construction of an open data portal using platforms for data repositories and catalogs. In the last few years, there has been a rapid proliferation of this type of portals, with domain or organization specific datasets being widely disseminated in platforms like CKAN. In these platforms, datasets are organized in thematic groups and described by keywords and other attributes assigned by the publisher. Usually described by metadata with poor semantics, these datasets very often remain as "data silos", with no explicit connection or data integration mechanism, making it difficult for the users to locate and interrelate relevant data sources. In contrast, the Semantic Web focuses on a way of modeling and representing data in an easier manner to establish interrelationships between data, accompanied by richer descriptors. Based on this scenario, this paper proposes LigADOS, an approach to create interconnections between datasets considering their content and related metadata. LigADOS is based on the principles of the Semantic Web and associated linked data solutions and technologies, to support rich access strategies to RDF data published using portal platforms like CKAN and others.

Keywords: Dataset interlinking · Semantic metadata interlinking · Open data portals platforms · FAIR Data Point

1 Introduction

The Open Data movement has been guided by the need to comply with laws to enforce transparency and accountability, which establish the need to make public sector activities data available to citizens and the society in general. Although these data can be available in different ways on the Web, the access to open data fostered the emergence of platforms

E. Garoufallou and M.-A. Ovalle-Perandones (Eds.): MTSR 2020, CCIS 1355, pp. 73–84, 2021.
https://doi.org/10.1007/978-3-030-71903-6_8

to support data portals development and deployment. Currently, it is possible to identify some possibilities of relations among published datasets, when they share some string utilized as descriptors. However, the basis of these possible relations are vulnerable, since it considers string syntax. It is not enough to know if two or more strings have the same meaning when applied to distinct situations.

The Semantic Web goes in the opposite direction. Its associated technologies provide possibilities for data access strategies capable of dealing with interrelationships between data, accompanied by richer descriptors. The core framework, coined as Resource Description Framework (RDF) extends the linking structure of the Web to name, identify and describe resources and the relationships between them. However, open data portals platforms are not able to explore the potential of RDF datasets. In addition, the machine processing capability of RDF datasets is underutilized, as there is no support, integrated or not, to access the data representation structures utilized.

Based on this scenario, this paper presents LigADOS, an approach to support rich access strategies to RDF data published on open data portal platforms. The approach contributes with richer access possibilities, exploring linked data dispositions for search, querying and navigation.

The remainder of this article is divided into seven sections. Section 2 discusses characteristics of open data portal platforms and explains the goals of an FDP. Section 3 presents the state of the art about indirect dataset interlinkage, considering metadata associated with them on open data portals. Section 4 discusses in detail the LigADOS approach. Section 5 contains an application of LigADOS prototype in The Brazilian Open Data Portal. And, finally, Sect. 6 concludes with final remarks and topics for further investigation.

2   Open Data Portals Platforms on the Semantic Web

The Semantic Web offers the fundamentals to interconnect, across the Web, information resources that are not originally associated, taking advantage of the Web infrastructure. Besides HTTP and URIs (Uniform Resource Identifier), the Semantic Web and, more specifically, linked data, use RDF (Resource Description Framework) as a data representation framework. This infrastructure is the basis of the Web of Data, which is focused on interlinking data published on the Web and machine processable semantic annotations on vocabularies and ontologies [1].

Several governmental and non-governmental organizations – at the local, regional, national and international levels – have made public some data produced by their internal processes. As examples of national level initiatives, several countries have launched their own Open Government Data Portals (OGDP) contributing to society participation and the understanding of government decisions.

Comprehensive Knowledge Archive Network (CKAN)[1], Socrata[2] and Opendata-soft[3] are platforms for developing portals focused on publishing open government data.

---

[1] https://ckan.org/.

[2] https://www.tylertech.com/products/socrata.

[3] https://www.opendatasoft.com/.

CKAN has been widely used in government portals in countries in Europe, South America, North America, Africa and Australia. Mainly local governments in the United States of America have used Socrata; and Opendatasoft is most popular with European organizations. However, Socrata and Opendatasoft are paid solutions. Dataverse[4] and DSpace[5] are open data portal platforms more focused on the support of the scientific community [2], that have been applied to organize data considering some scientific literature that references them, even structuring the quote.

Many open data initiatives associated with government processes use the CKAN platform as the support for their OGDPs. It is a free and open source tool, focused on creating websites for open data availability, developed and maintained by the Open Knowledge Foundation. A dataset comprises the metadata that describes it and the distributions that contain the data itself. A dataset can be composed of at least one and at most several distributions. These distributions can be of different formats, proprietary or not, such as XLSX, PDF, XML, CSV and RDF. CKAN does not impose rules on how to organize data distributions.

Natively, CKAN provides a series of descriptor options (metadata) for each dataset. Although RDF datasets have metadata in smaller grains than the set as a unit, CKAN does not exploit this advantage in the available mechanisms for assigning metadata or in its mechanisms for accessing the data. In fact, most of the available metadata options refer to structural metadata, that is, they refer to descriptive characteristics (title), storage (unique identifier) and management (use licenses). The option of metadata with semantic characteristics is limited to tags. Tags, in turn, are usually assigned by the data publishers themselves. This does not guarantee the best representativeness of the data, since there are no rules or restrictions in their assignment [3]. Furthermore, in CKAN, tags are assigned to each dataset, often referring to a thematic area, not necessarily representing the instances of the datasets. Several research have developed works to support and automate tag generation [3–5].

Currently, working groups associated with the GO FAIR initiative have recommended a kind of metadata organization perspective divided into five metadata schemes or levels [6]. FAIR is the acronym for "Findable", "Accessible", "Interoperable" and "Reusable", an initiative that recommends a set of guiding principles to make data generated and/or used by scientific research easier to be discovered, accessible, interoperable and reusable by both people and machines [7].

The possibility of developing and using extensions already coded and tested, associated with the fact that most OGDPs initiatives publish their open data using the CKAN platform, led to the choice of this platform for use in the experiments of the proposed approach.

Considering metadata spread in several repositories, there is a trend to the establishment of a federation of data points to improve data discoverability by human beings and by machines. As part of the FAIR initiative, these central points, coined FAIR Data Points (FDP), actually constitute repositories of metadata. The FDP architecture includes a Web-based graphical user interface (GUI) and an application programming interface

---

[4] https://dataverse.org/.

[5] https://duraspace.org/dspace/.

(API) for exposing its functionalities to the users. The Metadata Provider is a core component responsible for the provisioning of the metadata content available in the FDP. Aligned to the FAIR principles, five metadata schemes describe complementary layers of data organization. The five layers are FDP Metadata (level 1), Data Catalog Metadata (level 2), Dataset Metadata (level 3), Distribution Metadata (level 4) and Data Record Metadata (level 5)[6].

The metadata organization in five layers, a hierarchy from high-level less granular to bottom-level more granular, moves towards better dataset findability, as metadata are more detailed each level to better understand the data contents without the need of accessing the data instances. In addition, metadata includes the information about dataset licenses and access protocols. This facilitates interoperability and data reuse, as proposed by FAIR initiative. Further, it opens possibilities towards data interlinkage.

3 Open Data Interlinkage

Much work has been invested in developing approaches to make linked open data easily accessible. In this context, a link makes it possible to navigate in a seamless way between resources belonging to different datasets, possibly of different domains, giving access to richer and more complete information than the data at hand. There are approaches that focus on the quality of a linkset, a special kind of dataset containing only RDF links between two datasets. For this, they define measures like the *average linkset reachability*, which is a type of metric to evaluate the number of new concepts reached by crossing a linkset [8]. There are approaches that propose supporting the discovery of links to enrich new datasets to be published, or just connect available datasets without considering metadata associated to them [9–14]. This means that they do not consider including data that play the role of descriptors. In contrast, there are approaches that propose data interlinkage, considering metadata and indirect links between the datasets. Indirect in the sense that a moderating component mediates connections. Also, most often, the links are external to the portals, because the moderating component is not embedded in the data portals [3, 5–7, 15–17].

In this regard, when indirect data interlinkages use specialized vocabulary for descriptive metadata annotation, such as DCAT, VoID, Schema.org [6, 7, 15, 16], the portals contemplate a rich set of metadata. However, they are still limited to identify how a published dataset metadata was organized, with no support to content-related interlinkage processes. Although tags are usually included in these sets of metadata, they represent only a simple string.

When domain specific vocabularies are utilized, they are able to annotate only part of metadata: usually tags or the indication of the main dataset domain [3, 5, 17]. Indeed, it adds another semantic level, lifting simple strings to semantic expressions. Combining annotation using specialized vocabulary for descriptive metadata and domain specific vocabularies takes to richer descriptions allowing semantic interlinkage processes [17].

Anyway, this combination keeps metadata in dataset level or in distribution level, disregarding data instances. When data instances are considered to extract some level

---

[6] https://github.com/FAIRDataTeam/FAIRDataPoint-Spec

of metadata, the semantic lifting is higher [5, 7]. Moreover, it gives the ability to data consumers to grasp the dataset content without delving into data instances.

A track of investigation that has stood out in recent years involves the establishment of guidelines and the development of solutions to deal with FAIR data, emphasizing metadata interlinkage [7]. In this context, an approach is the development of a semantic proxy to collect and adapt existing metadata to this new reality [6].

In this paper, we explore data instances as sources to obtain a more granular level of metadata. Thus, we propose an approach that considers indirect RDF dataset interconnections, by defining and exposing data record level metadata interlinkage.

4   LigADOS Approach

LigADOS proposal aims to take advantage of the benefits offered by the Web of Data to interlink datasets published on open data portals, generate higher grained semantic metadata, as well as provide support for machine processing. The focus of the approach is the interconnection of datasets already aligned with the concepts of the Web of Data, that is, datasets modeled in RDF in any type of serializations. The interconnection between datasets are established by data instances semantic classifications, that is, extracting higher level semantic descriptors from their embedded semantic annotations. Data instances classifications form a kind of semantic metadata, aligned to FAIR principles. So, they serve as inputs to compose metadata schemes proposed by FDPs, while expanding the possibilities for interconnecting datasets published in different portals. LigADOS creates an interface, aimed at the general public, to visualize dataset interlinkages, from where it is possible to easily identify and access the datasets involved in the interconnections.

The approach is composed of five macro processes: (i) metadata extraction; (ii) semantic interlinkages generation; (iii) semantic tags generation; (vi) semantic interlinkages publication; and (v) semantic metadata generation to support data portal interlinkages (see Fig. 1). A technical agent triggers the whole process, transparently to the functioning of the portal instance. This technical agent can be an artefact programmed for this purpose or a human being. The execution process occurs without external agents interactions. The processes execution beneficiaries are the portal data consumers (users), as well as the applications able to process linked data.

The "**Metadata extraction**" macro process starts with the scanning of the entire portal instance in order to extract metadata from all published datasets, with at least one distribution modeled in RDF. The extraction generates a new dataset, represented in RDF, containing a set of metadata annotated with the DCAT vocabulary that is then persisted in a triplestore. This choice of vocabulary follows a trend used in other works [6, 7, 16], but which is, mainly, aligned with the FAIR recommendations [7], for clearly allowing the identification of dataset distributions.

The "**Semantic interlinkages generation**" macro process is the core of the interlinkage processes. Firstly, LigADOS extracts the URLs of the distributions represented in RDF from the set of metadata. After that, it reads all data in order to identify the triple subjects and objects that are identified by a URI, and that are annotated with some vocabulary, ontology or thesaurus. Thus, the approach triggers federated queries to find the URI of the

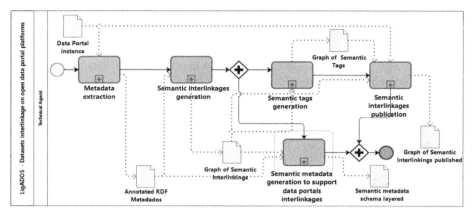

Fig. 1. Macro processes of LigADOS approach.

class or concept that categorizes the term and/or element used to annotate a triple resource of the dataset distribution. The identification of the class or concept considers the element exactly one level above, looking for relations such as skos:broader[7], rdf:type[8], rdfs:subClassOf[9]. Once the class or concept is identified, the query also extracts the class label looking for relations as skos:prefLabel[10] or rdfs:label[11]. These classes and/or concepts are used as inputs for assembling the triples that will be part of the *Graph of Semantic Interlinkings*, which is the output of this activities flow.

The *Graph of Semantic Interlinkings* is formed by nodes that represent: (i) the open data portal instance; (ii) the organizations that published the datasets; (iii) the datasets; (iv) the RDF datasets distributions; (v) the vocabularies, ontologies and thesaurus referenced in the datasets distributions; and (vi) the classes and/or concepts of the vocabularies, ontologies and thesaurus that classify the terms and/or elements used to annotate the triples of the datasets distributions. Note that the nodes, which represent vocabularies, ontologies and thesaurus, as well as those that represent the classes and/or concepts of these ontology resources, configure as metadata of data record level. This means they are aligned with the FAIR initiative and the metadata schema layers proposed in the specification of an FDP.

In short, the *Graph of Semantic Interlinkings* is a metadata graph. It aggregates in the same graph different metadata levels, when compared to the FDP metadata layered organization. Its prominence is given by the semantic descriptors of the data instances. The graph indicates the indirect interconnections between datasets and yet generates more granular semantic metadata than originally associated with datasets. Besides, aligned with the FAIR initiative, which recommends richly described metadata, this graph supports the identification of new possibilities for interoperability and reusability.

---

[7] skos:broader refers to the "broader" property of the SKOS vocabulary.

[8] rdf:type refers to "type" properties defined in the abstract syntax of the RDF vocabulary.

[9] rdfs:subClassOf refers to the "subClassOf" property of the RDFS Schema vocabulary.

[10] skos:prefLabel refers to the "prefLabel" property of the SKOS vocabulary.

[11] rdfs:label refers to the "label" property of the RDFS Schema vocabulary.

To define nodes, either as a subject or as an object, as well as to establish connections between these nodes, it is necessary to use specialized vocabularies. For the *Graph of Semantic Interlinkings* the following vocabularies are used: Friend of A Friend (FOAF)[12], Data Catalog Vocabulary (DCAT)[13], Dublin Core™ Metadata Initiative (DCMI) Metadata Terms[14], Vocabulary of A Friend (VOAF)[15], Vocabulary for Annotating Vocabulary Descriptions (VANN)[16] and, of course, the domain specific vocabularies from where class/concepts were extracted. An instance of a data portal must have only one associated graph generated.

Considering the approach defined in [5], the "**Semantic tags generation**" macro process generates triples using the "keyword" property of the DCAT vocabulary (`dcat:keyword`) in order to link the URIs of the datasets to the URIs of the extracted classes/concepts[17]. Thus, these triples are included in the *Graph of Semantic Tags*, also persisted in a triplestore. As a result, it is possible to browse the labels associated with a dataset in order to explore other potential datasets that use the same tags, thus discovering indirect links between them. The difference between LigADOS and that approach is that the former obtains semantic tags at a higher level of classification than the latter one, as it contemplates classes/concepts of elements/terms used in the annotation of the triples resources. This last point is also an advantage of LigADOS, since it considers datasets represented in RDF, while in [5] consider data in tabular formats. In LigADOS, it is essential that semantic metadata are accessible on the portal platforms used as catalogs or in any repositories used as an access point for open data: governmental, institutional or research. Thus, when proposing the use of an approach for the generation and availability of semantic tags on these platforms, it corroborates to the FAIR guidelines for data discovery (Findability), also facilitating accessibility (Accessibility).

The "**Semantic interlinkages publication**" macro process considers data consumers on open data portals with different knowledge profiles regarding the Web of Data technologies. Due to this heterogeneity of profiles, the major factor is to provide some intuitive support for the use of RDF datasets. A requirement to meet this demand involves an interface support that uses visual and interactive resources. As portal platforms are not yet able to provide these resources natively, whereas there are software solutions that already exploit these requirements, the LigADOS approach proposes the combination of both worlds.

---

[12] http://xmlns.com/foaf/spec/.

[13] https://www.w3.org/TR/vocab-dcat-2/.

[14] https://www.dublincore.org/specifications/dublin-core/dcmi-terms/.

[15] https://lov.linkeddata.es/vocommons/voaf/v2.3/.

[16] https://vocab.org/vann/.

[17] The latest version of the DCAT vocabulary (W3C Recommendation 04 February 2020) has made the domain of the "keyword" property flexible for any type of resource (`dcat:Dataset`, `dcat:DataService`), maintaining its range as a literal. Tags are also associated with datasets on portal platforms. Therefore, both the approach defined in [5] and the approach described here consider associating the generated tags to the dataset. However, both approaches experiment to make the range of the aforementioned property more flexible, in the sense of pointing to a class/concept of a common consensus vocabulary, which has an associated label.

This macro process makes available a download option, an interactive graph exploration option and a SPARQL endpoint to the *Graph of Semantic Interlinkings*. In addition, it publishes an interactive graph exploration option to the Graph of Semantic Tags.

The "**Semantic metadata generation to support data portal interlinkages**" macro process generates a set of extended metadata, which is aligned to the metadata profile defined for a FDP. That is, a profile defined for a metadata repository that provides access to federated data on open data portals. Systematically, LigADOS reads the set of metadata extracted from the portal instance, as well as the *Graph of Semantic Interlinkings* to extract four of five metadata organization levels for a FDP. These metadata need to be complemented with other metadata defined for a FDP profile. Since all metadata structure depends on a FDP installation, it is essential that LigADOS receives the FDP URL installation as data input.

Among the triples to complement the FDP profile, we can cite the one that establishes the metadata schema layers. Different from other metadata levels (catalog, dataset, distribution), where it is easy to perceive the identification level, the data record level requires some adjustments, as we need first to define how to identify this level.

The data record metadata is directly associated with a class/concept extracted from a vocabulary. This class/concept may be used by different dataset distributions, from the same dataset or from others. By itself, it is not able to characterize a single data record. A combination of data is necessary for its complete characterization.

In this context, the application of the alternative approach for RDF reification – RDF* – raises as an appropriate option. The RDF* approach allows nested triples, aiming to annotate triples resources with another metadata triple. Nested (embedded) triples can naturally correspond to the concept of triple identifiers [18].

Thus, the characterization of a data record occurs by combining the identification of the data distribution with the vocabulary classes/concepts that characterize terms/elements used to annotate its triples. This association represents the core of the interconnection process proposed by LigADOS. The following fragment represents the triple structure that identifies metadata of data record level. To compose it, LigADOS extracts data from the *Graph of Semantic Interlinkings* (using RDF* reification on subject) and assembles the relation to the parent metadata (object).

```
@prefix dcterms: <http://purl.org/dc/terms/> .
@prefix vocab: <http://namespacevocabulario.org/ns/> .

<<<FDP_URI_Distribution> dcterms:references vocab:URI_Class>>
dcterms:isPartOf <FDP_URI_ParentMetadata> .
```

LigADOS supports metadata extraction of catalog, dataset, distribution up to the level of data record metadata. The data steward must provide the metadata of the data record level, not the FDP owner. Thus, LigADOS automates this activity, also supporting portal data stewardship. At the FDP environment, the data record metadata level allows the identification of data interconnections managed by different portals without federated queries. The FDP Metadata Provider component can retrieve this graph through a SPARQL endpoint whenever required, to store in the FDP local triplestore. It should be noted that this macro process simplifies a set of activities for the inclusion of metadata that would be performed by the person in charge of the target FDP.

The data record level metadata carry the basis for indirect interconnections between datasets published in the same portal instance or between datasets published in different portals. The *Graph of Semantic Interlinkings* alone contains the interconnections within a portal. When this type of graph, belonging to different portal instances, is loaded in a FDP, it makes it possible to establish interconnections between portals. As the FDP structure is based on the cataloging of metadata to reach federated data, the interconnections between portals occur through the semantic metadata. This metadata central point makes it possible to query these interconnections in the FDP environment, without the need to use federated queries to source portals.

As LigADOS extracts instances classifications to generate data record metadata, it provides support to create indexes. As each class/concept extracted represents several resources (nodes) of the original datasets (graphs), one can detect certain kind of information without actually consulting the datasets. Although some generated benefits may be similar to those of RDF summarization [19], LigADOS does not apply any type of RDF summarization method, but creates a brand new dataset (graph) to represent non explicit data interlinkages between all datasets (graphs) published in a portal. In [19] was depicts a high-level taxonomy of the RDF summarization approaches, grouping the main methods of the algorithms into four main categories (structural, statistical, pattern-mining and hybrid), identifying subcategories whenever possible. LigADOS considers only annotated resources that is resources defined in vocabularies, ontologies or thesaurus, in any triple position, without concern about reducing datasets sizes.

5 LigADOS Approach Prototype and Evaluation

A prototype supporting the LigADOS approach was developed in Java, using the RDF4J framework and storing triples in GraphDB^{TM}. GraphDB^{TM} has features for users to explore and navigate graphs generated from the result of SPARQL queries, even providing interactive features. Two modules support the approach: one to construct and publish the interlinkages, as well as the semantic tags; and another to prepare metadata for the FDP. Both work without prompting the user, running in the background of the portal instance, even to publish the interlinkages at the portal. For this, the first module uses the CKANAPI.

An experimentation of the approach and prototype was carried out in instances of open data portals based on CKAN. The Brazilian Open Data Portal is used by the Brazilian public sector to provide data on many varied topics, from governmental agencies and administrative organizations at the federal level.

The approach was applied to a subset of datasets from the environmental domain extracted from this portal. At the Brazilian Open Data Portal, there were twenty-five publications represented in RDF. However, twenty-three of them were published by the same organization, which is not enough to demonstrate the approach developed. As a result, we extracted some datasets in their original formats; next, we triplified them to evaluate the approach. As an example, we considered two datasets published by different organizations. The original publication of the "Vegetation of Brazilian Mangrove"[18] dataset

---

[18] In this paper, the original descriptions of the datasets and its distributions were translated from Portuguese to English.

is composed of three distributions. The "National Forest Information System - SNIF" dataset is composed of twenty-eight distributions. Among the associated metadata are the title, the organization that published them, a brief textual description, administrative metadata and tags. For the "Vegetation of Brazilian Mangrove" dataset, there are only three associated tags. Although there are twenty associated tags for the "National Forest Information System - SNIF" dataset, there are no intersections between the sets of tags. In general, the datasets fall within the environmental domain, but there is no evidence of relationships between the distributions of the datasets. There are neither common labels, nor coincident descriptions that lead to consider the existence of any kind of relationship between them.

After applying the LigADOS approach, which generated semantic interconnections considering the semantics embedded in the data, it was possible to verify that both datasets shared the same common Aims-Agrovoc thesaurus concepts (in Portuguese): "Vegetação" (Vegetation), "Mato" (Scrub), "Floresta de regiões húmidas" (Rain Forest) e "Floresta tropical" (Tropical Forest) (see Fig. 2). In Fig. 2, the highlighted arrows show the dataset interlink through the Aims-Agrovoc" node and distribution interlinks by common thesaurus concepts utilized by dataset distributions.

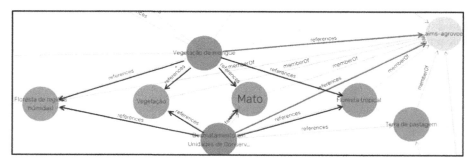

Fig. 2. Interconnections between dataset distributions by the use of a common thesaurus

Other interlinks were established on the Brazilian Open Data Portal. Table 1 depicts some dataset distributions interlinks for the environmental domain, including datasets published by distinct organizations, before and after the approach use. Some previous interconnections refer to the organization that published the dataset, others refer to some specific word utilized to describe the dataset or even the name of the file distribution. Just a few correspond to tags, and they do not even consider semantic aspects, because they are not linked to vocabularies, behaving as simple textual descriptions. In the "After" columns at Table 1, we disregard the original interlinkages, exposing only the brand new semantic interlinkings generated.

The numbers show that the LigADOS approach increases the number of interlinkages. However, this is not the most important aspect. The main aspect is that the new interlinkage points are considering the instances of data, namely, the semantic meaning resulting from the use of the same vocabulary, ontology or thesaurus, and not just free terms attributed at the dataset publication at the portal instance.

Table 1. Interlinkages established for the Brazilian Open Data Portal datasets

	Mangrove vegetation		Vegetation Suppression Authorization		Deforestation Conservation Units		Deforestation - Biome - States		Biome Conservation Units	
	Before	After	Before	After	Before	After	Before	After	Before	After
Mangrove vegetation	-	-	2	6	0	4	0	4	0	4
Vegetation Suppression Authorization	2	6	-	-	1	5	2	5	1	5
Deforestation Conservation Units	0	4	1	5	-	-	2	5	1	5
Deforestation - Biome - States	0	4	2	5	2	5	-	-	3	5
Biome Conservation Units	0	4	1	5	1	5	3	5	-	-

6   Conclusions and Future Works

This paper described LigADOS, an approach for interconnecting datasets on open data portal platforms on the Semantic Web. LigADOS explores characteristics of linked data representation and vocabulary based annotation as a strategy to support the interconnection of published RDF datasets. The main strategy is to increase the level of semantic expressiveness of the datasets, in order to establish and expose existing non-explicit interconnections among them, not previously perceived by their publishers. Also, LigADOS supplies semantic metadata to compose four of five metadata schema levels of a FDP, specially the data record metadata level, which expands the dataset interlinkages possibilities between data portals.

The results indicate that interconnections are easily established when datasets modeled in RDF make use of common vocabularies, ontologies or thesaurus. Additionally, they indicate that datasets published by different organizations and for different purposes may have hidden interconnections mainly due to the way in which data portal platforms currently handle linked data, and also because of the lack of semantic metadata. In contrast, the results of other experiments carried out indicate that datasets which, initially, seemed to deal with related issues (by observing the metadata cataloged at the time of their publications), may not actually have semantic interconnections when considering data instances. Finally, the prototype application showed that it is possible to integrate data portals platforms with triplestores like GraphDB, providing interfaces for graphical navigation in RDF.

As future work, we intend to use graph centrality measures to identify classes and/or concepts from which we can generate a subgraph. Centrality measures can be applied to quantify the nodes that most serve as hubs between datasets. Thus, semantic interconnections could be initially explored from several points and not from a single one (currently the initial points represent the "dcat:Catalog" and the "dcat:Dataset" type).

References

1. Hendler, J., Berners-Lee, T., Miller, E.: Integrating applications on the semantic web. J. Inst. Electr. Eng. Jpn. **122**(10), 676–680 (2002)
2. Langer, A., Bilz, E., Gaedke, M.: Analysis of current RDM applications for the interdisciplinary publication of research data. In: Proceedings of the 1st International Workshop on Approaches for Making Data Interoperable SEM4TRA-AMAR@ SEMANTICS (2019)

3. Tygel, A.A.: Semantic tags for open data portals: metadata enhancements for searchable open data. D.Sc. thesis. Federal University of Rio de Janeiro, Rio de Janeiro (2016)
4. de Lira, M.A.B.: Uma Abordagem Para Enriquecimento Semântico de Metadados Para Publicação de Dados Abertos. M.Sc. thesis. Federal University of Pernambuco, Pernambuco (2014)
5. Castro, B.P.C., Rodrigues, H.F., Lopes, G.R., Campos, M.L.M.: Semantic enrichment and exploration of open dataset tags. In: Proceedings of the 25th Brazillian Symposium on Multimedia and the Web, pp. 417–424. Association for Computing Machinery, New York (2019)
6. Moreira, J.L.R., et al.: Towards findable, accessible, interoperable and reusable (FAIR) data repositories: improving a data repository to behave as a FAIR data point. Liinc em Revista 15(2), 244–258 (2019). https://doi.org/10.18617/liinc.v15i2.4817
7. Wilkinson, M., et al.: Interoperability and FAIRness through a novel combination of Web technologies. PeerJ Comput. Sci. 3, e11 (2017). https://doi.org/10.7717/peerj-cs.110
8. Albertoni, R., De Martino, M., Podestà, P.: Linkset quality assessment for the thesaurus framework LusTRE. In: Garoufallou, E., Subirats Coll, I., Stellato, A., Greenberg, J. (eds.) MTSR 2016. CCIS, vol. 672, pp. 27–39. Springer, Cham (2016). https://doi.org/10.1007/978-3-319-49157-8_3
9. Leme, L.A.P.P., Lopes, G.R., Nunes, B.P., Casanova, M.A., Dietze, S.: Identifying candidate datasets for data interlinking. In: Daniel, F., Dolog, P., Li, Q. (eds.) ICWE 2013. LNCS, vol. 7977, pp. 354–366. Springer, Heidelberg (2013). https://doi.org/10.1007/978-3-642-39200-9_29
10. Caraballo, A.A.M., Nunes, B.P., Lopes, G.R., Leme, L.A.P.P., Casanova, M.A.: Automatic creation and analysis of a linked data cloud diagram. In: Cellary, W., Mokbel, M.F., Wang, J., Wang, H., Zhou, R., Zhang, Y. (eds.) WISE 2016. LNCS, vol. 10041, pp. 417–432. Springer, Cham (2016). https://doi.org/10.1007/978-3-319-48740-3_31
11. Achichi, M., Bellahsene, Z., Ellefi, M.B., Todorov, K.: Linking and disambiguating entities across heterogeneous RDF graphs. J. Web Semant. 55, 108–121 (2019)
12. Martins, Y.C., da Mota, F.F., Cavalcanti, M.C.: DSCrank: a method for selection and ranking of datasets. In: Garoufallou, E., Subirats Coll, I., Stellato, A., Greenberg, J. (eds.) MTSR 2016. CCIS, vol. 672, pp. 333–344. Springer, Cham (2016). https://doi.org/10.1007/978-3-319-49157-8_29
13. Gomes, R.V.A., Casanova, M.A., Lopes, G.R., Paes Leme, L.A.P.: A metadata focused crawler for linked data. In: Proceedings of the 16th International Conference on Enterprise Information Systems, vol. 2, pp. 489–500. SCITEPRESS, Lda (2014)
14. Kettouch, M., Luca, C., Hobbs, M.: SemiLD: mediator-based framework for keyword search over semi-structured and linked data. J. Intell. Inf. Syst. 52(2), 311–335 (2019). https://doi.org/10.1007/s10844-018-0536-1
15. Milić, P., Veljković, N., Stoimenov, L.: Linked relations architecture for production and consumption of linksets in open government data. In: Janssen, M., et al. (eds.) I3E 2015. LNCS, vol. 9373, pp. 212–222. Springer, Cham (2015). https://doi.org/10.1007/978-3-319-25013-7_17
16. Neumaier, S., Umbrich, J., Polleres, A.: Lifting data portals to the web of data. In: LDOW@WWW (2017)
17. Pesce, V., Maru, A., Archer, P., Malapela, T., Keizer, J.: Setting up a global linked data catalog of datasets for agriculture. In: Garoufallou, E., Hartley, R.J., Gaitanou, P. (eds.) MTSR 2015. CCIS, vol. 544, pp. 357–368. Springer, Cham (2015). https://doi.org/10.1007/978-3-319-24129-6_31
18. Hartig, O., Thompson, B.: Foundations of an alternative approach to reification in RDF. arXiv preprint arXiv:1406.3399v2 (2019)
19. Čebirić, Š., et al.: Summarizing semantic graphs: a survey. VLDB J. 28(3), 295–327 (2019)

Lifting Tabular Data to RDF: A Survey

Manuel Fiorelli[✉] and Armando Stellato

Department of Enterprise Engineering, University of Rome Tor Vergata, via del Politecnico 1, 00133 Roma, Italy
fiorelli@info.uniroma2.it, stellato@uniroma2.it

Abstract. Tabular data formats (e.g. CSV and spreadsheets) combine ease of use, versatility and compatibility with information management systems. Despite their numerous advantages, these formats typically rely on column headers and out-of-band agreement to convey semantics. There is clearly a large gap with respect to the Semantic Web, which uses RDF as a graph-based data model, while relying on ontologies for well-defined semantics. Several systems have been developed to close this gap, supporting the conversion of tabular data to RDF. This study is a survey of these systems, which have been analyzed and compared. We identified commonalities and differences among them, discussed different approaches and derived useful insights on the task.

Keywords: CSV · TSV · Excel · Conversion · RDF · Survey

1 Introduction

More and more organizations are going to share their data under open licenses with the aim of fostering their reuse. Usually, this kind of open data includes spreadsheets and, in general, tabular data, which combine wide tooling support, flexibility and conveniency. However, tabular data usually lack explicit semantics backed by a formal ontology, as they rely on column headers and out-of-band information. Therefore, they only enable a low grade in the five-star model of Linked (Open) Data [1].

Tabular formats are still convenient at the beginning of the path toward Linked Data, as almost any data management system can export to CSV or spreadsheets. Subsequent steps include data cleaning, data transformation and, finally, data upload to a new infrastructure based on RDF (Resource Description Framework). Another very frequent scenario involves dataset updates: dataset managers have already migrated to RDF, but they receive many updates from third parties expressed through (possibly heterogeneous) tabular formats (as in the AGRIS Dataset [2]).

Unsurprisingly, several systems have been developed to support this common use case of converting tabular data to RDF. Being interested in data integration and data management, we wanted to make sense of this offering. Accordingly, the contribution of this study is a review of these systems, highlighting their characteristics, similarities and peculiarities. In Sect. 2, we first described these systems individually. Then, in Sect. 3 we developed a comparative summary, which allowed us to better understand commonalities and differences among them, discuss different approaches and derive insights on the task. Finally, Sect. 4 provides the conclusions.

© Springer Nature Switzerland AG 2021
E. Garoufallou and M.-A. Ovalle-Perandones (Eds.): MTSR 2020, CCIS 1355, pp. 85–96, 2021.
https://doi.org/10.1007/978-3-030-71903-6_9

2 Reviewed Systems

2.1 Standalone Converters

Any23. Any23 [3] is a swiss-army knife supporting the conversion of several formats to RDF. It can be used as a library, web service or command line tool. Any23 can convert CSV files under the assumption that each row contains the description of one resource using a vocabulary generated systematically from the header of the table.

Grafter. Grafter [4] is a library that uses an internal DSL based on the functional language Clojure (https://clojure.org/). The laziness of Clojure allows Grafter to stream the execution of a processing pipeline, making it scalable to a large amount of data. Furthermore, a pipeline made exclusively of pure functions (i.e. free of side effects) can be executed any number of times without side effects. The functional nature of processing pipelines enables solutions, such as previewing the transformation on a subset of the input data. Grafter aims to separate different concerns in a pipeline, such as loading of input data, cleaning of such data and the actual transformation. Grafter has been integrated into the cloud-based platform DataGraft [5] for the transformation and publication of data as linked data. Grafter is accessed via Grafterizer, a web application that can represent transformation pipelines and RDF templates graphically instead of relying on the Clojure-based DSL. The application supports live preview of the data as these are cleaned and processed, as well as of the final RDF. Furthermore, transformations can be shared and subsequently reused.

Populous. Populous [6] uses OPPL (Ontology Pre-Processing Language) [7] as a mapping language. OPPL supports representation and execution of ontology design patterns [8]. Populous provides a simple tabular user interface for the population of an ontology by domain experts. The table is backed by a template for the given domain ontology, which is instantiated with the values in each row. In line with its goal, Populous supports constraining the columns with respect to an ontology and data catalogs.

RDF123. RDF123 [9] provides an application for writing mapping specifications, as well as a web service for executing them against spreadsheets. It strives to move away from the assumption of rows representing homogenous resources. While every row is transformed using the same graph pattern, the mapping language achieves the desired level of flexibility by having all components of the graph (i.e. vertices and edges) be computed via complex expressions (possibly containing conditionals): when they produce an empty value, the corresponding component is omitted from the generated graph. The mapping is represented as RDF graphs, the components of which may contain expressions interpreted by the RDF123 runtime. Figure 1 contains an excerpt of a mapping that uses the value of the second column to set the property vcard:street-address.

RMLEditor. RMLEditor [10] provides a graphical user interface for specifying the transformation of raw data to RDF, without knowledge of the underlying mapping language RML[1]. This system allows to lookup column names on LOV (Linked Open Vocabularies) [11] to find a suitable vocabulary property. While RMLEditor mostly deals with

---

[1] https://rml.io/specs/rml/.

CSV/TSV files organized in rows, its mapping language has explicit support for joins, even over different data sources.

SKOS Play!. SKOS Play! converter[2] is an open-source (web) application for converting Excel spreadsheets to SKOS thesauri or RDF datasets in general. The tool assumes that the spreadsheets are structured into rows and relies on information encoded in a heading row to customize the mapping of the cells: e.g. language, datatype, value separator, etc. SKOS Play! supports cross-row references based on a selectable column, and different columns can be associated with subjects generated from other columns.

Spread2RDF. Spread2RDF [12] is a command-line tool that supports Excel/Excelx, Google spreadsheets, OpenOffice, LibreOffice and CSV. It uses an internal DSL (Domain-Specific Language) based on Ruby (https://www.ruby-lang.org/) to specify the transformation, which is executed on blocks of columns. Within a block, a cell underneath a column is converted to an RDF node, which is then used as the object of a property (bound to the column) of the subject associated with the row. By defining further column blocks, it is possible to generate resources that are used both as objects in the context of the original column block as well as subjects in the context of the new column block. While the processing is mostly row-oriented, it is also possible to address specific cells in a worksheet, to pinpoint specific pieces of information. The DSL supports templates: named fragments that can be reused within a mapping specification. Spread2RDF can compile mapping specifications into standalone executables.

```
<rdf:RDF
xmlns:foaf="http://xmlns.com/foaf/0.1/"
xmlns:rdf="http://www.w3.org/1999/02/22-rdf-syntax-ns#">
  <rdf:Description rdf:about="Ex:$1">
    <rdf:type

rdf:resource="http://www.w3.org/2006/vcard/ns#Address"/>
    <vcard:street-address>Ex:$2</foaf:mbox>
...
</rdf:RDF>
```

Fig. 1. An excerpt of a mapping for RDF123

TabLinker. TabLinker [13] is thought for converting statistical data to RDF using the Data Cube [14] vocabulary. While most systems can seamlessly operate on diverse tabular formats, TabLinker depends on the features of spreadsheets, in particular Microsoft Excel, e.g. the use of cell styles as a way to describe the layout of the data: where are the headers (vertical and horizontal), how they are hierarchically decomposed, etc. Furthermore, the vocabulary Open Annotation [15] can be used to represent harmonization rules, e.g. how the various dimensions can be mapped to RDF properties.

```
<#address>
  a :Resource ;
  :identity [
    :source_column 1 ;
  ] ;
  :type vcard:Address ;
  :attribute[
    :property vcard:street-address;
    :source_column 2
  ]
  ...
  .
```

Fig. 2. An excerpt of a mapping for Vertere

Tarql. Tarql [16] is a command-line tool allowing for SPARQL queries over tabular data, interpreted as a table of variable bindings, i.e. a sequence of assignments of terms to variables (usually the result of matching the WHERE clause of a SPARQL query).

Vertere. Vertere [17] is a command-line tool that represents mapping rules in RDF and these rules are intended to be executed row by row: this data parallelism can be exploited for parallel execution. Figure 2 illustrates how to bind the second column to the property vcard:street-address.

XLWrap. XLWrap [18] is an RDF wrapper for spreadsheets, CSV and TSV files, which can be retrieved locally or fetched via HTTP. The transformation is driven by mappings expressed as RDF in Trig syntax using a dedicated mapping vocabulary. A mapping consists of templates, which are applied to portions of the input data depending on user-defined transformations. Transformations, templates and other parts of the mapping can contain expressions referencing the input data, much like what happens in spreadsheets. XLWrap is also available as a server that automates the execution of transformations (e.g. after a change in the input files or the mappings). Furthermore, the sever can optionally start a SPARQL endpoint using Joseki (now deprecated by Apache Fuseki[3]).

2.2 Database to RDF Solutions

Sparqlify. Sparqlify [19] is a system for mapping relational databases to RDF that also supports simpler tabular data formats. Its mapping language SML (Sparqlification Mapping Language) combines SQL (Structured Query Language) for querying the source data with the possibility to instantiate graph patterns (like the ones found in SPARQL) out of RDF terms computed based on the information extracted via SQL.

---

[2] https://labs.sparna.fr/skos-play/convert.

[3] https://jena.apache.org/documentation/fuseki2/.

2.3   Knowledge Development Environments

Mapping Master (M2). Mapping Master (M^2) [20] is a plugin for Protégé dealing with data in the financial domain with complex layouts. Its mapping language combines the Manchester Syntax for expressing complex OWL (Web Ontology Language) axioms with (possibly relative) references to cells of the tabular data. The application of a formula to an arbitrary area of the input data allows for handling different data layouts.

PoolParty's Spreadsheet Import. PoolParty [21] can import a thesaurus from a tabular representation in which the indentation of rows represents the hierarchical relationships between concepts.

Sheet2RDF. Sheet2RDF [22] (an early version of which was described in [23]) can be used as a library, a standalone command-line tool and as a tool integrated into the web-based collaborative knowledge development platform VocBench 3 [24]. The latter provides a graphical user interface with suggestions informed by the ontology and data already existing in a target dataset. Sheet2RDF offers different levels of mapping specification, which progressively trade ease of use for flexibility. At the highest level, Sheet2RDF interprets the input rows as descriptions of homogenous resources, whose properties should be found in the header. If the input file conforms to certain conventions[4] inspired by the ones of SKOS Play!, no configuration is requested at all. One interesting feature of Sheet2RDF is its ability to trigger specific customizations for certain modeling patterns requiring more complex property values (e.g. SKOS-XL [25] reified labels). The user can optionally provide hints, e.g. bind a column to a property with a non-matching name, a class, natural language, etc. Sheet2RDF uses an iterative approach, attempting the automatic conversion again considering user-supplied information. A third level consists in allowing users to define new heuristics, patterns and corresponding triggers. Under the hoods, Sheet2RDF repurposes the knowledge acquisition platform CODA [26] using its transformation language PEARL [27]. Indeed, PEARL editing (in a dedicated editor) is the lowest level for specifying transformations.

TopBraid Composer's Tabular Data Import. TopBraid Composer [28] provides wizards for importing tabular data: a table represents a class whose properties are associated with the different columns. It is possible to map that class and properties to an existing ontology, or to import both the new vocabulary items and their instances.

2.4   Data Wrangling Tools

GraphDB OntoRefine. GraphDB OntoRefine is a data transformation tool that has been available in Ontotext GraphDB [29] since version 8.0. OntoRefine is integrated into its management web application (i.e. workbench) and it is based on OpenRefine. It supports TSV, CSV, *SV, XLS, XLSX, JSON, XML, RDF as XML, and Google sheet: additional formats can be introduced through OpenRefine extensions. OntoRefine relies on a systematic conversion of the input data to RDF triples, which can be accessed through a SPARQL endpoint. SPARQL and SPIN (SPARQL Inference Notation) can be used to transform this raw data according to any target domain model.

---

[4] https://art.uniroma2.it/sheet2rdf/documentation/heuristics.jsf.

Karma. Karma [30] is an ontology-based web application for data integration supporting several input formats (including hierarchical ones). Karma assumes a row-oriented layout for tabular formats. The transformation to RDF is specified visually as a graph, which is really a template for the graph that will be instantiated for each input row. The transformation is internally implemented using an interpretation of the R2RML [31] language called KR2RML. Karma allows for creating new columns executing Python scripts over the content of other columns. This capability can be also found in Grafter. Karma follows the paradigm of programming-by-example, since the system learns from models previously constructed by users how to construct models in the future.

LODRefine. LODRefine extends Open Refine (https://openrefine.org/) to provide a web application for the generation of RDF and the interaction with existing RDF datasets, e.g. for the purpose of identity resolution. It inherits from Open Refine a range of facilities for data cleaning and the possibility to load different data formats into a common tabular structure. The mapping of cleaned data to RDF is expressed graphically, with user supporting facilities such as auto-completion of ontology terms. GREL (Google Refine Expression Language) enables complex value transformations.

2.5 Full-Fledged ETL Solutions

CSV2RDF. CSV2RDF [32] builds on Sparqlify, proposing an extension of Semantic MediaWiki [33] for crowdsourcing the generation of the mappings; these are generated through an iterative process seeded by an initial mapping suggested by the system. Mappings are expressed through a MediaWiki Template supporting a subset of SML. For visualization, CSV2RDF integrates CubeViz [34] (data cubes) and Facete [35] (spatial data).

Csv2rdf4lod-automation. Csv2rdf4lod-automation [36] represents mapping rules in RDF, formalizing the underlying language as an ontology. The idea of Csv2rdf4lod-automation is to start from a systematic conversion of the input data and to refactor this raw RDF by applying several enhancements: e.g. configure the property URIs and associate column groups to different resources. Concerned with provenance, the system updates data monotonically, adding process metadata. TabLinker has a similar concern.

DataLift. DataLift [37] firstly performs a systematic conversion to RDF, which is followed by further processing steps, including discovery of relevant ontologies on LOV [11], refactoring using SPARQL and linking to other datasets.

LinkedPipes ETL. LinkedPipes ETL [38] is an ETL (Extract Transform Load) framework for RDF aimed at overcoming some limitations of UnifiedViews concerning usability and integrability. LinkedPipes ETL has a more sophisticated debugging capability than UnifiedViews. Regarding the development of conversion pipelines, LinkedPipes ETL can suggest new components, based on input/output compatibility, likelihood of usage in a certain context, fulltext search in component metadata, etc. LinkedPipes ETL uses essentially the same approach to triplication of tabular data as UnifiedViews.

UnifiedViews. UnifiedViews [39] is an ETL framework supporting complex data transformation pipelines. These are composed of data processing units (DPUs) arranged into complex data flows, enabling data units (i.e. RDF, files and relational tables) to move from a DPU to another. DPU are classified into extractors (no input, obtain data from outside), transformers (transform input data unit into output ones), loaders (no output, deploy input data unit to some destination), quality assessors (like transformers, but output quality reports). Extensible through the implementation of new DPUs, the framework provides a lot of them out of the box. There is a DPU for turning CSV to RDF, which favors a systematic conversion: further processing is done using a SPARQL DPU. Another DPU can convert Excel spreadsheets to CSV. UnifiedViews has a web-interface with a graphical editor of pipelines. Users can debug a fragment of a pipeline, inspect the input data units, etc. The Semantic Integrator edition of PoolParty uses UnifiedViews to replace its native import mechanism.

3 Comparative Summary

Table 1 contains the systems described in Sect. 2 and aims at simplifying a comparison between them. We will also provide general considerations on the task.

A very discriminative feature lies in the way the mapping of input data to RDF is specified, allowing for different levels of customization. At the one extreme, Any23 does not support any customization, relying on a systematic mapping that generates property URIs from column headers. At the other extreme, there are systems providing a dedicated mapping language. Vertere and Csv2rdf4lod-automation represent the mapping in RDF, while RDF123 uses more straightforward RDF templates. A comparison between Fig. 1 and Fig. 2 (in the sections devoted to these systems) should make the difference clear. XLWrap combines templates like the ones used by RDF123 with transformations of the input data expressed in RDF. Grafter and Spread2RDF use an internal DSL in some general-purpose programming language. Advantages include falling back to the hosting language for coding some aspects of the process and reliance on the existing tools (e.g. IDEs, project managers and interactive consoles).

Users not acquainted with these programming languages might be annoyed by learning a new language and installing its runtime. Spread2RDF addresses the latter problem, by optionally compiling a mapping specification into a standalone executable. The familiarity problem with the mapping language is solved by using SPARQL, which is already well-known to semantic web practitioners. This is used, in particular, by those systems (DataLift, OntoRefine, LinkedPipes ETL and UnifiedViews) that adopt a two-step approach: systematic conversion, followed by RDF transformation. Tarql conflates these two steps by directly allowing the evaluation of SPARQL over tabular data. Sheet2RDF executes the conversion as a single step; however, it offers an incremental and layered approach to mapping specification. Moreover, its PEARL language is based on SPARQL for the specification of graph patterns.

Reuse is a concern in mapping specification (e.g. use the same pattern for SKOS-XL preferred and alternative labels): e.g. Spread2RDF templates, Sheet2RDF patterns and triggers or cascades of SPARQL queries in UnifiedViews and LinkedPipes ETL.

Most systems deal with data laid out in rows representing homogenous records, much like a table in a relational database. Accordingly, systems thought for mapping databases to RDF (e.g. Sparqlify) may optionally process CSV files and the like. The systematic mapping implemented by Any23 is analogous to the Direct Mapping [40] standardized for relational databases. Moreover, the latter is explicitly exploited by DataLift. Beyond Direct Mapping, R2RML [31] standardizes a way to express a custom mapping of relational databases to RDF. Karma's KR2RML extends it to support other (hierarchical) data sources. RML (used by RMLEditor) has a similar goal, extending R2RML to support heterogeneous data formats, including CSV, XML and JSON. This support consists on a default iteration logic and different reference formulation options (e.g. XPath for XML, JSONpath for Json, etc.).

TabLinker, Mapping Master and XLWrap are specialized in complex data layouts, which can be found in the statistical and financial domains. Following Langegger and Wöß [18], these layouts are just representation models for different information models.

Tabular data formats (e.g. CSV) are in fact bidimensional, and support for different formats is often achieved by merely extracting data along these two dimensions. Spreadsheets, however, allow for additional dimensions. Firstly, they may consist of multiple sheets: these can be considered as multiple tables (e.g. in UnifiedViews and LinkedPipes ETL) or may have a special interpretation (e.g. Sheet2RDF allows for a sheet declaring prefix mappings). Tools such as XLWrap even supports cross-sheet references. Furthermore, even individual sheets allow for additional dimensions: e.g. TabLinker uses cell style and comment to represent additional metadata beyond the two-dimensional grid of cells.

Mapping Master and Populous work at the level of OWL axioms: this approach is particularly suitable when the goal is not to populate an ontology (i.e. increase the A-box) but to extend the ontology vocabulary (i.e. increase the T-box).

Most systems are standalone converters, but we identified other scenarios: database mapping solutions (Sparqlify), knowledge development environments (MappingMaster, Sheet2RDF, PoolParty's and TopBraid Composer's importers), data wrangling tools (Karma, LODRefine and OntoRefine) and full-fledged ETL solutions (CSV2RDF, Csv2rdf4lod-automation, DataLift, LinkedPipes ETL, UnifiedViews).

Table 1. Comparative summary of reviewed systems

System name	Output	Input layout	Mapping	Assistance to Mapping	Integrations
Any23	RDF	rows	—	—	—
Csv2rdf	RDF	rows	MediaWiki template	skeleton mappings	Semantic MediaWiki, Facete, CubeViz, Sparqlify
csv2rdf4lod-automation	RDF	rows	Conversion ontology	—	—
DataLift	RDF	rows	—	—	LOV, Linking services
Grafter	RDF	rows	Clojure DSL	Grafterizer	DataGraft
GraphDB OntoRefine	RDF	rows	SPARQL, SPIN, GREL	SPARQL editor with syntax highlighting and completion	GraphDB Workbench
Karma	RDF	Hierarchical data	Graphical DSL, KR2RML	Learning techniques, Steiner tree optimization, lookup target ontology	Sesame Server and Workbench
LinkedPipes ETL	RDF	rows	SPARQL	debugging, component suggestion	—
LODRefine	RDF	rows	Graphical DSL, GREL	lookup in the target ontology	CrowdFlower, NER services, reconciliation with DBpedia
Mapping Master	OWL	varied layouts	M^2 Language	user interface	Protégé
PoolParty	RDF	indented rows	—	—	—
Populous	OWL	rows	OPPL	—	—

(*continued*)

Table 1. (*continued*)

System name	Output	Input layout	Mapping	Assistance to Mapping	Integrations
RDF123	RDF	rows	RDF template	—	—
RMLEditor	RDF	rows	Graphical DSL, RML	—	LOV
Sheet2RDF	RDF	rows	PEARL	PEARL editor, heuristics, lookup in the target ontology	VocBench 3
SKOS Play!	RDF	rows	structured header	—	—
Sparqlify	RDF	rows	SML	—	—
Spread2RDF	RDF	column blocks	Ruby DSL	—	—
TabLinker	Data Cube	data cubes	Annotated Excel file	—	—
Tarql	RDF	rows	SPARQL	—	—
TopBraid Composer	RDF	rows	Wizard	—	—
Unified Views	RDF	rows	SPARQL	debugging	PoolParty
Vertere-RDF	RDF	rows	RDF-based language	—	—
XLWrap	RDF	varied layouts	Conversion ontology + RDF template	—	Joseki

4   Conclusions

We surveyed several systems for the triplification of tabular data. After discussing them in isolation, we highlighted commonalities, differences and interesting insights. We identified different approaches to the conversion, the peculiarities of certain types of inputs and data formats, discussed easiness of use and different deployment scenarios. The summary provided by Table 1 reveals that complex layouts have not been explored by most tools yet; still, 25% of them support a non-row layout, with 2 of them explicitly supporting the most varied layouts. This feature can then be very selective if the input data is not conformant to the usual row series. Otherwise, the choice of a tool can be driven by the integration with other systems and the provided assistance to mapping.

Future work includes improving our survey in two directions: broadening the range of analyzed tools and extending the comparison framework with more detailed features, to facilities a systematic comparison between different mapping specification approaches.

References

1. Berners-Lee, T.: Linked Data. In: Design Issues (2006). https://www.w3.org/DesignIssues/LinkedData.html
2. Celli, F., Anibaldi, S., Folch, M., Jaques, Y., Keizer, J.: OpenAGRIS: using bibliographical data for linking into the agricultural knowledge web. In: Agricultural Ontology Services (AOS), Bangkok, Thailand (2011)
3. Apache Any23 - CSV Extractor. https://any23.apache.org/dev-csv-extractor.html
4. Grafter - Linked Data Machine Tools. https://grafter.org/
5. Roman, D., et al.: DataGraft: one-stop-shop for open data management. Semant. Web **9**(4), 393–411 (2018)
6. Jupp, S. et al.: Populous: a tool for building OWL ontologies from templates. BMC Bioinformatics **13**(1) (2012)
7. Egaña, M., Rector, A., Stevens, R., Antezana, E.: Applying ontology design patterns in bio-ontologies. In: Gangemi, A., Euzenat, J. (eds.) EKAW 2008. LNCS, vol. 5268. Springer, Heidelberg (2008). https://doi.org/10.1007/978-3-540-87696-0_4
8. Gangemi, A., Presutti, V.: Ontology design patterns. In: Handbook on ontologies. Springer Berlin Heidelberg (2009), pp.221–243
9. Han, L., Finin, T., Parr, C., Sachs, J., Joshi, A.: RDF123: from spreadsheets to RDF. In: Sheth, A., et al. (eds.) ISWC 2008. LNCS, vol. 5318, pp. 451–466. Springer, Heidelberg (2008). https://doi.org/10.1007/978-3-540-88564-1_29
10. Heyvaert, P., et al.: RMLEditor: a graph-based mapping editor for linked data mappings. In: Sack, H., Blomqvist, E., d'Aquin, M., Ghidini, C., Ponzetto, S.P., Lange, C. (eds.) ESWC 2016. LNCS, vol. 9678, pp. 709–723. Springer, Cham (2016). https://doi.org/10.1007/978-3-319-34129-3_43
11. Vandenbussche, P.-Y., Atemezing, G.A., Poveda-Villalón, M., Vatant, B.: Linked Open Vocabularies (LOV): a gateway to reusable semantic vocabularies on the Web. Semantic Web **8**(3), 437–452 (2017)
12. A DSL-based converter for spreadsheets to RDF. https://github.com/marcelotto/spread2rdf
13. TabLinker.: https://github.com/Data2Semantics/TabLinker
14. W3C: The RDF Data Cube Vocabulary. In: World Wide Web Consortium (W3C). Available at: https://www.w3.org/TR/vocab-data-cube/. Accessed 14 Jan 2014
15. Ciccarese, P., Soiland-Reyes, S., Clark, T.: Web annotation as a first-class object. IEEE Internet Comput. **17**(6), 71–75 (2013)
16. Tarql. https://github.com/cygri/tarql
17. Vertere-RDF. https://github.com/knudmoeller/Vertere-RDF
18. Langegger, A., Wöß, W.: XLWrap – querying and integrating arbitrary spreadsheets with SPARQL. In: Bernstein, A., et al. (eds.) ISWC 2009. LNCS, vol. 5823, pp. 359–374. Springer, Heidelberg (2009). https://doi.org/10.1007/978-3-642-04930-9_23
19. Sparqlify. https://aksw.org/Projects/Sparqlify.html
20. O'Connor, M.J., Halaschek-Wiener, C., Musen, M.A.: Mapping master: a flexible approach for mapping spreadsheets to OWL. In: Patel-Schneider, P.F., et al. (eds.) ISWC 2010. LNCS, vol. 6497, pp. 194–208. Springer, Heidelberg (2010). https://doi.org/10.1007/978-3-642-17749-1_13
21. In: PoolParty Semantic Suite - Semantic Technology Platform. https://www.poolparty.biz/

22. ART Group: Sheet2RDF. https://art.uniroma2.it/sheet2rdf/
23. Fiorelli, M., Lorenzetti, T., Pazienza, M.T., Stellato, A., Turbati, A.: Sheet2RDF: a flexible and dynamic spreadsheet import&lifting framework for RDF. In: Ali, M., Kwon, Y.S., Lee, C.-H., Kim, J., Kim, Y. (eds.) IEA/AIE 2015. LNCS (LNAI), vol. 9101, pp. 131–140. Springer, Cham (2015). https://doi.org/10.1007/978-3-319-19066-2_13
24. Stellato, A., et al.: VocBench 3: a collaborative semantic web editor for ontologies. Thesauri and Lexicons. Semantic Web 11(5), 855–881 (2020)
25. World Wide Web Consortium (W3C): SKOS Simple Knowledge Organization System eXtension for Labels (SKOS-XL). In: World Wide Web Consortium (W3C). https://www.w3.org/TR/skos-reference/skos-xl.html. Accessed 18 Aug 2009
26. Fiorelli, M., Pazienza, M.T., Stellato, A., Turbati, A.: CODA: computer-aided ontology development architecture. IBM J. Res. Dev. 58(2/3), 14:1–14:12 (2014)
27. Pazienza, M.T., Stellato, A., Turbati, A.: PEARL: ProjEction of annotations rule language, a language for projecting (UIMA) annotations over RDF knowledge bases. In: Proceedings of the Eighth International Conference on Language Resources and Evaluation (LREC'12), Istanbul, Turkey (2012)
28. TopBraid Composer. https://www.topquadrant.com/products/topbraid-composer/
29. Ontotext: Ontotext GraphDB. https://graphdb.ontotext.com/
30. Knoblock, C.A., et al.: Semi-automatically mapping structured sources into the semantic web. In: Simperl, E., Cimiano, P., Polleres, A., Corcho, O., Presutti, V. (eds.) ESWC 2012. LNCS, vol. 7295, pp. 375–390. Springer, Heidelberg (2012). https://doi.org/10.1007/978-3-642-30284-8_32
31. Das, S., Sundara, S., Cyganiak, R.: R2RML: RDB to RDF mapping language. In: World Wide Web Consortium - Web Standards. https://www.w3.org/TR/r2rml/. Accessed 27 Sept 2012
32. Ermilov, I., Auer, S., Stadler, C.: CSV2RDF: User-Driven CSV to RDF Mass Conversion Framework. In: Proceedings of the ISEM 2013, 04–06 September 2013, Graz, Austria (2013)
33. Krötzsch, M., Vrandečić, D., Völkel, M., Haller, H., Studer, R.: Semantic Wikipedia. Web Semantics Sci. Serv. Agents World Wide Web 5(4), 251–261 (2007)
34. Martin, M., Abicht, K., Stadler, C., Auer, S., Ngomo, A.-C.N., Soru, T.: CubeViz - exploration and visualization of statistical linked data. In: Proceedings of the 24th International Conference on World Wide Web, WWW 2015 (2015)
35. Stadler, C., Martin, M., Auer, S.: Exploring the web of spatial data with facete. In: Companion proceedings of 23rd International World Wide Web Conference (WWW), pp. 175–178 (2014)
36. Lebo, T., Williams, G.T.: Converting governmental datasets into linked data. In: Proceedings of the 6th International Conference on Semantic Systems, New York, NY, USA, pp. 38:1–38:3 (2010)
37. Scharffe, F. et al.: Enabling linked data publication with the Datalift platform. In: AAAI Workshop on Semantic Cities (2012)
38. Klímek, J., Škoda, P., Nečaský, M.: LinkedPipes ETL: evolved linked data preparation. In: Sack, H., Rizzo, G., Steinmetz, N., Mladenić, D., Auer, S., Lange, C. (eds.) ESWC 2016. LNCS, vol. 9989, pp. 95–100. Springer, Cham (2016). https://doi.org/10.1007/978-3-319-47602-5_20
39. Knap, T., et al.: UnifiedViews: an ETL tool for RDF data management. Semantic Web 9(5), 661–676 (2018)
40. World Wide Web Consortium (W3C): A Direct Mapping of Relational Data to RDF. In: World Wide Web Consortium (W3C). https://www.w3.org/TR/rdb-direct-mapping/. Accessed 27 Sept 2012

Automatic Human Resources Ontology Generation from the Data of an E-Recruitment Platform

Sabrina Boudjedar[1], Sihem Bouhenniche[1], Hakim Mokeddem[1(✉)],
and Hamid Benachour[2]

[1] Ecole Nationale Supérieure d'Informatique,
BP 68M, 16309 Oued-Smar, Algiers, Algeria
{fs_boudjedar,fs_bouhenniche,h_mokeddem}@esi.dz
[2] Laboratoire de Recherche En Intelligence Articifielle (LRIA), USTHB,
El Alia BP 32, Bab Ezzouar, Algiers, Algeria
hamid.benachour@gmail.com

Abstract. Over the last decade, several e-recruitment platforms have been developed, allowing users to publish their professional information (training, work history, career summary, etc.). However, representing this huge quantity of knowledge still limited. In this work, we present a method based on community detection and natural language processing techniques in order to generate a human resources "HR" ontology. The data used in the generation process is user's profiles retrieved from the Algerian e-recruitment platform *Emploitic.com*(www.emploitic. com). Data includes occupations, skills and professional domains. Our main contribution appears in the identification of new relationships between these concepts using community detection in each area of work. The generated ontology has hierarchical relationships between skills, professions and professional domains. In order to evaluate the relevance of this ontology, we used both the manual method with experts in human resources domain and the automatic method through comparisons with existing HR-ontologies. The evaluation has shown promising results.

Keywords: Ontology · E-recruitment · Occupation · Competence · Professional domain · Community detection

1 Introduction

The recent development of web technologies has revolutionized the world by offering permanent accessibility and high availability of data at the same time. Nevertheless, existing knowledge representation tools have shown their limits to fit with this huge revolution [7]. An ontology which is defined as "a formal and explicit specification of a shared conceptualization that is characterized by high semantic expressiveness" [2], can provide better knowledge representation that improves data exploitation.

© Springer Nature Switzerland AG 2021
E. Garoufallou and M.-A. Ovalle-Perandones (Eds.): MTSR 2020, CCIS 1355, pp. 97–109, 2021.
https://doi.org/10.1007/978-3-030-71903-6_10

In this context, using ontologies in human resources domain can be useful for both recruiters and candidates. In fact, an ontology can be used to create semantic search engines of job offers and candidate profiles. In addition, it can make easier for recruiters to select relevant candidates by matching between their profiles and job requirements.

The human resources domain is characterized by a huge quantity of concepts. For example, ESCO ontology (European Skills, Competences, qualifications and Occupations) created by the European Commission, provides 2942 occupations and 13.485 skills linked to these occupations [10]. In fact, creating a human resources ontology manually is a time-consuming task because it requires managing huge quantities of data that need to be processed and exploited automatically. In addition to that, human resources domain is a field that grows quickly. For this reason, using an automatic process to generate an HR ontology can help to manage its evolution. Thus, many research works studied the generation of HR ontologies such as AGOHRA (Automatic Generation of an Ontology for Human Resource Applications) [6] and HOLA (HR Ontology Learned Automatically) [1] -ontologies. However, these ontologies contain many information gaps and do not include many concepts.

In this paper, we propose a new method based on community detection and natural language processing techniques, for automatic generation of our HR-ontology using data provided by an Algerian e-recruitment platform named "Emploitic.com". It is structured as follows: in Sect. 2, we present some related works regarding HR ontologies and their generation process. Then, we describe our ontology generation process and its evaluation in Sect. 3.

2   Related Works

Several research works have been performed in order to create a valid HR-ontology. In this section, we go through the most interesting HR-ontologies. We present their structures and generation process.

ESCO [10], an ontology resulting from a European project, which brings together occupations, skills and qualifications. This ontology was created manually in order to provide a common European repository to be used in recruitment. The ontology includes 2942 occupations, 13485 skills/competences and 9455 qualifications available in 26 different languages. This knowledge is organized in a structure of three pillars:

1. Occupation pillar organizes occupation concepts. Each occupation concept is accompanied by a description, its related skills and essential knowledge for this occupation.
2. Skill pillar organizes skill concepts. Each skill concept is accompanied by a description and its occupations.
3. Qualification pillar organizes qualification concepts. Qualifications displayed in ESCO come from databases of national qualifications that are owned and managed by the European Member States.

Authors of [6] proposed a semi-automatic generation approach of the HR-ontology AGOHRA based on job offers collected from the Internet. The generation process of this ontology follows these steps: firstly, a standardization on job offers is performed to separate offers according to the language used and also to remove duplicate offers. Secondly, occupations are extracted from job titles of each offer and only occupations having a significant frequency are maintained. Thirdly, skills linked to each occupation are extracted and represented according to the n-gram word format. In order to filter skills, a comparison is made with a prefix tree containing about 25,000 skills from social media profiles. Finally, the ontology is generated in RDF (Resource Description Framework) format where each universe contains a set of occupations and each occupation contains a set of skills. For its validation, a manual evaluation was performed by experts in HR domain. The detailed analysis showed results of a good quality (average precision of 0.79).

More recently, authors of [1] generated automatically a human resource ontology named HOLA from Professional Social-Network Data (LinkedIn). Authors used data extracted from user's profiles and maintained only occupations and skills in the generation process of the HOLA ontology. This process follows these steps: first, data are extracted and represented in a graph where nodes represent either occupations or skills and edges represent the existing relationships between them. The weight of the edge between these two concepts represents the importance of the skill in a given occupation. Second, since data is entered by users, the noise level is probably very high. This step eliminates the noise and cleans data to keep only those that are useful in the creation. At the end, nodes are grouped into communities using Louvain algorithm in order to have more relationships in the graph. For the evaluation and validation, authors performed an automatic evaluation by doing a comparison between HOLA and ESCO. The evaluation results showed that HOLA contains more nodes and relations with 19,756 nodes and 154,259 edges.

3   Generation Process

AHROGA[1] is an HR-ontology generated automatically from data of the Algerian e-recruitment platform *emploitic.com*. We can define our ontology through the following characteristics:

1. **The Domain and The Goal of The Ontology**
   Our ontology is a human resources ontology. This ontology aims to provide useful services that enable to evaluate whether a candidate has required skills for an occupation, suggest to a candidate how to highlight his skills and propose most relevant profiles for recruiters.
2. **Data Used for Ontology Generation**
   For the ontology generation, we use candidate profiles of *emploitic.com*, that include occupations, skills and professional domains.

---

[1] **A**lgerian **H**uman **R**esources **O**ntology **G**enerated **A**utomatically.

3. **Concepts (classes)**

The concepts of our ontology are: Professional domain, Occupation, Community and Skill.

The generation process of our HR-Ontology is based on these three main aspects:

- Cleaning and validating data.
- Using professional domains in order to split our data in different clusters (representing sub-domains) and perform community detection on every cluster separately.
- Merging the resulting clusters into one cluster.

Our generation process is inspired from the process proposed by the authors of [2]. In addition to that, our generation process brings a new way to validate and evaluate the resulted ontology and its concepts using both automatic and manual methods. This process is described in the following pipeline (see Fig. 1).

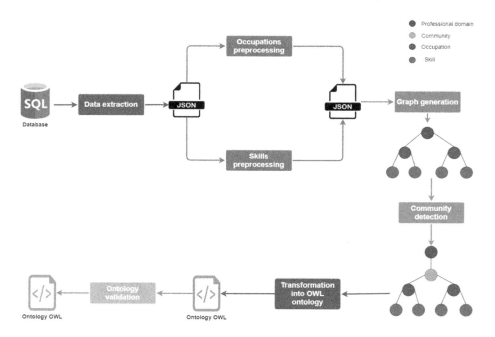

Fig. 1. Generation process

3.1   Extraction

This first step aims to extract necessary data to build AHROGA ontology and to perform preprocessing and cleaning.

Data Extraction. Our data corpus contains 300.000 profiles extracted in JSON format from *Emploitic.com* database. We identified for each profile three concepts that we consider essential to create AHROGA: Professional domain, occupation and skill.

There are many reasons to justify this choice. The most important are:

- The availability of these attributes in each profile.
- The strong semantic link between occupations, skills and professional domains.

Data Preprocessing. The data preprocessing phase is necessary in order to clean data and eliminate all types of noise.

Preprocessing concerns only occupations and skills because they are filled manually by users, which increases the probability of providing erroneous data, unlike professional domains which are proposed by the system.

Occupations Preprocessing. In order to standardize and validate occupations, we performed a preprocessing stage. This stage enables to identify the following problems:

- Existence of words/sentences that do not represent valid occupations, for example: curriculum vitae, without experience, 2019, never worked, etc.
- Use of locations inside occupations, for example: teacher at **bab ezzouar**, secretary **algiers**.
- Existence of occupations in multilingual, for example: web developer, développeur web.
- Using surnames and first names in occupations.
- Spelling errors.

In order to standardize and validate occupations, a preprocessing stage was done. This one goes through the following steps:

- Unifying the occupation format in lower case.
- Detecting the language of occupations to keep only ones written in French because 80% of job seekers use it.
- Removing special characters, accents, punctuation, numbers, stop words, verbs and proper names such as first and last names and Algerian localizations.
- Eliminating non-significant names that are very used by job seekers such as: CV, job search, profile, experience, curriculum vitae, internship.
- Grouping occupations that have the same stem.

After performing these tasks, many insignificant occupations which represent 3% of the data corpus were eliminated. In addition, we have identified through this step 290,458 occupations.

Skills Preprocessing. Preprocessing skills enables to identify two types of problems:

- Syntax problems such as wrong spelling.
- The validity problem of the skill itself. For example, internet is not a valid skill.

Among syntax problems we encountered we find: misspellings and multilingual skills, expressing skills in very long paragraphs (more than 6 words), using words that cannot be considered as skills like pc, internet, computer.

In order to fix these problems, we performed the same tasks used in occupations preprocessing.

3.2   Analysis

The purpose of the analysis stage is to extract existing relationships between data concepts. It goes through the three following steps.

Similar Jobs Detection. Similar jobs detection enables to create new relationships between occupations based on their syntax similarity in order to improve our final ontological structure. We link two occupations by using a distance calculated by Jaro-Winkler metric [4], which is a string metric measuring an edit distance between two sequences. This distance is a variant of Jaro distance metric proposed by William E Winkler [5]. It is based on the number and order of common characters between the two strings. It uses the length P of the longest common prefix of two strings s and t. Letting $P' = \max(P, 4)$ we define :

$$Jaro - Winkler(s,t) = Jaro(s,t) + \frac{P'}{10}(1 - Jaro(s,t)) \qquad (1)$$

For example, through this step we create syntax links between "Architect" and these occupations: "Urban planning architect", "Project manager architect", "Designer Architect", "Architect designer".

Initial Graph Generation. Before performing the community detection algorithm, we firstly represent cleaned data in a weighted graph. This graph is structured as follows :

- **Nodes:** to represent domains, occupations and skills.
- **Edges:** pairs of relations between two different nodes. There are three types of relations:
    - ☐ omain-Occupation.
    - ☐ ccupation-Occupation.
    - ☐ ccupation – Skill.
- **Edge Weight:** a numerical value assigned to an edge representing the importance of an occupation in its domain or the importance of a skill in its occupation, it is calculated by the occurrence frequency.

Community Detection. We had initially 27 large separated domain graphs that include a lot of occupations. In order to create small communities that have high semantic links, we splitted occupations into smaller communities by performing community detection on each of the 27 graphs separately.

We have tested two different community detection algorithms: Louvain [3] and Label Propagation Algorithm (LPA) [11]. A performance comparison we performed have shown that Louvain algorithm gives more exact results. The performance metric is calculated by using a confusion matrix. Each element m(i,j) of this matrix represents the number of nodes in the community i. The performance formula is as follows [8]:

$$I = \frac{-2\sum_i i \sum_j j m_{ij} log \frac{nm_{ij}}{m_{i+}m_{+j}}}{\sum_i log \frac{nm_{i+}}{n} + \sum_j log \frac{m_{+j}}{n}} \tag{2}$$

If the estimated community is correct, the measure takes 1 otherwise it takes 0.

In Table 1, we can see an example of obtained performances by applying Louvain and LPA algorithms on 3 different domains.

Table 1. Louvain and LPA Community detection performance on 3 domains

Professional domain	Louvain algorithm	LPA algorithm
IT, information systems, internet	0.876	0.875
Construction site, construction jobs, architecture	0.859	0.844
Engineering, studies, project, r&d	0.86	0.556

A second comparison based on a quantity and a quality of generated communities is shown in Table 2.

According to these results, we used Louvain algorithm for community detection because:

1. It generates partitions (set of communities) with better performance compared to LPA algorithm.
2. It generates fewer communities with better grouping of occupations.
3. It considers the importance of skills for each occupation as a parameter for grouping, which helps to group together occupations with significant numbers of common skills.

Table 2. Comparison between Louvain and LPA algorithms based on generated communities

Professional domain	Louvain algorithm		LPA algorithm	
	Communities	Some generated communities	Communities	Some generated communities
IT, information systems, internet	16	Community 0 : developer, web developer, IT developer, software developer, programmer	38	Community 0 : IT developer, developer, web developer
		Community 1 : software architect, software engineer		Community 1 : software architect
Construction site, construction jobs, architecture	17	Community 0 : project director, project manager, works manager	33	Community 0 : project manager, site manager, architect, project manager, state architect
		Community 1 : architect, project architect, state architect		Community 1 : Project leader

3.3 Generation

To enable computer programs to exploit the ontology and provide useful features to users, we transformed the resulting graph after the detection of communities into Ontology Web Language (OWL)[2] through the creation of ontological components which are: axioms, classes, instances and relations.

Listing 1.1. Structure of ontology owl file

```
<owl: ObjectProperty  rdf:about="#has_level">
  <rdfs:domain  rdf:resource="#Domain"/>
  <rdfs:range  rdf:resource="#Community"/>
</owl: ObjectProperty>

<owl: ObjectProperty  rdf:about="#has_job">
  <rdfs:domain  rdf:resource="#Community"/>
  <rdfs:range  rdf:resource="#Job"/>
</owl: ObjectProperty>

<owl: ObjectProperty  rdf:about="#has_skill">
  <rdfs:domain  rdf:resource="#Job"/>
  <rdfs:domain  rdf:resource="#Community"/>
  <rdfs:range  rdf:resource="#Skill"/>
</owl: ObjectProperty>
```

---

[2] https://www.w3.org/OWL/.

3.4   Validation

The validation is performed at the end of each previous step. It verifies that relationships and concepts are correct and checks if the generated ontology is consistent.

Confirmed Occupations. To validate occupations, we used only those having an occurrence frequency greater than a certain threshold, which is determined according to the percentage of valid occupations in each domain. Using a threshold of 1% allowed us to validate 43,110 profiles, which represent 15% of the total number of profiles.

Confirmed Skills. The purpose of this validation is to keep only correct skills. The approach that we followed is based on text classification. For that, we have firstly created the dataset by retrieving 5000 skills from profiles. Then, we used ESCO ontology API to get their descriptions. In addition, we have used Wikipedia for skills that did not have descriptions in ESCO. After that, we added a third attribute about the validity. The dataset that we have used in the skills classification is presented in the table below.

Table 3. Skills classification dataset

	Skill	Description	Validity
1	Apache Maven	The tool Apache Maven is a software program to perform configuration identification, control, status accounting and audit of software during its development and maintenance. (from ESCO)	1

As second step, we have used naïve Bayes classifier [9], which is recommended in text classification in order to classify skills into two different classes (valid, not valid). By applying this approach on our dataset, we got a model accuracy of 95% and we validated 77.10% of all skills.

Experts' Validation: The purpose of this evaluation is to validate with experts the ontology concepts of three professional domains: (1) IT, information systems, internet (2) construction site, construction jobs, architecture and (3) telecommunications, networks.

This evaluation was conducted with five experts in the human resources domain.

The evaluation is based on a questionnaire that has three sections where each section represents one professional domain. Questions of each domain concern the generated communities and the relationships between occupations and skills.

After analyzing experts' responses, we calculated for each occupation the average number of valid skills and the percentage of valid domain skills. The results are presented in the table below.

Table 4. Experts' evaluation

Domain	Occupation	Number of generated skills	Average number of valid skills	Valid domain skills
IT, information systems, internet	Computer science engineer	60	43	74%
	Web Developer	37	33	
	Mobile Developer	20	17	
	Database Administrator	20	9	
Construction site, construction jobs, architecture	Urban Architects	8	4	64%
	Civil engineer	14	9	
	Planning engineer	13	10	
	Site supervisor	10	6	
Telecommunications, networks	Network engineer	61	41	70%
	Telecommunication systems engineer	45	32	

We then calculated for each domain the percentage of community validation. The results are presented in the figure below.

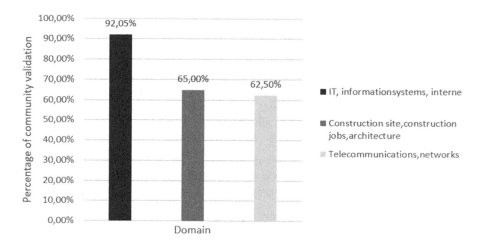

Fig. 2. Community validation

3.5   Evaluation

In order to evaluate the quality of our results, a comparison of our ontology was made with ESCO ontology. It is based on common concepts between the two ontologies. We have found that 68.20% of total skills and 73.61% of total occupations generated using our method exist in ESCO, which affirm that these instances are valid.

In order to ensure that our results are relevant, we applied the same approach used to generate HOLA ontology on our dataset and we compared it with our approach. (See Table 5)

Table 5. Comparison between our ontology and HOLA's ontology

	HOLA	AHROGA
Number of communities of level 1	20	27
Number of communities of level 2	108	392
Occupations of the same communities	Dentist doctor, veterinary doctor, bailiff, legal officer, personal representative, call center operator, waiter, receptionist, microbiologist, technical officer, professor, operator, nurse, machine operator	Dentist doctor, veterinarian doctor, doctor

This comparison shows that our approach performed better compared to HOLA's approach. Using professional domains as a concept in AHROGA allows better grouping of occupations in communities. For example, two occupations which are not in the same domain but share the same skills (depending on users) are assigned to the same community with HOLA approach.

4   Conclusion and Future Work

In this paper, we have proposed an automatic ontology generation method using data of the Algerian e-recruitment platform *Emploitic.com*. From 300,000 profiles collected, we have retrieved common data to build a structured hierarchy of concepts representing each professional domain. Our dataset contained many noisy data, we have started by a preprocessing step in order to clean it and keep only valid data. Then, we have represented these cleaned data in a weighted graph, on which we have applied the community detection using Louvain algorithm in order to create new relationships between concepts based on shared skills. Finally, this hierarchical structure was represented in OWL format in order to be used in useful use cases. For its evaluation and validation, we have used both of manual methods like validating ontology concepts by human resources domain experts, and automatic methods like comparing our ontology concepts with ESCO.

AHROGA contains 13606 instances and 113612 relationships, including 27 domains, 716 communities, 1437 occupations and 11,426 skills. The approach we proposed is generic and can be applied on every dataset that contains occupations, skills and professional domains.

As future works, we have proposed to make several improvements on our generation pipeline. Firstly, in order to enrich the ontology, we have planned to use a combination of job offers and profiles data rather than only using profiles data. Secondly, we believe that we can enrich also our ontology by adding multilingual instances since that most of data are provided in three languages (French, Arabic and English) and by considering more concepts in the creation of our ontology, such as professional experience and education qualifications. Finally, useful services based on the ontology need to be implemented. For example, matching automatically job offers and candidate profiles.

References

1. Alfonso-Hermelo, D., Langlais, P., Bourg, L.: Automatically learning a human-resource ontology from professional social-network data. In: Meurs, M.-J., Rudzicz, F. (eds.) Canadian AI 2019. LNCS (LNAI), vol. 11489, pp. 132–145. Springer, Cham (2019). https://doi.org/10.1007/978-3-030-18305-9_11
2. Bedini, I., Nguyen, B.: Automatic ontology generation: state of the art. PRiSM Laboratory Technical report. University of Versailles (2007)
3. Blondel, V.D., Guillaume, J.L., Lambiotte, R., Lefebvre, E.: Fast unfolding of communities in large networks. J. Stat. Mech. Theory Exp. **2008**(10), P10008 (2008)
4. Cohen, W.W., Ravikumar, P., Fienberg, S.E., et al.: A comparison of string distance metrics for name-matching tasks. In: IIWeb 2003, pp. 73–78 (2003)
5. Jaro, M.A.: Advances in record-linkage methodology as applied to matching the 1985 census of Tampa, Florida. J. Am. Stat. Assoc. **84**(406), 414–420 (1989)
6. Kessler, R., Lapalme, G.: Agohra: generation of an ontology in the field of human resources. Traitement Automatique des Langues **58**(1), 39–62 (2017)
7. Omelayenko, B., Fensel, D.: A two-layered integration approach for product information in B2B E-commerce. In: Bauknecht, K., Madria, S.K., Pernul, G. (eds.) EC-Web 2001. LNCS, vol. 2115, pp. 226–239. Springer, Heidelberg (2001). https://doi.org/10.1007/3-540-44700-8_22
8. Orman, G.K., Labatut, V.: A comparison of community detection algorithms on artificial networks. In: Gama, J., Costa, V.S., Jorge, A.M., Brazdil, P.B. (eds.) DS 2009. LNCS (LNAI), vol. 5808, pp. 242–256. Springer, Heidelberg (2009). https://doi.org/10.1007/978-3-642-04747-3_20
9. Rish, I., et al.: An empirical study of the Naive Bayes classifier. In: IJCAI 2001 Workshop on Empirical Methods in Artificial Intelligence, vol. 3, pp. 41–46 (2001)

10. le Vrang, M., Papantoniou, A., Pauwels, E., Fannes, P., Vandensteen, D., De Smedt, J.: ESCO: Boosting job matching in Europe with semantic interoperability. Computer **47**(10), 57–64 (2014)
11. Xie, J., Szymanski, B.K., Liu, X.: SLPA: uncovering overlapping communities in social networks via a speaker-listener interaction dynamic process. In: 2011 IEEE 11th International Conference on Data Mining Workshops, pp. 344–349. IEEE (2011)

Examination of NoSQL Transition and Data Mining Capabilities

Dimitrios Rousidis ⓘ, Paraskevas Koukaras ⓘ, and Christos Tjortjis$^{(\boxtimes)}$ ⓘ

The Data Mining and Analytics Research Group, School of Science and Technology,
International Hellenic University, Thermi, 570 01 Thessaloniki, Greece
{d.rousidis,p.koukaras,c.tjortjis}@ihu.edu.gr

Abstract. An estimated 2.5 quintillion bytes of data are created every day. This data explosion, along with new datatypes, objects, and the wide usage of social media networks, with an estimated 3.8 billion users worldwide, make the exploitation and manipulation of data by relational databases, cumbersome and problematic. NoSQL databases introduce new capabilities aiming at improving the functionalities offered by traditional SQL DBMS. This paper elaborates on ongoing research regarding NoSQL, focusing on the background behind their development, their basic characteristics, their categorization and the noticeable increase in popularity. Functional advantages and data mining capabilities that come with the usage of graph databases are also presented. Common data mining tasks with graphs are presented, facilitating implementation, as well as efficiency. The aim is to highlight concepts necessary for incorporating data mining techniques and graph database functionalities, eventually proposing an analytical framework offering a plethora of domain specific analytics. For example, a virus outbreak analytics framework allowing health and government officials to make appropriate decisions.

Keywords: NoSQL · Graph databases · Machine Learning (ML) · Data Mining (DM)

1 Introduction

On March 6th, 1972 when the paper titled "Relational Completeness of Data Base Sublanguages" by E.F. Codd, was published few could expect its impact. The first paragraph of its abstract *"This paper attempts to provide a theoretical basis which may be used to determine how complete a selection capability is provided in a proposed data sublanguage independently of any host language in which the sublanguage may be embedded"* proved prophetic [1]. Since the late 70s with the launch of Oracle, the first commercially available Relational Database Management System (RDBMS) the Relational Model (RD) dominated software applications. Since then, nearly everything changed in IT, while nowadays the world is living the Big Data era. According to the 'TechJury' website, in 2020 every person will generate 1.7 MByte in just a second, whilst Internet users generate about 2.5 quintillion bytes (2.5 Exabytes) of data each day [2]. Social Media (SM) and Cloud Computing skyrocketed the volume of data and forced the IT industry

© Springer Nature Switzerland AG 2021
E. Garoufallou and M.-A. Ovalle-Perandones (Eds.): MTSR 2020, CCIS 1355, pp. 110–115, 2021.
https://doi.org/10.1007/978-3-030-71903-6_11

to search for alternative databases (DB) and Database Management Systems (DBMS). Along with the data, there is a simultaneous growth to the structured, encoded set of data than describes and aids to the discovery, management, assessment of the described entities, the metadata. However, metadata in DBMS are handled today in ad-hoc ways [19]. Therefore, NoSQL, a term used by C. Strozzi in 1998 [3], introduced a mechanism that enhances the functionalities of the typical tabular-based RDBMS for all simple and complex data and metadata.

The goal of this paper is to elaborate on benefits of NoSQL DBs as well as the opportunities and new possibilities by combining Machine Learning (ML) methods and supplying practitioners and researchers with enough arguments for the necessity of NoSQL DBs. Therefore, what types can be utilized based on various occasions and what are the Data Mining (DM) tasks that can be performed.

The rest of the paper is structured as follows: Sect. 2 presents the characteristics, and the categorization of NoSQL DBs. Section 3 provides an analysis of the most common DM tasks with the utilization of graph DBs. The last section introduces an ongoing research project that utilizes Graph NoSQL DB for the development of a virus outbreak decision making framework.

2 NoSQL Databases

2.1 Characteristics of NoSQL

NoSQL is based on the BASE (Basically Available, Soft State and Eventually Consistent) model in contrast to the ACID (Atomicity, Consistency, Isolation, Durability) model. Its main advantage is the ease of storing, handling and manipulating, providing access to huge volumes of data, becoming ideal for data intensive applications [4].

The main characteristics of NoSQL DBs are: 1. Non-relational: not fully supporting relational DB features, such as joins, 2. Schema-less (lacking a fixed data structure), 3. Fault-tolerance as data are duplicated to multiple nodes, 4. Horizontally scalable (connecting multiple hardware or software entities to work as a single logical unit), 5. Open source (they are cheap and easy to implement), 6. Massive write-read-remove-get performance, 7. Strong Consistency (all users see the same data), 8. High Availability (all users have access to at least one copy of the requested data) and 9. Partition-Tolerance (the total system keeps its characteristics even when deployed on different servers).

According to [5] the main use of NoSQL in industry is: 1. Session Store (managing session data), 2. User Profile Store (enabling online transactions and user-friendly environments), 3. Content and Metadata Store (building a data and metadata warehouse and storage of multitype data), 4. Mobile Applications, 5. Internet of Things (aiding the concurrent expansion, access and manipulation of data from billions of devices), 6. Third-Party Aggregation (with the ease of managing huge amounts of data, with access by third-party organizations), 7. E-commerce (storing and handling enormous volumes of data), 8. Social Gaming, 9. Ad-Targeting (enabling tracking user details quickly).

The main advantages of NoSQL DBs are: i) non-relational, ii) schema-less, iii) data are replicated to multiple nodes and can be partitioned, iv) horizontally scalable, v) provide a wide range of data models, vi) database administrators are not required, vii) less hardware failures, viii) faster, more efficient and flexible, ix) high pace evolution,

x) less time writing queries, xi) less time debugging queries, xii) code is easier to read, xiii) Big Data compliant (high data velocity, variety, volume, and complexity) xiv) they have huge volumes of fast changing structured, semi-structured, and unstructured data. On the other hand, there are some disadvantages i) Immaturity, ii) no standard query language, iii) Some DBs are not ACID compliant and iv) no standard interface [6].

2.2 Categorization

There is a debate in the bibliography about the number of categories that NoSQL DBs can be grouped. Most sources group them in four categories, but there is a number of experts that group them in five categories which are: i) Column, ii) Document, iii) Key-value, iv) Graph and v) Multimodel, the latter being the extra one added to the four category division. In [7] authors refer to 15 categories; the five main ones (1–5) and 10 others, which are denoted as Soft NoSQL Systems (6–15): 1. Wide Column Store/Column Families, 2. Document Store, 3. Key Value/Tuple Store, 4. Graph DB, 5. Multimodel DB, 6. Object DB, 7. Grid & Cloud DB Solutions, 8. XML DB, 9. Multidimensional DB, 10. Multivalue DB, 11. Event Sourcing, 12. Time Series/Streaming DB, 13. Other NoSQL related DB, 14. Scientific and Specialized DBs, 15. Unresolved and uncategorized [8].

The five most popular categories are:

(i)   *Key-Value stores.* Key-Value, based on Amazon's Dynamo paper [9] are designed to handle massive associated arrays which consist of pairs of keys and values, and they also can retrieve values as long as a key is known. The most popular key value DB are Redis, Amazon DynamoDB, MS Azure Cosmos DB (considered a multi-model DB), Memcashed, and Hazelcast.

(ii) *Wide column stores.* Also called Extensible Record Stores, are based on Google's BigTable paper [10], can store data in records than can hold huge numbers of dynamic columns. Their data model consists of a collection of column families, key and value where the value is a set of related columns and they are indexed by the triple combination of row key, column key and timestamp. The most popular ones are Cassandra, HBase, MS Azure Cosmos DB, Datastax Enterprise and MS Azure Table Storage.

(iii) *Graph databases.* Data are represented by graphs, inspired by graph theory. Their data model consists of nodes and edges linked with relationships. The most popular graph DBs are Neo4j, MS Azure Cosmos DB, ArangoDB, OrientDB, and Virtuoso.

(iv) *Document stores.* In a document store, data are stored in so-called documents. The term "documents" refers to arbitrary data in a schema-free organization of data. The most popular document DBs are MongoDB, Amazon DynamoDB, Microsoft Azure Cosmos DB, Couchbase and CouchDB.

(v)   *Time Series.* A Time Series Database (TSDB) is a DB optimized for time-stamped or time series data; each entry is associated with a timestamp. A TSDB is used for measuring change over time and the properties that distinguish them are data lifecycle management, summarization, and large range scans of many records. The most popular TSDBs are InfluxDB, Kdb +, Prometheus, Graphite and RRDtool.

2.3 Popularity

The rise of the popularity of NoSQL DBs can be demonstrated by their extensive development and use by IT colossi. For instance, Apache's Cassandra is used by Facebook, Reddit, Twitter, Digg and Rockspace, amongst others. Baidu is using Hypertable. Google has developed BigTable. Amazon has developed DynamoDB and LinkedIn is using Project Voldemort. According to the ranking of DB-Engines, *"an initiative to collect and present information on DMS"* which ranks DBMSs according to their popularity (updated monthly), NoSQL DB are constantly on the rise, whereas relational DBs, although still on top, remain unchanged or face minor decline. DB-engines methodology for measuring the popularity of a system is based on the following 6 parameters: 1) Number of mentions of the system on website, 2) General interest in the system, 3) Frequency of technical discussions about the system, 4) Number of job offers, in which the system is mentioned, 5) Number of profiles in professional networks, in which the system is mentioned, and 6) Relevance in social networks.

According to the DB-engines ranking (https://db-engines.com/en/ranking) for the period from November 2012 until September 2020, it is evident, that despite occupying the first four positions, the popularity of relational DB is disputed. NoSQL DBs are on the rise. MongoDB is in 5th place demonstrating a 339% increase on popularity, the most popular Key-Vale DB is Redis (7th place), Cassandra, the most popular Wide Column DB, is 10th overall, Neo4j is leading the Graph DBs in 21st place and finally InfluxDB is the most popular Time Series DB in 29th place.

3 Data Mining Tasks Utilizing Graphs

Complex Information Networks are an emerging field in this era of powerful complex data organizations and web-based media mining. The DM tasks linked with Heterogeneous Information Networks (HIN) ought to adapt to the new demanding requests on this field of studies. The main DM tasks utilizing graphs are being presented while being categorized as follows [11]:

Similarity is a method for discovering how similar objects are. It offers the foundations for a plethora of other DM techniques, like clustering, classification, web search etc.

Clustering is notable for carrying DM tasks that require big data objects to be fragmented and grouped into smaller clusters that share a degree of similarity, but at the same time maintaining dissimilarity from objects in neighboring clusters. Modern datatypes and objects, like networked data diverge from the 'traditional' data where clustering is based on the unique and consistent object characteristics [12].

Classification is useful when possible class marks need to be ascertained, which is attainable through a classifier or an appropriate new model. In ML, classification is carried out on indistinguishably structured objects. However, the new emerged needs of modern object types, require to also take into account their relationships (associations). Hence, a linked based object classification occurs when entities related with each other are structured in this way, forming unique graphs. Conventional strategies are regularly reused or stretched out to have the option to deal with this sort of associations [13].

Link Prediction is one of the most demanding DM tasks. It investigates whether possible connections between nodes exist, utilizing rules, such as: a) the examination of nodes and b) hub attributes. Literature refers to link prediction by examining the structural attributes of social networks with predictors, or attribute information [11].

Ranking features are significant since they can quantify an object's significance within a social network. For instance, RankClus manages bipartite networks creating clusters of objects maintaining the equality of significance both on clustering and ranking. NetClus, is an optimal solution for star-type schema clustering, whilst other popular frameworks are HeProjI, OcdRank etc. [11].

Recommendation and related systems comprise of a wide range of algorithms from various domains. The goal is to recommend suitable services and objects to users. This can be accomplished using similarity features. In contrast to older recommendation systems that were utilizing user specific feedback information measurements, recent techniques have become more astute and functional, by utilizing collaborative filtering, matrix factorization or circle-based techniques [11].

Information Fusion is one of the main concerns that characterize HINs. The goal is to combine data from many variant HINs and improve intricacy and scrutiny of the information retrieved. Robust algorithms combine objects regardless if they belong to the same networks or they have identical semantic meaning. SM networks are brimming with this type of data, making them proper candidates for this kind of task [11].

4   Discussion – Future Work

The aim of this paper is to offer an insight about NoSQL DBs. A brief background on the reasons for their introduction and development is given. Next, their powerful characteristics and features are highlighted. Then, their many advantages over mainly RDs, especially their enhanced data and metadata management, along with their disadvantages are being grouped and analyzed [20]. The main categories with the most popular DB by category are presented, as well as the most widely used categories. Finally, according to popularity statistics, relational DBs are losing their users as four out of five demonstrate a decrease in their popularity (three of them from 10% up to 15%) and at the same time these users are transferring their trust to NoSQL DBs. This trend is also demonstrated by the fact that enterprise and IT colossi like Amazon, Apache and Google are leading their development.

This paper presents ongoing research related with the use of SM as a source for information retrieval and forecasting with the aid of DM techniques [14–17]. The next step of the project is to incorporate the use of graph DB (Neo4j) to provide a forecasting mechanism in healthcare [18]. The framework to be created will take into account more than 30 different parameters such as population characteristics (gender percentages, life expectancy, density, etc.), indexes (economic and medical, freedom of press etc.), policies applied (lockdown), including sentiment analysis related to COVID-19 on data retrieved mainly from Twitter, as well as other SM platforms. The goal is to assign weights to these parameters, to provide a hands-on formula and mechanism to health and government officials, enabling them to make appropriate decisions during a pandemic.

References

1. Codd, E.F.: Relational completeness of data base sublanguages, pp. 65–98. IBM Corporation (1972)
2. Petrov, C.: 25 Big Data Statistics - How Big It Actually Is in 2020? (2020) https://techjury. net/blog/big-data-statistics/. Accessed 3 Aug 2020
3. NoSQL, 1 August 2020. https://en.wikipedia.org/wiki/NoSQL. Accessed 4 Aug 2020
4. Moniruzzaman, A.B.M., Hossain, S.A.: NoSQL database: new era of databases for big data analytics-classification, characteristics and comparison. arXiv preprint arXiv:1307.0191 (2013)
5. Vaghani, R.: Use of NoSQL in industry, 17 December 2018. https://www.geeksforgeeks.org/ use-of-nosql-in-industry. Accessed 5 Aug 2020
6. Nayak, A., Poriya, A., Poojary, D.: Type of NOSQL databases and its comparison with relational databases. Int. J. Appl. Inf. Syst. **5**(4), 16–19 (2013)
7. NoSQL Databases List by Hosting Data - Updated 2020, 03 July 2020. https://hostingdata. co.uk/nosql-database/. Accessed 5 Aug 2020
8. Zollmann, J.: NoSQL databases. Software Engineering Research Group (2012). https://www. webcitation.org/6hA9zoqRd
9. DeCandia, G., et al.: Dynamo: Amazon's highly available key-value store. ACM SIGOPS Oper. Syst. Rev. **41**(6), 205–220 (2007)
10. Chang, F., et al.: Bigtable: a distributed storage system for structured data. ACM Trans. Comp. Syst. (TOCS) **26**(2), 1–26 (2008)
11. Shi, C., Li, Y., Zhang, J., Sun, Y., Philip, S.Y.: A survey of heterogeneous information network analysis. IEEE Trans. Knowl. Data Eng. **29**(1), 17–37 (2016)
12. Jain, A.K.: Data clustering: 50 years beyond K-means. Pattern Recogn. Lett. **31**(8), 651–666 (2010)
13. Lafferty, J., McCallum, A., Pereira, F.C.: Conditional random fields: probabilistic models for segmenting and labeling sequence data (2001)
14. Koukaras, P., Tjortjis, C., Rousidis, D.: Social media types: introducing a data driven taxonomy. Computing **102**(1), 295–340 (2019). https://doi.org/10.1007/s00607-019-00739-y
15. Koukaras, P., Tjortjis, C.: Social media analytics, types and methodology. In: Tsihrintzis, G.A., Virvou, M., Sakkopoulos, E., Jain, L.C. (eds.) Machine Learning Paradigms. LAIS, vol. 1, pp. 401–427. Springer, Cham (2019). https://doi.org/10.1007/978-3-030-15628-2_12
16. Rousidis, D., Koukaras, P., Tjortjis, C.: Social media prediction: a literature review. Multimedia Tools Appl. **79**(9–10), 6279–6311 (2019). https://doi.org/10.1007/s11042-019-082 91-9
17. Koukaras, P., Berberidis, C., Tjortjis, C.: A semi-supervised learning approach for complex information networks. In: Hemanth, J., Bestak, R., Chen, J.I.Z. (eds.) Intelligent Data Communication Technologies and Internet of Things. Lecture Notes on Data Engineering and Communications Technologies, vol. 57, pp. 1–13. Springer, Singapore (2021). https://doi. org/10.1007/978-981-15-9509-7_1
18. Koukaras, P., Rousidis, D., Tjortjis, C.: Forecasting and prevention mechanisms using social media in health care. In: Maglogiannis, I., Brahnam, S., Jain, L.C. (eds.) Advanced Computational Intelligence in Healthcare-7. SCI, vol. 891, pp. 121–137. Springer, Heidelberg (2020). https://doi.org/10.1007/978-3-662-61114-2_8
19. Gupta, I., Raghavan, V., Ghosh, M.: Leveraging metadata in no SQL storage systems. In: 2015 IEEE 8th International Conference on Cloud Computing, pp. 57–64. IEEE (2015)
20. Lofstead, J., Ryan, A., Lawson, M.: Adventures in NoSQL for metadata management. In: Weiland, M., Juckeland, G., Alam, S., Jagode, H. (eds.) ISC High Performance 2019. LNCS, vol. 11887, pp. 227–239. Springer, Cham (2019). https://doi.org/10.1007/978-3-030-34356-9_19

Entity Linking as a Population Mechanism for Skill Ontologies: Evaluating the Use of ESCO and Wikidata

Lino González, Elena García-Barriocanal, and Miguel-Angel Sicilia[(✉)]

Computer Science Department, University of Alcalá, Polytechnic Building. Ctra. Barcelona km. 33.6, 28871 Alcalá de Henares, Madrid, Spain
{lino.gonzalez,elena.garciab,msicilia}@uah.es

Abstract. Ontologies or databases describing occupations in terms of competences or skills are an important resource for a number of applications. Exploiting large knowledge graphs thus becomes a promising direction to update those ontologies with entities of the latter, which may be updated faster, especially in the case of crowd-sourced resources. Here we report a first assessment of the potential of that strategy matching knowledge elements in ESCO to Wikidata using NER and document similarity models available at the Spacy NLP libraries. Results show that the approach may be effective, but the use of pre-trained language models and the short texts included with entities (labels and descriptions) does not result in sufficient quality for a fully automated process.

Keywords: Entity linking · ESCO · Skill ontologies

1 Introduction

Competence/skill databases and knowledge bases are an important component for different applications. Notably, matching training and job offers to candidate profiles requires some kind of expression of the available capacities and the competence or skill gap, that can be used as the basis for building models, e.g. models that match needs in projects [1].

While there are some mature and curated occupational databases that connect job positions to competence components, the lexical resources they contain require in some sectors a constant update to adapt to the changing job market as expressed in job offerings, since the latter are nowadays mostly posted and disseminated in the form of semi-structured text.

A promising approach for the update of those competences is that of reusing other, non-occupational or general-purpose open knowledge bases that are curated as crow-sourced resources, as for example, Wikipedia-related projects. This could be useful in reducing update time, and enrich the databases, and may also support other applications or related functionality that could exploit the

E. Garoufallou and M.-A. Ovalle-Perandones (Eds.): MTSR 2020, CCIS 1355, pp. 116–122, 2021.
https://doi.org/10.1007/978-3-030-71903-6_12

knowledge graphs that such kind of general purpose resources provide. Entity linking techniques become thus a promising approach to complement expert curation in occupational databases with entities matched in open general purpose knowledge graphs. However, this requires an assessment of the effectiveness of those tools, with regards to the quality and usefulness of the links produced.

In this paper, we present the results of an experiment in entity linking for occupational databases. Concretely, we provide results of the use of state of the art entity linking algorithms between the large effort of ESCO, the *European Skills, Competences, Qualifications and Occupations* ontology [3] and Wikidata. The rationale for using ESCO is that the structure of skills includes fine-grained knowledge items, that are more likely to produce matches that may be useful in bringing more elements to the database. For example, a match of a programming language or some concrete industrial machine may be used to extract more potential knowledge items by traversing Wikidata relations, and hopefully, some of them would reflect novel or recent skills that have been incorporated to Wikidata as part of the continuous process of crowd-sourcing by volunteer curators.

The rest of this paper is structured as follows. Section 2 provides background information on occupational models and ESCO, and briefly surveys related research. Section 3 describes the materials and methods used and their rationale. Then, results are discussed in Sect. 3. Finally, conclusions and outlook are provided in Sect. 5.

2 Background

Occupational databases containing competences and skills have been developed in the last years, principally as a way to support statistics and policy on the labour market. These databases are typically of a national scope, and follow diverse schemas for the description of competences and skills.

The European Commission is developing ESCO (European Skills, Competences, Qualifications and Occupations) together with stakeholders as employment services, employer federations, trade unions, and professional associations. ESCO [3] is an attempt to provide vocabularies for the labour market, with concepts as subclasses of SKOS concepts[1]. It covers three different domains: occupations, knowledge, skills and competences, and qualifications. Here we are concerned with the second. Concretely, we deal with the definition of ESCO skills. The ESCO skills pillar distinguishes between (a) skill/competence concepts and (b) knowledge concepts by indicating the skill type. There is however no distinction between skills and competences. Since skill/competence concepts are usually described as short phrases describing some work-related ability or performance, we focus here on mapping only "knowledge"-type skills, since they contain in many cases proper nouns (e.g. names of computer languages, software tools or machines) that are better candidates for an unambiguous mapping to resources in publicly available knowledge graphs. A central use case for ESCO is matching job offers [2], and for that task, having a rich and updated list of concrete entities is critical.

---

[1] https://www.w3.org/TR/2009/REC-skos-reference-20090818/.

While ongoing editorial work of the ESCO Reference Groups was the primary method for initial content creation, mining external resources is considered a potential method for update. Previous work has already combined ESCO with other models or assets for particular purposes. For example, Sibarani et al. [7] combine ESCO and Schema.org[2] for the task of job market analysis. Shakya and Paudel [6] use ESCO in candidate matching as a schema to integrate disparate data. However, to the best of our knowledge, enriching ESCO with open knowledge graphs has not been addressed in previous work.

3   Materials and Methods

The method for linking skills consisted on three steps: entity recognition, entity linking and extracted candidate entities. A pre-trained Named Entity Recognition (NER) model (described below) was used for the first step. First, the entities obtained were filtered based on the manual inspection of each of the matchings and their type. Then, the filtered skills were matched against a Wikidata dump. Finally, the resulting Wikipedia resources matched were examined manually and a final extraction step involved a search for related instances that were candidates to be added to ESCO.

The NER model provided in SpaCy is based on state of the art neural models [8], that uses convolutional networks and built on GloVe vectors. We used the `en_core_web_lg` model, based on the large Ontonotes 5[3] corpus comprising various genres of text (news, conversational telephone speech, weblogs, usenet newsgroups, broadcast, talk shows). The NER f-score reported in Spacy documentation is 85.36.

The documents for the matching were the result of the concatenation of the fields `preferredLabel`, `description` and `altLabels` found in the file containing the skills obtained from the ESCO website (version 1.0.3), in English language. Only skills of ESCO type `knowledge` were used for the matching, since the departure assumption is that names of concrete entities appear in that kind of ESCO resources. A file with the matchings was produced, including information on the matched skill and the text and type of the entity identified.

Entity linking was carried out by disambiguation of entities in the large Wikibase knowledge graph [4].

We used SPARQL queries that match the strings of the terms found, we look for entities whose descriptions are similar to the `preferredLabel` and `description` fields extracted from ESCO. A direct `FILTER` query on labels is not feasible as the queries timeout, however, Wikibase provides a way of using the MediaWiki API, with all labels in words indexed as in the following query (where `<label>` is a parameter):

```
SELECT ?item ?label ?itemDescription
WHERE{
```

---

[2] https://schema.org/.
[3] https://catalog.ldc.upenn.edu/LDC2013T19.

```
SERVICE wikibase:mwapi
{
  bd:serviceParam wikibase:endpoint "www.wikidata.org";
                  wikibase:api "Generator";
                  mwapi:generator "search";
                  mwapi:gsrsearch "inlabel:<label>";
                  mwapi:gsrlimit "max".
  ?item wikibase:apiOutputItem mwapi:title.
}
?item rdfs:label ?label.
?item rdfs:description ?desc
FILTER CONTAINS(?label, <label>)
SERVICE wikibase:label { bd:serviceParam wikibase:language "en". }
}
```

However, the above query produces many false positives that have to be disambiguated. The approach was based on document similarity using the same Spacy word embedding mentioned for the NER task. The documents compared were the skill preferred label concatenated with the description on one hand, and the Wikibase label concatenated with the description on the other (all in their English versions).

4   Results and Discussion

4.1   Recognition of Entities

The results of the NER step produced 2520 matches over 962 different skills. The average number of matches per skill is 2.6, with 5.0 as 90% quantile. The matches were distributed across reuse levels in the following way: around 20% cross-sector and 56% sector specific, near 15% transversal, and less than 1% occupation-specific.

Regarding Spacy entity types[4], 51% correspond to ORG, i.e. "companies, agencies, institutions, etc.", 14% to NOPR ("nationalities or religious or political groups.") and 7% to PERSON. Others between 1% and 5% in descending order of appearance are PRODUCT ("objects, vehicles, foods, etc. – not services"), CARDINAL, LANGUAGE, GPE ("countries, cities, states."), LAW ("named documents made into laws."), LOC ("non-GPE locations, mountain ranges, bodies of water."), DATE and ORDINAL.

The mappings were manually evaluated and labelled according to the following values:

- RELEVANT for matches that appear correct and relevant as skills.
- IRRELEVANT for matches that appear correct but are not relevant as skills. These include for example dates, cardinals or ordinals.
- INCORRECT for matches that appear errors of the NER model.

---

[4] https://spacy.io/api/annotation#named-entities.

Table 1. Types of entities found and description

Entity type	Percentage	Description
ORG	51%	Companies, agencies, institutions, etc.
NOPR	14%	Nationalities or religious or political groups
PERSON	7%	Person
OTHERS	1%–5%	Product, cardinal, language, gpe, law, loc, date, ordinal

Further, each of the correct matches was evaluated with regards to the entity type as CORRECT or INCORRECT.

A total of 683 matches were labelled as RELEVANT, 80% sector specific, 13% cross-sector and only 6% occupation specific. Of those, only 264 were unique matches.

4.2   Entities Linked

From the collection of relevant skills, the process of automated mapping with Wikibase was carried out. The manual inspection of the results showed correct matches for around 50% of the distinct entities relevant coming from the NER process.

However, the results included a significant amount of false positive links, for a cosine similarity threshold of 0.8 (this was adjusted manually). These include for example:

– Resources about the skill, as in the case of books or articles. An example is Wikidata Q56114813 which is an article titled "A principled approach to operating system construction in Haskell" and has as the date of this writing almost no descriptive elements in Wikidata. This is a match for the programming skill in Haskell contained in ESCO.
– Errors in disambiguation of entities, as in the case of the match for Haskell to Oxford's PhD thesis *Avenues of art history: recent developments in English art history, with special reference to the works of Francis Haskell and their possible application to the study of Chinese art history* Q59574327.

The inspection of cases shows that most of incorrect matches are to Wikidata entities lacking description or with short description texts. This suggests some filtering of potential matches based on the amount of lexical descriptions available to increase accuracy.

4.3   Extracted Candidate Entities

The inspection of the entities correctly linked resulted in the following categories of elements, when traversing a generalization up in Wikidata. The path to more general classes is traversing up the instance-of property (P31) or the subclass of property (P279).

- `programming language` (Q9143), as Erlang, Haskell or Java.
- `methodology` (Q185698). It should be noted that this is defined generically as "scientific method of accumulating data" as Kanban.
- `software` (Q7397) as Apache Tomcat.

However, the way of incorporating new instances is also not straightforward, since it can follow different paths. For example, the Haskell language is an instance of eight other terms, some of them controversial as `interpreted language` or `lazy evaluation`.

The lack of consistent semantic use of Wikidata is thus a problem that makes needs to be addressed separately. Figure 1 shows the graph representation of the `instance of` relations for Haskell. The graph illustrates the semantic consistence problems of the resource.

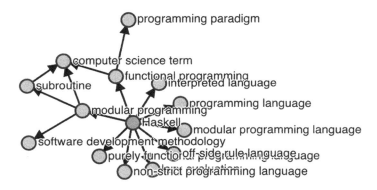

Fig. 1. Graph with the `instance of` relations of entity *Haskell*

Semantic inconsistencies hamper the possibility of automatically populating the ESCO skill model with terms obtained by property traversal. Other knowledge graphs with more constrained semantics may be an alternative, or some kind of manual pre-selection of traversal paths need to be used to guarantee the quality of the updates. This aspect of the accuracy and trustworthiness of Wikidata is under-researched according to [5], and is of special importance in tasks that attempt to bridge manually curated resources as ESCO with community-curated resources.

5   Conclusions and Outlook

We have reported the use of pre-trained language models for the task of extracting and then linking entities from the ESCO database of concrete skills to Wikidata terms for the specific purpose of extracting potential additional knowledge items to be integrated in ESCO. The performance of state of the art pre-trained models produces a small set of relevant matches for the use case, that have to be manually filtered.

While the results produce a limited number of mappings and is prone to errors of different kinds, the extraction of related knowledge elements are still potentially relevant, and may be considered as a promising mechanism to keep the skill database updated, as a complement to manually curated additions. However, this also requires some kind of quality control on the entities being extracted from Wikidata, since its crowdsourced nature entails a degree of errors that prevent the direct inclusion of new knowledge items.

Future work may proceed in different directions. The limited success of the results in the NER task suggest that an application-specific NER model may be required for the domain of the labour market. In a different direction, the errors in the entity linking with Wikidata may be mitigated by exploiting the relations inside the knowledge graph as a lexical resource.

References

1. Bandini, S., Mereghetti, P., Merino, E., Sartori, F.: Case–based support to small–medium enterprises: the Symphony Project. In: Basili, R., Pazienza, M.T. (eds.) AI*IA 2007. LNCS (LNAI), vol. 4733, pp. 483–494. Springer, Heidelberg (2007). https://doi.org/10.1007/978-3-540-74782-6_42
2. Colombo, E., Mercorio, F., Mezzanzanica, M.: AI meets labor market: Exploring the link between automation and skills. Inf. Econ. Policy **47**, 27–37 (2019)
3. Le Vrang, M., Papantoniou, A., Pauwels, E., Fannes, P., Vandensteen, D., De Smedt, J.: ESCO: boosting job matching in Europe with semantic interoperability. Computer **47**(10), 57–64 (2014)
4. Mora-Cantallops, M., Sánchez-Alonso, S., García-Barriocanal, E.: A systematic literature review on Wikidata. Data Technol. Appl. **53**(3), 250–268 (2019)
5. Piscopo, A., Simperl, E.: What we talk about when we talk about Wikidata quality: a literature survey. In: Proceedings of the 15th International Symposium on Open Collaboration, pp. 1–11 (2019)
6. Shakya, A., Paudel, S.: Job-candidate matching using ESCO ontology. J. Inst. Eng. **15**(1), 1–13 (2019)
7. Sibarani, E.M., Scerri, S., Morales, C., Auer, S., Collarana, D.: Ontology-guided job market demand analysis: a cross-sectional study for the data science field. In: Proceedings of the 13th International Conference on Semantic Systems, pp. 25–32 (2017)
8. Strubell, E., Verga, P., Belanger, D., McCallum, A.: Fast and accurate entity recognition with iterated dilated convolutions. arXiv preprint arXiv:1702.02098 (2017)

Implementing Culturally Relevant Relationships Between Digital Cultural Heritage Objects

Carlos H. Marcondes[(✉)] [iD]

Information Science School, Federal University of Minas Gerais,
Belo Horizonte 31270-191, MG, Brazil
ch_marcondes@id.uff.br

Abstract. A vocabulary of culturally relevant relationships – CRR - between cultural heritage objects in Library, Archive, and Museum (LAM) was proposed with the aim of interlinking digital collections using the Linked Open Data (LOD) technologies. The CRR vocabulary was proposed to be used by culture curators, teachers, historians, etc. to enable them to interlink such digital resources to provide a richer context and to reveal new senses of such resources. This paper aims at testing and evaluating the CRR vocabulary, as follows. Wikipedia articles about remarkable cultural heritage objects as the painting Mona Lisa and the book Dom Casmurro are used to create RDF triples where the heritage object is the subject, relationships of the CRR vocabulary are the predicates, and links found in each Wikipedia article to other LAM digital objects, or other Web resources are the objects of each triple. The RDF graphs thus generated are presented and discussed. The necessity of improvements in the proposed CRR vocabulary is outlined and suggestions of these changes are proposed.

Keywords: Heritage objects · Digital collections · Interlinking · Culturally relevant relationships

1 Introduction

Since 2000's cultural heritage collections of LAM are being published on the Web. The Web catalog technology makes such collection information silos because, although held by different institutions, many of such collections are complementary. Many of them have thematic intersections or are related to other web resources as authorities, historic events, subjects, exhibitions, or to articles in Wikipedia and its sibling resources DBpedia and Wikidata. The emergence of Digital Humanities (Zeng 2019) poses new challenges to libraries, archives, and museums (LAM). It requires that digital cultural heritage objects – HO - be machine-processable.

Some of these collections are now being published as structured data using LOD technologies. As more cultural heritage datasets are published according to LOD technologies the web of culture data [16]. The publishing of LAM digital collections according to LOD technologies will achieve their full potential as the published resources became structured interlinked and queried (Tim Berners-Lee 2006).

© Springer Nature Switzerland AG 2021
E. Garoufallou and M.-A. Ovalle-Perandones (Eds.): MTSR 2020, CCIS 1355, pp. 123–133, 2021.
https://doi.org/10.1007/978-3-030-71903-6_13

Aiming at exploring the synergies between such collections, and between them and other web resources, a research project (Marcondes 2019) proposed a vocabulary of culturally relevant relationships – CRR - between HO with the aim of interlinking such collections using the LOD technologies. The CRR vocabulary used as sources and inspiration of its relationships cases suggested by culture curators (Marcondes 2019, 125) [15] and ICA (2017) RIC-CM among others (Marcondes 2019, 122). Many relationships in such vocabularies are similar to the intended meaning of the CRR relationships that emerge from the cases suggested by culture curators which are the raw material for the development of the CRR vocabulary, but few of them have exactly the same meaning. A comprehensive description of the CRR vocabulary, including the meaning of each relationship, relationships with similar meaning in other vocabularies as Dublin Core, ICOM/CIDOC (2014) namespace/URI specification are detailed in the former cited paper; it was not included in the present paper due to its number of pages limitations. A table with the CRR vocabulary relationships is included in Sect. 3.

There are several LAM projects using LOD technologies (Marcondes 2019, 123) but few of them interlink collections hosted by different institutions. Related work highlight the value of initiatives to interlink LAM data and enrich metadata. Such practice is being increasingly recognized as one that adds value to LAM data [17], (Klein and Kyrios 2013), [2], (Zeng 2019), (McKenna, Debruyne and O'Sullivan 2020), [1]. The aim o CRR vocabulary is to provide a tool to interlink and enrich of LAM data.

The proposed interlink vocabulary is conceived as a tool to be used by culture curators in their work of contextualizing, commenting, evaluating, and make sense of HO, and improve their reuse for educational and cultural purposes. The CRR vocabulary now needs to be tested for its adequacy to interlink several HO and interlink them with other web resources, forming complex conceptualizations of events, works, agents, and themes of cultural relevance.

This phase of the research aims at testing the proposed vocabulary in real cases of sets of HO for which the relationships between them are remarkable and recognized in the academic literature on culture. The cases related in this paper are one of several test rounds planned.

This paper addresses the following questions. Are the proposed of CRR relationships complete and comprehensive to describe the different cases of culturally relevant relationships found/known in culture? Are the proposed relationships simple and intuitive so to be used by culture curators without special training?

2   Material and Method

There are many difficulties to test CRR vocabulary. To our knowledge, there is no standard methodology for testing vocabularies As proposed the vocabulary was conceived to be used by culture curators in their work to interlink HO available throughout the web. The CRR vocabulary was conceived to be simple and intuitive to be used by culture curators without any special training. Such aims guided its development.

Although conceived with such aims it is hard to summon up culture curator that understand the need for such vocabulary and are aware of LOD technologies and their potentials. In the face of this difficulty, we opt to use as test cases articles of Wikipedia about largely recognized examples of HO. Such Wikipedia articles are full of links to other related HO, thus constituting conceptualizations similar to those that may be developed in real cases of interlinked HO by culture curators. Such test methodology seems to be objective and verifiable, therefore adequate to this phase of the research.

Cases of sets of digital HO with their interrelationships that are remarkable and recognized in the academic literature on culture were selected. The corresponding Wikipedia articles texts about such objects were used to identify other heritage objects linked (to simulate the CRR relationship) to the Wikipedia article, along with Agents, Concepts, Events/Processes, Time, and Places, which comprise the entities of the ontology proposed in this research project (Marcondes 2020, 133). Such links are manually extracted from the Wikipedia article's text. Two cases of remarkable heritage objects are chosen, the painting Mona Lisa, https://en.wikipedia.org/wiki/Mona_Lisa, and the book Dom Casmurro, https://pt.wikipedia.org/wiki/Dom_Casmurro, by the Brazilian author Machado de Assis.

Links within each article text are indicative of a possible CRR relationship with such entities. The entities identified were then tentatively interlinked using the CRR vocabulary, forming a conceptualization. For each Wikipedia article were developed two tables, one with all links found within the article introduction paragraph (such paragraph is "pasted" as it is in the original Wikipedia article) and the other with chosen links found within the remainder of the article (not exhaustive); these are representatives of typical links between the HO corresponding to the Wikipedia article and other HO as books, paintings, documents, or entities as Agents, Concepts, Events/Processes, Time, and Places.

Results of each conceptualization are presented as several RDF (RDF Primer 2004) triples in a two columns table where the table title represents the subject of a triple, the 1st column represents the predicate and the 2nd column represents the object of each triple. Links used are not necessarily URI used in LOD since they are used just to demonstrate the interlinking features of the CRR vocabulary. Within the 2nd column, when an appropriate CRR relationship is not identified, a text from the Wikipedia article is quoted. Within the 2nd column when the triple object is a reference to a publication within the Wikipedia article, it is cited in the References with a note "(Wikipedia reference)". When there is not an adequate CRR relationship to interlink the subject and the object of a triple, the corresponding 1st column of the Table is filled with the observation "There is not a foreseen CRR relationship".

3 The CRR Vocabulary

A table with all of the CRR vocabulary relationships extracted from Marcondes (2019) follows. When the vocabulary was conceived there was an intention to reuse relationships from other vocabularies. Most of the time this intention was not carried out because the concepts in the original vocabulary have a slightly different meaning or were not relationships. This is the case of the CRR relationships 0021 Created_by/0022 Creator. Such relationships are somehow similar to Dublin Core element dc:creator, but dc:creator (see http://purl.org/dc/elements/1.1/creator) is not a relationship. In such cases, similar concepts are annotated within the CRR relationships (Table 1).

Table 1. CRR vocabulary relationships

Relationship	Inverse Relationship
Id: 0011 Based_on	Id: 0012 Base_for
Id: 0021 Created_by	Id: 0022 Creator
Id: 0031 Design_or_Procedure_for	Id: 0032 Design_or_Procedure
Id: 0041 Documents	Id: 0042 Documented_by
Id: 0051 Has_Contribution_of	Id: 0052 Contributor
Id: 061 Has_Subject	Id: 0062 Is_Subject
Id: 0071 Influenced	Id: 0072 Influenced_by
Id: 081 Inspired	Id: 0082 Inspired_by
Id: 0091 Is_Illustrated_by	Id: 092 Illustrated
Id:0101 Link_to_Agent	Id: 0102 Link_Agent_to_Object
Id: 0121 Link_to_Event_Process	Id: 0122 Link_Event_Process_to_Object
Id: 0131 Mentined_by_in	Id: 0132 Mentions
Id: 0141 Part_of	Id: 0142 Has_part
Id: 0151 Portrays	Id: 0152 Is_Portrayed_by
Id: 0161 Provenance	Id: 0162 Place_of_Provenance
Id: 0171 Similar_item	

4   Results

This section presents the two cases used to evaluate the CRR vocabulary

4.1   Da Vinci's Mona Lisa Case, Mona Lisa (2020)

Links in the article introduction:
The *Mona Lisa* (/ˌmoʊnə ˈliːsə/; Italian: *Monna Lisa* [ˈmɔnna   ˈliːza] or *La Gioconda* [la dʒoˈkonda]; French: *La Joconde* [la ʒɔkɔ̃d]) is a half-length portrait painting by the Italian artist Leonardo da Vinci. It is considered an archetypal masterpiece of the Italian Renaissance [3, 4], and has been described as "the best known, the most visited, the most written about, the most sung about, the most parodied work of art in the world" [5]. The painting's novel qualities include the subject's expression, which is frequently described as enigmatic [6], the monumentality of the composition, the subtle modeling of forms, and the atmospheric illusionism [7].

The painting is likely of the Italian noblewoman Lisa Gherardini [8] the wife of Francesco del Giocondo, and is in oil on a white Lombardy poplar panel. It had been believed to have been painted between 1503 and 1506; however, Leonardo may have continued working on it as late as 1517. Recent academic work suggests that it would not have been started before 1513 [9–12]. It was acquired by King Francis I of France and

Table 2. Triples in the article Mona Lisa

Subject: https://en.wikipedia.org/wiki/Mona_Lisa		
ln	Predicate (CR Relationship)	Object
1	0131 Mentioned_in	- Guinness World Record, https://en.wikipedia.org/wiki/Guinness_World_Records
2	There is not a foreseen CRR relationship	- Italian Renaissance, https://en.wikipedia.org/wiki/Italian_Renaissance
3	0021 Created_by	- Leonardo da Vinci, https://en.wikipedia.org/wiki/Leonardo_da_Vinci
4	0151 Portrays	- Lisa Gherardini, https://en.wikipedia.org/wiki/Lisa_del_Giocondo
5	"… is in oil on a white", there is not a foreseen CRR relationship	- Lombardy poplar, https://en.wikipedia.org/wiki/Populus_nigra
6	0101 Link_to_Agent	- King Francis I of France, https://en.wikipedia.org/wiki/Francis_I_of_France
7	"… is now the property of the", there is not a foreseen CRR relationship	- French Republic, https://en.wikipedia.org/wiki/France
8	"… on permanent display at", there is not a foreseen CRR relationship	- Louvre Museum, https://en.wikipedia.org/wiki/Louvre

is now the property of the French Republic itself, on permanent display at the Louvre Museum in Paris since 1797 [13].

The *Mona Lisa* is one of the most valuable paintings in the world. It holds the Guinness World Record for the highest known insurance valuation in history at US$100 million in 1962 [14] (equivalent to $650 million in 2018).

Other links found in the article to typical types of Heritage objects - books, documents, museum objects - in LAM collections, or to entities as Agents, Concepts, Events/Processes, Time, and Places, which comprise the entities of the proposed ontology (Marcondes 2019, 133), are also considered. Such links follow.

"Florence, Italy", "Prado Museum La Gioconda, Wikipedia article: Mona Lisa (Prado's version)", "Isleworth Mona Lisa, Wikipedia article: Isleworth Mona Lisa", "Mona Lisa at the Encyclopædia Britannica", "Raphael Sanzio's drawing after Leonardo's Mona Lisa al Louvre Museum", "The Heidelberg Document at Heidelberg University", "Secrets of the Mona Lisa, Discovery Channel documentary on YouTube", "Kemp, Martin; Pallanti, Giuseppe (2017), *Mona Lisa: The people and the painting.* Oxford: Oxford University Press ISBN 9780198749905", "Discussion by Janina Ramirez and Martin Kemp: Art Detective Podcast, 18 Jan 2017", "Research in 2003 by Professor Margaret Livingstone of Harvard University said that Mona Lisa's smile disappears when observed with direct vision" (Table 3).

Table 3. Additional triples in the article Mona Lisa

Subject: https://en.wikipedia.org/wiki/Mona_Lisa		
ln	Predicate (CR Relationship)	Object
1	0162 Place_of_Provenance	- Florence, Italy, https://en.wikipedia.org/wiki/Florence
2	0012 Base_for	- Prado Museum La Gioconda, https://en.wikipedia.org/wiki/Mona_Lisa_(Prado)
3	0012 Base_for	- Isleworth Mona Lisa, https://en.wikipedia.org/wiki/Isleworth_Mona_Lisa
4	0062 Is_Subject	- Mona Lisa at the Encyclopædia Britannica, https://www.britannica.com/EBchecked/topic/388735
5	0012 Base_for	- Raphael Sanzio's drawing after Leonardo's Mona Lisa al Louvre Museum, https://www.louvre.fr/en/oeuvre-notices/head-and-shoulders-woman-three-quarters-profile-facing-left-folded-arms
6	0131 Mentioned_in	- The Heidelberg Document at Heidelberg University, http://monalisa.org/2012/09/11/302/
7	0131 Mentioned_in	- *Secrets of the Mona Lisa*, Discovery Channel documentary on YouTube, https://www.youtube.com/watch?v=viHQRGpQ2w4
8	0131 Mentioned_in	- Kemp, Martin; Pallanti, Giuseppe (2017). *Mona Lisa: The people and the painting.* Oxford: Oxford University Press ISBN 9780198749905, https://en.wikipedia.org/wiki/Special:BookSources/9780198749905
9	0131 Mentioned_in	- Discussion by Janina Ramirez and Martin Kemp: Art Detective Podcast, 18 Jan 2017, https://web.archive.org/web/20170401070045/https://www.acast.com/artdetective/monalisabyleonardodavinci-withmartinkemp
10	0131 Mentioned_in	- Research in 2003 by Professor Margaret Livingstone of Harvard University, http://news.bbc.co.uk/2/hi/entertainment/2775817.stm

4.2 Machado de Assis's Dom Casmurro Case, Dom Casmurro (2019)

Links in the article introduction:

Dom Casmurro is an 1899 novel written by Brazilian author Joaquim Maria Machado de Assis. Like The Posthumous Memoirs of Bras Cubas and Quincas Borba, both by Machado de Assis, it is widely regarded as a masterpiece of realist literature. It is written as a fictional memoir by a distrusting, jealous husband. The narrator, however, is not a reliable conveyor of the story as it is a dark comedy. Dom Casmurro is considered by critic Afranio Coutinho "a true Brazilian masterpiece, and maybe Brazil's greatest representative piece of writing" and "one of the best books ever written in the Portuguese language, if not the best one to date." The author is considered a master of Latin American literature with a unique style of realism (Jackson 1998).

Other links are found in the article as follows.

"Machado de Assis' life as a translator of Shakespeare, and also his influence from French realism, especially Honoré de Balzac, Gustave Flaubert and Émile Zola", "The Brazilian writer Dalton Trevisan once noted that *Dom Casmurro* is

Table 4. Triples in the article Dom Casmurro

Subject: https://en.wikipedia.org/wiki/Dom_Casmurro		
ln	Predicate (CR Relationship)	Object
1	0021 Created_by	- Joaquim Maria Machado de Assis, https://en.wikipedia.org/wiki/Machado_de_Assis
2	there is not a foreseen CRR relationship	- *The Posthumous Memoirs of Bras Cubas*, https://en.wikipedia.org/wiki/The_Posthumous_Memoirs_of_Bras_Cubas
3	there is not a foreseen CRR relationship	- *Quincas Borba*, https://en.wikipedia.org/wiki/Quincas_Borba
4	there is not a foreseen CRR relationship	- masterpiece, https://en.wikipedia.org/wiki/Masterpiece
5	there is not a foreseen CRR relationship	- Literary Realism, https://en.wikipedia.org/wiki/Literary_realism
6	there is not a foreseen CRR relationship	- literature, https://en.wikipedia.org/wiki/Literature
7	there is not a foreseen CRR relationship	fictional, https://en.wikipedia.org/wiki/Fiction
8	there is not a foreseen CRR relationship	- memoir, https://en.wikipedia.org/wiki/Memoir
9	there is not a foreseen CRR relationship	- narrator, https://en.wikipedia.org/wiki/Narrator
10	"... is not a reliable conveyor", there is not a foreseen CRR relationship	- ... is not a reliable conveyor, https://en.wikipedia.org/wiki/Unreliable_narrator
11	"... it is a dark comedy", there is not a foreseen CRR relationship	- comedy, https://en.wikipedia.org/wiki/Comedy
12	there is not a foreseen CRR relationship	- Afranio Coutinho, https://en.wikipedia.org/wiki/Afranio_Coutinho
13	there is not a foreseen CRR relationship	- Portuguese language, https://en.wikipedia.org/wiki/Portuguese_language
14	there is not a foreseen CRR relationship	- Latin American, https://en.wikipedia.org/wiki/Latin_American
15	there is not a foreseen CRR relationship	- Literature, https://en.wikipedia.org/wiki/Literature
16	061 Has_Subject, Is_Subject	- Realism [6]

not to be read as the story of Capitu betraying Bentinho, but as a story of jealousy itself", https://en.wikipedia.org/wiki/Dalton_Trevisan. "A television miniseries titled Capitu, the feminine character of Dom Casmurro, was released in 2008", "MetaLibri Digital Library's Dom Casmurro".

Table 5. Additional triples in the article Dom Casmurro

Subject: https://en.wikipedia.org/wiki/Dom_Casmurro		
ln	Predicate (CR Relationship)	Object
1	Id: 0072 Influenced_by	- Shakespeare, https://en.wikipedia.org/wiki/Shakespeare
2	Id: 0072 Influenced_by	- Othello, https://en.wikipedia.org/wiki/Othello
3	Id: 0072 Influenced_by	- Honoré de Balzac, https://en.wikipedia.org/wiki/Honoré_de_Balzac
4	Id: 0072 Influenced_by	- Gustave Flaubert, https://en.wikipedia.org/wiki/Gustave_Flaubert
5	Id: 0072 Influenced_by	- Émile Zola, https://en.wikipedia.org/wiki/Émile_Zola
6	There is not a foreseen CRR relationship	- Dalton Trevisan, https://en.wikipedia.org/wiki/Dalton_Trevisan
7	Id: 0011 Based_on	- Television miniseries titled Capitu, https://memoriaglobo.globo.com/entretenimento/minisseries/capitu/
8	There is not a foreseen CRR relationship	- MetaLibri Digital Library's Dom Casmurro, http://metalibri.wikidot.com/title:dom-casmurro

5   Discussion

In the sequel are presented and discussed sequentially, ordered by Table and line within each Table, the cases where an adequate CRR relationship is not found as a predicate (column 1) to interlink the subject of the triple corresponding to the Table to the HO described in column 2.

Table 2, line 2, there is not a foreseen CRR relationship between a heritage object and the artistic movement, style, or artistic period to which it is associated. The CIDOC CRM (2014) has is a similar entity, the *E 4 Period* for entities as the Jurassic, The European Bronze Age, the Italian Renaissance.

Table 2, line 5, there is not a foreseen CRR relation for material or technique used for a heritage object. There is a similar property in the CIDOC CRM (2014), the *P33 used specific technique* property.

Table 2, line 7, 8, there are not foreseen CRR relationships for ownership of a heritage object or its belonging to a collection of a heritage institution. Again there are some similar properties in the CIDOC CRM (2014), as the *P52 has current owner* and *P54 has current permanent location*. Especially the relationship expressed in Table 2, Line 8 should be included in the CRR vocabulary, as such a relationship is more specific and implies the relationship expressed in Table 2, Line 7.

Table 4, lines 2, 3, there is not a foreseen CRR relationship between two works of the same author.

Table 4, lines 4, 6, 8, 9, 10, 11, 12, 13, 14, 15, there is not a foreseen CRR relationship similar to a thesaurus Associative Relationship.

Table 4, lines 5, 7, 16, there is not a foreseen CRR relationship between a heritage object and entities such as artistic movements or periods to which it is associated. The same relationship appears in Table 2, Line 2. Maybe the addition of such a relationship to the CRR vocabulary would be useful.

Table 5, line 8, there is not (it was not foreseen) a CRR relationship similar to the thesaurus Associative Relationship. As in Table 4 Lines 4, 6, 8, 9, 10, 11, 12, 13, 14, 15, maybe the adding of an Associative Relationship would enable curators to interlink HO and them with external entities without adding more specific relationships that could make the CRR vocabulary hard to be used by culture curators.

Table 5, line 8, there is not (it was not foreseen) a CRR relationship for a downloadable version of the HO. Such a type of relationship might be useful to ease the reuse of such an HO.

Wikipedia offers many pages describing culturally relevant HO, as the Hamlet (https://en.wikipedia.org/wiki/Hamlet), the Michelangelo's david (https://en.wikipedia.org/wiki/David_(Michelangelo), The Notre-Dame Cathedral (https://en.wikipedia.org/wiki/Notre-Dame_de_Paris) and many others. Such pages are full of links to other resources.

The choice of Wikipedia pages seemed appropriate as avoided the neet of training and explaining curators the aim of CRR vocabulary and LOD technologies. Mona Lisa page has 348 external links and Dom Casmurro page has 37 external links, according to https://www.duplichecker.com. Links within a Wikipedia page are divided in Bibliography, i.e. the bibliographic support to the claims made within the page, and External links, i.e. links to resources other than Wikipedia pages. Most of the links in each page are to other Wikipedia pages and documents thus simulating a LOD environment and the adequacy of CRR vocabulary to assign meaning to such links. The result tables can also be easily converted in RDF N triples and loaded in triplestores, thus opening up a new and wide perspective of tests to be done.

6 Conclusion

The results of the test described above suggest the inclusion of the CRR vocabulary of the following relationships: *Belongs to the collection of the cultural heritage institution*, *Link to the artistic movement or period*, *Link to a downloadable version*, and a generic *Associative Relationship*.

Two more cases are foreseen to be tested, the romance Don Quijote de La Mancha by the Spanish writer Miguel de Cervantes Saavedra, https://es.wikipedia.org/wiki/Don_Quijote_de_la_Mancha, and the panel painting Guerra e Paz by the Brazilian painter

Candido Portinari that decorates United Nations headquarters in New York, https://pt.
wikipedia.org/wiki/Guerra_e_Paz_(Candido_Portinari).

A further test of the potentialities of the CRR vocabulary would be to convert the
tables of each case into the triples that make up each one and load the corresponding
datasets into a triple store. This will enable the conceptualization to be queried using
SPARQL and the results evaluated according to its potentialities to answer queries that
retrieve relevant facts about each case. After such tests, we intend to release a new version
of CRR vocabulary.

There is another question in the development of the CRR vocabulary, how to implement a tool that enables culture curators to easily and friendly use the CRR vocabulary to
annotate and interlink cultural heritage collections to create enhanced cultural resources
made up of HO of collections in different institutions.

The proposed CRR vocabulary may be useful to enable the construction of new,
curated, and innovative resources as virtual exhibitions, virtual classes, etc., build on
the bases of digital resources from different LAM collections. As a project requisite the
CRR vocabulary must be kept small and concise as to be used intuitively and without
the need for any special training by culture curators.

As the number of LOD dataset available on the web grows the success the value
aggregated by interlinking cultural heritage digital collections as proposed by Berners-
Lee (2006) will be highlighted. The success of such an enterprise depends on cooperation
among heritage institutions to interlink their LOD collections.

Acknowledgments. This work was carried out with the support of the Brazilian agencies CAPES
- Financing Code 001, and CNPq, grant number 305253/2017-4

References

1. Alemu, G., Garoufallou, E.: The future of interlinked, interoperable and scalable metadata.
   Int. J. Metadata Semant. Ontol. **14**(2), 81–87 (2020)
2. Alexiev, V.: Museum linked open data: ontologies, datasets, projects. Digital Present. Preserv.
   Cult. Sci. Herit. **VIII**, 19–50 (2018)
3. Dom Casmurro article in Wikipedia (2019). https://en.wikipedia.org/wiki/Dom_Casmurro.
   Accessed 12 Mar 2020
4. Europeana Data Model Primer. Europeana (2011). https://pro.europeana.eu/files/Europe
   ana_Professional/Share_your_data/Technical_requirements/EDM_Documentation/EDM_
   Primer_130714.pdf
5. ICA: International Council on Archives. Experts Group on Archival Description (2016).
   Records in Context: a conceptual model for archival description (Consultation Draft v0.1).
   ICA. http://www.ica.org/sites/default/files/RiC-CM-0.1.pdf. Accessed 2016/12/12
6. ICOM/CIDOC: CIDOC Conceptual Reference Model Version 5.1.12 (2014). http://www.
   cidoc-crm.org/docs/cidoc_crm_version_5.1.2.pdf
7. IFLA. International Federation of Library Associations and Institutions. Study Group on
   Functional Requirements for Bibliographic Records: Final Report. UBCIM Publications New
   Series. K.G. Saur, München (1998)
8. Jackson, K.D.: Madness in a Tropical Manner. The New York Times (1998). (Wikipedia
   reference). Accessed 05 Jan 2014

9. Klein, M., Kyrios, A.: VIAFbot and the integration of library data on Wikipedia. Code4Lib **2**, 85–107 (2013)
10. The Linked Open Data Cloud (2020). https://lod-cloud.net/. Accessed 02 Aug 2020
11. Marcondes, C.H.: Towards a vocabulary to implement culturally relevant relationships between digital collections in heritage institutions. Knowl. Organ. **47**(2), 122–137 (2020). https://doi.org/10.5771/0943-7444-152020-2-122
12. McKenna, L., Debruyne, C., O'Sullivan, D.: NAISC: an authoritative linked data inter-linking approach for the library domain. Europeana Tech (SWIB 2019), 15. Hamburg, Leibniz-Informationszentrum Wirtschaft, HBZ (2020)
13. Mona Lisa article in Wikipedia (2020). https://en.wikipedia.org/wiki/Mona_Lisa. Accessed 12 Mar 2020
14. RDF Primer. W3C (2004). https://www.w3.org/TR/rdf-primer/. Accessed 22 Dec 2011
15. Riva, P., Le Boeuf, P., Žumer, M.: A Conceptual Model for Bibliographic Information. IFLA Library Reference Model, Netherlands (2017)
16. SPARQL Query Language for RDF. W3C (2008). https://www.w3.org/TR/rdf-sparql-query/. Accessed 04 Mar 2014
17. Volz, J., Bizer, C., Gaedke, M., Kobilarov, G.: Silk – a link discovery framework for the web of data. LDOW, 538 (2009)
18. Zeng, M.L.: Semantic enrichment for enhancing LAM data and supporting digital humanities. El profesional de la información **28**(1), e280103 (2019)

An Introduction to Information Network Modeling Capabilities, Utilizing Graphs

Paraskevas Koukaras⬤, Dimitrios Rousidis⬤, and Christos Tjortjis^(✉)⬤

The Data Mining and Analytics Research Group, School of Science and Technology,
International Hellenic University, 570 01 Thermi, Thessaloniki, Greece
{p.koukaras,d.rousidis,c.tjortjis}@ihu.edu.gr

Abstract. This paper presents research on Information Network (IN) modeling using graph mining. The theoretical background along with a review of relevant literature is showcased, pertaining the concepts of IN model types, network schemas and graph measures. Ongoing research involves experimentation and evaluation on bipartite and star network schemas, generating test subjects using Social Media, Energy or Healthcare data. Our contribution is showcased by two proof-of-concept simulations we plan to extend.

Keywords: Linked data · Information Networks · Graph modeling · Data mining · Social data · NoSQL

1 Introduction

Complex Information Networks (IN) have recently drawn a lot of research interest. The structural and semantic information contained in such networks offer various new capabilities for innovation. This work reports on ongoing research including the state-of-the-art methodologies on this field of informatics and data science. Focus is given on describing aspects of complex IN, such as network schema modeling and graph measures.

Recent research addresses graph theory and Heterogeneous Information Networks (HIN) [1], both suitable for modeling multi-typed data, while exposing multiple connections and pertaining their semantic nature during any Data Mining (DM) analysis. In such structures, data objects or entities interact with many different networks, generating multilayer networks [2].

This paper presents the necessary baseline concepts for performing information modeling and testing on real or artificially generated networks, which are highly populated by multi-typed entities. For example, Social Media (SM), Energy or Healthcare/medical IN. To that end, IN analysis becomes a necessity highlighting the importance of preserving the structural integrity of these networks [3]. This type of analysis involves concepts such as network analysis, graph mining, link mining, web mining etc. [4]. The theoretical background is presented for a transition to a more practical elaboration on IN mining. Section 2 presents the problem and approach, Sect. 3 expands on IN modeling while referring to commonly utilized network schemas and graph measures.

E. Garoufallou and M.-A. Ovalle-Perandones (Eds.): MTSR 2020, CCIS 1355, pp. 134–140, 2021.
https://doi.org/10.1007/978-3-030-71903-6_14

Section 4 presents ongoing and future research utilizing the abovementioned concepts for extracting knowledge from complex IN.

2 Problem and Approach

Most data objects, people, groups, or elements are interrelated or co-operate keeping their abstract essence. Such networks that contain non-trivial informative features are complex IN. Paradigms of IN, involve world wide web, SM, Sociopolitical, Energy, Healthcare and Academic domains while more are included in Linked Open Data Cloud[1] such as Geography, Government, Life Sciences, Linguistics etc. [4]. Semantic stores, such as OpenLink Virtuoso[2] merge RDBMS, ORDBMS, Virtual Databases etc. functionalities into a system, highlighting the importance for research on effective IN modeling and generating approaches for better data handling and knowledge extraction. Many such models and frameworks based on IN have been introduced and utilized. Despite that clustering and classification problems have benefited from IN application, just few of the proposed approaches consider network structures as they primarily focus on textual information.

This paper aims to introduce a coherent set of methods with state-of-the-art concepts that aid understanding of complex IN. It lays the foundation for the development of an approach, successfully and efficiently employing any given DM task, like forecasting [5], incorporating tools and metrics for processing data from any given domain, retrieving information and presenting results with state-of-the-art visualization tools of the fast growing graph database technologies.

One of the benefits of the proposed approach is that there are no commitments/obligations regarding the database and programming language to be used, as any NoSQL multi-model graph database can be combined with any programming language. Thus, this paper envisions the generation of two simulations, presented in Sect. 4, for further experimentation and elaboration on complex IN. These integral parts of any graph database approach related with Big Data, in the previously mentioned domains, IN models, network schemas and graph measures providing the necessary baseline for exploiting various possibilities for innovative DM tasks. However, a wide series of tests is necessary for evaluating this theoretical approach.

3 Background

3.1 Information Network Modeling

Modeling complex IN is demanding. Real world data handling involves manipulation of data and abstract object entities that may form multilayer networks. These raw data need to be structured in a way to facilitate interactions between multiple interconnected object types, composing IN that are semi-structured. Various projects (such as KONECT[3]) address the area of network science for data collection, analysis and visualization.

---

[1] https://lod-cloud.net/.

[2] https://virtuoso.openlinksw.com/.

[3] https://konect.cc/.

Real World Networks (RWN). IN display some unique characteristics. The accuracy of the model depends on how well the model mimics real world conditions. Features amongst interconnected networks are of great importance. They associate with attributes, network analysis and statistics. In graphs networks, the degree of a node is defined as the number of the connections the node has, whilst degree distribution is the probability distribution of these degrees, scattered within the network. Clustering coefficient quantifies how close the degrees are to each other. Finally, to calculate the average path length, the average of the lengths of the shortest paths amongst all possible pairs of the network nodes is calculated [6].

Random Graphs (RG): In RG, modeling presumes that all edges connecting nodes create random relationships. This assumption though does not impose a rule and cannot always apply to real-world networks. Thus, by utilizing that model, it is assumed that all random graph relations generated always correspond to real-life networks. These networks exhibit a Poisson degree distribution, a small clustering coefficient and a normal average path [6].

Small World Model (SWM): The SWM introduces an improvement to resolve issues met within RG and more specifically issues related to the real-world representation due to issues with the clustering coefficient [7]. In SWM the average shortest path between nodes increases proportionally as a function of the number of the nodes within the network. For instance, in RWN such as SM, a person entity has a finite number of relationships (connections) like friends, groups, pages, etc. SWM approach suggests that for all entities, the number of connections is the same; therefore, all entities have the same number of neighbors. Even though SWM leads to better modeling for the clustering coefficient of RWN, there are disadvantages i.e. the unrealistic hypothesis of same number of neighboring entities and the decreased precision since the SWM produces a degree distribution similar to the Poisson degree distribution of RG.

Preferential Attachment Model (PAM). PAM seems to be the optimal and most functional model in IN modeling [8]. PAM suggests that the new nodes added to networks prefer to connect to existing ones as they share common characteristics and some already display more connections. As a node's degree increases, the probability that new nodes connect to that node increases too. Even though a PAM offers more realistic conditions (e.g. in terms of average path lengths), there are still issues with the clustering coefficient, which is very small and does not approximate the values from RWN.

3.2 Network Schemas

Multi-relational Networks with Single Typed Object. The elementary attribute of this schema is that the object type is distinct, but its relationships are always one to many. Facebook and Twitter data, along with other SM utilize this multi-relational network schema as it is more efficient for connecting, analyzing and depicting billions of links and attributes. They represent actions like messaging, sharing, connecting, publishing and many other applications [9].

Bipartite Network. This schema is common in HIN and represents a relation or interaction amongst two different types of objects such as multimedia files. Bipartite networks utilize k-relations of objects creating links with other neighboring objects [10].

Star-Schema Network. This network schema is the most widely used conversion of relational databases where an object produces a HIN acting as a hub, where other objects connect to it. Often, relational database models such as bibliographic networks with objects of authors, books, articles etc. utilize star-schema networks [11].

Multiple-Hub Network. Multiple-hub networks introduce an upgrade and enhancement on star-schemas in terms of information complexity. They represent multifaceted network structures comprising many hubs, requiring increased precision in data visualization. Often, complex sciences as bioinformatics, astrophysics, theoretical mathematical structures, etc. utilize multi-hub networks where wide disintegration of network objects is required [12].

3.3 Graph Measures

Centrality's goal is to identify the central node in a graph and demonstrate the importance of vertices in graphs. Degree centrality computes a degree value defining the most central node, outlining the one with the greatest degree value. Eigenvector centrality computes the most significant node as the one with the most connections with other significant nodes. Katz centrality introduces an upgrade for the eigenvector centrality for directed graphs involving a bias term. According to betweenness centrality, the whole graph is created by multiple node hubs where the origin of these hubs are always the central nodes. Closeness centrality assumes that the nodes that proximate to the rest of the nodes are central. These measures are applied in a more common form; nodes are clustered, group degree centrality, group betweenness centrality and group closeness centrality can be distinguished [6].

Transitivity and Reciprocity. Regarding SM, manipulating the relationship between nodes (e.g. linking of nodes) is vital. Transitivity uses closed triads of edges, while reciprocity is a simpler version considering only closed loops (with length of two), that occur in directed graphs. Clustering coefficient formulas investigate the occurrences that discriminates global clustering coefficient and local clustering coefficient. These methods aid at calculating transitivity of the whole network, as well as transitivity for stand-alone nodes [6].

Similarity Similarity is measured by referring to structural equivalence in complex IN, DM and analytics [13]. It denotes the degree to which two nodes are similar when having common neighboring nodes. An interpretation of high similarity is that nodes share the same social environments along common attributes, properties, and attitudes. Similarity levels can be computed by applying Cosine and Jaccard similarity measures [6].

Communities and Interactions. Communities can be explicit (emic) or implicit (etic) also called clusters, groups, subgroups and are vital in complex IN (e.g. Sociopolitical, Healthcare, Energy and SM DM). They involve features and dynamics that lead to the optimization of an organization's entities, representing users [14].

4   Discussion and Ongoing Research

This study showcases in an abstract way the essential theoretical background on complex IN modeling, while referring to graphs. IN modeling combined with a multi-model database, using the characteristics of a NoSQL database (e.g. Neo4J or OrientDB) [15] can offer various DM capabilities. Transitioning from SQL to NoSQL databases comes with benefits such as: 1. Import documents as with other DBMSs but also utilize relationships between objects and new data types. This is achieved by using default pointers which are persistent, enabling very fast querying, 2. Elastic linear scalability for better expanding (common master-slave architecture incommodes servers with increasing requests), 3. Open source with no limitations on development and bug reporting, 4. They support SQL querying although they are modified to work with graphs and tree structures. 5. Improved visualization with the use of graphs. 6. Enhances RDBMS capabilities by introducing concepts such as graph measures, presented in Sect. 3.3.

To demonstrate the theoretical background of ongoing research it refers to recent literature, IN model types, network schemas and graph measures. To that end, this study prepares a baseline approach for knowledge discovery in complex IN. Contributions of this work are attributed to ongoing research, yielding two simulations for further experimentation, elaboration and result evaluation. Each simulation exposes a different notion regarding complex IN modeling, generating test subjects modeled by the concepts presented.

The *first simulation* defines a bipartite network schema while modeling and populating a database abiding with the bipartite schema and testing the validity of the model. Such a network schema displays the following characteristics: exactly two object types (nodes) with one or more relations (links) while forming a k-partite graph [10]. The dataset to be utilized refers to business reviews[4] with over 1.4 million business attributes, such as hours, parking, availability and more.

The *second simulation* defines a star network schema while modeling and populating a database implementing queries and calculating graph measures. Such a schema displays the following characteristics: two or more object types (nodes) with two or more relations (links) while using a HIN having the target object as a hub node. The dataset to be utilized refers to movie ratings[5] with 25 million ratings and one million tag applications applied to 62,000 movies by 162,000 users.

Current research progress attempts to inform about the key concepts that need to be considered before moving on to an effective IN analysis. Once established, future work is envisioned to involve:

A. Domain specific experimentations, such as SM, Energy or Healthcare/Medical datasets, live or historical, where user objects exist, exposing complex relations, attributes and characteristics. For example, perform sentiment analysis on SM data in comparison with identified user relationships or association rule mining or forecasting, exposing complex relationships among them.

---

[4] https://www.yelp.com/dataset/.

[5] https://grouplens.org/datasets/movielens/.

B. The incorporation of bi-functional novel algorithms like the one detailed in [16] for information extraction from very large datasets or knowledge discovery according to user specified prompts performing ranking and clustering on graphs at the same time.
C. Elaboration and evaluation of common graph measures, such as the ones presented in Sect. 3.3, attempting to perceive new measures or metrics offering more practical applications involving user related data objects or comparing use cases with multiple graph measures.

References

1. Han, J.: Mining heterogeneous information networks by exploring the power of links. In: Gama, J., Costa, V.S., Jorge, A.M., Brazdil, P.B. (eds.) DS 2009. LNCS (LNAI), vol. 5808, pp. 13–30. Springer, Heidelberg (2009). https://doi.org/10.1007/978-3-642-04747-3_2
2. Kivelä, M., Arenas, A., Barthelemy, M., Gleeson, J.P., Moreno, Y., Porter, M.A.: Multilayer networks. J. Complex Netw. **2**(3), 203–271 (2014)
3. Sun, Y., Han, J.: Mining heterogeneous information networks: a structural analysis approach. ACM SIGKDD Explor. Newsl. **14**(2), 20–28 (2013)
4. Koukaras, P., Tjortjis, C., Rousidis, D.: Social media types: introducing a data driven taxonomy. Computing **102**(1), 295–340 (2019). https://doi.org/10.1007/s00607-019-00739-y
5. Koukaras, P., Rousidis, D., Tjortjis, C.: Forecasting and prevention mechanisms using social media in health care. In: Maglogiannis, I., Brahnam, S., Jain, L.C. (eds.) *Advanced Computational Intelligence in Healthcare*-7. SCI, vol. 891, pp. 121–137. Springer, Heidelberg (2020). https://doi.org/10.1007/978-3-662-61114-2_8
6. Zafarani, R., Abbasi, M.A., Liu, H.: Social Media Mining: An Introduction. Cambridge University Press, Cambridge (2014)
7. Watts, D.J., Strogatz, S.H.: Collective dynamics of 'small-world' networks. Nature **393**(6684), 440–442 (1998)
8. Barabási, A.L., Albert, R.: Emergence of scaling in random networks. Science **286**(5439), 509–512 (1999)
9. Zhong, E., Fan, W., Zhu, Y., Yang, Q.: Modeling the dynamics of composite social networks. In: Proceedings of 19th ACM SIGKDD International Conference on Knowledge Discovery and Data Mining, pp. 937–945, August 2013
10. Long, B., Wu, X., Zhang, Z., Yu, P.S.: Unsupervised learning on k-partite graphs. In: Proceedings of 12th SIGKDD International Conference on Knowledge Discovery and Data Mining, pp. 317–326, August 2006
11. Shi, C., Kong, X., Yu, P.S., Xie, S., Wu, B.: Relevance search in heterogeneous networks. In: Proceedings of 15th International Conference on Extending Database Technology, pp. 180–191, March 2012
12. Kong, X., Cao, B., Yu, P.S.: Multi-label classification by mining label and instance correlations from heterogeneous information networks. In: Proceedings of 19th ACM SIGKDD International Conference on Knowledge Discovery and Data Mining, pp. 614–622, August 2013
13. Koukaras, P., Tjortjis, C.: Social media analytics, types and methodology. In: Tsihrintzis, G.A., Virvou, M., Sakkopoulos, E., Jain, L.C. (eds.) Machine Learning Paradigms. LAIS, vol. 1, pp. 401–427. Springer, Cham (2019). https://doi.org/10.1007/978-3-030-15628-2_12
14. Papadopoulos, S., Kompatsiaris, Y., Vakali, A., Spyridonos, P.: Community detection in social media. Data Min. Knowl. Disc. **24**(3), 515–554 (2012)

15. Fernandes, D., Bernardino, J.: Graph Databases Comparison: AllegroGraph, ArangoDB, InfiniteGraph, Neo4J, and OrientDB. In: DATA, pp. 373–380, July 2018
16. Koukaras, P., Berberidis, C., Tjortjis, C.: A semi-supervised learning approach for complex information networks. In: Proceedings of 3rd International Conference Intelligent Data Communication Technologies and Internet of Things (ICICI 2020), p. 13, August 2020

Track on Metadata and Semantics for Digital Libraries, Information Retrieval, Big, Linked, Social and Open Data

Using METS to Express Digital Provenance for Complex Digital Objects

Christy Chapman[(✉)] [iD], Seth Parker [iD], Stephen Parsons [iD], and W. Brent Seales [iD]

University of Kentucky, Lexington, KY 40506, USA
{cychapman,c.seth.parker,stephen.parsons,seales}@uky.edu

Abstract. Today's digital libraries consist of much more than simple 2D images of manuscript pages or paintings. Advanced imaging techniques – 3D modeling, spectral photography, and volumetric x-ray, for example – can be applied to all types of cultural objects and can be combined to create complex digital representations comprising many disparate parts. In addition, emergent technologies like virtual unwrapping and artificial intelligence (AI) make it possible to create "born digital" versions of unseen features, such as text and brush strokes, that are "hidden" by damage and therefore lack verifiable analog counterparts. Thus, the need for transparent metadata that describes and depicts the set of algorithmic steps and file combinations used to create such complicated digital representations is crucial. At EduceLab, we create various types of complex digital objects, from virtually unwrapped manuscripts that rely on machine learning tools to create born-digital versions of unseen text, to 3D models that consist of 2D photos, multi- and hyperspectral images, drawings, and 3D meshes. In exploring ways to document the digital provenance chain for these complicated digital representations and then support the dissemination of the metadata in a clear, concise, and organized way, we settled on the use of the Metadata Encoding Transmission Standard (METS). This paper outlines our design to exploit the flexibility and comprehensiveness of METS, particularly its `behaviorSec`, to meet emerging digital provenance metadata needs.

Keywords: Metadata · Digital provenance · Digital libraries · METS · Cultural heritage · Herculaneum papyri · 3D modeling · Virtual unwrapping

1 Introduction

As GLAM (Galleries, Libraries, Archives, and Museums) institutions increasingly move their collections online, and as technological advances make it easier, safer, and cheaper to create digital versions of practically any type of cultural heritage object, the metadata needs surrounding digital libraries (DLs) are increasingly complex. Today's DL objects consist of computation- and data-intensive components that are combined and manipulated in a multitude of ways to create enhanced digital representations of heritage materials. Examples range from complex 3D models built from x-ray scans or photogrammetry point clouds to layered images of objects captured with spectral photography under different wavelengths of light that reveal features invisible to the naked

© Springer Nature Switzerland AG 2021
E. Garoufallou and M.-A. Ovalle-Perandones (Eds.): MTSR 2020, CCIS 1355, pp. 143–154, 2021.
https://doi.org/10.1007/978-3-030-71903-6_15

eye [1]. Other emergent technologies like virtual unwrapping [2, 3] and inpainting [4] use AI to create "born digital" versions of texts and paintings, thereby exposing features "hidden" by damage but lacking analog counterparts that can be used to verify the integrity of the digitally produced rendition.

While it is tempting to gather the various files and outputs from these technologies and simply provide them as-is to scholars and patrons, most archivists agree that a digital object should be more durable, designed, and structured than the somewhat accidental collection of files produced by software. Given the "behind-the-scenes" nature of the computations that generate these representations, how can scholars, reviewers, and GLAM patrons trust that such complex digital objects faithfully render what they claim to render and can serve as objects worthy of scholarly study? Provenance metadata should provide the answer, but traditional structures that simply outline descriptive details about an object and provide basic information about its digital capture are no longer sufficient. Instead, we need durable, robust mechanisms capable of depicting all of the algorithmic steps and file combinations used to create complicated digital representations.

As one of its digital restoration projects, EduceLab[1] is creating 3D compilations of papyri fragments from the collection of opened Herculaneum scrolls carbonized by the eruption of Mount Vesuvius in 79 AD.[2] In 2017, we piloted the project using the historical images of P.Herc.118, a set of scroll fragments housed in 12 "pezzi" or frames (Pezzo 1-Pezzo 12, see Fig. 1) at the University of Oxford's Bodleian Library [1]. Our 3D compilations of P.Herc.118 comprise various versions of different types of files generated over the years using five different imaging modalities – multispectral and hyperspectral photography under numerous wavelengths of light; digitization of color analog photographs; digitization of hand-drawn sketches; and 3D photogrammetry models built using hundreds of 2D photos. These data undergo various computational processes, such as segmentation, stitching, image registration, and machine learning-based contrast enhancement, during the process of creating the compilation[3]. One of the primary goals of the project is to develop a transparent method for depicting and disseminating the digital provenance of these born-digital objects in a clear, concise, and organized way. In this paper, we describe our conceptual model for using METS, in particular its `behaviorSec`, to accomplish this goal.

2   EduceData and METS

Described as "the one metadata schema to rule them all," [5], METS (the Metadata Encoding Transmission Standard, http://www.loc.gov/standards/mets/) serves as a comprehensive container that can enumerate various types of files; show how they are interconnected and work together to create a complex digital object; and provide all of the

---

[1] EduceLab, inspired by the Digital Restoration Initiative at the University of Kentucky (UK), is a research group in UK's Computer Science department. EduceData refers to the image data used to build EduceLab's complex born-digital objects and the accompanying digital provenance metadata.

[2] Funded by the Andrew W. Mellon Foundation, grant number G-1810-06243.

[3] For a comprehensive description of the P.Herc.118 project, see Bertlesman et al. (2021) and https://www.thinking3d.ac.uk/Seales/.

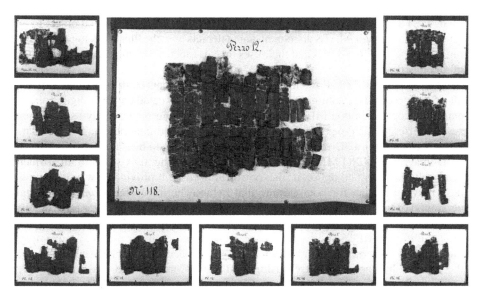

Fig. 1. The 1998 color photos of the P.Herc.118 pezzi. The scroll was peeled apart in 1883, resulting in twelve pieces, or "pezzi" in Italian, each consisting of several smaller sections.

relevant metadata for each file, either embedded within the document itself or linked to a location outside of the document. A key benefit of METS is that it allows users to combine elements from different schemata [6], an important characteristic when various types of files are required to construct a complex digital object like that of P.Herc.118. Unrolled by Italian scholars in 1883, P.Herc.118 has been the subject of various attempts over the years to create a visually accessible facsimile. In addition to the hand-drawn "disegni" sketches of the visible text made by artists as the scroll was first unfurled, the image record also includes a 1998 set of high-resolution color digital photographs, as well as a series of multispectral images captured using infrared lighting in 2005 [7, 8]. In 2017, our team added a hyperspectral stack of some 370 images per pezzo that range from near ultraviolet to infrared lighting. We also captured 3D scans of each of the 12 pezzi using photogrammetry. Our project compiled all of these images into one unified data set, so that the best visual representations from each facsimile could be combined and viewed at the same time.

It has been documented that METS is less useful for *interchanging* digital objects among institutions than it is for *packaging* the information for digital objects [9], and that may be particularly true when it comes to the complicated provenance of complex digital objects. But by offering a balance between expressiveness, which allows complex representations of various types resulting from complicated processes such as volumetric x-ray and AI tools, and proscriptive structure, which simplifies and leads to predictable, canonical sections, METS is a useful packaging tool for achieving our EduceData goals for P.Herc.118 and other digital restoration projects.

- First, METS allows all of the files that go into creating a complex digital object to be referenced in a single METS document, and it depicts how the files work together. Seeing at a glance the list of files and their uses reveals much about the digital provenance of an object.
- Second, because METS allows the user to combine elements from different schemata, all of the descriptive, administrative, and preservation metadata for a digital object can be collocated in one METS document. This attribute is extremely useful when several different file types combine to create a particular digital object. The metadata schema chosen for a 3D mesh (i.e. CARARES) is likely to be different from that of a 2D image (i.e. NISO MIX), yet both are included in the 3D version of an artifact. The multiple schemata option is also powerful because it provides a way to include descriptive metadata for both the original cultural heritage object *and* the digital version(s) of that object. Catalogers often struggle to disambiguate descriptive details about the two conceptual entities (physical artifact versus digital representation), but the flexibility of METS successfully addresses this issue. In our profile, for example, the dmdSec (descriptive metadata section) for a digital object will be used to describe the physical heritage object itself using the Dublin Core standard. Basic descriptive and technical metadata for the image files, on the other hand, will be included in the amdSec (administrative metadata section) as techMD using the NISO MIX and PREMIS standards.
- Third, because METS allows one to point externally to files, we can develop tools that automatically collect and compile technical metadata as computational operations are performed. Most of the technical metadata generated by our software tools will be collected and stored as JSON files, which are not compatible with XML-based METS. To avoid having to crosswalk all of the JSON metadata to XML, most of the technical metadata (other than basic descriptive details such as date/time captured, etc.) will reside outside the METS document but will be referenced using the mdRef element in the amdSec as techMD, allowing users to peruse the easier-to-read JSON files or crosswalk them to XML if they so desire.
- Finally, by using the behaviorSec, we can delineate, describe, and enable the execution of specific computational actions to both create and recreate a final digital object. The behaviorSec has generally been limited to such uses as indicating how a digital object should be displayed – the order of pages with page turning behaviors, for example. Our METS profile goes a step further, however, and uses the behaviorSec to make explicit for analysis and review the algorithmic steps imposed upon the referenced files. These computational processes are depicted through visualizations that are enabled through executable code referenced in the <mechanism> element of the behaviorSec. This final point is the most powerful, and perhaps most unconventional, use of METS in our profile.

3 Related Work

Several thorough overviews of METS extol its flexibility and simplicity [10, 11]. However, little research has been conducted on best practice usage of the METS behaviorSec itself. One exception is that of Gartner [12], who suggested using METS as an "Intermediary XML Schema" for digital objects that result from experiments in live cell protein studies. In these studies, a variety of biological nanoimaging experiments generate a series of raw images that must be combined and processed with various software tools before being delivered to the biology research team. Gartner proposes using METS documents as "mediating encoding mechanisms" from which data or metadata for archival or delivery can be generated by Extensible Stylesheet Language Transformations (XSLT). According to Gartner, "the intermediary schema technique may be used to define templates, similar to a content model, from which the final METS files to be delivered can be constructed," [12]. This technique is similar to the one we describe, in that it uses the behavior section "to invoke the XSLT transformation by which a METS template file is to be processed and to define the software necessary to co-process the raw image experiment files for delivery," [12].

4   The METS File

To demonstrate EduceLab's planned usage of METS, consider a small part of the P.Herc.118 3D model compilation process – the creation of a 3D version of the 2005 infrared (IR) photographs of Pezzo 4. Creating this DL object involved the following source files (Fig. 2):

1. The set of 2005 infrared (IR) images (Fig. 2, Column 1). The multispectral team in 2005 photographed each pezzo in tiny square sections so as to achieve the highest resolution possible and reveal the greatest amount of visible text [7]. To create a composite, complete image of Pezzo 4, the resulting 35 small, square photos had to be painstakingly stitched together digitally by finding the overlaps and linking them (Fig. 2, A).
2. The 1998 color image of Pezzo 4 (Fig. 2 Column 2), which provided the color information for the 3D model and served as the base to which everything was registered (Fig. 2, D).
3. The 2017 photogrammetry files acquired using an Artec Space Spider handheld scanner (Fig. 2, Column 3). The proprietary Artec software generated three digital artifacts from the scans that combine to create the 3D model – a mesh (`.obj`) that represents the geometric shape of the surface; a texture (`.png`) that applies the color to that mesh; and a materials file (`.mtl`) that incorporates reflectance information. Many iterative steps to create the final 3D mesh and texture occur within the Artec software, proprietary processes we call `ArtecStudioReconstruct` (Fig. 2, B) and `ReorderTexture` (Fig. 2, C).

Pipelines and processes applied to these files to combine them into one composite image include `Stitching`, `ArtecStudioReconstruct`, `ArtecReorderTexture`, and `2D-3DRegistration`.

Although a complete list of files and transformations could be considered to be a kind of comprehensive catalogue of an object's digital provenance, the METS `behaviorSec` creates an opportunity for designing a kind of structural guide to the many pieces of data, metadata, and data transformations at play. This additional design opportunity goes well beyond what many times passes for packaged digital objects. Rather

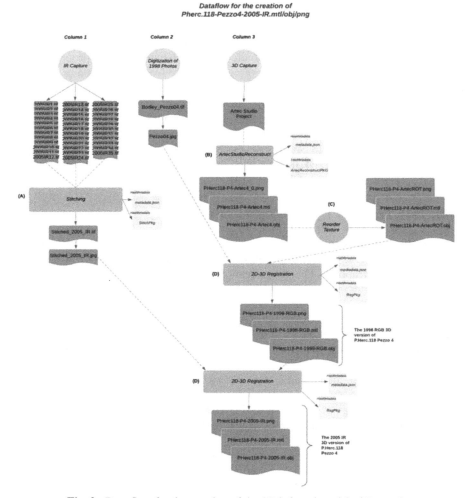

Fig. 2. Data flow for the creation of the 3D infrared model of Pezzo 4.

than merely listing inside a single METS document all of the composite files, along with all of the intermediate files and data transformations that occurred "behind the scenes" to create the composite 3D model, the METS `behaviorsSec` feature can serve as a powerful design tool for structuring all kinds of interpretive operations, such as displaying and visualizing the digital provenance chain of any given digital object.

4.1 EduceData Behaviors

We employ various working pieces of software internally to create ad hoc visualizations of our processes and their outputs (to view an example using the P.Herc.118 data, see http://infoforest.cs.uky.edu/pherc118/). We refer to these behaviors as EduceData Visualizations and are in the process of transforming these tools into the METS behaviors format. Applying the METS structure to our tools will afford them greater portability, scalability, and searchability so that they and the digital objects we create can achieve widespread distribution and use.

According to the METS primer [13], the METS behavior section "provides a means to link digital content with applications or computer programming code that can be used in conjunction with the other information in the METS document to render or display the digital object, or to transform one or more of its component content files." For our digital objects, the METS `behaviorSec` will include a set of behavior mechanism `xlink:href` pointers to code that, when invoked, will assemble all of the files and interface information necessary to execute the behavior. The various behavior mechanisms will launch visualizations that (1) explain how input files were manipulated at various iterations, (2) enable the replication of such manipulations, and (3) depict all of the processes and associated metadata.

Various users of the P.Herc.118 compilations will benefit from these EduceData Visualizations. For example, allowing one transparently to "see" the parameter settings and human judgements that play a role in the creation of a digital object will help engender the researcher's trust in the object as a resource for scholarly study. The casual museum patron might like to see if they can improve upon the visibility of a text by making their own contrast or color adjustments. Or, a peer reviewer of research produced using the born-digital object may want to inspect the quality of the registration process to assess the validity of resulting scholarly claims.

For example, the following behaviors will produce EduceData Visualizations for examining and reproducing the creation of the 2005 IR 3D version of P.Herc.118 Pezzo 4:

- **VisualizeImage:** Allows a user to view any 2D image with adjustments, such as color and contrast.
- **VisualizeMesh:** Allows one to view a particular 3D model. Behaviors in this example would enable simple viewing of the 3D version of P.Herc.118 Pezzo 4's 1998 color image or the 3D version of the 2005 infrared image.
- **VisualizeMetadata:** Behavior that aggregates all metadata for a particular digital object from the various sections of the METS file, such as the `dmdSec` (descriptive metadata) and `amdSec` (`techMD`, `digiprovMD`, `rightsMD`, etc.), and presents it in graphical form.
- **VisualizePipeline:** Shows connections inside of a single pipeline or process. The referenced code will use the software-generated `metadata.json` files to visualize a graph produced by a processing pipeline, such as those for `Stitching` and `2D-3D Registration`.
- **VisualizeHistory:** Uses all of the components of a digital object to depict the entire digital object's history in graphical form. This is an extension of the `VisualizeMetadata` and `VisualizePipeline` behaviors, in that it will render the connections *between* pipelines, such as between `Stitching` and `Registration`, or between `ArtecReconstruction` and `Registration`, in a fashion similar to that of Fig. 2.

- **Register2Dto2D, Register3Dto3D, and Register2Dto3D** (three different behaviors): Replicates the specified registration process by using the intermediate files along with the fixed and moving images stored in a `.regpkg` project file to recreate a registered digital object, such as the 2D 1998 color photo registered to the Artec 3D mesh. In the future, this behavior will give users the ability to perform a new registration of any 2D or 3D object referenced in the METS document to any other 2D or 3D object also so referenced, generating a new transform file that stores the chosen registration parameters.
- **ExploreRegistration:** Allows one to inspect the intermediate results of all steps for a selected registration pipeline.
- **StitchImage:** Draws from a Photoshop metadata file to replicate the stitching process, such as that of the 35 2005 IR images, that composes a single image from multiple images that possess overlapping field-of-views.
- **ArtecReconstruct or PGReconstruct:** `ArtecReconstruct` uses the files from the Artec Studio Project directory created by the Artec Spider capture event to replicate the rendering of the 3D meshes used to create the 3D models. `PGReconstruct` is the same behavior, but one associated with our 3D modeling pipeline going forward. A new custom designed photogrammetry kit will enable a simplified dataflow and processing pipeline, which will in turn create a cleaner, more straightforward METS file and behavior mechanism.

A truncated, conceptual draft of a METS file for the 3D version of the 2005 IR image of P.Herc.118 Pezzo 4 is available for viewing at https://tinyurl.com/y57dfonp. Once METS files have been constructed for the compiled image of each of the 12 pezzi, a consolidated METS file can be created by using the `mets:fptr` element in the `structMap` section to aggregate each pezzo's representative METS file, thereby creating a complete catalog and digital provenance chain for the entire set of 3D models for P.Herc.118.

5   Extending the Behaviors

Because of the flexibility and extensibility of METS, we can add behaviors that provide different functionalities as needed or desired by various stakeholders. For example, the use of METS behaviors as described opens up possibilities for much more interactivity with the source files used to create complex digital objects. With all of the component files clearly delineated and organized, we can establish groups of behaviors that not only serve as the blueprint for how a digital object *was constructed*, but also provides the building blocks for *future digital objects*. New complex digital object visualizations can be created on the fly, eliminating the need for extensive image processing that creates a static digital object. Instead, the user can see the output of a new "virtual" digital object with all of its relevant metadata generated and maintained in a new project file for examination.

For example, two additional image sets can be registered to the P.Herc.118 Pezzo 4 3D mesh: the original disegni drawings and the 2017 hyperspectral images. While the process outlined in this paper does not include these images, most scholars will want to view the disegni images registered to the 2005 IR 3D model. Or, a museum patron might like to see how a papyrus fragment has changed since 2005 by registering the stitched 2005 IR image to the 2017 IR version. The visualization behaviors proposed below provide a better option for achieving such goals, rather than creating and storing a new digital object each time a new need arises to view the images or the data in a different way.

- **GenerateCompositeImage:** For combining one or more spectral images into a single output image. The type of composite is user-defined, and examples might include false color rendering, color mapping, contrast enhancement, etc.
- **GenerateRGBImage:** Same process as `GenerateCompositeImage`, but with a predefined operation for generating an RGB image, a popular spectral combination based on red, green, and blue values that results in a full-color rendition.
- **VisualizeSegmentation:** For P.Herc.118 Pezzo 4, there are nine disegni drawings which must be isolated from each other digitally through a process called segmentation before they can be registered to any other 2D images or 3D meshes. This behavior enables one to examine the segmentation process applied to the original digital images of the disegni.
- **RegistrationSuite:** Allows the user to select a stack of images or a `.regpkg` project file referenced in the METS document and execute a selected registration pipeline (`Register2Dto2D`, `Register3Dto3D`, or `Register2Dto3D`) to create one or more newly aligned images. For example, a user could select all of the segmented disegni files and register them to the 1998 color 3D mesh, and then do it again to create a registration package for the disegni to the 2005 IR mesh.
- **VisualizeLayers:** For viewing and manipulating the newly registered images in 3D. One could, for example, view the disegni registered to the 1998 color 3D mesh, then to the 2005 IR 3D model.
- **ExplorationHeaven:** For visualizing *and* modifying a digital object by tweaking any step in the digital object's history.
- **FlattenObject:** Allows the user to virtually flatten the surface of a 3D mesh, essentially ironing out all of its wrinkles and undulations, then use that information to create a new 2D photo showing all of the wrinkles removed.

Each of these custom visualizations will generate a new project file containing all of the relevant metadata produced by each new process as it is applied to the selected image files. If desired, systems could provide version control, allowing users to save locally the entire project package along with the new digital object for further study and use. By using the METS document to house all relevant information about a digital object, from descriptive details about the physical source to technical details about its electronic capture to digital provenance details about the final digital object's computational construction, users have everything they need at their fingertips to recreate and investigate claims arising from the study of these digital objects as well as expand upon them by creating their own new versions.

6   Additional Applications

Image registration is one of the simplest types of digital restoration that EduceLab performs. As noted earlier, other more complex digital objects are created using our virtual unwrapping software pipeline and by applying new AI techniques. METS behaviors can also be used to describe these computational actions.

For example, virtual unwrapping applies a series of algorithmic steps to micro-CT scans of manuscripts that cannot be opened and renders the hidden text within. This process of identifying and isolating the writing surfaces that contain text, flattening them, and then rendering the writing on those layers can be made explicit using EduceData Visualization behaviors similar to those described above for registration. Behaviors could be created, for example, to visualize the volume of slice images generated from a micro-CT scan from which a virtually unwrapped image is constructed, and then replicate the entire virtual unwrapping process. Another possible use is to visualize aligned objects in the same 3D space, such as examining a virtually unwrapped 3D mesh showing writing with a multispectral photograph registered to it. Another behavior might allow users to inspect the intermediate results of each step in a specific virtual unwrapping pipeline, a visualization that would enable the backtracking of results to the inputs and that could eventually be expanded to allow one to see how results change when different parameters are chosen or steps are implemented.

AI also enables new complex digital analysis tasks, such as machine-based recognition of artistic styles and recto/verso determinations from x-ray scans, all using large labeled data sets and tools like trained Convolutional Neural Networks (CNNs) or Generative Adversarial Networks (GANs). METS can be used to not only track the provenance of how images are created, but it can also be used to track these black-box analyses to ascertain how researchers come to expert scholarly conclusions about these digital objects (i.e., how a particular style determination was made using CNNs).

We are currently using machine learning techniques in two areas: contrast enhancement of spectral images and ink identification in micro-CT data. Potential relevant behaviors could analyze an entire spectral suite of images and generate a single image with the ideal contrast or other AI-enabled enhancements. A graphical visualization of all the steps and intermediate results in a chosen spectral enhancement pipeline could be displayed. For ink identification pipelines, a behavior could access the complete training dataset for specified ink type, along with the specific parameters (i.e. the model architecture, training algorithm, and hyperparameters) captured automatically and stored in metadata.json files to replicate the training of the ink identification and texturing model. Another behavior could replicate the creation of a textured 3D mesh showing the text by applying a trained ink-ID model to a selected writing surface from a micro-CT volume.

7   Conclusion

At EduceLab, we want our digital objects to be easy to exchange, validate, and reuse. Today's digital library represents a big data problem in need of careful organization through imposed structure in order for these goals to be achieved. Future work will incorporate the CIDOC-CRM ontology in our METS files to improve their semantic interoperability. But as noted by Doerr [14], METS is without a competitor when it comes to providing syntactic interoperability for information exchange.

This paper describes our effort at building complex digital objects, which we believe must be designed and packaged with intentionality to support access, all kinds of intended uses, and scholarly analysis. The METS mechanism is expressive enough to capture the complexity of new algorithms and big-data applications, yet still respects the important standards that have emerged around descriptive, technical, and provenance metadata and their accepted standards.

We seek to move beyond a process where almost all the care and design is focused on developing the *software* – creating tools that generate interesting results, like image enhancements or virtual unwrapping – only to produce a digital object that is merely a wrapped set of file lists and links that were likely produced through the ad hoc happenstance of software parameters and outputs. While that could be considered to be a comprehensive archival record of the process, it misses a very important opportunity. The structuring of complex digital objects using METS brings a new level of intentionality and design to the overall process, building a structural guide for the users of those objects, and giving the software a meaningful target for what to produce and how those results can and should be combined to support a durable digital object.

References

1. Bertelsman, A., et al.: The Digital Compilation of P.Herc.118. Accepted for publication in Manuscript Studies 6.1 (2021)
2. Parker, C.S., Parsons, S., Bandy, J., Chapman, C., Coppens, F., Seales, W.B.: From invisibility to readability: recovering the ink of Herculaneum. Public Libr. Sci. (PLoS) ONE **14**(5), e0215775 (2019). https://doi.org/10.1371/journal.pone.0215775
3. Seales, W.B., Parker, C.S., Segal, M., Tov, E., Shor, P., Porath, Y.: From damage to discovery via virtual unwrapping: reading the scroll from En-Gedi. Sci. Adv. **2**, 9 (2016). https://doi.org/10.1126/sciadv.1601247
4. Jboor, N.H., Belhi, A., Al-Ali, A.K., Bouras, A., Jaoua, A.: Towards an inpainting framework for visual cultural heritage. In: Jaber, K.M. (ed.) 2019 IEEE Jordan International Joint Conference on Electrical Engineering and Information Technology (JEEIT), pp. 602–607. IEEE, Piscataway (2019). https://doi.org/10.1109/jeeit.2019.8717470
5. Pomerantz, J.: Metadata. In: MIT Press Essential Knowledge Series, p. 112. The MIT Press, Cambridge, London (2015)
6. Dulock, M., Cronin, C.: Providing metadata for compound digital objects: strategic planning for an institution's first use of METS, MODS, and MIX. J. Libr. Metadata **9**(3–4), 289–304 (2009). https://doi.org/10.1080/19386380903405199
7. Stepp, R.A., Ware, G.: Application of astronomical imaging techniques to P.Herc.118. Am. Stud. Papyrol. 733–746 (2010). Accessed https://quod.lib.umich.edu/i/icp/XXV_Congress_Proceedings.pdf
8. Macfarlane, R.T.: P.Herc.817 from facsimiles to MSI: a case for practical verification. Am. Stud. Papyrol. 455–462 (2010). Accessed https://quod.lib.umich.edu/i/icp/XXV_Congress_Proceedings.pdf
9. Gartner, R.: The digital object in context: using CERIF With METS. J. Libr. Metadata **12**(1), 39–51 (2012). https://doi.org/10.1080/19386389.2012.661689

10. Cantara, L.: METS: the metadata encoding and transmission standard. Catalog. Classif. Q. **40**(3–4), 237–253 (2005). https://doi.org/10.1300/J104v40n03_11
11. Guenther, R., McCallum, S.: New metadata standards for digital resources: MODS and METS. Bull. Am. Soc. Inf. Sci. Technol. **29**(2), 12–15 (2003). https://doi.org/10.1002/bult.268
12. Gartner, R.: METS as an intermediary schema for a digital library of complex scientific multimedia. Inf. Technol. Libr. (Online) **31**(3), 24–35 (2012). https://doi.org/10.6017/ital.v31i3.1917
13. Metadata Encoding and Transmission Standard: Primer and Reference Manual, Version 1.6. https://www.loc.gov/standards/mets/METSPrimer.pdf. Accessed 29 Aug 2020
14. Doerr, M.: METS and the CIDOC CRM – a comparison, (2011). Accessed http://culturalheritageimaging.org/What_We_Do/Publications/mets-crm-doerr/mets_crm.pdf

How Can a University Take Its First Steps in Open Data?

Yannis Tzitzikas[1,2]([✉]) [iD], Marios Pitikakis[1] [iD], Giorgos Giakoumis[1] [iD],
Kalliopi Varouha[1] [iD], and Eleni Karkanaki[1]

[1] University of Crete, Heraklion and Rethymnon, Greece
{tzitzik,pitikakis}@csd.uoc.gr, geokop7@gmail.com,
{kvarouha,eleni.karkanaki}@uoc.gr
[2] Information Systems Laboratory, FORTH-ICS, Heraklion, Greece

Abstract. Every university in Greece is obliged to comply with the national legal framework on open data. The rising question is how such a big and diverse organization could support open data from an administrative, legal and technical point of view, in a way that enables gradual improvement of the open data-related services. In this paper, we describe our experience, as University of Crete, for tackling these requirements. In particular, (a) we detail the steps of the process that we followed, (b) we show how an Open Data Catalog can be exploited also in the first steps of this process, (c) we describe the platform that we selected, how we organized the catalog and the metadata selection, (d) we describe extensions that were required, and (e) we discuss the current status, performance indicators, and possible next steps.

Keywords: University open data · Directive 2013/37/EU.

1 Introduction

Open access has been a core strategy in the European Commission for several years now and aims at improving knowledge circulation and thus innovation. In 2012, the European Commission encouraged all EU Member States, via a Recommendation, to put public-funded research results in the public sphere in order to make science more efficient and strengthen their knowledge-based economy. It is widely recognized that making data and research results more accessible contributes to advancements in science and innovation in the public and private sectors. For example, the EU Open Data Portal[1] and European Data Portal[2] provide access to the European Union open data, categorized by subject and/or application domain.

In Greece, starting from October of 2014 with the law 4305 (amending the law 3448/2006) each public organization is obliged to comply with the Directive

---

[1] http://data.europa.eu/euodp/en/home.
[2] https://www.europeandataportal.eu/.

E. Garoufallou and M.-A. Ovalle-Perandones (Eds.): MTSR 2020, CCIS 1355, pp. 155–167, 2021.
https://doi.org/10.1007/978-3-030-71903-6_16

2013/37/EU[3] of the European Parliament (amending Directive 2003/98/EC) on the *re-use of the public sector information* and this includes higher education area. Responding to this requirement is a challenging endeavor for a university because (a) a university is a big organization, (b) it comprises schools, departments and units of different characteristics and mindset, (c) the legal framework should be fully respected. The rising question is: how a university could support open data administratively, legally and technically in a *flexible* way that allows for the *gradual* improvement of the open data provided? In this paper we describe what University of Crete has done so far for responding to the requirements of the national legal framework on open data. The key contributions of this (case study) paper are: (a) we detail the steps of the process that we followed (also from an administrative point of view), (b) we show how an Open Data Catalog can be exploited also in the first steps of this process, (c) we describe the platform that we selected, how we organized the catalog and what metadata we included, (d) we describe extensions that were required, (e) we discuss the current status, performance monitoring, and possible next steps. The rest of this paper is organized as follows. Section 2 describes the general context and related work in national and international level, Sect. 3 describes the process that we followed and the envisioned ecosystem, Sect. 4 describes the Open Data Catalog, Sect. 5 describes supporting related activities, and finally, Sect. 6 concludes the paper.

2   Context and Related Work

General Context. [1] contains an interesting discussion and analysis of the challenges the universities face for stewarding the data they collect and hold in ways that balance accountability, transparency, and protection of privacy, academic freedom, and intellectual property, while [8] investigates possible open data partnerships between universities and firms. In general, the potential of open data is unlimited. Just indicatively [4] describes an approach for interlinking educational information across universities through the use of Linked Data principles, while [6] describes an approach for ranking universities using Linked Open Data. Below we list a few indicative universities that follow good practices as regards open data. The Harvard College Open Data Project (HODP) (https://hodp.org/) is a student-faculty group that aims to increase transparency and solve problems on campus using public Harvard data, featuring dozens of publicly-available datasets from around Harvard University. The University of Southampton catalog (https://data.southampton.ac.uk/datasets.html) provides datasets in (at least) Turtle and RDF/XML formats, as well as an HTML description, and it also offers a SPARQL endpoint. In general, we observe a gap in the literature as regards the processes that a university can follow as regards open data.

---

[3] https://eur-lex.europa.eu/legal-content/EN/TXT/PDF/?uri=CELEX:32013L0037&from=EN/.

National Level (Greek Universities). In Greece there are 24 universities. 3 of them, namely, University of Crete (http://opendata.uoc.gr/), Aristotle University of Thessaloniki (https://opendata.auth.gr/) and University of Macedonia (http://data.dai.uom.gr/data/) have set up a catalog for open data. University of Macedonia has also selected CKAN platform to develop their catalog which contains 22 organizations and 132 datasets. Other universities have not set up a catalog, but have decided to directly publish their data in the central Greek Government portal for open data. Indeed, in that catalog we can find datasets from 9 universities. The number of datasets per university that are published is rather low, it ranges from 3 to 14. Overall, we can understand that we are still in the first steps of the path of open academic data, as more than the half of Greek Universities (14/24 = 58%) have not published any dataset. However, it is worth mentioning, that in June 2020, a proposal for a "National Plan for Open Science" was released [2], focusing on open science.

3 The Process Followed and the Envisioned Ecosystem

Below we describe the five main steps of the overall process that UoC (University of Crete) has followed.

- $\mathcal{S}_{①}$: A *Task Force for Open Data*, for short TFOD, was appointed (June 2017) which prepared a *feasibility study* about Open Data and the goals/needs of the institution.
- $\mathcal{S}_{②}$: The task force (TFOD) then performed an *inventory of the documents and datasets in the possession of the university*. For this purpose, an Open Data Catalog was installed and customized accordingly (the catalog is described in detail in Sect. 4).
- $\mathcal{S}_{③}$: The *ODEDIAD*, acronym in Greek of "Clarity and Open Data Project Management Team" was formally appointed (Dec 2018), in compliance with the circular DHD/F.40/2369 of 24 January 2017 from the Ministry of Administrative Reform and Electronic Governance. To enhance flexibility, a small scheme was decided, comprising a general coordinator, and coordinators for the *administrative* aspect, the *technical* aspect and the *open data catalog* aspect. Moreover, each department/unit of the university has appointed a contact person with whom ODEDIAD communicates. ODEDIAD then (a) *harmonized and characterized* the dataset descriptions collected in step $\mathcal{S}_{②}$, and prepared the *Decision on Open Data* that was formally approved by the University (April 18, 2019) and was submitted to the Ministry of Education and Religious Affairs.
- $\mathcal{S}_{④}$: The Open Data Catalog was improved and *aligned with the decision* (in $\mathcal{S}_{③}$), and the Departments/Units were encouraged to start uploading the actual datasets in the catalog.
- $\mathcal{S}_{⑤}$: The Open Data Catalog became *public* (Oct 18, 2019) and ODEDIAD is responsible for *maintaining and continuously improving* the catalog.
  The envisioned ecosystem is shown in Fig. 1 in the form of a Use Case Diagram that depicts the main Actors and the main Use Cases. The role of catalog-related actors is discussed in Sect. 4.3.

It is worth noting that the process started in a *bottom-up* manner (at step $\mathcal{S}_{\textcircled{2}}$), for engaging all departments/units of the university, and then we applied a *top-down* harmonization step (at Step $\mathcal{S}_{\textcircled{3}}$), for achieving completeness and uniformity.

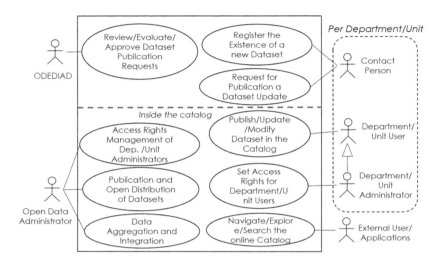

Fig. 1. The envisioned open data ecosystem of the University of Crete

4   The UoC Open Data Catalog

Here we describe: how the platform was selected (in Sect. 4.1), how we customized CKAN (in Sect. 4.2), how we organized the catalog in department/units (in Sect. 4.3), what metadata we selected to include (in Sect. 4.4), what access services are offered (in Sect. 4.5), and an analysis of the uploaded content so far (in Sect. 4.6).

4.1   Selecting the Platform

For selecting the UoC Open Data Catalog we investigated several options based on the platform characteristics, the technology considerations and the options that were available (Oct 2017). The cost of data catalogs is a key evaluation criterion. Products distributed as "open source" software are generally preferred because they are essentially "free" and can be modified or customized without restriction or licensing fees. However, open source software still requires management costs (hosting, maintenance, updates and security patches, training etc.). On the other hand, SaaS products typically are proprietary; a vendor provides the software, the setup and hosting services, at a monthly or annual fee. Under the SaaS delivery model, the vendor is responsible for maintenance, server availability and reliability, scalability and performance according to a contract.

For making our decision we considered the following: (a) Self-managed, open source catalogs can provide a high degree of customization and autonomy. Most open source catalogs are designed to run in combination with other open source software and therefore technical proficiency in these areas is required. (b) The open data catalog must be hosted on reliable and relatively fast server architecture. Slow response times or periods of unavailability will discourage users. (c) Institution policies and/or laws regarding the open data catalog. (d) Scalability. As datasets are added, the catalog must be able to handle the additional load and must be easily extensible (have the flexibility to include additional functionality). (e) How datasets are managed and stored in the data catalog: "All-in-One" vs "Federated" catalogs. In an "All-in-One" model, datasets are stored in the catalog's architecture, with the main benefit of hosting and managing from a single platform and thus exercising strong oversight over the entire catalog infrastructure. Alternatively, in "Federated" catalogs datasets can reside on any publicly accessible location and the catalog includes a link (URL) to the dataset, as opposed to including the dataset itself. (f) Communities of support, support models or user communities. Below we list and summarize the leading open data platforms.

CKAN (http://ckan.org) is a web-based open source management system for the storage and distribution of open data, formally supported by Open Knowledge International (http://okfn.org). It can be installed on any Linux server, including cloud-hosted configurations, and it has a modular architecture through which additional or custom features may be added. Many national governments (like the United Kingdom, the United States, Austria, Brazil, Canada, Germany, Netherlands, Norway etc.) use CKAN to power their open data portals and it is also used by international portals such as the EU Open Data Portal (https://open-data.europa.eu/).

DKAN (https://getdkan.org/) is also open-source and takes a different approach by integrating the open data catalog features of CKAN into a content management system (CMS), namely Drupal. This can be more appealing to organizations that have already invested in Drupal-based websites since DKAN can also be enabled in existing Drupal sites so that anyone can easily start to publish open data in standards compliant ways.

Junar (http://www.junar.com) delivers a cloud-based open data platform and manages its content based on the Software-as-a-Service (SaaS) model. This platform is frequently selected because of its ease of deployment and because it provides an "All-in-One" infrastructure. Junar can either provide a complete data catalog or can provide data via an API to a separate user catalog.

JKAN (https://jkan.io/) is using Jekyll (https://jekyllrb.com/) (a simple static site generator) and allows for a quick deployment of static pages from underlying files. This data portal is based on CKAN and it is aimed at data publishers that need to deploy their data quickly. It is also open source, lightweight and can be easily customized with themes.

The Open Government Platform[4] (OGPL), like DKAN, is an open-source Drupal-based data catalog, but not designed to be CKAN-compatible at the API level. OGPL was jointly developed by the Government of India and the U.S. Government.

Socrata[5] is a cloud-based SaaS open data catalog platform that provides API, catalog, and data manipulation tools. One distinctive feature of Socrata is that it allows users to create views and visualizations based on published data and save those for others to use. Additionally, Socrata is proprietary but offers an open source version of their API, intended to facilitate transitions for customers that decide to migrate away from the SaaS model.

Our review revealed that the format in which metadata are published depends highly on the open data portal that publishes it. Open data portal software frameworks are either built on their own standards or use an already existing standard. The two predominant platforms – CKAN and Socrata – have each been developed on their own respective frameworks that are coming from major standards such as Dublin Core[6] and RDFS[7]. The platforms tend to use either one standard to generate metadata or a combination of a few. The most commonly used metadata standards in Open Data catalogs are based on some version of the Data Catalog Vocabulary (DCAT[8]) standard. DCAT has gained popularity due to its flexibility and elegant design, and aims at improving the data catalogues' interoperability so applications can easily consume metadata (even from multiple catalogs).

CKAN stores the datasets as a folder that hosts datasets or resources. Metadata are presented at a dataset level using Dublin Core, DCAT and INSPIRE geospatial format[9]. Junar uses the RDF metadata standard as presented in Dublin Core and DCAT, it does not support structural metadata. JKAN is based on CKAN, therefore it supports the same metadata standards as previously mentioned for CKAN. Socrata is based on the RDF metadata (Dublin Core and DCAT) with enrichment from custom metadata fields.

4.2 Adopting and Customizing CKAN

For the UoC Open Data Catalog we have selected CKAN to publish, store and manage open datasets. A dataset is a "unit" of data and contains two things: *metadata* (i.e. information about the data) and any number of *resources*, which hold the data itself. CKAN can store a resource internally, or store it simply as a link (i.e. the resource itself could be elsewhere on the web). It allows the creation of custom metadata fields, supports Dublin Core/DCAT for publishing metadata and provides data in open, non-proprietary formats such as CSV, XML, and JSON.

---

[4] http://ogpl.github.io/index-en.html.
[5] https://www.tylertech.com/products/socrata.
[6] http://dublincore.org/documents/dces/.
[7] https://www.w3.org/TR/rdf-schema/.
[8] https://www.w3.org/TR/vocab-dcat/.
[9] https://inspire.ec.europa.eu/data-specifications/2892.

CKAN provides a *full-text search* for dataset metadata as well as filtering and sorting of results. It is possible to restrict the search to datasets with particular tags, data formats etc. or targeted search within an organization/department. When a dataset is found and selected, CKAN displays the dataset page, which includes the name, description, and other information about the dataset, and links to and brief descriptions of each of the resources that belong to the dataset. On-site data/resource preview is also available for known data formats (like csv, xls, xlsx, rdf, xml, rdf+xml, owl+xml, atom, rss, json, geojson, png, jpeg, gif).

CKAN offers flexibility to integrate or embed the data catalog with other websites, add additional pages, layouts, color schemes, logos and generally easy customization. It has a large community of users and support, and offers extensibility with many additional or custom features developed regularly via extensions. CKAN also provides multi-language support and internationalization.

Plug-ins. CKAN provides a DCAT extension/plug-in[10] to export and harvest RDF serializations of datasets based on DCAT. The Data Catalog Vocabulary (DCAT) is "an RDF vocabulary designed to facilitate interoperability between data catalogs published on the Web". The extension defines the mapping of metadata for CKAN datasets and resources to the corresponding DCAT classes, mainly `dcat:Dataset` and `dcat:Distribution`, which is compatible with DCAT-AP v1.1. DCAT-AP was designed to meet the metadata publishing needs in the context of the European Commission's Interoperability Solutions for European Public Administrations (ISA) programme: "Improving semantic interoperability in European eGovernment systems".

Other CKAN extensions that are used for the UoC Open Data catalog are:

- A geospatial viewer[11] for CKAN resources, which contains view plugins to display geospatial files and services in CKAN. More specifically, we are using the Leaflet GeoJSON viewer plugin.
- The pages extension[12] that provides an easy way to add simple pages to CKAN. Using this extension we added a "featured datasets" page and Twitter feed page (for embedding Twitter content, news, dissemination activities etc.)
- An LDAP plugin[13] which provides LDAP authentication for CKAN and integration with our existing UoC LDAP user service. This extension allows us to import existing username/full name/email/description, and add LDAP users to a given organization automatically.
- An extension[14] that integrates Google Analytics into CKAN.

In addition, some custom made extensions were created for the purposes of our UoC Open Data Catalog. For example, normally each dataset is owned by an "Organization" in a CKAN instance. A plugin was created to rename

---

[10] https://github.com/ckan/ckanext-dcat.
[11] https://github.com/ckan/ckanext-geoview.
[12] https://github.com/ckan/ckanext-pages.
[13] https://github.com/NaturalHistoryMuseum/ckanext-ldap.
[14] https://github.com/ckan/ckanext-googleanalytics.

the default "Organization" of CKAN into "Department". Another plugin was developed to easily export the list of all datasets from a "Department". Some required additional metadata fields were inserted with another plugin and finally the appearance/theme of the catalog was customized.

4.3 Organization of the Catalog

Currently (July 2020), there are 47 "departments" (16 academic, 22 administrative and 9 other) inserted into the catalog that correspond to the actual structure of the University of Crete. We have created another "department" for the UoC OpenData Task Force, which contains instructions and reference material shared between the OpenData team, the dataset administrators and the catalog users.

Each catalog "department" has its own administrator and multiple members (which can be either editors or simple users). Depending on each user's role in the department, users can perform different actions. A department administrator can edit the department's information, add/edit a dataset or add individual users to the department, with different roles depending on the level of authorization needed. An editor can create a dataset owned by that department. By default, a new dataset is initially private, and visible only to other users in the same department. When it is ready for publication, it can be published by the department administrator (this may require a higher authorization level within the department). A simple user in a department can only view private (and public) datasets. During the $\mathcal{S}_{(2)}$ inventory phase, all users (contact persons, local administrators, department/unit users) were allowed to insert datasets. The uploaded datasets/resources were reviewed by the ODEDIAD and the University DPO in order to be compliant with the data protection directive. After phase $\mathcal{S}_{(5)}$, when the catalog became public, new datasets/resources can still be uploaded to the catalog but need to be reviewed, evaluated and approved by ODEDIAD and the DPO before they become available for public consumption and use. In addition, there is an annual validation and update procedure of all the UoC open datasets.

4.4 Selected Metadata

The metadata fields (per category) for each set of documents, information and data are shown in Table 1.

4.5 Access Services

The user can *search* the catalog, can *browse* the catalog by department, and can *explore* in a faceted-search manner the available datasets (through tags, file formats, access rights) as shown in Fig. 2 (right). Apart from the above *programmatic access* is supported. The native CKAN API allows users, providers, consumers and developers to write code that interacts with the CKAN site and its data. CKAN's Action API is a RPC-style API that exposes all of CKAN's core features to API clients. All of a CKAN website's core functionality (everything you can do with the web interface and more) can be used by external code that calls the CKAN API.

Table 1. Metadata fields: general, right-related, for digital files, for physical files

	General fields
1	Title
2	Description
3	File Owner/Location (e.g. Office, Department, Address)
4	Quantity of data (indicative) e.g. number, size in GB, number of documents etc.
5	Refresh rate (approx.)
6	Is it geospatial data? (YES/NO)
	Rights of use and licences
7	Availability (YES/NO)
8	If already available, way of accessibility (e.g. website, on request etc.)
9	If available through on request (either electronic or printed application) method of accessibility (e.g. by mail, in person, electronically etc.)
10	Is there a privacy/personal data restriction? (YES/NO)
11	Are the other restrictions? (national security issues, tax secrecy etc.) (YES/NO)
12	Available through fees? (YES/NO)
13	Available through licensing? (YES/NO/If YES, type of licence)
14	File Type (Physical/ Digital/Physical and Digital)
	For digital file/dataset
15	Automatically machine processable & editable format (e.g. txt, csv, html, xml, rdf, odt, ods, doc, xls, docx, xlsx)
16	Non automatically processable format (e.g. jpeg, tiff, gif, pdf, scanned documents etc.)
17	Access through URL (e.g. website if available)
18	API (if available)
	For physical file/dataset
19	Format (e.g. A4 document, photographic archive etc.)
20	Location (e.g. file cabinet 5 in room 123)
	Additional information
21	Content topic or tag (e.g. health, environment, economy, specific science etc.)

4.6   Analysis of the Uploaded Contents

After several rounds of discussions with all the academic department contact persons (during $\mathcal{S}_{③}$), we arrived to a commonly agreed upon collection of datasets (homogenization/harmonization) that every department should provide openly (and preferably using in a machine processable format). This collection includes the 22 datasets for the 16 Departments of UoC that are shown in Table 2. Similarly, for the 5 Schools of UoC, a 5 list of common datasets were identified. The rest of the University units had not any common dataset.

The Open Data Decision of the University of Crete, that contains the harmonized descriptions of all datasets of the organization is publicly available[15]. As mentioned in Sect. 3 (Step $\mathcal{S}_{④}$), following the issuance of this decision, the Open

---

[15] https://rb.gy/0rqbdu.

Table 2. The datasets of an academic department

1	Open Courses	12	Internship Programs
2	Course Outlines	13	Photo Gallery
3	Undergraduate and Postgraduate Study Guides	14	Events, Summer Schools, Meetings, Conferences, Competitions
4	Course Schedules	15	Alumni information (after explicit consent of the graduates)
5	Admission and Study Statistics	16	Announcements and News
6	ist of Publications of the Teaching, Scientific and Research staff	17	List of Personnel
7	MSc and PhD theses	18	Elections of collective bodies
8	Internal/external Evaluations and Accreditation	19	Financial information and data
9	Distinctions and Achievements	20	Decisions on committees establishment
10	Building facilities, maps, infrastructure	21	Decisions related to studies
11	Promotional/Dissemination material	22	Decisions on Tender Notices

Data Catalog was improved and aligned with that decision. Subsequently, the Departments/Units were encouraged to start uploading the actual datasets in the catalog or add links to the related web resources in case they are available in other systems. Currently (July 2020), the UoC Open Data Catalog[16] hosts 509 descriptions of datasets, and 104 (20,76%) of them contain at least one resource or external link to a web page or institutional system. In machine processable formats (CSV, JSON, GeoJSON, XLS), we have 9 (1,8%) datasets. Note that some datasets are offered in more than one formats.

Some especially useful datasets, are those that provide statistics about the UoC student population from 2006 up to now (gender, age, nationality, duration of studies etc.). Another, is the "Research Directory" that contains information about all labs of the University, categorized by research field, department, position, or name. Finally, the Computer Science Department has posted many datasets in CSV and JSON format. Currently, the number of *tags* inserted into the CKAN catalog are 118.

5   Supporting and Ongoing Activities

Training and Outreach Activities. A manual with examples of how to use the catalog was created and published in the unit of ODEDIAD in the catalog (also for the needs of the step $\mathcal{S}_{(2)}$ as described in Sect. 3). The catalog became public on Oct 18, 2019 (Fig. 2 show the first page of the UoC Open Data catalog website) and all members of the university were informed through email and public announcements on the UoC website. To support also notification services to those interested in the updates of the catalog, a twitter account (https://twitter.com/UoC_OpenData) was created on April 2020. The engagement of the

---

[16] http://opendata.uoc.gr/.

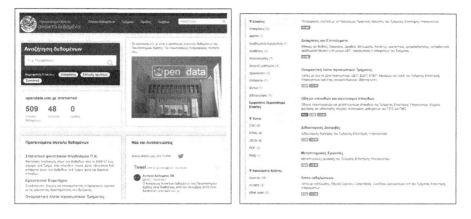

Fig. 2. The UoC Open Data Catalog website

community is rather low, however we have to note that no outreach action took place during the covid-19 pandemic period.

Monitoring and KPIs. We decided a number *Key Performance Indicators* (KPIs) for measuring and monitoring the performance. Their definition, and 2020 value, are described next.

- K1: Number of Datasets in the Open Data Decision of the University of Crete (April 2020 value: 501).
- K2: Number (and Percentage) of Datasets in the Open Data Catalog with at least one resource or external link to a web page or institutional system (April 2020 value: 104 (20,76%)).
- K3: Number (and percentage) of Datasets in the Catalog available in machine-processable form (April 2020: 9 (1,8%)).
- K4: Number of Visits to the Catalog (we started counting the visitors on April 2020). (April 2020 value: not available).
  Possible Next Steps. Our short term goal is to increase K2 and K3. To this end, we have categorized the possible next steps into three main categories:
- *Training and Good Practices.* Good practices for each individual type of dataset (news, personnel lists, etc.), for increasing the percentage of datasets that are in a machine-processable format. This is also related to suggestions for increasing the interoperability of the information systems of the university, so that some information to be automatically exported in the catalog without any human intervention.
- *Advancing the Services of the Catalog.* Currently we are working on providing a bulk and/or automated dataset upload (and export) procedure, combined with a custom data interface to other internal UoC systems. Another important advancement concerns the *search* service: since the one offered by CKAN exploits only the metadata of the datasets, we investigate the provision of an additional search service over the *contents* of the datasets. Another challenging direction is the automatic production of a *Knowledge Graph (KG)* based

on the contents of all datasets, an endeavor that requires applying methods for large scale integration (see [7] for a survey). The availability of such a KG, would also enable the application of the *multi-perspective keyword search* services described in [5], for providing a user friendly search system over RDF data. In the future, the KG could be enriched with scholarly data (e.g. as in [3]) for covering also the research output of the institution.

- *Connections with External Systems.* This includes communication and integration with http://data.gov.gr/, which is the central directory of public data of all Greek government agencies and contains more than 10K datasets and 340 organizations, as well as connection with repositories of scientific data, specifically HELIX (the Hellenic Data Service) (https://hellenicdataservice. gr) with aims to be the national e-Infrastructure for data-intensive research.

6 Concluding Remarks

The provision of an organizational and technical framework for Open Data in a big organization, like a university, is a challenging task. In this paper we described the *five-steps process* that the University of Crete has followed and the outcomes of this process so far, as well as the forthcoming steps. In brief, we adopted a mixed, *bottom-up and top-down* approach, in which the catalog played a central role in the entire process. Even if the majority of the data are not in a common, easily processable form, the catalog contains the *placeholders* for the *entire spectrum of the datasets* in the possession of the organization, and we have realized even in its current form serves as a *global index* of the various resources that are published in the various websites of the university. To set up priorities and plan our next actions, we have identified a few KPIs. We hope this will be useful in other organizations that have similar obligations and characteristics.

References

1. Borgman, C.L.: Open data, grey data, and stewardship: universities at the privacy frontier. Berkeley Tech. LJ **33**, 365 (2018)
2. Athanasiou, S., et al.: National plan for open science. Technical report (2020). https://doi.org/10.5281/zenodo.3908953
3. Färber, M.: The Microsoft academic knowledge graph: a linked data source with 8 billion triples of scholarly data. In: Ghidini, C., et al. (eds.) ISWC 2019. LNCS, vol. 11779, pp. 113–129. Springer, Cham (2019). https://doi.org/10.1007/978-3-030-30796-7_8
4. Fernandez, M., d'Aquin, M., Motta, E.: Linking data across universities: an integrated video lectures dataset. In: Aroyo, L., et al. (eds.) ISWC 2011. LNCS, vol. 7032, pp. 49–64. Springer, Heidelberg (2011). https://doi.org/10.1007/978-3-642-25093-4_4
5. Kadilierakis, G., Nikas, C., Fafalios, P., Papadakos, P., Tzitzikas, Y.: Elas4RDF: multi-perspective triple-centered keyword search over RDF using elasticsearch. In: Harth, A., et al. (eds.) ESWC 2020. LNCS, vol. 12124, pp. 122–128. Springer, Cham (2020). https://doi.org/10.1007/978-3-030-62327-2_21

6. Meymandpour, R., Davis, J.G.: Ranking universities using linked open data. In: LDOW (2013)
7. Mountantonakis, M., Tzitzikas, Y.: Large-scale semantic integration of linked data: a survey. ACM Comput. Surv. (CSUR) **52**(5), 1–40 (2019)
8. Perkmann, M., Schildt, H.: Open data partnerships between firms and universities: the role of boundary organizations. Res. Policy **44**(5), 1133–1143 (2015)

Linked Vocabularies for Mobility and Transport Research

Susanne Arndt$^{(\boxtimes)}$ ⓘ and Mila Runnwerth

TIB – Leibniz Information Centre for Science and Technology, 30167 Hannover, Germany
{Susanne.arndt,Mila.runnwerth}@tib.eu

Abstract. The paper describes the creation of a vocabulary for a domain-specific information service platform (*SIS move*) by vocabulary re-use and linking. Source vocabularies differ with respect to several factors (domain-specificity, accessibility, data model). We address why vocabularies should be considered for a domain-specific vocabulary and how they are brought under a common modelling paradigm with standards for knowledge organization systems and alignment of schemata. We also discuss the creation and validation of alignments. Eventually, we give an outlook on the vocabulary's further evolution and application.

Keywords: Thesaurus · SKOS · Terminology · Mobility · Transport

1 Introduction

The *Specialized Information Service Mobility and Transport Research (SIS move)* [1] is a platform providing researchers from academia and industry with international (open access) literature, information about the European landscape of researchers, and research data. Covering a field with several disciplines and terminologies, SIS move needs a controlled vocabulary for information retrieval (cf. Sect. 2). Instead of building from scratch, we design a system of linked vocabularies from existing sources. New concepts, definitions, labels, or relations can expand these linked vocabularies. We evaluate several candidates against requirements to be met in SIS move (cf. Sect. 4). With reference to related work and best practices (cf. Sect. 3), we demonstrate how to prepare candidates for integration (cf. Sect. 5), and close with discussing application and further development of the Linked Vocabularies for SIS move (cf. Sect. 6).

We use the terms *concept*, *term* and *terminology* consistent with [2]: A *concept* is a mental unit, a *term* a linguistic expression referring to a concept, and a *terminology* the set of all concepts of an area of expertise, their relations and terms. Terminologies are an object of linguistics as well as terminology science, information science and computer science. Having unique theories and methods for terminology modelling, these disciplines create terminology resources differing in content scope and data modelling approach, e.g. *(technical) dictionaries, vocabularies, terminologies, terminological resources, thesauri, controlled vocabularies, ontologies, glossaries*. We do not want to exclude any type of terminology documentation as a potential source. Throughout the paper, we will hence use the term *vocabulary* to refer to terminology documentation

© Springer Nature Switzerland AG 2021
E. Garoufallou and M.-A. Ovalle-Perandones (Eds.): MTSR 2020, CCIS 1355, pp. 168–179, 2021.
https://doi.org/10.1007/978-3-030-71903-6_17

regardless of format or degree of formalization. Specific vocabularies will be referred to by the proper term, e.g. *thesaurus* for a "controlled and structured vocabulary in which concepts are represented by terms, organized so that relationships between concepts are made explicit, and preferred terms are accompanied by lead-in entries for synonyms or quasi-synonyms" used for subject indexing and information retrieval [3].

2 SIS Move's Thesaurus Use Case

The main use case for the vocabulary is linguistic assistance in a library information discovery system that indexes textual publications, research data, and audiovisual media. Features include word completion while typing a query in the search bar, discovering new information indexed according to a controlled vocabulary, similarity search, disambiguation, or query expansion by synonym or broader/narrower terms.

Especially in mobility and transport research technical languages of social sciences and engineering may cause misapprehensions. Discovering scientific literature from another field within the knowledge space of transport science can be facilitated by (visual) exploration of the vocabulary's content (both terms and relations). Another relevant target group in this context is politics and the general public. A transformation of today's mobility towards a more socially and economically sustainable behavior is prominent in most governments' agendas. A crucial aspect in scientific counselling is finding a widely understood language. A vocabulary listing colloquial terms may play the role of a "negotiator" between researchers and laypeople.

3 Related Work

Section 3.1 introduces standards for vocabulary development; Sect. 3.2 discusses best practices and tools. More than 100 domain-relevant vocabularies of different type are available for mobility and transport research. We discuss these types in Sect. 4 where we address their suitability for re-use in SIS move on prototypic examples.

3.1 Standards

Table 1 gives an overview of standards and data models from different disciplines. Two approaches for vocabulary development can be distinguished, concept-orientation and term-orientation. In term-orientation, an entry represents a single term referring to one or more concepts, all of which need to be described by the entry. Different term-oriented entries may describe the same concept. In concept-orientation an entry represents a single concept which is referred to by one or more terms, all of which need to be described by the entry. Different entries may contain the same term. In terminology science, concept-orientation is complemented by term autonomy, the option to describe terms with term-specific data types [4].

The Linked Vocabularies for SIS move adhere to RDF, RDFS and OWL. To establish a controlled vocabulary, we follow concept-orientation supported by TBX or SKOS. Many thesauri come as RDF-based SKOS or SKOS-like representations, so SKOS was

Table 1. Standards for vocabulary development.

Resource type	Standards
Thesauri	- ISO 25964 [3] - MARC 21 [5]
Terminologies	- Term Base Exchange (TBX) [6] - ISO 1087 [2] - ISOCat [7]
Linked data	- Resource Description Framework (RDF) [8] - RDF Schema (RDFS) [9]
Ontologies	- Web Ontology Language (OWL) [10]
Simple knowledge organization systems	- Simple Knowledge Organization Systems (SKOS) [11] - iso-thes [12] - SKOS-XL [13]
Lexical resources	- LexInfo [14] - Lexicon Model for Ontologies (lemon) [15] - ISO 1951:2007 [16] - General Ontology for Linguistic Description (GOLD) [17]

our first choice. We want to implement term-autonomy, but to model terms as entities, an expansion of SKOS is needed, e.g. SKOS-XL. Some more sophisticated linguistic models are available as well, e.g. *lemon* or *LexInfo*, providing means to describe terms as lexical entries. To give an adequate description of terms both need to be accompanied by ontologies for lexical characteristics (e.g. part of speech, case, gender, etc.). Appropriate classes and properties can be found in ISOCat or the GOLD ontology.

3.2   Best Practices and Tools

Another guide-post for vocabulary re-use and transformation are showcases defining best practices. Practical considerations for transforming legacy vocabularies into semantic web resources often revolve around thesauri. For example, [18, 19] discuss the modelling of an excerpt of the thesaurus *Technology and Management* (TEMA) [20]. SIS move follows some modelling decisions of this project, e.g. using SKOS, treating labels as entities, but does not follow others, e.g. treating vocabulary concepts as instances of `owl:Class`. Similarly, [21] describes a semantic web version of the AGROVOC thesaurus discussing the differences between an application of OWL and an application of SKOS. Here, the alignment of concepts to other vocabularies also plays a crucial role. Another project that focused on making several domain-specific legacy thesauri fit for the semantic web was FinnONTO. Here, it was not only attempted to align a vocabulary with others but to integrate thesauri describing different domains into a single resource (*KOKO*) [22, 23]. The creation of KOKO is comparable to that of the Linked Vocabularies for SIS move, e.g. source vocabularies had to be transformed into a semantic web format, they had to be harmonized according to a common schema and their shared contents had to be identified and mapped (cf. Sect. 5). Other aspects of FinnONTO are not transferable to SIS move, e.g. directly involving source vocabulary developers in the development of the Linked Vocabularies for SIS move. In comparison to aforementioned projects, SIS move also tries to consider less structured sources that show lexical orientation rather than conceptual orientation. We are not aware of showcases for this kind of integration.

The group working on KOKO also developed the Skosmos software stack – a tool for publishing interlinked SKOS vocabularies [24–26]. A range of other tools for the presentation of vocabularies are available, e.g. LOV [27], LODC [28], Bartoc [29], BARTOC Fast [30], Ontology Lookup Service [31].

4 Finding the Right Vocabulary

We analyzed existing vocabularies covering mobility and transport research for qualitative criteria that can be quantitatively expressed. The first five apply to vocabularies in general, the latter two are subject-specific.

- Exhaustivity. The vocabulary should have high domain coverage.
- Specificity. It should contain specific concepts.
- Currency. It should contain concepts of current research.
- Multilinguality. It should at least contain German and English terms.
- Accessibility. It should have an open license and standardized format.
- Multidisciplinarity. It should cover all mobility- and transport-related disciplines.
- Prominence. It should be known by SIS move's target group.

None of our source vocabularies covers all criteria. With regard to exhaustivity and multidisciplinarity, traditional thesauri and authority files are a good source, e.g. the approximately 250,000 subject headings of the *Integrated Authority File (GND)* [32]. Due to cooperative maintenance by German-speaking libraries under the *German National Library's* editorial sovereignty, it covers a great number of concepts from several subjects. With regard to multilinguality, specificity and prominence, there are some limitations: The GND is mainly developed in German, but mapped automatically to the US-American and French national authority files, thereby gaining some degree of multilinguality (cf. MACS project [33]). Its subject headings are applied in subject indexing of literature. Historically and logistically, the use case scenario of in-depth domain-specific indexing is not covered by the GND. Since the vocabulary gradually opens to other resources and use cases, its role as a vocabulary hub for interlinked vocabularies is now discussed. The GND is distributed as RDF under a CC0 license. Mobility and transport experts, SIS move's primary target group, may not be aware of it, though.

Specialized thesauri for mobility and transport research include the *Transportation Research Thesaurus (TRT)* [34]. It is used for subject indexing titles in the *Transportation Research Board Publications Index*[1] [35] and well established in the international

---

[1] The Transportation Research Board is a division of the National Academy of Sciences, Engineering, and Medicine. It promotes innovation and progress in transportation [35].

research community. The subject-specific TRT has approx. 9,500 concepts. Nevertheless, the TRT is diverse regarding its topics. Next to *transportation* and *transportation operations* it includes topics like *environment, economic and social factors* or *materials*. The same limitations regarding specificity and multilinguality that apply to the GND are visible here, though. Furthermore, the TRT comes in custom XML and even though its reuse is encouraged by its creators it is not under an explicit open license.

Ontologies are also candidates for the Linked Vocabularies for SIS move. They are knowledge representations that make use of formalized languages like RDF [8], RDFS [9] and OWL [10]. They are not topically exhaustive since they define small sets of concepts with explicit semantics based on description logic. Their main focus is on conceptual, not on linguistic description. Since ontologies are often developed in research projects, they are close to current research questions. Their degree of multidisciplinarity depends on their context of origin. Successful re-utilization depends on their developers' reputation and communication towards the community. We identified approximately 30 mobility- and transport-related ontologies in scope of SIS move. For a survey on recent domain ontologies cf. [36–38]. Unfortunately, quite a number of ontologies from research are not re-used and short-lived [37]. Examples for active domain ontologies are the Transmodel Ontology [39], the Transport Disruption Ontology [40] or the extension of schema.org by the Automotive Ontology Community Group [41].

Terminologies, compared to ontologies, are almost always multilingual since their main area of application is the translation of technical documents: they are close to the text and therefore include many very specific concepts from their given domain. Since terminology databases are often created for corporate communication, especially product documentation, they may not include concepts relevant in research and development. As corporate knowledge, they are often not publicly available for reuse (even though their exchange is possible with TBX [6], a standardized XML dialect).

Another source are vocabularies from the scientific community that are unstructured with respect to standards listed in Sect. 3.1. These are rather rare since scientific considerations about a field's terminology are usually semantically implicit parts of research papers, not provided in dedicated digital records like online glossaries, e.g. [42]. Re-using semi- and unstructured vocabularies requires adaptation (cf. Sect. 5.1). Coming from the active research community, such vocabularies are very specific but may become out of date once their initial context of origin ceases to exist. Multilinguality is important for research-related vocabulary development for international communication of research results that often requires researchers to use English instead of their native language and their respective terminology. Multidisciplinarity can also be a goal, but managing an exhaustive number of concepts for several domains is out of scope. Community vocabularies might not be openly available, for example because they are part of proprietary projects, or simply because open licenses are not considered.

In conclusion, none of the resources discussed here sufficiently support SIS move's services (cf. Sect. 2) on their own. We therefore re-use selected vocabularies and propose a multi-modular structure for SIS move's Thesaurus.

5   A Multi-modular Thesaurus for SIS Move

To meet the criteria (cf. Section 4) we build a system of linked vocabularies realized as an ontology importing several other ontologies. We started with [34] since it is a comparatively large thesaurus recommended by our community, and [42] since it is a glossary compiled by an active researcher. The overall structure of the Linked Vocabularies for SIS move is illustrated in Fig. 1. Two steps of preprocessing were necessary:

1) Choosing modelling paradigm and formats. Making vocabularies comparable is not just a file format conversion but requires harmonization of modelling approaches. Terminologies, thesauri and authority files are typically concept-oriented; glossaries and researcher resources term-oriented, an approach well known from dictionaries. RDF, RDFS and OWL provide means to formalize either. We use concept-orientation (cf. Sect. 5.1), semantic web formats and RDF serializations since ontologies and thesauri adhere to these, while terminologies are mostly offered in TBX and researcher vocabularies in unstructured formats (CSV, DOCX).

2) Mapping of data models and vocabulary content: Vocabularies may be described by individual, non-standardized schemata, the GND, for example, allows only elements defined by the GND Ontology [43]. We consider these schemata as structural modules in the Linked Vocabularies for SIS move whose function is the description of content modules. Schemata are often compatible so we can identify equivalent classes and properties by mappings. Further, a mapping of content modules is needed: Different vocabularies make statements about the same concept and to get a full account about it, equivalent concepts in different vocabularies need to be mapped (cf. Sect. 5.2).

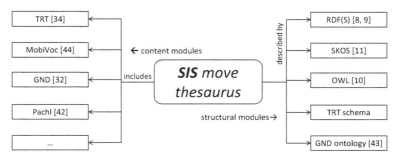

Fig. 1. Intended overall structure of the Linked Vocabularies for SIS move.

5.1   Skosification of Vocabularies

We demonstrate the transformation of a concept-oriented XML-based vocabulary and of a text-based term-oriented vocabulary into SKOS data.

Skosifying[2] a Concept-Oriented Vocabulary. The aforementioned TRT is concept-oriented and each entry comprises several elements: obligatorily, a notation, a preferred term, and a superordinate concept; optionally, a definition and its reference, a scope

---

[2] We use the term *skosify* (v.) to refer to all processes necessary to transform any representation of concept-related information to a SKOS representation of concepts.

note, alternative terms and subordinate or related concepts[3]. In RDF, we would like to depict the information as a triple structure comprising of subject, predicate and object. Each TRT entry has at least one subject: the concept the entry is about. Modelling the TRT according to RDF requires aligning the TRT XML elements with RDF classes and properties. Since SKOS is an RDF-based standard for modelling controlled vocabularies, this is a straightforward task: all TRT elements map to SKOS as shown in Table 2.

Table 2. Mapping of TRT XML elements to SKOS classes and properties.

TRT xml tag	SKOS classes and properties
<TermInfo>	skos:Concept[a]
<DF>	skos:definition
<T>	skos:prefLabel
<UF>	skos:altLabel
<RT2>	skos:related
<NN>	skos:notation
<SN>	skos:scopeNote

[a]Alternatively, one could introduce a class: TermInfo as a subclass of skos:Concept as an easy way to distinguish TRT concepts from other concepts.

Only TRT's <Date Added> element does not mirror a SKOS term and thus needs to be mapped to an element from a different schema, e.g. dcterms:date. All in all, with some slight adjustments the SKOS standard fits the TRT rather well. To semanticize the TRT in practice, we used the tool *jxml2owl* [45, 46], a java application which provides a GUI. We receive the following triple structure for the TRT entry in Turtle (the definition is abbreviated and no namespace prefix is given for TRT content):

```
:Aet a :TermInfo , skos:Concept;
    dcterms:date "01/01/1999"^^xsd:string ;
    skos:prefLabel "Public transit"@en-us ;
    skos:altLabel "Local transit"@en-us ,
        "Mass transit"@en-us , "Transit"@en-us ;
    skos:notation "Aet"^^xsd:string ;
    skos:definition "Transportation service
        [...]"^^xsd:string ;
    ftrts:source "AASHTO Glossary"^^xsd:string ;
    skos:related :Afma , :Afna .
```

---

[3] For an exemplary entry on *public transit* cf. https://tib.eu/cloud/s/qtKsWFMWtXF96Z2.

Missing both in the XML entry and in the Turtle entry are the hierarchical relations of the thesaurus. These are implicitly expressed via the notation but not via an XML attribute, therefore these relations could not be obtained with *jxml2owl*. To make all information in the TRT explicit, we had to do some post-processing with *Protégé* [47]: With a SPARQL query [48] that compares the notation strings, the implicit hierarchical relations can be added as triples with the respective concept as their subject.

Skosifying a Term-Oriented Vocabulary. Skosifying a term-oriented vocabulary, e.g. the *Glossary of Railway Operation and Control* [42], is not as straightforward as skosifying a thesaurus: it needs remodeling as a concept-oriented resource. In term-oriented resources, conceptual information is "spread" over several entries and usually not explicitly identified or related. Making the informal connections between entries explicit requires intellectual processing, e.g. comparing concept descriptions, consulting external resources, or interpreting informal cues, such as:

- The phrase "another term for" indicates synonymy: different terms refer to the same concept and can be subsumed in the same conceptual entry.
- The use of defined terms in term descriptions indicates conceptual relations[4]. For example, *cyclic timetable* in [42] is defined as "a *timetable* in which trains that belong to the same route are scheduled with fixed time intervals between their train paths". The use of the term *timetable* in the definition indicates a relation of super-/sub-ordination between *cyclic timetable* and *timetable*.
- The phrase "see also" indicates several conceptual relation types: super-/subordination, coordination, association. It is not used consistently in [42], e.g. the entries for *gravity yard* and *hump yard* should make mutual reference to each other since they are coordinate concepts.

Once the conceptual structure was implemented, a similar skosification as with the concept-oriented TRT had been performed.

5.2   Mapping of Vocabularies

The mapping of vocabularies is necessary from two practical viewpoints: First, vocabularies can be structured by non-standardized schemata with comparable, but differently named classes. Here, a mapping of structural modules (see the beginning of this section) is needed; e.g. to retrieve all labels from the Linked Vocabularies for SIS move with a single, simple query, proprietary label properties should be mapped to standardized label properties (e.g. `gndo:preferredNameForTheSubjectHeading` to `skos:prefLabel`). Data models of legacy thesauri are, however, often more expressive than SKOS so that the issue is not just a naming difference, but a matter of (semantic) incompatibility requiring more elaborate standards, as also observed by [49].

Second, vocabularies may have "conceptual overlaps", i.e. any two vocabularies can describe the same concept. Here, a mapping of content modules is needed. We decided to map domain-specific vocabularies (starting with the *TRT* [34] and the *Glossary of*

---

[4] In [42] defined terms used in definitions are marked by hyperlinks, here represented by italics.

Railway Operation and Control [42]) to GND subject headings which is the standard vocabulary for subject indexing in German-speaking libraries (cf. Section 4). The design of the sources influenced our choice of the mapping mechanism. Since there is no third-party vocabulary with existing mapping information to both TRT and the *Glossary of Railway Operation and Control*, transitivity-based inference was not applicable as a mapping mechanism. An approach based-on (semantic) word similarity (e.g. embeddings, cf. [50]) is also not promising since the vocabulary entries often do not contain definitions or other information that allows to create a sense-specific semantic representation for the vocabulary entry. This sparsity forced us to use a naïve label-based mapping approach. For this, we first had to make the labels comparable: the TRT is American English and the GND is German, thus there had to be a translation. We used DeepL [51] to generate German labels for the smaller TRT. Second, we needed to compare the labels and set a `skos:mappingRelation` between all concepts with string-identical labels. This simple mapping technique had the advantage that it could be done with a SPARQL CONSTRUCT query in Protégé. With this query around 4,400 mappings between TRT and GND were created. Due to the ambiguity of terms these relations are, however, only proposals. Each match has to be validated for correctness within the domain and confirmed as one of SKOS' sub-properties of `skos:mappingRelation`. We are currently conducting an intellectual mapping review process in which mapping proposals are evaluated against unstructured semantic information from the mapped vocabularies. Since the semantic information of vocabulary items is sometimes sparse, validation also needs to rely on external sources defining domain-specific concepts. In cases where mappings cannot be confirmed, validation is supported by subject specialists at TIB. This process is slow but will result in high-quality mappings. Furthermore, it helps identify conceptual gaps within the GND that could be addressed by the creation of new domain-specific concepts in this central resource for subject indexing in the library landscape in Germany.

6 Summary and Outlook

This paper introduces SIS move's strategy for the creation of a domain-specific network of linked vocabularies to be used in an information discovery system for transport and mobility research. Instead of re-inventing the wheel, we build on existing vocabularies established in the mobility and transport research community. It currently comprises three sources, the *Integrated Authority File* [32], the *Transportation Research Thesaurus* [34] and the *Glossary of Railway Operation and Control* [42]. An ongoing mapping process resulted in about 2,800 semantically confirmed mappings so far. The mappings between single vocabularies resulting from the SIS move project will be made publicly available for re-use in other projects [52]. Eventually, the semantic integration of sources will result in an aggregated resource that better addresses the criteria introduced in Sect. 4 than the single vocabularies on their own. Single vocabularies can be updated regularly and new community-driven sources (e.g. MobiVoc [44]) can be integrated on demand. In the future, we also want to enable domain experts to participate in thesaurus development. However, we do not expect them to learn semantic web languages, or to work with ontology editors or SPARQL endpoints. The threshold for participation should be low and making a contribution straightforward. The strategy for vocabulary re-use of SIS move will also be applied in future projects, e.g. the newly established SIS for Civil Engineering, Architecture and Urban Studies [53]).

On a technical level, this paper addressed the challenges of creating a thesaurus from different sources. It gave an overview of the range of standards related to distinct types of resources like thesauri, ontologies and controlled vocabularies. It focused on the topic of bringing unstructured vocabularies to machine-readable formats: The effort of intellectual processing is higher when sources are term-oriented, when they have unstructured formats and when their data model is not standardized.

Last, we would like to give an outlook on the thesaurus' future applications in SIS move's service portfolio [1]. Its main strength lies in supporting exploratory search utilizing thesaurus relations. Here, exploration has two dimensions. First, researchers may want to explore the concept system itself to find information on a concept or on a term (e.g. a definition or an equivalent expression). Second, exploring the thesaurus structure helps researchers to discover information on publications, research data and researchers that are linked with the thesaurus concepts. This is not the case for all SIS move resources yet, but automatic indexing is planned with annif [54]. Thesaurus data will be employed in functionalities in SIS move's discovery system, for example search term expansion (based on synonyms, equivalent terms, or super-/sub-ordinate terms) and autocomplete (based on thesaurus terms). An evaluation of the linked vocabularies for SIS move in information retrieval is still pending since the integration is still ongoing work. In all implementations, thesaurus/user interactions need to be as effortless as possible, e.g. by offering user-friendly visualizations of thesaurus information.

Acknowledgements. SIS move is funded by grant number 393261503 of the Deutsche Forschungsgemeinschaft (DFG).

References

1. Specialized information service mobility and transport research (SIS move). https://www.fid-move.de. Accessed 13 Jul 2020
2. ISO 1087:2019 terminology work and terminology science – Vocabulary
3. ISO 25964 information and documentation – thesauri and interoperability with other vocabularies
4. Drewer, P., Schmitz, K.-D.: Terminologiemanagement. Grundlagen - Methoden - Werkzeuge. Springer Vieweg, Berlin, Heidelberg (2017). https://doi.org/10.1007/978-3-662-53315-4
5. Library of congress: MARC 21 format for bibliographic data. https://www.loc.gov/marc/bibliographic/. Accessed 13 Jul 2020
6. ISO 30042:2019 management of terminology resources — TermBase eXchange (TBX)
7. ISO 12620:2019 management of terminology resources — data category specifications
8. Schreiber, G., Raimon, Y.: RDF 1.1 Primer (2014). https://www.w3.org/TR/rdf11-primer/. Accessed 13 Jul 2020
9. Brickley, D., Guha, R.: RDF Schema 1.1 (2014). https://www.w3.org/TR/rdf-schema/. Accessed 13 Jul 2020
10. W3C OWL Working Group: OWL 2 Web Ontology Language Document Overview (Second Edition) (2012). https://www.w3.org/TR/owl2-overview/. Accessed 13 Jul 2020

11. Miles, A., Bechhofer, S.: SKOS simple knowledge organization system reference (2019). https://www.w3.org/TR/skos-reference/. Accessed 13 Jul 2020
12. ISO 25964 SKOS extension (iso-thes). http://pub.tenforce.com/schemas/iso25964/skos-thes. Accessed 13 Jul 2020
13. Miles, A., Bechhofer, S.: SKOS simple knowledge organization system eXtension for labels (SKOS-XL) namespace document – HTML variant (2009). https://www.w3.org/TR/skos-ref erence/skos-xl.html. Accessed 13 Jul 2020
14. LexInfo ontology. https://github.com/ontolex/lexinfo. Accessed 13 Jul 2020
15. Lemon – the lexicon model for ontologies. http://lemon-model.net/lemon. Accessed 13 Jul 2020
16. ISO 1951:2007 presentation/representation of entries in dictionaries — requirements, recommendations and information
17. General ontology for linguistic description (GOLD) (2010). http://linguistics-ontology.org/. Accessed 13 Jul 2020
18. Kasprzik, A.: Cleaning up a legacy thesaurus to make it fit for transformation into a semantic web KOS. In: Mayr, P., et al. (eds.) TPDL 2018. LNCS, vol. 11057, pp. 64–70. CEUR Workshop Proceedings, Aachen (2018)
19. Bernauer, E., Mehlberg, M., Runnwerth, M., Schmidt, G.: Towards a comprehensive knowledge organisation system for the engineering domain. In: Workshop on Classification and Subject Indexing in Library and Information Science in Conjunction with the European Conference on Data Analysis (ECDA 2015) (2015)
20. WTI-Frankfurt-digital GmbH: Thesaurus Technik und Management (TEMA)
21. Caracciolo, C., Morshed, A., Stellato, A., Johannsen, G., Jaques, Y., Keizer, J.: Thesaurus maintenance, alignment and publication as linked data: the AGROOVOC use case. In: Metadata and Semantic Research. MTSR 2011. Communications in Computer and Information Science, vol 240, pp. 489–499 (2011). https://doi.org/10.1007/978-3-642-24731-6_48
22. Frosterus, M., Tuominen, J., Pessala, S., Seppälä, K., Hyvönen, E.: Linked open ontology cloud KOKO – managing a system of cross-domain lightweight ontologies. In: Cimiano, P.; Fernández, M., Lopez, V., Schlobach, S, Völker, J. (eds.) ESWC 2013. LNCS, vol. 7955, pp. 296–297. Springer, Berlin, Heidelberg, (2013). https://doi.org/10.1007/978-3-642-41242-4_49
23. Frosterus, M., Tuominen, J., Pessala, S., Hyvönen, E.: Linked open ontology cloud: managing a system of interlinked cross-domain lightweight ontologies. Int. J. Metadata Semant. Ontol. 10(3), 189–201 (2015). https://doi.org/10.1504/ijmso.2015.073879
24. Suominen, O., Ylikotila, H., Pessala, S. et al.: Publishing SKOS vocabularies with Skosmos. Article Manuscript (2005). http://skosmos.org/publishing-skos-vocabularies-with-skosmos.pdf. Accessed 13 Jul 2020
25. Skosmos. http://skosmos.org/. Accessed 13 Jul 2020
26. Finto. https://finto.fi/en/. Accessed 13 Jul 2020
27. Linked open vocabularies. https://lov.linkeddata.es/dataset/lov. Accessed 13 Jul 2020
28. Linked open data cloud. https://lod-cloud.net/. Accessed 13 Jul 2020
29. Basel register of thesauri, ontologies & classifications. https://bartoc.org/. Accessed 13 Jul 2020
30. Bartoc federated asynchronous search tool. https://bartoc-fast.ub.unibas.ch/bartocfast/. Accessed 13 Jul 2020
31. Ontology look-up service. https://github.com/EBISPOT/OLS. Accessed 10 Mar 2020
32. Integrated authority file (GND). https://www.dnb.de/EN/gnd. Accessed 13 Jul 2020
33. Multilingual access to subjects (MACS). https://www.dnb.de/voclink. Accessed 13 Jul 2020
34. Transportation research thesaurus (TRT). https://trt.trb.org/trt.asp?. Accessed 13 Jul 2020
35. TRB Publications Index. https://pubsindex.trb.org/. Accessed 13 Jul 2020

36. Katsumi, M., Fox, M.: Ontologies for transportation research: a survey. Transp. Res. Part C Emerg. Technol. **89**, 53–82 (2018). https://doi.org/10.1016/j.trc.2018.01.023
37. Ontology catalog LOV4IoT-Transport. http://lov4iot.appspot.com/?p=lov4iot-transport. Accessed 13 Jul 2020
38. Gyrard, A., Atemezing, G., Bonnet, C., Boudaoud, K., Serrano, M.: Reusing and unifying background knowledge for Internet of Things with LOV4IoT. In: Proceedings of IEEE 4th International Conference on Future Internet of Things and Cloud (FiCloud), pp. 262–269 (2016). https://doi.org/10.1109/ficloud.2016.45
39. Transmodel ontology. https://github.com/oeg-upm/transmodel-ontology. Accessed 13 Jul 2020
40. Transportation disruption ontology. https://github.com/transportdisruption/transportdisruption.github.io/. Accessed 13 Jul 2020
41. Automotive ontology community group: auto section of schema.org. https://auto.schema.org/docs/auto.home.html. Accessed 13 Jul 2020
42. Pachl. J.: Glossary of railway operation and control (2020). http://www.joernpachl.de/glossary.htm. Accessed 13 Jul 2020
43. GNDontology. https://d-nb.info/standards/elementset/gnd. Accessed 13 Jul 2020
44. Open mobility vocabulary (MobiVoc). https://www.mobivoc.org/. Accessed 20 Jul 2020
45. Rodrigues, T., Rosa, P., Cardoso, J.: Moving from syntactic to semantic organizations using JXML2OWL. Comput. Ind. **59**(8), 808–819 (2008). https://doi.org/10.1016/j.compind.2008.06.002
46. JXML2OWL on sourceforge. https://sourceforge.net/projects/jxml2owl/. Accessed 13 Jul 2020
47. Musen, M.A.: The protégé project: a look back and a look forward. AI Matters **1**(4), 4–12 (2015). https://doi.org/10.1145/2557001.25757003
48. Harris, S., Seaborne, A: SPARQL 1.1 query language (2013). https://www.w3.org/TR/2013/REC-sparql11-query-20130321/. Accessed 13 Jul 2020
49. Martínez-González, M., Alvite-Díez, M.: Thesauri and semantic web: discussion of the evolution of thesauri toward their integration with the semantic web. IEEE Access **7**, 153151–153170 (2019). https://doi.org/10.1109/access.2019.2948028
50. Chandrasekaran, D., Mago, V.: Evolution of semantic similarity – a survey (preprint) (2020). https://arxiv.org/abs/2004.13820. Accessed 13 Jul 2020
51. DeepL translator. https://www.deepl.com/translator. Accessed 20 Jul 2020
52. Vocabulary mappings of SIS move. https://github.com/SArndt-TIB/SIS-move-mappings
53. Specialized information service for civil engineering, architecture and urban studies. http://fid-bau.de/. Accessed 20 Jul 2020
54. Suominen, O., et al.: NatLibFi/Annif: Annif 0.48 (Version v0.48.0) (2020). https://doi.org/10.5281/zenodo.3921043

Linking Author Information: EconBiz Author Profiles

Arben Hajra(✉) ⓘ, Tamara Pianos ⓘ, and Klaus Tochtermann

ZBW - Leibniz Information Centre for Economics, Kiel/Hamburg, Germany
{a.hajra, t.pianos, k.tochtermann}@zbw.eu

Abstract. Author name ambiguity represents a real obstacle in the world of digital library (DL) information retrieval. The search with an author's name almost always casts doubt on whether all publications in the result list belong to that author or another author sharing the same name. In several other cases, the scholar is interested in having additional information about a selected author, such as a short biography, affiliations, metrics, or co-relations with other authors. The main purpose of this work is the integration and usage of diverse data, based on Linked Data approaches and authority records, to create a comprehensive author profile inside a DL. We are proposing and deploying an approach that provides such author profiles by using the available data, on-the-fly, i.e., harvesting the available sources for this purpose. The proposed approach - developed as a fully functional prototype - has been introduced for evaluation to a group of authors, scholars, and librarians. The results indicate acceptance of such an approach, underlining the benefits and limitations that come with it.

Keywords: Authority files · Identifiers · Researcher profiles · Wikidata · LOD

1 Introduction

Author name ambiguity represents a real obstacle in DL information retrieval. Namely, the search based on the author's name almost always casts doubt on whether the result i.e. all publications in the result list belongs to that author. The problem, therefore, arises with the persons sharing the same name, e.g. Joachim Wagner [1980] vs Joachim Wagner [1954]. On the other side, searching with an author name does not provide a complete list of results either because of different name variations e.g. Judžin F. Fama, Eugene Francis Fama, Gene Francis Fama.

Furthermore, on several occasions when a scholar is searching for a particular author, there is a concern in further details, to ensure a comprehensive overview of the author. The information, such as birth year, affiliations, profession, biography, and metrics would provide a broad picture of the author and help the scholar in that regard. However, retrieving such kind of data will cost the scholar several navigations, clicks, and is thus time-consuming. Besides biographical information, the author profiles would be more inclusive if they displayed different content analyses based on the author's research output. Such kinds of analyses, with a potential visualization of main topics and concepts

© Springer Nature Switzerland AG 2021
E. Garoufallou and M.-A. Ovalle-Perandones (Eds.): MTSR 2020, CCIS 1355, pp. 180–191, 2021.
https://doi.org/10.1007/978-3-030-71903-6_18

from their research output e.g. "income distribution", "climate change", "behavioral economics", may provide a clearer outlook of the authors' covered topics.

Another important issue that usually represents the interest of scholars is the list of co-authors with whom a particular author has collaborated, i.e. to know with whom the author has collaborated mostly, and to have an immediate switch to their profile. Moreover, let us assume that a scholar found an author whose research is closely related to their research field. They would be interested in finding other authors working on similar topics, besides the co-author network.

In addition, author metrics are an important indicator for showing the impact of authors' research output. The presence of an h-index or i10 index for measuring the citation impact and productivity may help the scholar to quickly assess the work. The author's opinion on recent topics may also be of interest. For this purpose, the scholar would need to search and browse for any blog post or any other posts on social media.

Finding, harvesting, and consuming the information needed for these purposes is possible only by navigating through many websites and spending a considerable amount of time. The main purpose of this work is the integration and usage of various data, based on Linked Data approaches and authority records, with the aim of creating a comprehensive author profile inside a Digital Library (DL). Such a profile helps the scholarly process, by reducing the time and effort of manually finding and collecting data, and increases the quality of data in the sense of accuracy. Our approach focuses on researchers in business and economics, based on the data sources used in the EconBiz[1] environment. A service like the one presented here can be used by scholars to find more information on specific authors. Authors themselves can use it to see how others make use of named entities or linked data. For this approach, we make use of the available data by harvesting as many sources as possible.

The paper begins by presenting some of the concerns that have motivated us in this regard. Section 2 describes our proposed approach, as well as examining several services and methods that are used in our development, such as authority files and linked open data. The deployment of the proposed approach, the design, and the main features are described in Sect. 3. The collected results, evaluations, and limitations are described in Sect. 4. The paper concludes with the Sect. 5.

2   Proposed Approach and Background Research

The goal of this work is to overcome most of the issues tackled in the previous section, by proposing to generate author profiles for every author in a particular DL. Scholars will find the following information aggregated in one place, such as a comprehensive list of publications, co-authorship relations, a short bio about the author, affiliations, professions, topics covered in their research output, and everything else that can be found by linking further sources. Our intention in this regard is to make use of the available data, on the fly, by harvesting the available sources for this purpose. Hence, instead of creating and storing the data locally - creating another isolated silo of data - we intend to use the data by exploiting the existing data or by creating links.

---

[1] https://www.econbiz.de.

Harvesting the data from other sources is almost impossible if we rely only on the author's name, for the reasons stated in the previous sections. Therefore, we rely on any available persistent identifier (PID). Nowadays, there are several efforts for generating authority profiles for aggregating and uniquely identifying resources and authors.

2.1 Authority Control

The benefits of authority controls have been a topic in research and many discussions [1]. Therefore, one of the major benefits is precisely the appearance of a single entity in one name, which can often be presented differently elsewhere, as well as the ability to create interlinks among them [2]. Authority files integrate data from several sources such as name variations, biographical info, affiliations, and represent them into separate clusters. Hence, for each cluster i.e. authority record a unique id is assigned.

As most prominent Authority files we may distinguish the Virtual International Authority File (VIAF) and the Integrated Authority File (GND). VIAF integrates multiple name authority files from many institutions and national libraries, around the world [3]. Initially, the main contributors were the Library of Congress (LC)[2], the German National Library (DNB)[3], and OCLC[4]. Currently, the service is hosted by OCLC.

The Integrated Authority File (GND) known as Gemeinsame Normdatei in German, is a service for facilitating the use and administration of authority data. The GND is managed by the German National Library (DNB)[5], all library networks of the German-speaking countries and their participating libraries, the German Union Catalogue of Serials (ZDB), and many other institutions [4]. Similar to VIAF, it integrates information about different entities such as persons, corporate bodies, conferences, events, geographic information, topics, and works. Each entity is identified with a specific id, known as GND ID. Presently, the GND contains over 15 million authority records.

In addition to classical authority controls, there are several other initiatives for clustering and identifying authors with a persistent identifier. The usage of ORCID, RePEc, SSRN, Google Scholar, Wikidata ID, offers many opportunities in this regard.

2.2 Linked Data and Linking PIDs

The deployment of Linked Data principles and Semantic Web technologies increases the visibility, interoperability, and accessibility of the data [5, 6], in comparison to the MARC format which does not offer much in that direction [7, 8]. Publishing the data as linked open data (LOD) is getting more and more acceptance [9, 10]. Today we can find the entire catalogs of bibliographical and authority records serialized in any of the resource description frameworks (RDF) formats and accessible as dump files, API, or SPARQL endpoints. Such a case is the German National Library (DNB) that is offering several linked data services for authority or bibliographic records [11, 12]. One of these linked data services is Entity Facts, which provides all the bibliographic data from DNB

---

[2] https://www.loc.gov/.

[3] https://www.dnb.de.

[4] https://www.oclc.org.

[5] https://www.dnb.de/.

and the authority data from GND free of charge [13]. Besides the GND data, Entity Facts also contain links to other data providers such as VIAF, ISNI, BNF, LoC, Wikipedia, Wikidata, Wikimedia Commons, etc., and in some cases, it harvests information from their side (like the author pictures from Wikimedia Commons).

An interesting fact is the presence of other identifiers as part of the authority files. In this respect, VIAF also provides links to sources such as GND, LC, BNF, Wikidata, etc. The same is the case with the GND, where among other PIDs, identifiers like the ORCID ID can be found. As of June 2019, there were more than 50.000 GND records connected with ORCID IDs [14].

Another example of linked open data implementation in the domain of libraries and authority files is the LOBID[6] services from the North Rhine-Westphalian Library Service Centre (hbz)[7]. Among the services, the "lobid-gnd" provides a search interface for searching the GND and a web API that is based on JSON-LD. The web API application of lobid-gnd is used in our approach [15].

RePEc (Research Papers in Economics) is a bibliographic database of working papers, journal articles, books, book chapters, and software components [16]. It provides several remarkable and up to date ranking services, e.g., rankings of individuals, journals, institutions[17]. Among the several services that are using the RePEc data, CitEc represents an example of showing various metrics, such as a number of citations, h-index, i10 index, for a given author [18].

Wikidata represents a free and open knowledge base that can be accessed and edited by both humans and machines [19]. It is the main data management platform for Wikipedia, and where the community-created knowledge is of essential importance [20]. The growth of Wikidata is enormous, with new records added every minute. Currently, it counts around 90 million data items, i.e. things in human knowledge, including topics, concepts, and objects. Each of the items is identified with a unique id that starts with "Q", and basically, each item consists of a particular page with the editable details, such as a label, a description and aliases.

Among the tools and services that are using Wikidata, Scholia is an interesting example of how to handle scientific bibliographic information. Scholia is a Web service that aggregates on-the-fly data from Wikidata with the purpose to create scholarly profiles for researchers, organizations, journals, publishers, individual scholarly works, and research topics [21].

In addition to the diverse information provided, Wikidata plays a very important role as the central hub for linking identifiers and authority records [22]. Moreover, there are many advantages of creating and storing such kinds of interlinks in public and community-curated linking hubs like Wikidata, rather than in closed local databases [23].

The presence of authority identifiers and other PIDs' statements inside the Wikidata items is growing rapidly. At present, around 2.6 million humans in Wikidata contain a VIAF property, and more than one million a GND ID. Other identifiers, such as RePEc, ORCID, and SSRN are also included. Hence, by knowing at least one of the identifiers, the list can be extended with several others through Wikidata.

---

[6] https://lobid.org.

[7] https://www.hbz-nrw.de/.

2.3   The Subject Portal EconBiz

EconBiz is a free search portal for economics and business studies, provided by the ZBW - Leibniz Information Centre for Economics[8]. It has a disciplinary focus on business, economics, and related subjects. EconBiz includes more than 10 million records from different databases (ECONIS, OLC EcoSci, RePEc, USB Cologne, EconStor, etc.). The integration of the Standard Thesaurus for Economics (STW)[9] supports researchers by suggesting keywords and related terms. EconBiz content is also accessible through a RESTful API, with the base URL https://api.econbiz.de/v1/.

Metadata in EconBiz is partially disambiguated, i.e. around 0.5 Million authors in several bibliographical records are identified with a unique identifier such as a GND ID (Fig. 1). In addition, through an ongoing project, we aim to extend the number of uniquely identified authors through co-authors analyses. Furthermore, when existing metadata within a DL are incapable to accurately identify an author, the authority file approaches are considered, such as the usage of VIAF clusters.

Fig. 1. Author's disambiguation state in EconBiz records

3   Author Profiles - EconBiz as a Use Case

The proposed approach is developed as a prototype for generating author profiles for the subject portal (DL) EconBiz. For each author in EconBiz, where a GND ID is assigned, a comprehensive profile is created. As explained in the previous section, especially in part 2.3, the GND ID is accepted as the central identifier for this purpose.

3.1   The Approach

In the intention to create profiles for authors, the main idea is to make use of the data available from other sources. Instead of creating and storing the data locally, which will require additional effort on creation, collection, and curation, we are harvesting the data from several sources, on the fly. The ever-increasing publication of open data, as well as the adaptation of linked data principles, provides some relief in this regard. Hence, today metadata or entire catalogs are accessible without any cost or manual input. In our approach, we make use of several sources and services for different purposes. The harvesting process is made through the consumption of already provided APIs and

---

[8] https://www.zbw.eu.

[9] https://zbw.eu/stw/version/latest/about.en.html.

various SPARQL queries. An example of such a query is shown in Listing 1, for retrieving all the prizes that a particular author has won in economics, based on Wikidata input. Figure 2 provides an overview of the flow and data sources used for this approach.

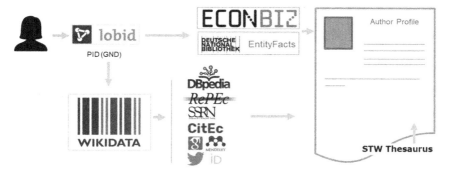

Fig. 2. The flow chart for creating EconBiz author profiles

Initially, we are targeting one of the LOBID services (lobid-gnd) for searching the appropriate GND ID, given that searching by name is easier for the scholar than with a particular ID. With the GND ID, the Entity Facts service can be consumed to retrieve diverse information about the author, e.g. alternative names, profession, picture, profession, affiliations, and some external identifiers. In all the cases when other identifiers like RePEc ID or ORCID are available but the GND ID is missing, Wikidata is used as a hub for extending the range of identifiers. More identifiers increase the possibility to target more sources i.e. DBpedia, Wikidata, ORCID, or RePEc.

The usage of EconBiz content is of crucial importance for further data processing and visualizations. The EconBiz API is consumed for listing the results, author's topics, and co-authors network. Besides, for further terms and concepts enrichment, the STW thesaurus is considered.

Listing 1. SPARQL query to Wikidata for getting author's prizes in economics

```
SELECT DISTINCT ?label WHERE {
      wd:{WID}  p:P166 ?statement.
      ?statement ps:P166 ?award.
      ?award wdt:P31 wd:Q17701409.
      ?award rdfs:label ?name.
   OPTIONAL {?statement pq:P585 ?date.BIND(YEAR(?date) AS ?year) }
   SERVICE wikibase:label {bd:serviceParam wikibase:language "en"}
   BIND(CONCAT(STR(?year), " - ", str(?name) ,"" )  AS ?label ).
   FILTER (LANG(?name) = "en").
}ORDER BY ASC(?awardLabel) ASC(?year)
```

3.2   The Implementation of EconBiz Author Profiles

The developed prototype, the EconBiz Author Profiles[10], integrate various sets of data from several sources. The users have the possibility to initiate a search from a search bar, which integrates the LOBID search service and enables the search with the author's

---

[10] https://authors.econbiz.de.

name with a combination of several parameters such as the birth year. In addition to the previous functionally, users have the possibility to select an author from already generated lists of Nobel laureates in economics and the top 1,000 RePEc economists. The list of Nobel laureates in Economics is generated through the Nobel API[11] and Wikidata, while the list of the top 1,000 economists is generated through the RePEc API[12]. It is worth mentioning, that the RePEc API provides the name of the author, the ranking position, and the short RePEc ID. Since our system is relying on GND IDs, we are using the Wikidata hub for assigning the GND ID to the authors. During our first check at Wikidata for this kind of mapping (RePEc to GND), August 2018, around 97% of the authors from RePEc top 1,000 were already part of Wikidata. Hence, with just a minimal effort all the top 1,000 RePEc authors are now mapped with a GND ID. If the ranking changes, as usually happen, the system automatically updates the list with the most recent names and positions.

The display of information is organized in three main areas, as shown in Fig. 3.

Area 1: displays the main details about the author. By harvesting the data from sources such as Entity Facts, DBpedia, Wikidata, etc., we are able to retrieve essential information about the author. Through Entity Facts the author profile is enriched with the information such as the academic title, alternative spellings, living years and places, short bio, a picture (if available), professions, affiliations, and part of the external links. Authors' pictures, - if available - are provided by Entity Facts in most of the cases, while in other cases we are checking Wikidata with a simple SPARQL Query, where "12365291X" is the GND ID of the selected author.

In addition to the Entity Facts, information from other sources are retrieved. The abstract below the picture originates from DBpedia (denoted as c.), is retrieved by querying the DBpedia SPARQL endpoint[13]. At the same time, DBpedia offers the possibility for other data enrichments. The second element is the citation metrics at the beginning of the author's details. The number of citations (5.480 in this case), the h-index, and i10 are derived from the CitEc service, based on RePEc content (see a.).

Moreover, through Wikidata the author profile integrates several other links and pages related to the author, such as ORCID, Google Scholar, SSRN, and RePEc. By including the Twitter ID, the author's Twitter timeline shows the tweets which in many cases represent the most up-to-date information on recent topics (Fig. 4).

Area 2: the second area shows the terms and concepts used in the author's research output (a.) and the co-authorship network (part b). The data in this area is generated only from the EconBiz content, i.e. all the publications where the GND ID of the corresponding author is present. The view of terms/concepts is extracted and calculated from titles, abstracts and subjects/keywords of publications by the respective author, as a result of term frequencies methods [6]. Through the usage of a word tag cloud, the representation is visualized by providing an instant overview of the main terms/topics used in the author's research output and indicating the fields in which the author's contribution is most prominent. In addition, by clicking the "Single terms" button, the view

---

[11] https://nobelprize.readme.io.

[12] https://ideas.repec.org/api.html.

[13] https://dbpedia.org/sparql.

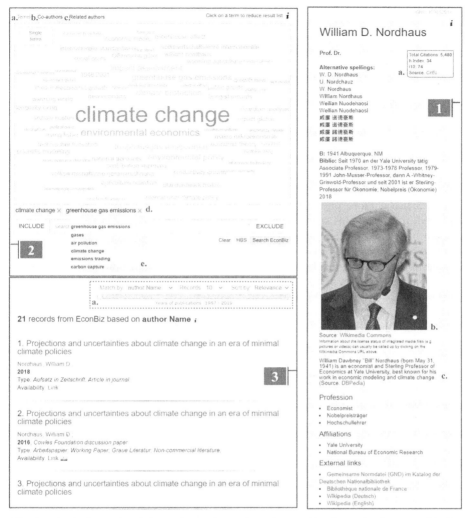

Fig. 3. Displaying author information on EconBiz author profiles [https://authors.econbiz.de]

is changing to the terms that contain just a single word. Hence, the scholar may perform quick analyses through the offered visualizations.

Moreover, this kind of visualization is used in the next steps for narrowing down the list of results and effortlessly finding the publications needed, as presented in part d. of the same area. More details about this feature are provided in the next section, while a general overview can be found in our previous research about visual search in DLs [24].

Part b. of this area two is related to the list of co-authors associated with the selected author, based on EconBiz content where the author's GND ID is used. The collaboration with others is visualized by calculating the frequency of co-authorship. In addition to providing a snapshot, this also provides possible navigation to other authors. The tab

Fig. 4. Other author profiles and Twitter timeline

option in c., denoted as "Related authors", triggers the view to authors working in related fields by analyzing the entire authors' list.

Area 3: lists authors' publications indexed in EconBiz, accessed through the API. As mentioned in the previous section, the proposed approach makes it possible to narrow the result list through different query formulations. In this regard, the use of the word tag cloud from the area 2a provides comfortable search options. Hence, just by clicking on the term/concept, the results will be limited to the records matching the criteria, as for example the selection of concepts "climate change" and "greenhouse gas emission" results in a list of 21 records. In addition to this option, i.e. formulating the search query from the tag-cloud, the scholar is able to include and exclude terms by using the text-box below the tag-cloud. Excluding a term, by inserting a term through the "exclude" button, means to list all the publications where that term does not appear on the indexed fields.

All search terms, added from the tag-cloud or manually through the text-box, appear in a panel below the tag-cloud. From there, the scholar is able to extend the panel with new entries or remove any of them. In addition, the already inserted terms may be extended with related terms through the usage of external thesauri [24]. This feature in our model is set to the hover event, by prompting a box with the most related terms based on the STW thesaurus (see area 2e.). Moreover, the list may be extended with additional machine learning generated terms through word embedding approaches, as we have exposed in our previous studies [6, 24].

Besides the presented features, the list of results could be filtered and sorted using several criteria, through the interactivity in the area 3a.

In addition to the content indexed in EconBiz, the approach makes use of different other services to provide more related and up-to-date information. Such a scenario represents the usage of Harvard Business School Working Knowledge[14] for recommending similar articles based on the query that the scholar has formulated.

4   Evaluations

Up to the time of writing this text, the proposed approach- developed as fully functional prototype- has been introduced for evaluation to a group of persons reaching 50. The group consists of experts in the field of economics and business, authors that can find themselves in the service, students and other scholars. In addition, a number of subject

---

[14] https://hbswk.hbs.edu/.

librarians had a look at the service. All the subjects who participated in the evaluation have provided overall feedback about the service, including the approach, the selection of the data, and the way how the information was presented and visualized. For this purpose, we have followed some of the UX methods for collecting the data, such as interviews, focus groups, and questionnaires. In general, the provided feedbacks reflect the overall design and implementation, while on several occasions the feedbacks are very specific, related to a particular design or functionality.

4.1 Results

The collected feedbacks are divided into two groups, according to the authors who find themselves in the service, and the others who see the service from users' point of view. All evaluators consider that an approach, as we have presented here, represents a useful instrument to facilitate scientific communication. A positive assessment is given to the integration and display of information, by linking a large number of data about the author. The idea of building a comprehensive profile in a single place, without having to navigate different locations and without input by the author, is one of the benefits in almost every received feedback. In addition to biographical information, the word tag-cloud generated from the most frequently used terms in the author's work is also an important element that brings a new dimension to the profile. Thus, they estimate that the information provided through such visualizations gives good overviews of the areas covered by the author. The co-authorship network is also considered a very important service in order to understand in greater detail the cooperation between authors and to navigate to the relevant author easily. The functionalities to narrow down the results, through query formulations or even within the publication years, represent a crucial component in regard to the interactivity with the service.

There have been several occasions where through the usage of the tool various metadata mistakes were identified (i.e. false authorship, duplicate names, etc.). Hence, such a service can also serve as a tool for quality control of bibliographical records.

Despite the positive reflections from all participants, there are some limitations evident which are emphasized in the following section.

4.2 Limitations

One of the main limitations that continue to be an obstacle in many cases is the incompleteness of the author's disambiguation with relevant identifiers in all publications where the author's name appears. The application of this approach would be much more productive in an environment where all authors in the corresponding publications and in the entire collection are uniquely identified. In any situation where there is a lack of identifiers, or even when some of the authors have identifiers, the following problems are observed: the list of results may be incomplete i.e., the list of publications may not include the publications where the author is not connected to the identifiers, the visualization of concepts that reflect the author's contribution to the relevant fields and co-authorship networks are not comprehensive. This also makes it difficult to set a default for the EconBiz-search because a search for a name may retrieve too many results not belonging to the author while a GND-search may retrieve few results.

Given the fact that our approach utilizes existing data from different sources, despite many advantages, some deficiencies are present in several situations. Since we do not own the data, we do not have complete control over it, hence the process of updating or adding new facts is complex and update-cycles may take long. Such kind of complexity is present when the Entity Facts data are considered, which are based on GND authority records. Hence, we can positively respond to part of the requests addressed by the authors for changes in the data obtained from that service, however, some detailed changes can only be done by specific GND editors. Data from Wikidata is handled in a completely different manner, where anyone can add or update any statement, normally by following the set rules.

5 Conclusion and Future Work

In our approach, the creation of author profiles consists of steps such as: proper identification of an author and a persistent identifier, harvesting data from various sources, presentation of that data in a comprehensive and structured way, as well as the analysis of publications (mainly indexed in EconBiz) to produce visualizations. Such a profile is a useful tool in the hands of scholars and provides a number of benefits, by making numerous clicks and navigation to several other sites superfluous. To this end, scholars can explore the research output of individual authors, get quick overviews on the research interests of an author, navigate to more information like co-authors or related authors, identify other authors who work in a similar field, find publications relevant to their field of interest, etc.

The data harvesting process relies on the linked data principles that attempt to make use of already existing data, instead of requesting from the author/librarian to re-create the same again. This reduces the effort of manually finding and collecting data. If more authority files are used and openly linked in the future, this approach will be even more beneficial to authors and researchers alike.

In order to provide authors with greater control over the presented data, the use of ORCID can be done analogously to GND authority records. In fact, such an idea has been introduced since the beginning of our approach, however, despite the advantages of using ORCID data - created by the authors themselves - it has been found that most authors do not possess an ORCID profile yet, or their profile has a lack of information.

In addition, as future work, we are considering to increase the functionality in terms of adjustment of some visualization. One example would be the adjustment of the word tag-cloud to different time segments, that only the topics of that timeframe would be displayed, e.g. only early publications by the author or only the most recent years.

The creation of topic pages is an idea that can be explored in the future. Such an approach is already applied for generating the COVID-19 page[15], an experimental proof of concept that allows finding publications or authors publishing on this topic.

References

1. Tillett, B.B.: Authority control: state of the art and new perspectives, pp. 51–98 (2012). https://doi.org/10.4324/9780203051092-8

---

[15] https://authors.econbiz.de/1206288906.

2. Taylor, A.G.: Authority files in online catalogs: an investigation of their value. Cat. Classif. Q. **4**, 1–17 (1984). https://doi.org/10.1300/J104v04n03_01
3. Loesch, M.F.: VIAF (the virtual international authority file). Tech. Serv. Q. **28**, 255–256 (2011). http://viaf.org https://doi.org/10.1080/07317131.2011.546304
4. DNB - The Integrated Authority File (GND). https://www.dnb.de/EN/gnd
5. Heath, T., Bizer, C.: Linked data: evolving the web into a global data space. Synth. Lect. Semant. Web Theory Technol. **1**, 1–136 (2011). https://doi.org/10.2200/S00334ED1V01Y20 1102WBE001
6. Hajra, A., Tochtermann, K.: Linking science: approaches for linking scientific publications across different LOD repositories. Int. J. Metadata Semant. Ontol. **12**, 121–141 (2017). https://doi.org/10.1504/ijmso.2017.10011833
7. Gonzales, B.M.: Linking libraries to the web: linked data and the future of the bibliographic record. Inf. Technol. Libr. **33**, 10–22 (2014). https://doi.org/10.6017/ital.v33i4.5631
8. Zhu, L.: The future of authority control: issues and trends in the linked data environment. J. Libr. Metadata. **19**, 215–238 (2019). https://doi.org/10.1080/19386389.2019.1688368
9. Downey, M.: Assessing author identifiers: preparing for a linked data approach to name authority control in an institutional repository context. J. Libr. Metadata **19**, 117–136 (2019). https://doi.org/10.1080/19386389.2019.1590936
10. Hallo, M., Luján-Mora, S., Maté, A., Trujillo, J.: Current state of linked data in digital libraries. J. Inf. Sci. **42**, 117–127 (2016). https://doi.org/10.1177/0165551515594729
11. DNB: linked data service. https://www.dnb.de/EN/lds
12. Hannemann, J., Kett, J.: Linked data for libraries. In: Proceedings of the World Library and Information Congress: 76 International Federation of Library Associations and Institutions (IFLA), pp. 1–11 (2010)
13. DNB - Entity Facts. https://www.dnb.de/EN/entityfacts
14. Vierkant, P.: Mehr als 50.000 Personendatensätze der Gemeinsamen Normdatei (GND) mit ORCID-Records verknüpft. https://www.orcid-de.org/mehr-als-50-000-personendatensa etze-der-gemeinsamen-normdatei-gnd-mit-orcid-records-verknuepft/
15. Pohl, A., Steeg, F., Christoph, P.: lobid – Dateninfrastruktur für Bibliotheken. Information-spraxis, p. 4 (2018). https://doi.org/10.11588/ip.2018.1.52445
16. RePEc: research papers in economics. http://repec.org/
17. Zimmermann, C.: Academic rankings with RePEc. Econometrics **1**, 249–280 (2013). https://doi.org/10.3390/econometrics1030249
18. CitEc: citations in economics. http://citec.repec.org/
19. Wikidata. https://www.wikidata.org/wiki/Wikidata:Main_Page
20. Vrandečić, D., Krötzsch, M.: Wikidata: a free collaborative knowledgebase. Commun. ACM **57**, 78–85 (2014). https://doi.org/10.1145/2629489
21. Nielsen, F.Å., Mietchen, D., Willighagen, E.: Scholia, scientometrics and Wikidata. In: Blomqvist, E., Hose, K., Paulheim, H., Ławrynowicz, A., Ciravegna, F., Hartig, O. (eds.) ESWC 2017. LNCS, vol. 10577, pp. 237–259. Springer, Cham (2017). https://doi.org/10.1007/978-3-319-70407-4_36
22. Van Veen, T.: Wikidata: from "an" identifier to "the" identifier. Inf. Technol. Libr. **38**, 72–81 (2019). https://doi.org/10.6017/ital.v38i2.10886
23. Neubert, J.: Wikidata as a linking hub for knowledge organization systems? Integrating an authority mapping into wikidata and learning lessons for KOS mappings. In: NKOS@TPDL 2017, pp. 14–25, Thessaloniki, Greece (2017)
24. Hajra, A., Tochtermann, K.: Visual search in digital libraries and the usage of external terms. In: 2018 22nd International Conference Information Visualisation (IV), pp. 396–400. IEEE (2018). https://doi.org/10.1109/iv.2018.00074

OntoBelliniLetters: A Formal Ontology for a Corpus of Letters of Vincenzo Bellini

Salvatore Cristofaro[(✉)] and Daria Spampinato

Istituto di Scienze e Tecnologie della Cognizione - CNR, Catania, Italy
salvatore.cristofaro@istc.cnr.it, daria.spampinato@cnr.it

Abstract. In this paper the formal OntoBelliniLetters ontology is described concerning the corpus of Vincenzo Bellini's correspondence letters kept at the Belliniano Civic Museum of Catania. This ontology is part of a wider project - the BelliniInRete project - one of whose aims is the development of a more general and complete ontology for the whole Vincenzo Bellini's legacy preserved in the Museum.

The main concepts and relations building up the ontology knowledge base are described and discussed and hints for their implementation by means of the standard OWL-2 description language are presented. The ontology schema is inspired by the *CIDOC Conceptual Reference Model* (CIDOC CRM).

Keywords: Vincenzo Bellini · Correspondence letters · Ontology

1 Introduction

In this paper the formal OntoBelliniLetters ontology is described concerning the semantic organization of the corpus of Vincenzo Bellini's correspondence letters kept at the Belliniano Civic Museum of Catania. OntoBelliniLetters partially stems from the TEI-encodings of Bellini letters developed as part of the BelliniInRete project which aims at renewing and creating a lasting change in the exploitation and enhancement of the Belliniano Museum (see [2,3]); however, OntoBelliniLetters is not purely the result of a mapping grounded into the set of particular TEI constructs used for the letters: certain semantic specificities are involved that are not explicitly and directly undertaken within the TEI-encodings.

Conceptually, the OntoBelliniLetters ontology is made up of *entities*, provided with *attributes*, and *relations* (see Sect. 3). The ontology schema has been conceived with "CIDOC CRM mappability" in mind,[1] with entities definable in terms of CIDOC CRM (sub)classes, and relations in terms of CIDOC CRM (sub)property chains. CIDOC CRM is the international standard for information integration and exchange in the cultural heritage domain. It consists of two main types of *primitives*, namely, the *classes*, identified by names $E1, E2, \ldots$ and the *properties*, named $P1, P2, \ldots$, which serve to model objects and relationships underlying a

---

[1] http://www.cidoc-crm.org/.

© Springer Nature Switzerland AG 2021
E. Garoufallou and M.-A. Ovalle-Perandones (Eds.): MTSR 2020, CCIS 1355, pp. 192–203, 2021.
https://doi.org/10.1007/978-3-030-71903-6_19

given reality. In fact, entities involved in the OntoBelliniLetters ontology which describe real-world instances (such as persons, places, dates, etc.) can be represented in terms of subclasses of corresponding CIDOC CRM **E**n primitives, e.g., the classes **E21** (Person), **E53** (Place), **E50** (Date), etc., whereas relationships between entities can be implemented by linking CIDOC CRM classes through chains of CIDOC CRM **P**n properties, as in the case of the relationship "P has birth date D", linking a person P to its date of birth D, which can be modelled (e.g.) as the chain **E21** (Person) $\rightarrow$ **P98** (was born) $\rightarrow$ **E76** (Birth) $\rightarrow$ **P4** (has time-span) $\rightarrow$ **E52** (Time-span) $\rightarrow$ **P78** (is identified by) $\rightarrow$ **E50** (Date).

In the literature, some proposals of manuscript digitisation, and digital data sharing and exploitation are presented that involve semantic organisation of letter corpora; see, for instance, [5], which presents a digital edition of a collection of letters of Vespasiano da Bisticci, and [7], where a linked data approach is described for the creation of a digital infrastructure for publishing, sharing and analysing correspondence based on EMLO.[2] We mention also that, originally, an experimentation has been undertaken by the authors concerning the possibility of exploiting RDA (*Resource Description and Access*)[3] framework for the development of an ontology of the whole Bellini's legacy, including, in particular, the letter corpus (see [1]). However, due to data representation issues, which made things unnecessarily complicated, this task was abandoned in favour of the idea of exploiting CIDOC CRM instead.

The paper is organized as follows. Section 2 briefly reviews some notions and concepts used in the paper. Then, leading Sect. 3 provides a conceptual descriptions of the main *ontology items* (entities and relations) involved in OntoBelliniLetters; some domain specific *axioms* are even described as well, and their OWL-2 implementations are presented (cf. Sect. 3.4). Conclusions and future works are discussed in Sect. 4.

2   Background Notions and Concepts

The notion of an *entity* and other related ones are often used in this paper. For convenience we briefly review them below for future reference.

An entity (in the present context) is a formal representation of an homogeneous collection C of concrete or abstracts object within a given universe or domain of the discourse. Conceptually, an entity (for the collection C) consists just of a list (i.e., a finite ordered sequence) of *features* or *properties* shared by all objects in C. Any particular tuple of *values* of these features is intended to uniquely identify a specific, well determined object of C.

A feature is conceptually represented by the set of its values, called an *(entity) attribute*. So, an entity has the form $(\mathsf{att}_1, \mathsf{att}_2, \dots, \mathsf{att}_n)$ where $\mathsf{att}_1, \mathsf{att}_2, \dots, \mathsf{att}_n$ are the attributes carrying out the information about the object features. A sequence of values $(v_1, v_2, \dots, v_n)$, where $v_i \in \mathsf{att}_i$, for $i = 1, 2, \dots, n$, is called an

---

[2] EMLO (*Early Modern Letters Online*) is a collaborative, open source union catalogue of early modern correspondence (http://emlo.bodleian.ox.ac.uk/).

[3] http://www.rda-rsc.org/.

(entity) instance which is thus meant to represent a specific object of the collection C. Note that, the *role* of an attribute att_i, i.e., the particular feature it represents, is determined by just its position i in the sequence $\mathsf{att}_1, \mathsf{att}_2, \ldots, \mathsf{att}_n$; however, usually, specific names are associated to attributes that exemplify their roles. Entity attributes can be basically divided into two main classes: *atomic attributes* and *non-atomic attributes*. Atomic attributes carry out a unique, unstructured type of information, whereas non-atomic attributes are defined in terms of atomic ones and correspond by themselves to entities; i.e., each of them is in fact the instance set of some entity.

A more formal definition of an entity can be provided recursively as follows. Note that below we denote with $\langle\!\langle \mathcal{E} \rangle\!\rangle$ the instance set of an entity $\mathcal{E}$. Let $\mathcal{A}_1, \mathcal{A}_2, \ldots, \mathcal{A}_m$ data item sets representing atomic attributes.[4] Then:

(1) each 1-tuple $\mathcal{E} =_{Def} (\mathcal{A}_j)$, where $1 \leqslant j \leqslant m$, is an entity (a *primitive entity*), and we put $\langle\!\langle \mathcal{E} \rangle\!\rangle =_{Def} \mathcal{A}_j$;
(2) if $\mathcal{E}_1, \mathcal{E}_2, \ldots, \mathcal{E}_k$ are any k entities, where $k \geqslant 2$, then the k-tuple $\mathcal{E} =_{Def} (\langle\!\langle \mathcal{E}_1 \rangle\!\rangle, \langle\!\langle \mathcal{E}_2 \rangle\!\rangle, \ldots, \langle\!\langle \mathcal{E}_k \rangle\!\rangle)$ is an entity, ad we put

$$\langle\!\langle \mathcal{E} \rangle\!\rangle =_{Def} \langle\!\langle \mathcal{E}_1 \rangle\!\rangle \times \langle\!\langle \mathcal{E}_2 \rangle\!\rangle \times \cdots \times \langle\!\langle \mathcal{E}_k \rangle\!\rangle \,,$$

(i.e., the cartesian product of the instance sets $\langle\!\langle \mathcal{E}_1 \rangle\!\rangle, \langle\!\langle \mathcal{E}_2 \rangle\!\rangle, \ldots, \langle\!\langle \mathcal{E}_k \rangle\!\rangle$);
(3) nothing else is an entity.

Note that the representation provided by an entity is essentially conceptual: in particular, in the case an entity $\mathcal{E}$ is used to represent a collection C of concrete objects of the real world, not all possible combinations of attribute values (i.e., not all entity instances) necessarily correspond to objects actually existing within the collection C.

For example, the collection C of the letters sent by Vincenzo Bellini to its father Rosario Bellini or to its uncle Vincenzo Ferlito, with each letter being characterized by its own written text content, can be conceptualized in terms of an entity and, specifically, represented as the triple $\mathcal{E} =_{Def} (\mathsf{sender}, \mathsf{recipient}, \mathsf{text})$, where: (i) the attribute sender is used to represent the property that someone (i.e., some person) is the sender of a letter, with its values identifying letter senders; (ii) the attribute $\mathsf{recipient}$ similarly concerns letter recipients; and, finally, (iii) the attribute text carries out information about letter texts. If there are altogether n different letters, and we stipulate to represent the text of the i-th letter by means of a string T_i, we may put $\mathsf{text} =_{Def} (\{T_1, ..., T_n\})$, with text thus being a primitive entity composed of only the atomic attribute $\{T_1, ..., T_n\}$. Next, if we assume that a person is determined solely by just its first and last names, we may represent the collection of all of the involved persons (i.e., letter senders/recipients) by the entity $(\mathsf{firstName}, \mathsf{lastName})$, where the two (atomic) attributes $\mathsf{firstName}$ and $\mathsf{lastName}$ provide in fact the information about persons' first and last names, respectively; formally, we may put:

$$\mathsf{firstName} =_{Def} \{\mathbf{Vincenzo}, \mathbf{Rosario}\} \quad \text{and} \quad \mathsf{lastName} =_{Def} \{\mathbf{Bellini}, \mathbf{Ferlito}\}.$$

---

[4] Formally, the data items referred to here correspond to strings over some fixed alphabet.

Summing up we may write

$$\mathcal{E} = (\ $$
$$\{\mathbf{Vincenzo, Rosario}\} \times \{\mathbf{Bellini, Ferlito}\},$$
$$\{\mathbf{Vincenzo, Rosario}\} \times \{\mathbf{Bellini, Ferlito}\},$$
$$\{T_1, ..., T_n\}$$
$$)\ .$$

Note that (e.g.) the entity instance

$$((\mathbf{Vincenzo, Ferlito}), (\mathbf{Rosario, Bellini}), T_i)\ ,$$

where $i \in \{1, \ldots, n\}$, does not correspond to any letter of the collection C as it would represent a letter whose sender is Vincenzo Ferlito (and hence not included in C).

3   Conceptualizing Bellini's Correspondence

We conceptually represent the whole collection of Bellini's letters kept at the Belliniano Museum as an entity (the *letter-entity*).

As dictated by the examination and analysis of this letter collection, the letter-entity involves various groups of attributes determined by the consideration of different aspects of the letters. A group of *standard attributes* identify who wrote a letter and to whom the letter is addressed to, and carry information about postal shipping/delivery of letters, such as:

– author (person(s) that wrote a letter);
– addresse (person(s) a letter content (i.e., meaning) is addressed to);
– sender (sender of a letter);
– recipient (recipient of a letter).

Similarly there are even attributes about letter preservation and archiving, e.g., the organization keeping a letter and how and where it is archived there; these include:

– repository (organization keeping the letter);
– inventory (inventory number);
– collocation (physical collocation of the letter);
– title (letter title).

Besides the letter-entity, the OntoBelliniLetters ontology involves several other entities and relations concerning such aspects as physical letter structure, letter texts arrangement and letter text contents, as well as other types of entities and relations, as described in the following sections.

Note that, in the OWL-2 formalization of the ontology, all these entities and relations correspond to OWL-2-(sub)classes and OWL-2-(sub)properties, respectively, with the role of an attribute att of an entity $\mathcal{E}$ implemented by means of a specific property linking the class corresponding to $\mathcal{E}$ to the class corresponding to att.

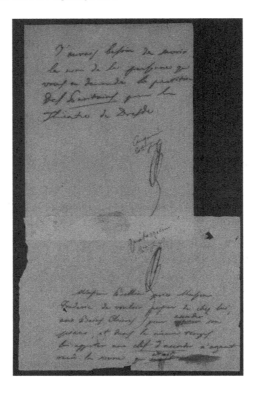

Fig. 1. Glued letter-sheets.

3.1 Physical Letter Structure

Letter texts are written on sheets of paper (*letter-sheets*): certain texts spread across two or more letter-sheets (possibly glued along edges, as shown in Fig. 1) and/or lie on opposite sides of the same sheet (say, the front side and the back side).

Each letter-sheet is conceptualized as a rectangle with its own width and height *dimensions*; is made up of a certain *material* (e.g., the type of paper with its thickness) and has a given *condition state*. Opposite sides of letter-sheets – the *(letter-)pages* - are the elementary physical support units bearing letter texts. Thus each letter-sheet is composed of two (opposite) pages and a letter (text) may spans one or more pages. Each page acquires the dimensions and the material of the letter-sheet it is a side of, and two opposite pages have thus the same dimensions and the same material; however, condition state of opposite pages may be different (e.g., due to stains, abrasions, discolorations, etc.). A page thus corresponds to an entity provided of (at least) the following attributes: dimension, conditionState and material; moreover, two page-entities P_1 and P_2 may be related by the hasOpposite relation meaning that P_1 and P_2 are opposite sides of the same letter-sheet. A letter L is related to a page P bearing

Fig. 2. An example of a Bellini's letter containing overlappig text parts following different writing orientations.

(part) of L's text by means of the relationship L hasSupport P. Note that the hasOpposite relation is *symmetric*, since sides of a paper sheet are opposite each other; moreover any page cannot have more than one opposite (see Sect. 3.4).

3.2 Letter Text Arrangement

A peculiar property of Bellini's correspondence is the presence, within the same letter page, of written text parts that follow different writing orientations and/or that partially overlap each other. See for instance Fig. 2. These peculiarities represent useful information about writing modalities and preferences in Bellini's letters. We take care of them by conceptually wrapping the written text parts into 2-dimensional rectangular boxes - the *wboxes* - that virtually lie within letter pages, and to each wbox D we associate the cartesian coordinate system (x_D, y_D) where the positive direction of the x_D-axis follows the writing direction of the text within D, and the positive direction of the y_D-axis goes from the baseline

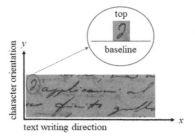

Fig. 3. The (x, y) cartesian coordinate system associated to a wbox.

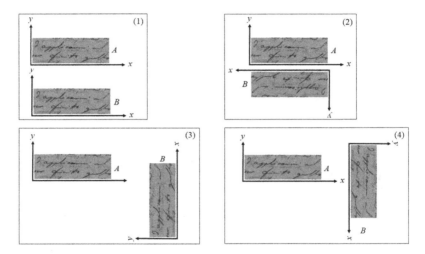

Fig. 4. Graphical representations of the relationships A hasRight B (1), A hasLeft B (2), A hasTop B (3) and A hasBottom B (4), where A and B denotes wboxes.

to the top of the written characters (see Fig. 3). Then, we consider the following 5 kind of relationships between two wboxes A and B:

(1) A hasRight B: axes x_A and x_B have the same positive directions;
(2) A hasLeft B: axes x_A and x_B have opposite positive directions;
(3) A hasTop B: axes y_A and x_B have the same positive directions;
(4) A hasBottom B: axes y_A and x_B have opposite positive directions;
(5) A hasOverlap B: a portion of A overlaps over a portion of B.

(Figure 4 provides graphical representations of the relationships (1), (2), (3) and (4) above.) In fact, from an examination of Bellini's correspondence, it turns out that the five relations above cover all possible cases of mutual arrangement of the various text parts in terms of writing orientation and overlapping.

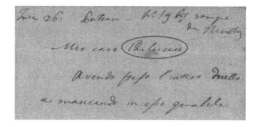

Fig. 5. The use of diminutives within Bellini's letter texts: "Carluccio" refers to the person Carlo Pepoli, the librettist of Bellini's Opera *I Puritani*.

For a wbox D and a page P we define the relationship D hasPage P meaning that D lies within P. Note that we intend a wbox as being uniquely identified by the particular text part it wraps and the letter page it lies within. Thus, each wbox D has associated a unique text part T and lies within one and only one page P; hence in particular, if P_1 and P_2 are pages such that D hasPage P_1 and D hasPage P_2 both hold, then P_1 and P_2 are identical. Below we will discuss other properties relating pages and wboxes (cf. Sect. 3.4).

3.3 Letter Text Contents

The text of a letter expresses concepts and describes situations and facts about everyday life. Certain single words, or, more generally, word sequences W occurring within the written texts of Bellini's letters are interpreted as referring to relevant entities $\mathcal{E}$ of which it is useful to keep track of the information about their involvement into the various text parts and how they are in fact referred to (i.e., the word sequences W); such information is relevant to the museum context and for education purposes. We call these entities $\mathcal{E}$ the *named-entities*, and the word sequences W above that refer to them, their respective *internal-names*. Named-entities corresponds to persons, places, organizations, (manifestations and types of) musical works, etc. For example, in its letters, Bellini sometimes uses diminutives for naming persons, such as for instance the word "Carluccio" with which he refers to Carlo Pepoli, the librettist of its Opera *I Puritani* (see Fig. 5). Also, mentions to musical works (such as *Puritani* or *Capuleti*) frequently occur within the text of Bellini's letters, as well as the use of specific terms related to the musical domain (such as *aria, atto, cantata, cavatina, coro, duetto, opera, sortita*, etc.); even specific places and/or organizations are referred to in various parts of the letters, such as cities and theatres. Note that the correlation between a named-entity $\mathcal{E}$ and an internal-name W of it, does not always follow "by per se" from solely the information contained within W (e.g., as in the case above of the diminutive "Carluccio" correlated to the person Carlo Pepoli), but is sometimes the result of a contextual analysis of the various text parts of the letter(s) where W occurs and/or other information available on the life of Vincenzo Bellini.

Named-entities have their own attributes. Note that certain specific attributes provide external linkings of these entities to corresponding authority file entries, and similar informative resources and repertories, such as VIAF,[5] Geonames,[6] Wikipedia,[7] Treccani encyclopedia,[8] RISM,[9] and LesMU [6]. Besides these *link-attributes*, owned by all named-entities, other characterizing attributes are specific to the particular type of named-entity they are involved in. For instance, in the case of a person-entity, there are the attributes foreName, surName and addName carrying out information about the forename, the surname and aliases (or nicknames) of persons, respectively, as well as the attributes birthDate (resp. deathDate) and birthPlace (resp. deathPlace) holding the date and the place of birth (resp. of death). Also, attributes concerning social role and status of persons are involved. In the case of the place-entity, the attributes settlement, district and country are involved which correspond to the urban-type settlement, urban district and belonging country of geographic places, respectively.

3.4   Domain Axioms

Besides entities and relations described above, for a fruitful modelling of our domain of interest, i.e., the Bellini's correspondence, certain (domain) specific axioms are to be introduced ruling the way entities are related each other. Below we present and describe some of these axioms. Note that for notational convenience we use *First Order Logic* (FOL) to formally state the axioms. However, we point out that the full machinery of FOL is not actually required for this purpose; in fact, the *Description Logic* (DL) underlying OWL-2 (i.e., $\mathcal{SROIQ}$, see [4]) suffices. We use FOL notation as it is more easy and intuitive than DL (at least to our opinion), and allows to express a deeper level of detail.

To begin with, we recall from Sect. 3.1 that the supports for text letters are the pages which correspond to the sides of the sheets of paper where the texts are actually written. As noted, if two pages A and B are opposite, then they must have (I) the same material and (II) the same dimensions; moreover, (III) for each page P there can be at most a unique page Q which is the opposite of P; i.e., the relation hasOpposite must be *functional*. Formally, we can readily state conditions (I) and (II) within FOL, respectively, as follows:

$$(\forall A)(\forall B)(\forall M)(A \text{ hasOpposite } B \wedge B \text{ hasMaterial } M \Rightarrow A \text{ hasMaterial } M) \quad (A1)$$

and

$$(\forall A)(\forall B)(\forall D)(A \text{ hasOpposite } B \wedge B \text{ hasDimension } D \Rightarrow A \text{ hasDimension } D), \quad (A2)$$

---

[5] http://viaf.org/.
[6] https://www.geonames.org/.
[7] https://www.wikipedia.org/.
[8] http://www.treccani.it/enciclopedia/.
[9] http://www.rism.info/home.html.

whereas conditions (III) states as:

$$(\forall A)(\forall B)(\forall C)(A \text{ hasOpposite } B \wedge A \text{ hasOpposite } C \Rightarrow B = C). \quad (\text{A3})$$

Observe further, that if a page A has a page B as its opposite then the converse should even holds true, i.e., B has A as its opposite; thus, the relation hasOpposite is *symmetric*:

$$(\forall A)(\forall B)(A \text{ hasOpposite } B \Rightarrow B \text{ hasOpposite } A). \quad (\text{A4})$$

Additionally, it is quite reasonable to assume that hasOpposite is an *irreflexive* relation, namely, no page can be the opposite of itself:

$$(\forall A)(\neg(A \text{ hasOpposite } A)). \quad (\text{A5})$$

Also, since a page conceptually identifies a side of a paper sheet bearing some letter text, one should postulate that any page is the support of some letter:

$$(\forall P)(\exists L)(L \text{ hasSupport } P). \quad (\text{A6})$$

Further axioms involve (e.g.) wboxes. Recall that wboxes are conceptualized as specific parts of letter texts wrapped into rectangular containers that are intended to be matched against writing directions and/or overlapping. Thus, any wbox D must lie within exactly one page P; a condition which corresponds to the (conjunction of the) following two statements, the second of which expresses *functionality* of the relation hasPage:

$$(\forall D)(\exists P)(D \text{ hasPage } P) \quad (\text{A7})$$

and

$$(\forall D)(\forall P)(\forall Q)(D \text{ hasPage } P \wedge D \text{ hasPage } Q \Rightarrow P = Q). \quad (\text{A8})$$

Also, relation hasOverlap (cf. Sect. 3.2) could be postulated as *irreflexive* (i.e., no wbox D overlaps with itself):

$$(\forall D)(\neg(D \text{ hasOverlap } D)), \quad (\text{A9})$$

and, since any wboxes agrees with itself in terms of text writing direction, we further have that hasRight relation is *reflexive*:

$$(\forall D)(D \text{ hasRight } D). \quad (\text{A10})$$

Furthermore, given that writing directions within two wboxes X and Y can mutually arrange X and Y in one and only one way, the relations hasRight, hasLeft, hasTop and hasBottom should be pairwise *disjoint*; formally, this can be stated as an *axiom-schemata* as follows:

$$(\forall X)(\forall Y)(X \text{ rela } Y \Rightarrow \neg(X \text{ relb } Y)), \quad (\text{A11})$$

where

$$\text{rela} \in \{\text{hasRight}, \text{hasLeft}, \text{hasTop}, \text{hasBottom}\}$$

(A1)	SubObjectPropertyOf(
	    ObjectPropertyChain(:hasOpposite :hasMaterial)
	    :hasMaterial
	)

(A2)	SubObjectPropertyOf(
	    ObjectPropertyChain(:hasOpposite :hasDimension)
	    :hasDimension
	)

(A3)	FunctionalObjectProperty(:hasOpposite)
(A4)	SymmetricObjectProperty(:hasOpposite)
(A5)	IrreflexiveObjectProperty(:hasOpposite)

(A6)	EquivalentClasses(
	    :LETTER
	    ObjectSomeValuesFrom(:hasSupport :PAGE)
	)

(A7)	EquivalentClasses(
	    :WBOX
	    ObjectSomeValuesFrom(:hasPage :PAGE)
	)

(A8)	FunctionalObjectProperty(:hasPage)
(A9)	IrreflexiveObjectProperty(:hasOverlap)
(A10)	ReflexiveObjectProperty(:hasRight)
(A11)	DisjointObjectProperties(:hasRight :hasLeft :hasTop :hasBottom)

Fig. 6. OWL-2 Functional-Style representation of the domain axioms (A1)–(A11).

and
$$relb \in \{hasRight, hasLeft, hasTop, hasBottom\} \setminus \{rela\}.$$

As remarked above, axioms (A1)–(A11) are expressed by means of FOL syntax. For completeness we report in the table represented in Fig. 6 the corresponding translations into OWL-2 Functional-Style Syntax, where LETTER, PAGE and WBOX represent the OWL-2-classes corresponding to the letter-entity, the page-entity and the wbox-entity, respectively.

4   Conclusions and Future Work

In this paper, the OntoBelliniLetters ontology has been described concerning the corpus of Vincenzo Bellini's correspondence letters kept at the Belliniano Civic Museum of Catania. The ontology schema has been devised and formalized within the logical apparatus provided by the OWL-2 description language for semantic knowledge representation; however, it is currently under refinement, and the ontology has not been fully populated yet, as a subset of letters is being processed for the purposes of the formal extraction and analysis of the relevant information to be inserted into the ontology. Completion of the ontology is planned for the near future.

Acknowledgements. This work has been partially supported by the BelliniInRete project, funded by the Patto per Catania under the Fondo Sviluppo e Coesione 2014–2020: Piano per il Mezzogiorno.

References

1. Cristofaro, S., Spampinato, D.: Una proposta di ontologia basata su RDA per il patrimonio culturale di Vincenzo Bellini. In: Marras, C., Passarotti, M., Franzini, G., Litta, E. (eds.) Quaderni di Umanistica Digitale: AIUCD 2020, pp. 82–88 (2020). https://doi.org/10.6092/unibo/amsacta/6316
2. Del Grosso, A.M., Capizzi, E., Cristofaro, S., De Luca, M.R., Giovannetti, E., Marchi, S., Seminara, G., Spampinato, D.: Bellini's Correspondence: a Digital Scholarly Edition for a Multimedia Museum. Umanistica Digitale 3(7), 23–47 (2019). https://doi.org/10.6092/issn.2532-8816/9162
3. Del Grosso, A.M., Capizzi, E., Cristofaro, S., Seminara, G., Spampinato, D.: Promoting Bellini's legacy and the Italian opera by scholarly digital editing his own correspondence, September 2019. https://doi.org/10.5281/zenodo.3461673. Poster paper presented at the TEI Conference and Members' Meeting 2019. "What is Text, really? TEI and beyond." September 16–20, 2019, Graz, Austria
4. Rudolph, S.: Foundations of description logics. In: Polleres, A., d'Amato, C., Arenas, M., Handschuh, S., Kroner, P., Ossowski, S., Patel-Schneider, P. (eds.) Reasoning Web 2011. LNCS, vol. 6848, pp. 76–136. Springer, Heidelberg (2011). https://doi.org/10.1007/978-3-642-23032-5_2
5. Tomasi, F.: L'edizione digitale e la rappresentazione della conoscenza. Un esempio: Vespasiano da Bisticci e le sue lettere. Ecdotica **9**(2012), 264–286 (2013)
6. Trovato, P., Nicolodi, F., Di Benedetto, R., Rossi, F., Aversano, L.: LesMu: lessico della letteratura musicale italiana : 1490–1950. Filologia e ordinatori, Franco Cesati (2007)
7. Tuominen, J., Mäkelä, E., Hyvönen, E., Bosse, A., Lewis, M., Hotson, H.: Reassembling the republic of letters - a linked data approach. In: Mäkelä, E., Tolonen, M., Tuominen, J. (eds.) Proceedings of the Digital Humanities in the Nordic Countries 3rd Conference (DHN 2018), pp. 76–88. CEUR Workshop Proceedings (2018)

Creative Data Ontology: 'Russian Doll' Metadata Versioning in Film and TV Post-Production Workflows

Christos A. Dexiades[(✉)] and Claude P. R. Heath

Royal Holloway, University of London, Egham TW20 0EX, UK
`Christos.Dexiades.2015@live.rhul.ac.uk`, `Claude.Heath@rhul.ac.uk`

Abstract. A 'Russian doll' is a decorative painted hollow wooden figure that can be contained in a larger figure of the same sort, which can, in turn, be contained in another figure, and this can be repeated as many times as needed. This paper describes the development of an OWL-based ontology designed for metadata versioning in the media post-production industry. This has been implemented using the same Russian doll principle: of a 'record' being able to "wrap" (or contain) another record, one which relates to the versioning of that metadata, repeated as often as needed. Our ontology for metadata used in the media industry distinguishes itself from others by addressing the full range of post-production processes, rather than the archiving of a finished product. The ontology has been developed using metadata fields provided by high profile UK-based post-production companies, informed by ethnographic and co-design work carried out with them. This is the basis for a prototype metadata management tool for use in both media post-production and on media productions. We present central design principles emerging from our collaborative research, and describe the process of co-developing this ontology with our partners.

Keywords: Creative metadata ontologies · Post-production workflows · Film & tv media

1 Introduction

The Creative Data team was formed as part of the StoryFutures research project to respond to the need, expressed by our post-production media industry partners, for a unified approach to how metadata is handled in the sector. The aim of Creative Data research is to stimulate and support innovation while providing a common approach where none currently exists, thus addressing the difficulties created by mishandling and loss of the metadata that is crucial to successful and

This research has been supported by AHRC project StoryFutures, part of the The Creative Industries Clusters Programme funded by UK Industrial Strategy. Website: https://www.storyfutures.com.

E. Garoufallou and M.-A. Ovalle-Perandones (Eds.): MTSR 2020, CCIS 1355, pp. 204–215, 2021.
https://doi.org/10.1007/978-3-030-71903-6_20

efficient post-production of media projects. The particular contribution of the ontology we describe in this paper is to handle dynamic changes to metadata - to feed into the Creative Data vision for an open access metadata management solution encompassing the numerous permutations enacted on metadata, during both the media production process and also the post-production of this media into a finished product.

The Creative Data team includes world-leading post-production industry partners based in the UK. Our collective aim is to create a new open source digital tool addressing technical and industry issues that currently inhibit metadata persistence, accuracy and reliability. Creative Data has documented the industry 'pain points' concerned with metadata, which add significant time, cost, and difficulty to post-production workflows. There is currently a great deal of disruptive technical and business remodelling taking place in the industry - also a window of opportunity for new approaches such as ours to be adopted. It therefore has become increasingly important that the provenance and reliability of metadata can be guaranteed to practitioners in all areas of the industry.

The handover of creative data, including metadata, from the production to post-production company, is carried out either physically or digitally, and occurs at different stages of a project's production cycle. In an ideal scenario, data should be ingested into the systems of a post-production company in such a way that metadata is reliably stored, and is made accessible to those tasked to process it - with the aim of delivering the finished product back to the client in a timely fashion. However, in current practice, metadata often becomes separated from the source media itself, and what is therefore sought is a means of linking records of metadata on a centralised database, using what we have called the 'Russian doll' data design principle:

A record should be able to 'wrap' or contain another record relating to the versioning of that metadata.

While post-production practitioners rightly pride themselves on being trusted to untangle metadata issues, and to deliver to schedule, there are a range of obstacles that frequently have to be overcome by practitioners in order to do this, and a number of these are described in more detail in Sect. 4.1.

Practitioners generally extract and read metadata off from media files, and perform a variety of specialised searches and queries in order to compile and sort through the available information. There are often situations where documents and databases consulted do not conform to expected standards or have not been updated - resulting in metadata mismatches. Missing pieces of information sometimes have to be reverse engineered from snippets of other information available where guidance from production-side is unobtainable. There is currently no single point of reference across the industry for post-production pipelines to access metadata.

Practitioners are required to handle vast quantities of creative data appearing in a bewildering variety. This includes essential "hard" technical metadata: concerning camera lens type, make, serial number, focal length, roll number, exposures, duration of clip, frame-rates, and so on. The 'ingest' of data also includes equally important "soft" metadata (a term used by a post-production partner). This relates to creative content: 'Slate' (the clapper board with chalked information concerning takes, shots, roll numbers and so on), reference photographs of sets and costumes, notes of camera positions, GPS, annotated scripts, shoot schedules, call sheets, character descriptions, editorial selections and decisions, handwritten notes from camera crews and script supervisors, and other tags and annotations associated with the media files - but not currently travelling with them. These types of metadata are key to supporting both the creative and the technical post-production processes - and have been made and added to audio-visual data captured on set or location (added by humans but also increasingly by machine learning).

Compounding the lack of a single point of reference for metadata is the absence of a common vocabulary across the industry - very often there are different terms being used for the same data elements. This applies equally to "hard" and "soft" metadata. The Creative Data team has therefore gathered from our partners an extensive set of metadata fields deemed to be common across the industry, upon which it is possible to build a common vocabulary (concept ontology) to help fashion suitable tooling to support centralised and universal access to metadata.

2 Related Work

When reviewing the literature in the area of ontologies for film and TV production, we elicited information from the perspective of researching previous work on ontology-based solutions for the media industry, focusing on those that manage metadata during all stages of the production process.

COMM is a core ontology for annotating multimedia in order to explain the composition of media objects and what its parts represent by using DOLCE as a foundation ontology [5]. Loculus is a metadata wrapper for managing, distributing, and reusing motion pictures. The Loculus schema enables information about an artifact from different stages of the production process to be encapsulated together [11]. The Creative Works Ontology is similar in that it is used to capture relationships between creative works and other relevant entities, initially focusing on film and television. Each work has metadata assigned to it such as awards nominated for or won and information about a specific release [7]. Although metadata from the various stages of the workflow are present in Loculus, this metadata is attached to a final product rather than being available for use during each stage of the production process. Similarly, COMM and the Creative Works Ontology does not focus on the production process but instead annotates the finished product to describe its features or attributes.

OntoFilm is a core ontology that conceptualises the domain of film production and its accompanying workflows using Semantic Web Rule Language (SWRL). It was developed in consultation with industry professionals after collaborative meetings confirming the need for a common ontological framework to bridge the semantic gap between pre-production concepts and post-production metadata [6]. The Deep Film Access Project (DFAP) also researched the role of semantic technology in film production, focusing on how it could contribute to the integration of the data and metadata generated during the production life-cycle. Later versions of the DFAP ontology uses COMM and contains a remodelled version of Loculus for multimedia, foundational, and film production terminology [8]. Although OntoFilm and DFAP does connect metadata to each stage of the production workflow, it focuses solely on film production and, in the case of OntoFilm, aims to incorporate gaming animation production into future work. However, in addition to film production, the Creative Data team place a an emphasis on addressing VFX, immersive and unscripted television workflows (see Sect. 4.2). This aims to support practitioners in the widest possible range of creative industry post-production scenarios.

3   Objectives

As described above, the aim of the Creative Data research is to revise how metadata is loaded, tracked, shared and used in the media industry - by developing a cloud-based database solution, to standardise the handling of metadata, and increase its reliability and assurance on its provenance. Our open-source approach to this problem will allow businesses to then create bespoke tooling on top of this open-source kernel. The preferred technology for the tool was identified as context-aware database design (for more information about the 'Context Broker' API, see [2]) and the metadata ontology described in the following sections. The creation of bespoke tools and sub-tools is already a common practice within this industry. The specific objectives for the tool can be summarised in three design principles which were carried forward into our subsequent tool development work:

1. **Log metadata against project data**: Unique identifiers can potentially link media-files to a complete history of any given data-item and its versions, including any associated metadata. This can be stored in and accessed via the cloud. This will be a fundamental reorientation of how metadata is referenced, ending the industry's previous dependence on metadata that travels with but is not intrinsically linked into the production data itself.
2. **Track all of the technical amendments across a given project**: Unique identifiers can be used to follow the progress of data through its many versions, establishing whether metadata has been altered or omitted.
3. **Support a common vocabulary**: The industry employs many new specialist terminologies, as well as degree of legacy language. Without a common vocabulary, this terminology will continue to be a source of misunderstanding about metadata, causing further confusion and creating financial cost.

4   Methodology

The Creative Data Semantic Model (or Concept Ontology) was formed as part of a scoping exercise with our partners, over a period of time. It seeks to rationalise the various concepts and terms currently employed in the field, many of which have overlapping meanings and can cause misunderstandings across disciplinary boundaries. The model supports a common vocabulary by providing a prioritised set of post-production concepts for our database tool, using a sample set of metadata fields. These were identified by our partners as essential for supporting the use cases given in Sect. 4.2. It is important to mention here that the sharing of these fields represents a significant first step towards the more integrated approach sought by the Creative Data team described in the Introduction. Notably, the original set of fields numbered several thousand, reflecting the complexity of the many workflows. However, for the purposes of creating an initial prototype the partners identified a smaller and key subset of fields (numbering approximately 350 fields), which were used as a building block during the development of the first iteration of the digital tool. This is referred to here as the sub-ontology - feedback from our partners upon this sub-ontology is constantly fed into the main and full ontology with its many more classes. Detailed information about the sub-ontology is available at: http://cs.rhul.ac.uk/home/zcva113/mtsr2020.

Segments of the sub-ontology are also shown in Figs. 1, 2, 3 and 4. It is worth noting that the full ontology has a wide reach, encompassing metadata fields used not only in VFX, but also for immersive media projects in VR and AR.

After the initial scoping of the sub-ontology, work began by defining it with the Protégé ontology editing tool [4]. The sub-ontology could then be refined and visualised using the Cameo Concept Modeler plugin [1] for MagicDraw [3], taking advantage of it's extensive features. This methodology allowed us to use diagrammatic outputs, such as those shown in this paper, to gather feedback from our partners at different stages of the ethnographic research, and also during collaborative meetings where the requirements of our metadata management tool was specified. In this way, the veracity of the modelling was authenticated by domain experts, and the capturing of domain-specific information regarding several specialised areas of post-production was assured.

4.1 'Russian Doll' Metadata Versioning

Metadata versioning has been implemented in this project using principles that are analogous to Russian dolls. That is, a record should be able to 'wrap' or contain another record relating to the versioning of that metadata. The sub-ontology has two top-level classes aimed at linking metadata and connecting records that describe the transitions that metadata typically undergoes:

DataItems, Record

The former is an umbrella class for all entities in the ontology that can have metadata associated with it whilst the *Record* class encapsulates versioning metadata, including temporal details about a data item. Each instance of *Record* can be thought of as a record, tracking metadata adaptations of a *DataItems* instance which is, in turn, a record of a real-world entity.

To enable metadata versioning, every instance of *DataItems* and its sub-classes should have an instance of *Record* assigned to it upon creation, using the object properties *dataItemHasRecord* and *recordIsAboutDataItem*. Instances of *Record* have a creation date, which is implemented through the *recordCreatedOn* data property. This schema is shown in Fig. 1.

Fig. 1. Segment diagram of the creative data semantic model (sub-ontology), showing the implementation of metadata versioning.

Table 1. Table of ontology components for the implementation of metadata versioning.

Entity name	Description
DataItems	Represents any entity that has metadata associated with it
Record	Encapsulates versioning metadata about an entity
recordIsAboutDataItem	Links a record and the data item it is about
dataItemHasRecord	The inverse of *recordIsAboutDataItem*
hasRecordVersion	Links two versions of an entity record together to keep track of changes in metadata

When the metadata of a *DataItems* instance is changed, a copy of that instance of *DataItems* is made with the metadata adjustments applied and a new *Record* instance is also created for the new *DataItems* instance. These are again connected using the *dataItemHasRecord* and *recordIsAboutDataItem* properties. The two instances of *Record* - the original and the updated - are connected using the symmetric object property *hasRecordVersion* (See Table 1).

4.2   Use Cases, and Their Supporting Ontology Features

Below we provide details on how the semantic model described in the previous section has been applied to three Use Cases - these have been identified by our partners as being representative of key metadata generation and metadata sharing practices in the industry. 'Pain-points' associated with these use-cases are also described using quotes from our ethnographic research.

Use Case 1: Television Post-production, Media Support

Media support operatives prepare the data received from production clients, ready for use in the later stages of post-production - for edit support, where media files are aligned into 'sync maps', which can then edited by a team of creatives (sound, colour, and picture editors). Workflows in media support begin with accepting media from the in-house librarian and sending "tech receipts" to clients - containing a hard drive snapshot of the contents of the drives delivered. The operative then makes a copy of this data, conforms it according to the desired format and finally ingests it into the workflow.

Pain points in the media support role centre on the absence of key metadata required for data ingestion and for the workflows. For various reasons, the required input from production teams is omitted or made in error. In the current state of affairs, fixing this requires a great deal of "back and forth" communications between post-production and production, taking up the time of media support: "a lot of people [on the production side] don't understand why we need roll numbers for example", says one practitioner, and so "there's a lot of feedback looping, a lot of people involved in getting media set up properly."

Ontology representation: The *Asset* class has the following three subclasses - *Email*, *EmailReceipt* and *HardDriveSnapshot* - to allow communications and email receipts sent to the client to be represented in the ontology. Like instances of other subclasses of *Asset*, all instances of these subclasses are also assigned to an instance of *File*, which encapsulates the metadata that describes how an asset is stored on the file system. They can also be linked to an instance of the *Client* class to indicate who it has been sent to. This is shown in Figure 2. When ingesting data, a new instance of a subclass of *Asset* - typically *Clip* - is created and the values of its data type properties are entered either automatically (by importing the existing metadata) or manually. Importantly, this supports practitioners by enabling them to keep track of communications with clients in relation to a production and thereby creating a contact log.

Use Case 2: Television Post-production, Descriptive Logging

Unscripted and documentary content requires the addition of descriptive tags to the unedited footage, in order to be able to find and edit content in vast collections of data captured on camera 'rigs' set up on locations. This process is referred to as 'live logging' because it involves logs written by people trained by the post-house. These loggers write annotations into a bespoke timestamped tool. The aim is to record the relevant facts of a given capture, as to what the footage depicts. The post-production staff and editors are then able to search for, recover and create edits with specific content. The proposed tool allows users to carry through the descriptive metadata added by logging, so that this metadata can be accessed at any time during post-production, on the project timeline and database. Unlike the existing workflow, no exports of metadata selection are needed. The edit producer can search, read, create and send a list of clips and timecodes

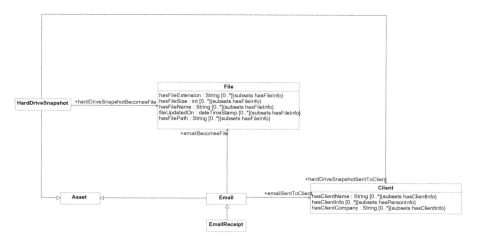

Fig. 2. Use Case 1: Segment diagram of the creative data semantic model (sub-ontology) showing the implementation of client email and receipt tracking.

within these clips, derived from the search from the descriptive metadata, to an editor.

Pain points for this use case are connected with the lack of persistence of metadata across post-production re-edits, for example, when descriptive logs are lost after a near-final edit has been made. Hence, if and when a creative tweak to the final edit is needed, this requires the link to the descriptive logs to be painstakingly re-established.

Ontology representation: Each instance of *Clip* can have any number of instances of *LoggingTag* assigned to it to describe its contents. Each tag is given a name and type which would enable the user to search for and generate a list of clips that match these attributes. Each entry in this list would have details of the clip and the timecode associated with the tag that matched the search criteria. Multiple instances of the *LoggingTag* can have both the same name and be allocated to the same *Clip* so they are distinguished by their combination of *Clip* and timecode. This is shown in Figure 3. This supports practitioners by enabling them to quickly generate lists of clips and timecodes by tag, which allows them to efficiently find the content that they require later in the post-production stage and preventing such content from being lost.

Use Case 3: Visual Effects for Film and TV, On-Set Shoot Data

During the pre-production phase of a feature film, the production company may secure one or more vendors, to supply visual effects (VFX). This may involve the VFX company being on set to acquire the additional data

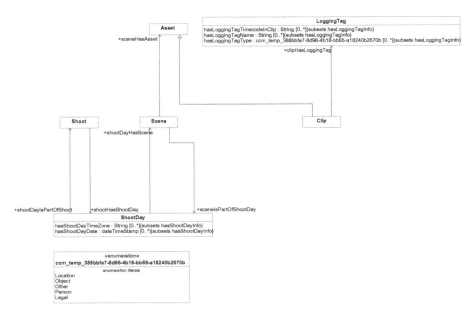

Fig. 3. Use Case 2: Segment diagram of the creative data semantic model (sub-ontology) showing the implementation of live logging.

and associated metadata required for VFX. This process is referred to as 'Shoot'. This metadata is then collated into an on-set VFX database, which must be organised in such a way that it can be passed on to the larger central data management database for users throughout the companies' internal VFX pipeline. The proposed tool allows data-organising activities to take place while still on-set, using laptops and other devices, respecting the data schema in use within businesses. The user utilises the unique IDs of metadata items, knowing that IDs are always updated with current information. After clean-up this data is made accessible to other areas of the VFX pipeline.

Pain points connected to this use case are similar to those in Use Case 1 regarding the absence of key metadata. An ingest practitioner stated: "We troubleshoot a lot, with conversions, if something's wrong, they come to us first." In one example, it was said: "Well I had a producer once, and I asked them this, 'Can you ask them if these shots are anamorphic or spherical? At the moment, my screen is frozen, I can't see them'. And then, I had to say to them [as the question was not understood], 'It means squishy or non-squishy!'"

Ontology representation: Data types such as clips, 3D models, and reference materials are represented as subclasses of the *Asset* class. All instances of *Asset* are also assigned to an instance of *File*, which encapsulates the metadata that describes how an asset is stored on the file system.

These instances of *Asset*, and in turn the instances of *File*, are then associated with a *Shoot* by assigning them to a *Scene* which in turn belongs to a *Shoot*. This supports practitioners by connecting any given *Asset* to its associated metadata and also to the *Scene* and to the *Shoot* that it has originally come from. In the design of a metadata management tool, this feature of the sub-ontology improves the process whereby metadata of interest is located - often at later stages of post-production where finding or re-acquiring this information requires a great deal of back-and-forth communications.

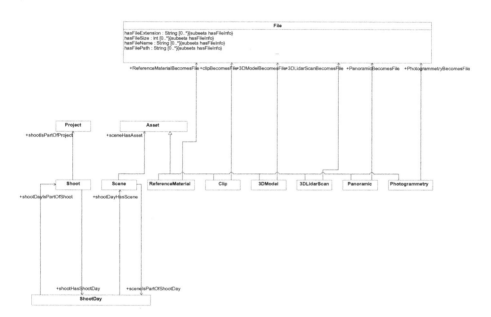

Fig. 4. Use Case 3: Segment diagram of the creative data semantic model (sub-ontology) showing the implementation of on-set VFX data management.

5 Discussion

Improving access to and correct understanding of metadata, and ensuring the persistence of metadata during the editing process, is the primary goal of implementing the Russian doll principle: that a *Record* should be able to 'wrap' or contain another *Record* relating to the versioning of that metadata. Our objective is to facilitate the communication channels needed to accomplish metadata coherence and consistency within workflows, by providing the underlying ontology and data model to support this.

Through metadata versioning, we can track the technical modifications across a project to identify when a data item has been modified and quickly trace where and when errors were introduced. The project data itself is represented as a file on a computer and each have an instance of the *File* class which identifies the file through its data type properties *hasFilePath* and *hasFileName*. Each instance of *File* can then be allocated to an instance of *Asset* or one of its subclasses, which have their own set of metadata fields and values where appropriate. This means we can link files stored on disk to its ontological representation and its associated metadata, including the metadata history.

While we have extended the metadata wrapping approach, as has been seen in Sect. 4.1, we acknowledge that the deliberately limited scope of the sub-ontology, which covers three specifically chosen use-cases, does leave a number of questions open as to how to scale our approach. However, our technology testing and prototyping work has highlighted the potential for ontology-based solutions for metadata management in post-production. We have identified three main goals for our tool and have successfully developed a limited-scope prototype for a semantic model that could be used to achieve these overarching goals. As our prototyping work continues, we can observe that media metadata is itself wrapped in a larger 'universe' of metadata, a wider ecology of metadata sharing [9,10]. We may anticipate that our technical and design principles, including those of metadata versioning shown in Fig. 1, can be made to transfer to other fields and domains beyond that of production and post-production.

6   Conclusion

Unlike other media ontologies, the Creative Data Semantic Model has the capacity to manage the ebb and flow of metadata changes across film, unscripted television production, and VFX. As the media industry continues to reshape itself it is essential that the provenance and reliability of metadata can be guaranteed across workflows, and that this can also be addressed in new workflows.

In future work, Creative Data will extend the data management tool, using the sub-ontology to manage metadata about digital assets in production, ensuring consistency and correctness is applied to creative content in the selected scenarios. This can then be merged with the full ontology of the entire range of metadata fields, integrating this with the data management tool. Other avenues of research include: 1. New efficiencies in workflow designs; 2. New services relating to metadata usage to be conceived and delivered; 3. Show clients the knock-on effects of creative and technical decisions made early-on; 4. Training resources built on ontologies; 5. Venn diagram generators visualising the ontology and metadata - the latter two being especially under-researched areas.

References

1. Cameo concept modeler. https://www.nomagic.com/product-addons/magicdraw-addons/cameo-concept-modeler-plugin, cATIA No Magic
2. Context broker Api walkthrough. https://fiware-orion.readthedocs.io/en/master, fiware-Orion

3. Magicdraw. https://www.nomagic.com/products/magicdraw, cATIA No Magic
4. Protégé (5.5.0), stanford University (2019). https://protege.stanford.edu
5. Arndt, R., Troncy, R., Staab, S., Hardman, L.: COMM: a core ontology for multimedia annotation. In: Staab, S., Studer, R. (eds.) Handbook on Ontologies. IHIS, pp. 403–421. Springer, Heidelberg (2009). https://doi.org/10.1007/978-3-540-92673-3_18
6. Chakravarthy, A., Beales, R., Matskanis, N., Yang, X.: Ontofilm: a core ontology for film production. In: Chua, T.S., Kompatsiaris, Y., Mérialdo, B., Haas, W., Thallinger, G., Bailer, W. (eds.) Semantic Multimedia, pp. 177–181. Springer, Berlin Heidelberg (2009)
7. Inc., M.P.L.: Seeinga creative works ontology for the film and television industry (2018). https://movielabs.com/creative-works-ontology
8. Lehmann, J., Atkinson, S., Evans, R.: Applying semantic technology to film production. In: Gandon, F., Guéret, C., Villata, S., Breslin, J., Faron-Zucker, C., Zimmermann, A. (eds.) ESWC 2015. LNCS, vol. 9341, pp. 445–453. Springer, Cham (2015). https://doi.org/10.1007/978-3-319-25639-9_55
9. Riley, J.: Seeing standards: a visualization of the metadata universe (2009). http://jennriley.com/metadatamap
10. Riley, J.: Understanding Metadata: What is Metadata, and What is it For?: A Primer. NISO, Baltimore (2017)
11. (Tinni), S.C., Pham, B., Smith, R., Higgs, P.: Loculus: a metadata wrapper for digital motion pictures. In: Proceedings of the Eleventh IASTED International Conference on Internet and Multimedia Systems and Applications (IMSA 2007), pp. 151–156, ACTA Press, USA (2007)

Machine Learning Models Applied to Weather Series Analysis

Francesca Fallucchi[1](✉) ⓘ, Riccardo Scano[2](✉) ⓘ,
and Ernesto William De Luca[1](✉) ⓘ

[1] Guglielmo Marconi University, 00193 Rome, Italy
f.fallucchi@unimarconi.it
[2] Council for Agricultural Research and Economics, 00198 Rome, Italy

Abstract. In recent years the explosion in high-performance computing systems and high-capacity storage has led to an exponential increase in the amount of information, generating the phenomenon of big data and the development of automatic processing models like machine learning analysis. In this paper a machine learning time series analysis was experimentally developed in relation to the paroxysmal meteorological event "cloudburst" characterized by a very intense storm, concentrated in a few hours and highly localized. These extreme phenomena such as hail, overflows and sudden floods are found in both urban and rural areas. The predictability over time of these phenomena is very short and depends on the event considered, therefore it is useful to add data driven methods to the deterministic modeling tools to get the anticipated predictability of the event, also known as nowcasting. The detailed knowledge of these phenomena, together with the development of simulation models for the propagation of cloudbursts, can be a useful tool for monitoring and mitigating risk in civil protection contingency plans.

Keywords: Machine learning · Nowcasting · Cloudburst

1 Introduction

In this paper regression models were applied to a meteorological time series with the aim of identifying a physical correlation that could possibly be integrated into a nowcasting system [27]. The volume and "speed" of the data used in this study are characteristic of the big data domain [4], whose analysis requires massive processing models provided by machine learning.

In particular the rain data collected at the Manziana weather station north of Rome was analyzed with the aim of identifying a possible correlation between the event of extreme rain and the monitored meteorological quantities (temperature, humidity, pressure) [19]. These meteorological measures have characterized the minutes just before the phenomenon of the rainstorm, assuming that they were the "trigger" of the phenomenon itself. A rainstorm is defined as serious if the intensity is 80–100 mm per hour, with durations of about ten minutes. Unfortunately it is very difficult to establish the point where rainstorms occur because they are very concentrated and sometimes there

© Springer Nature Switzerland AG 2021
E. Garoufallou and M.-A. Ovalle-Perandones (Eds.): MTSR 2020, CCIS 1355, pp. 216–227, 2021.
https://doi.org/10.1007/978-3-030-71903-6_21

are no detection tools in the points where the intensities are maximum [2]. The rains of the storms instead have longer durations and are more extensive, therefore better measurable.

Current monitoring systems are doppler radars, multispectral satellites and ground stations that measure physical quantities directly. As a result, there are large amounts of meteorological data observed available for forecasting models, including for example the Nation Oceanic and Atmospheric Administration (NOAA) which is reaching 100 TB per day. The main current forecasting approach for these phenomena is based on applications that make use of the information obtained from the weather-radar network which detects the movement of storms in real time [19, 20].

Specifically, the weather radar is an instrument designed for the detection of atmospheric precipitation carried out by means of a rotating antenna that sends a pulse signal in the microwave band. The presence of raindrops along the signal path generates a change in reflectivity which is detected by the antenna itself and from which an estimate of the intensity of precipitation can be obtained.

The data thus recorded (on average every 10 min) are used to create georeferenced maps of reflectivity and therefore of intensity of precipitation with a resolution of about 1 km and with greater reliability than other detection systems (satellites and ground stations).

Nowday available tools, capable of explicitly simulating the non-hydrostatic dynamics of convective phenomena, are aimed at large-scale and medium-long time atmospheric forecasting (cf. European Center for Medium-Range Weather Forecasts - ECMWF) [19]. The classic numerical models produce long-term forecasts of 1 to 10 days and for large areas of about 5 km.

On the other hand, nowcasting is oriented towards high resolution (1 km × 1 km) and short-term (max 1 h) forecasts, therefore usable for immediate emergency decisions in response to extreme phenomena. Due to climate changes and orographic reasons [3], the consequent flash floods can take on a particularly violent character being triggered by rainfall which in a few hours reaches cumulative values above 500 mm, thus increasing the level of risk.

In order to improve the tools for forecasting extreme weather events, such as heavy rainfall, ensemble forecasting systems have been developing for some years to be used in parallel with classic systems with limited area [5, 9]. These high resolution models are able to provide a probabilistic forecast of the state of the atmosphere on a small scale by simulating the convective phenomena with a horizontal resolution of about 1.5 to 2.2 km. The forecasting ability of these phenomena is very short and depends on the event considered, it is therefore necessary to combine data driven modeling tools with physical methods that allow to simulate the event with greater precision [2, 5]. In general the use of different data sources could allow a level of reliability of the warning system, for example the social media analysis with NLP methods and information extraction could improve strategies of disaster management, but in this case the time scale would be of the order of days [10].

2 Related Works

The evolution of high-performance computing systems has enabled the development of machine learning based on big data [Changhyun C. et al. 2018] especially with meteorological data as explanatory variables [Dueben P. et al. 2018][Abrahamsen E. B. et al. 2018]. By learning the models' strengths and weaknesses [17], the climate community is starting to adopt AI algorithms as a way to help improve forecasts, but some researchers don't rely on these 'black boxes' deep-learning systems to forecast imminent weather emergencies such as floods. Nevertheless some AI algorithms are proving useful for weather forecasting, indeed in 2016 researchers reported the first use of a deep-learning system to identify weather fronts showing that the algorithm could replicate human expertise [Liu, Y. et al. 2016]. After 2016 test, computer scientists have incorporated an AI algorithm into the weather service's hail forecasts. [McGovern, A. et al. Bull, 2017]. Machine learning techniques have demonstrated promising results for forecasting chaotic systems purely from past time series measurements of system state variables (training data) without prior knowledge of the system dynamics, filling the gaps in underlying mechanistic knowledge [Pathak J. et al. 2018]. The prediction of extreme weather events depends on the formulation and analysis of complex dynamical systems characterized by high intrinsic dimensionality of the underlying attractor to which are not applicable the classical order-reduction methods through projection of the governing equations. Alternatively, data-driven techniques aim to quantify the dynamics of specific critical modes. [Wan Z. et al. 2018][Sebastian Scher et al. 2016]. The occurrence of natural disasters such as floods and cloudbursts is increasing due to the climate change, moreover the damage is becoming larger and larger due to the rapid urbanization over the world [Gozzini B, 2017]. By using big data and the machine learning model to predict the occurrence of heavy rain damage, it's possible greatly reduce the damage through proactive disaster management [Changhyun C. et al. 2018]. High-resolution nowcasting for extreme weather is an essential tool needed for effective adaptation to climate change and in particular deep learning techniques have shown dramatic promise in high-resolution (1 km × 1 km) short-term (1 h) predictions of precipitation [Agrawal S., Hicdkey J., Xingjian S. et al. 2019]. Lastly, to be able to model a trigger of geospatially localized natural adverse events, is also useful to implement an ontology interoperable disaster risk reduction system (DRR) and to organize an Emergency Response System (ERS) [1, 8, 16, 21].

3 Theoretical Background

The machine learning analysis [18] developed in this work makes extensive use of fundamental mathematical models [22, 24, 26] and the statistical theories supporting data analysis [6, 7, 13].

In general a machine learning method assigns an x point (feature) of a R_k space to an y point (pattern) of another R_h space. The features are usually numerical vectors while the patterns are labels, sortable or non-sortable, appropriately coded with real numbers. The supervised approach requires that the algorithm receives sample reports (training set) before the test.

Classification is a supervised method for assigning data (x_n, y_n) to predefined classes through the likelihood function with which it is possible to classify the n data by separating them linearly through a hyperplane.

In general in a set of points of the n-dimensional space, the classifier is a subspace of dimension $n - 1$, obtained by applying a projection function P from the space with k dimensions to one $k + h$ dimensions, where the additional dimensions h are the weights that reassign the labels of the training set $(P(x_k), y_k)$ in order to make the points of the plane separable.

A binary classifier is the Naive Bayes classifier able to decide whether the binary hypothesis $y = (1,0)$ is much probable for a vector of features (x) observed by applying the Bayes theorem:

$$p(y|x) = p(x|y)\,p(y)\,/\,p(x) \tag{1}$$

where $p(y)$ is the prior probability of hypothesis y, while the likelihood $p(x|y)$ is estimated from a training set.

The data driven algorithms and techniques used in this analysis have the aim of modeling time series problem starting from the data sampling (x, y) of the physical process itself. The inductive model used here is part of the general techniques commonly designated with the term of soft computing that find application in the treatment and processing of uncertain or incomplete information [12, 13, 25].

In particular the supervised machine learning process was divided into the following analysis phases:

- pre-processing of the categorized (labeled) data has been carried out through normalization, smoothing (rounding and cleaning), reduction of dimensionality (selection of specific main attributes) and finally the choice of the algorithm parameters such as threshold values and cross-validation in which the parts of the training set are recombined for the next training;
- division of the data into two sets with which is performed the training and test algorithm model, verifying its predictive capacity by comparing the output with the real data (see Fig. 1).

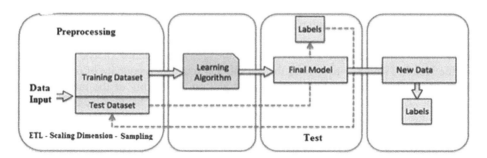

Fig. 1. Supervised machine learning algorithm.

The model's performance was determined with the use of the RSME (root mean square error), the accuracy measurement ((VP + VN) / (P + N)) and with the confusion matrix in which the four classification results are identified in true positives (VP), false positives (FP), true negatives (VN) and false negatives (FN).

On the other hand the adoption of the artificial neural networks (RNA) mathematical model to find relationships between the data, would have been computationally expensive in terms of calculation time and sample size in particular for the training phase [14].

4   Methodology

The use of machine learning models for "physics-free" data driven meteorological forecasts in small-scale areas, have the advantage of being computationally economic and allow short-term forecasts for already trained inference models. Deep learning procedure was not adopted due to the small size of the selected dataset that would produce overfitting, which is a typical problem of low bias and high variance models implemented by tensorflow.

The analysis carried out here is theoretically based on the inferential model of the precipitation ($R_t^{lat,lon}$) conditional probability (P) at time t compared to each physical variable ($V_{t-1}^{lat,lon}$) (same latitude and longitude) measured at soil and with a retrograde temporal lag (t − 1), such as to be considered as a physical trigger factor of the rainstorm (r):

$$P\left(R_t^{lat,lon} > r \Big/ V_{t-1}^{lat,lon}\right) \tag{2}$$

The considerable amount of data would make the Bayesian approach too complex [14, 15] compared to the regression and classification models of the time series used here.

The pluviometric datasets refer to a tipping rain gauge with electronic correction of the values and to a thermo-hygrometer for temperature and humidity measurements, provided by the civil protection of the Lazio region, documented and of known information quality comparable over time and space.

The temporal coverage of the dataset used in this work refers to the range of years from 2015 to 2019 with an update frequency of 15 min. The 15th minute interval is bounded by the maximum radio transmission frequency of the weather station data.

The spatial coverage is punctual and refers to the "Manziana" weather station (see Fig. 2) which provided representative data for the area being analyzed. The choice of a specific weather station was mainly due on the theoretical prerequisite of the physical uniformity (omogeneus boundary conditions) and on the quality of the measurement equipment (99% data availability). Over the period considered, the average annual temperatures are of the order of 15 °C while the average annual precipitation is about 998 mm.

The rainiest period is concentrated between August and November when the Italy Tyrrhenian coasts are affected by intense storms. The rainfall dataset allows us to characterize the extreme events recognized as storms with the parameter of the cumulative rainfall over 15-min intervals. The indicators chosen for the analysis (station location,

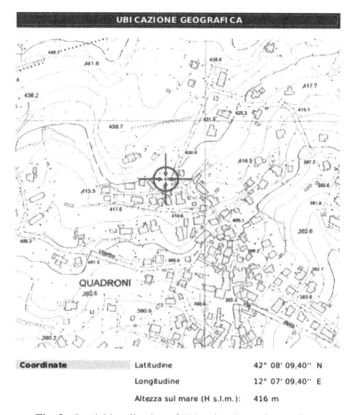

Fig. 2. Spatial localization of "Manziana" weather station.

precipitation, temperature, humidity, pressure and time interval) provide the necessary information on the meteorological phenomenon analyzed [23].

The time interval (2015–2019) was chosen to have the maximum continuity of the gapless series and considering the presence of various cloudburst phenomena due to global warming [3, 23], indeed the time span considered was marked by several paroxysmal meteorological events, characterized by high quantities of rain often concentrated over a day. The indicators were chosen to obtain a possible data-driven correlation between the parameters characterizing the physical phenomenon.

Conversely the possible limitations of the indicators are due to the limited number of years of the historical series and to the absence of a physical analysis of the same meteorological phenomenon [3, 5].

Below (see Fig. 3) there is the class diagram that represents the general preprocessing algorithm developed.

The above detailed algorithm consisting of:

– dataset reading and indexing;

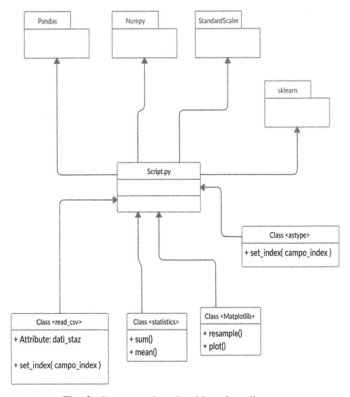

Fig. 3. Preprocessing algorithm class diagram.

- cleaning and normalization with the deletion of missing data (Null), incorrect or meaningless (Nan) for the forecast;
- conversion of variables in numeric (float) and date format;
- computation of average values for all variables over the entire time span;
- daily resample and scaling for plotting and visual verification of the variables trend;
- calculation of the scatter matrix (see Fig. 4) which provides the graphic distribution and the variables relationship;
- computation of the heatmap-type correlation matrix between the dataset variables (see Fig. 5), from which it is already clear the greatest correlation between precipitation and temperature.

The following flow diagram (see Fig. 6) represents the general algorithm of the entire processing scheme:

- backward translation of the series by a time step (15′) for the variables (temperature, pressure, humidity) whose correlation with the precipitation must be verified;

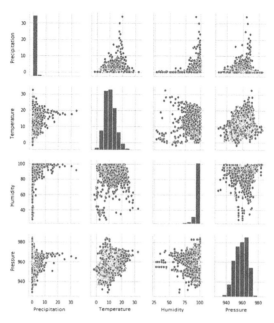

Fig. 4. Scatter matrix.

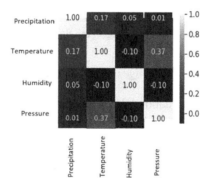

Fig. 5. Correlation matrix.

- regression path definition with the application of the linear and random forest cross-validation models (with 2 training sets and 1 test set (cv = 3)) and with the RSME (root mean squared error) as performance metric;
- RMSE computation for the null model: (average number of precipitation minus precipitation values), which must be major of the error obtained with the linear and random forest models;
- definition of the classification path by transforming the precipitation into a categorical variable {1,0} by calculating the percentage variation over a time step (precipitation

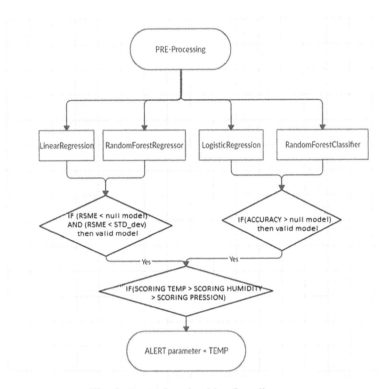

Fig. 6. Processing algorithm flow diagram.

percentage change greater than average percentage change produces true (1) otherwise false (0));
- Application of the cross-validation logistic and random forest classification model (with 2 training sets and 1 test set (cv = 3)) and with the accuracy as performance metric;
- calculation of the null model accuracy: average number of precipitation values classified as significant (greater than average percentage change) compared to the total (100%), which must be less than accuracy obtained with the logistic and random forest models.
- extraction from the historical series of the record corresponding to the maximum precipitation value, from which is obtained the temperature drop ($\Delta t = t_i - t_{i-15}'$) in the case of extreme precipitation event (mm max).

5   Results and Discussion

Three summary tables are reported (see Table 1, 2, 3) which represent the results obtained for each model (classification, regression) applied to the current case and the discriminating value for each corresponding metric (major accuracy for classification and minor RSME for regression).

Table 1. Correlation with precipitation.

Temperature	0.17
Pression	0.01
Humidity	0.05

Table 2. Correlation with precipitation.

Analysis type (response variable = Precipitation) (characteristic variables = Temperature, Humidity, Pression)

	Classification			Regression			
	ML model			ML model			
	Random forest	Logistic	Null	Random Forest	Linear	Null	Standard deviation
Accuracy	0.755	0.76501188	0.76501189				
RSME temperature				1.462	**1.395**	1.4114	1.4115
RSME humidity				1.407			
RSME pression				1.414			

Table 3. Temperature threshold (supposed as trigger meteorological value for the cloudburst).

	Precipitation (mm max cumulated in 15′)	Temperature
t_{i-1}	–	23.8
$t_i (= t_{i-1 +15'})$	34.0	19.6
Threshold (Δt)		−4.2

Therefore cross-validation model (logistic, random forest) of the classification path obtains accuracy values lower than null model. On the other hand, the linear model of the cross-validation regression path obtains RMSE error values lower than random forest model, null model and the simple standard deviation. Then from the comparison of the results obtained for the cross-validation linear regression model applied to each atmospheric parameter (temperature, humidity, pressure) temporally anticipated (15′), it is clear that the temperature is the variable that predicts the trend of the precipitation better than the others (lower RSME) and therefore also possible extreme phenomena such as cloudbursts. Moreover the temperature jump that anticipates the cloudburst event is obviously linked to the geomorphological characteristics of the analyzed area, but the correlation between the two physical variables, temperature jump and severe precipitation, can have a general validity.

6 Conclusions

In this paper meteorological time series analysis has been described, focusing in particular on the paroxysmal cloudburst weather event. Then data driven methods were implemented based on machine learning models to analyze the temporal propagation of the cloudburst. It has been experimentally verified that the data-driven approach, with the use of machine learning models, could improve the results of the forecast analysis of extreme meteorological phenomena, in particular when combined with traditional physical forecasting models [5, 9, 11].

Data Availability. Data used to support the findings of this study are available from the corresponding author upon request.

Conflicts of Interest. Authors declare that there are no conflicts of interest regarding the publication of this paper.

References

1. Simas, F., Barros, R., Salvador, L., Weber, M., Amorim, S.: A data exchange tool based on ontology for emergency response systems. In: Garoufallou, E., Virkus, S., Siatri, R., Koutsomiha, D. (eds.) MTSR 2017. CCIS, vol. 755, pp. 74–79. Springer, Cham (2017). https://doi.org/10.1007/978-3-319-70863-8_7
2. Li, J., Liu, L., Le Duy, T., Liu, J.: Accurate data-driven prediction does not mean high reproducibility. Nat. Mach. Intell. (2020). https://doi.org/10.1038/s42256-019-0140-2
3. Almanacco della Scienza CNR, n. 9 (2017)
4. Rezzani A.: Big Data. Maggioli editore (2013)
5. Wan, Z., Vlachas, P., Koumoutsakos, P., Sapis, T.: Data assisted reduced-order modeling of extreme events in complex dynamical systems. Plos One **13**, e0197704 (2018)
6. Ozdemir, S.: Data Science, Apogeo (2018)
7. Virkus, S., Garoufallou, E.: Data science from a perspective of computer science. In: Garoufallou, E., Fallucchi, F., William De Luca, E. (eds.) MTSR 2019. CCIS, vol. 1057, pp. 209–219. Springer, Cham (2019). https://doi.org/10.1007/978-3-030-36599-8_19
8. Zschocke, T., Villagrán de León, J.C., Beniest, J.: Enriching the description of learning resources on disaster risk reduction in the agricultural domain: an ontological approach. In: Sánchez-Alonso, S., Athanasiadis, Ioannis N. (eds.) MTSR 2010. CCIS, vol. 108, pp. 320–330. Springer, Heidelberg (2010). https://doi.org/10.1007/978-3-642-16552-8_29
9. Hosni, H., Vulpiani, A.: Forecasting in light of big data. Physics **31**, 557–569 (2017)
10. Gründer-Fahrer, S., Schlaf, A., Wustmann, S.: How social media text analysis can inform disaster management. In: Rehm, G., Declerck, T. (eds.) GSCL 2017. LNCS (LNAI), vol. 10713, pp. 199–207. Springer, Cham (2018). https://doi.org/10.1007/978-3-319-73706-5_17
11. Pathak, J., et al.: Hybrid forecasting of chaotic processes: using machine learning in conjunction with a knowledge-based model. American Institute of Physics (2018)
12. Mandrioli, D.: Paola Spoletini P.: Informatica Teorica. CittàStudi edizioni (2011)
13. Melucci, M.: Information retrieval. Franco Angeli (2013)
14. Russell, S., Norvig, P.: Intelligenza Artificiale, vol. 1-2. Pearson, London (2010)

15. Sipser, M.: Introduzione alla teoria della computazione, Maggioli Editore (2016)
16. Fallucchi, F., Tarquini, M., De Luca, E.W.: Knowledge management for the support of logistics during humanitarian assistance and disaster relief (HADR). In: Díaz, P., Bellamine Ben Saoud, N., Dugdale, J., Hanachi, C. (eds.) ISCRAM-med 2016. LNBIP, vol. 265, pp. 226–233. Springer, Cham (2016). https://doi.org/10.1007/978-3-319-47093-1_19
17. David, S., Hrubes, P., Moran, S., Shipilka, A., Yehudayoff, A.: Learnability can be undecidable. Nat. Mach. Intell. **1**, 44–48 (2019)
18. Raschka, S.: Machine Learning con Python. Apogeo (2015)
19. Libelli, S.M.: Modelli matematici per l'ecologia. Pitagora editrice (1989)
20. Banbura, M., Giannone, D., Modugno, M., Reichlin, L.: Now-casting and the real-time data flow. European central bank (2013)
21. Santos, L., Sicilia, M., Padrino, S.: Ontologies for emergency response: effect-based assessment as the main ontological commitment. MTSR, 93-104 (2011)
22. Comincioli, V.: Problemi e modelli matematici nelle scienze applicate. Casa editrice Ambrosiana (1993)
23. Report annuario dei dati ambientali. ISPRA (2017)
24. Cammarata, S.: Reti neuronali. Dal Perceptron alle reti caotiche e neurofuzzy. Etas Libri (1997)
25. Cusani, R., Inzerilli, T.: Teoria dell'Informazione e Codici. Ed. Ingegneria 2000 (2008)
26. Bergomi, M.G., Frosini, P., Giorgi, D., Quercioli, N.: Towards a topological geometrical theory of group equivariant non-expansive operators for data analysis and machine learning. Nat. Mach. Intell. **1**(9), 423–433 (2019)
27. Hickey, J.: Using machine learning to "Nowcast" precipitation in high resolution. Google AI Blog (2020)

EPIC: A Proposed Model
for Approaching Metadata Improvement

Hannah Tarver$^{(\boxtimes)}$ and Mark Edward Phillips

University of North Texas Libraries, Denton, TX, USA
{hannah.tarver,mark.phillips}@unt.edu

Abstract. This paper outlines iterative steps involved in metadata improvement within a digital library: Evaluate, Prioritize, Identify, and Correct (EPIC). The process involves evaluating metadata values system-wide to identify errors; prioritizing errors according to local criteria; identifying records containing a particular error; and correcting individual records to eliminate the error. Based on the experiences at the University of North Texas (UNT) Libraries, we propose that these cyclical steps can serve as a model for organizations that are planning and conducting metadata quality assessment.

Keywords: Metadata evaluation · Metadata quality · Processes

1 Background

The Digital Collections at the University of North Texas (UNT) Libraries comprise over 3 million records and represent more than fifteen years of digitization, web harvesting, and metadata activities. Publicly, users can access a wide range of materials – printed and handwritten text; photos and other images; large maps and technical drawings; audio/video recordings; physical objects; and other items – from three public interfaces: The Portal to Texas History (materials from partner institutions and collectors across the state), the UNT Digital Library (materials owned by UNT or created at the university), and the Gateway to Oklahoma History (materials from organizations in Oklahoma, managed by the Oklahoma Historical Society). Although many of the items have been digitized and described in-house, the Digital Collections also include items and metadata harvested from government databases, or provided by partner institutions; additionally, editors include a wide range of highly-trained specialists, trained students of various expertise, and volunteers who may have little-to-no experience.

Given the size and scope of the Digital Collections, we have conducted extensive quality-control and clean-up projects, as well as research related to methods of determining metadata quality system-wide (e.g., evaluating dates [9], overall change [10], and interconnectedness of values [7]). While there has been extensive research about metadata quality as a concept, most of it has focused on

© Springer Nature Switzerland AG 2021
E. Garoufallou and M.-A. Ovalle-Perandones (Eds.): MTSR 2020, CCIS 1355, pp. 228–233, 2021.
https://doi.org/10.1007/978-3-030-71903-6_22

frameworks and metrics for evaluating the quality of metadata in an individual record or in a larger collection; most notably the quality frameworks put forth by Moen et al. in 1998 [3], by Bruce and Hillmann in 2004 [1], and by Stvilia et al. in 2007 [8]. In each case, these papers outlined specific aspects of metadata quality – such as accuracy or completeness – and how these aspects ought to be defined as distinct and important when evaluating metadata records.

This case study outlines a model based on the experiences at UNT with practical metadata evaluation and correction, but has wide applications for other digital libraries. Rather than focusing on how to determine quality or the best methods of evaluation, the proposed model encompasses the overarching process of iterative metadata improvement, breaking assessment and mitigation into discrete steps in a replicable way.

2   EPIC Model

The model comprises four steps (EPIC): Evaluate (determine quality and identify errors), Prioritize (order errors according to resources and impact), Identify (connect an error to the affected record/s), and Correct (make appropriate changes to affected records and eliminate the error). These steps function as an ongoing, repeatable cycle (see Fig. 1).

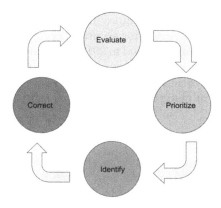

Fig. 1. Illustration of the EPIC model.

The first two steps – evaluate and prioritize – occur primarily at a system or aggregated collection level, to determine what errors or issues exist, and to make decisions about which problems should be corrected immediately. The third and fourth steps – identify and correct – refer to individual records as issues are remediated. Although this is a cyclical process, not all steps necessarily take the same amount of time, or happen with the same frequency.

2.1 Evaluate

The key component for assessment is to evaluate the existing level of quality in records and to identify areas that need improvement. Organizations may employ various processes, e.g., "Methods of conducting assessment can include focus groups, surveys, benchmarking, observational analyses, interviews, and methodologies that we borrow from other disciplines such as business" [4]. Ideally, this would cover a range of quality types – e.g., accuracy, accessibility, completeness, conformance to expectations, consistency, provenance, timeliness – as well as content and structural elements. Realistically, some aspects are more easily evaluated or verified than others. Many repositories rely on manually checking records [2] and some problems can *only* be found by looking at a record – e.g., mismatches between the item and record values. However, as a primary method of analysis, manual checks do not scale to large collections and require a significant time commitment. Additionally, manual checks may not be the best method to evaluate overall consistency within a collection(s); however usage of system-wide tools depends on the digital infrastructure an organization is using.

At UNT, we do not have to evaluate structural aspects of metadata (e.g., whether XML is well-formed) because validation happens as part of our upload processes. Similarly, we use the same fields and qualifiers for all records, so it is easy to validate the metadata format. For descriptive content, we use tools (called count, facet, and cluster) that are integrated directly into our system [6]. These are based on similar operations in command-line functions and in OpenRefine, to rearrange metadata values in ways that assist editors to identify records needing correction or review for accuracy, completeness, and consistency.

Before these tools were implemented in 2017, we used a Python-based program (metadata breakers [5]) to evaluate values after harvesting records via OAI-PMH. Other organizations also use the metadata breakers as well as tools based in various programming languages or made to evaluate metadata in spreadsheets [2].

2.2 Prioritize

System-wide, there are likely to be a large number of identified issues, ranging from relatively simple fixes that affect only a handful of records (e.g., typos), to larger issues across entire collections (e.g., legacy or imported values that do not align with current standards). A number of possible criteria may determine which issues are fixed immediately or addressed in the future, based on local needs. In our system, we place higher priority on values that directly affect public-facing functionality or search results – such as coverage places and content descriptions – versus fields that are less-frequently used, or not browseable (e.g., source or relation). Other criteria may include the amount of expertise or time required, number of records affected, available resources/editors, or information known about the materials. At UNT, determining the most useful criteria for prioritization is an ongoing process.

2.3   Identify

This step requires connection between values or attributes and unique identifiers for the relevant records. When we used tools outside of our system, one challenge was determining which records contained errors found during evaluation. Although we had unique identifiers and persistent links in the harvested records, an editor would have to track down every record from a list of identifiers for a particular error. This made the process complicated if an error occurred in a large number of records. Organizations that can export and reload corrected records may not have this problem; however, not all systems have this capability, which means that a specialized process may be necessary to coordinate between value analysis and affected records. Once our tools were integrated into the system, editors had a direct link between attributes and records, although we do have to manually edit individual records to change values.

2.4   Correct

The final step is to correct records identified with a particular issue. Although we encourage editors to change other, obvious errors that they might see in the records, the priority is on fixing specific issues rather than more comprehensive reviews. This process promotes relatively quick, precise editing system-wide, resulting in iterative improvements. With tool integration, any editor in our system may access the tools (e.g., for self-review) and managers can link to records containing an error – or to a tool with set criteria for multiple errors – to distribute review and corrections. Other organizations could choose to approach correction more comprehensively, or according to methods that work within their systems; the essential purpose of this step is to ensure that records are improved, even if further edits are needed.

3   EPIC as a Cycle

We have described metadata editing in stages, but we approach it as an ongoing cycle, where some stages take longer – or happen more often – than others. Higher-priority issues or small issues affecting few records may be fixed immediately while others are documented for later correction. Additionally, we add thousands of items every month and complete most records after ingest, so the possibility of new errors is a constant concern. Organizations that employ more rigorous review prior to upload or that add new materials less frequently, might evaluate and prioritize issues periodically, or on a schedule (e.g., annually, biannually, or quarterly).

Evaluation can also inform managers about the work of less-experienced students and mitigate problems related to individual editors. Additionally, we start with the premise that a metadata record is never "done," i.e., there may always be new information, updated formatting or preferred guidelines, or the identification of errors. Under this approach, a single record may be edited or "touched" many times and/or by many editors, but the overarching goal is always that metadata improves over time.

3.1 Benefits of EPIC

We use and suggest this approach for several reasons:

The Cycle Works at Scale. Iterative metadata editing works for collections of any size; but, importantly, it is functional even as a system gets extremely large, when it is more difficult to determine record quality and to direct resources. Evaluating quality at the system level ensures meaningful changes that can improve consistency, findability, and usability across large numbers of records, even when quality in individual records may remain less than ideal.

Individual Processes Allow for Planning. Although we are presenting this model as distinct steps in the cycle, in practical use some components may overlap or only occur occasionally – e.g., an editor evaluating records at a collection level may identify a small number of records containing a problem and correct them without "prioritizing." However, it is difficult to plan ongoing work that would be required for system-level issues affecting thousands of records without breaking down the components. Some problems are more systemic or less important than others and we need a way to discuss and determine the best approach – i.e., prioritization – as well as methods within each step that are most appropriate for a particular digital library or institution. The model also provides a way to contextualize the experiences and research within the metadata quality domain from various organizations.

Division of Labor. Fixing systemic problems requires a large number of people over time. By determining specific issues and documenting them – preferably with some level of priority – we can assign records to editors based on a number of criteria. For example, some errors are time consuming (e.g., they affect a large number of records) but are easy to correct without training or expertise by new editors, volunteers, or editors working outside their area. Other problems may affect fewer records but require familiarity with metadata or a subject area; those could be assigned to appropriate editors as time permits.

This has been particularly useful during the COVID-19 pandemic when we offered metadata editing tasks to library staff who could not perform their usual duties from home. Approximately 100 new editors were added to our system and assigned to metadata work with relatively little training. Those editors can make inroads on some of the simple, yet frequently-occurring problems (such as name formatting in imported records).

4   Conclusion

This proposed model explicates discrete steps in metadata improvement to disambiguate conversations around these activities. For example, discussions about how to evaluate metadata (or specific fields) is sometimes conflated with prioritization of issues or relative importance of individual fields. We have found these to be two distinct and equally important facets of metadata quality. Likewise, identifying records within a large collection that have a specific set of metadata characteristics can be challenging by itself, sometimes requiring specialized tools, indexing, or analysis separate from other components. Organizing planning activities and methods within individual steps provides additional context and more productive discourse. At UNT, we are continuing our research around metadata evaluation and prioritization of quality issues, and also plan work to test and apply the EPIC model in a more structured way. By presenting this model, we hope to encourage other researchers and practitioners to explore these components individually as they create tools, workflows, and documentation that supports metadata improvement.

References

1. Bruce, T.R., Hillmann, D.: The continuum of metadata quality: defining, expressing, exploiting. In: Hillmann, D., Westbroooks, E.L. (eds.) Metadata in Practice. ALA Editions, Chicago (2004). ISBN 9780838908822. https://ecommons.cornell.edu/handle/1813/7895
2. Gentry, S., Hale, M., Payant, A., Tarver, H., White, R., Wittmann, R.: Survey of benchmarks in metadata quality: initial findings (2020). https://digital.library.unt.edu/ark:/67531/metadc1637685/
3. Moen, W.E., Stewart, E.L., McClure, C.R.: Assessing metadata quality: findings and methodological considerations from an evaluation of the US Government Information Locator Service (GILS). In: Proceedings IEEE International Forum on Research and Technology Advances in Digital Libraries, pp. 246–255 (1998). https://doi.org/10.1109/ADL.1998.670425
4. Mugridge, R.L.: Assessment of cataloging and metadata services: introduction, pp. 435–437 (2017). https://doi.org/10.1080/01639374.2017.1362913
5. Phillips, M.E.: Metadata analysis at the command-line (2013). https://journal.code4lib.org/articles/7818
6. Phillips, M.E., Tarver, H.: Experiments in operationalizing metadata quality interfaces: a case study at the University of North Texas libraries, pp. 15–23 (2018). https://digital.library.unt.edu/ark:/67531/metadc1248352/
7. Phillips, M.E., Zavalina, O., Tarver, H.: Using metadata record graphs to understand digital library metadata, pp. 49–58 (2019). https://digital.library.unt.edu/ark:/67531/metadc1616551/
8. Stvilia, B., Gasser, L., Twidale, M.B., Smith, L.C.: A framework for information quality assessment. J. Am. Soc. Inf. Sci. Technol. **58**(12), 1720–1733 (2007)
9. Tarver, H., Phillips, M.E.: Lessons learned in implementing the extended date/time format in a large digital library, pp. 60–67 (2013). https://digital.library.unt.edu/ark:/67531/metadc174739
10. Tarver, H., Zavalina, O., Phillips, M.E., Alemneh, D.G., Shakeri, S.: How descriptive metadata changes in the UNT Libraries' collection: a case study, pp. 43–52 (2014). https://digital.library.unt.edu/ark:/67531/metadc406345/

Semantic Web Oriented Approaches for Smaller Communities in Publishing Findable Datasets

Nishad Thalhath[1] , Mitsuharu Nagamori[2] , Tetsuo Sakaguchi[2] ,
Deepa Kasaragod[3(✉)] , and Shigeo Sugimoto[2]

[1] Graduate School of Library, Information and Media Studies,
University of Tsukuba, Tsukuba, Japan
nishad@slis.tsukuba.ac.jp
[2] Faculty of Library, Information and Media Studies,
University of Tsukuba, Tsukuba, Japan
{nagamori,saka,sugimoto}@slis.tsukuba.ac.jp
[3] Department of Neurobiology, Graduate School of Biomedical and Health Sciences,
Hiroshima University, Hiroshima, Japan
deepa@hiroshima-u.ac.jp
https://www.slis.tsukuba.ac.jp

Abstract. Publishing findable datasets is a crucial step in data interoperability and reusability. Initiatives like Google data search and semantic web standards like Data Catalog Vocabulary (DCAT) and Schema.org provide mechanisms to expose datasets on the web and make them findable. Apart from these standards, it is also essential to optionally explain the datasets, both its structure and applications. Metadata application profiles are a suitable mechanism to ensure interoperability and improve use-cases for datasets. Standards and attempts, including the Profiles (PROF) and VoID vocabularies, as well as frameworks like Dublin core application profiles (DCAP), provide a better understanding of developing and publishing metadata application profiles. The major challenge for domain experts, especially smaller communities intending to publish findable data on the web, is the complexities in understanding and conforming to such standards. Mostly, these features are provided by complex data repository systems, which is not always a sustainable choice for various small groups and communities looking for self-publishing their datasets. This paper attempts to utilize these standards in self-publishing findable datasets through customizing minimal static web publishing tools and demonstrating the possibilities to encourage smaller communities to adopt cost-effective and simple dataset publishing. The authors express this idea though this work-in-progress paper with the notion that such simple tools will help small communities to publish findable datasets and thus, gain more reach and acceptance for their data. From the perspective of the semantic web, such tools will improve the number of linkable datasets as well as promote the fundamental concepts of the decentralized web.

Keywords: Metadata · Data publishing · Datasets · Findable datasets · Static publishing · Semantic web

© Springer Nature Switzerland AG 2021
E. Garoufallou and M.-A. Ovalle-Perandones (Eds.): MTSR 2020, CCIS 1355, pp. 234–242, 2021.
https://doi.org/10.1007/978-3-030-71903-6_23

1   Introduction

1.1   Significance of Publishing Findable Datasets

Good data management practices are a prerequisite in any research or scientific quest for finding new knowledge or reusing existing knowledge. This is of significant importance to various data stakeholders including academia, industry, government agencies, funding bodies, journal publishers. Interoperability and reusability of data allows for transparency, reproducibility and extensibility of the data and hence the scientific knowledge.

One of the underlying guidelines for data management that ensures data findability is the FAIR principle [17]: —Findability, Accessibility, Interoperability, and Reusability formulated by FORCE11 – The Future of Research Communications and e-Scholarship. FAIR principles are not protocols or standards but are underlying guidelines that relies on data/metadata standards to allow for data to be reused by machines and humans [8].

The data citation principles from Data Citation Synthesis Group: Joint Declaration of Data Citation Principles by FORCE11 highlights the necessity of creating citation practices that are both human understandable and machine-actionable [5]. A recent trend of clear emerging consensus to support the best data archiving and citation policies with different stakeholders interest in view and comprising the privacy, legal and ethical implications has been seen [4]. The life sciences community are also warming up to idea of the need for better metadata practices in terms of annotating the experiments; for example, the information accompanying the nucleic acid sequencing data [13].

1.2   Standards in Defining Datasets

Dublin Core, Data Catalog Vocabulary(DCAT) [2], VOID -Vocabulary for Interlinked Data [9], schema.org[1], etc. are some of the standards and vocabularies for defining data/metadata. These are based on FAIR principles and ensure data longevity and stewardship. W3C's DCAT is an resource description file (RDF) vocabulary for data catalogs. It is based on six main classes and is designed to facilitate interoperability between data catalogs published on the Web. Dublin Core[TM] Metadata Element (Dublin Core) and additional vocabularies referred to as "DCMI metadata terms" from Dublin Core[TM] Metadata Initiative (DCMI) is described for use in RDF vocabularies for making data linkable[2]. The heterogeneity of metadata standards required across different dataset maintenance combining the Dublin Core vocabularies and SKOS vocabularies is addressed by DCAT. VOID is complementary to the DCAT model, uses RDF based schema for describing metadata. Schema.org provides framework to provide supporting information descriptions of data which makes data discovery easier through services like Google Dataset Search engine [15].

---

[1] https://schema.org/.

[2] https://www.dublincore.org/specifications/dublin-core/dcmi-terms/.

1.3   Explaining the Data

Metadata application profiles (MAP) provide a means to express the schema customising the metadata instance by documenting the elements, policies, guidelines, and vocabularies for that particular implementation along with the schemas, and applicable constraints [6] including specific syntax guidelines and data format, domain consensus and alignment [1,7].

Data profiles are profiles that express the structure and organization data sources like CSV and JSON. Frictionless data DataPackage [16] is another example of data profiles which provides JSON schemas mostly on tabular data. Although CSVW is used in expressing data profiles of tabular data, it is more suitable in explaining linkable data from tabular data resources [14].

Profiles vocabulary [3] is an RDF vocabulary to semantically link datasets with the related profiles. Profile resources may be human-readable documents (PDFs, textual documents) or machine-actionable formats (RDF, OWL, JSON, JSON-LD), constraint language resources used by specific validation tools (SHACL, ShEx), or any other files that define specific roles within profiles.

1.4   Challenges for Smaller Communities

The major challenge for domain experts in smaller communities say researchers in small labs or data journalists, intending to publish findable data on the web, is the complexities in understanding and conforming data publishing standards. Mostly, these features are provided by complex data repository systems, which is not always a sustainable choice for various small groups and communities looking for self-publishing their datasets [12].

This is a work in progress paper which aims to incorporate FAIR based concepts into a minimal and sustainable digital publishing platform for data from smaller communities like small research labs, independent data journalists as well as organization or individuals who prefer not to depend on big data sharing platforms for political and technical reasons or for the sake of platform ownership.

2   Methods

2.1   Addressing the Problems in Self-publishing Datasets

Dataset publishing systems need to cater to more specific requirements than general digital repositories or web publishing platforms. They need to address emerging specifications and use cases on finding and curating datasets. One of the significant challenges for smaller stakeholders in adapting such a sophisticated system is its resource requirements. Most of the regular data publishing systems demand a bigger scale of resources, such as server-side processing and database dependency. Maintaining such infrastructure for a long time poses monetary overheads.

Along with its resource requirement, ensuring the security and updating the software stacks demands further resources. In the long run, any such unmaintained systems may expose security vulnerabilities and often causes dependency conflicts on its hosted infrastructure. Due to various challenges in maintaining such resource-intensive data publishing platforms, stakeholders with minimal resources will face challenges in ensuring the longevity of their datasets. For post-project datasets such as data collected from data journalism projects or crowdsourcing projects which prefer to self publish their data, than depending on a centralized data repositories may also find it challenging to maintain the platform for an uncertain duration.

2.2   Guidelines for Findable Dataset Publishing

There are different dataset indexing services built on various standards, principles, and interests. Data search services like Google Dataset Search[3] and Socrata Open Data API[4] are some of the emerging search systems designed for dataset searching. This attempt at this stage is primarily focusing on Google Dataset Search recommendations[5] as a guideline and expand the scope to cover more standards and specifications from the Semantic Web perspective. Google Dataset Search helps to find datasets irrespective of the publishing platform. The guidelines are intended for the providers to describe their data in a machine-actionable way that can better help the search engines and indexers understand the content of the resource. Some of the salient requirements are the provenance, rights, and basic descriptive metadata of the datasets [10]. Some of the key challenges addressed by these recommendations are defining the constitutes of datasets, identifying the datasets, relating datasets to each other, linking metadata between related datasets, and finally describing the content of datasets [11].

As a minimal prototype for the proposal, and Google Dataset Search as the initial focus of finding services, the authors included schema.org Dataset[6] markup as main JSON-LD expression and DCAT with DublinCore as RDFa expression within the rendered HTML to explain the dataset. Since Schema.org is evolving as a well-accepted and unified vocabulary in describing resources for search engines, this approach has added advantage of better search engine visibility. The alternate DCAT and DublinCore RDF/RDFa expressions will also increase the reachability in other types of data finding mechanisms.

2.3   Extending a Static Publishing System

Hugo web publishing framework has emerged as one of the fastest framework for building websites[7]. Hugo, written in Go language, is open source based static

---

[3] https://datasetsearch.research.google.com/.

[4] https://dev.socrata.com/.

[5] https://developers.google.com/search/docs/data-types/dataset.

[6] https://schema.org/Dataset.

[7] https://gohugo.io/.

site generator which is fast and flexible and supports different content types and taxonomies which are extensible into multiple content output formats. Dynamic JSON format based i18n provide translation module for multilingual publishing.

Under static publishing, files are updated on the file system thus making it easily scalable and less resource intensive. Static publishing also allows for easier management of content backups without having to deal with security issues or server side maintenance involving CMS based approaches.

The advantage of extending existing frameworks for static publishing allows communities to 1). Integrate data publishing to their existing websites, 2). Extend an existing open source projects, thereby reducing the risks of longevity of the proposal, 3). Remove the redundant dependency on the efforts, thus supporting the growth of the depending project 4). Allow minimal resource requirements for development and maintenance.

2.4 Template Driven Output Formats

Template driven output formatting are easier to customise, share and reuse. They can be adapted to any similar system. Hugo's Go-based templating[8] supports logic to build templates for any level of complex design. Go language's html and text templates are capable of generating virtually any text based formats[9, 10]. Different output formats include 1). HTML and embedded JSON-LD, 2). RDF files for content negotiation.

2.5 Semantically Linking Published Profiles and Catalogues

The proposed solution uses Profiles vocabulary [3] to semantically link datasets, and data catalogs to corresponding profiles. Schema.org based JSON-LD expression is used in linking datasets to data catalogs. DCAT and Dublin Core based RDF expression is used to provide an alternative RDF expression of the published item. This multi-level semantic linking will help the published instance to be findable in different ways. Semantically linking datasets to data catalogues and collections also links datasets to its corresponding profiles (Fig. 1). Generating RDF and JSON-LD helps to support finding profiles of the data.

2.6 Similar Attempts

Some of the similar approaches are enlisted below with the advantages and disadvantages: 1). Quire[11] from J. Paul Getty Trust is a Hugo based multiformat publishing format which is customised for book publishing and not datasets. 2). DKAN[12] is a Drupal 8-based, microservice-architectured, schema-centered, API-first, front-end decoupled, open data platform. It requires a web-server with PHP

---

[8] https://gohugo.io/templates/.
[9] https://golang.org/pkg/text/template/.
[10] https://golang.org/pkg/html/template/.
[11] https://gettypubs.github.io/quire.
[12] https://getdkan.org/.

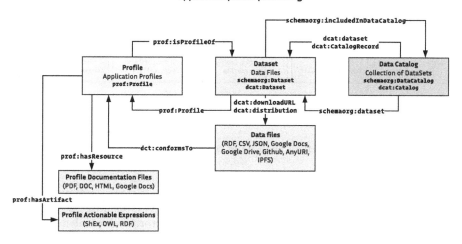

Fig. 1. Semantic relationship of dataset and application profile

support and a database. 3). JKAN[13] is a Jeykll based small footprint backend-free open data portal, which work with GitHub pages as well. However, it doesn't have semantic web features. 4). CKAN[14] is designed for bigger data portals and is less semantic web friendly. It requires enormous resources to maintain the portal. 5). Invenio[15] which is Python based and developed for larger digital repositories like zenodo. However, it is an overkill for smaller communities.

3   Resulting Project

3.1   HuDot: A Minimalist Publishing System

This is a work in progress project that proposes to integrate these concepts into a reusable implementation based on the Hugo web publishing framework. The work in progress project is titled HuDot and shall be made available under MIT license. Content within HuDot is organized on items and collections. Page types are initially dataset, collection, profiles, and a text type for regular pages. A general overview and the relationship of these pages are illustrated in Fig. 2.

The proposed minimalist publishing system is an open-source project under MIT license, which is a permissible license. The project's longevity is maintained as long the Hugo dependencies are maintained. The authors intend to keep the templates interoperable with any Hugo implementation so that the data publication can be seamlessly integrated with any Hugo based websites. The emerging

---

[13] https://jkan.io/.

[14] https://ckan.org/.

[15] https://invenio-software.org/.

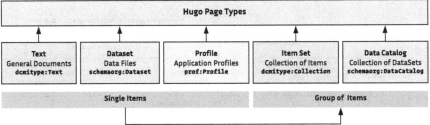

Fig. 2. Hugo page types organised in HuDot

popularity of Hugo as a static publishing solution for various communities can make easy adoption of these templates in independently publishing datasets. The whole HuDot systems is designed by limiting any external dependencies other than Hugo. This may help the adapters in keeping their sites irrespective of the longevity of the HuDot project. As the project progresses, detailed documentation explaining the semantic web approaches in developing these templates and customizing them will also be added.

4 Discussion

4.1 Novelty and Impact

This approach brings in the newly proposed Profiles vocabulary for semantically linking and expressing profiles of datasets and encourages stakeholders in publishing metadata application profiles and data profiles along with their datasets. The most crucial gap this attempt tries to fill in is proposing an easier option to deal with the complex requirements in resource and knowledge for publishing findable datasets. Limited resource communities and independent data publishers find it challenging to create essential semantic web oriented resources in expressing a findable dataset. Most of the time, such datasets end up in cloud file storage or linked to web pages, which may not express the content and nature of the dataset. Eventually, this makes it difficult to be exposed as a data resource. Creating adaptable and less resource-intensive tools which support semantic web technologies by design will increase the adaptability of such technologies. This may also reduce the cost and efforts for individuals and resource-limited communities in integrating semantic web concepts.

4.2 Limitations of the Approach and Future Work

Our approach is not a replacement for any full-fledged data archival and data curation systems like Dkan or hosted systems like zenodo. To use a content management framework like Hugo and customize the templates requires certain level of technical expertise and it can be a challenge for many users. Many of the communities may find it difficult to customize templates for non HTML outputs. Extending the utility with improved HuDot based tooling to generate linkable and linked (open) data from datasets using associated profiles is to be considered. This will also involve providing extended documentation and theme support for easier adaptation.

5   Conclusion

The authors have described a work-in-progress project on developing a simple static site publishing tool based on Hugo to help smaller data stakeholders like data journalists, individual research labs to publish findable data. This would help towards promoting more reach and acceptance of dataset in terms of self-publishing. From the perspective of the semantic web, such tools will improve the number of linkable datasets as well as promote the fundamental concepts of the decentralized web.

Acknowledgements. This work was supported by JSPS KAKENHI Grant Numbers JP18K11984 (to Nagamori) and 19K206740A (to Kasaragod).

References

1. Baca, M.: Introduction to metadata (2016). http://www.getty.edu/publications/intrometadata
2. Browning, D., Perego, A., Albertoni, R., Cox, S., Beltran, A.G., Winstanley, P.: Data catalog vocabulary (DCAT) - version 2. W3C Recommendation, W3C (2020). https://www.w3.org/TR/2020/REC-vocab-dcat-2-20200204/
3. Car, N.: The profiles vocabulary. W3C Note, W3C (2019). https://www.w3.org/TR/2019/NOTE-dx-prof-20191218/
4. Cousijn, H., et al.: A data citation roadmap for scientific publishers. Sci. Data **5**(1), 180259 (2018). https://doi.org/10.1038/sdata.2018.259
5. Crosas, M.: Joint declaration of data citation principles - FINAL (2013). https://www.force11.org/datacitationprinciples
6. Heery, R., Patel, M.: Application profiles: mixing and matching metadata schemas. Ariadne **25** (2000). http://www.ariadne.ac.uk/issue/25/app-profiles/
7. Hillmann, D.: Metadata standards and applications. Metadata Management Associates LLC (2006). http://managemetadata.com/
8. Jacobsen, A., et al.: FAIR principles: interpretations and implementation considerations. Data Intelligence **2**(1–2), 10–29 (2019). https://doi.org/10.1162/dint_r_00024
9. Alexander, K., Cyganiak, R., Hausenblas, M., Zhao, J.: Describing linked datasets with the VoID vocabulary. https://www.w3.org/TR/void/
10. Noy, N.: Making it easier to discover datasets (2018). https://blog.google/products/search/making-it-easier-discover-datasets/, library Catalog: www.blog.google
11. Noy, N., Brickley, D.: Facilitating the discovery of public datasets (2017). http://ai.googleblog.com/2017/01/facilitating-discovery-of-public.html, library Catalog: ai.googleblog.com

12. Sansone, S.A., et al.: FAIRsharing as a community approach to standards, repositories and policies. Nature Biotechnol. **37**(4), 358–367 (2019). https://doi.org/10.1038/s41587-019-0080-8

13. Stevens, I., Mukarram, A.K., Hörtenhuber, M., Meehan, T.F., Rung, J., Daub, C.O.: Ten simple rules for annotating sequencing experiments. PLoS Comput. Biol. **16**(10), e1008260 (2020). https://doi.org/10.1371/journal.pcbi.1008260

14. Tennison, J.: CSV on the web: a primer. W3C Note, W3C (2016). https://www.w3.org/TR/2016/NOTE-tabular-data-primer-20160225/

15. Thalhath, N., Nagamori, M., Sakaguchi, T.: MetaProfiles - a mechanism to express metadata schema, privacy, rights and provenance for data interoperability. In: Ishita, E., Pang, N.L.S., Zhou, L. (eds.) ICADL 2020. LNCS, vol. 12504, pp. 364–370. Springer, Cham (2020). https://doi.org/10.1007/978-3-030-64452-9_34

16. Walsh, P., Pollock, R.: Data package. https://specs.frictionlessdata.io/data-package

17. Wilkinson, M.D., et al.: The FAIR guiding principles for scientific data management and stewardship. Sci. Data **3**(1), 160018 (2016). https://doi.org/10.1038/sdata.2016.18. https://www.nature.com/articles/sdata201618

Track on Metadata and Semantics for Agriculture, Food and Environment (AgroSEM'20)

Ontology-Based Decision Support System for the Nitrogen Fertilization of Winter Wheat

Ingmar Kessler$^{(\boxtimes)}$, Alexander Perzylo , and Markus Rickert

fortiss, Research Institute of the Free State of Bavaria associated with
Technical University of Munich, Guerickestraße 25, 80805 Munich, Germany
{ikessler,perzylo,rickert}@fortiss.org

Abstract. Digital technologies are already used in several aspects of agriculture. However, decision-making in crop production is still often a manual process that relies on various heterogeneous data sources. Small-scale farmers and their local consultants are particularly burdened by increasingly complex requirements. Regional circumstances and regulations play an essential role and need to be considered. This paper presents an ontology-based decision support system for the nitrogen fertilization of winter wheat in Bavaria, Germany. Semantic Web and Linked Data technologies were employed to both reuse and model new common semantic structures for interrelated knowledge. Many relevant general and regional data sources from multiple domains were not yet available in RDF. Hence, we used several tools to transform relevant data into corresponding OWL ontologies and combined them in a central knowledge base. The GUI application of the decision support system queries it to parameterize requests to external web services and to show relevant information in an integrated view. It further uses SPARQL queries to automatically generate recommendations for farmers and their consultants.

Keywords: OWL · SPARQL · DSS · Data integration · Agriculture

1 Introduction

The digital transformation of agriculture is an ongoing process whose progress differs for various regions, organizations, and activities. The regional circumstances in Bavaria for instance include the following factors [3]: It has both the most farm holdings and the smallest area per holding compared to the national average in Germany. 106 718 farm holdings in Bavaria are sole proprietorships and account for 87% of the agricultural area in the state. 61% of them are part-time holdings and 81% of their personnel are family members. Winter wheat has the largest share of the cereal production by area with 47%.

Farmers typically aim at optimizing their crop yield while remaining within the limits set by agricultural best practices and local legal regulations. Small agricultural holdings in particular may still often rely on paper documents or

E. Garoufallou and M.-A. Ovalle-Perandones (Eds.): MTSR 2020, CCIS 1355, pp. 245–256, 2021.
https://doi.org/10.1007/978-3-030-71903-6_24

homemade spreadsheets to manage their fields. Their decision-making depends on finding, combining, and interpreting heterogeneous data sources that are published by various organizations. These data sources often have different formats such as paper documents, PDF documents, websites, and spreadsheets, which contain informal identifiers and implicit definitions. As the number and complexity of regulations increase, e.g., regarding the environment, water protection, pesticides, and fertilizers, this becomes increasingly difficult for small-scale farmers in particular. Many farmers need to call a small number of local consultants about similar routine concerns, which is time-consuming and cost-intensive.

Digital technologies may become necessary to support farmers in their knowledge management and decision-making. The presented system uses Semantic Web and Linked Data technologies such as OWL ontologies to integrate heterogeneous data sources and create a decision support system (DSS). Due to its local significance, our initial use case focuses on the automatic generation of recommendations for the nitrogen (N) fertilization of winter wheat. Farmers can already use software tools such as a website called *Bodenportal* by an association for Bavarian farmers (LKP) to calculate the legal upper limit for the total required N fertilization (N_{req}) for a given field, crop, and year. It is usually not applied to the field all at once, but rather split into three separate applications to optimize the results. Farmers and their consultants must decide on how much fertilizer to apply and when, while complying with this legal upper limit. The presented DSS uses this N_{req} value and other parameters from various data sources to automatically recommend an application time and rate (kg N ha^{-1}).

The rest of the paper is structured as follows. Section 2 discusses related work including existing semantic resources and other ontology-based DSS. Section 3 describes the overall concept and architecture of the presented system and gives an overview of regional data sources. Section 4 presents an evaluation of the DSS for a particular N fertilization recommendation. Section 5 concludes the paper.

2   Related Work

The Semantic Web and Linked Data ecosystem includes ontologies and vocabularies to encourage common semantic structures, data sources using these structures, and applications consuming these data sources. Unit ontologies [9] such as QUDT (Quantities, Units, Dimensions and Types) [7] specify how to semantically describe measurements. The GeoSPARQL [16] standard consists of a vocabulary and SPARQL extensions to describe and work with geographic information. EU Vocabularies [19] provides several authority tables including one for administrative territorial units (ATU). GeoNames [21] contains semantic geospatial features and, e.g., their names, coordinates, and hierarchical relations. Wikidata [23] is an open knowledge base about a wide variety of topics. In GovData [11], the open data portal of the German government, the most common formats are PDF, HTML, and CSV, whereas RDF is very rare for actual data. However, metadata is often provided in RDF according to DCAT-AP.de [20], the German adaptation of the Data Catalog Vocabulary Application Profile (DCAT-AP) for data portals in Europe.

An overview and a survey of Semantic Web technologies in agriculture are provided in [2] and [6]. AGROVOC [5] is a multilingual SKOS-XL thesaurus that covers many topics such as environment, agriculture, food, and nutrition. AgroPortal [8] is a repository for hosting, searching, versioning, and aligning agricultural ontologies and vocabularies. The Crop Ontology [13] is a community-based platform for creating OBO ontologies and vocabularies in RDF to provide common semantic structures for phenotypes, breeding, germplasms, and traits.

Agricultural data sources, including German and Bavarian ones, are often not available in RDF, but there have been efforts to change that. The SPARQL endpoint in [12] provides reference data to estimate the costs of machine use. Similarly, the SPARQL endpoint in [1] provides requirements regarding water protection based on the database of the *Federal Office of Consumer Protection and Food Safety* (BVL) on authorized plant protection products. This database uses EPPO codes[1] as plant and pest identifiers.

The ontology-based DSS in [14] and [22] use SWRL rules to generate recommendations for wheat production in Syria and for home gardens in Ecuador. In [17], existing semantic resources are reused and new ontologies are modeled to integrate heterogeneous data sources, so that SPARQL queries can calculate answers to questions of farmers in Nepal. The DSS presented here, which is based on our previous work [15], is similar to [17] to some extent, but focuses on a different region with different data sources and questions. The data sources also include GeoTIFF, relational databases, and web services. GeoSPARQL is used extensively to model and query geospatial data to show relevant information in a GUI application and to automatically generate recommendations.

3   Concept

The aim of the presented DSS is to assist farmers and consultants in a GUI application by retrieving and showing relevant information and automatically generating fertilization recommendations. This requires the integration of various heterogeneous data sources with different formats (CSV, PDF, SHP, SQL, etc.) and structures from multiple organizations, as well as of human expert knowledge. In order to provide a solid foundation for the system and potential future applications, common semantic structures were reused or modeled as OWL ontologies based on regional data sources. Relevant data was transformed into additional ontologies and combined in a central knowledge base. This way, SPARQL queries provide unified access to interrelated knowledge from multiple data sources.

Several agricultural experts collaborated with us on this work by gathering and preparing relevant data sources and posing competency questions that the system should be able to answer. These data sources were not available in RDF and ranged from general agricultural, geospatial, and weather information to data, definitions, and regulations specific to Bavaria. They also interviewed two local consultants about their decision-making regarding N fertilization to create corresponding decision trees.

---

[1] https://www.eppo.int/RESOURCES/eppo_databases/eppo_codes.

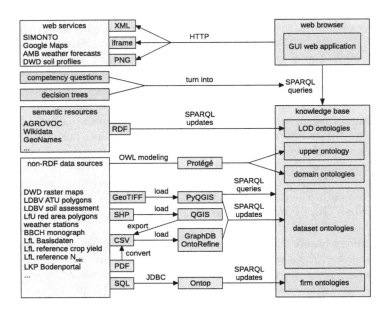

Fig. 1. Architecture of the DSS: OWL ontologies are created from data sources (bottom-left) and stored in a knowledge base (bottom-right) that is queried via SPARQL by a GUI web application (top-right), which also accesses external web services (top-left).

In our approach (Fig. 1), various tools are used to integrate non-RDF data sources and existing semantic resources by creating corresponding OWL ontologies that contain common semantic structures or actual data (Sect. 3.2). The created ontologies are consistent with OWL 2 DL. As a result, they are compatible with DL reasoners and in principle other DL ontologies. The ontologies are stored in corresponding named graphs in a GraphDB triplestore[2], which features OWL 2 RL inference and acts as the central knowledge base of the system. The competency questions and decision trees were turned into parameterizable SPARQL queries (Sect. 3.3). A web-based GUI application was built for farmers to intuitively interact with the DSS (Sect. 3.4). It parameterizes predefined SPARQL queries to the knowledge base with both automatically derived values and user input to show relevant information to the user, to parameterize requests to external web services, and to automatically generate recommendations.

3.1   Semantic Representation of Agricultural Knowledge

The OWL ontologies in the knowledge base can be grouped into different categories and usually import several higher-level ontologies. Since not all relevant existing semantic resources provide SPARQL endpoints and to improve performance and maintainability, relevant subsets were extracted from them

---

[2] https://www.ontotext.com/products/graphdb/.

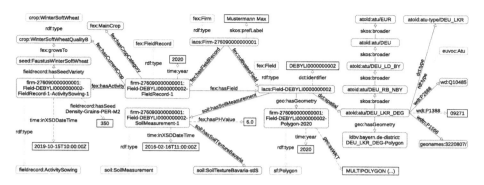

Fig. 2. Excerpt from the OWL ontologies showing several core entities.

using SPARQL updates and saved as Linked Open Data (LOD) ontologies. This includes crops from AGROVOC, ATU individuals from EU Vocabularies, ATU interrelations from GeoNames, and additional ATU labels as well as German regional keys from Wikidata. The structures in the non-RDF data sources were modeled as common semantic structures in the form of OWL entities, i.e., classes, properties, and individuals, in one upper and several domain ontologies, while also taking the LOD ontologies into account. The upper ontology consists of top-level classes, common properties, and individuals that are shared among several domains. The domain ontologies group together entities related to topics such as weather, soil, crops, seed varieties, field records, fertilizers, or pesticides. Each dataset ontology is usually created from a single data source using the tools shown in Fig. 1 as described in Sect. 3.2. Finally, the data of farm holdings are saved in separate firm ontologies.

The core entities (Fig. 2) in the OWL ontologies include *fex:Firm*, *fex:Field*, and *fex:FieldRecord*, i.e., a firm has a record on the cultivation of a crop on a field. Accordingly, a field record corresponds to a period of time that usually starts with soil preparation and sowing activities and ends with a harvesting activity. In the ontologies, sowing activities for instance are characterized by, e.g., their date, seed density, and seed variety, which grows into a certain kind of crop. If multiple crops are grown simultaneously in different parts of a field, it has multiple *fex:FieldRecord* individuals for a given year and each may have its own geospatial polygon. If multiple crops are grown sequentially as main, second, or catch crops in a given year, this is indicated by the *fex:hasCropCategory* property of each *fex:FieldRecord* individual.

Each *fex:Field* individual is linked not only to *fex:FieldRecord* individuals, but also to additional entities such as soil measurements (*soil:SoilMeasurement*) from laboratory results, which are characterized by, e.g., their date, soil texture, humus class, and pH value. The geospatial polygon (*sf:Polygon*) of a field provides its location and boundary and may change over the years. Polygons are not just available for fields, but also for rural and urban districts as well as areas with fertilization restrictions (Fig. 3). Therefore, SPARQL queries can determine in which district a field is located (Listing 1), which affects for instance

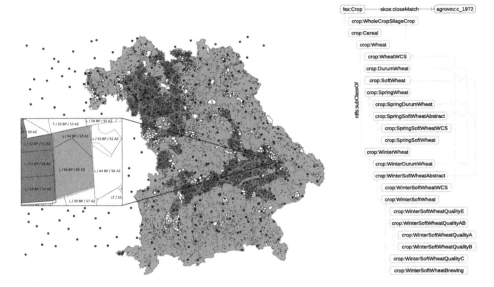

Fig. 3. Map of Bavaria showing areas with fertilization restrictions (red, white, and green), rural and urban districts (gray lines), DWD and AMB weather stations (blue and red dots), soil assessment polygons (black lines and labels), and fields (yellow). (Color figure online)

Fig. 4. Wheat class hierarchy modeled based on regional data sources.

reference crop yields (Listing 2). The IRIs of districts and other administrative territorial units (*euvoc:Atu*) were reused from EU Vocabularies and aligned with other semantic resources. This can simplify information exchange and queries to additional semantic resources that share the same IRIs.

The soil textures in the soil ontology are one of the new common semantic structures that have been modeled in the various domain ontologies for our initial use case based on regional data sources. While there already are other ontologies that describe soil textures, they do so in general or for other countries. However, data sources and regulations in Germany and in Bavaria use two different definitions of soil textures. The soil texture (*soil:SoilTextureAlkis*) of a polygon in the soil assessment map has the same definition as the ones in ALKIS (Authoritative Real Estate Cadastre Information System) and is a parameter of the automatic generation of N fertilization recommendations. The soil texture (*soil:SoilTextureBavaria*) of a soil measurement in Bavaria is different and affects many fertilization requirements other than N such as CaO and K_2O.

Similarly, local farmers and data sources use regional terms and definitions for crops that focus more on the regional crop usage than on botanical definitions. For example, *crop:WinterSoftWheatQualityE* indicates in simplified terms that a farmer intends to achieve a protein content of more than 14%, while *crop:WinterSoftWheatWCS* indicates that he intends to produce silage from the harvest. The distinction is important, as they each have different N requirements and reference values in the regional data sources. Additionally, while both crops are still the same botanical species Triticum aestivum, certain seed varieties are often more suitable for different purposes than others. The class hierarchy (Fig. 4) in the crop ontology was modeled based on tables of reference values called *Basisdaten* by the *Bavarian State Research Center for Agriculture* (LfL), the code list for grant applications (FNN) by the StMELF, the database on authorized plant protection products by the BVL, and the *Descriptive Variety Lists* by the *Federal Plant Variety Office* to represent how the various concepts relate to each other. This way, a dataset ontology can unambiguously assert to which specific concept each datum from a data source refers. This is important, as data referring to a concept applies to all of its subclasses as well.

3.2   Integration of Regional Data Sources

The following non-RDF data sources are relevant to agriculture in Bavaria in general and to our initial use case in particular. Figure 1 shows the tools that were used to create corresponding OWL ontologies, which were made available to the DSS via a central knowledge base.

A CSV file from the *German Meteorological Service* (DWD) includes 490 local weather stations that provide soil temperature and moisture profiles at various depths below the ground over time as well as station attributes such as their geographic coordinates. A second CSV file from an agrometeorological service in Bavaria (AMB) includes 150 stations with weather forecasts that provide agriculturally relevant data such as the air temperature 5 cm above the ground instead of the usual 2 m and the soil temperature 10 cm below the ground. Both CSV files were loaded into GraphDB OntoRefine to create virtual SPARQL endpoints and then transformed by SPARQL updates into OWL ontologies.

A shapefile (SHP) from the StMELF contains polygons of 1947 red areas and 3207 white areas, which were defined by the *Bavarian State Office for the Environment* (LfU) and specify certain fertilization restrictions for water protection. It was loaded into QGIS[3], exported as a CSV file containing the polygons in the well-known text (WKT) format as well as their attributes, and then loaded into GraphDB OntoRefine. Similarly, a shapefile from the *Bavarian State Office for Digitization, Broadband and Surveying* (LDBV) contains 376 196 polygons from the official soil assessment map and their attributes soil texture, field value, and soil value. Additional shapefiles from the LDBV contain polygons of the borders of the Bavarian state, its 7 governmental districts, and its 71 rural and 25 urban districts. We used SPARQL updates to match the German regional keys from the shapefiles to the ones from Wikidata to link the polygons to the ATUs from EU Vocabularies. The SPARQL query in Listing 1 returns the rural or urban district in which a field is located and covers the edge case where a field may intersect with two or more districts by comparing the sizes of the intersections. GeoSPARQL itself does not specify a function to calculate the area of a polygon, but several triplestores provide extension functions such as *ext:area*.

---

[3] https://www.qgis.org/en/site/.

```
SELECT ?district
WHERE {
  ?field dct:identifier "DEBYLI0000000002" ; geo:hasGeometry ?fieldPolygon .
  ?fieldPolygon a sf:Polygon ; geo:asWKT ?fieldWkt ; geo:sfIntersects ?districtPolygon .
  ?districtPolygon a sf:Polygon ; geo:asWKT ?districtWkt .
  ?district dct:type ?type ; geo:hasGeometry ?districtPolygon .
  FILTER (?type IN (atold:atu-type\/DEU_LKR, atold:atu-type\/DEU_KRFS))
  BIND (ext:area(geof:intersection(?fieldWkt, ?districtWkt)) AS ?area)
}
ORDER BY DESC(?area)
LIMIT 1
```

Listing 1: SPARQL query returning district with largest intersection with field.

GeoTIFF files from the DWD contain raster maps for the monthly average temperature and precipitation in Bavaria. Since GeoSPARQL is not well suited for working with raster maps, they and the field polygons from the knowledge base were loaded into PyQGIS. The average pixel value for each polygon was calculated in each map and added to the OWL ontology containing the polygon.

PDF documents on the website of the LfL such as the *Basisdaten* contain, e.g., tables of reference values. This includes the crop yield in the rural and urban districts of Bavaria, the mineral N available in the soil (N_{min}) for various crops in the governmental districts, and the nutrient contents of various organic fertilizers. Tables from PDF documents were first converted into CSV files and then loaded into GraphDB OntoRefine. The SPARQL query in Listing 2 returns the reference crop yield for the district returned by the query in Listing 1.

The relational database of the *Bodenportal* by the LKP contains data about agricultural firms in Bavaria. This includes for instance the name, official ID, and location of a firm; the names, official IDs, sizes, and polygons of its fields; laboratory results of the fields' soil; and the calculated N_{req} value as well as its various input parameters. Ontop [4] supports R2RML Direct Mapping [18] as well as custom mappings to create a virtual SPARQL endpoint to access a relational database. The data of several firms, which agreed to participate in the evaluation of the DSS, were exported as separate firm ontologies. During the export, PyQGIS was used to convert field polygons from the Gauss-Krüger coordinate system to WGS 84, as the latter usually has better GeoSPARQL support in triplestores. Additionally, SPARQL updates were used to categorize numeric laboratory results of various nutrients into qualitative soil content levels. In doing so, the updates used knowledge that had been modeled in the OWL ontologies based on agricultural literature such as the LfL's guide for the fertilization of arable and grassland.

```
SELECT ?referenceCropYield
WHERE {
  agrovoc:c_8412 skos:closeMatch/qudt:hasQuantity ?quantity . # winter wheat
  ?quantity qudt:hasQuantityKind agrovoc:c_10176 ; # crop yield
            dct:spatial atold:atu\/DEU_LKR_DEG ; time:year 2020 ;
            qudt:quantityValue ?quantityValue .
  ?quantityValue qudt:unit unit:KiloGM-PER-M2 ; qudt:numericValue ?referenceCropYield .
}
```

Listing 2: SPARQL query returning reference yield for crop, district, and year.

3.3   Explicit Modeling of Human Expert Knowledge

One aspect of our work was the formalization of relevant knowledge of human experts. This way, the DSS can use not only institutional data sources (Sect. 3.2) but also the implicit knowledge of local consultants gained through years of experience. For this purpose, the agricultural experts collaborating with us interviewed two Bavarian consultants about the decision-making processes underlying their recommendations to farmers about the appropriate N application time and rate for winter wheat. This showed that their recommendations differ in regard to both the required parameters and the results for each of the three separate N applications. Therefore, the agricultural experts created for each of the two consultants one set of three decision trees. We then turned these decision trees into parameterizable SPARQL queries and related knowledge in the OWL ontologies, so that the DSS can automatically calculate the time and rate for each N application. Farmers may choose their preferred consultant in the GUI application when using the DSS, which determines what recommendations and corresponding queries are used.

3.4   Web-Based Decision Support System Application

The GUI application of the DSS was implemented as a web application using the Angular framework. It sends SPARQL queries to the knowledge base to retrieve agricultural information and the data of several firms, which agreed to participate in the evaluation of the DSS. After a user has selected a firm, one of its fields, and one of its field records, the GUI displays the view depicted in Fig. 5(left). It shows a map of the field and its surroundings, information about the field, its vegetation, and its soil. This includes the BBCH code, which indicates the current growth stage of the crop, and its description from the BBCH monograph. To do so, the GUI application queries the knowledge base for the current crop, the sowing date and the geographic coordinates of the field. It then sends them to the external SIMONTO web service, which simulates and returns the BBCH code. Four expandable panels at the bottom contain the field's photo gallery as well as embedded external diagrams of the soil temperature profile, the soil moisture profile, and the weather forecast at the closest weather station to the selected field. The input mask for the automatic N fertilization recommendation changes depending on which consultant and which of the three N applications have been selected. There, the user can inspect and modify automatically derived

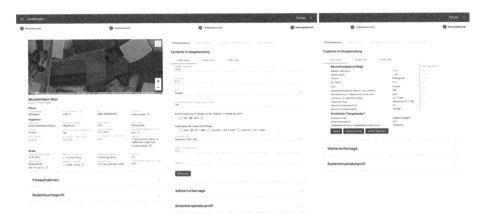

Fig. 5. GUI application of the DSS showing relevant information about a field from various heterogeneous data sources (left), an input mask for the automatic N fertilization recommendation (middle), and its results (right).

parameters, fill in any remaining ones, and trigger the calculation. Accordingly, SPARQL queries (Sect. 3.3) are parameterized and sent to the knowledge base to calculate the recommendation results, which replace the input mask.

4   Evaluation

The presented DSS and its GUI application were tested during their development by agricultural experts, Bavarian farmers, and their consultants, so that their feedback could be taken into account. Feature requests included, e.g., the weather forecast, the soil temperature profile, the SIMONTO web service, the photo gallery, and displaying city names in the map view. Their suggestions also provided an agricultural perspective to make the phrasing of the labels in the GUI more familiar and understandable to farmers and consultants. The agricultural experts checked that the automatically generated recommendations match the results of their decision trees, which they updated based on field tests.

The following qualitative evaluation shows the parameterization and the results for the first N application for the field depicted in Fig. 5. Many parameters of the input mask for the N fertilization recommendation are automatically filled in by the GUI using knowledge that has been asserted or inferred in the knowledge base. This includes quantitative parameters such as the N_{min} value as well as qualitative parameters such as whether a field is at a *warm* or *cool* location. As part of the work described in Sect. 3.3 this qualitative parameter was defined quantitatively. The agricultural experts interviewed consultants and determined that a specific threshold for the average temperature in a certain month at the field's location determines whether it is *warm* or *cool*. Hence, the GUI queries the field's average value from one of the DWD raster maps to auto-

Table 1. Parameters of the automatic recommendation for the first N application.

N_{req} (kg ha^{-1})	Previous crop	N_{min} (kg ha^{-1})	Seed variety	Stand density (shoots m^{-2})	Location	Organic time	Organic fertilizer	Organic rate (t ha^{-1})
172.0	Winter barley	61.5	Faustus	700	Warm	Before first application	Chicken manure	2.0

matically fill in the corresponding parameter. If multiple sources are available for a parameter, data of the firm is preferred to generic reference values.

Table 1 shows the parameters and their values, which include the N_{req} and N_{min} values, the seed variety, whether the field's location is *warm* or *cool*, and the crop cultivated in the previous year. Some parameters cannot be automatically derived from the currently available data sources and still need to be manually entered by the user. This includes the current stand density of wheat shoots and the optional use of an organic fertilizer, i.e., its type, application rate, and relative time. The recommendation results are shown in Fig. 5(right) and consist of the parameter values, their effects, the application time and rate, and the remainder of the N_{req} value. The DSS has calculated an organic N rate of 15.8 kg ha^{-1} due to 2.0 t ha^{-1} chicken manure and recommends for the first N application a mineral N rate of 52.5 kg ha^{-1} at the beginning of the vegetation period.

5 Conclusion and Outlook

In this work, common semantic structures were reused or newly modeled in OWL ontologies for various regional data sources. These structures were used to transform heterogeneous data into OWL ontologies that were stored in a central knowledge base. The presented DSS and its GUI application use SPARQL queries to display information relevant to crop production and to automatically generate recommendations. In this way, farmers may become less reliant on external help.

The agricultural experts plan to present the results of a UEQ-based [10] user study with farmers and consultants in a subsequent paper. The scope of the system could be extended, since its approach and much of its knowledge are not strictly limited to its initial use case, i.e., the N fertilization of winter wheat in Bavaria. Potential candidates include a DSS for pesticide applications, a GUI application to semantically manage field activities, and supporting other regions. All of them would entail integrating additional agricultural data sources. This work and many others could be simplified, if more organizations were to provide their data as semantic resources.

Acknowledgments. The research leading to these results has been funded by the Bavarian State Ministry of Food, Agriculture and Forestry (StMELF) under grant agreement no. D/17/02 in the project FarmExpert.

References

1. Albrecht, K., Martini, D., Schmitz, M.: Linked open data im Pflanzenschutz. In: GIL, pp. 19–24 (2019)

2. Aubin, S., Caracciolo, C., Zervas, P.: Landscaping the use of semantics to enhance the interoperability of agricultural data. Agrisemantics WG report (2017)
3. Bavarian State Ministry of Food, Agriculture and Forestry: Bavarian agricultural report. https://www.agrarbericht-2018.bayern.de. Accessed 16 Jul 2020
4. Calvanese, D., et al.: Ontop: answering SPARQL queries over relational databases. Semant. Web **8**(3), 471–487 (2017)
5. Caracciolo, C., et al.: The AGROVOC linked dataset. Semant. Web **4**(3), 341–348 (2013)
6. Drury, B., Fernandes, R., Moura, M.F., de Andrade Lopes, A.: A survey of semantic web technology for agriculture. IPA **6**(4), 487–501 (2019)
7. Hodgson, R., Mekonnen, D., Price, D., Hodges, J., Masters, J.E., Cox, S., Ray, S.: Quantities, units, dimensions and types (QUDT). http://www.qudt.org. Accessed 26 Feb 2020
8. Jonquet, C., et al.: AgroPortal: a vocabulary and ontology repository for agronomy. COMPAG **144**, 126–143 (2018)
9. Keil, J.M., Schindler, S.: Comparison and evaluation of ontologies for units of measurement. Semant. Web **10**(1), 33–51 (2019)
10. Laugwitz, B., Held, T., Schrepp, M.: Construction and evaluation of a user experience questionnaire. In: USAB, pp. 63–76 (2008)
11. Marienfeld, F., Schieferdecker, I., Lapi, E., Tcholtchev, N.: Metadata aggregation at GovData.de: an experience report. In: OpenSym, pp. 1–5 (2013)
12. Martini, D.: Webservices auf heterogenen Datenbeständen - Methoden der Umsetzung am Beispiel der KTBL-Planungsdaten. In: GIL, pp. 155–158 (2018)
13. Matteis, L., et al.: Crop ontology: vocabulary for crop-related concepts. In: S4BioDiv (2013)
14. Mawardi, S.Y., Abdel-Aziz, M.H., Omran, A.M., Mahmoud, T.A.: An ontology-driven decision support system for wheat production. IJCST **4**(8), 11–17 (2013)
15. Nafissi, A., et al.: Wissensbasierte digitale Unterstützung in der Pflanzenbauberatung. In: GIL, pp. 145–150 (2019)
16. Perry, M., Herring, J.: GeoSPARQL - a geographic query language for RDF data. OGC Standard (2012)
17. Pokharel, S., Sherif, M.A., Lehmann, J.: Ontology based data access and integration for improving the effectiveness of farming in Nepal. In: WI-IAT, pp. 319–326 (2014)
18. Prud'hommeaux, E., Sequeda, J., Arenas, M., Bertails, A.: A direct mapping of relational data to RDF. W3C Recommendation (2012)
19. Publications Office of the European Union: EU vocabularies. https://op.europa.eu/en/web/eu-vocabularies. Accessed 3 Feb 2020
20. Sklarß, S., Gattwinkel, D., Göldner, A., Horn, C., Wittig, C., Koroyin, O.: DCAT-AP.de Spezifikation: Deutsche Adaption des "Data Catalogue Application Profile" (DCAT-AP) für Datenportale in Europa. DCAT-AP.de Specification (2019)
21. Vatant, B., Wick, M., Kendall, E.: GeoNames ontology. https://www.geonames.org/ontology/documentation.html. Accessed 18 Feb 2020
22. Vergara-Lozano, V., Medina-Moreira, J., Rochina, C., Garzón-Goya, M., Sinche-Guzmán, A., Bucaram-Leverone, M.: An ontology-based decision support system for the management of home gardens. In: CITI, pp. 47–59 (2017)
23. Vrandečić, D., Krötzsch, M.: Wikidata: a free collaborative knowledgebase. Commun. ACM **57**(10), 78–85 (2014)

Semantic Description of Plant Phenological Development Stages, Starting with Grapevine

Catherine Roussey[1]([✉]) [iD], Xavier Delpuech[2] [iD], Florence Amardeilh[3] [iD], Stephan Bernard[1] [iD], and Clement Jonquet[4,5] [iD]

[1] Université Clermont Auvergne, INRAE, UR TSCF, Aubière, France
`{catherine.roussey,stephan.bernard}@inrae.fr`
[2] French Wine and Vine Institute, Pôle Rhône-Méditerranée, Montpellier, France
`xavier.delpuech@vignevin.com`
[3] Elzeard R&D, Pessac, France
[4] MISTEA, University of Montpellier, INRAE, Institut Agro, Montpellier, France
`florence.amardeilh@elzeard.co`
[5] LIRMM, University of Montpellier, CNRS, Montpellier, France
`clement.jonquet@inrae.fr`

Abstract. The French project Data to Knowledge in Agronomy and Biodiversity (D2KAB) will make available a semantically-enabled French agricultural alert newsletter. In order to describe/annotate crop phenological development stages in the newsletters, we need a specific semantic resource to semantically represent each stages. Several scales already exist to describe plant phenological development stages. BBCH, considered a reference, offers several sets of stages –one per crop called 'individual scales'–and a general one. The French Wine and Vine Institute (IFV) has aligned several existing scales in order to identify the most useful grapevine development stages for agricultural practices. Unfortunately these scales are not available in a semantic form preventing their use in agricultural semantic applications. In this paper, we present our work of creating an ontological framework for semantic description of plant development stages and transforming specific scales into RDF vocabularies; we introduce the *BBCH-based Plant Phenological Description Ontology* and we illustrate this framework with four scales related to grapevine.

Keywords: Semantics resources · RDF vocabularies · Semantic description · Phenological stages · Phenology · Agricultural semantics · Grapevine

1 Introduction

Agronomy and agriculture face several major societal, economical, and environmental challenges, a semantic data science approach will help to address. The

© Springer Nature Switzerland AG 2021
E. Garoufallou and M.-A. Ovalle-Perandones (Eds.): MTSR 2020, CCIS 1355, pp. 257–268, 2021.
https://doi.org/10.1007/978-3-030-71903-6_25

French ANR project *Data to Knowledge in Agronomy and Biodiversity* (D2KAB – www.d2kab.org) illustrates how semantic data science helps the development of innovative agricultural applications. D2KAB's objective is to create a framework to turn agronomy and biodiversity data into semantically described, interoperable, actionable, and open knowledge. To build such a framework, we rely on semantic resources (e.g., terminologies, vocabularies, ontologies) to describe our data and publish them as Linked Open Data [10]. We use AgroPortal repository (http://agroportal.lirmm.fr) [17] to find, publish and share semantic resources then we exploit those semantic resources for applications in agriculture or environment. One of D2KAB's driving agri-food scenario is to build an augmented, semantically-enabled, reading interface for the official French agricultural alert newsletters, called *Bulletin de Santé du Végétal* (Plant Health Bulletins, later abbreviated PHB). The prototype will be developed with an archive of preexisting PHB PDF files semantically enriched –or annotated– using text mining techniques and transformed into linked data. The annotations will be described using the Semantic Sensor Network ontology combined with the Web Annotation Data Model as presented in [7]. References to phenology are frequently found in PHB, for instances, in order to identify the periods of grapevine sensitivity to abiotic factors (e.g., spring frost from bud break), or to biotic factors (e.g., diseases). In order to describe/annotate crops phenological development stages, we need a specific semantic resource to represent each stages and their relations for any specific crops but also interrelate similar stages between different crops.

Several scales exist to describe plant phenological development stages such as the BBCH general scale [3] and other crop specific scales. Unfortunately, these scales are not available in a semantic form (i.e., described with a semantic Web language such as SKOS, RDF-S or OWL) preventing their use in agricultural semantic applications, such as the one we want to develop for PHB. Indeed, our corpus of PHB shows different scales were idiosyncratically used to refer phenological development stages in observed plots. For example, in a grapevine related PHB, we find the sentence: *bourgeon dans le coton (stade 03 ou B ou BBCH 05) dans les secteurs tardifs*, which is both a reference to a 'label' ("bourgeon dans le coton" translated as "bud in wool") and a semi-formal mention to several scales: (i) 03 is a code from Eichhorn-Lorenz scale [18]; (ii) B is a code from the Baggiolini scale [9]; (iii) and BBCH 05 is a code from the BBCH-grapevine-individual scale [3]. These codes inside the text are first extremely hard to identify and second, they need to be transformed into a formal concept identifying the stage inside a semanticized scale. Plus, it appears the most frequent labels used are IFV's, but this scale does not offer any coding system (only labels). From our analysis and experience working on the PHB use case, there is a clear need to build a set of aligned vocabularies to semantically describe the stages of the different scales.

In this paper, we present our work in transforming French Wine and Vine Institute (IFV)'s French labels and other related scales: BBCH general and individual scales [3], Baggiolini grapevine specific scale [9], Eichhorn-Lorenz [18] grapevine specific scale into RDF vocabularies. We present the first version of the *BBCH-based Plant Phenological Description Ontology*, an ontological framework which encodes in the same semantic resource the BBCH generic scale (as OWL classes) and each crop specific scales (as SKOS instances in respective concept schemes) aligned one another. The rest of the paper is organized as follow: Sect. 2 presents the scales to semanticize; Sect. 3 reviews existing vocabularies/ontologies to capture phenological development stages; Sect. 4 illustrates the methodology used to build a RDF vocabulary for grapevine development stages based on BBCH scale; Sect. 5 discusses pros and cons for publication of phenological information as linked open data before concluding the paper.

2   Phenological Development Scales

The extended BBCH (*Biologische Bundesanstalt, Bundessortenamt und CHemische Industrie*) scale uniformly codes phenologically similar development stages of different plant species. BBCH describes several sets of development stages: one per plant species ('individual scales') and a general one [3]. The general scale forms the framework within which the individual scales are developed. It can also be used for plant species for which no individual scale are available: « *The entire developmental cycle of the plants is subdivided into ten clearly recognizable and distinguishable longer-lasting developmental phases. These principal development stages are described using numbers from 0 to 9 in ascending order (...) The principal development stages alone are not sufficient to precisely define application or evaluation dates (...); Secondary stages are used when points of time or precise steps in plant development must be identified. Secondary stages are defined as short developmental steps (inside a principal stage) characteristic of the respective plant species. They are also encoded with a single digit. The combination of the principal and the secondary stages, results in a two-digit code –e.g., "51" stands for "Inflorescence or flower buds visible". The scale allows precisely defining all phenological development stages for the majority of plant species.* » [3]. BBCH is considered a reference to describe stages and the monography is available in English, French, German and Spanish [1–4].

For grapevine, the first phenological scale was proposed by Baggiolini [8] in 1952. It initially had 10 stages that were completed in 1993 by Baillod and Baggiolini [9] to reach 16 stages. In 1977, Eichhorn and Lorenz (EL) proposed a more detailed scale of 24 stages for grapevine. In 1992, a universal scale known as BBCH for cultivated mono and dicotyledonous plants was proposed by Hack et al., then adapted to grapevine in 1995 by Lorenz et al. [18]. The BBCH grapevine individual scale allows comparison with other species, both annual and perennial, and has gradually established itself as a reference scale in the scientific community. In 1995, Coombe [11] proposed an alignment between the different existing scales for grapevine while proposing modifications to EL's. However, in the French agricultural technical community, different phenological scales are sometimes used according to the habits of the technicians and the territories. IFV had therefore produced a technical sheet [15] to synthesise the most useful and relevant grapevine development stages and their correspondences with the BBCH grapevine individual scale, the EL and the Baggiolini scales. The definitions of each stage were enriched by specific French expressions.

Even if there exists other scales for other crops, such as Zadoks (1974), there is clearly no universally agreed-upon "phenological stages"; however, because of its wide adoption, BBCH scale works well as a pivot language to describe crop specific development stages. In other terms, crop specific RDF vocabularies will have to be formally aligned to the BBCH generic scale (either via instantiation or via explicit mappings between scales.

3 Resources for Phenological Development Stages

None of the aforementioned scales are published as semantic resources by their producers. However, some existing vocabularies or ontologies do encompass parts of them. Searching "BBCH" on AgroPortal returned mostly matches in 3 vocabularies: the Crop Ontology, Plant Ontology and SOY, a specific trait ontology for soy, irrelevant for us for now. Other semantic resources we identified would contain development or phenological descriptors include the AGROVOC thesaurus and the Plant Phenology Ontology [25] or crop specific resources like the Banana Anatomy Ontology.

3.1 AGROVOC

AGROVOC thesaurus is published by the Food and Agriculture Organization of the UN (FAO) [22]. It is edited by a worlwide community of experts and covers all FAO's areas of interest, including agriculture, forestry, fisheries, food and related domains. It is available in 29 languages, with an average of 35,000 terms and developed in SKOS-XL. The strength of this thesaurus is its multilingual lexical coverage and therefore it is often used to annotate or index agricultural documents or images [24]. AGROVOC contains some phenological stages. The `skos:Concept` individual "plant developmental stages" is the root of a broader/narrower hierarchy of 38 development stages. For example the URI http://aims.fao.org/aos/agrovoc/c_2992 identifies the 'flowering' stage. We note that the reference to an existing scale is not mentioned –i.e., it does not refer to BBCH or any other scale either directly or through its mappings–, neither the crop which this stage occurred, and many stages are missing. For these reasons, AGROVOC is not precise enough for our purpose, despite offering 38 stages for alignments.

3.2 Plant Ontology and Crop Ontology

The Crop Ontology (CO) [23] and Plant Ontology (PO) [12] are two efforts to develop reference ontologies for plants genomics and phenomics developed and maintained during the Planteome project [16]. CO is actually a set of several crop specific traits dictionaries all connected to PO and Plant Trait Ontology (TO).

One of the crop specific trait dictionary is the Vitis Ontology,[1] but it does not contain any development stage. PO however covers all plants; it contains standardized terms, definitions, and logical relations describing plant anatomy, morphology and development stages [26]. In PO, a development stage is represented as a class. A stage corresponds to a time interval in the growth of the corresponding plant structure. Thus, a shorter stage is defined as a subclass of a longer stage. A stage is related to a plant anatomical entity using `has_participant` object property. Some (49) references to the BBCH scale (or to other scales e.g. 38 references to Zadoks) can be found in the `has_related_synonym` annotation property. For example, the URI http://purl.obolibrary.org/obo/PO_0007086 corresponds to the stage at which five nodes or five internodes are visible. This stage corresponds to the BBCH stage 35. As most OBO ontologies, PO is based on the Basic Formal Ontology (BFO) [6] and reuses some properties defined in the Relation Ontology (RO). Interesting object properties, such as *precedes* and *preceded_by* indicate that the end of a stage happens before the beginning of another, but these properties defines some domain and range restrictions related to BFO constructs. Thus reusing these properties means reusing BFO constructs. PO, which was designed to annotate genomic and phenotypic data, is more detailed than the BBCH scale which was designed for agricultural practices and thus not really relevant for our use case.

3.3   Plant Phenology Ontology (PPO)

The Plant Phenology Ontology (PPO) provides a standardized vocabulary useful for large-scale integration of heterogeneous plant phenology data from around the world [25]. It relies on PO as well as on the Phenotype and Trait Ontology (PATO). Phenology studies do not really observe phenological stages, which usually occur over a period of days; they rather observe physical traits of plants, which provides information such as whether a plant has leaves or fruits. Thus, PPO defines phenological traits and does not focus on plant development stages. PPO enables to describe precisely the presence or absence of some plant anatomical entities that is modelled as phenological traits.

To conclude, among the semantic resources identified, we have not found any solution to adopt directly in our use case. Although BBCH is often referenced, which confirms its role of corner stone, we have not found a semantic resource which would rely on BBCH and offer a means to semantically encode phenological development stages for any crops. Therefore, we decided to propose a new ontological framework to describe the BBCH scales: this framework will contain an OWL ontology to represent BBCH generic scale as well as several specific vocabularies (or datasets of SKOS individuals) for each crop specific scales – in our grapevine use case: BBCH individual, IFV labels, EL and Baggiolini scales.

---

[1] http://agroportal.lirmm.fr/ontologies/CO_356.

4   An Ontological Framework for Phenological Development Stages

We have followed the *Linked Open Terms* method, an ontology engineering methodology inspired by Agile software development [20]. This methodology focuses on the reuse of terms (classes, properties and attributes) existing in already published vocabularies or ontologies and the publication of the ontology following the linked data principles. The method defines iterations over the following four activities: (1) ontological requirements specification, (2) ontology implementation, (3) ontology publication, and (4) ontology maintenance.

4.1   Ontological Requirements Specification

Our ontological requirements were specified by several competency questions:

- What are the French/English preferred and alternative labels for a specific development stage?
- What is the definition in French/English of a specific development stage?
- What are the principal and secondary development stages for grapevine in a specific scale (BBCH individual, IFV, EL or Baggiolini)?
- Which BBCH principal stage is linked to a specific secondary stage S of the R scale (IFV, EL or Baggiolini)?
- Which BBCH secondary stage is equivalent to a specific secondary stage S of the R scale (IFV, EL or Baggiolini)?
- Which BBCH secondary stage is mapped (broad or narrow match) to the secondary stage S of the R scale (IFV, EL or Baggiolini)?
- How to order (with follow/precede relations) the primary and secondary stages of a specific scale?

4.2   Ontology Implementation

We have chosen to specialize the SKOS model [5] to represent development stages in our ontology; it is a W3C Recommendation with the appropriate semantic constructs, and it can address most of our competency questions, especially related to the use of labels and mappings properties. A phenological development stage will be a subclass of a `skos:Concept` and will be described with multilingual preferred and alternative labels. A stage will belong to a specific scale which will be represented by a set of instances in a `skos:ConceptScheme`. A secondary stage will be linked to its principal stage using a `skos:broader` relation. The ontology will be an OWL file which can possibly imports each scale defined in a specific file (to build a knowledge base) or be imported by any other ontology which want to build atop our model.

BBCH General Scale Model. We represent the BBCH stages from the general scale as a set of classes; each specific stages in an crop specific scale (BBCH individual scale or IFV scale) will therefore be instances of the classes. For example, the class secondary stage 'BBCH 01' of the general scale represents the set of secondary stages 'BBCH 01' of every individual scale. As shown in Fig. 1, we created a class `ppdo:GrowthStage`, subclass of `skos:Concept` that will be the top of the BBCH stages hierarchy. This class is then specialized in two subclasses for principal and secondary stages. Both are defined as classes to express that all their individuals should be linked to one specific instance of the class `ppdo:StageDivision` with the `ppdo:hasRank` property. Thus all the instances of `ppdo:GrowthStage` linked to the individual `principal`, will be automatically classified as instances of `ppdo:PrincipalGrowthStage` and all the instances of `ppdo:GrowthStage` linked to the individual `secondary` will be automatically classified as instances of `ppdo:SecondaryGrowthStage`. Figure 1 presents examples of principal and secondary stages specializing the classes.

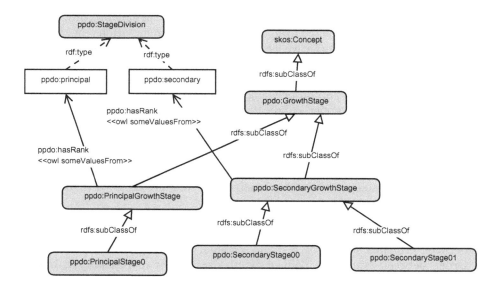

Fig. 1. BBCH general scale model and examples of classes –the prefix `ppdo` currently means http://ontology.inrae.fr/ppdo/ontology.

BBCH Individual Scale Model. A development stage for grapevine is represented as an instance of one of the subclasses of `ppdo:GrowthStage` in the general BBCH model e.g., Fig. 2 presents an instance of `ppdo:SecondaryStage01`. The URI identifying the development stage follows the pattern:

<scaleName:cropName_typeOfStage_stageCode>

Several SKOS properties or specific relations are used to describe the stage:

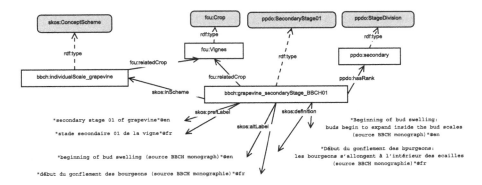

Fig. 2. Example of instantiation of the BBCH general scale model with the grapevine specific scale (stage BBCH 01) –the prefix `bbch` currently means http://ontology.inrae. fr/ppdo/bbch.

- Labels are described using `skos:prefLabel` and `skos:prefLabel` properties. Preferred labels are extracted from the associated documentation (e.g., BBCH monograph) whereas alternative labels are taken from the text definition when possible;
- Definitions are described using `skos:definition` property. The BBCH monograph provides one definition per language;
- The `skos:inScheme` property indicates the scale which the stage belongs to. Each BBCH individual scale or any other scale will be represented as instances of `skos:ConceptScheme`.
- The crop associated to the development stage –or the whole scale– is described using `fcu:relatedCrop` property which comes from the French Crop Usage thesaurus,[2] a resource created to classify crops and already used to annotate PHB [21];
- Relations between principal and secondary stages are described using `skos: broader/narrower` properties. Figure 3 illustrates use of this property between principal stage BBCH 0 and secondary stage BBCH 00;
- Order between stages, as defined by the scale, are represented with the `ppdo:precedes` and `ppdo:follows` properties. Figure 3 presents an example between secondary stage BBCH 00 and secondary stage BBCH 01.

IFV Scale Model. We model IFV labels as a new formal scale following the same guidelines used for BBCH individual scale of grapevine. Here, the main new point was to formally align the BBCH individual scale with the IFV one. To do so we used SKOS mapping properties:

- Because IFV labels describe only secondary stages, each IFV stage is mapped to one BBCH principal stage using the `skos:broadMatch` property;

---

[2] http://agroportal.lirmm.fr/ontologies/CROPUSAGE_FR (`fcu` on the Figures).

– Similarly, each IFV stage is mapped to one BBCH secondary stage using the `skos:exactMatch` property.

Figure 3 presents an example of the alignment of IFV stage 00 to its corresponding BBCH stages. Even if not presented here, we would use the same approach to develop and map other scales (EL, Baggiolini).

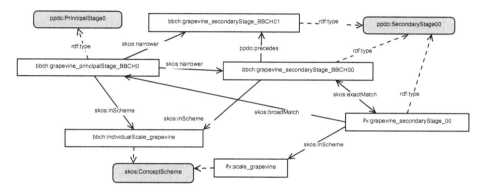

Fig. 3. Alignment between stage BBCH 01 of grapevine and corresponding IFV stage –the prefix `ifv` currently means http://ontology.inrae.fr/ppdo/ifv.

RDF Encoding. Once the models were designed, they were encoded as classes and instances in RDF using constructs from RDFS, SKOS and OWL. We used the Protégé ontology editor (v5.1.0) [19] with Cellfie plugin.[3] We have first created the general model as an `owl:Ontology` defining the classes (Fig. 1) from the BBCH general scale. We also added metadata descriptions (e.g., authors, dates, licenses) as recommended by [14] or [13]. Second, we populated the ontology with instances from all the stages from the BBCH individual scale of grapevine, IFV labels, the Baggiolini scale and the EL scale to produce different OWL knowledge bases (i.e., datasets importing the ontology and adding individuals.) We used different sources to populate the ontology. The BBCH monographs provided the information (labels and descriptions) in four languages (French, English, Spanish and German) for the general scale and the grapevine individual scale. Scientific publication of Baggiolini scale and the Eichhorn-Lorenz scale provided the information in English. And finally, IFV provided us with one CSV file gathering the information in French and English. Then, we extracted the data semi-automatically to different spreadsheets before loading them in the knowledge bases using Cellfie transformation rules. Cellfie was also used to generate individuals, each of them as an instance of one of the stage classes; transformation rules

---

[3] Cellfie (https://github.com/protegeproject/cellfie-plugin) allows to import spreadsheets content inside OWL ontologies in Protégé.

enabled to create links using object properties: `ppdo:precedes`, `ppdo:follows`, `skos:broader`, `skos:broadMatch`, `skos:exactMatch`, `rdf:type`. To improve the coherency of the final resource, we used a SWRL rule to inferred all inverse properties. A final check was performed using the SKOS Play! tool (http://labs. sparna.fr/skos-play): it enabled to visualize and control the SKOS model and detected some errors.

The result is an ontological framework (and ontology and several knowledge bases) with an ontology that specializes the SKOS model, of 98 classes –most of them being stages in the BBCH generic scale– and 125 individuals –coming from grapevine scales only– and 1208 object property assertions and 1696 annotation property assertions. Within this ontology, each encoded scale is accessible by a specific SKOS concept scheme. We named this ontology *BBCH-based Plant Phenological Description Ontology*, tagged it as v1.0.

4.3   Ontology Publication and Maintenance

The BBCH-based Plant Phenological Description Ontology v1.0 is publicly available: https://gitlab.irstea.fr/copain/phenologicalstages. This file is also loaded into a Jena Fuseki triple store and can be queried at: http://ontology.inrae.fr/ppdo/sparql/. The current implementation contains 98 classes, 21 object properties, 1 datatype property and 125 individuals and it imports all the individuals from the French Crop Usage thesaurus. The issue tracker provided by Gitlab is the tool used to receive feedback and control issue lists. In a near future, we plan to complete the metadata descriptions, choose a perennial URI pattern, and upload the BBCH-based Plant Phenological Description Ontology including authorized and properly credited specific scales to the AgroPortal ontology repository [17].

5   Discussion and Conclusion

This transformation (RDFization) of the grapevine phenological development scales is a collaborative work between an IFV expert and computer scientists expert in ontology engineering. The result shall enhance the value and reusability/interoperability of the currently existing phenological development scales, once lifted to RDF. For example, IFV labels were improved as the French labels and definitions were translated in English thanks to the BBCH monograph. Also, some inconsistencies/errors were detected. For instance, IFV scale mentions BBCH 88 of grapevine which does not exist in the BBCH monograph. The semantic of mappings between the stages of different scales are defined using SKOS properties thus clarifying the alignment and overlap between the different scales with semantic web properties with clear semantics. We have already populated the ontology with stages from the Baggiolini scale and the Eichhorn-Lorenz scale. In the future, we plan to publish several wheat scales (e.g., Zadoks) using the same framework.

The mixture of SKOS and OWL allows to include and interlink in one ontology model all the stages in all the scales as instances of the relevant classes. But in addition, the `skos:inScheme` and `skos:ConceptScheme` constructs enable to capture the set of stages of each specific scale in a same scheme that can be described with its specific metadata (authors, dates, etc.). The mix of `owl:subClassOf` and `skos:broader/skos:narrower` hierarchies allows to respectively represent groups of generic stages and relations between stages in a specific scale only.

The semantic resource produced is currently available through a SPARQL endpoint at INRAE. By the end of our project, we expect to store and make available our PHB archive in the same environment and published all these interlinked datasets and ontology as Linked Open Data. Then, in order to improve the interlinking of the BBCH-based Plant Phenological Description Ontology, some alignments could be proposed. First, we could link the `ppdo:GrowthStage` individuals that represent crop specific stages to some AGROVOC individuals. AGROVOC proposes some generic stage not related to a specific crop, thus a `skos:broadMatch` property could be used.[4] Second, we could link those individuals to more precise description that are proposed in the Plant Phenotype Ontology and the Plant Ontology. The type of mapping should be well studied due to the fact that the point of view between these two models are quite different: PPO and PO represent precise development processes of each plant organ, phenological development scales are just a snapshot of some typical plant development stages useful to schedule agricultural practices.

Acknowledgements. This work was achieved with support of the Data to Knowledge in Agronomy and Biodiversity (D2KAB – www.d2kab.org) project that received funding from the French National Research Agency (ANR-18-CE23-0017); as well as with help of French Wine and Vine Institute (www.vignevin.com). We also thanks Thibaut Scholasch (Fruition Sciences) for help translating the labels.

References

1. Entwicklungsstadien mono- und dikotyler Pflanzen: BBCH Monografie
2. Etapas de desarrollo de las plantas monocotiledóneas y dicotiledóneas: BBCH Monografia
3. Growth stages of mono- and dicotyledonous plants: BBCH Monograph
4. Stades phénologiques des mono-et dicotylédones cultivées: BBCH Monographie
5. Alistair, M., Sean, B.: SKOS simple knowledge organization system. W3C Recommendation, W3C, August 2009. http://www.w3.org/2004/02/skos/core.html
6. Arp, R., Smith, B., Spear, A.D.: Building Ontologies with Basic Formal Ontology. MIT Press, Cambridge (2015)
7. Aubin, S., Bisquert, P., Buche, P., Dibie, J., Ibanescu, L., Jonquet, C., Roussey, C.: Recent progresses in data and knowledge integration for decision support in agri-food chains. 30èmes Journées Francophones d'Ingénierie des Connaissances. IC 2019, Toulouse, France, pp. 43–59, July 2019

---

[4] Or, to be more generic, we need a mechanism to map a `skos:Concept` in AGROVOC to a `owl:Class` in our ontology.

8. Baggiolini, M.: Les stades repères dans le développement annuel de la vigne et leur utilisation pratique. Revue Romande d'Agriculture, de Viticulture et d'Arboriculture **1**, 4–6 (1952)

9. Baillod, M., Baggiolini, M.: Les stades repères de la vigne. Rev. Suisse Vitic. Arboric. Hortic **25**(1), 7–9 (1993)

10. Bizer, C., Heath, T., Berners-Lee, T.: Linked data - the story so far. Semantic Web Inf. Syst. **5**(3), 1–22 (2009)

11. Coombe, B.G.: Growth stages of the grapevine: adoption of a system for identifying grapevine growth stages. Australian J. Grape Wine Res. **1**(2), 104–110 (1995)

12. Cooper, L., et al.: The plant ontology as a tool for comparative plant anatomy and genomic analyses. Plant Cell Physiol. **54**(2), e1 (2012)

13. Dutta, B., Toulet, A., Emonet, V., Jonquet, C.: New generation metadata vocabulary for ontology description and publication. In: Garoufallou, E., Virkus, S., Siatri, R., Koutsomiha, D. (eds.) MTSR 2017. CCIS, vol. 755, pp. 173–185. Springer, Cham (2017). https://doi.org/10.1007/978-3-319-70863-8_17

14. Garijo, D., Poveda Villalon, M.: A checklist for complete vocabulary metadata. Technical report WIDOCO, April 2017

15. IFV: Les stades phénologique de la vigne (2017). https://www.vignevin.com/wp-content/uploads/2019/05/Poster-stades-ph%C3%A9nologiques-de-la-vigne.pdf

16. Jaiswal, P., et al.: Planteome: a resource for common reference ontologies and applications for plant biology. In: 24th Plant and Animal Genome Conference, PAG 2016. San Diego, USA, January 2016

17. Jonquet, C., et al.: AgroPortal: a vocabulary and ontology repository for agronomy. Comput. Electron. Agri. **144**, 126–143 (2018)

18. Lorenz, D., Eichhorn, K., Bleiholder, H., Klose, R., Meier, U., Weber, E.: Growth stages of the grapevine: phenological growth stages of the grapevine (Vitis vinifera L. ssp. vinifera)—codes and descriptions according to the extended BBCH scale. Australian J. Grape Wine Res. **1**(2), 100–103 (1995)

19. Musen, M.A.: The protégé project: a look back and a look forward. AI Matters **1**(4), 4–12 (2015)

20. Poveda-Villalón, M.: A reuse-based lightweight method for developing linked data ontologies and vocabularies. In: Simperl, E., Cimiano, P., Polleres, A., Corcho, O., Presutti, V. (eds.) ESWC 2012. LNCS, vol. 7295, pp. 833–837. Springer, Heidelberg (2012). https://doi.org/10.1007/978-3-642-30284-8_66

21. Roussey, C., et al.: A methodology for the publication of agricultural alert bulletins as LOD. Comput. Electron. Agri. **142**, 632–650 (2017)

22. Sachit Rajbhandari, J.K.: The AGROVOC concept scheme a walkthrough. Integr. Agri. **11**(5), 694–699 (2012)

23. Shrestha, R., et al.: Multifunctional crop trait ontology for breeders' data: field book, annotation, data discovery and semantic enrichment of the literature. AoB Plants **2010**, plq008 (2010)

24. Stefano, A., Yves, J., Fabrizio, C., Armando, S., Johannes, K.: Migrating bibliographic datasets to the semantic web: the AGRIS case. Semantic Web **6**(2), 113–120 (2015)

25. Stucky, B.J., Guralnick, R., Deck, J., Denny, E.G., Bolmgren, K., Walls, R.: The plant phenology ontology: a new informatics resource for large-scale integration of plant phenology data. Front. Plant Sci. **9**, 517 (2018)

26. Walls, R.L., et al.: The plant ontology facilitates comparisons of plant development stages across species. Front. Plant Sci. **10**, 631 (2019)

On the Evolution of Semantic Warehouses: The Case of Global Record of Stocks and Fisheries

Yannis Marketakis[1]([✉])[ID], Yannis Tzitzikas[1,2][ID], Aureliano Gentile[3][ID],
Bracken van Niekerk[3][ID], and Marc Taconet[3][ID]

[1] Institute of Computer Science, FORTH-ICS, Heraklion, Greece
{marketak,tzitzik}@ics.forth.gr
[2] Computer Science Department, University of Crete, Heraklion, Greece
[3] Food and Agriculture Organization of the United Nations, Rome, Italy
{aureliano.gentile,bracken.vanniekerk,marc.taconet}@fao.org

Abstract. Semantic Warehouses integrate data from various sources for offering a unified view of the data and enabling the answering of queries which cannot be answered by the individual sources. However, such semantic warehouses have to be refreshed periodically as the underlying datasets change. This is a challenging requirement, not only because the mappings and transformations that were used for constructing the semantic warehouse can be invalidated, but also because additional information (not existing in the initial datasets) may have been added in the semantic warehouse, and such information needs to be preserved after every reconstruction. In this paper we focus on this particular problem in a real setting: the Global Record of Stocks and Fisheries, a semantic warehouse that integrates data about stocks and fisheries from various information systems. We propose and detail a process that can tackle these requirements and we report our experiences from implementing it.

1 Introduction

The Web of Data contains thousands of RDF datasets available online (see [12] for a recent survey), including cross-domain Knowledge Bases (e.g., DBpedia and Wikidata), domain specific repositories (e.g., WarSampo [5], DrugBank [21], ORKG [6], life science related datasets [14] and recently COVID-19 related datasets [8,13]), as well as Markup data through schema.org. One important category of domain specific semantic repositories, are the semantic warehouses, those produced by integrating various evolving datasets. Such warehouses aim at offering a unified view of the data and enabling the answering of queries which cannot be answered by the individual datasets. However, such semantic warehouses have to be refreshed because the underlying datasets change since they are managed by different stakeholders and operating information systems. This is a challenging requirement, not only because the mappings and transformations that were used for constructing the semantic warehouse can be invalidated, but

© Springer Nature Switzerland AG 2021
E. Garoufallou and M.-A. Ovalle-Perandones (Eds.): MTSR 2020, CCIS 1355, pp. 269–281, 2021.
https://doi.org/10.1007/978-3-030-71903-6_26

also because additional information, that does not exist in the initial datasets, may have been added in the semantic warehouse, and such information needs to be preserved after every reconstruction. In this paper we focus on that particular problem. We study this problem in a real setting, specifically on the Global Record of Stocks and Fisheries (for short GRSF) [19], a semantic warehouse that integrates data about stocks and fisheries from various information systems. In brief, GRSF is capable of hosting the corresponding information categorized into uniquely and globally identifiable records. Instead of creating yet another registry, GRSF aims at producing its records by using existing data. This approach does not invalidate the process being followed so far, in the sense that the organizations that maintain the original data are expected to continue to play their key role in collecting and exposing them. In fact, GRSF does not generate new data, rather it collates information coming from the different database sources, facilitating the discovery of inventoried stocks and fisheries arranged into distinct domains.

In this paper, we focus on the evolution of this domain-specific semantic warehouse. Although, GRSF is constructed by collating information from other data sources, it is not meant to be used as a read-only data source. After its initial construction, GRSF is being assessed by GRSF administrators who can edit particular information, like for example the short name of a record, update its connections, suggest merging multiple records into a new one (more about the merging process is given in Sect. 2.1), or even provide narrative annotations. The assessment process might result in approving a record, which will make it accessible from a wider audience through a publicly accessible URL. In general, GRSF URLs are immutable, and especially if a GRSF record becomes public then its URL should become permanent as well.

The challenge when refreshing it, is that we want to be able to preserve the immutable URLs of the catalogue, especially the public ones. In addition, we want to preserve all the updates carried out from GRSF administrators, since their updates are stored in GRSF and are not directly reflected to the original sources. To do this, we need to identify records, and so we exploit their identifiers at different levels. In a nutshell, the key contributions of this paper are: (a) the analysis of the requirements for preserving updates in aggregated records that are not reflected in the original data, (b) the identification of aggregated records in different versions of a semantic warehouse, (c) the definition of a process for managing the evolution while preserving updates in the aggregated records.

The rest of this paper is organized as follows: Sect. 2 discusses background and requirements, Sect. 3 describes related work, Sect. 4 details our approach, and Sect. 5 reports our experience on the implementation. Finally Sect. 6 concludes the paper and elaborates with future work and research.

2   Context

Here we provide background information about the domain-specific warehouse GRSF (in Sect. 2.1) and then discuss the evolution-related requirements (in Sect. 2.2).

2.1   Background: GRSF

The design and the initial implementation of the Global Record of Stocks and Fisheries have been initiated in the context of the H2020 EU Project Blue-BRIDGE[1]. It integrates data from three different data sources, owned by different stakeholders, in a knowledge base (the GRSF KB), and then exposes them through a catalogue of a Virtual Research Environment (VRE), operated on top of D4Science infrastructure[1]. These data sources are: (a) Fisheries and Resources Monitoring System (FIRMS)[2], (b) RAM Legacy Stock Assessment database[3], and (c) FishSource[4]. They contain complementary information (both conceptually and geographically). Specifically, FIRMS is mostly reporting about stocks and fisheries at regional level, while RAM is reporting stocks at national or subnational level, and FishSource is more focused on the fishing activities. All of them contribute to the overall aim to build a comprehensive and transparent global reference set of stocks and fisheries records that will boost regional and global stocks and fisheries status and trend monitoring as well as responsible consumer practices. GRSF continues its evolvement and expansion in the context of the ongoing H2020 EU Project BlueCloud[5].

GRSF intents to collate information in terms of *stocks* and *fisheries records*. Each record is composed of several fields to accommodate the incoming information and data. The fields can be functionally divided into *time-independent* and *time-dependent*. The former consists of identification and descriptive information that can be used for uniquely identifying a record, while the latter contains indicators which are modeled as dimensions. For example for the case of stock records such dimensions are the abundance levels, fishing pressure, biomasses, while for fishery records they are catches and landings indicators.

The process for constructing the initial version of GRSF is described in [19]. Figure 1 shows a Use Case Diagram depicting the different actors that are involved, as well as the various use cases. In general there are three types of users: (a) *Maintainers* that are responsible for constructing and maintaining GRSF KB, as well as publishing the concrete records from the semantic warehouse to the VRE catalogues. They are the technical experts carrying out the semantic data integration from the original data sources. (b) *Administrators*, that are responsible for assessing information of GRSF records through the VRE catalogues, in order to validate their contents, as well as for spotting new potential merges of records. They are marine experts familiar with the terminologies, standards, and processes for assessing stocks and fisheries. Upon successful assessment they approve GRSF records and they become available to external users. (c) *External users* for querying and browsing it. To ease understanding, Table 1 provides some background information about the terminologies of GRSF that are used in the sequel.

---

[1] BlueBRIDGE (H2020-BG-2019-1), GA no 675680.
[2] http://firms.fao.org/firms/en.
[3] https://www.ramlegacy.org/.
[4] https://www.fishsource.org/.
[5] BlueCloud (H2020-EU.3.2.5.1), GA no: 862409.

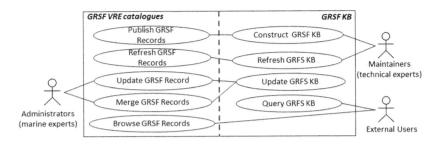

Fig. 1. Use Case Diagram describing the GRSF Ecosystem

Table 1. Explanation of the Terminology in GRSF

Term	Description
Source record	A record that has been derived by transforming its original contents, with respect to a core ontology, specifically MarineTLO [17]. For each record harvested from the original sources, we create a single source record and ingest it in GRSF KB
GRSF record	A new record that has been constructed taking information from one or more source records. GRSF records are described in a similar manner with source records (i.e. as ontology-based descriptions), however during their construction they adopt GRSF rules, and use global standard classification as much as possible (e.g. where possible, instead of a species common name use the FAO ASFIS classification), generate new attributes (e.g. semantic ID), flags, citations, etc.
Semantic ID	They are *identifiers* assigned to GRSF records that are generated following a particular pattern and are meant to be both human and machine understandable. They are called semantic identifiers in the sense that their values allow identifying several aspects of a record. The identifier is a concatenation of a set of predefined fields of the record in a particular form. To keep them as short as possible it has been decided to rely on standard values or abbreviations whenever applicable. Each abbreviation is accompanied with the thesaurus or standard scheme that defines it. For GRSF stocks the fields that are used are: (1) species and (2) water areas (e.g. `ASFIS:SWO+FAO:34`). For GRSF fisheries the fields that are used are: (1) species, (2) water areas, (3) management authorities, (4) fishing gears, and (5) flag states (e.g. `ASFIS:COD+FAO:21+authority:INT:NAFO+ISSCFG:03.1.2+ISO3:CAN`)
Merge	A process ensuring that source records from different sources having exactly the same attributes that are used for identification, are both used for constructing a single GRSF Stock record. The same attributes that are used for constructing the Semantic ID, are used for identifying records. An example is shown in Fig. 4
Dissect	A process applied to aggregated source fishery records so that they will construct concrete GRSF fishery records compliant with the standards. The process is applied on particular fields of the aggregated record (i.e. species, fishing gears, and flag states) so that the constructed GRSF record is uniquely described and suitable for traceability purposes. An example is shown in Fig. 4
Approved record	After their construction GRSF records, appear with status *pending*. Once they are assessed from GRSF administrators, they can be approved (if they are valid) and as a result their status is changed to *approved*. Approved records are then made publicly available

Figure 2 shows the different activities that are carried out. Initially, information from the data sources are transformed and ingested into the GRSF KB, as source records, which are afterwards used for constructing the GRSF records, based on a set of well defined GRSF rules and after applying the corresponding activities (i.e. merging and dissection). Both the source records and GRSF records are published in the catalogue of a VRE. The former for provenance reasons and the latter for inspection and validation from GRSF administrators. When a GRSF record is approved, it becomes publicly available by replicating its contents in a public VRE.

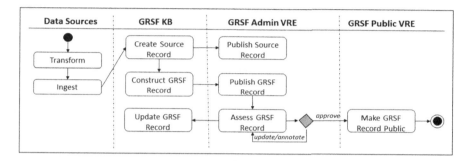

Fig. 2. The process of constructing, publishing and assessing GRSF records

2.2 Evolution Requirements

The following list provides the key requirements for refreshing GRSF:

• (R1): *Refresh* the contents of GRSF with up-to-date information from the underlying sources for updating all the time-dependent information, as well as bringing potential fixes in the original records in GRSF.

• (R2): *Remove obsolete records* from GRSF and VRE catalogues: If their status is approved, then instead of removing them, change their status to *archived* and archive them in the VRE catalogue with a proper annotation message.

• (R3): *Preserve the immutable URLs* that are generated for GRSF records when they are published in VRE catalogues. These URLs should be preserved (instead of generating new ones) to avoid the creation of broken links.

• (R4): *Maintain* all the updates that have been carried out in GRSF records from GRSF administrators. These updates are performed in GRSF KB and are not applied back to the data sources (e.g. an update in the name of a record).

• (R5): *Maintain all the annotations* made by GRSF admininstrators to GRSF records (annotations are small narratives describing their observations during the assessment of the records).

• (R6): *Preserve all the merges* that are used for constructing GRSF records. Although GRSF merges are applied using a set of well-defined rules (as described in Sect. 2.1), GRSF administrators can propose and apply the merging of records manually. Since the latter might not be re-producable it is important to preserve them when refreshing GRSF.

3   Related Work and Novelty

There are several works that deal with the problem of evolution in ontology-based access in general. A survey for ontology evolution is given in [4]. The problem of query answering in mediators (virtual integration systems) under evolving ontologies without recreating mappings between the mediator and the underlying sources is studied in [9] where query re-writing methods are proposed. The losses of specificity of ontology-based descriptions, when such descriptions are migrated to newer versions of the ontology has been studied in [18]. Finally, there are various methods that focus on monitoring the "health" of various RDF-based systems, e.g. [11] focuses on the connectivity monitoring in the context of a semantic warehouse over time, [7] focuses on monitoring Linked Data over a specific period of time, [2] focuses on measuring the dynamics of a specific RDF dataset, and [15] proposes a framework that identifies, analyses and understands such dynamics. $SPARQLES$ [20] and $SpEnD$ [22] focus on the monitoring of public SPARQL endpoints, $DyKOSMap$ framework [3] adapts the mappings of Knowledge Organization Systems, as the data are modified over time.

[14] is the one closest to our work. In that paper, the authors analyze the way change operations in RDF repositories correlate to changes observed in links. They investigated the behaviour of links in terms of complex changes (e.g. modification of triples) and simple ones (e.g. addition or removal of links). Compared to this work, and for tackling the GRSF requirements, in our work we focus on identifying and analyzing the evolution of each concrete record which is part of the GRSF dataset. Therefore instead of analyzing the evolution in terms of triples, we do it in terms of a collection of triples (e.g. a record). Furthermore, we exploit the semantics of the links of a record by classifying them in different categories. For example, triples describing identifiers or URLs are classified as immutable and are not subject to change, while links pointing to time-dependent information are frequently updated. In addition, in our work we deal with the requirement of preserving manually provided information and various several human-provided updates and activities in the dataset, during its evolution.

4   An Approach for Semantic Warehouse Evolution

In Sect. 4.1 we elaborate on the identification of resources, while in Sect. 4.2 we detail the GRSF refresh workflow.

4.1   Uniquely Identifying Sources

Before actually refreshing information in GRSF KB, it is required to identify and map the appropriate information from the source databases, with information in the VRE catalogues and the GRSF KB. To do so, we will rely on identifiers for these records. The main problem, however, is raised from the fact that although data had identifiers assigned to them from their original sources, they were valid only within the scope of each particular source. As they have been integrated they were assigned a new identifier (i.e. in GRSF KB), and as they have been published in the VRE catalogues they have been assigned additional identifiers (i.e. in VRE catalogues). As regards the latter, it is a mandatory addition due to the different technologies that are used for GRSF. We could distinguish the identifiers in three distinct groups:

Data Source Identifiers. They are identifiers assigned to each record from the stakeholders of each source. If r denotes a record, let use $r.sourceID$ to denote its identifier in a source. For the cases of FIRMS and FishSource, they are short numbers (e.g. 10086), while for the case of RAM they are codes produced from the record details (e.g. PHFLOUNNHOKK). Furthermore, the first two sources have their records publicly available, through their identifiers with a resolvable URL representation (e.g. http://firms.fao.org/firms/resource/10089/en, https://www.fishsource.org/stock_page/1134).

GRSF KB Identifiers. After the data have been harvested, they are transformed and ingested in GRSF KB. During the transformation they are assigned URIs (Uniform Resource Identifier), which are generated, by applying hashing over the data source identifier of the corresponding record, i.e. we could write $r.URI = hash(r.sourceID)$. This guarantees the uniqueness of the URIs and avoids connecting irrelevant entities. Obviously, the data source identifiers are stored in GRSF KB, as well. For source records, URIs are generated based on the hashing described above, while for GRSF records a unique random URI is generated.

GRSF VRE Catalogue Identifiers. All the records from the GRSF KB, are published in the VRE catalogue, which enables their validation and assessment from GRSF Administrators. After publishing them in the catalogue, they are assigned a resolvable URL. The generated URL, denoted by $r.catalogID$, is stored in GRSF KB. These URLs are used for disseminating records, therefore they should be preserved when refreshing GRSF, because the generation of new ones, would break the former links.

4.2 Refreshing Workflow

Figure 3 shows the GRSF refreshing workflow. Similarly to the construction process, which has been described in [19], and is also shown in the activity diagram in Fig. 2, everything starts by harvesting and transforming data from the original data sources. Specifically, they are downloaded and transformed as ontology-based instances of the extended top level ontology MarineTLO [17]. These instances are then ingested into a triplestore for constructing the new GRSF records (GRSF KB - V2). These activities are carried out by reusing or adapting existing software modules like MatWare [16], and X3ML Framework

[10], and using software that has been implemented for the problem at hand, i.e. grsf-services and grsf-publisher[6].

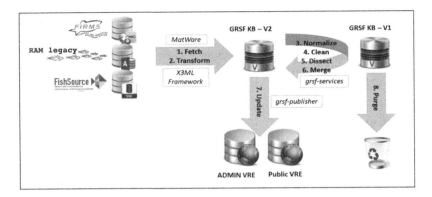

Fig. 3. The workflow for refreshing GRSF, while preserving particular information from the previous version

Algorithm 1 shows how the VRE catalogue URLs and the manually-edited information are preserved across the two versions of GRSF KBs. More specifically, $GRSF\_new$ which is the new version and $GRSF\_pre$ which is the previous one. It traverses through the records in the new version of GRSF KB and finds their older instances in the previous version by inspecting their $r.sourceID$. If the record is of type $Stock$ then it replicates the catalogue URLs (i.e. $r.catalogID$), as well as all the editable information that have been updated by GRSF administrators in $GRSF\_pre$ (denoted by $r.info$). $r.info$ embodies all the fields of a record that can be edited by administrators. Since these updates are kept in GRSF KB and are not reflected in the original sources, their preservation in GRSF is crucial. Furthermore, administrators have the ability to propose merging multiple records into a new one, bypassing therefore the default merging algorithm that is being used.

For the case of records of type *fishery* an alternative approach is being followed, because of the dissection process carried out when constructing GRSF *fishery* records. Unlike *stock* records, if a source *fishery* record has multiple values over some specific fields, then they are dissected to construct GRSF fishery records, as depicted in Fig. 4. The fields considered for the dissection process are species, fishing gears and flags states. Considering that the source fishery record example contains two different species, the dissection process produces two distinct GRSF fishery records.

As a result, because of the dissection procees, the original ID of the fishery record is not enough for identifying the referring GRSF fishery record. For this

---

[6] https://wiki.gcube-system.org/index.php?title=GCube_Data_Catalogue_for_GRSF.

Algorithm 1: Refreshing GRSF KB

Input: Collection $GRSF\_new$, Collection $GRSF\_pre$
Output: Collection $GRSF\_new$

1 **forall** $r\_new \in GRSF\_new$ **do**
2   **forall** $r\_pre \in GRSF\_pre$ **do**
3   **if** $r\_new.sourceID == r\_pre.sourceID$
4   **if** $r\_new.type == Stock$
5                  $r\_new.catalogID = r\_pre.catalogID$
6                  $r\_new.info = r\_pre.info$
7   **else if** $r\_new.type == Fishery$
8   **if** $partialMatch(r\_new.semanticID, r\_pre.semanticID)$
9                      $r\_new.catalogID = r\_pre.catalogID$
10                     $r\_new.info = r\_pre.info$
11 **Return** $GRSF\_new$

---

reason, we are using the semantic ID as well. As described in Sect. 2.1, the semantic ID of fishery records is the concatenation of the values of five particular fields. Therefore, we compare those and identify a positive match if $r\_new.semanticID$ is an expansion of $r\_pre.semanticID$. An indicative example of such a partial match is given below, where the previous version of the semantic ID did not contain values for the last two fields. We should note here that this is usual, since as the data sources themselves evolve, missing information are added to them.

$r\_pre.semanticID$: `asfis:GHL+rfb:NEAFC+auth:INT:NEAFC++`

$r\_new.semanticID$: `asfis:GHL+rfb:NEAFC+auth:INT:NEAFC+iso3:GRL+isscfg:03.29`

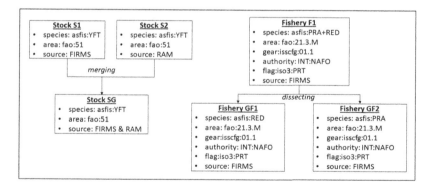

Fig. 4. Merging multiple stock records in a single GRSF stock record (left part) and dissecting a single fishery record in multiple GRSF fishery records (right part)

The activities carried out so far, resulted in the creation of a new version of the GSF KB. Now, we have to update the VRE catalogues. There are three sub-activities at this point: (a) updating the records that are already published, (b) publishing new records that do not exist in the catalogues (c) remove or archive obsolete records.

The first group contains all the GRSF records, for which, we have identified their catalogue URLs, while the second one contains new records not yet assigned a catalogue URL. The former are updated (using their catalogue URLs), and the latter are published (a new catalogue URL is generated). The third group contains the obsolete records. The decision we have taken for obsolete records is to remove them from the catalogue, only if their status was not approved. The approved records are not removed from the catalogue with the rationale, that an approved record might have been disseminated publicly to external users or communities, so removing it would be an arbitrary decision. On the contrary, they are archived with a proper annotation message. We do not apply this for records under pending status; those records can be safely removed, since their status (pending) reveal that they have not been assessed by GRSF administrators.

5   Results and Evaluation

The refresh workflow that we propose meets all requirements described in Sect. 2.2. Obviously it tackles the refresh requirement *R1*. Most importantly, it preserves the work carried out by GRSF administrators, so as to maintain all of their inputs after refreshing and re-constructing GRSF. For example, updates in record names, traceability flags, connections, proposed merging, addition of narrative annotations, etc. (*req. R4, R5, R6*). In addition, the records that are obsolete are removed from GRSF KB and VRE catalogues (*req. R2*). Regarding obsolete records that were publicly available, they are properly archived. As a result, they are still publicly available, however their status, which is archived, reveals that they might not be valid any more. They are only kept in order to avoid creating broken URLs and as an historical evidence of their existence (*req. R3*).

From a technical perspective, the technical architecture of the refresh workflow relies on loosely-coupled technical components that are extensible and easy to maintain. Moreover, the entire process runs in a semi-automatic manner, which requires little human intervention: the only step that human intervention is required is during the archival of obsolete records (e.g. for drafting a proper annotation message). This allows the entire process to be executed periodically.

Table 2 shows some statistics about the refresh. The original version was constructed on December 2018, and the refresh was carried out on July 2020. Figure 5 shows the time that is needed for each step of the refresh workflow. The most time-consuming step is the last one (i.e. Publish / Update) that publishes or (re-publishes) records in VRE catalogues because records are published in sequential manner, through the a set of VRE publishing services that unavoidably perform several validity checks, and each record takes around 2 s to be published. It is worth mentioning however, that when publishing/updating takes place, GRSF KB has already been refreshed, and this (last step of the entire process) just makes the records visible in GRSF catalogues. Another remark is that the actual refreshing activities that are part of the Refresh Source, Construct GRSF and Delete Archive steps, are performed rather quickly. Overall, the refresh workflow has a similar efficiency with the GRSF construction process.

Table 2. Refresh statistics

	Number of records		
Source	Refreshed	New	Obsolete
FIRMS	928	122	5
RAM	1,290	84	1
FishSource	4,094	975	117
GRSF	6,690	7,318	2,998

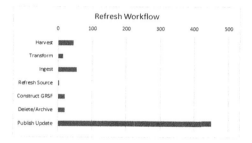

Fig. 5. Refresh time (in minutes)

6   Concluding Remarks

We have focused on the evolution requirements of a semantic warehouse about fish stocks and fisheries. We analyzed the associated requirements and then we described a process for tackling them. A distinctive characteristic of the approach is that it preserves all the manually added/edited information (at warehouse level), while at the same time it maintains the automation of the refresh process. The proposed solution is currently applied in the context of the ongoing EU Project BlueCloud, where the aim for GRSF per se, is to to continue its evolution, as well as its expansion with more data sources and concepts (e.g. fish food and nutrition information). Despite the fact, that we focused on the case of stocks and fisheries, the same approach can be useful also in other domains where edits are allowed at the level of aggregates/integrated data.

Issues that are worth further work and research include: the partial refreshing of the semantic warehouse, which would be useful if there are data sources that are more frequently updated compared to others, the addition of generated information from the semantic warehouse (i.e. unique identifiers) back to the original sources in order to support the refreshing workflow and enforce their preservation, the automatic identification of the existence of updates in the underlying source which would trigger the refreshing workflow as well as the estimation of the refreshing period based on the update frequency of a data source that would enable the fully automatic trigger and execution of the refresh workflow.

Acknowledgements. This work has received funding from the European Union's Horizon 2020 innovation action BlueCloud (Grant agreement No 862409).

References

1. Assante, M., et al.: Enacting open science by d4science. Futur. Gener. Comput. Syst. **101**, 555–563 (2019)
2. Dividino, R.Q., Gottron, T., Scherp, A., Gröner, G.: From changes to dynamics: dynamics analysis of linked open data sources. In: Proceedings of PROFILES@ESWC. CEUR-WS.org (2014)
3. Dos Reis, J.C., Pruski, C., Da Silveira, M., Reynaud-Delaître, C.: Dykosmap: a framework for mapping adaptation between biomedical knowledge organization systems. J. Biomed. Inform. **55**, 153–173 (2015)
4. Flouris, G., Manakanatas, D., Kondylakis, H., Plexousakis, D., Antoniou, G.: Ontology change: classification and survey. Knowle. Eng. Rev. **23**(2), 117–152 (2008)
5. Hyvönen, E., et al.: WarSampo data service and semantic portal for publishing linked open data about the second world war history. In: Sack, H., Blomqvist, E., d'Aquin, M., Ghidini, C., Ponzetto, S.P., Lange, C. (eds.) ESWC 2016. LNCS, vol. 9678, pp. 758–773. Springer, Cham (2016). https://doi.org/10.1007/978-3-319-34129-3_46
6. Jaradeh, M.Y., et al.: Open research knowledge graph: next generation infrastructure for semantic scholarly knowledge. In: Proceedings of the 10th International Conference on Knowledge Capture, pp. 243–246 (2019)
7. Käfer, T., Abdelrahman, A., Umbrich, J., O'Byrne, P., Hogan, A.: Observing linked data dynamics. In: Cimiano, P., Corcho, O., Presutti, V., Hollink, L., Rudolph, S. (eds.) ESWC 2013. LNCS, vol. 7882, pp. 213–227. Springer, Heidelberg (2013). https://doi.org/10.1007/978-3-642-38288-8_15
8. Kohlmeier, S., Lo, K., Wang, L.L., Yang, J.: Covid-19 open research dataset (cord-19) (2020). https://doi.org/10.5281/zenodo.3813567
9. Kondylakis, H., Plexousakis, D.: Ontology evolution without tears. Web Semant. Sci. Serv. Agents World Wide Web **19**, 42–58 (2013)
10. Marketakis, Y., et al.: X3ml mapping framework for information integration in cultural heritage and beyond. Int. J. Digit. Libr. **18**(4), 301–319 (2017). https://doi.org/10.1007/s00799-016-0179-1
11. Mountantonakis, M., Minadakis, N., Marketakis, Y., Fafalios, P., Tzitzikas, Y.: Quantifying the connectivity of a semantic warehouse and understanding its evolution over time. IJSWIS **12**(3), 27–78 (2016)
12. Mountantonakis, M., Tzitzikas, Y.: Large-scale semantic integration of linked data: a survey. ACM Comput. Surv. (CSUR) **52**(5), 103 (2019)
13. R. Gazzotti, F. Michel, F.G.: Cord-19 named entities knowledge graph (cord19-nekg) (2020)

14. Reis, R.B., Morshed, A., Sellis, T.: Understanding link changes in LOD via the evolution of life science datasets (2019)
15. Roussakis, Y., Chrysakis, I., Stefanidis, K., Flouris, G., Stavrakas, Y.: A flexible framework for understanding the dynamics of evolving RDF datasets. In: Arenas, M., et al. (eds.) ISWC 2015. LNCS, vol. 9366, pp. 495–512. Springer, Cham (2015). https://doi.org/10.1007/978-3-319-25007-6_29
16. Tzitzikas, Y., et al.: Matware: constructing and exploiting domain specific warehouses by aggregating semantic data. In: Presutti, V., d'Amato, C., Gandon, F., d'Aquin, M., Staab, S., Tordai, A. (eds.) ESWC 2014. LNCS, vol. 8465, pp. 721–736. Springer, Cham (2014). https://doi.org/10.1007/978-3-319-07443-6_48
17. Tzitzikas, Y., et al.: Unifying heterogeneous and distributed information about marine species through the top level ontology marineTLO. Program **50**(1), 16–40 (2016)
18. Tzitzikas, Y., Kampouraki, M., Analyti, A.: Curating the specificity of ontological descriptions under ontology evolution. J. Data Semant. **3**(2), 75–106 (2013). https://doi.org/10.1007/s13740-013-0027-z
19. Tzitzikas, Y., et al.: Methods and tools for supporting the integration of stocks and fisheries. In: Salampasis, M., Bournaris, T. (eds.) HAICTA 2017. CCIS, vol. 953, pp. 20–34. Springer, Cham (2019). https://doi.org/10.1007/978-3-030-12998-9_2
20. Vandenbussche, P.Y., Umbrich, J., Matteis, L., Hogan, A., Buil-Aranda, C.: SPARQLES: monitoring public SPARQL endpoints. Semantic web **8**(6), 1049–1065 (2017)
21. Wishart, D.S., et al.: Drugbank 5.0: a major update to the drugbank database for 2018. Nucleic Acids Res. **46**(D1), D1074–D1082 (2018)
22. Yumusak, S., Dogdu, E., Kodaz, H., Kamilaris, A., Vandenbussche, P.: Spend: linked data SPARQL endpoints discovery using search engines. IEICE Trans. Inf. Syst. **100**(4), 758–767 (2017)

A Software Application
with Ontology-Based Reasoning
for Agroforestry

Raphaël Conde Salazar[1]([✉])(iD), Fabien Liagre[2], Isabelle Mougenot[3](iD),
Jéôme Perez[1], and Alexia Stokes[1](iD)

[1] AMAP, University of Montpellier, CIRAD, CNRS, INRAE, IRD,
Montpellier, France
`raphael.condesalazar@free.fr`
[2] AGROOF, Anduze, France
`liagre@agroof.net`
[3] UMR 228 ESPACE-DEV, Espace pour le Développement,
University of Montpellier, Montpellier, France
`espace-dev@ird.fr`
`http://amap.cirad.fr`
`https://agroof.net/`
`http://www.espace-dev.fr/`

Abstract. Agroforestry consists of combining trees with agriculture, both on farms and in the agricultural landscape. Within a context of sustainable development, agroforestry can improve soil conservation and reduce the use of toxic chemicals on crops, as well as improving biodiversity. Interdisciplinary by nature, the field of agroforestry mobilizes a large body of knowledge from environmental and life sciences using systemic approaches. In this framework, field observation data are acquired in partnership with several categories of stakeholders such as scientists, foresters, farmers, breeders, politicians and land managers. For data management efficiency, we propose the software application AOBRA (a software Application with Ontology-Based Reasoning for Agroforestry). The core of AOBRA is a domain ontology called "Agroforestry" which serves as a basis for capitalizing and sharing knowledge in agroforestry. By exploiting the capabilities of inference and linkages to other areas of expertise on the Web offered by the use of an ontology model, it aims to provide a broad view of agroforestry designs, and to allow the comparison between different spatial layouts of trees and crops.

Keywords: Agroforestry · Knowledge management system · Ontology · OWL

1 General Introduction

The development of intensive agriculture in Europe has led to a gradual depletion of soil over the last 50 years [2]. Combined with modifications in climate, leading

E. Garoufallou and M.-A. Ovalle-Perandones (Eds.): MTSR 2020, CCIS 1355, pp. 282–293, 2021.
https://doi.org/10.1007/978-3-030-71903-6_27

to more frequent extreme weather events, crop yields are decreasing [11]. Nevertheless, a worldwide increase in the human population and the necessity to feed up to 10 billion people in 2050 has resulted in the creation of a new paradigm in agriculture, to enable the preservation of resources and use of sustainable techniques, whilst increasing crop production. Among the proposed alternatives to intensive agriculture, is agroforestry. Agroforestry consists in the reintroduction of trees in the agricultural sector. Its most common forms are i) agrisilviculture, where trees intended for wood production are intercropped with cereals such as maize (*Zea mays*) and barley (*Hordeum vulgare*) and ii) sylvopastoralism, when silvicultural and pastoral activities are integrated in the same area. Agroforestry is not a simple planting of trees, but the close association between trees and agriculture that provides a beneficial synergy [5]. This synergy allows the limitation of inputs such as water, fertilizers and pesticides with a view to sustainable development. To better manage ressources within a modern and integrated agroforestry, we need diverse data, indicators and guidelines, to assist farmers in the transition from monospecific to plurispecific agriculture.

Field observations and data collected by different stakeholders such as biologists, foresters, farmers and breeders, in the framework of scientific agroforestry experiments have been accumulating [9]. The management and reuse of these data are made difficult by the multiplicity of media and formats used and by the diversity of stakeholders and their professional vocabularies. In addition, agroforestry studies require systemic approaches to understand in particular how to better manage a site in response to climate change, pests, or soil pollution. These responses must take into account the close links with other fields of knowledge such as climatology, zoology and pedology. To use and share these data and to report on the development and efficiency of the structural organisation of a agroforestry plot, we propose an application AOBRA, that used ontology-based reasoning. AOBRA will provide a global overview of the experiments already carried out and will allow the comparison of data in terms of tree and crop production. "Agroforestry" is the core ontology of the application, it will enable to describe the elements and its organization for the most common patterns available in agroforestery. In this paper we present a general view of the system, followed by the "Agroforestry" knowledge model. We will also discuss the implementation of AOBRA and the technological choices made. Finnaly, we illustrate the functioning of AOBRA using data from the monitoring of tree biomass in agroforestry plots at the Restinclières estate in the South of France.

2   Application Overview

Our approach consists of three parts (Fig. 1) described below:

Modelling: The data provided by farmers and researchers are in the form of an Excel sheet or database organized in a classical form of relational database. At this stage, we will transform these data into formal descriptions that can now be used as semantic data. These data are stored in an OWL serialization

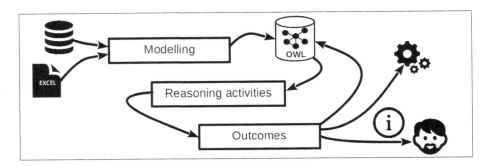

Fig. 1. The AOBRA software application.

format. The adoption of the semantic web standards will help to link easily our data with other knowledge database available of the web.

Reasoning activities: Inference mechanisms are applied to the semantic data in order to deduce new knowledge. During this phase, the data are aggregated in space and time, and several calculations are carried out, leading to the consolidation of quantitative data for the creation of qualitative indicators.

Outcomes: The data inferred from the reasoning activities are new semantic data that can be reused to participate in new deductions, thus amplifying the creation of new knowledge. Native and inferred data are then extracted using the SPARQL query language, to answer user queries via the application interface or to feed into other applications (e.g. a website via APIs).

During the modeling phase, we used the "Agroforestry" framework ontology that we have developed. The "Agroforestery" model use not only the physical description of the biotic and abiotic elements present on a agroforestery plot but also the interactions between them and the impact on the plot.

3   The "Agroforestry" Model

As presented in green in Fig. 2 the **StructuralElement** class is central. We distinguish the separate **SimpleElement** and **CompositeElement** daughter classes, which allow us to state that one element will admit other structural elements within it, or on the contrary, be a "leaf" element of the model. These modeling elements are disconnected from any temporal consideration. The **StructuralElement** class is associated via the *hasProperty* association to the **PropertyOfElement** class, that allows the enriching of the structural elements with various characteristics that evolve over time. The *PropertyOfElement* property is this time reified and will be specialized by exploiting different terminological references to the example of the total plant size in Trait Ontology (TO:1000012, named "whole plant size"). A superclass named **Resources** is used to generalize **StructuralElement** but also **PropertyOfElement**. The interest of this superclass is to be able to semantically enrich any resource of the model with terms borrowed from ontoterminological resources made available on the Web. For this purpose, the **Term** class also specializes the **Resource** class and its instances complement and standardize the way of describing the other resources in the model. For example, the notes within the UML class diagram (Fig. 2) include terms from terminology ontologies that can be used to qualify the elements of an agroforestry site, as well as their properties and interrelationships. We created the "Agroforestry" knowledge base using existing ontologies and terminologies model, that have already been validated.

Integration of the SOSA ontology SOSA (Sensor, Observation, Sample, and Actuator)

In order agroforestry practitioners to capitalize on the various observations made in the field, the SOSA ontology [8] was integrated with the "Agroforestry" ontology. If some properties of our agroforestry elements have immutable values (such as site location), other properties (such as soil acidity through the measurement of soil pH), are quantified or qualified using a specific observation procedure. These data may vary over time and are dependent on the measurement method. It is essential to take into account this variability to obtain a rigorous outcome when comparing and analysing data from multiple observations. SOSA is the central (but self-contained) module of the SSN (Semantic Sensor Network) [6] ontology which allows the describing of "sensors" (including humans) and the observations acquired by these sensors. The SOSA core ontology places the observation (**sosa:Observation**) at the centre of its model: an observation then informs the value of a descriptive property for an element of interest, at a given instant or time interval. The observation is linked to an individual of the class **sosa:FeatureOfInterest** by the relation *sosa:hasFeatureOfInterest*. The observed property of the element (class **sosa:ObservableProperty**) is related to an observation by the relation *sosa:observedProperty* and the value of this property is related to observation by the relation *sosa:hasResult*. In the "Agroforestry" model, the **StructuralElement** class specialises in **sosa:FeatureOfInterest**, and will naturally benefit from all the modelling around the notion of observation. We can therefore, organize the information around the growth of a tree, considering it as an instance of the **sosa:FeatureOfInterest** class, and inform its size at regular intervals through several observations. The **ssn:Property** class (superclass of **sosa:ObservableProperty**) and extended by the **PropertyOfElement** class so that it can write in a complementary way the properties involved in the description of the key elements of agroforestry. The idea is to be able to have in the longer term, pairs of elements/collections of properties relevant to agroforestry and thus facilitate their reuse by the agroforestry community. We also extended the **PropertyOfElement** through **RelationshipBetweenElements**, to support relationships other than structural relationships between elements of agroforestry management. These relationships can be valued and dated in time, and will allow us to capture the interactions between biotic elements found in the same plots. Pilot sites in agroforestry allow us to highlight the effects of agroforestry practices through experiments conducted on test plots.

The classes **sosa:Sample** and **sosa:Sampling** will therefore also be useful; an experimental plot can be seen as a **sosa:Sample** individual. In purple inside Fig. 2, we resume the UML class diagram of the main SOSA classes, some of which are extended in the "Agroforestry" model.

Extension of GeoSPARQL Ontology and OWL-Time Ontology

A double spatial and temporal dimension is necessary for any entity of the "Agroforestry" model if one wants to account for the evolution of a system where proximity relationships over time are of the utmost importance. Agroforestry systems and in particular, agrosilvicultural systems, are by their nature spatial, where the place of each element (tree, cereal plant and tree line) is of prime importance in the context of plant-plant interactions. The geographical location of the data of interest is able to bring together and link data from different fields such as hydrology or pedology. As an example, a river could border an agroforestry plot and so limit competition for water between trees and cereal plants. GeoSPARQL [1] is proposed by the OGC (Open Geospatial Consortium) international consortium, to provide the necessary elements for the representation and querying of spatialized data in the context of the semantic web. GeoSPARQL is organized in a modular way, and can offer services both to systems based on qualitative spatial reasoning and to those based on quantitative spatial calculations. Quantitative spatial calculations, such as distance calculations, require precise knowledge of the geometry of the elements studied (Euclidean geometry), whereas systems based on qualitative spatial reasoning rely on topological relationships between elements. These relationships (such as adjacency, intersection or inclusion) are, for example, described through the formalism "region connection calculus" (RCC8) [12]. GeoSPARQL also offers the possibility of associating one to several geometries, for example a point or a polygon, to any geographical entity through the **geo:Geometry** class, that represents the super class of all possible geometries. In the "Agroforestry" model, the **StructuralElement** class is subsumed by **geo:Feature** allowing us to take advantage of all the modeling proposed by GeoSPARQL around geometries. Time is an equally important notion in the context of agroforestry developments in which, for example, the annual seasonality of crops is confronted with the multi-annual life of trees. In order to better understand the interactions between trees and crops over time, we must precisely define the planting dates and the periods of the specific presence of each agroforestry element. Therefore, the **StructuralElement** class subsumed by **sosa:FeatureOfInterest** will be able to mobilize the modeling retained in SOSA, i.e., to maintain a *sosa:phenomenonTime* type relationship with a **time:TemporalEntity** temporal entity of the OWL-Time ontology [7]. The class **time:TemporalEntity** is then specialized in **time:Instant** and **time:Interval**, and so it is possible to introduce an agroforestry management element in a period of time, based on a precise time interval; or to define a temporal pattern for a specific observation (Fig. 2).

We have presented both the conceptual model corresponding to the minimum foundation for structuring knowledge specific to forest management, and portions of conceptual models of framework ontologies conveying three concepts that are

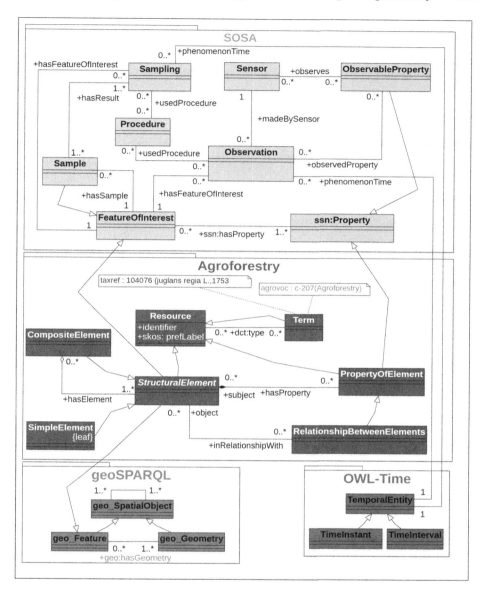

Fig. 2. Integrated class diagram: "Agroforestry", SOSA, GeoSPARQL and OWL-Time models and their relationships

of primary interest, i.e., observation, space and time. Figure 2 illustrates the articulations defined between these different models SOSA, GeoSPARQL, OWL-Time and "Agroforestry", for the specific needs of agroforestry management. The color code allows to visualize the origin of each modeled element.

4   Implementation

For the implementation, we have chosen the Java Jena framework [10] for RDF graph editing and management and more specifically for:

- Permanent storage of RDF triplets in the TDB triplestore.
- The support of RDFS and OWL formalisms for the construction of ontologies and SPARQL for their consultation.
- The choice among different reasoners that take advantage not only of OWL and RDFS formalisms, but also of rule-based languages such as SWRL or the specific language "Jena Rule".

For the reasoning activities, the general process is presented in Fig. 3. The inference mechanism takes place in several successive steps:

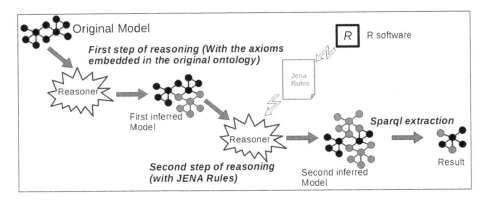

Fig. 3. Diagram of the process for obtaining and extracting inferred data from the AOBRA application.

First step: Inferences with the PELLET tool and OWL axioms
The original model comprising a merger between the "Agroforestry" ontology (Tbox) and the data on amenities (Abox) is submitted to the PELLET inference engine. This procedure will have the effect of making explicit some implicit information by generating additional RDF triplets based on the properties (e.g., reflexivity and transitivity) of the predicates initially present in our model. For example, the transitivity and reflexivity of the *bfo:hasPart* relation and its inverse *bfo:partOf*, will be used to make explicit the content/container relations not expressed in the original model (Fig. 4). This mechanism of inference is made possible by the use of the OWL language which provides a formalization for the description of the properties of a predicate used in an RDF triplet. OWL is inspired by description logic and so has formal semantics defined in first order logic.

Second step: inferences based on the "JENA Rules" The possibilities of inference based on the OWL language are limited. In the interest of generating new data, we have developed a rules-based mechanism. Jena has its own rule-based reasoner (JENA Rules). JENA Rules are in line with Horn clauses (head and body) and have a syntax close to SWRL rules. Functions created by users or other programs (such as the statistics oriented R software) can be called up by the rules, allowing complex calculations to be performed, the results of which can be used when applying the rules.

The algorithms in the form "IF ... THEN" will subsequently be transposed into JENA Rules. The transition to JENA rules is facilitated by the fact that these characteristics are represented through properties that are usually described in a standardised manner in terminology repositories. Thus, instances of the class **afy:StructuralElement** are associated with a set of properties via the relation *ssn:hasProperty*. Similarly, the instances of the **sosa:Observation** class are linked to a property via the *sosa:observedProperty* relation. However, the instances of the class **afy:StructuralElement** are linked by the relation *sosa:isFeatureOfInterestOf* to the instances of the class **sosa:Observation** to translate the link between the observations and the observed entity. Figure 5 shows the example of an algorithm for the identification of the properties to be studied and the expression of the JENA rule derived therefrom (Fig. 6).

Third step: data extraction The SPARQL language allows us to query and manage graph data, whether native or inferred.

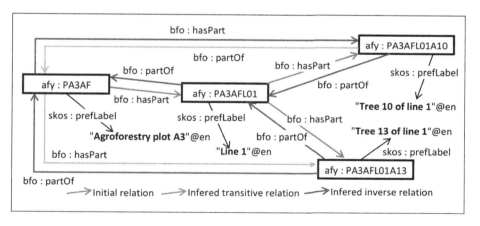

Fig. 4. "Inference with the PELLET engine:" Example of the exploitation of the transitivity and reflexivity of the relation *hasPart* and its inverse *PartOf*.

> For all elements, properties and observations, **IF** there is an element who have a property **AND** that there is an observation whose observe this property **AND** that this observation has as feature of interest this element **THEN** this property is a property to study .

Fig. 5. Algorithm for retrieving the studied properties.

```
[RetrievingProperties:      (?structuralElement ssn:hasProperty ?property)
                            (?observation sosa:observedProperty ?property)
                            (?observation sosa:hasFeatureOfInterest ?structuralElement)
                            ->
                            (?property :isPropertyToStudy 'true'^^xsd:Boolean)          ]
```

Fig. 6. JENA rule to identify the studied properties.

5 Case Study: The Restinclières Agroforestry System

Our application was tested in Restinclières domain [3], that has the particularity to be a research site that enables to acquire tree related data as well as data on the performance of agriculture practices in experimental and controls plot [4]. At this field station, we can compare the growth of trees without crops (forest controls) and crops without trees (agricultural controls). The data used were collected between 2015 and 2018 and collected from the agroforestry plot (PA3AF) and the associated control plot (PA4TF). The dendrometric data available for these two plots are total tree height, the height from the base of the trunk to the lower branches of the crown (height at which tree is pruned) and diameter at breast height (DBH, at 1.3 m). These measurements were taken annually at the same time over three consecutive years in 2015, 2016 and 2017. Due to their close proximity, it is considered that the climatic and soil conditions are identical for both plots. All trees are walnut hybrids (*Juglans nigra* x *J.regia*) and were planted in the same year (1994), for the production of ornamental wood. There are 140 trees on the PA3AF plot and 224 trees on the PA4TF plot. The data are made compliant with the "Agroforestry" model.

As a first analysis, we launched a **statistical evaluation of the data**.

We focused on the values of the trees different characteristics that are recorded as observations.

- First, we retrieve all values of the same characteristic shared by all the trees of the same plot for one year.
- Second, we create of a vector with the retrieved values of the same characteristic shared by all the trees of the same plot for a year. The different values are grouped as vectors (c(33.1, 24.2, 42.3...)) by plot and year.
- Third, we calculate the quantiles distribution of a vector with the retrieved values of the same characteristic shared by all the trees of the same plot for one year. These vectors are then processed by functions of the R software used for statistical data processing. The later is carried out by different JENA rules which are able to call external functions during their execution.

Other JENA rules using other R-functions allowed us to also calculate the median, standard deviation and variance of tree property values by plot and year.

Our results showed and in particular when looking at the quantiles distribution of tree height and diameter for the agroforestry plot PA3AF and the forest control PA4TF (Table 1) that tree growth more in the agroforestry plot.

Table 1. Distribution of quantiles of tree diameters and heights for plots P3AF and P4TF for the year 2016.

Statistics 2016 trunk diameters			
Plot	Quantile 25	Quantile 50	Quantile 75
<http://www.afy.fr/Restinclieres/PA3AF>	25.6	29.7	32.5
<http://www.afy.fr/Restinclieres/PA4TF>	14.9	19.9	23.9
Statistics 2016 trunk heights			
Plot	Quantile 25	Quantile 50	Quantile 75
<http://www.afy.fr/Restinclieres/PA3AF>	410.0	420.0	440.0
<http://www.afy.fr/Restinclieres/PA4TF>	298.7	380.0	420.0

In light of these results, we continued our analysis for the **tree biomass**. We investigated whether we observed a stronger tree growth under agroforestry conditions. We studied the tree biomass by diameter category on the total tree biomass of a plot in order to confirm this phenomenon of increased production. Improved growth of agroforestry trees would imply a useful reduction in the operating time required to market the trees for the production of ornamental wood. There are several tree categories used in the ornamental timber trade, that are determined by the DBH. The categories add to the knowledge base and are defined using JENA rules. For a specified year and plot, we calculate the ratio between the tree biomass for a given category and the total tree biomass. For the calculation of this ratio, it is necessary to aggregate the calculation of biomass at the spatial and temporal level. Therefore, we obtain confimation that agroforestry-grown trees grow faster than those in monospecific forestry plots, as shown by the ratio of average trees (Category II, Table 2) The presence of Category III trees for the PA3AF agroforestry plot and their absence for the PA4TF forest control reinforces this result over the three years studied.

Table 2. Ratio of the biomass of one tree category to the biomass of all trees per plot per year.

Ratio of biomass of trees eligible for trading Category II/ total biomass per plot for the year 2015	
Plot	Ratio
<http://www.afy.fr/Restinclieres/PA3AF>	0.78
<http://www.afy.fr/Restinclieres/PA4TF>	0.46

To determine why there was a large difference in growth of trees between the agroforestry plot compared to the forest control plot, even though meterological and soil conditions were the same, we examined whether the location of a river (River Lez) adjacent to plots, could influence tree growth. Table 3 show the mean value of the distances between the trees and the River Lez for each plot, tree category and year (Table 3). For the control forest plot, the average distance to the river was slightly lower for the tallest trees categories (38 m for category II versus 46 m for category I). On the contrary, for the agroforestry plot, the ratio was reversed, as the tallest trees were the furthest from the river (187 m for category III versus 173 m for category II and 169 m for category I). Taking into account the additional fact that the trees in the forest control were on average closer to the River Lez than their counterparts in the agroforestry plot (40 m versus 170 m on average), we can reject the hypothesis that the proximity of the river has an effect on tree growth. Results suggest therefore that other mechanisms occur that enhance agroforestry-grown trees, such as less competition for resources and access to fertilizer applied to the seasonal crops.

Table 3. Average distances between trees and the river Le Lez by plot, tree category and year.

Average distances to Le Lez by category in 2017			
Plot	Category I	Category II	Category III
<http://www.afy.fr/Restinclieres/PA3AF>	169.6	173.4	187.3
<http://www.afy.fr/Restinclieres/PA4TF>	46.0	38.46	

Our knowledge base showed that agroforestry-grown trees had enhanced height and biomass production compared to forestry-grown trees. For agro-foresters, this result means that the end product will be obtained more quickly, and so the economic value of individual trees will be higher. The agroforester will also benefit from the intercropped cereals. Using our knowledge base, it is also possible to estimate the relative yield of successive crops grown on the agroforestry plot (*Pisum sativum*, pea in 2016, *Triticum durum*, durum wheat in 2017 and *Hordeum vulgare*, barley in 2018), compared to their agricultural-grown controls. Analysing data of relative yields measured at harvest time, we found that the there was a decrease in yield for agroforestry-grown crops (peas - 18%, durum wheat - 34% and barley - 39%). The variability of these yields depend partially on tree age (the trees increasingly shade the crops as they grow) and motivated us to set up indicators combining agricultural yield and tree growth evolution. The constitution of simple rules on the principle of Horn rules and supported by reusable user functions, allows us to infer not only indicators, but also new observations such as those concerning the category of a tree that can be exploited again by other rules.

6   Conclusion

Our case study demonstrated that an application centered around a knowledge modele can provide evidences for agroforestery management. We were able to generate indicators for size and crop yields from an agroforestry plot, and to compare the data with control plots or other (agro)forestry plots with similar conditions (i.e., pedology, climatology, crop and identical planting period) using available data and ontologies. We chose to use ontologies already developed and selected those that were recognized and adopted by various communities of experts. In this case study, we used the SOSA framework ontology to express the observations and extracted the definitions of our elements and properties in terminological ontologies such as Agrovoc. Thus, the particularity of our model is to be above all a generic model, usable by all skateholders and visible on the semantic web. Our application and model may one hand aid agroforesters, skateholders and decision makers in managing ressources and taking decisions when planning their future tree-crop mixtures and on the other hand any individuals interested in the elements description on these plots.

References

1. Battle, R., Kolas, D.: Enabling the geospatial Semantic Web with Parliamentand GeoSPARQL. Semantic Web **3**(4), 355–370 (2012).https://doi.org/10.3233/SW-2012-0065, https://content.iospress.com/articles/semantic-web/sw065
2. Calame, M.: Comprendre l'agroécologie: origines, principes et politiques. ECLM (2016)
3. Domaine de Restinclières: Domaine de Restinclières et agroforesterie (2020). https://restinclieres.herault.fr/549-l-agroforesterie.htm
4. Dufour, L.: Tree planting and management in agroforestry. In: Agroforestry for sustainable agriculture, p. 480 p. Burleigh Dodds Science Publishing, Cambridge (united kingdom) (2019). https://hal.archives-ouvertes.fr/hal-02439981
5. Dupraz, C., Liagre, F.: Agroforesterie: des arbres et des cultures. France Agricole Editions (2008)
6. Haller, A., et al.: The modular SSN ontology: a joint W3C and OGC standard specifying the semantics of sensors, observations, sampling, and actuation. Semant. Web **10**(1), 9–32 (2018). https://doi.org/10.3233/SW-180320
7. Hobbs, J.R., Pan, F.: An ontology of time for the semantic web. ACM Trans. Asian Language Inf. Process. (TALIP) **3**(1), 66–85 (2004). https://doi.org/10.1145/1017068.1017073
8. Janowicz, K., Haller, A., Cox, S.J., Le Phuoc, D., Lefrançois, M.: SOSA: a lightweight ontology for sensors, observations, samples, and actuators. J. Web Semant. **56**, 1–10 (2019). https://doi.org/10.1016/j.websem.2018.06.003
9. Labelle, R.: Ten years of work in agroforestry information and documentation. Agroforestry Syst. **5**(3), 339–352 (1987)
10. McBride, B.: Jena: a semantic web toolkit. IEEE Internet Comput. **6**(6), 55–59 (2002)
11. O'Neill, B.C., et al.: IPCC reasons for concern regarding climate change risks. Nat. Climate Change **7**(1), 28–37 (2017). https://doi.org/10.1038/nclimate3179
12. Randell, D.A., Cui, Z., Cohn, A.G.: A spatial logic based on regions and connection. KR **92**, 165–176 (1992)

Track on Metadata and Semantics for Open Repositories, Research Information Systems and Data Infrastructures

HIVE-4-MAT: Advancing the Ontology Infrastructure for Materials Science

Jane Greenberg[(✉)], Xintong Zhao, Joseph Adair, Joan Boone, and Xiaohua Tony Hu

Metadata Research Center, Drexel University, Philadelphia, PA 19104, USA
{jg3243,xz485,jda57,jpb357,xh29}@drexel.edu

Abstract. This paper introduces Helping Interdisciplinary Vocabulary Engineering for Materials Science (HIVE-4-MAT), an automatic linked data ontology application. The paper provides contextual background for materials science, shared ontology infrastructures, and knowledge extraction applications. HIVE-4-MAT's three key features are reviewed: 1) Vocabulary browsing, 2) Term search and selection, and 3) Knowledge Extraction/Indexing, as well as the basics of named entity recognition (NER). The discussion elaborates on the importance of ontology infrastructures and steps taken to enhance knowledge extraction. The conclusion highlights next steps surveying the ontology landscape, including NER work as a step toward relation extraction (RE), and support for better ontologies.

Keywords: Materials science · Ontology · Ontology infrastructure · Helping interdisciplinary vocabulary engineering · Named entity recognition · Knowledge extraction

1 Introduction

A major challenge in materials science research today is that the artifactual embodiment is primarily textual, even if it is in digital form. Researchers analyze materials through experiments and record their findings in textual documents such as academic literature and patents. The most common way to extract knowledge from these artifacts is to read all the relevant documents, and manually extract knowledge. However, reading is time-consuming, and it is generally unfeasible to read and mentally synthesize all the relevant knowledge [26,28]. Hence, effectively extracting knowledge and data becomes a problem. One way to address this challenge is through knowledge extraction using domain-specific ontologies [18]. Unfortunately, materials science work in this area is currently hindered by limited access to and use of relevant ontologies. This situation underscores the need to improve the state of ontology access and use for materials science research, which is the key goal of the work presented here.

Supported by NSF Office of Advanced Cyberinfrastructure (OAC): #1940239.

E. Garoufallou and M.-A. Ovalle-Perandones (Eds.): MTSR 2020, CCIS 1355, pp. 297–307, 2021.
https://doi.org/10.1007/978-3-030-71903-6_28

This paper introduces Helping Interdisciplinary Vocabulary Engineering for Materials Science (HIVE-4-MAT), an automatic linked data ontology application. The contextual background covers materials science, shared ontology infrastructures, and knowledge extraction applications. HIVE-4-MAT's basic features are reviewed, followed by a brief discussion and conclusion identifying next steps.

2 Background

2.1 Materials Science

Materials science is an interdisciplinary field that draws upon chemistry, physics, engineering and interconnected disciplines. The broad aim is to advance the application of materials for scientific and technical endeavors. Accordingly, materials science researchers seek to discover new materials or alter existing ones; with the overall aim of offering more robust, less costly, and/or less environmentally harmful materials.

Materials science researchers primarily target solid matter, which retains its shape and character compared to liquid or gas. There are four key classes of solid materials: metals, polymers, ceramics, and composites. Researchers essentially process (mix, melt, etc.) elements in a controlled way, and measure performance by examining a set of properties. Table 1 provides two high-level examples of materials classes, types, processes, and properties.

Table 1. Examples of Materials classes and types, processes, and properties

Material class & type	Manufacturing process	Properties (examples)
Class: Polymer Type: Polyethylene [21]	Polymerization (distillation of ethane into fractions, some of which are combined with catalysts)	Melt temperature Tensile strength Flexurile strength (or bend strength) Shrink Rate
Class: Metal Type: Steel	Iron ore is heated and forged in blast furnaces, where the impurities are altered and carbon is added	Yield strength Tensile strength Thermal conductivity Resistance to wear/corrosion Formability

The terms in Table 1 have multiple levels (sub-types or classes) and variants. For example, there is stainless steel and surgical steel. Moreover, the universe of properties, which is large, extends even further when considering nano and kinetic materials. This table illustrates the language, hence the ontological underpinnings, of materials science, which is invaluable for knowledge extraction. Unfortunately, the availability of computationally ready ontologies applicable to materials science is severely limited, particularly compared to biomedicine and biology.

2.2   Ontologies: Shared Infrastructure and Knowledge Extraction Applications

Ontologies have provided a philosophical foundation and motivation for scientific inquiry since ancient times [15]. Today, computationally ready ontologies conforming to linked data standards [9] offer a new potential for data driven discovery [14]. Here, the biomedical and biology communities have taken the lead in developing a shared infrastructure, through developments such as the National Center for Biological Ontologies (NCBO) Bioportal [4,29] and the OBO foundry [6,25]. Another effort is the FAIRsharing portal [1,23], providing access to a myriad of standards, databases, and other resources [31].

Shared ontology infrastructures help standardize language and support data interoperability across communities. Additionally, the ontological resources can aid knowledge extraction and discovery. Among one of the best known applications in this area is Aronson's [8] $MetaMap$, introduced in 2001. This application extracts key information from textual documents, and maps the indexing to the metathesaurus ontology. The $MetaMap$ application is widely-used for extraction of biomedical information. The HIVE application [16], developed by the Metadata Research Center, Drexel University, also supports knowledge extraction in a same way, although results are limited by the depth of the ontologies applied. For example, biomedicine ontologies, which often have a rich and deep network of terms, will produce better results compared to more simplistic ontologies targeting materials science [32,33].

Overall, existing ontology infrastructure and knowledge extraction approaches are applicable to materials science. In fact, biology and biomedical ontologies are useful for materials science research, and researchers have been inspired by these developments to develop materials science ontologies [7,11,17]. Related are nascent efforts developing shared metadata and ontology infrastructures for materials science. Examples include the NIST Materials Registry [5] and the Industrial Ontology Foundry [2]. These developments and the potential to leverage ontologies for materials science knowledge extraction motivate our work to advance HIVE-4-MAT. They have also had a direct impact on exploring the use of NER to assist in the development richer ontologies for materials science [33].

2.3   Named Entity Recognition

The expanse and depth of materials science ontologies is drastically limited, pointing to a need for richer ontologies; however, ontology development via manual processes is a costly undertaking. One way to address this challenge is to through relation extraction and using computational approaches to develop ontologies. To this end, named entity recognition (NER) can serve as an invaluable first step, as explained here.

The goal of Named Entity Recognition (NER) is to recognize key information that are related to predefined semantic types from input textual documents [20]. As an important component of information extraction (IE), it is widely applied in tasks such as information retrieval, text summarization, question answering and knowledge extraction.

The semantic types can vary depending on specific task types. For example, when extracting general information, the predefined semantic types can be location, person, or organization. NER approaches have been also proven effective to biomedical information extraction; an example from SemEval2013 task 9 [24] about NER for drug-drug interaction is shown in Fig. 1 below.

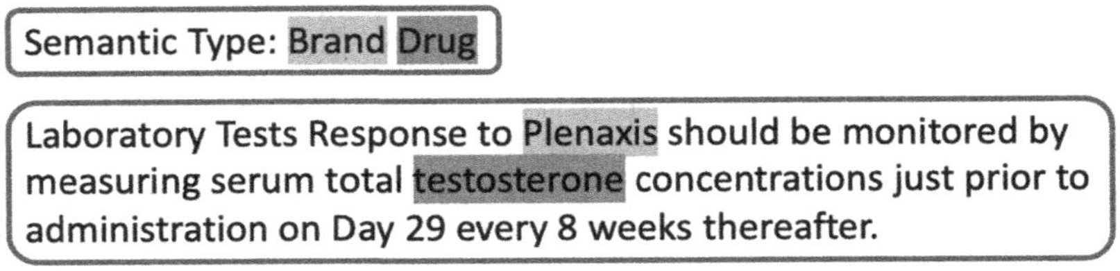

Fig. 1. An NER example from a SemEval task

As shown in the Fig. 1, the NER pharmaceutical model receives the textual input (e.g. sentences), and returns whether there are important information entities that belong to any predefined labels, such as brand name and drug name.

A similar undertaking has been pursued by Weston et al. [28], with their NER model designed for **inorganic materials** information extraction. Their model includes seven entity labels and testing has resulted in an overall f1-score of 0.87 [28]. This work has inspired the HIVE team to use NER, as a step toward relation extraction, and the development of richer ontologies for materials science.

3   Purpose and Goals

Goals of this paper are to:

1. Introduce HIVE
2. Demonstrate HIVE's three key features Vocabulary browsing, term search and selection, and knowledge extraction/indexing
3. Provide an example of our NER work, as a foundation for relation extraction.

4   HIVE-4-MAT: Prototype Development and Features

Hive is a linked data automatic metadata generator tool developed initially as a demonstration for the Dryad repository [16,30], and incorporated into the DataNet Federation Consortium's iRODS system [12]. Ontologies encoded in the Simple Knowledge Organization System (SKOS) format are shared through a HIVE-server. Currently, HIVE 2.0 uses Rapid Automatic Keyword Extraction (RAKE), an unsupervised algorithm that processes and parses text into a set of candidate keywords based on co-occurrence [22]. Once the list of candidate keywords is selected from the SKOS encoded ontologies, the HIVE system matches candidate keywords to terms in the selected ontologies. Figure 2 provides an overview of the HIVE model.

HIVE-4-MAT builds on the HIVE foundation, and available ontologies have been selected for either broad or targeted applicability to materials science. The prototype includes the following ten ontologies: 1)Bio-Assay Ontology (BioAssay), 2) Chemical Information Ontology (CHEMINF), 3) Chemical Process Ontology (prochemical), (4) Library of Congress Subject Headings (LCSH), 5) Metals Ontology, 6) National Cancer Institute Thesaurus (NCIT), 7) Physico-Chemical Institute and Properties (FIX), 8) Physico-chemical process (REX), 9) Smart Appliances REFerence Ontology (SAREF), and 10) US Geological Survey (USGS).

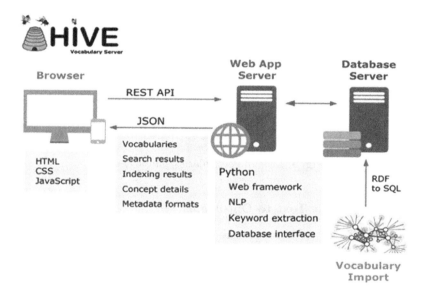

Fig. 2. Overview of HIVE structure

Currently, HIVE-4-MAT has three main features:

- Vocabulary browsing (Fig. 3 and Fig. 4)
- Term search and selection (Fig. 5)
- Knowledge Extraction/Indexing (Fig. 6)

The vocabulary browsing feature allows a user to view and explore the ontologies registered in HIVE-4-MAT. Figure 3 presents the full list of currently available ontologies, and Fig. 4 provides an example navigating through the hierarchy of the Metals ontology. The left-hand column (Fig. 4) displays the hierarchical levels of this ontology; the definition, and the right-hand side displays the alternative name, broader concepts and narrow concepts.

Helping Interdisciplinary
Vocabulary Engineering for
Materials Discovery (HIVE-4-MAT)

NSF-HDR# 1940239

Vocabularies Search Index

Vocabulary	Short name	Concepts	Last Updated
BioAssay Ontology	BioAssay	7211	02/03/2020
Chemical Information Ontology	CHEMINF	915	08/21/2019
Chemical Process	procchemical	53	01/07/2016
Library of Congress Subject Headings	LCSH	421572	07/26/2018
Metals	Metals	44	01/01/2016
National Cancer Institute Thesaurus	NCIT	156172	02/24/2020
Physico-Chemical Methods and Properties	FIX	1163	02/11/2014
Physico-chemical process	REX	552	12/11/2017
Smart Appliances REFerence ontology	SAREF	112	02/10/2015
US Geological Survey	USGS	968	01/01/2016

Metadata Research Center, College of Computing & Informatics at Drexel University

Fig. 3. Lists of vocabularies/ontologies

4.1   Mapping Input Text to Ontologies

The term search and selection feature in Fig. 5 allows a user to select a set
of ontologies and enter a search term. In this example, eight of the 10 ontologies are selected, and the term thermoelectric is entered as a search concept.
Thermoelectrics is an area of research that focuses on materials conductivity of
temperature (heat or cooling) for energy production. In this example, the term
was only found in the LCSH, which is a general domain ontology. The lower-half
of Fig. 5 shows the term relationships. There are other tabs accessible to see the
JSON-LD, SKOS-RDF/XML and other encoding. This feature also allows a user
to select an encoded term for a structure database system, such as a catalog, or
for inclusion in a knowledge graph.

Figure 6 illustrates the Knowledge Extraction/Indexing Feature. To reiter-
ate, reading research literature is time-consuming. Moreover, it is impossible for
a researcher to fully examine and synthesize all of the knowledge from existing
work. HIVE-4-MAT's indexing functionality allows a researcher or a digital content curator to upload a batch of textual resources, or simply input a uniform
resource locator (URL) for a web resource, and automatically index the textual
content using the selected ontologies. Figure 6 provides an example using the

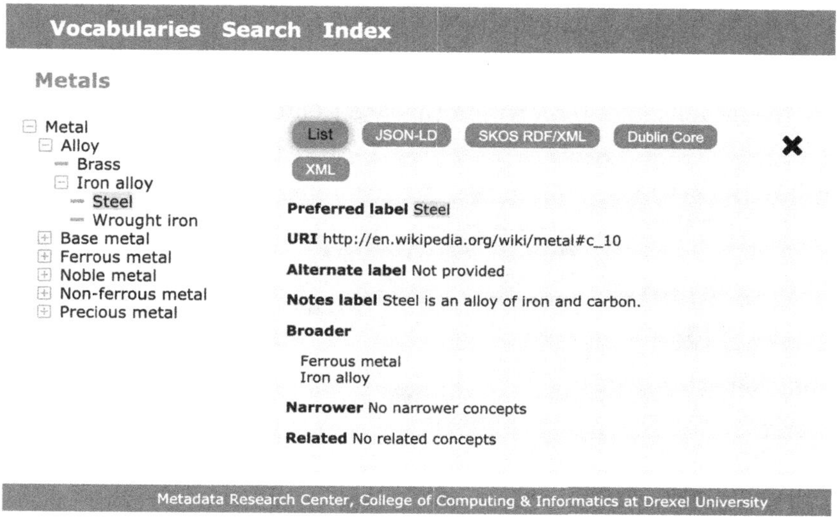

Fig. 4. Vocabularies/ontologies structure

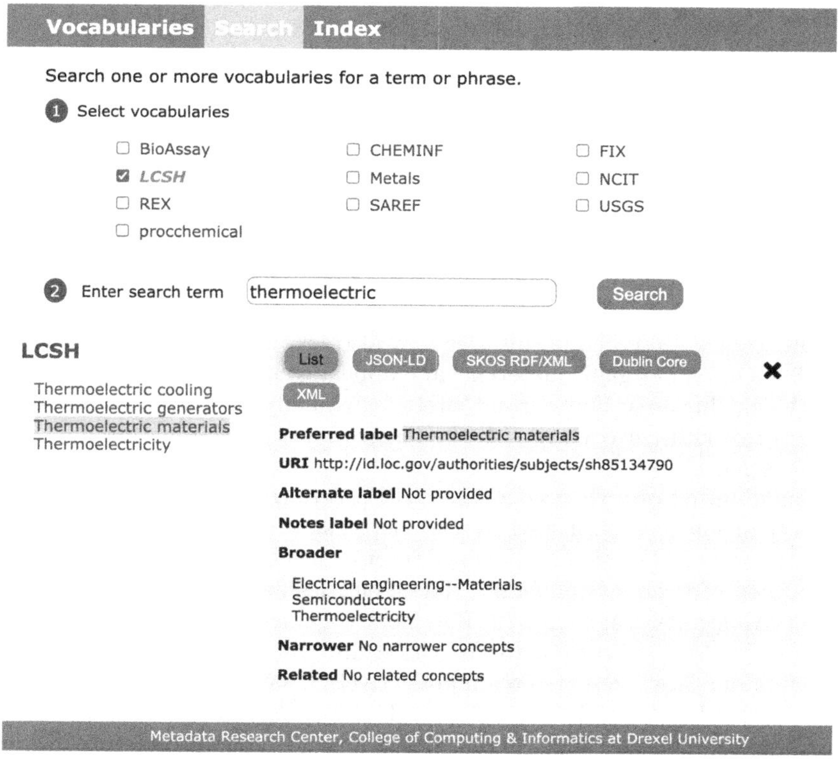

Fig. 5. Term search

Wikipedia content for Wikipedia page on Metal [3]. The visualization of the HIVE-4-MAT's results helps a user to gain an understanding of the knowledge contained within the resource, and they can further navigate the hypertext to confirm the meaning of a term within the larger ontological structure.

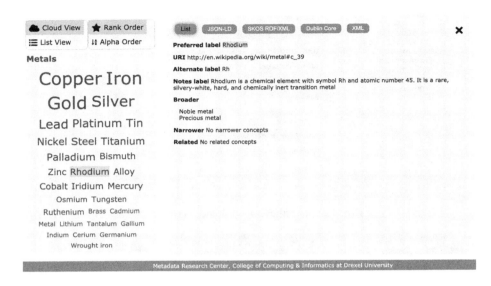

Fig. 6. Keyword extraction

4.2   Building NER for Information Extraction

Inspired by the work of Weston et al. [28], the HIVE team is also exploring the performance and applications of NER as part of knowledge extraction in materials science. Research in this area may also serve to enhance HIVE. Weston et al. [28] focus on inorganic materials, and appear to be one of the only advanced initiative's in this area. Our current effort focuses on building a test dataset for **organic materials** discovery, with the larger aim of expanding research across materials science.

To build our corpus, we used Scopus API [27] to collect a sample of abstracts from a set of journals published by Elsevier that cover organic materials. The research team has identified and defined a set of seven key entities to assist with the next step of training our model. These entities have the following semantic labels: (1) Molecules/fragments, (2) Polymers/organic materials, (3) Descriptors, (4) Property, (5) Application, (6) Reaction and (7) Characterization method. Members of our larger research team are actively annotating the abstracts using these semantic labels as shown in Fig. 7. The development a test dataset is an important research step, and will help our team move forward testing our NER model and advancing knowledge extraction options for materials science in our future work.

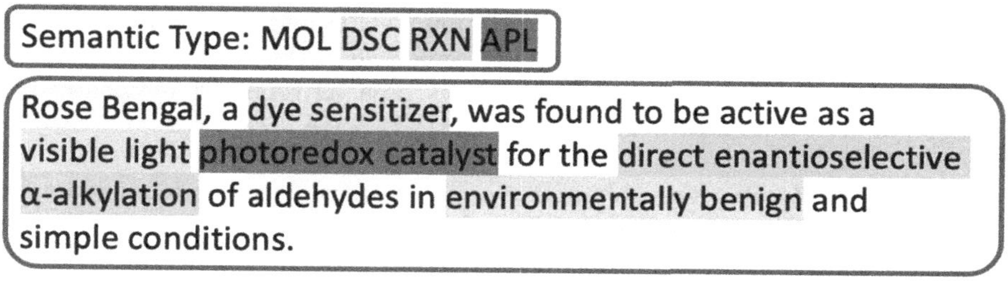

Semantic Type: MOL DSC RXN APL

Rose Bengal, a dye sensitizer, was found to be active as a
visible light photoredox catalyst for the direct enantioselective
α-alkylation of aldehydes in environmentally benign and
simple conditions.

Fig. 7. Example from our in-progress organic dataset

5   Discussion

The demonstration of HIVE and reporting of initial work with NER is motivated
by the significant challenge materials science researchers face gleaning knowledge
from textual artifacts. Although this challenge pervades all areas of scientific
research, disciplines such as biology, biomedicine, astronomy, and other earth
sciences have a much longer history of open data and ontology development,
which drives knowledge discovery. Materials science has been slow to embrace
these developments, most likely due to the disciplines connection with competitive industries. Regardless of the reasons impacting timing, there is clearly
increased interest and acceptance of a more open ethos across materials science,
as demonstrated by initiatives outlined by Himanen et al. in 2019 [19]. Two key
examples include NOMADCoE [13] and the Materials Data Facility [10], which
are inspired by the FAIR principles [13,31]. These developments provide access
to structured data, although, still the majority of materials science knowledge
remains hidden in textually dense artifacts. More importantly, these efforts recognize the value of access to robust and disciplinary relevant ontologies. HIVE-4-
MAT complements these developments and enables materials science researchers
not only to gather, register, and browse ontologies; but, also the ability to automatically apply both general and targeted ontologies for knowledge extraction.
Finally, the HIVE-4-MAT output provides researchers with a structured display
of knowledge that was previously hidden within unstructured text.

6   Conclusion

This paper introduced the HIVE-4-MAT application, demonstrated HIVE's
three key features, and reported on innovative work underway exploring NER.
The progress has been encouraging, and plans are underway to further assess the
strengths and limitation of existing ontologies for materials science. Research
here will help our team target areas where richer ontological structures are
needed. Another goal is to test additional algorithms with the HIVE-4-MAT
application, as reported by White, et al. [30]. Finally, as the team moves forward,
it is critical to recognize that ontologies, alone, are not sufficient for extracting knowledge, and it is important to consider other approaches for knowledge

extraction, such as Named Entity Recognition (NER) and Relation Extraction (RE) can complement and enrich current apporaches. As reported above, the HIVE team is also pursuing research in this area as reported by Zhao [33], which we plan to integrate with the overall HIVE-4-MAT.

Acknowledgment. The research reported on in this paper is supported, in part, by the U.S. National Science Foundation, Office of Advanced Cyberinfrastructure (OAC): Grant: #1940239. Thank you also to researchers in Professor Steven Lopez's lab, Northeastern University, and Semion Saiki, Kebotix for assistance in developing the entity set for organic materials.

References

1. Fairsharing. https://fairsharing.org/
2. Industrial ontology foundry. https://www.industrialontologies.org/
3. Metal-wikipedia entry. https://en.wikipedia.org/wiki/Metal/
4. Ncbo bioportal. http://bioportal.bioontology.org/
5. Nist materials registry. https://materials.registry.nist.gov/
6. Obo foundry. http://www.obofoundry.org/
7. Anikin, A., Litovkin, D., Sarkisova, E., Petrova, T., Kultsova, M.: Ontology-based approach to decision-making support of conceptual domain models creating and using in learning and scientific research. In: IOP Conference Series: Materials Science and Engineering, vol. 483, page 012074 (2019)
8. Aronson, A.R.: Effective mapping of biomedical text to the umls metathesaurus: The metamap program (2001)
9. Bizer, C.: The emerging web of linked data. IEEE Intell. Syst. **24**(5), 87–92 (2009)
10. Blaiszik, B., Chard, K., Pruyne, J., Ananthakrishnan, R., Tuecke, S., Foster, I.: The materials data facility: data services to advance materials science research. JOM **68**(8), 2045–2052 (2016)
11. Cheung, K., Hunter, J., Drennan, J.: MatSeek: an ontology-based federated search interface for materials scientists. IEEE Intell. Syst. **24**(1), 47–56 (2009)
12. Conway, M.C., Greenberg, J., Moore, R., Whitton, M., Zhang, L.: Advancing the DFC semantic technology platform via HIVE innovation. In: Garoufallou, E., Greenberg, J. (eds.) MTSR 2013. CCIS, vol. 390, pp. 14–21. Springer, Cham (2013). https://doi.org/10.1007/978-3-319-03437-9_3
13. Draxl, C., Scheffler, M.: Nomad: the fair concept for big data-driven materials science. MRS Bull. **43**(9), 676–682 (2018)
14. Eisenberg, I.W., et al.: Uncovering the structure of self-regulation through data-driven ontology discovery. Nat. Commun. **10**(1), 1–13 (2019)
15. Greenberg, J.: Philosophical foundations and motivation via scientific inquiry. In: Lee, H.-L., Smiraglia, R. (eds.) Ontology in Knowledge Organization, pp. 5–12. Würzburg : Ergon (2015)
16. Greenberg, J., Losee, R., Agüera, J.R.P., Scherle, R., White, H., Willis, C.: Hive: Helping interdisciplinary vocabulary engineering. Bull. Am. Soc. Inf. Sci. Technol. **37**(4), 23–26 (2011)
17. Greenberg, J., Zhang, Y., Ogletree, A., Tucker, G.J., Foley, D.: Threshold determination and engaging materials scientists in ontology design. In: Garoufallou, E., Hartley, R.J., Gaitanou, P. (eds.) MTSR 2015. CCIS, vol. 544, pp. 39–50. Springer, Cham (2015). https://doi.org/10.1007/978-3-319-24129-6_4

18. Haendel, M.A., Chute, C.G., Robinson, P.N.: Classification, ontology, and precision medicine. N. Engl. J. Med. **379**(15), 1452–1462 (2018)
19. Himanen, L., Geurts, A., Foster, A.S., Rinke, P.: Data-driven materials science: status, challenges, and perspectives. Adv. Sci. **6**(21), 1900808 (2019)
20. Li, J., Sun, A., Han, J., Li, C.: A survey on deep learning for named entity recognition (2020)
21. Rogers, T.: Everything you need to know about polyethylene (pe), creative mechanisms (2015)
22. Rose, S., Engel, D., Cramer, N., Cowley, W.: Automatic keyword extraction from individual documents. Text Min. Appl. theory **1**, 1–20 (2010)
23. Sansone, S.-A., et al.: Fairsharing as a community approach to standards, repositories and policies. Nat. Biotechnol. **37**(4), 358–367 (2019)
24. Segura-Bedmar, I., Martínez, P., Herrero-Zazo, M.: SemEval-2013 task 9: extraction of drug-drug interactions from biomedical texts (DDIExtraction 2013). In: Second Joint Conference on Lexical and Computational Semantics (*SEM), Volume 2: Proceedings of the Seventh International Workshop on Semantic Evaluation (SemEval 2013), Atlanta, Georgia, USA, June 2013, pp. 341–350. Association for Computational Linguistics (2013)
25. Smith, B., et al.: The obo foundry: coordinated evolution of ontologies to support biomedical data integration. Nat. Biotechnol. **25**(11), 1251–1255 (2007)
26. Tshitoyan, V., et al.: Unsupervised word embeddings capture latent knowledge from materials science literature. Nature **571**(7763), 95–98 (2019)
27. Wan, K.: What are Scopus APIs and how are these used? (2019). Accessed 17 Oct 2020
28. Weston, L., et al.: Named entity recognition and normalization applied to large-scale information extraction from the materials science literature, June 2019
29. Whetzel, P.L., et al.: Bioportal: enhanced functionality via new web services from the national center for biomedical ontology to access and use ontologies in software applications. Nucleic Acids Res. **39**(suppl_2), W541–W545 (2011)
30. White, H., Willis, C., Greenberg, J.: The hive impact: contributing to consistency via automatic indexing. In: Proceedings of the 2012 iConference, pp. 582–584 (2012)
31. Wilkinson, M.D., et al.: The fair guiding principles for scientific data management and stewardship. Sci. Data **3**(1), 1–9 (2016)
32. Zhang, X., Zhao, C., Wang, X.: A survey on knowledge representation in materials science and engineering: an ontological perspective. Comput. Ind. **73**, 8–22 (2015)
33. Zhao, X., Greenberg, J., Menske, V., Toberer, E., Hu, X.: Scholarly big data: computational approaches to semantic labeling in materials science. In: Proceedings of the Workshop on Organizing Big Data, Information, and Knowledge at JCDL 2020 (2020)

Institutional Support for Data Management Plans: Five Case Studies

Yulia Karimova$^{(\boxtimes)}$ ⬤, Cristina Ribeiro⬤, and Gabriel David⬤

INESC TEC, Faculty of Engineering, University of Porto,
Rua Dr. Roberto Frias, 4200-465 Porto, Portugal
ylaleo@gmail.com,{mcr,gtd}@fe.up.pt

Abstract. Researchers are being prompted by funders and institutions to expose the variety of results of their projects and to submit a Data Management Plan as part of their funding requests. In this context, institutions are looking for solutions to provide support to research data management activities in general, including DMP creation. We propose a collaborative approach where a researcher and a data steward create a DMP, involving other parties as required. We describe this collaborative method and its implementation, by means of a set of case studies that show the importance of the data steward in the institution. Feedback from researchers shows that the DMP are simple enough to lead people to engage in data management, but present enough challenges to constitute an entry point to the next level, the machine-actionable DMP.

Keywords: Research data management · Data management plan · Research workflow

1 Introduction

The 17 Sustainable Development Goals [24] require the development of information infrastructures, directed to sharing and reusing data [9] that contribute to reproducible research, advance science and foster collaboration, while promoting researchers' work [17]. Along with this, Research Data Management (RDM) activities also became important in the daily work of researchers. Thus, both the SDG and the management of research projects require an alignment with RDM best practices and recommendations, as proposed by initiatives for Open Data such as the Research Data Alliance (RDA) [18].

In this context, data should be described with as much detail as possible and conform to the FAIR principles [26]. Moreover, with new RDM and funder requirements for grant applications, researchers need adequate, user-friendly tools to help them from the early stages of their projects, namely on the creation of Data Management Plans (DMP), as they are now required for most grant applications [3,9].

A good DMP must include detailed information about data management and preservation during and after the project. Moreover, the context of the project,

E. Garoufallou and M.-A. Ovalle-Perandones (Eds.): MTSR 2020, CCIS 1355, pp. 308–319, 2021.
https://doi.org/10.1007/978-3-030-71903-6_29

people in charge of RDM, and possible ethical and legal issues are also part of a good plan [22,25]. A DMP can be regarded as a living document that is useful for structuring the course of research activities, integrating with other systems and workflows [22], and leading the entire strategy of the project [4]. However, the creation of a DMP requires some effort, specific knowledge, some data publication experience and appropriate tools [20]. This is why many institutions are looking for solutions to help researchers in DMP creation and RDM activities in general [2,5,27].

At the Institute for Systems and Computer Engineering, Technology and Science (INESC TEC), under the TAIL project [19], we collaborate with researchers from different scientific domains, analyzing the difficulties they face in RDM activities and DMP creation. This led us to build an RDM workflow, taking into account researchers' needs and existing RDM and funder requirements, while exploring the integration of the available RDM tools and services, and developing our own. The collaborative DMP-building method is part of a workflow with the overall objective of improving the DMP quality while reducing the effort and time required from researchers on the creation of the detailed plan [11], and will be described and illustrated with a set of case studies.

2   Supporting Researchers on DMP Creation

Currently, institutions have different ways to support researchers on RDM activities during the life cycle of their project, seeking both the engagement of researchers and the establishment of RDM infrastructures according to their needs. The consultation services and training sessions that provide an overview of metadata, data standards, ethical issues and data repositories are the most common initiatives to support researchers with DMP creation. The provision of lists of data repositories, license models and guidelines, the explanation of the funding requirements, the creation of DMP templates and the review of DMP written by the researchers are also proposed as institutional support. Examples of support materials are the Guide to DMP used at the Digital Repository of Ireland[1] and the MOOC [16] and DMP template[2] created for the University of Edinburgh.

Libraries are reported as one of the services where researchers can ask for RDM support [1,5,6,23]. Although libraries are still in the early stages of connecting to RDM infrastructures and need staff with RDM skills, this represents an expansion of their traditional mission. Some of them already provide consultation services and include RDM support as a new internal working group [6]. Meetings at researcher's office, lab, or other location, attending researchers on the library, providing feedback by email forms, and collaborating with the departmental grant administrators and project managers, are some specific ways to support researchers at libraries [6].

---

[1] https://guides.lib.unc.edu/researchdatatoolkit/home.
[2] https://tinyurl.com/y7tbv3b4.

Another source of support are the IT departments at universities and research centres. Partnerships between libraries and other hired support teams have become common and their goal is to develop new services to inform, train and support researchers [1,5,6,21]. At the University of Melbourne, for example, there is a digital scholarship program [8], while Cornell University implemented the Research Data Management Service [13], the University of Glasgow [7,15] developed a system for contacting researchers with approved projects and controlling requests for RDM support with automatically generated email if a DMP is required, and the University of Sydney organised eResearchUnit[3] that sends researchers a pre-filled DMP template, based on the abstract of the funded grant application.

Despite the existence of different tools and workflows to help researchers in the creation of DMP, all of them aim to facilitate the researcher's daily work, to simplify the process of DMP creation, to decrease the time spent on it and to improve the quality of the results. The work developed in this area showed that the diversity of scientific domains and respective plans requires people in charge of RDM support, able to help with a multitude of requirements [15].

3 The Collaborative Method Between Data Steward and Researchers in the Preparation of a DMP

An RDM workflow has to take into account researchers' needs and institutional and funder requirements. The set of tools illustrated in Fig. 1 covers important stages of the data lifecycle. The DMPOnline tool[4] is used to create the plans, the LabTablet[5] for data collection, the Dendro platform[6] for data organization and description, and the INESC TEC research data repository[7] [10,12] for data publishing.

Given the requirement of DMP submission with grant applications, we proposed a collaborative method between data stewards and researchers in the preparation of a DMP [11]. The method has been tested with researchers from different scientific domains and includes several activities (see Fig. 2).

First of all, the data steward makes an interview to understand the data and how they can be managed. Typically, researchers don't understand how they can organize the data. Another common issue is the existence of sensitive, private, or personal data. In one of the cases, researchers were not aware that the data collected by interviews involved personal data, with specific management requirements. This interview also collects information about publications and published data related to the project, if any. This helps to identify data repositories and metadata standards that are more appropriate for the project.

---

[3] https://eresearch.uts.edu.au/.
[4] https://dmponline.dcc.ac.uk/.
[5] https://github.com/feup-infolab/labtablet.
[6] https://github.com/feup-infolab/dendro.
[7] https://rdm.inesctec.pt/.

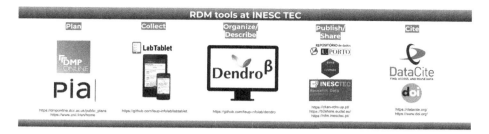

Fig. 1. The set of RDM tools used at INESC TEC

Often researchers don't know of any repositories or metadata standards for their domain.

After that, the data steward proceeds with an analysis of the existence of sensitive, private or personal data that may be collected during the project, and therefore the necessity of a Data Protection Impact Assessment (DPIA). In cases where a DPIA is required, besides the examples of DMP, the data steward also surveys DPIA examples for the corresponding domain.

The next step of the method involves the analysis of prior publications related to the project, by the researchers in the team. This step helps the steward find detailed information about methodology, software, type and names of the instruments that can be used on the project and suggest what documents can be created besides datasets, for example agreements between partners, that also need to be preserved or published. The same analysis occurs with research data related to the project and data description requirements. The data steward proposes an appropriate metadata scheme, assesses the amount of space required on the repository and what formats and file types will be used.

As a result, the necessary information is collected and the first version of the DMP is created by the data steward. In some cases, interaction with the Ethics Committee is promoted. And interaction with the Data Protection Officer (DPO) is proposed in case a DPIA is required.

At the next step, the first DMP is presented to the researchers for validation and improvement. This step also includes clarification of the authorship and ownership of the data, and possible embargo periods, which in turn may involve iterations between project partners. Neither the DMP (nor the DPIA in case there is one) are public at this point. They will be open to the public only after the authorization for publication of the final version DMP by all the project partners. The project leaders and the data steward will decide where the DMP will be published, for example through DMPOnline, or on Zenodo.

After the DMP publication, it is added as a formal project document for further monitoring. The data steward recommends that researchers keep the DMP synchronized with changes occurring in the project, regarding it as a "living document".

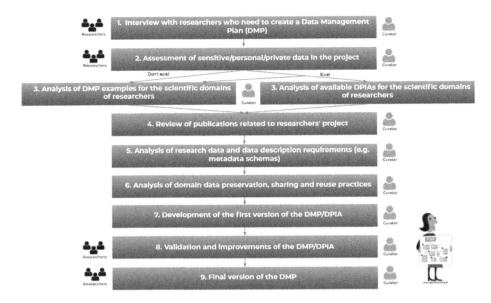

Fig. 2. The collaborative method in the preparation of a DMP

4   DMP Created with the Collaborative Method

INESC TEC is a research institute with over 700 researchers, from different areas that range from energy to computer science, from manufacturing to communications. For more than 5 years, INESC TEC has been nurturing experimental activities in RDM, partly as a research endeavour, but having in mind the development of new services to support RDM in the context of running projects and to expose datasets in the institutional data repository. The strategy to support DMP creation is part of this commitment, and currently involves 2 part-time people (one data steward and one repository manager) that promote awareness of RDM and process requests for DMP.

The DMP creation starts with the request sent by email to the INESC TEC data steward. The collaborative method is therefore tested on real cases, allowing us to evaluate the method in different scientific domains and identify any specific requirements. The DMP is typically created at the beginning of the project, but sometimes also halfway through the project and very rarely at the end. At the moment, eight plans were created for projects in Environmental radioactivity, Biodiversity, Education, Oceanography, Psychology, Environmental engineering, Health and Statistics domains. Some of them are complete and published, some are in preparation or in monitoring. In the following we go into the details of the DMP-creation process for 5 case studies, highlighting aspects that may be transferable to other cases. These 5 cases are in an advanced stage of preparation and give us more information for analysis.

Environmental Radioactivity: This project was focused on the study of the concentration of the noble gas radon (Rn-222); the aim is to examine how meteorological conditions influence it, how it impacts the local atmospheric electric field and its association with the atmosphere's ionization and aerosol concentration[8]. The Principal Investigator (PI) of this project already had experience in RDM activities, but not on the creation of the DMP. The data steward held an interview with the PI, to understand the context of the project and to collect data and papers related to the project. After the interview, their analysis continued, identifying the absence of sensitive data, and studying specific requirements for data management and description in this domain. At the same time, several examples of plans in similar domains were analyzed, as well as some DMP templates, and the first version of the DMP was created. A list with specific questions for verification and confirmation with the PI was created on the second meeting. Not all questions from the list were used on the DMP, however many of them helped to add more specific details about tools used during the project, their calibration method, specific software used for processing, data analysis, measurement method, detailed description of the data transfer process from the station, and even information about what happens to the project data in case the PI leaves. This DMP was created on the final phase of the project and does not require monitoring[9].

Biodiversity: The FARSYD project[10] aims to examine the relation between farming systems, biodiversity and ecosystem services in high nature value farmlands. The PI had little experience in RDM, and for this project she created an Excel file with the detailed description of each experience. This file and description of the project helped the data steward understand the context of the project and identify the existence of private and sensitive data that cannot be publicly exposed. Following the collaborative methodology, the data steward analysed all obtained information, collected examples of DMP in the biodiversity domain, and experimented with the GFBio DMP Tool[11] and the Best Practice Guide [14], promoted by the German Federation for Biological Data. This analysis helped to prepare the new list with specific questions that were validated with the PI. Two existing checklists were verified: one prepared for the Environmental Radioactivity and the one specific to the Biodiversity domain. Although the questions from the first list are not immediately applicable to this plan, some of the points were used with adaptation. This led to the inclusion of the description of the specific tools used during the project, specific software, training areas for habitat mapping, several approaches to obtain data, depending on the specific target, and the location. Moreover, this project contained private data provided by the Portuguese Institute of Financing Agriculture and Fisheries, the Integrated Administrative and Control System and the Land Parcel Information Systems, so the data steward helped to add detailed information on the management of

---

[8] https://www.arm.gov/research/campaigns/ena2015grm.
[9] https://dmponline.dcc.ac.uk/plans/29718/export.pdf.
[10] https://cibio.up.pt/projects-1/page/552.
[11] https://www.gfbio.org/plan.

this kind of data and the corresponding preservation rules with restrictions and different access levels. The first version of the DMP was created halfway through the project, and was improved, detailed and publicly shared through DMPOnline[12]. Monitoring and improvement of DMP happened twice since the plan's publication and the last monitoring action was scheduled for August 2020.

Education: The project SCReLProg[13] aims to develop a pedagogical approach to overcome programming difficulties and effective strategies for self- and co-regulation of e-learning. The researchers of this project did not have experience with RDM. They sent, together with the request for support, a lot of documentation about the project before the first meeting with the data steward. These elements were valuable to provide an overview of the project, prepare a list of questions, identify the existence of personal data and prepare information related to informed consent, ethics committee approval and the need for a DPIA, according to the General Data Protection Regulation. All meetings were conducted via Skype with the researcher in charge of RDM, not the PI of the project. The version for publication of the DMP[14] was shared, corrected and approved by the researchers in charge of project activities. Six months after the start, it was publicly open and the first monitoring session scheduled for March 2020. The specificity of this DMP lied in the necessity of the DPIA, that was also created as a collaboration between the data steward and the institution's DPO. The DMP process also led to the correction of the existing informed consent form, the detailed analysis of all tools, software and data collection methodologies, and the inclusion of recommendation for processing and preservation of personal data. Due to the small risks and threats estimated by the DPO, the publication of the DPIA was replaced by a signed agreement between the project partners. The data steward suggested changing the Google Drive storage by the institutional Drive at INESC TEC[15], and Google Forms by UESurvey. Moreover, the DMP creation helped prevent complicated situations related to personal data before data collection, preparation and sharing, and provided the project team with all the required documentation. The next DMP monitoring was scheduled for August 2020.

Oceanography: The DMP of the SAIL project[16] is the most complex and detailed plan created at INESC TEC, due to the diversity of data, tools, software, internal procedures and the number of institutions involved. Moreover, this is the first plan that comprises several scientific domains: biodiversity, oceanography and robotics. This DMP is not finished yet; it is under validation by the project team. The first version of the DMP was created faster than others, because the project was due to start. This DMP is regarded as a project output and will be published on Zenodo[17]. It is possible to publish new versions of the DMP after

[12] https://dmponline.dcc.ac.uk/plans/47150/export.pdf.
[13] https://www.inesctec.pt/en/projects/screlprog.
[14] https://dmponline.dcc.ac.uk/plans/36851/export.pdf.
[15] https://drive.inesctec.pt/.
[16] https://tinyurl.com/ydgy6lng.
[17] https://zenodo.org/communities/sail/.

the monitoring actions, as Zenodo provides version control. The DMP is pending agreement by the members of the project team, and corrections and monitoring will follow.

Psychology: Project "Identification of learning and development conditions at/through work: challenge the paradoxes of technological introduction and life-long learning" focuses on learning about production processes, involves several types of data and data collection techniques, and will deal with personal and sensitive data. Although the project is currently under evaluation, the first version of the DMP was already created. The specificity of this case study is the existence of a researcher in charge of the RDM tasks, that will plan, organize and answer the RDM questions of researchers. This person had experience in data management, but not in DMP creation. This resulted in their request for help in this process. In this case, the DMP creation took an abbreviated path. A first version of the DMP has been directly sent to the data steward for evaluation and correction. In two days, the data steward analyzed the plan, added comments, and identified the points that needed more detail. As the project will deal with sensitive data, the data steward also raised issues regarding the informed consent and DPIA, the corresponding contact with the institution's DPO, and the approval by the ethics committee. The DMP is in preparation using DMPOnline tool and is not public yet. Work on it will proceed in case the project is approved. This case study is included, although the project is not funded, to illustrate the commitment of researchers to a DMP in the planning stage of the project. The fact that more and more project calls require DMP in the submission phase is evidence of the importance of the data steward services.

Environmental Engineering, Health, Statistics: These projects are also under preparation and already have the first versions of the DMP. The concern of researchers with RDM issues is visible from their contacts. Like the previous case, the PI emailed us and sent a DMP draft for validation. Finalization, publication and monitoring of these plans are expected by October 2020.

5 Preliminary Results

The proposal for a collaborative method for DMP creation at INESC TEC is intended as the first approach to establish a DMP workflow for research projects and to ingrain RDM into the project activities. The establishment of this workflow will introduce RDM-related activities in the internal project proposal and execution processes aiming at a double goal. It will enforce the compliance with the project funders requirements and it will also improve the quality of the research methods in the project, by making the data life cycle explicit, by assigning appropriate effort to data management activities and by avoiding misunderstandings among the project partners. This is expected to have a positive impact on the institutional research maturity. Although the collaborative method can be improved, the case studies show that the expertise of a data steward and RDM skills are essential in the institution. The researchers might create DMP based on existing examples from their domain on their own, but besides requiring more time, the final version would likely not have an adequate level of detail and possibly omit the monitoring of the plan. The results of the questionnaire[18] submitted after each DMP process also proved the importance of the existence of the data steward. Some researchers declared: "It is essential to have specialized staff to assist researchers in these tasks", and all stated that it is very important to have a data steward that responds to RDM issues at the institution, and helps prevent errors during the planning stage that might influence the course of the project.

The results showed that the identification of sensitive and personal data is one of the main aspects where unexpected difficulties may arise. The experience from the cases described here led to a better articulation between the data steward, the DPO and the Ethics Committee. The RDM workflow can be seen as a more general one, as every research project is expected to have a DMP. Only projects with personal data demand the collaboration with the DPO and the elaboration of a DPIA requires prior knowledge of the data processing steps. Thus the DMP precedes the DPIA. However, the recommendations from the DPIA may lead to a revision of the DMP, and therefore an iterative approach is suggested. The Ethics Committee deals with more fundamental issues like the appropriateness of the project purpose and of its research methods. Although the DMP and a possible DPIA could be informative for the Ethics Committee, the level of analysis and the timings of a project proposal suggest that the ethics analysis may be performed in parallel, the details of the interaction among the three institutional roles being determined by the specificity of each project.

Metadata schemes, the choice of a repository, data organization and preservation rules, and the scheduling of RDM tasks among the project partners are other complex issues where researchers need support. To describe all DMP elements, it is necessary to collaborate with specific teams, such as project managers and IT staff who know the institution's technical settings, such as repository capacity and internal regulations. In our case studies, the data steward is aware of these rules and is expected to follow the practices in specific fields, monitor RDM developments and good practices, international and institutional laws and policies, and suggest improvements in the institutional RDM workflow. Moreover, the data steward can help create DMP with more detail, satisfying FAIR requirements, anticipate problems with project partners, and monitor the resulting DMP. One of the researchers confirmed that the collaboration with the data steward was very useful and that, from now on, no project with their group will start without a DMP, to avoid difficulties related to the data, their organization, management and ownership.

Considering the answers, researchers considered DMP monitoring also very important, and that it needs to be carried out "every 6 months", upon notification by email. The existence of a pre-filled DMP for a specific domain or "a generic template, that can be adapted for specific DMP" was also mentioned by researchers in the questionnaire. User support, RDM tools and good practices

---

[18] https://forms.gle/zZMVVbRp9z77XXBA8.

were indicated as important for the whole institution. With each new plan created, both the data steward and the researcher acquire new knowledge, skills and engage more with research data management. In other words, the collaboration and proposed method positively affect all of the institute's stakeholders.

6   Future Work

To take the INESC TEC DMP support to the next level, we will continue with the collaboration with researchers from different domains on their concrete projects. The DMP monitoring mechanisms will be detailed and evolve to conform to the Machine Actionable DMP standard (maDMP) proposed by the RDA DMP Common Standards Working Group[19], that we have engaged with during the maDMP Hackathon[20], mapping our DMP to the maDMP scheme. The results of the Hackathon are the starting point to incorporate tasks complying with the maDMP standard[21] in our proposal for the research project workflow. To this end, we will analyze the information collected during the Hackhathon, improve our DMP scheme and its implementation, and test it with researchers.

The development of a DMP system, based on cases studies of researchers from different scientific domains and institutions, is planned as part of the improvement of the INESC TEC RDM workflow. The system will simplify DMP creation, help with its monitorization, and link research data with the corresponding projects and the monitoring mechanisms of the DMP, thus keeping DMP as a "live" document during of the project. Due to the diversity of scientific domains of INESC TEC, during the creation of the system, we will also be able to compare the experiences and requirements of different scientific domains to identify possible differences and contribute to the Data Domain Protocol proposed by Science Europe[22], a flexible metadata models for DMP creation on different scientific domains. All in all, the interest and availability of researchers in this collaboration promotes an in-depth analysis of DMP issues, the application and testing of existing solutions and the development of our own.

References

1. Ahokas, M., Kuusniemi, M.E., Friman, J.: The Tuuli project: accelerating data management planning in Finnish research organisations. Int. J. Digit. Curation **12**(2), 107–115 (2017). https://doi.org/10.2218/ijdc.v12i2.512
2. Clare, C., et al.: The Cookbook, Engaging Researchers with Data Management (2019). https://doi.org/10.11647/OBP.0185
3. European Commission: Annex L. Conditions related to open access to research data (2017)

---

[19] https://www.rd-alliance.org/groups/dmp-common-standards-wg.
[20] https://github.com/RDA-DMP-Common/hackathon-2020.
[21] https://tinyurl.com/y6evw2ed.
[22] https://www.scienceeurope.org/.

4. Cox, A., Verbaan, E.: Data management planning. In: Exploring Research Data Management (2018). https://doi.org/10.29085/9781783302802.013
5. Dressler, V.A., Yeager, K., Richardson, E.: Developing a data management consultation service for faculty researchers: a case study from a large Midwestern public university. Int. J. Digit. Curation **14**(1) (2019). https://doi.org/10.2218/ijdc.v14i1.590
6. Fearon, D., Gunia, B., Lake, S., Pralle, B.E., Sallans., A.L.: SPEC kit 334: research data management services (2013). https://doi.org/10.29242/spec.334
7. Graham., P.: Managing research data (2012)
8. Managing Data@ Melbourne Working Group: Managing data@ Melbourne: an online research data management training program (2017). https://minerva-access.unimelb.edu.au/handle/11343/225138
9. Hodson, S., Mons, B., Uhlir, P., Zhang, L.: The Beijing Declaration on Research Data. CODATA, Committee on Data of the International Science Council (2019). https://doi.org/10.5281/zenodo.3552330
10. Karimova, Y., Castro, J.A., Ribeiro, C.: Data deposit in a CKAN repository: a Dublin core-based simplified workflow. In: Manghi, P., Candela, L., Silvello, G. (eds.) IRCDL 2019. CCIS, vol. 988, pp. 222–235. Springer, Cham (2019). https://doi.org/10.1007/978-3-030-11226-4_18
11. Karimova, Y., Ribeiro, C.: The collaborative method between curators and researchers in the preparation of a Data Management Plan and Privacy Impact Assessment. 5 Forum Gestão de Dados de Investigação, Aveiro (2019). https://forumgdi.rcaap.pt/wp-content/uploads/2019/12/09_5ForumGDI__Yulia_Karimova.pdf
12. Karimova, Y., Castro, J.A., da Silva, J.R., Pereira, N., Ribeiro, C.: Promoting semantic annotation of research data by their creators: a use case with B2NOTE at the end of the RDM workflow. In: Garoufallou, E., Virkus, S., Siatri, R., Koutsomiha, D. (eds.) MTSR 2017. CCIS, vol. 755, pp. 112–122. Springer, Cham (2017). https://doi.org/10.1007/978-3-319-70863-8_11
13. Ray, J.M.: Research data management: Practical strategies for information professionals (2013). https://doi.org/10.2307/j.ctt6wq34t
14. Cadman, M.J.: GBIF-ICLEI best practice guide for publishing biodiversity data by local governments. Global Biodiversity Information Facility, Copenhagen (2012). http://links.gbif.org/gbif_best_practice_guide_data_publishing_by_local_governments_en_v1
15. Anne, K.M.: Managing research data. Research methods (2018). https://doi.org/10.1016/b978-0-08-102220-7.00021-2
16. Molloy, L.: JISC research data MANTRA project at EDINA, Information Services, University of Edinburgh: Evaluation. Information Processing and Management (2012). https://eprints.gla.ac.uk/71435/
17. Pasquetto, I.V., Randles, B.M., Borgman, C.L.: On the reuse of scientific data. Data Sci. J. **16**(8) (2017). https://doi.org/10.5334/dsj-2017-008
18. RDA: RDA for the Sustainable Development Goals. Introduction: Fit with the overall RDA vision and mission (2019). https://www.rd-alliance.org/groups/rda-sustainable-development-goals
19. Ribeiro, C., da Silva, J.R., Castro, J.A., Amorim, R.C., Lopes, J.C.: Research data management tools and workflows: experimental work at the University of Porto. IASSIST Q. **42**(2), 1–16 (2018)
20. Sayogo, D.S., Pardo, T.A.: Exploring the determinants of scientific data sharing: understanding the motivation to publish research data. Gov. Inf. Q. **30**, 19–31 (2013). https://doi.org/10.1016/j.giq.2012.06.011

21. Schöpfel, J., Ferrant, C., André, F., Fabre, R.: Research data management in the French national research center (CNRS). Data Technol. Appl. (2018). https://doi.org/10.1108/DTA-01-2017-0005
22. Simms, S., Jones, S.: Next-generation data management plans: global, machine-actionable, FAIR. Int. J. Digit. Curation **12**(1) (2017). https://doi.org/10.2218/ijdc.v12i1.513
23. Tenopir, C., et al.: Research data services in European academic research libraries. Liber Q. **27**(1) (2017). https://doi.org/10.18352/lq.10180
24. Tomáš, H., Janoušková, S., Moldan, B.: Sustainable development goals: a need for relevant indicators. Ecol. Indicators **60** (2016). https://doi.org/10.1016/j.ecolind.2015.08.003
25. Vitale, C.H., Sandy, H.L.M.: Data management plans: a review. DESIDOC J. Libr. Inf. Technol. **39**(6) (2019). https://doi.org/10.14429/djlit.39.06.15086
26. Wilkinson, M.D., et al.: The FAIR Guiding Principles for scientific data management and stewardship. Sci. Data **3** (2016). https://doi.org/10.1038/sdata.2016.18
27. Wittenberg, J., Elings, M.: Building a research data management service at the University of California, Berkeley: a tale of collaboration. IFLA J. **43**(1) (2017). https://doi.org/10.1177/0340035216686982

Track on Metadata and Semantics for Digital Humanities and Digital Curation (DHC2020)

Building Linked Open Date Entities
for Historical Research

Go Sugimoto(✉)

Austrian Centre for Digital Humanities and Cultural Heritage, Austrian Academy of Sciences,
Sonnenfelsgasse 19, Vienna, Austria
go.sugimoto@oeaw.ac.at

Abstract. Time is a focal point for historical research. Although existing Linked Open Data (LOD) resources hold time entities, they are often limited to modern period and year-month precision at most. Therefore, researchers are currently unable to execute co-reference resolution through entity linking to integrate different datasets which contain information on the day level or remote past. This paper aims to build an RDF model and lookup service for historical time at the lowest granularity level of a single day at a specific point in time, for the duration of 6000 years. The project, Linked Open Date Entities (LODE), generates stable URIs for over 2.2 million entities, which include essential information and links to other LOD resources. The value of date entities is discussed in a couple of use cases with existing datasets. LODE facilitates improved access and connectivity to unlock the potential for the data integration in interdisciplinary research.

Keywords: Historical date · Entity model · URI · Lookup · Time Ontology in OWL

1 Introduction

Time is one of the most fundamental concepts of our life. The data we deal with often contain time concepts such as day and year in the past, present, and future. There is no doubt that historical research cannot be done without notations of time. On the other hand, the advent of Linked Open Data (LOD) has changed the views on the possibility of data-driven historical research. Indeed, many projects have started producing a large number of LOD datasets. In this strand, entity linking has been considered as a critical ingredient of LOD implementation. Digital humanities and cultural heritage communities work on co-reference resolution by means of Named Entity Linking (NEL) to LOD resources with an expectation to make connections between their datasets and other resources [1–4]. It is often the case that they refer to globally known URIs of LOD such as Wikidata and DBpedia for the purpose of interoperability. Historical research datasets include such fundamental concepts as "World War I" (event), "Mozart" (person), "the Dead Sea Scrolls" (object), "the Colosseum" (building), and "Kyoto" (place). However, rather surprisingly, time concepts/entities are not fully discussed in this context. One reason is that the availability of LOD entities are limited to meet the needs of historians. Moreover,

© Springer Nature Switzerland AG 2021
E. Garoufallou and M.-A. Ovalle-Perandones (Eds.): MTSR 2020, CCIS 1355, pp. 323–335, 2021.
https://doi.org/10.1007/978-3-030-71903-6_30

they may not be well known and use cases are largely missing. It is also likely that entity linking is simply not executed. In the following sections, we discuss those issues and solutions in detail.

The primary goal of this paper is to foster LOD-based historical research by modelling and publishing time concepts/entities, called "Linked Open Date Entities (LODE)", which satisfies the preliminary requirements of the target users. In particular, we 1) design and generate RDF entities to include useful information, 2) provide a lookup and API service to allow access to the entities through URI, 3) illustrate a typical implementation workflow for entity linking ("nodification"), and 4) present use cases with existing historical resources.

2 Related Work and Unsolved Issues

Firstly, we examine published temporal entities in LOD. In terms of descriptive entities, DBpedia holds entities including the 1980s, the Neolithic, the Roman Republic, and the Sui dynasty. PeriodO[1] provides lookups and data dumps to facilitate the alignment of historical periods from different sources (the British Museum, ARIADNE, etc.). Semantics.gr has developed LOD vocabularies for both time and historical periods for SearchCulture.gr [5]. However, the lowest granularity is early, mid, and late period of a century. As descriptive time entities are already available, this article concentrates on numeric time entities that could connect to the descriptive ones. In this regard, DBpedia contains RDF nodes of numeric time such as 1969. They hold literals in various languages and links to other LOD resources, and can be looked up. However, year entities[2] seem to be limited in the span between ca. 756 BC and ca. AD 2071, while years beyond this range tend to be redirected to the broader concepts of decade. Moreover, there seem to be no or only few entities for a month and day of a particular year. SPARQL queries on Wikidata suggest that the year entities are more or less continuously present between 2200 BC and AD 2200.[3] Year-month entities seem to be merely available for a few hundred years in the modern period[4], and day-level entities are scarce.[5] Situations are normally worse in other LOD datasets.[6] Therefore, it is currently not possible to connect datasets to the time entities comprehensively for a day and month, or a year in the remote past. This is not satisfactory for historical research. For instance, we could easily imagine how important time information could be in a situation in which the day-to-day reconstruction of history in 1918 during World War I is called for. The same goes for prehistory or medieval history, although lesser time precision would be required.

---

[1] https://perio.do (accessed July 20, 2020).
[2] See also https://en.wikipedia.org/wiki/List_of_years. (accessed July 20, 2020).
[3] Currently the lower and upper limit would be 9564 BC and AD 3000.
[4] A SPARQL query only returns 218 hits between AD 1 to AD 1600, while 5041 entities are found between AD 1600 and 2020.
[5] A SPARQL query returns no hit before October 15 1582 (on the day when the Gregorian calendar was first adopted), and only returns 159691 hits between AD 1 to AD 2020.
[6] For example, rare cases include https://babelnet.org/synset?word=bn:14549660n&details=1&lang=EN. (accessed July 20, 2020).

Secondly, we look for ontologies in order to represent temporal information in RDF. [6] study TimeML to annotate historical periods, but its XML focus is out of our scope. Time Ontology in OWL[7] reflects classical works of [7, 8] and [9], overcoming problems of the original OWL-Time[8] that defined instant (point of time) and interval (period of time), but limited itself to the Gregorian calendar [10]. Thus, the use of different temporal reference systems (e.g. the Jewish calendar, radiocarbon dating) for the same absolute point in time can be modelled nicely [11]. The specifications also state some advantages of their approach over a typed literal, echoing the vision of our proposal (Sect. 3.1). In the Wikidata ontology, two streams of temporal concepts are present. One is concepts for the unit of time, or time interval, including millennium, century, decade, year, month, and day. The other is considered as the instances of the former. For example, the second millennium is an instance of millennium, while August 1969 is an instance of month. In the field of historical research, CIDOC-CRM[9] has similarity to Time Ontology in OWL, defining temporal classes and properties influenced by [8]. [12] apply Time Ontology in OWL for the ancient Chinese time, which demonstrates the importance of developing ontologies for non-Gregorian calendars.

Thirdly, a few examples are found along the line of data enrichment and entity linking. During the data aggregation process of Europeana, data enrichment is performed [2]. Some Europeana datasets include enriched date information expressed via edm:TimeSpan in relation to a digital object.[10] It contains URIs from semium.org, labels, and translations.[11] Those URIs connect different resources in the Europeana data space. A time concept links to broader or narrower concepts of time through dcterms:isPartOf. Another case is Japan Search.[12] In its data model, schema:temporal and jps:temporal function as properties for time resources.[13] The SPARQL-based lookup service displays time entities such as https://jpsearch.go.jp/entity/time/1162 and https://jpsearch.go.jp/entity/time/1100-1199, which often contain literal values in Japanese, English, and gYear, as well as owl:sameAs links to Wikidata and Japanese DBpedia. The web interface enables users to traverse the graphs between time entities and cultural artifacts in the collection.

3   Implementing the Linked Open Date Entities

3.1   Nodification

We shall now discuss why RDF nodes are beneficial. Time concepts in historical research datasets are normally stored as literal values, when encoded in XML or RDF. In fact, those

---

[7] https://www.w3.org/TR/owl-time/ (accessed July 20, 2020).

[8] https://www.w3.org/TR/2006/WD-owl-time-20060927/ (accessed July 20, 2020).

[9] https://www.cidoc-crm.org/ (accessed July 20, 2020).

[10] The DPLA Metadata Application Profile (MAP) also uses edm:TimeSpan (https://pro.dp.la/hubs/metadata-application-profile) (accessed July 20, 2020).

[11] See an example record at https://www.europeana.eu/portal/en/record/9200434/oai_baa_onb_at_8984183.html. For example, https://semium.org/time/1900 represents AD 1900. (accessed July 20, 2020).

[12] https://jpsearch.go.jp/ (accessed July 20, 2020).

[13] https://www.kanzaki.com/works/ld/jpsearch/primer/ (accessed July 20, 2020).

literals are often descriptive dates, such as "early 11th century", "24 Aug 1965?", "1876 年", and "1185 or 1192", to allow multilingualism, diversity, flexibility, and uncertainty [5]. [6] report that less than half of dates in the ARIA database of Rijksmuseum are 3 or 4 digit year. Sometimes literal values are more structured and normalised like 1789/7/14. However, they could be only a fraction. The syntax of "standardised" dates also varies in different countries (10/26/85 or 26/10/85). The tradition of analogue data curation on historical materials may also contribute to this phenomenon to a certain extent. Whatever the reasons are, literals in RDF have three major disadvantages over nodes: a) new information cannot be attached, b) they are neither globally unique nor referable, and c) they cannot be linked. Since LOD is particularly suited to overcome those shortcomings, literals alone may hinder historical research in the LOD practices. This is the forefront motivation of the transformation of literals with or without data type into nodes/entities/resources. We may call it "nodification". Figure 1 visualises a real example of nodification. ANNO[14] and the Stefan Zweig dataset[15] can be interlinked and the graph network is extended to other global LOD resources.

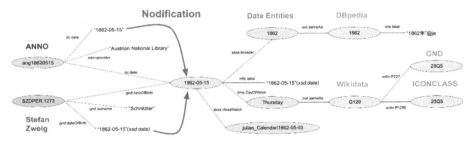

Fig. 1. Interlinking of nodes by nodification of two datasets

Some may still argue that nodification is redundant and/or problematic, because typed literals are designed for time expressions, and XMLSchema-based (e.g. xsd:date) calculations by queries cannot be done with nodes. But, this is not entirely true. First of all, the nodification of this project does not suggest a replacement of literals. When LOD datasets include typed literals, they can be untouched and/or fully preserved in rdfs:label of the new nodes. The temporal calculations are still fully supported, and are encouraged for mathematical operations. It is possible to use SPARQL to obtain not only dates in typed literals, but also dates without data types. It is also noted that the year entities in DBpedia do not seem to support data types for literals, thus arithmetic calculations may not be possible, while Wikidata does for the year, month and day entities.[16] Secondly, as literals are intact, this proposal is a data enrichment and hence not a duplication. The enrichment provides additional possibilities to attach new information, which cannot be achieved by typed literals. Thirdly, a lookup service of LODE serves as a *global and*

---

[14] https://anno.onb.ac.at/ (accessed July 20, 2020).

[15] https://www.stefanzweig.digital (accessed July 20, 2020).

[16] However, there would be a problem, because it sets January 1 as the value of xsd:dateTime for a time interval entity (e.g. 1987 is represented as 1987–01-01T00:00:00Z).

permanent reference point for the links across datasets. It encourages data owners to include the entity URIs in their datasets, so that they are able to connect to other datasets that refer to the same URIs. In addition, users often need data browsing before and/or without data querying, in order to understand the scope of data (e.g. data availability, coverage, connectivity, structure) by traversing graphs. Whilst the nodification offers an optimal use case for easy data exploration, literals have limited possibility. Lastly, without the nodification, LOD users have to connect datasets via date literals on the fly whenever they need to. Although it is possible to generate RDF nodes out of literals only when needed, URIs may not be assigned permanently for the nodes in this scenario. Therefore, long-term references are not assured. In addition, it is critical to openly declare and publish URIs a priori through the lookup. Otherwise, it is unlikely that NEL is conducted widely. In a way, the nodification also has a similar scope to materialisation[17] with regard to pre-computing of data for performance. In Table 1, several advantages of our approach (preprocessed nodification) are outlined over 1) the use of only literals, and 2) on-demand nodification.

3.2 URI Syntax Principles

In order to execute the nodification, URIs are required. This section briefly highlights the design principles for the URI syntax of LODE. The date URIs consist of a base URI and a suffix. The base URI is set as https://vocabs.acdh.oeaw.ac.at/date/ as a part of an institutional vocabulary service, although it is misleading to be called vocabulary. As for the suffix, we follow the most widely accepted standard, ISO8601, which is the convention of many programming languages (SQL, PHP, Python) and web schemas (XMLSchema 1.1). The most common format should look like YYYY (2020), YYYY-MM (2020-01), and YYYY-MM-DD (2020-01-01). An important factor of adopting the subset of ISO8601 is that it can provide non-opaque numeric-based URIs. It enables human users to conjecture or infer any dates, including dates in a remote past and future, even if look ups are not available. In contrast, it is very hard for them to infer dates from opaque URIs such as the Wikidata URIs.[18] ISO8601-based URIs are also language independent, as opposed to the DBpedia URIs. Those consideration helps researchers who deal with time spanning tens of thousands of years.

The use of ISO8601 also implies that the Gregorian calendar and proleptic Gregorian calendar are applied. The latter is the extension of the Gregorian calendar backward to the dates before AD 1582. Although ISO8601 allows it, the standard also suggests that there should be an explicit agreement between the data sender and the receiver about its use. Therefore, we provide a documentation to explain the modelling policy.[19] In addition, the ISO8601 syntax is applied for BC/BCE and AD/CE, although there is complicated

---

[17] Materialiastion is the term used in Semantic Web to generate graphs based on inferences. Implicit knowledge is materialised in order to make it explicit for the purpose of query performance.

[18] For instance, https://www.wikidata.org/entity/Q2432 represents AD 1984.

[19] Full details are available at https://vocabs.acdh.oeaw.ac.at/date/ together with the syntax principles.

Table 1. Pros and cons of three approaches

	Preprocessed nodification (our approach)	Only literals	On-demand nodification
Connects to nodes in RDF	✓	✗	❗[a]
Includes literals	✓	✓	✓
Possibility to add other information	✓	✗	✗
Time calculation by XSD typed literals	✓	✓	✓
Stable URIs	✓	✗	✗
Lookup service	✓	✗	✗
Graph data browsing	Optimal	Not optimal	Not optimal
Access and query performance	Depends (probably better)	Depends	Depends
RDF data size (after enrichment)	Bigger	Smaller	Smaller
Data processing tasks for enrichment	Much more[b]	No, or much less	No, or much less

[a]Only on demand for selected datasets.
[b]This may not be a disadvantage, if one would like to execute other types of data enrichment and normalisation to improve data quality in parallel.

discussions and controversy.[20] Year Zero does not exist, thus "0000" means 1 BC[21] and "−0001" is 2 BC. More than 4 digits ("−13000") allow time concepts in prehistory. As

[20] See https://phabricator.wikimedia.org/T94064. There are confusing specifications in XML Schema Part 2: Datatypes Second Edition (https://www.w3.org/TR/xmlschema-2/#isoformats), XML Schema Definition Language (XSD) 1.1 Part 2: Datatypes (https://www.w3.org/TR/xmlschema11-2/#dateTime), and the HTML living standard (https://html.spec.whatwg.org/#global-dates-and-times). (accessed July 20, 2020).

[21] As seen in Wikidata (https://www.wikidata.org/entity/Q25299). (accessed July 20, 2020).

the syntax is the subset of ISO8601, exactly 3 digits (YYY) and 2 digits (YY) can be also used, representing a decade and century respectively.[22]

In order to accommodate other calendars (e.g. Julian, Islamic) and dating systems (carbon-14 dating), one can add a schema name between the base URI and the date. For example, we could define URIs for the Japanese calendar as follows: https://vocabs. acdh.oeaw.ac.at/date/japanese_calendar/平成/31.

3.3 Modelling LODE in RDF

The first implementation of our RDF model should at least include entities at the lowest granularity level of a single day for the duration of 6000 years (from 3000 BC to AD 3000). From the perspectives of historians and archaeologists, day-level references would be required for this temporal range. The number implies that there will be over 2.2 million URIs, counting the units of the whole hierarchy from days to millennia. In any case, this experiment does not prevent us from extending the time span in the future.

Regarding the RDF representation of time entities, we adopt properties from Time Ontology in OWL, RDFS, and SKOS. However, there is a clear difference between LODE and Time Ontology in OWL. The former aims to create historical dates as stable nodes, rather than literals that the latter mostly employs. The latter also does not have properties expressing broader semantic concepts than years; decades, centuries, and millennia are not modelled by default. Therefore, we simply borrow some properties from the ontology for specific purposes, including time:DayOfWeek, time:monthOfYear, time:hasTRS, time:intervalMeets, and time:intervalMetBy. In LODE, the URLs of DBpedia, YAGO, Wikidata, semium.org, and Japan Search are included in our entities as the equivalent or related entities, where possible, especially for the entities of years and upward in hierarchy. Figure 2 illustrates a typical date entity for the day-level.

In order to generate 2.2 million entities, we have created dozens of Perl scripts, producing entities in RDF/XML for days, months, years, decades, centuries, and units of time, because of the complexity of generating the DBpedia and YAGO URIs as well as literal variations for different units of time. As there are only 6 millennia, they are manually created as the top level entities. The Perl library of DateTime[23] is primarily used to calculate, for example, the day of a week, the day of a year, and the corresponding day of the Gregorian calendar in the Julian calendar. Some small functions are also developed to generate variations of descriptive dates in English and German and to calibrate entities for BC and AD as well as leap years.

The overall structure of various entities in LODE is visualised in Fig. 3. There were two choices to create links between the date entities. One is the SKOS vocabulary and the other is an ontology using RDFS/OWL. According to the SKOS Reference specifications[24], a thesaurus or classification scheme is different from a formal knowledge representation. Thus, facts and axioms could be modelled more suitably in an ontology,

---

[22] For example, "196" means the 1960s, and "19" is the 19th century. They should not be confused with "0196" (AD 196) and "0019" (AD 19). Years less than 5 digits must be expressed in exactly 4 digits.

[23] https://metacpan.org/pod/DateTime (accessed July 20, 2020).

[24] https://www.w3.org/TR/skos-reference/ (accessed July 20, 2020).

```
@prefix skos: <http://www.w3.org/2004/02/skos/core#> .
@prefix time: <http://www.w3.org/2006/time#> .
@prefix rdfs: <http://www.w3.org/2000/01/rdf-schema#> .
@prefix xsd: <http://www.w3.org/2001/XMLSchema#> .
@prefix acdhdate: <https://vocabs.acdh.oeaw.ac.at/date/> .
@prefix acdhut: <https://vocabs.acdh.oeaw.ac.at/unit_of_time/> .


acdhdate 1900-02-01
  a acdhut February_1, acdhut Day, skos:Concept ;
  rdfs:label "1900-02-01"^^xsd:date ;
  skos:prefLabel "1900-02-01"@en ;
  skos:altLabel "1 February 1900"@en, "1st February 1900"@en, "01-02-1900"@en, "02/01/1900"@en,
  "01/02/1900"@en ;
  skos:definition "1900-02-01 in ISO8601 (the Gregorian and proleptic Gregorian calendar). 1st February
  1900."@en ;
  skos:inScheme acdhdate conceptScheme ;
  time:hasTRS <http://www.opengis.net/def/uom/ISO-8601/0/Gregorian> ;
  skos:closeMatch acdhdate julian_calendar/1900-01-20 .
  time:intervalMetBy acdhdate 1900-01-31 ;
  time:intervalMeets acdhdate 1900-02-02 ;
  skos:broader acdhdate 1900-02 ;
  time:DayOfWeek <http://www.w3.org/ns/time/gregorian/Thursday>, acdhut Thursday ;
  time:monthOfYear <http://www.w3.org/ns/time/gregorian/February>, acdhut February ;
  skos:note "With regard to Date Entity modelling, documentation should be consulted at
  https://vocabs.acdh.oeaw.ac.at/date/. It includes information about URI syntax, ISO8601 conventions, and
  data enrichment among others." ;
```

Fig. 2. The 1901-02-01 entity in Turtle

as the formal logic is required. The date entities seem to be facts and axioms, as we are dealing with commonly and internationally accepted ISO8601. However, from a historical and philosophical point of view, one could also argue that they are also heavily biased toward the idea of the Christian culture. Therefore, the decision to adopt SKOS or OWL was not as simple as it seemed. This paper primarily uses SKOS for two reasons: a) the implementation of a lookup service is provided by SKOSMOS which requires SKOS, b) it is preferred to avoid debates on the ontological conceptualisation of time for the time being. It is assumed that the even Wikidata ontology (Sect. 2) could be a subject of discussion. Moreover, there would be potential problems to use semantic reasoners, for example, due to the inconsistency of our use of decades and centuries.[25] In this sense, SKOS is more desirable thanks to its simple structure and loose semantics.

---

[25] For example, a popular usage is that a decade starts from a year ending in a 0 to a year ending in a 9, while a decade starts from a year ending in a 1 to a year ending in a 0 in a rarer version. Wikidata adopts the former, resulting the 0s and 0s BC consisting of only 9 years. A similar conflict of constructs exists for the use of century.

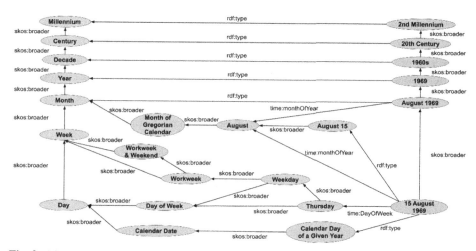

Fig. 3. The structure of LODE based on the Wikidata ontology, in which the unit of time concepts (in blue) and its instances (in red) are linked each other (Color figure online)

Nevertheless, we adopted the same structure of the Wikidata ontology for interoperability reasons, by simply replacing all its proprietary properties with **skos:broader** and **skos:narrower** and a couple of Time Ontology in OWL. This builds a hierarchy of time concepts such as day, month, and year. Similarly, we separate the units of time from instances, with **rdf:type** connecting them. The sequence of the same time unit is encoded by **time:intervalMetBy** and **time:intervalMeets**.

A lookup service is implemented with SKOSMOS[26] (Fig. 4). Once SKOS compliant RDF files are imported to a Jena Fuseki server, one can browse through a hierarchical view of the vocabulary and download an entity in RDF/XML, Turtle, and JSON-LD.

Fig. 4. Date Entity Lookup in SKOSMOS

---

[26] https://skosmos.org/ (accessed July 20, 2020).

4 Use Cases

One benefit of LODE is the capability of handling multilingualism and different calendars. In a use case of Itabi: Medieval Stone Monuments of Eastern Japan Database[27], one may like to align the Japanese calendar with the Western one, when expressing the temporal information in the dataset as LOD. A trouble is that most records hold the accurate date (i.e. day and month) in the Japanese calendar, and only the equivalent year in the Western calendar. Thus, while preserving the original data in literals, it would be constructive to use nodification and materialisation techniques to connect relevant date entities to the artifact (Fig. 5). LODE helps substantially in this scenario, because it allows us to discover the corresponding day both in the proleptic Gregorian calendar and the Julian calendar by inferences/materialisation, as well as the day of the week. The implementation is not possible yet, however, LODE plans to include mapping between the Japanese and Western calendar in the future. By extending this method, we could expect that LOD users can query LODE to fetch a literal in a specific language and use it for querying a full-text database that is not necessarily RDF-compliant, and does

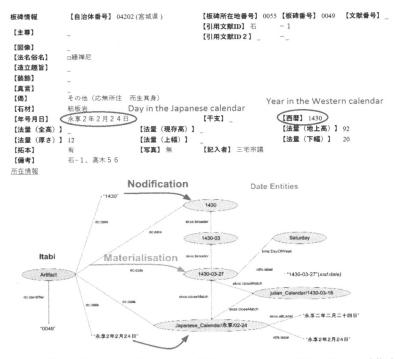

Fig. 5. A record containing the Japanese and Western calendar (https://www.rekihaku.ac.jp/doc/itabi.html (accessed July 20, 2020)) (above) and an example of its simplified RDF model connecting date entities (below)

---

not support the Western alphabet and/or calendars. Such a use case is not possible with literals alone.

A more typical pattern of nodification is data enrichment. The Omnipot project in our institute aims to create an extremely large knowledge graph by ingesting local and global LOD into one triple store. The project evaluates the connectivity of heterogeneous graphs through LODE and the usability of data discovery and exploration. During the nodification of 1.8 million literals in ANNO, not only dates but also data providers and media types are nodified. In this regard, the nodification is not a labour-intensive obstacle, but a part of a data improvement and NEL. A similar nodification is conducted for the Schnitzler-LOD datasets[28] and PMB[29] by Regular Expression. This practice verifies our approach with human inferable non-opaque URIs. Unlike the Wikidata URIs, the LODE and DBpedia URIs were embedded with little effort. The simplicity of implementation incentivises data owners to nodify their data in the future.

Research Space[30] displays incoming and outgoing node links in the Omnipot project *automatically*. Figure 6 showcases connections between them, via the 1987 entity. Users could interactively compare art objects in Europeana with art works in Wikipedia from the same year via Wikidata.[31] This view is currently not possible with literals alone. By default many visualisation software offer a graph view enabling users to focus on nodes as a mean to traverse graphs. Therefore, they do not have to worry about query formulations. As it is not trivial to construct the same view by a query using literals, user friendliness should be considered as a selling point of nodification.

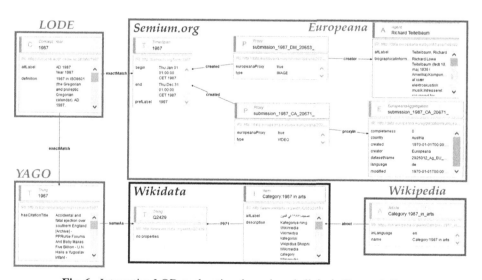

Fig. 6. Interactive LOD exploration through node links in Research Space

---

[28] https://schnitzler-lod.acdh-dev.oeaw.ac.at/about.html (accessed July 20, 2020).

[29] https://pmb.acdh.oeaw.ac.at/ (accessed July 20, 2020).

[30] https://www.researchspace.org/ (accessed July 20, 2020).

[31] As Wikipedia is not LOD, only links to Wikipedia articles are shown and clickable.

5 Future Work and Conclusion

Future work would be more case studies which the use of literals alone cannot easily replicate. An RDF implementation of TEI[32] could bring interesting use cases by normalising and nodifying date literals in various languages, scripts, and calendars in historical texts. In addition, LODE could align with the Chinese, Islamic, Japanese, and Maya calendars, and add more information about festivities and holidays that literals cannot fully cover. Consequently, event-based analyses by SPARQL may uncover unknown connections between people, objects, concepts, and places in a global scale. It could even connect to pre-computed astronomical events at various key locations such as the visibility of planets on a specific day, with which interdisciplinary research can be performed. Further, detailed evaluation of use cases is also needed. For instance, query performance and formulation, and usability could be measured and analysed more systematically. We are also fine-tuning the LODE model by properly modelling the concepts of instants and intervals based on the Time Ontology in OWL.

LODE attempts to solve two problems of existing LOD: a) It tries to meet the needs for greater coverage and granularity of date entities for historical research. b) By designing a simple model and suggesting a straightforward method of nodification, it helps to reduce the complexity of LOD by automatically connecting/visualising vital information in a big Web of Data. Although the research focused exclusively on cultural heritage, many science domains deal with some conception of time, and thus, this study could be an impetus to acknowledge the necessity and the impact of time entities in a broader research community. Since time is one of the most critical dimensions of datasets, we would be able to unlock more potential of LOD.

References

1. van Veen, T., Lonij, J., Faber, W.J.: Linking named entities in Dutch historical newspapers. In: Garoufallou, E., Subirats Coll, I., Stellato, A., Greenberg, J. (eds.) MTSR 2016. CCIS, vol. 672, pp. 205–210. Springer, Cham (2016). https://doi.org/10.1007/978-3-319-49157-8_18
2. Stiller, J., Petras, V., Gäde, M., Isaac, A.: Automatic enrichments with controlled vocabularies in Europeana: challenges and consequences. In: Ioannides, M., Magnenat-Thalmann, N., Fink, E., Žarnić, R., Yen, A.-Y., Quak, E. (eds.) EuroMed 2014. LNCS, vol. 8740, pp. 238–247. Springer, Cham (2014). https://doi.org/10.1007/978-3-319-13695-0_23
3. van Nispen, A.: EHRI Vocabularies and Linked Open Data: An Enrichment? ABB: Archives et Bibliothèques de Belgique - Archief- en Bibliotheekwezen in België 106, 117–122 (2019)
4. Zeng, M.L.: Semantic enrichment for enhancing LAM data and supporting digital humanities. Revi. Article. EPI 28 (2019). https://doi.org/10.3145/epi.2019.ene.03.
5. Georgiadis, H., Papanoti, A., Paschou, M., Roubani, A., Hardouveli, D., Sachini, E.: The semantic enrichment strategy for types, chronologies and historical periods in searchculture.gr. In: Garoufallou, E., Virkus, S., Siatri, R., Koutsomiha, D. (eds.) MTSR 2017. CCIS, vol. 755, pp. 211–223. Springer, Cham (2017). https://doi.org/10.1007/978-3-319-70863-8_20
6. de Boer, V., van Someren, M., Wielinga, B.J.: Extracting historical time periods from the Web. J. Am. Soc. Inf. Sci. 61, 1888–1908 (2010). https://doi.org/10.1002/asi.21378

---

[32] https://tei-c.org/ (accessed July 20, 2020).

7. Allen, J.F.: Maintaining knowledge about temporal intervals. Commun. ACM. **26**, 832–843 (1983). https://doi.org/10.1145/182.358434
8. Allen, J.F., Ferguson, G.: Actions and Events in Interval Temporal Logic. In: Stock, O. (ed.) Spatial and Temporal Reasoning. pp. 205–245. Springer Netherlands, Dordrecht (1997). https://doi.org/https://doi.org/10.1007/978-0-585-28322-7_7.
9. Hobbs, J.R., Pan, F.: An ontology of time for the semantic web. ACM Trans. Asian Lang. Inf. Process. (TALIP). **3**, 66–85 (2004). https://doi.org/10.1145/1017068.1017073
10. Cox, S., Little, C., Hobbs, J., Pan, F.: Time ontology in OWL (2017). https://www.w3.org/TR/2017/REC-owl-time-20171019/
11. Cox, S.J.D.: Time ontology extended for non-Gregorian calendar applications. SW. **7**, 201–209 (2016). https://doi.org/10.3233/SW-150187
12. Zou, Q., Park, E.G.: Modelling ancient Chinese time ontology. J. Inf. Sci. **37**, 332–341 (2011). https://doi.org/10.1177/0165551511406063

Wikidata Centric Vocabularies and URIs for Linking Data in Semantic Web Driven Digital Curation

Nishad Thalhath[1]([✉]) [iD], Mitsuharu Nagamori[2] [iD], Tetsuo Sakaguchi[2] [iD], and Shigeo Sugimoto[2] [iD]

[1] Graduate School of Library, Information and Media Studies, University of Tsukuba, Tsukuba, Japan
`nishad@slis.tsukuba.ac.jp`
[2] Faculty of Library, Information and Media Studies, University of Tsukuba, Tsukuba, Japan
{`nagamori,saka,sugimoto`}`@slis.tsukuba.ac.jp`
`https://www.slis.tsukuba.ac.jp`

Abstract. Wikidata is evolving as the hub of Linked Open Data (LOD), with its language-neutral URIs and close adherence to Wikipedia. Well defined URIs help the data to be interoperable and linkable. This paper examines the possibilities of utilizing Wikidata as the means of a vocabulary resource for promoting the use of linkable concepts. Digital curation projects are vibrant with varying demands and purposes, which makes them less suitable for adopting any common vocabularies or ontologies. Also, developing and maintaining custom vocabularies are expensive processes for smaller projects in terms of resources and skill requirements. In general, Wikidata entities are well documented with Wikipedia entries, and Wikipedia entries express the conceptual and hierarchical relations in detail with provisions to modify or create. The authors explain the concept of using Wikidata as a vocabulary source with a proof of concept module implementation for Omeka-S, a widely adapted open source digital curation platform. This paper is expected to show some practical insights on reliable an reasonable vocabulary development for social informatics as well as cultural heritage projects, with a notion to improve the quality and quantity of linkable data from digital curation projects.

Keywords: Metadata · Wikidata · URI · Vocabulary · Semantic web · Digital curation · Omeka

1 Introduction

Wikidata is evolving as the hub of Linked Open Data (LOD), with its language-neutral URIs and close adherence to Wikipedia and as the core project of Wikimedia's data management strategy [9]. This paper examines the possibilities of utilizing Wikidata as a vocabulary resource for promoting the use of linkable

© Springer Nature Switzerland AG 2021
E. Garoufallou and M.-A. Ovalle-Perandones (Eds.): MTSR 2020, CCIS 1355, pp. 336–344, 2021.
https://doi.org/10.1007/978-3-030-71903-6_31

concepts. The authors evaluate this proposal in the context of social informatics (SI) scenarios. SI projects are vibrant with varying demands and purposes, which makes them less suitable for adopting any common vocabularies or ontologies. Also, developing and maintaining custom vocabularies are expensive processes for smaller projects in terms of resources and skill requirements. In general, Wikidata entities are well documented with Wikipedia entries, and Wikipedia entries express the conceptual and hierarchical relations in detail with provisions to modify or create. These detailed articles act as documentation for the Wikidata entity and help the domain experts to use precise entities than abstract concepts. Wikidata as a vocabulary is not a novel concept, but there are less practical and easy to use integration for less skilled users and communities. This paper explains the concept of using Wikidata as a vocabulary source and a proof of concept implementation by developing an open source module for Omeka-S[1], a semantic web digital curation system, to easily find and use Wikidata URIs and use it as a linkable and comprehensive vocabulary.

1.1 Significance of Wikidata in Linked Data

Wikidata Project is growing along with the acceptance of Wikipedia. Wikidata is tightly bound to Wikipedia, and that makes it a sustainable project. Community driven model prompts it to be integral and well maintained with accurate content and reviewable contributions. Wikipedia eventually became the de-facto standard of open knowledge. Wikipedia collects and maintains multilingual unstructured textual information through community contributions. Whereas the Wikidata process and present structured information from unstructured Wikipedia entries. Wikidata also provides multilingual information, but still maintain language-neutral cool URIs [10].

Similar to Wikipedia, Wikidata is organized as pages. Every subject is called an entity, and every entity has its own editable page. There are two types of entities; they are items, and properties. Wikidata organise information as entities and these entities can be either an item or a property. Items are individuals and classes, but properties are similar to RDF properties. Wikipedia article in any language has a Wikidata item, which represents the subject of the article [2]. Wikidata accepts corrections and contributions from its community the same way as it does with Wikipedia. The corrections or changes can be real-time, which makes it acceptable to changes and additions faster than any other knowledge systems. Wikidata is not just a datasource, but a platform as well [12] and in the last couple of years, Wikidata is moving closer to the center of the LOD cloud by surpassing similar Wikipedia driven projects.

1.2 Wikidata as a Vocabulary Source for Digital Curation

Wikidata can be treated as a controlled vocabulary resource in places where we can use it to replace literals. Multi-lingual labels in Wikidata permits the use of

---

[1] https://omeka.org/s/.

any Wikidata entity to be mapped with a persistent URI irrespective of the language. In the context of Social Informatics projects, the stakeholders can always find the relevant resources from Wikipedia and use the corresponding Wikidata entity as a URI, with suitable labels. Concepts are always linked to the same URI resources irrespective of the language or domain of the project. A higher level of interoperability with precise concept mapping can be obtained from this approach. Wikidata, so as Wikipedia is a domain-independent knowledge graph and the URIs serve valid machine-actionable as well as human-interpretable resources. The machine actionability gives the possibility of using these URIs to further automated knowledge extraction processes.

2   Related Works

Product ontology[2] described a way to develop ontologies for e-commerce definitions using Wikipedia [7]. Product ontology uses Wikipedia, and Wikipedia based URIs in Product Ontology namespace [8]. This paper proposes similar attempts using Wikidata entities instead of Wikipedia and emphasizes a clear language-neutral URI concept with a more LOD cloud oriented perspective. Another related work is using Wikidata as a semantic framework for the Gene Wiki. This attempt created a fully open and extensible data resource for human and mouse molecular biology and biochemistry data [1]. Gene Wiki resource enriches all the Wikipedias with structured information and serves as a new linking hub for the biological semantic web.

Organisations like Europeana encourages users to adapt linkable URIs from Wikidata as a vocabulary to semantically enrich the open data[3]. Using URIs as identifiers will enhance the reusability and interoperability of the data. Studies were conducted on describing digital objects within the context of Europeana with Wikidata [3]. Various projects uses Wikidata as an authority record for obtaining persistent concept URIs to use within ontologies and linkable datasets [5,6]. General purpose ontologies like schema.org makes such process simple, seamless and efficient[4]. There were studies to evaluate the linkage between Library of Congress Subject Heading (LCSH) and Wikidata [11] for vocabulary alignment. Wikidata was also used as a work authority for video games [4].

OpenRefine[5], an open-source data cleansing and transforming tool utilizes Wikidata reconciliation APIs to align datasets to Wikidata items[6].

This paper proposes more broader approaches than being domain specific, by developing a plugin for Omeka-S, a general purpose digital curation system.

---

[2] http://www.productontology.org/.
[3] https://pro.europeana.eu/page/get-your-vocabularies-in-wikidata.
[4] https://schema.org/.
[5] https://openrefine.org/.
[6] https://wikidata.reconci.link/.

2.1 Manually Finding URIs from Wikipedia and Wikidata

The most simple and straightforward method to use Wikidata is to find the corresponding entities from Wikipedia. Every article in Wikipedia has an entity mapped in Wikidata. These Wikidata articles can act as good documentation for the Wikipedia entry. However this process is cumbersome for maintaining bigger digital curation projects, especially in digital humanities, cultural heritage and social informatics.

Domain experts can always create new articles within Wikipedia to obtain more precise URIs in Wikidata namespace. When a specific Wikidata entry is not exist for any given concepts, the users can create it by editing Wikidata. If any specific properties are not available, users have to propose new properties in the Wikidata ontology, which is a systematic process, and the decision is taken by the Wikidata maintainers. This option to create new articles promotes bi-directional growth by increasing the number of articles as well as in return, obtaining precise concept URIs.

3 Methods

Using Wikidata URIs to describe resources is getting acceptance from the Semantic Web communities. Developing and integrating a ready to use and extensible system will help the adaptation process smoother for communities with limited resources. Omaka S is versatile and easy to use Semantic Web digital curation systems. We anticipate that implementing our proposal within Omeka will be beneficial for many. Omeka S is widely used in cultural heritage and digital humanities curation. Omeka S is developed with PHP, and it is easy to install, configure, and maintain. Omeka Team also provides a module name ValueSuggest[7] to search and auto-populate vocabularies within Omeka S. Our implementation is based on ValueSuggest module, which is under GPLv3. ValueSuggest module provides an excellent framework to develop a vocabulary search tool that can be used within Omeka ecosystem.

Wikidata offers different APIs to query and retrieve data. The primary interface for querying Wikidata is its SPARQL endpoint[8]. Wikidata also provides a MediaWiki API[9], which is fast and powerful for basic operations. Wikidata community provides a Wikidata reconciliation web service API for OpenRefine[10]. This API can be used to align datasets to Wikidata items in OpenRefine. As per the Reconciliation Service API specification[11], the API has different querying, recommendations, and preview endpoint implementations. This module utilizes all these endpoints to form a querying and previewing system effectively. Due to the performance advantages, main querying interfaces are built on top of the

---

[7] https://omeka.org/s/modules/ValueSuggest/.
[8] https://query.wikidata.org/.
[9] https://www.wikidata.org/w/api.php.
[10] https://wikidata.reconci.link/.
[11] https://reconciliation-api.github.io/specs/latest/.

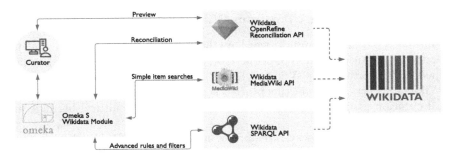

Fig. 1. Overview of the modules querying flow and corresponding API services

MediaWiki API and reconciliation API than with Wikidata SPARQL API. However, for advanced scenarios and use-cases, a SPARQL based querying system will be efficient than the other two. A detailed overview of the modules querying flow and corresponding API services are illustrated in Fig. 1.

The querying is dealt through the module interface within Omeka, and the previews are obtained from the preview endpoint of the reconciliation API directly from the web browser. As a default nature, the APIs' response is cached within the Omeka server using file cache for an hour, this improves performance and reduces response time[12]. Caching helps collaborative editing for bigger projects stable and saves resources. The module provides extensible filter samples for MediaWiki API, OpenRefine reconciliation API, and Wikidata SPARQL API. A detailed matrix of default filters and interfaces are provided in Table 1. The examples are sufficient enough to cover most of the general use-cases. Users can modify or add more filters based on the given examples for specific use cases or create more complex filters to cater to their particular use-cases.

Table 1. Default filters and interfaces

List type	Description	API service	API type	Constraint
All	All Wikidata items	MediaWiki	wbsearchentities	
Entities	All Wikidata entities	OpenRefine	Suggest	Entity
Properties	All Wikidata properties	OpenRefine	Suggest	Property
Persons	Persons from Wikidata	OpenRefine	Reconciliation	Q5
Locations	Locations from Wikidata	OpenRefine	Reconciliation	Q2221906
Languages	Languages from Wikidata	OpenRefine	Reconciliation	Q315
Custom	Custom filter example	OpenRefine	Reconciliation	
SPARQL	SPARQL example	SPARQL	Query	

---

[12] https://docs.zendframework.com/zend-cache/.

4   Results

The authors successfully implemented the concepts discussed in this paper and developed a wikidata module for Omeka-S, with which digital curators can easily search and populate relevant terms and URIs from Wikidata. This module is released as an opensource software under GNU General Public License v3. Omeka-S users can easily install and use this module within their Omeka-S instances. The entire installable source code is accessible from the project GitHub repository at https://github.com/nishad/omeka-s-wikidata. The module is listed in Omeka-S website at https://omeka.org/s/modules/Wikidata/.

Once installed and activated, preconfigured wikidata data types can be selected for properties in resource templates within the Omeka-S control panel. By default, the module provides ready to use configurations for all Wikidata items, entities, properties, places, persons, and languages. Data type selection for properties is shown in Fig. 2.

Fig. 2. Preconfigured Wikidata data types for properties in resource templates

Fig. 3. Example of searching for entities indicating a person

Users can directly type in the search terms within the property fields for the items, and the module will provide an easy to access list of search results to pick the proper term. To avoid the confusion of similar labels, further information can be viewed on mouse hovering individual results. A default search for a person is demonstrated in Fig. 3.

The module is multi-lingual by default. Wikidata names in available languages can be retrieved by setting the language field for every entry. Multi-lingual capability of the module is demonstrated in Fig. 4.

Fig. 4. Wikidata names in available languages can be retrieved by setting the language field

Upon selecting the appropriate entry, the module automatically populates the URI and label in the selected language, as demonstrated in Fig. 5.

Fig. 5. Automatically populated Wikidata URI and label

5   Conclusion

Linking data from different domains will help to develop new possibilities of information-driven knowledge discovery. Linking concepts through URIs will improve the quality and availability of linkable data. In terms of semantic web based digital curation, the impact of such projects can be increased drastically by introducing linkable URIs. More practical approaches and utilities will help implementers and users to adapt Wikidata centric URIs in their curation platforms and Content Management Systems.

Acknowledgments. This work was supported by JSPS KAKENHI Grant Number JP18K11984.

The authors acknowledge the Omeka Team, for developing Omeka-S, a wonderful open-source Semantic Web digital curation platform software, and the ValueSuggest module.

This paper uses icon of 'computer user' (https://thenounproject.com/term/computer-user/1577369) by bezier master from the Noun Project, licensed under Creative Commons CCBY.

References

1. Burgstaller-Muehlbacher, S., et al.: Wikidata as a semantic framework for the Gene Wiki initiative. Database 2016, January 2016. https://doi.org/10.1093/database/baw015. https://academic.oup.com/database/article/doi/10.1093/database/baw015/2630183
2. Erxleben, F., Günther, M., Krötzsch, M., Mendez, J., Vrandečić, D.: Introducing Wikidata to the linked data web. In: Mika, P., et al. (eds.) ISWC 2014. LNCS, vol. 8796, pp. 50–65. Springer, Cham (2014). https://doi.org/10.1007/978-3-319-11964-9_4
3. Freire, N., Isaac, A.: Wikidata's linked data for cultural heritage digital resources: an evaluation based on the Europeana data model. In: Proceedings of the 2019 International Conference on Dublin Core and Metadata Applications, DCMI 2019, Dublin Core Metadata Initiative, pp. 59–68 (2019)
4. Fukuda, K.: Using Wikidata as work authority for video games. In: Proceedings of the 2019 International Conference on Dublin Core and Metadata Applications, DCMI 2019, Dublin Core Metadata Initiative, pp. 80–87 (2019)
5. Gelati, F.: Archival Authority Records as Linked Data thanks to Wikidata, schema.org and the Records in Context Ontology, September 2019. https://doi.org/10.5281/zenodo.3465304
6. Gelati, F.: Personen-Datenbank Zeitgeschichte: Code Pre- Release, October 2019. https://doi.org/10.5281/zenodo.3484706
7. Hepp, M.: GoodRelations: an ontology for describing products and services offers on the web. In: Gangemi, A., Euzenat, J. (eds.) EKAW 2008. LNCS (LNAI), vol. 5268, pp. 329–346. Springer, Heidelberg (2008). https://doi.org/10.1007/978-3-540-87696-0_29
8. Hepp, M., Siorpaes, K., Bachlechner, D.: Harvesting wiki consensus: using Wikipedia entries as vocabulary for knowledge management. IEEE Internet Comput. **11**(5), 54–65 (2007). https://doi.org/10.1109/MIC.2007.110
9. Malyshev, S., Krötzsch, M., González, L., Gonsior, J., Bielefeldt, A.: Getting the most out of Wikidata: semantic technology usage in Wikipedia's knowledge graph. In: Vrandečić, D., et al. (eds.) ISWC 2018. LNCS, vol. 11137, pp. 376–394. Springer, Cham (2018). https://doi.org/10.1007/978-3-030-00668-6_23
10. Sauermann, L., Cyganiak, R.: Cool URIs for the semantic web. W3C note, W3C, December 2008. https://www.w3.org/TR/2008/NOTE-cooluris-20081203/

11. Snyder, E., Lorenzo, L., Mak, L.: Linked open data for subject discovery: assessing the alignment between library of congress vocabularies and Wikidata. In: Proceedings of the 2019 International Conference on Dublin Core and Metadata Applications, DCMI 2019, Dublin Core Metadata Initiative, pp. 12–20 (2019)
12. Ogbuji, U.: Introduction to Wikidata as a platform and data source, November 2018. https://developer.ibm.com/technologies/artificial-intelligence/articles/use-wikidata-in-ai-and-cognitive-applications-pt1/

A Linked Data Model for Data Scopes

Victor de Boer[1]([✉]) [iD], Ivette Bonestroo[1], Marijn Koolen[2] [iD],
and Rik Hoekstra[2] [iD]

[1] Vrije Universiteit Amsterdam, Amsterdam, The Netherlands
v.de.boer@vu.nl
[2] Huygens ING, Amsterdam, The Netherlands
{rik.hoekstra,marijn.koolen}@di.huc.knaw.nl

Abstract. With the rise of data driven methods in the humanities, it becomes necessary to develop reusable and consistent methodological patterns for dealing with the various data manipulation steps. This increases transparency, replicability of the research. Data scopes present a qualitative framework for such methodological steps. In this work we present a Linked Data model to represent and share Data Scopes. The model consists of a central Data scope element, with linked elements for data Selection, Linking, Modeling, Normalisation and Classification. We validate the model by representing the data scope for 24 articles from two domains: Humanities and Social Science.

Keywords: Scholarly data · Linked Data · Data scope

1 Introduction

In recent years, digital tools and methods have permeated the humanities domain [4]. With more collections and archives being digitized as well as the growth of 'digital born' data, a Digital Humanities (DH) movement has gained popularity [2]. While digital data and tools can make humanities research more effective and efficient and uncover new types of analyses, as long as the methods used are transparent and reproducible methods. Adhering to principles of FAIR data management [11] will not only increase the reusability of digital data and methods, but also ensure that they can be subjected to the same rigorous criticism of tools and data as is common in humanities research [7].

The paper 'Data scopes for digital history research' introduces the concept of "data scopes" to alleviate a lack of transparency and replicability with regards to the data manipulation steps in historical research. Data scopes are proposed to "characterize the interaction between researchers and their data and the transformation of a cluster of data into a research instrument" [6].

The original Data scopes paper presents a qualitative model including the five data manipulation activities. We here present an open standardised machine readable format for data scopes to further increase transparency and reproducibility by allowing for (semi-)automatic analysis and replication. It also moves

© Springer Nature Switzerland AG 2021
E. Garoufallou and M.-A. Ovalle-Perandones (Eds.): MTSR 2020, CCIS 1355, pp. 345–351, 2021.
https://doi.org/10.1007/978-3-030-71903-6_32

the model even more towards the FAIR principles, making the data scopes a method to publish data manipulation steps as findable, accessible, interoperable and reusable. The model we present here is expressed using Linked Data principles [5], where we use the Resource Description Framework (RDF) to define an ontology defining the concepts and relations for the model based on [6].

Next to presenting the ontology and its design decisions, we also provide an initial validation of the model in Sect. 4 by manually annotating articles from two research domains, that of (computational) humanities and social science.

2 Related Work

The Nanopublications ontology allows for FAIR and machine-readable representations of scientific claims and assertions [3]. This has created more incentives for researchers to use this standard format which increases the accessibility and interoperability of the information. Related to this is the PROV model that allows for specifying (data) provenance [8]. The combination of Nanopublications and PROV provides a powerful mechanism to express generic scientific statements and their provenance. The model we present here is compatible with these models, yet provides more specific detail towards DH use cases.

SPAR (Semantic Publishing and Referencing) is a comprehensive set of ontologies describing concepts in the scholarly publishing domain [10]. These include the Document Components Ontology (DoCo) that describes different aspects related to the content of scientific and scholarly documents. DoCo consist of three parts: document components, discourse elements and a pattern ontology. This ontology improves interoperability and shareability of academic documents. The model we present here can be used in combination with SPAR and DoCo to not only describe a research document, but also the data manipulation steps taken in the research, and the context in which the conclusions are valid.

3 Design of the Data Scope Ontology

The central concept of a "data scope" as introduced by Hoekstra and Koolen [6], describes a view on research data as well as the process that results in this view. The process is inherently iterative and includes modelling decisions, interpretations and transformations on the data. The datascope takes shape through five activities:

- **Selection:** which data and sources are selected? This matches the process of forming a corpus for a specific research question.
- **Modelling:** how are the relevant elements in sources represented? With the increased use of digital tools, these models become more and more explicit.
- **Normalization:** how are surface forms mapped to a normalized form? (e.g. the mapping of person names to a "Firstname, Lastname" form.)

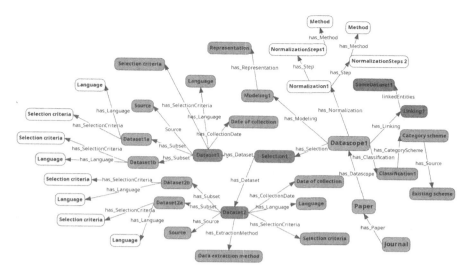

Fig. 1. The data scope model. Boxes show class instances and arrows depict object relations. The colors show the five parts of the model. Classes and namespaces are omitted for brevity. (Color figure online)

- **Linking:** what explicit internal and external connections are established? This includes actions like deduplication, named entity resolution etc.
- **Classification:** how are objects grouped or categorized? This includes categorization using internal or external schemes or theories.

For our ontology, we used the data scope and five activities as the basis of the model. Further classes and properties are derived from the activities descriptions in [6] of the components to help establish the steps or classes that can be linked to each component. Finally, we selected six research articles of digital humanities and computational social science articles as samples to adapt and adjust the model. These articles come from the same pool as our evaluation data set, which we describe in Sect. 4.

The resulting ontology contains 14 classes, 14 object properties and 4 datatype properties. Its classes include those for the Data scope itself, the five activities, and subactivities such as dsont:NormalizationStep, to define a separate step in the normalization procedure. Classes for research articles allow for associating a data scope to a publication. Figure 1 shows the ontology by means of an abstract example, where class instances are depicted (for example, "Datascope1" is an instance of dsont:DataScope). A DataScope instance links to instances of each of the five activities. Each activity allows for further specifications. For example the selection part links to the selection of the datasets. These datasets link for example to the date in which they have been collected etc.

The ontology is expressed in RDFS and is available on github[1]. The data-model uses permanent w3id identifiers for its dereferenceable URIs (namespace https://w3id.org/datascope/). The ontology, example data and annotation results (see Sect. 4) can be queried using SPARQL at https://semanticweb.cs.vu.nl/test/user/query. The sample query below counts for each data scope the number of datasets for which a normalization step is registered.

```
PREFIX dsont: <https://w3id.org/datascope#>
SELECT ?s ?norm (COUNT(?ds) as ?dscount) WHERE
{ ?s rdf:type dsont:DataScope .
?s dsont:has_Selection ?sel .
?sel dsont:has_Dataset ?ds .
?s dsont:has_Normalization ?norm }
GROUP BY ?s ?norm
```

4 Model Validation

We perform an initial validation of the model by manually annotating 24 articles using the model.

We selected 24 articles from two related domains: humanities and social science, focusing on publications that include digital data as part of the methodology. To this end, we selected two research journals that focus specifically on digital methods in these two fields: Digital Scholarship for the Humanities (DSH)[2] and Computational Social Science (CSS)[3]. We selected articles published after 2018, resulting in an initial selection of 124 articles from DSH and 58 articles from CSS. These articles were filtered on the inclusion of a clear data section, which resulted in 71 articles. Of those selected articles, we randomly chosen 15 articles of each journal. 6 of the 30 articles were used in the design phase of the model (Sect. 3). The remaining 24 articles have been used for the validation.

For the annotation, a set of coding guidelines were established based on the data scopes paper as well as the data scopes ontology description. Two independent coders then each annotated the data sections of the 12 articles using these coding schemes. Each article is mapped to the ontology and expressed as RDFS instances of the classes. If activities or steps are not explicitly identified in the text, they are not represented as RDF triples. This gives us an indication of the coverage of the various classes and properties in current articles. Every step in an article that did not quite fit the model or the concept of data scope was noted in a document. We have only looked at the sections describing the data and did not look at other sections. In some cases, that meant that pre-processing steps were not recorded. In cases where such pre-processing steps actually make changes to the data, these should be considered part of the datascope. This shows that it is not always straightforward to identify the limit of a data scope (this was already identified in [6]).

---

[1] https://github.com/biktorrr/datascope_ontology.

[2] https://academic.oup.com/dsh.

[3] https://www.springer.com/journal/42001.

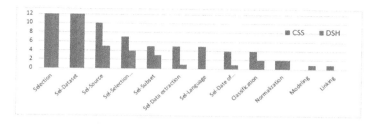

Fig. 2. Results of the annotation using the data scopes ontology for 24 articles.

Figure 2 shows for the main classes how many articles of the two journals have *at least* one element that was identified in the annotation. This includes the five main activities plus the main sub-elements of the Selection class ("Sel-").

Regarding the five main classes, we can see that the selection part is described in all articles, classification in 8, normalization in 4 and linking and modelling are both described in only one article. This matches the prediction by Hoekstra and Koolen that the Selection is most likely the element that is most often described currently. The figure does not show large differences between the two journals, the main discrepancy being one or two counts in either direction for classification, linking, and modelling. Looking at the Selection elements, we can see that the classes of the first dataset in the selection components are used by all the articles. We here identify some differences: articles from CSS mention all the steps within the selection part of our model more often than articles of DSH. Articles of DSH almost never mention language in the steps of the first dataset.

While each of the classes is used at least once in our 24 articles, many steps are not represented in the current papers. This can be a reflection of a lack of these activities, or of expressing these activities explicitly in the resulting papers.

5   Discussion

In our annotation effort, we have seen that in some cases it is unclear for some data manipulation step to which data scope elements they should be mapped. One example is the article by Badawy and Ferrara [1], where an identification step occurs before the selection process. Here the authors identify which Twitter accounts belong to ISIS sympathizers before selecting the data. This could be mapped to a selection or classification activity. Other such choices occur between for example normalization and classification. For replicability, clear guidelines on how the different elements of the model are used should be provided.

Currently, the ontology is quite high-level with a limited amount of classes and properties. It can be further specified towards concrete cases. For example, the research by Mantzaris et al. [9] uses multiple classification schemes because of changes in vote distribution for Eurovision throughout the years. This complexity does not fit our model yet but classes for this could be added.

Further possible extensions identified in the articles include classes about the data timeframe, specific information about dataset contents, filter options for data extraction, definitions of classifications, multiple classification schemes and interconnection between components.

Our model is compatible with models such as PROV and DoCo. DoCo information can be linked through the elements component which includes data and method in which the data scope is described. It is future research to combine the data scopes ontology with that of NanoPublications, that can be used to publish data scopes, further increasing the findability and verifiability of the research.

We here only provide an initial validation of the data model for a limited number of articles. These articles are selected to have data manipulation steps. We expect that in non-digital humanities articles, we will see hardly any occurrences of explicit data manipulation steps and therefore, the statistics presented before cannot be extrapolated beyond this selection. However, with the growing interest in digital tool criticism [7] and comprehensive virtual research environments, we expect that more such information will be made available. Current research consists of integrating the model in such a virtual research environment.[4] With more and more scholars using such environments and other digital tools and data, the data model we present in this paper represents a considerable step towards transparent and reproducible digital humanities and social science.

Acknowledgements. The research for this article was made possible by the CLARIAH-PLUS project financed by NWO (http://www.clariah.nl). The authors would like to thank Gard Ruurd for his contributions to the research.

References

1. Badawy, A., Ferrara, E.: The rise of Jihadist propaganda on social networks. J. Comput. Soc. Sci. **1**(2), 453–470 (2018)
2. Berry, D.M.: Introduction: understanding the digital humanities. In: Berry, D.M. (ed.) Understanding Digital Humanities, pp. 1–20. Palgrave Macmillan UK, London (2012). https://doi.org/10.1057/9780230371934_1
3. Groth, P., Gibson, A., Velterop, J.: The anatomy of a nanopublication. Inf. Serv. Use **30**(1–2), 51–56 (2010)
4. Haigh, T.: We have never been digital. Commun. ACM **57**(9), 24–28 (2014)
5. Heath, T., Bizer, C.: Linked data: evolving the web into a global data space. Synth. Lect. Semant. Web Theory Technol. **1**(1), 1–136 (2011)
6. Hoekstra, R., Koolen, M.: Data scopes for digital history research. Hist. Meth. J. Quant. Interdisc. History **52**(2), 79–94 (2019)
7. Koolen, M., Van Gorp, J., Van Ossenbruggen, J.: Toward a model for digital tool criticism: reflection as integrative practice. Digit. Scholarship Humanit. **34**(2), 368–385 (2019)
8. Lebo, T., et al.: PROV-O: The PROV ontology. W3C recommendation 30 (2013)
9. Mantzaris, A.V., Rein, S.R., Hopkins, A.D.: Preference and neglect amongst countries in the eurovision song contest. J. Comput. Soc. Sci. **1**(2), 377–390 (2018)

---

[4] http://mediasuite.clariah.nl.

10. Peroni, S., Shotton, D.: The SPAR ontologies. In: Vrandečić, D., et al. (eds.) ISWC 2018. LNCS, vol. 11137, pp. 119–136. Springer, Cham (2018). https://doi.org/10.1007/978-3-030-00668-6_8
11. Wilkinson, M.D., Bourne, P.E., et al.: The fair guiding principles for scientific data management and stewardship. Scientific data **3**(1), 1–9 (2016)

Track on Metadata and Semantics for Cultural Collections and Applications

Representing Archeological Excavations Using the CIDOC CRM Based Conceptual Models

Manolis Gergatsoulis[1]([✉]), Georgios Papaioannou[2], Eleftherios Kalogeros[1], and Robert Carter[2]

[1] Department of Archives, Library Science and Museology, Ionian University, Ioannou Theotoki 72 49100, Greece
{manolis,kalogero}@ionio.gr

[2] University College London in Qatar, Education City, Doha, Qatar
{g.papaioannou,robert.carter}@ucl.ac.uk

Abstract. This paper uses CIDOC CRM and CRM-based models (CRMarchaeo, CRMsci) to represent archaeological excavation activities and the observations of archaeologists during their work in the excavation field. These observations are usually recorded in documents such as context sheets. As an application of our approach (case study), we used the records of the recent archaeological excavations in Fuwairit in Qatar, part of the Origins of Doha and Qatar Project. We explore issues related to the application of classes and properties as they appear in the latest versions of the aforementioned models, i.e. CIDOC CRM, CRMarchaeo, and CRMsci. The proposed data model could be used as the basis to create an automated system for archaeological documentation and archeological data integration.

Keywords: Archaeology · Excavation · Context sheet · Archaeological documentation · CIDOC CRM · CRMarchaeo · CRMsci · Ontologies

1 Introduction

CIDOC CRM and CIDOC CRM based models such as CRMarchaeo have been recently used to model archaeological work. Archaeologists excavate, observe patterns, collect finds, keep notes, and produce records (such as handwritten excavation notebooks, filled-in context sheets, photographs, sketches drawings.) CIDOC CRM and CRMarchaeo aim to aid their digital documentation. Can CIDOC CRM and CIDOC CRM based models sufficiently represent archaeological records? To what extent are they able to provide a framework to assist archaeological work, documentation and interpretation? We address these issues by working towards an automated CRM-based system to assist archaeologists

This work was made possible thanks to a research fellowship by UCL Qatar/Qatar Foundation in 2020.

E. Garoufallou and M.-A. Ovalle-Perandones (Eds.): MTSR 2020, CCIS 1355, pp. 355–366, 2021.
https://doi.org/10.1007/978-3-030-71903-6_33

in modeling excavation works and research. Real time digital documentation of data from excavations, integrated with other semantically described data, will help archaeologists to more effectively evaluate and interpret their work results.

To this end, we have represented archaeological context sheets (first page of the two-page context sheet, see Fig. 4) from recent archaeological excavation works at Fuwairit in Qatar (2016–2018), part of the Origins of Doha and Qatar Project (ODQ), by successfully employing classes and properties of CIDOC CRM, CRMarchaeo and CRMsci models.

2   Related Work

In the last decade, CIDOC CRM-related research and work has been done to integrate archaeological data, given the need of documenting archaeological science [20]. The ARIADNE project [17] and its continuation ARIADNEplus project[1] have systematically attempted to integrate different European archaeological datasets by using CIDOC CRM and by developing the CRMarchaeo and CRMsci extensions. Other attempts involved the extensions CRMsci and CRMdig to document scientific archaeological experiments and results [20] or just the CIDOC CRM (without any of its extensions) in an effort to describe archaeological objects but without an evaluation of this approach [6].

The English Heritage has also developed a CIDOC CRM extension, the so-called CRM-HE[2], to model archaeological concepts and their properties. To the same end, the STAR project (Semantic Technologies for Archaeology Resources) [2] investigated the suggested extension on archaeological data integration. Additionally, they proposed a semi-automatic tool for archaeological dataset mapping to CRM-HE [3] as well as an approach for archaeological data creation from grey literature semantic search [23].

In terms of describing archaeological excavation records, there is an approach similar to the one presented in this paper [12]. This approach focused on CRMarchaeo classes and properties to model data derived from the daily archaeological excavation notebooks. Data in the archaeological notebooks related to describing the timespan of the works in an archaeological trench, defining and establishing elevation points, measuring the depths of archaeological strata, addressing the trench's stratigraphy, recording the archaeological findings from the works in the trench, and publishing the results of excavation and the archaeological work.

This work lies within the overall theme of integrating various types of cultural metadata and encoding them in different metadata schemas using CIDOC CRM. Approaches relate to mapping the semantics of archival description expressed through the Encoded Archival Description (EAD) metadata schema to CIDOC CRM [4], semantic mappings of cultural heritage metadata expressed through the VRA Core 4.0 schema to CIDOC CRM [9, 10], and mapping of the semantics of Dublin Core (DC) metadata to CIDOC CRM [14]. These mappings consider the CIDOC CRM as the most appropriate conceptual model for interrelations

---

[1] https://ariadne-infrastructure.eu/.

[2] https://crmeh.wordpress.com/.

and mappings between different heterogeneous sources [11] in the information science fields.

3   Preliminaries

3.1   Archaeology, Excavations, Strata, Contexts

Archaeology is the study of past material remains, aiming to comprehend past human cultures. From fossils dating millions of years ago to last decade's fizzy drink cans, archaeologists try to discover evidence of past phenomena, cultures and societies. Archaeology lies within humanities and social sciences, but it can also involve other scientific disciplines, depending on the nature of discoveries [21]. Archaeological work is a process of continuous discovery and recording. Archaeological finds are preserved and stored for interpretation, study, and exhibitions. In terms of methodology, archaeologists work in:

1. *recording* visible remains of past human activity (i.e. buildings and ruins),
2. *surveying* the surface of an area to spot, report and collect artifacts (i.e. human-made objects, e.g. fragments of pottery, glass and metal objects) and ecofacts (i.e. natural remains deposited as a result of human activity, e.g. animal bones, seeds etc.), and
3. systematically *excavating*the ground to discover artifacts and ecofacts. In archaeological excavations, archaeologists remove layers of soil (strata) within well-defined and oriented *trenches*. As soil is removed, distinct concentrations of soil and artifacts are revealed. These are called *contexts* and are reported in the diaries of the archaeologists or via filling in '*context sheets*'. Archaeological diaries and/or context sheets form the basis of documenting the excavation process and comprise the starting point for archaeological analysis and interpretation.

3.2   CIDOC CRM and CRMarchaeo

CIDOC Conceptual Reference Model (CIDOC CRM)[3], is a *formal ontology* intended to facilitate the integration, mediation and interchange of heterogeneous cultural heritage information. CIDOC CRM intends to provide a model of the intellectual structure of cultural documentation in logical terms.

Several extensions of CIDOC CRM suitable for documenting various kinds of cultural information and activities have been proposed so far. CRMarchaeo[4] is an extension of CIDOC CRM created to support the archaeological excavation process and all the various entities and activities related to it, while the CRMsci (Scientific Observation Model)[5] is an extension of CIDOC CRM intended to be used as a global schema for integrating metadata about scientific observations,

---

[3] http://www.cidoc-crm.org.
[4] http://new.cidoc-crm.org/crmarchaeo.
[5] http://www.cidoc-crm.org/crmsci.

measurements and processed data in descriptive and empirical sciences such as biodiversity, geology, geography, archaeology, cultural heritage conservation and others in research IT environments and research data libraries.

This work applies CIDOC CRM, CRMarchaeo and CRMsci to document archaeological data and reports, which will offer valuable experience concerning the documentation needs of these data. We test our approach by using archaeological data in Qatar. This research will, in turn, influence the process of further developing and refining these models. This work is based on CIDOC CRM version 6.2.7 (October 2019), CRMarchaeo version 1.5.0 (February 2020), and CRMsci version 1.2.8 (February 2020).

4 The Origins of Doha and Qatar Project, and the Archaeological Works at Fuwairit

The Origins of Doha and Qatar Project (ODQ) started in 2012[6]. It aims to investigate the history and archaeology of Doha, the capital of Qatar, and the other historic towns of Qatar, as well as the lives and experiences of their inhabitants. ODQ was run by University College London in Qatar (UCL Qatar) in collaboration with Qatar Museums (QM), funded by the Qatar Foundation through Qatar National Research Fund (QNRF), under grants NPRP5-421-6-010 and NPRP8-1655-6-064. Given the rapid development of Doha in the last few decades, which transformed the city from a pearl fishing town at the beginning of the 20th century [5] to a vivid modern capital city thanks to oil revenues since the 1950s [1,7,8], ODQ employed a multidisciplinary methodology. This included recording of historical buildings, excavations, recording oral histories of local people, GIS analysis for pre-oil and early oil Doha [16,18,19], archival research and study in historical documents on Doha's founding and growth. Preliminary Results have been publicly presented in Qatar and the world by the project leaders. The project has also produced educational material for schools in Qatar. From 2016 until 2018, ODQ expanded its works in Fuwairit, about 90 km north of Doha in Qatar, with recordings of historical buildings, excavations and surface surveys, as the area consists of a historic village with buildings of historical architecture, as well as rock art and inscriptions, and the archaeological site itself (the remains of a pearl-fishing town of the 18th-early 20th c. AD). Works included mapping/surveying, excavations, recording of historical buildings, archaeological surface survey in both Fuwairit and the neighboring Zarqa, and pottery analysis [15]. For the purposes of this paper, we used context sheets from the archaeological excavation works in Fuwarit during the first season (2016) and specifically from Trench 1. In Fig. 1 we see the representation in CIDOC CRM of the overall structure of the Origins of Doha Project.

---

[6] https://originsofdoha.wordpress.com/.

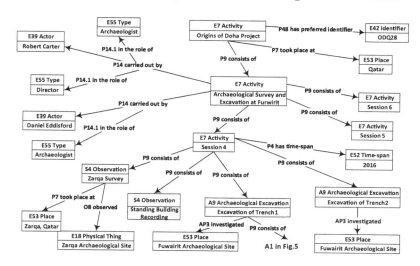

Fig. 1. Describing the *Origins of Doha Project* in CIDOC-CRM.

5   Describing the Structure of a Stratigraphic Matrix

5.1   Stratigraphy in Archaeology and the Stratigraphic Matrix

The process of layers (strata) of soil and debris laid on top of one another over time is called *stratigraphy*. Archaeologists and geologists are particularly interested in the stratigraphy of an area, as strata determine sequences of human-related or geological events. As a rule, when a stratum lies above another, the lower one was deposited first. Let's think of earth strata as layers in a chocolate cake. To make a cake, first we put the sponge base, then a chocolate cream layer, then another layer of sponge cake, then one more layer of chocolate cream, then the chocolate frosting, and last (but not least) a cherry on top. This is a sequence of cake-making events with the base being the earliest and the cherry being the latest event in the process. Archaeologists prefer to eat their cakes from top to bottom, from the cherry to the base! First, they define the contour of a specific space to excavate, which is usually a square or rectangular space of x metres by x metres. The excavation space is called an *archaeological* or *excavation trench*. Then they start to carefully and meticulously remove the top layer (stratum) of the trench, and they keep on excavating within this area stratum by stratum. The content of each stratum in the trench may include evidence of human activity, such as fragments of clay, glass and metal objects, roof tiles, bricks, fossils, remains of a fire, animal bones etc. These objects help towards dating the strata and interpreting past events that have formed the strata. When the excavation of a trench is finished, the sequence of excavated deposits and features can be arranged in a stratigraphic matrix according to their chronological relationship to each other, i.e. whether the events that created them occurred before or after each other. This matrix is also described as a *Harris Matrix* from the book on archaeological stratigraphy by E. C. Harris [13]. Usually, earth strata are not as straightforward as chocolate cake strata. Archaeological strata may contain formations such as post holes, pits, walls, and burrows which disturb natural layers but often indicate human activity and are the results of human behaviour. Archaeologists number each stratum and each feature (e.g. a built structure or pit cut) on the stratigraphic matrix, and they try to interpret past events by co-relating strata and objects found within stata. Each stratum and each feature are called *contexts*. It is important to note that contexts do not always have direct stratigraphic relationships with others even if they are close to each other or likely to be contemporary. For example, two deposits which have built up on either side of a wall have no direct stratigraphic link, though they might both have a relationship with the same context below (e.g. the wall, which is stratigraphically below both deposits). In such cases the matrix branches. For every context, archaeologists fill in a *context sheet* described below.

5.2 Describing a Stratigraphic Matrix in CRMarchaeo

In CRMarchaeo, each context on the stratigraphic matrix is member of the class A8 Stratigraphic Unit. Stratigraphic units are related via the property AP11 has physical relation, further refined by the property of property AP11.1 has type. The type can be 'above', 'below', 'within', 'next to' or other, depending on the relation of a context with another context in the stratigraphic matrix. In Fig. 2 we can see a fragment of the stratigraphic matrix of Trench 1, while in Fig. 3 we see the representation of a part of this stratigraphic matrix in CRMarchaeo.

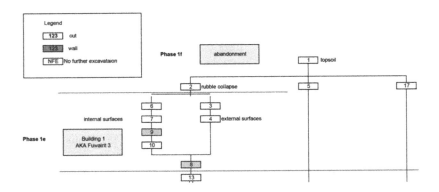

Fig. 2. A fragment of the stratigraphic matrix of trench 1.

6 Describing the Content of a Context Sheet

6.1 The Context Sheet

Archaeologists working for the Origins of Doha Project, and therefore at Fuwairit, have used context sheets to record their excavation work in the archaeo-

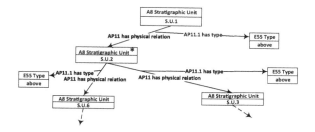

Fig. 3. Representation of the fragment of the stratigraphic matrix appearing in Fig. 2.

logical trenches. The context sheet is the report describing each context unheartened and, therefore, it is critical for archaeological research and interpretation. Every context sheet offers:

- Reference information (site codes, trench and context numbers, relation to other contexts, date, names of archaeologists recording, related photo and drawing numbers)
- Information on the context's soil deposit and its characteristics.
- Information about finds in the context.
- Space for archaeological interpretation.
- Space for recording levels and an accompanying sketch (back sheet[7]).

In Fig. 4 we see the front page of a context sheet from the excavation of Trench 1.

6.2   Modelling a Context Sheet in CRMarchaeo

A context sheet is an instance of the class E31 Document. A context sheet documents (P70 documents) an instance of the class A1 Excavation Process Unit (in our example this instance is Excavation of Stratigraphic Unit 2). The relation between the context sheet and the excavation of the stratigraphic unit that it documents is expressed through the path (see Fig. 5, in which the CRM representation of most of the fields of the context sheet appearing in Fig. 4 is depicted):

E31 Document → P70 documents → A1 Excavation Process Unit

Reference Information: The field *Site Code* contains a code (an instance of the class E42 Identifier which identifies the project (ODQ in our case). This identifier is related to the Origins of Doha Project (instance of the class E7 Activity (see Fig. 1) through a path of the form:

E7 Activity → P48 has preferred identifier → E42 Identifier

Concerning the values of the fields *Trench* and *Context Number*, we observe that the trench appears as an instance of the class A9 Excavation (see Fig. 1) while

---

[7] Note that the representation of the back sheet of the context sheet is out of the scope of this paper.

362   M. Gergatsoulis et al.

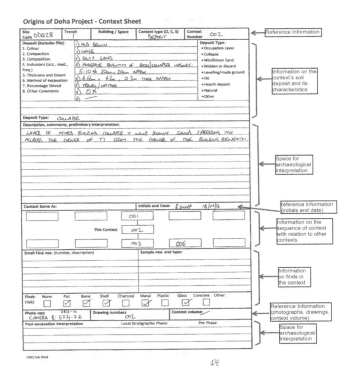

Fig. 4. A context sheet from the excavation of trench 1.

Context Number appears as an instance (in our example Excavation of Stratigraphic Unit 2) of A1 Excavation Process Unit (see Fig. 5). These two instances
should be related with the property P9 consists of through a path:

A9 Excavation → P9 consists of → A1 Excavation Process Unit

Information on the Context's Soil Deposit and its Characteristics:
There are several fields of the context sheet which are represented in CRM by
directly connecting the instance of A1 Excavation Process Unit with the instance
of other CRM classes through appropriate properties.

Concerning the items 1) *Colour*, 2) *Compaction* and 3) *Composition*, we
observed that *Colour* and *Compaction* can be seen as properties of the material
in *Composition*. These items are represented as follows: the value in *Compaction*
can be regarded as an instance (silty sand in our example) of the CRMsci class S11
Amount of Matter which consists of (P45 consists of) an instance (sand in our example) of the class E57 Material. The values of the properties of these material are
instances of the CIDOC CRM class E26 Physical Feature. Each feature is related to
the material with the property P56 bears feature. An instance of the class E55 Type
is also connected through the property P2 has type to each instance of E26 Physical
Feature to denote the type of the feature (compaction or colour in our case).

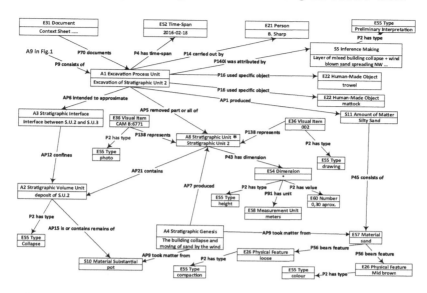

Fig. 5. Representation of the contents of part of the context sheet appearing in Fig. 4.

The field *Method of Excavation* (item 6) is represented through the CRM paths of the form:

A1 Excavation Process Unit → P16 used specific object → E22 Human-Made Object

which relate the instance Excavation of Stratigraphic Unit 2 with the tools used in this excavation (i.e. the trowel and the mattock). These tools are instances of the class E22 Human-Made Object.

Concerning the *Deposit Type* field of the context sheet, it gets one of the values listed in the right side of the context sheet under the title *Deposit Type*. In our model this is represented by creating an instance of the class E55 Type with the selected value (collapse in our example) and connecting this instance to the corresponding instance of A2 Stratigraphic Volume Unit through the path:

A2 Stratigraphic Volume Unit → P2 has type → E55 Type

Reference Information (Initials and Data): This specific instance of the A1 Excavation Process Unit (in our example Excavation of Stratigraphic Unit 2) was performed at a specific time, represented as an instance of E52 Time-span, and carried out by an instance of E21 Person. This information is modeled in CRM by the following paths:

A1 Excavation Process Unit → P4 has time-span→ E52 Time-span
A1 Excavation Process Unit → P14 carried out by → E29 Person

This information is recorded in *Initials and Date* field of the Context Sheet.

Information on the Sequence of Context with Relation to Other Contexts: The information on the sequence of context is depicted in the CIDOC CRM representation of the stratigraphic matrix (see Fig. 3). In this Figure we see that the context S.U.2 (i.e. the context described by context sheet of our example) is below the context S.U.1 and above the contexts S.U.3 and S.U.6. Notice that the instance S.U.2 of the class A8 Stratigraphic Unit coincide in both figures (Fig. 3 and Fig. 5).

Information on Finds in the Context: The finds in the context can be represented as instances of the CRMsci class S10 Material Substantial. Each instance of this class is then related to the deposit of the stratigraphic unit in which it is contained through a path of the form:

A2 Stratigraphic Volume Unit → AP15 is or contains remains of → S10 Material Substantial

Reference Information (photographs, drawings, context volume): Each photograph taken or a drawing designed during the excavation process is an instance of the class E36 Visual Item. The photograph/drawing is related to the corresponding instance of the A8 Stratigraphic Unit CRMarchaeo class through the property P138 represents. To distinguish between photographs and drawings we relate to the corresponding instance of E36 Visual Item an appropriate instance of E55 Type (i.e. an instance whose value is either photo or drawing).

Space for Archaeological Interpretation: To represent the content of the context sheet field *Description, Comments, Preliminary Interpretation* as well as the field *Post Excavation Interpretation* we use a set of paths of the form:

A1 Excavation Process Unit → P140i was attributed by → S5 Inference Making → P2 has type → E55 Type

where a specific interpretation is encoded as instance of S5 Inference Making while the corresponding instance of the class E55 Type (which may be one of the values 'Description', 'Comment', 'Preliminary Interpretation', 'Post-excavation Interpretation:Local Stratigraphic Phase', 'Post-excavation Interpretation:Pot Phase') describes the type of this interpretation.

Concerning the field *Context Same As* it relates the current context (instance of A8 Stratigraphic Unit with another context (i.e. another instance of A8 Stratigraphic Unit) which has the same features as the current context. This relation is expressed with the following path:

A8 Stratigraphic Unit → P130 shows features of → A8 Stratigraphic Unit

Such paths can be added in Fig. 3.

7   Conclusions and Future Work

This work has used CIDOC CRM and its extensions CRMarchaeo and CRMsci to represent archaeological work and assist archaeologists in documenting and managing archaeological and cultural heritage information. It also adds to the theoretical discussion on common grounds among humanities, computing, and information studies. We put emphasis on representing the contents on the first page of the two-page context sheets used by archaeologists in their systematic excavation works on archaeological trenches. As future work, we aim to extend the proposed model with the CRMba [22] classes and properties, to allow adding representations of architectural remains and their relations. Also, we will use CRMgeo to describe trench recordings of levels (the second page of the two-page context sheet) to complete the context sheet description. Another next step is to design an automated system for documenting excavation works. This will provide archaeologists with the capacity to document their work in the field (archaeological contexts, findings, interpretation) in real time and make the most of the system's data entry and information searching facilities as well as explore the reasoning capabilities of the relevant ontologies.

References

1. Adham, K.: Rediscovering the island: doha's urbanity. from pearls to spectacle. In: Elsheshtawy, Y. (ed.) The Evolving Arab City. Tradition, Modernity and Urban Development, pp. 218–257. Routledge (2011)
2. Binding, C., May, K., Souza, R., Tudhope, D., Vlachidis, A.: Semantic technologies for archaeology resources: results from the STAR project. In: Contreras, F., Farjas, M., Melero, F.J. (eds.) Proceedings 38th Annual Conference on Computer Applications and Quantitative Methods in Archaeology, BAR International Series 2494, pp. 555–561. BAR Publishing (2013)
3. Binding, C., May, K., Tudhope, D.: Semantic interoperability in archaeological datasets: data mapping and extraction via the CIDOC CRM. In: Christensen-Dalsgaard, B., Castelli, D., Ammitzbøll Jurik, B., Lippincott, J. (eds.) ECDL 2008. LNCS, vol. 5173, pp. 280–290. Springer, Heidelberg (2008). https://doi.org/10.1007/978-3-540-87599-4_30
4. Bountouri, L., Gergatsoulis, M.: The semantic mapping of archival metadata to the CIDOC CRM ontology. J. Archival Organ. **9**(3–4), 174–207 (2011)
5. Carter, R.A.: Sea of Pearls: Seven Thousand Years of the Industry that Shaped the Gulf. Arabian Publishing (2012)
6. Deicke, A.J.E.: CIDOC CRM-based modeling of archaeological catalogue data. In: Luca, E.W.D., Bianchini, P. (eds.) Proceedings of the First Workshop on Digital Humanities and Digital Curation co-located with the 10th Conference on Metadata and Semantics Research (MTSR 2016), *CEUR Workshop Proceedings*, vol. 1764. CEUR-WS.org, Goettingen, Germany (2016).http://ceur-ws.org/Vol-1764/4.pdf
7. Fletcher, R., Carter, R.A.: Mapping the growth of an arabian gulf town: the case of Doha, Qatar. J. Econ. Soc. History Orient **60**, 420–487 (2017)
8. Fuccaro, N.: Pearl towns and oil cities: migration and integration in the arab coast of the persian gulf. In: Freitag, U., Fuhrmann, M., Lafi, N., Riedler, F. (eds.) The City in the Ottoman Empire: Migration and the making of urban modernity, pp. 99–116. Routledge (2010)
9. Gaitanou, P., Gergatsoulis, M.: Defining a semantic Mmapping of VRA Core 4.0 to the CIDOC conceptual reference model. Int. J. Metadata, Seman. Ontol. **7**(2), 140–156 (2012)
10. Gergatsoulis, M., Bountouri, L., Gaitanou, P., Papatheodorou, C.: Mapping cultural metadata schemas to CIDOC conceptual reference model. In: Konstantopoulos, S., Perantonis, S., Karkaletsis, V., Spyropoulos, C.D., Vouros, G. (eds.) SETN 2010. LNCS (LNAI), vol. 6040, pp. 321–326. Springer, Heidelberg (2010). https://doi.org/10.1007/978-3-642-12842-4_37

11. Gergatsoulis, M., Bountouri, L., Gaitanou, P., Papatheodorou, C.: Query transformation in a CIDOC CRM based cultural metadata integration environment. In: Lalmas, M., Jose, J., Rauber, A., Sebastiani, F., Frommholz, I. (eds.) ECDL 2010. LNCS, vol. 6273, pp. 38–45. Springer, Heidelberg (2010). https://doi.org/10.1007/978-3-642-15464-5_6

12. Giagkoudi, E., Tsiafakis, D., Papatheodorou, C.: Describing and revealing the semantics of excavation notebooks. In: Proceedings of the CIDOC 2018 Annual Conference, 19 September–5 October, Heraklion, Crete, Greece (2018)

13. Harris, E.C.: Principles of Archaeological Stratigraphy, 2nd edn. Academic Press (1989)

14. Kakali, C., et al.: Integrating dublin core metadata for cultural heritage collections using ontologies. In: Proceedings of the 2007 International Conference on Dublin Core and Metadata Applications, DC 2007, Singapore, August 27–31, 2007, pp. 128–139 (2007)

15. Kuzbari, D.: The Language of Ancient Pottery. An Analytical Study for the 18th - early 20th Century Pottery from the Site of Fuwairit, Qatar: Unpublished BA thesis. University of Leicester, U.K. (2020)

16. Marras, A.: DOHA—Doha Online Historical Atlas. Come le Carte Raccontano un (2016). https://medium.com/@annamao/doha-doha-online-historical-atlas-come-le-carte-raccontano-un-territorio-bf8c85df5e3d. Accessed 2 April 2020

17. Meghini, C., et al.: ARIADNE: a research infrastructure for archaeology. ACM J. Comput. Cultural Heritage 10(3), 18:1–18:27 (2017). https://doi.org/10.1145/3064527

18. Michalski, M., Carter, R., Eddisford, D., Fletcher, R., Morgan, C.: DOHA—doha online historical atlas. In: Matsumoto, M., Uleberg, E. (eds.) Oceans of Data. Proceedings of the 44th Annual Conference on Computer Applications and Quantitative Methods in Archaeology CAA 2016, Oslo 30 March–3 April, 2016, pp. 253–260 (2016)

19. Morgan, C., Carter, R., Michalski, M.: The origins of doha project: online digital heritage remediation and public outreach in a vanishing pearling town in the Arabian Gulf. In: Conference on Cultural Heritage and New Technologies (CHMT 2020), November 2–4, 2015, Stadt Archaeologie Wien, pp. 1–8 (2016)

20. Niccolucci, F.: Documenting archaeological science with CIDOC CRM. Int. J. Dig. Libraries 18(3), 223–231 (2017). https://doi.org/10.1007/s00799-016-0199-x

21. Renfrew, C., Bahn, P.: Archaeology: Theories, Methods, and Practice, 6th edn. Thames and Hudson (2012)

22. Ronzino, P., Niccolucci, F., Felicetti, A., Doerr, M.: CRMba a CRM extension for the documentation of standing buildings. Int. J. Digital Libraries 17(1), 71–78 (2016)

23. Vlachidis, A., Binding, C., May, K., Tudhope, D.: Automatic metadata generation in an archaeological digital library: semantic annotation of grey literature. In: Przepiórkowski, A., et al. (eds.) Computational Linguistics - Applications, Studies in Computational Intelligence, vol. 458, pp. 187–202. Springer, Heidelberg (2013). https://doi.org/10.1007/978-3-642-34399-5_10

Generating and Exploiting Semantically Enriched, Integrated, Linked and Open Museum Data

Sotirios Angelis[✉] and Konstantinos Kotis[✉]

Intelligent Systems Lab, Department of Cultural Technology and Communication,
University of the Aegean, 81100 Mytilene, Greece
{sang,kotis}@aegean.gr

Abstract. The work presented in this paper is engaging with and contributes to the implementation and evaluation of Semantic Web applications in the cultural Linked Open Data (LOD) domain. The main goal is the semantic integration, enrichment and interlinking of data that are generated through the documentation process of artworks and cultural heritage objects. This is accomplished by using state-of-the-art technologies and current standards of the Semantic Web (RDF, OWL, SPARQL), as well as widely accepted models and vocabularies relevant to the cultural domain (Dublin Core, SKOS, Europeana Data Model). A set of specialized tools such as KARMA and OpenRefine/RDF-extension is being used and evaluated in order to achieve the semantic integration of museum data from heterogeneous sources. Interlinking is achieved using tools such as Silk and OpenRefine/RDF-extension, discovering links (at the back-end) between disparate datasets and other external data sources such as DBpedia and Wikidata that enrich the source data. Finally, a front-end Web application is developed in order to exploit the semantically integrated and enriched museum data, and further interlink (and enrich) them (at application run-time), with the data sources of DBpedia and Europeana. The paper discusses engineering choices made for the evaluation of the proposed framework/pipeline.

Keywords: Semantic data integration · Semantic enrichment · Museum LOD

1 Introduction

Museums and other cultural heritage organizations, while documenting artworks, artists and cultural heritage objects, are creating a great amount of data. In the past decade, there have been numerous attempts to take advantage of Semantic Web Technologies for linking and opening this (meta)data to the public as Linked Open Data (LOD). Based on the lessons learned from this experience, the work presented in this paper utilizes and evaluates related Semantic Web technologies with museum (meta)data, aiming at: a) integrating (combining the museum data stored in different sources to provide a unified view of them), enriching (adding relevant information to data records) and interlinking (finding similarities between datasets and connecting similar entities) datasets

E. Garoufallou and M.-A. Ovalle-Perandones (Eds.): MTSR 2020, CCIS 1355, pp. 367–379, 2021.
https://doi.org/10.1007/978-3-030-71903-6_34

form multiple heterogeneous museum collections, b) developing an application that allows end-users (humans and machines) to exploit artworks and artists from an integrated and enriched dataset, and c) discussing related challenges and engineering choices made towards proposing a framework/pipeline for exploiting semantically integrated and enriched museum LOD.

Specifically, the stages followed in the proposed framework/pipeline are presented in Fig. 1, depicting two distinct parts, the "data-preparation and application back-end" part (orange rectangle) and the "application front-end" part (green rectangle).

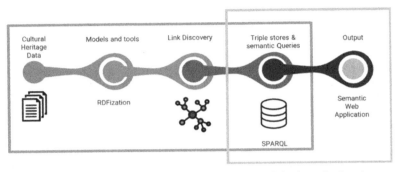

Fig. 1. The proposed pipeline for semantic integration and exploitation of cultural museum data (Color figure online)

In order to semantically integrate multiple datasets from different and heterogeneous sources, resulting to a single source with unified information, the first part of the pipeline is responsible for a) the selection of a data model that sufficiently describes cultural heritage data, b) the RDFization process i.e., transforming data to the Resource Description Framework (RDF) format, c) the Link Discovery (LD) process, and d) the management of the semantic queries. The model used in this current work is the Europeana Data Model (EDM) [1], which is a widely-used model designed to describe the Europeana Collection [2]. RDFization is the process followed to convert the raw data from their original format (e.g., CSV, XML) into RDF and store them in a single RDF graph, semantically enriched with cultural metadata through the selected data model (ontology). LD is the process followed to discover similarities and create links between entities that are stored in the RDF graph and links to other external data sources that promote the enrichment of source data.

The second part of the framework/pipeline concerns the design and development of the front-end application that provides a user interface for exploiting information in the semantically integrated and enriched dataset. The front-end application is designed to be data-centric and drive the user to discover information and relations about artworks and artists by querying the interlinked museum data in a unified manner. It provides internal hyperlinks that present the details of each entity that is requested by the user (e.g., Pablo Picasso, The Starry Night), as well as external hyperlinks to DBpedia [3], Wikidata [4], and Europeana. The external links are created and stored during the LD process, and they can be updated. New links can be discovered in real-time by the application.

The main contribution of this work is to utilize and evaluate Semantic Technologies towards shaping an efficient framework/pipeline for exploiting semantically enriched, integrated, linked and open museum data. Furthermore, this work contributes a functional and reusable application for the exploitation of such data by human and software agents. This paper is structured as follows: Sect. 2 presents selective related work in cultural heritage semantic data integration and exploitation. Section 3 presents the datasets used for the evaluation of the proposed framework/pipeline, the RDFization process, the front-end Web application infrastructure, and its implementation. Section 4 presents the Semantic Technologies and tools used in the evaluation scenario and system. Section 5 discusses the engineering choices made for this work. Finally, Sect. 6 presents key achievements and future work.

2 Related Work

As the interest in Semantic Web Technologies for the cultural domain is growing, there have been several attempts and projects for converting cultural heritage raw data into LOD. We evaluate and compare our work with a representative set of ones that are relatively recent and closely related to ours.

In the work of Dragoni et al. [5], authors present the process of mapping the metadata from small size collections with little-known artists to the LOD cloud, exposing the created knowledge base by using LOD format, making it available to third-party services. A framework is proposed for a) the conversion of data to RDF with the use of a custom ontology that extends the Europeana Data Model, and b) the enrichment of metadata from content found on the Web. The metadata enrichment is then succeeded by linking to external knowledge bases such as DBpedia and with the use of Natural Language Processing (NLP) methods for information extraction from Web pages containing relevant details for the records.

In Szekely et al. [6], authors describe the process and the lessons learned in mapping the metadata of the Smithsonian American Art Museum's (SAAM) objects to a custom SAAM ontology, that extends EDM with subclasses and sub-properties to represent attributes unique to SAAM. In this work the mapping is done by KARMA integration tool, while the linking and enrichment was focused to the interrelation of the museum's artists with entities in DBpedia, Getty Union List of Artist Names and the Rijksmuseum dataset. The paper also discusses the challenges encountered in data preparation, mapping columns to classes, connecting the classes and mapping based on field values.

In the work of Stolpe et al. [7], the conversion of the Yellow List of architecturally and culturally valuable buildings in Oslo, from Excel spreadsheets to Linked Open Data, is presented. The data was mapped in the CIDOC Conceptual Reference Model [8] and converted by XLWrap4 package, a spreadsheet-to-RDF wrapper. The entities of the RDF graph were linked to DBpedia and exposed via a SPARQL endpoint based on a Joseki triple store. A Web application that plots the results of SPARQL queries onto a Google Map based on the coordinates in the Yellow List, was developed to help users to explore the data.

These related works start with raw cultural data and convert them to RDF. Their main goal is to expose the data of a single dataset as LOD, while the main goal of our work is to semantically integrate, enrich and link disparate and heterogeneous cultural data in a way that it can be queried in a unified manner. Each of the related works have a single dataset to deal with, while two of them aim to achieve more detailed (enriched) descriptions of their data by engineering and using custom ontologies. Another difference is that, while dealing only with one dataset, related works do not need a LD process for interlinking between heterogeneous museum data, as needed in our case.

We also acknowledge the related work of Amsterdam Museum Linked Open Data [9] and The REACH Project [10], which present well-defined methodologies, the first on generating Linked Open museum Data and the latter on semantically integrating cultural data and exposing them via a web application. Each of them covers in detail parts of our proposed pipeline while working with data from one source (in contrast to our work).

3   The Approach

To evaluate the proposed framework/pipeline for exploiting semantically enriched, integrated, linked and open museum data, we designed and implemented a prototype system. This system is engineered in two distinct parts (or sub-systems), the back-end one that supports the data preparation and the application infrastructure, and the front-end one that supports the functionality of the Web application for querying and presenting the interlinked and enriched museum data in a unified and open manner (for human and software agents to exploit).

3.1   Back-End

The main goal here is to convert cultural data into RDF format so they can be easily integrated and linked. The datasets that were chosen for evaluation purposes are published as research datasets by two well-known museums, the Museum of Modern Art and the Carnegie Museum of Art.

MoMA Collection. The collection of the Museum of Modern Art – MoMA [11], includes almost 200.000 artworks from all over the world. This collection extents in the field of visual arts, such as paintings, sculptures, photographs, architectural designs etc. In order to contribute and help in the understanding of its collection, MoMA created a research dataset. The dataset contains 138.000 records, representing all the works that have been accessioned into MoMA's collection and cataloged in its' database. It contains basic metadata for each artwork, including title, artist, date of creation, medium etc. The dataset is available in CSV and JSON format and it is published in the public domain using a CC0 License.

Carnegie Collection. The Carnegie Museum of Art – CMoA has published a dataset [12] that contains information and metadata for almost every artwork from the museum's collection and counts over 28.000 artworks. The dataset includes artworks from all the departments of the museum, that divides to fine arts, photography, modern art and architecture. The dataset is available in CSV and JSON format and it is published under CC0 License.

RDFization Process. In order to reduce the heterogeneity of the available evaluation data and to combine the datasets in one unified RDF graph, the selection of the characteristics for the conceptual model for semantically enriching the RDF data with cultural metadata was based on two assumptions/limitations: a) to be present in both of the datasets and b) to match a semantic type that is described in the EDM. Additionally, following directions of the EDM and common principles/guidelines for the LOD, new classes and URIs were created, based on the unique identifiers of every record in the datasets. The properties that were mapped to semantic types for each collection are the following: Title, Date, Medium, ObjectID, Classification, URL, ThumbnailURL, ConstituentID, Artist, ArtistBio, BeginDate, EndDate, AggregationID, Aggregation_uri, Artist_uri, Artwork_uri. The resulted, after the mapping, model is shaped in Fig. 2.

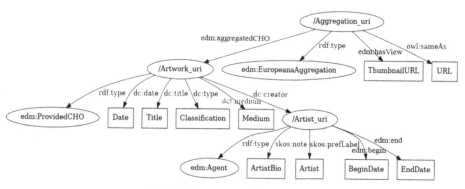

Fig. 2. The proposed Data Model

After the model was defined, the next step in the process was the conversion of data into RDF format. This was accomplished with the selection (among others) and use of the semantic integration tools KARMA [13] and OpenRefine [14]. Using both these tools we created the RDF graph based on the model and populated it with RDF data generated from each collection's dataset. The generated graphs were both stored in the same RDF triple store, forming a single integrated graph.

Links Discovery Process. The LOD standard [15] indicates firstly the conversion of data in a machine-readable format through an expressive model and consequently the discovery of relative information and the creation of external links to it. The linking tools that were chosen (among others) for evaluating the discovery of relative information to the data were the SILK Framework [16] and the OpenRefine Reconciliation Service [17]. The linking tasks that created were targeted at the model's main classes, i.e., Artwork and Artist. The first linking attempts were aiming to discover semantic similarities between entities of the two graphs, stored in the local triple store. Subsequently, the LD tasks searched and created links to the knowledge graphs of DBpedia [3] and Wikidata [4]. The similarity metrics were equality or string-matching metrics (Levenshtein distance), comparing a) for Artists: the attributes name, birth date, death date, and nationality, and b) for Artworks: the attributes title, creation date and creator.

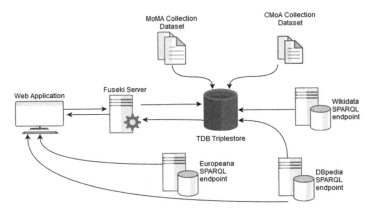

Fig. 3. System architectural design

3.2 Front-End

The developed front-end Web application is a type of single page application and it is compatible with modern desktop and mobile browsers. The application's infrastructure, as depicted in the overall systems' architectural design of Fig. 3, includes: a) the storage of the integrated and interlinked cultural datasets and their external connections to the Knowledge Graphs of DBpedia and Wikidata, b) a server that receives the requests and allows the interaction with the stored data, at the back-end and c) the Graphical User Interface (GUI) with the embedded functionality at the front-end.

The whole functionality of the front-end application is developed at the client-side and, although it is connected to a Fuseki server (for the proof-of-concept system evaluation), it can be functionally connected to any SPARQL endpoint that exposes the integrated datasets and supports federated queries. The chosen triple store for the evaluation system is the TDB2 [18] which is a part of the Apache Jena platform [19] and is configured to be integrated with the Fuseki2 server [20]. The evaluated graph that is stored at the TDB and includes the linked data (RDF data that created in the RDFization process for all artworks and artists from MoMA and CMoA collections process, plus the sameAs triples that generated during the LD process) from the museum collections alongside the external connections (sameAs triples to DBpedia and Wikidata that discovered in LD process), contains more than 1.645.000 triples.

Front-end Web Application Implementation. The front-end Web application was developed with the use of two mainstream front-end frameworks: React.js and Bootstrap 4. The design is following a reusable component-based approach, in which interdependent blocks are developed and they compose to build the UI of the application. Therefore, each component was developed to satisfy the needs of each distinct functionality of the application.

The front-end Web application is a template-driven search form that allows users to create semantics-based queries about artists and their artworks. The values of each field of the search form are gathered and synthesized in such a way that a SPARQL query is formed, which is then submitted for execution by the Fuseki Server. Each field is shaping a form that is configured properly to implement different criteria based on given attributes. During the form submission, a part of the final SPARQL query is built automatically.

To make search easier, text suggestions with possible matched entries are automatically filling the text fields, while users are typing, based on the entities that are present in the datasets. This is accomplished each time the user types a character in the search field, by forming and submitting a query for checking its match against the semantic types of the stored graph.

The query results are received from the server in JSON format and converted to tabular and triples format, as well as presented graphically as a directed graph. The graphical representation uses the D3.js library and a modified version of D3RDF[1] tool to create a directed graph based on the SPARQL query results.

The application creates pages dynamically in order to present the details of each resource and to perform additional linking tasks, discovering connections with external sources. The additional linking process searches for same resources in Europeana and DBpedia graphs by creating a federated SPARQL query based on the semantic type of the resource and the attribute that describes it. If results are returned, they are filtered based on chosen similarity metric (Jaro-distance), and a *sameAs* triple is added in the graph (if not present already). This feature is currently implemented only for the Artist entities.

Front-end Application Use Case Scenario. For demonstration reasons, let assume the user searches information about "Portraits painted by Andy Warhol". The generated SPARQL query for this search is presented below:

```
PREFIX rdf: <http://www.w3.org/1999/02/22-rdf-syntax-ns#>
PREFIX edm: <http://www.europeana.eu/schemas/edm/>
PREFIX dc: <http://purl.org/dc/elements/1.1/>
PREFIX skos: <http://www.w3.org/2004/02/skos/core#>
PREFIX dct: <http://purl.org/dc/terms/>
SELECT distinct * WHERE{
    ?cho dc:title ?title.
    ?cho dc:creator ?artist.
    ?artist skos:prefLabel ?name.
    ?cho dc:type ?classification.
FILTER regex(?title, "Portrait", "i")
FILTER regex(?name, "Andy Warhol", "i")
FILTER regex(?classification, "Painting", "i") }
```

The results that are returned from the server for the SPARQL query (Fig. 4) contain the cultural heritage object's URI, title and classification, the artist's URI and name, displayed in table format. The results demonstrate that users are able to search the museum data in a unified manner, as the information about the artworks are retrieved from both CMoA and MoMA collections. The details of the resource returned when the user selects the URI of the artist are presented in Fig. 5. Apart from the information about

---

[1] [https://github.com/Rathachai/d3rdf].

the artist, the details present the discovered external links, in this case link to DBpedia and to Wikidata.

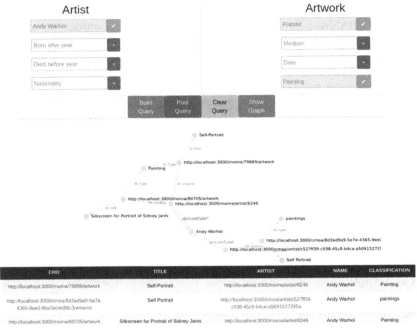

Fig. 4. Search results for query "Portraits painted by Andy Warhol"

PROPERTY	OBJECT
owl:sameAs	http://dbpedia.org/resource/Andy_Warhol
owl:sameAs	http://localhost:3000/cmoa/artist/c527ff39-c938-45c8-b4ca-a5091527295a
owl:sameAs	https://www.wikidata.org/wiki/Q5603
rdf:type	http://www.europeana.eu/schemas/edm/Agent
edm:begin	1928
edm:end	1987
skos:note	(American, 1928–1987)
skos:prefLabel	Andy Warhol

Fig. 5. Details of the resource "Andy Warhol"

4   Framework and System Evaluation

The Semantic Web technologies and tools used for the implementation of the framework's evaluation system can be organized in three types: a) RDFization tools, b) Link Discovery tools, c) Infrastructure and Storage technologies. All the experiments ran on Ubuntu 18.04 laptop, with i7 2nd Gen CPU and 6 GB of RAM.

4.1   RDFization

EDM. Europeana Data Model (EDM) was designed as a tool for collection, connection and enrichment of the metadata that describe the objects offered to Europeana Collection. In order to avoid management of a collection that every content provider uses different description metadata, EDM uses a well-defined set of elements which includes classes and attributes from commonly used vocabularies as well as some that were developed for this specific reason.

KARMA. KARMA [13] is an open-source tool for data integration. It has features to process and semantically integrate data provided by different sources, such as databases, Web APIs, or XML, CSV, JSON files.

Data processing was performed with use of expressions written in Python, called PyTransforms. They were applied to the data for cleaning and the creation of new columns with the URIs based on the identifiers of the records in order to be mapped to the classes that are defined accordingly to EDM. Consequently, with the use of KARMA's graphical interface, the data were mapped to their semantic types. The last step was to export the data in RDF format. The conversion of MoMA dataset (~128.000 records) form CSV to RDF lasted 1 min and 55 s, while the conversion of CmoA dataset (~28.000 records) from JSON to RDF, lasted 50 s.

OpenRefine. OpenRefine [14] is a platform for data exploration, cleaning and linking. It offers a variety of features for exploration, classification, and transformation of data. The data processing tasks run General Refine Expression Language – GREL, which comes embedded to OpenRefine. RDF-extension provides tools and features to OpenRefine to convert data into RDF format. Specifically, it adds a graphical interface and allows the user to import ontologies and vocabularies and to map the data with their attributes.

The data were cleaned, and new URI columns were created with use of GREL expressions. Afterwards, the model that the RDF graph will be based on, was created in the GUI of RDF-extension. Every potential node of the graph was mapped to the values of a column and assigned to a value type, such as text, number, date, URI etc. The conversion of MoMA dataset (~128.000 records) form CSV to RDF lasted 1 min and 45 s, while the conversion of CMoA dataset (~28.000 records) from JSON to RDF, lasted 35 s.

Other Tools. We have also experimented with RDF-gen [21] and DataBearing [22] tools that use their custom SPARQL-like domain-specific languages for data integration and RDFization process. Their main advantages are the quick implementation of the data model for common types and the good performance on big datasets. However, due to incomplete results obtained based on lack of resources, we decided not to include them in this paper.

4.2   Link Discovery Process

OpenRefine. One feature that is provided in OpenRefine platform is the Reconciliation Service. This feature allows LD between different data sources and it can work either with

RDF files or with SPARQL endpoints. The user must define the entity type, the resource class and optionally attributes that will provide higher precision at the discovered links.

The linking process between Artists from MoMA and CMoA collections lasted about 2 h and the results were 28.184 links for the whole datasets, from which the 640 were unique. The linking process between Artists from MoMA collection andDBpedia endpoint did not return any results, while the one between Artists from MoMA collection and Wikidata endpoint lasted about 12 h and the results were 82.185 links for the whole dataset, from which the 6.800 were unique.

SILK. Silk [16] is an open-source platform for data integration of heterogeneous sources. Silk is using a declarative language for the definition of the linking type and the criteria based on which the discovered entities will be matched successfully to the resources. Silk uses SPARQL protocol to send queries to local and external endpoints. The LD process runs linking tasks that are created with use of the declarative language or the graphical interface. Every Linking tasks defines the necessary data transformations and the similarity metrics that are used to discover relation between two entities.

The linking process between Artists from MoMA and CMoA collections lasted about 12 s and the results were 1.042 links. The linking process between Artists from MoMA collection and DBpedia endpoint lasted about 35 min and the results were 760 links. The linking process between Artists from CMoA collection and DBpedia endpoint lasted about 7 min and 25 s and the results were 452 links.

Example triples stored in the RDF graph, after LD process are presented below:

```
<http://localhost:3000/moma/artist/4609>
        a                <http://www.w3.org/2000/01/rdf-schema#Resource>,
                         owl:Thing , edm:Agent ;
        edm:begin        "1881" ;
        edm:end          "1973" ;
        owl:sameAs       <http://dbpedia.org/resource/Pablo_Picasso> ,
<https://www.wikidata.org/wiki/Q5593> ,
<http://localhost:3000/moma/artist/4609> ,
<http://localhost:3000/cmoa/artist/b7eaca81-9a3a-404a-866e-05844d616971>
;
        skos:note        "(Spanish, 1881-1973)" ;
        skos:prefLabel   "Pablo Picasso" .
<http://localhost:3000/moma/76281/artwork>
        a                edm:ProvidedCHO ;
        dc:creator       <http://localhost:3000/moma/artist/5471> ;
        dc:date          "1905" ;
        dc:title         "Fifth Avenue Critics" ;
        dc:type          "Print" ;
        dct:medium       "Etching" ;
        ore:isAggregatedBy  <http://localhost:3000/moma/76281> ;
        owl:sameAs          <http://localhost:3000/cmoa/776ffb7d-e37b-
4dce-8dcc-745786a17d95/artwork> .
```

4.3 Infrastructure and Data Storage

Fuseki2 [20] is a server that accepts SPARQL queries and is part of Apache Jena platform. It can be used as service, Web application or standalone server. Fuseki2 offers an environment for server management and it is designed to cooperate with TDB2 [18] triple-store to provide a reliable and functional storage level. Fuseki2 also supports SOH service (SPARQL over HTTP), in order to accept and execute SPARQL queries from HTTP requests. The design of the developed application was based on this feature. TDB2 is a part of the Apache Jena platform and is configured to integrate with the Fuseki2 server for storing RDF graphs.

5 Discussion

In order to propose a specific pipeline that fulfills the purpose of this research, several decisions had to be made about the choices of tools and technologies used in each stage. As a lesson learned, it must be stated that every stage of this pipeline is independent, and the choice made in each stage could be altered without significant impact on the performance of the overall process.

First of all, the datasets selected were in different formats (CSV and JSON) and were relatively big, containing together more than 150.000 records. This decision was made in order to be able to check integration and scalability issues and discover limitations on the approach. One limitation that we faced was during the attempt to apply semantic reasoning on the integrated data to infer new relations between the data and make the query results more efficient. Due to lack of computational power, chosen tool inefficiency and data model design issues, the inferencing process with the integrated reasoning services of Fuseki could not be completed for our RDF graphs.

The EDM is proposed for the semantic enriching because it is a widely-used and well-known model, it is a combination of commonly used vocabularies, it was designed for integration of heterogeneous museum data, and lastly because the integrated RDF data would be compatible with the Europeana Collection.

The tools were selected based on the criteria of efficiency, usability, cost, and reliability, and the majority of those that were evaluated were free, non-commercial, open-source and widely used. OpenRefine is proposed for the RDFization process, for its ease of use, mistakes avoidance design, usability on data manipulation and efficiency on data conversion from original data format to RDF. On the other hand, OpenRefine lacks on performance and choices during the LD process, so the proposal here is the Silk framework for its efficiency and variety of option that provides. Another lesson learned from limitations was related to the linking tasks that we've created on Silk: while were successfully discovered links between the museum datasets and DBpedia, they could not complete against the Europeana Collection. That was one of the reasons (as a workaround) that we've designed the front-end Web application instead to perform those LD tasks in a customized way.

Finally, Apache Jena platform is proposed for the infrastructure (RDF triple-store and SPARQL server) because it is one of the commonly used open-source and free Semantic Web frameworks, supports SPARQL queries over HTTP, and integrates TDB which is a high-performance triple store.

The source code of the developed application along with the integrated RDF data can be found on https://github.com/sotirisAng/search-on-cultural-lod.

6 Conclusion

This paper presented our contribution for an efficient framework/pipeline for semantically integrating, enriching, and linking open museum data as well as for exploiting such data (by end-users and by other applications) using a functional and reusable Web application. As presented in Fig. 6 (updated version of Fig. 1), the aim of the presented work is to propose a specific technological pipeline for efficient semantic integration and enrichment of museum data that can be queried either from humans or machines. Our future plans on this research line include:

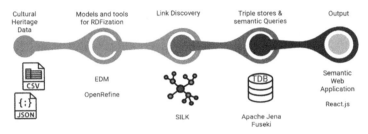

Fig. 6. Selected technologies for the proposed framework/pipeline

- publish the data online (public URIs)
- expand the data model/ontology used for wider coverage of the metadata provided by the museum collections,
- experiment with the integration of more datasets in formats other than JSON and CSV (e.g., data in relational databases or in XML formats),
- update the linking tasks by adding more sophisticated similarity metrics, to achieve better results on the linking process
- expand the functionality of the Web application to perform linking tasks to more entities, not only between Artists.

References

1. Europeana: Definition of the Europeana Data Model (2017)
2. Europeana Collections. https://www.europeana.eu/portal/en. Accessed 11 Feb 2020
3. DBpedia, https://wiki.dbpedia.org/, last accessed 2020/08/23
4. Wikidata. https://www.wikidata.org/wiki/Wikidata:Main_Page. Accessed 23 Aug 2020
5. Dragoni, M., Cabrio, E., Tonelli, S., Villata, S.: Enriching a small artwork collection through semantic linking. In: Lecture Notes in Computer Science, pp. 724–740. Springer, Heidelberg (2016). https://doi.org/10.1007/978-3-319-34129-3_44

6. Szekely, P., et al.: Connecting the smithsonian american art museum to the linked data cloud. Lect. Notes Comput. Sci. **7882**, 593–607 (2013). https://doi.org/10.1007/978-3-642-38288-8-40

7. Skjæveland, M.G.: From Spreadsheets to 5-star Linked Data in the Cultural Heritage Domain : A Case Study of the Yellow List Audun Stolpe. (2011)

8. CIDOC CRM. http://www.cidoc-crm.org/. Accessed 29 Sept 2020

9. De Boer, V., et al.: Amsterdam museum linked open data. Semant. Web. **4**, 237–243 (2013). https://doi.org/10.3233/SW-2012-0074

10. Doulaverakis, C., Kompatsiaris, Y., Strintzis, M.G.: Ontology-based access to multimedia cultural heritage collections - the REACH project. In: EUROCON 2005 - International Conference Computer as a Tool. I, pp. 151–154 (2005). https://doi.org/10.1109/eurcon.2005.1629881

11. The Museum of Modern Art (MoMA) collection data. https://github.com/MuseumofModernArt/collection. Accessed 11 Feb 2020

12. The collection data of the Carnegie Museum of Art in Pittsburgh, Pennsylvania. https://github.com/cmoa/collection. Accessed 11 Feb 2020

13. Knoblock, C.A., et al.: Semi-automatically mapping structured sources into the semantic web. Lect. Notes Comput. Sci. **7295**, 375–390 (2012). https://doi.org/10.1007/978-3-642-30284-8_32

14. OpenRefine, https://openrefine.org/. Accessed 11 Feb 2020

15. Linked Data - Design Issues. https://www.w3.org/DesignIssues/LinkedData. Accessed 23 Aug 2020

16. Volz, J., Bizer, C., Gaedke, M., Kobilarov, G.: Silk - a link discovery framework for the web of data. In: CEUR Workshop Proceedings, p. 538 (2009)

17. Reconciliation Service. https://github.com/OpenRefine/OpenRefine/wiki/Reconciliation-Service-API. Accessed 26 Aug 2020

18. TDB2. https://jena.apache.org/documentation/tdb2/. Accessed 26 Aug 2020

19. Apache Jena https://jena.apache.org/getting_started/index.html. Accessed 12 Feb 2020

20. Apache Jena Fuseki. https://jena.apache.org/documentation/fuseki2/. Accessed 12 Feb 2020

21. Santipantakis, G.M., Vouros, G.A., Kotis, K.I., Doulkeridis, C.: Rdf-gen: Generating RDF from streaming and archival data. ACM Int. Conf. Proc. Ser. (2018). https://doi.org/10.1145/3227609.3227658

22. DataBearings. https://sites.google.com/site/databearings/home. Accessed 03 Oct 2020

Track on European and National Projects

Metadata Aggregation via Linked Data: Results of the Europeana Common Culture Project

Nuno Freire[1]([✉]) [ID], Enno Meijers[2] [ID], Sjors de Valk[2] [ID], Julien A. Raemy[3,4] [ID],
and Antoine Isaac[5,6] [ID]

[1] INESC-ID, Lisbon, Portugal
nuno.freire@tecnico.ulisboa.pt
[2] Dutch Digital Heritage Network, The Hague, The Netherlands
enno.meijers@kb.nl, sjors@sjorsdevalk.nl
[3] HES-SO University of Applied Sciences and Arts Western Switzerland, Haute école
de gestion de Genève, Geneva, Switzerland
julien.raemy@hesge.ch
[4] University of Zurich, Zurich, Switzerland
[5] Europeana Foundation, The Hague, The Netherlands
antoine.isaac@europeana.eu
[6] Vrije Universiteit Amsterdam, Amsterdam, The Netherlands

Abstract. Digital cultural heritage resources are widely available on the web through the digital libraries of heritage institutions. To address the difficulties of discoverability in cultural heritage, the common practice is metadata aggregation, where centralized efforts like Europeana facilitate discoverability by collecting the resources' metadata. We present the results of the linked data aggregation task conducted within the Europeana Common Culture project, which attempted an innovative approach to aggregation based on linked data made available by cultural heritage institutions. This task ran for one year with participation of twelve organizations, involving the three member roles of the Europeana network: data providers, intermediary aggregators, and the central aggregation hub, Europeana. We report on the challenges that were faced by data providers, the standards and specifications applied, and the resulting aggregated metadata.

Keywords: Data aggregation · Linked data · Datasets · Cultural heritage · Semantic web

1 Introduction

Nowadays, digital cultural heritage (CH) collections from libraries, museums and archives are widely available on the web. Many of these collections do not contain natural language texts (e.g., pictures, videos, music), and others that are of textual nature often lack machine-readable representation that can be used for indexing by search engines. In order to make these resources findable, CH institutions have traditionally turned to creating and exploiting metadata (that is, data records describing the resources).

© Springer Nature Switzerland AG 2021
E. Garoufallou and M.-A. Ovalle-Perandones (Eds.): MTSR 2020, CCIS 1355, pp. 383–394, 2021.
https://doi.org/10.1007/978-3-030-71903-6_35

CH comprises very diverse, transnational communities, which results in scattered collections that use many resource description standards and data models that are specific to a context (e.g., a country or a set of institutions). Discoverability of CH resources is typically addressed by forming networks, where a central organization (a CH institution or another kind of organization) provides search and access services based on collecting the metadata associated with these resources. Such central organizations are in a position to enable wider discovery and reuse of the resources, by applying practices and technologies that cannot be applied sustainably at the level of each single digital collection.

Within CH, this collecting approach, called metadata aggregation, uses data aggregation technologies that are different from the ones used in other domains, such as by internet search engines or in the Web of Data. The Open Archives Initiative Protocol for Metadata Harvesting (OAI-PMH) [1] has been the dominant technology, since it is specialized for the aggregation of datasets of metadata.

Business models for scalable and sustainable metadata aggregation have been implemented in the CH domain by organizations and networks such as Europeana in Europe, DPLA in the United States of America, Trove in Australia, the National Digital Library of India, and DigitalNZ in New Zealand. The implementation of such networks is costly, however.

In the meantime, the CH community has spent a lot of effort on redefining the traditional metadata models for cultural heritage resources into novel models based on semantic technology. Nowadays, many digital libraries and online catalogues publish metadata about CH resources as linked data (LD).

Our research sets out to investigate the feasibility of using LD for aggregation, which may bring cost benefits. If aggregators were able to make use of the available LD, data providers already making available LD would more easily share their metadata with cultural heritage aggregators. And for providers that are not yet publishing LD, participation in CH aggregation based on LD would make the adoption of LD publication more valuable. They would reuse the LD with other use cases than aggregation, and with other domains besides cultural heritage, as for example with Internet search engines (if Schema.org, the data model used by search engines for harvesting structured data on the web[1], is also used for LD publication).

This paper presents a case study on the LD aggregation task conducted within the Europeana Common Culture project[2]. This task ran from May 2019 to June 2020, and involved twelve organizations, representing the three member roles of the Europeana network: data providers, intermediary aggregators, and the central aggregation hub, Europeana. We report on the challenges that were faced by data providers, the standards and specifications applied in the case study, and the aggregated LD that resulted at the end of the task.

We follow, in Sect. 2, by describing related work on LD aggregation. Section 3 presents the requirements that underlie the design of our method of LD aggregation in

---

[1] For more information about the role of Schema.org for structured data on the web, please consult: https://schema.org/docs/about.html.

[2] For information about the Europeana Common Culture project, consult https://pro.europeana.eu/project/europeana-common-culture.

Europeana, and Sect. 4 follows with an overview of our workflow. Section 5 presents the software toolset that was implemented. Section 6 presents the results and their analysis. Section 7 highlights the main conclusions and presents future work.

2 Related Work

LD has received attention from many CH researchers and practitioners. However, we find in most cases that the main focus of the literature concerns the publication of LD [2–4] and does not investigate in detail how the metadata aggregation can be deployed on top of available LD[3]. One noticeable exception is the Research and Education Space project (RES) that finished in 2017 and has successfully aggregated a considerable number of LD resources from the CH, education and academic data sources. The resulting aggregated dataset can be accessed online, but an evaluation of its aggregation procedures and results has not been published. The project's available technical documentation [5] addresses some of the required functionality that is relevant to our work. Some tasks, however, were not fully documented in the final specifications published by the project.

Solutions have been proposed by others for aggregation of LD (for example [6]) that tried to tackle the issue with generic solutions. None of the work in this area resulted in a standardized approach, however, and we could not find any sustainable application within cultural heritage.

The work we present here was conducted in the context of a line of research within Europeana, which aims at improving the efficiency of its network and sustainability. Our earlier studies on this topic identified LD as a potential technical solution for these objectives in metadata aggregation [7].

An important point is that LD provides a technological basis for metadata aggregation, which brings new options for data synchronization and data modelling. Some of the participants of the Europeana Common Culture LD task have recently engaged in a smaller pilot (the National Library of the Netherlands, the Dutch Digital Heritage Network (NDE) and Europeana Foundation) [8], whose positive results have led to the setup of this larger scale LD aggregation that we describe in this paper. NDE, the technical lead in our current task, is a Dutch national program aiming to increase the social value of the collections maintained by libraries, archives and museums in the Netherlands by improving their visibility, usability and sustainability. Designing and implementing a discovery infrastructure for LD is one of NDE's main efforts [9].

Our case study focused on a scenario of LD aggregation using mostly the Schema.org vocabulary [10] to represent cultural heritage object (CHO) metadata. Schema.org is an initiative which encourages the publication and consumption of structured data on the web. It is a cross-domain vocabulary originally created by the major Internet search engines, but nowadays evolves as a community-based effort. Europeana has researched the best practices for publication of Schema.org CH metadata [11] and makes available Schema.org metadata within the webpages of its portal. Schema.org has also been applied successfully in our earlier LD pilot [7]. Also directly related to our current work is our earlier evaluation of Schema.org usage in CH institutions for aggregation by Europeana

---

[3] In fact, the related LD work here has not changed since our earlier papers.

[12], whose positive outcome has been a support for also researching Schema.org for LD aggregation.

3 Requirements of the Europeana Network

This task was conducted under the current requirements for metadata aggregation in the Europeana network, which are based on the metadata harvesting functionality of OAI-PMH, and the Europeana Data Model (EDM) [13].

Although LD, by definition, uses well-known standards, these standards are defined for establishing wide interoperability of data. When building a solution based on LD for a particular interoperability use case, such as the one of Europeana, additional specifications are required. These serve the purpose of specifying how particular functional and informational requirements should be fulfilled by LD publishers and consumers. In the case of Europeana, such specifications guide how data providers and aggregators should exchange metadata in a LD-based solution.

In this case study, we have further elaborated the specification for defining a LD dataset for Europeana, from earlier work [8]. In short, the revised specification [14] allows data providers to provide dataset-level metadata as a LD resource, and makes use of well-known vocabularies for this kind of metadata. A key aspect of this specification is that it includes the types of dataset distributions that data providers can use, including the required metadata for each kind of distribution.

The significant number of data providers interested in participating in the LD aggregation task, motivated the creation of another specification that addresses the use of Schema.org LD for describing CHOs according to the requirements of Europeana and EDM [15]. Currently, Europeana only supports ingestion of metadata in EDM, but experiments on applying Schema.org to metadata descriptions of CHOs have shown that it can provide good quality data that is capable of fulfilling the requirements of Europeana. This specification provides a general level of guidance for usage of Schema.org metadata that, after conversion to EDM, will result in metadata that is suitable for aggregation by Europeana. This specification guides the functionality of the Schema.org to EDM converter that is part of the toolset developed in the project. This converter is described in Sect. 5.

A non-functional requirement also drives the design of our solution. This line of research aims at improving the efficiency and sustainability of the Europeana network. Whenever possible, we applied mature software supported by a community of developers and users instead of developing new software.

4 Overview of the Approach to Linked Data Aggregation

Our approach to LD aggregation is based on the publication of several LD resources by data providers and in aggregation systems run by aggregators as well as Europeana. Data providers must publish LD about their CHOs and also a LD description of the dataset these CHOs belong to. The systems of aggregators must be able to access and interpret the providers' dataset descriptions and apply the appropriate LD harvesting mechanism to collect the metadata about the providers' CHOs.

Figure 1 presents additional details of this approach. The data provider's LD publication must comprise the following:

- Resolvable CHO metadata - the CHOs that comprise the dataset to be aggregated must have either have resolvable URIs that lead to RDF data according to HTTP content negotiation [16], or be available via a data dump. In this case study, the focus for the CHO's metadata was mainly on Schema.org and EDM. Two additional data models were used by two data providers to test the mapping capabilities of our LD aggregation toolset.
- Resolvable Dataset description - the dataset to be aggregated must be described as a LD resource and have a resolvable URI. The dataset's metadata must have a title and specify the mechanism through which aggregators can harvest the dataset. For dataset's metadata, data providers may use three data models: DCAT [17], VoID [18] and Schema.org.
- Dataset Distribution - the distribution mechanism for the dataset, such as a data dump (file), a SPARQL endpoint, or a listing of resource URIs.

The systems of an aggregator comprise the following:

- Dataset Description Validator - a software component able to validate dataset descriptions according to the Europeana requirements.
- LD Harvester - a software component to transfer the datasets from data providers into the aggregator's system. The harvester must be able to interpret the providers' dataset descriptions and implement all the distribution mechanisms covered in the Europeana guidelines.
- Mapper Service - a software component that implements a conversion of CHOs' metadata from Schema.org to EDM, according to the Europeana guidelines.
- EDM Validator - a software component able to validate CHOs' metadata according to the Europeana requirements.

Next to these, aggregators generally use a data repository to maintain the aggregated dataset. Our effort however focuses only on the steps that precede the loading of datasets into such repositories.

The flow of data for the aggregation of a LD dataset is also shown of Fig. 1. It consists of the following five steps:

1. The aggregator validates the provider's dataset description for compliance with the Europeana guidelines.
2. If valid, the dataset description is passed on to the LD Harvester.
3. The LD Harvester reads the metadata about the distribution included in the dataset description and executes the appropriate harvesting mechanism for the type of distribution (described in Sect. 5).
4. When the CHO's metadata requires conversion to EDM, the Mapper Service converts it to EDM. When the metadata is in EDM, we proceed directly to the next processing task.

5. The EDM Validator verifies the compliance of the CHO's EDM metadata with the Europeana requirements.

After the last step, the resulting (EDM) metadata can be passed to the aggregator's other systems for integration into its aggregated dataset.

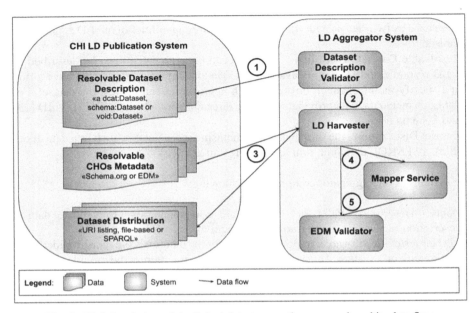

Fig. 1. High-level view of the linked data aggregation approach and its data flow.

5   System Implementation

Our task has produced a toolset that implements the workflow described in the previous section. The toolset was developed having in mind its usage by any aggregator in the Europeana network, therefore it makes use of mature software supported by a community of developers and users.

Figure 2 presents the high-level architecture of this toolset. The software components introduced in the previous section are implemented with a Docker configuration constituted by two independent Docker containers that host them. The exchange of data between the Docker containers happens via the file system (i.e., the file system of the Docker host is used by both containers). Docker containers preserve the technical independence of each of the tools, thus resulting in greater portability and flexibility of deployment. Aggregators can deploy only part of the toolset, according to their needs. Docker containers also provide greater scalability, enabling the toolset to be applied by aggregators with small and large collections.

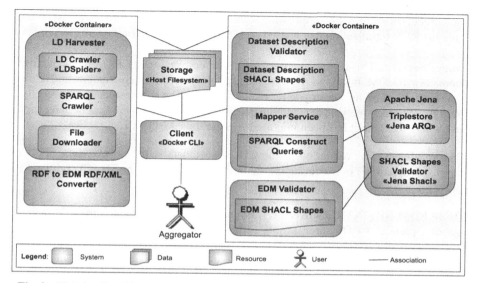

Fig. 2. High-level architecture of the toolset for linked data aggregation in cultural heritage.

The components of the aggregation system are implemented as follows.

Dataset Description Validator. The validation of the dataset descriptions, in RDF, is performed via a SHACL Shapes [19] specification. For executing the validation, the Apache Jena SHACL validator is used.

LD Harvester. To transfer the datasets from data providers into the aggregation system, the LD Harvester has three subcomponents, each implementing one of the supported types of dataset distribution:

- **LD Crawler.** A LD dataset is harvested via HTTP content negotiation of the URIs specified in the dataset RDF description. The crawler may be configured to continue crawling any URIs found in the harvested data, and stop crawling when a configured depth[4] is reached. This component combines our own software for processing the dataset descriptions with the LDSpider [20] software for LD crawling.
- **SPARQL Crawler.** A LD dataset is harvested by first querying the SPARQL endpoint of the data provider with a query specified in the dataset description. The query outputs the list of URIs that are part of the dataset. This component combines software that interprets the dataset description, executes the SPARQL queries and commands LDSpider. The URIs obtained via the SPARQL query are used for the crawling process.
- **File Downloader.** A LD dataset is harvested via downloading of file-based distributions (also known as data dumps) that contain the complete dataset. This component was developed for this specific system. It interprets the dataset description, downloads

---

[4] The maximum depth is a parameter of crawlers that defines when they should stop following newly found links, based on distance from the resource where the crawl started.

and processes the files, uncompressing them if necessary, and transforms the RDF data into the RDF serialization that is used within the LD aggregation system (N-Triples).

Mapper Service. This component implements the conversion of CHOs' metadata from Schema.org to EDM. It follows the Europeana guidelines for this conversion, and allows for customization of the conversion for each collection. The conversions are specified as SPARQL construct queries [21], and the queries are executed on an Apache Jena triple store, where the dataset has been imported, via the Jena ARQ API.

EDM Validator. The validation of the CHOs' metadata is performed via a SHACL Shapes specification. For executing the validation, the Apache Jena SHACL validator is used.

RDF to EDM RDF/XML Converter. The current data ingestion system of Europeana requires a particular RDF serialization, compatible with RDF/XML but guided by an XML Schema that Europeana applies to validate all datasets it receives[5]. Our converter transforms well-known RDF serializations into the RDF/XML required by Europeana.

The software is open for reuse and its source code is publicly available in a GitHub repository[6]. Its most relevant parts are the source code of the interpreter of dataset descriptions and the LD Crawler, the SHACL Shapes for validation of dataset descriptions and CHOs in EDM and the conversion of Schema.org to EDM as SPARQL Construct queries. Reusers of the software may adapt the mapping and validation functionalities by providing their specific SPARQL Construct Queries or SHACL Shapes definitions.

The key specifications for the LD aggregation process are published in Zenodo: the specification for defining a LD dataset for Europeana [14] and the guidelines for preparation of Schema.org metadata about CHOs for Europeana data providers [15].

6   Results

A LD aggregation task was presented to all partners of the Europeana Common Culture project. Ten partners expressed interest in participating as data providers and, at a later stage, two additional external organizations also joined[7]. Out of these twelve data providers, seven were able to provide a LD dataset, sometimes only for a very small proportion of their collections as not all their assets are available in the required LD format(s) – in fact, for some providers, publication of LD is still in experimental phase.

---

[5] For details consult the section 'EDM XML Schema and EDM validation in Oxygen' at https://pro.europeana.eu/page/edm-documentation.
[6] The GitHub repository of the software resulting from this task: https://github.com/netwerk-digitaal-erfgoed/lod-aggregator.
[7] The data providers of the LD aggregation task were the following: erfgoedplus.be (Belgium), National Library of Finland, German Digital Library, National Documentation Centre (Greece), DigiPhil (Hungary), CulturaItalia (Italy), National Library of Latvia, National Library of Portugal, National Library of the Netherlands, Nationaal Museum van Wereldculturen (The Netherlands), UMA information technology gmbh (Austria), Swedish National Heritage Board.

Two of the datasets, provided in Schema.org, were delivered with CHO metadata that lacked the elements required for a successful conversion to EDM. Six datasets were aggregated successfully. Out of these, three were provided in Schema.org, one in EDM, one in a "flattened" subset of EDM[8], and one using its own data model[9] (Table 1).

Table 1. The outcome of the data providers participation in the LD aggregation task.

Total data providers	Outcome				
	Not delivered	With insufficient CHO metadata	Delivered in Schema.org	Delivered in EDM	Delivered in other data model
12	4	2	3	2	1

Our analysis of the unsuccessful cases is that most data providers were publishers of LD, but some were not applying Schema.org, or were using it for describing other entity types than CHOs (for example, for contextual entities such as agents, places and concepts) and underestimated the effort of creating Schema.org metadata for CHOs. The two cases whose CHO metadata was not complete correspond to the Schema.org output provided out-of-the-box by the providers' digital library system - Fedora. Their metadata in Schema.org describes generic repository items (i.e. digital representations), lacking the descriptive detail required for CHOs (i.e. the original object). Both organizations considered the effort of implementing all the requirements for Schema.org to be beyond their available resources for our time frame. In the six unsuccessful cases the participation of the organization was indeed purely voluntary: they did not receive any resources to prepare and publish their metadata as LD.

Regarding the six successful cases, five data providers had previous experience with Schema.org or EDM for describing CHOs. They focused their implementation efforts on any aspects their LD was lacking. A sixth data provider published its metadata as linked data for the first time. It published it in EDM during the course of this task by re-using its past work on EDM metadata mappings for delivering EDM to Europeana via OAI-PMH.

The resulting data, after being harvested and processed by the LD infrastructure, amounted to approximately 17.2 million triples, describing around 909 thousand CHOs (Table 2). Regarding the quality of the linked data, we observed that data providers use mostly literal values (i.e. simple strings) to describe the CHOs. The statistics of contextual entities compared to CHOs illustrate that some providers are more advanced in converting their metadata to "richer" models, especially regarding the representation

---

[8] The LD published by the Nationaal Museum van Wereldculturen is not 100% valid according to the Europeana requirements, conversion into valid EDM was achieved by using the Mapping Server of our LD toolset.

[9] The LD published by the Swedish National Heritage Board is publish KSAMSÖK ontology. For the purposes of the pilot, it served as a test for the capabilities of the Mapper Service component to function with other different ontologies. A mapping from KSAMSÖK to EDM was available and it was reimplemented with SPARQL construct queries for execution by the Mapper Service.

of entities from subject vocabularies and named authority lists as RDF resources as opposed to mere strings.

RDF resources representing fully-fledged contextual entities (persons, concepts, etc.) were only consistently found in the data of three providers.

Table 2. Amount of aggregated data for the LD aggregation task.

Data provider	Number of triples	Number of CHO instances	Number of contextual entities
National Library of the Netherlands	27,488	1,255	0
National Documentation Center	1,882	79	87
National Library of Portugal	2,458,660	105,365	2
National Library of Finland	1,205,754	37,195	19,157
Nationaal Museum van Wereldculturen	12,878,876	731,780	0
Swedish National Heritage Board	661,886	33,730	16,409
Total	**17,234,546**	**909,404**	**35,655**

7   Conclusion and Future Work

We have presented a case study where we have applied an approach for metadata aggregation via LD, which had previously been successful for a small-scale pilot. During this LD aggregation task of the Europeana Common Culture project, we have built a toolset for LD aggregation that is designed for deployment by aggregators of the Europeana network or other similar networks. Although the toolset includes functionality that is tailored for EDM (especially the specifications for conversion from Schema.org and data validation), aggregators using other data models may add their own conversions and validations using the standards implemented by the toolset - SPARQL Construct queries and SHACL Shapes.

The toolset is based on Docker containers, allowing to preserve the technical independence of its tools, making the solution more portable to different environments and more scalable, giving the possibility to apply the toolset to small or large collections.

The participation of data providers was voluntary, but many have shown interest in participating. Twelve data providers joined the LD aggregation task at the beginning but not all of them were fully aware of the technical challenges that this novel approach would bring. Four of the providers were not able to deliver a dataset as LD, and two other providers delivered datasets with insufficient data for aggregation into Europeana. In the six successful cases, five providers already had in-house knowledge or an existing implementation of LD, and for one, it was its first effort in publishing LD. Our overall conclusion is that there is much interest in implementing LD among data providers. Nevertheless, it requires a significant level of resources when the organization does not have any previous experience.

We have identified three areas for future work. First, we believe that data providers need supporting tools for preparing their LD. The validation tools implemented in the toolset may also be used in the creation of services for data providers, allowing them to check the validity of their data at earlier stages of LD publication. A second line of work should focus on components for interoperability and integration of the toolset into the aggregators' systems, so that our components may be called from within these systems. A third one could explore the publication of Schema.org data within the web pages of the data providers' digital libraries. This approach is not based on LD content negotiation but on other technologies employed by Internet search engines, namely Sitemaps and Microformats. Our toolset could be applied to these kinds of sources if it is complemented with a Sitemaps crawler and an HTML Microdata extractor. For data providers, this would bring the benefit of a common solution for making their metadata available for indexing by search engines and for aggregation by Europeana and other CH networks.

Acknowledgments. We would like to acknowledge the support given by the participants of the pilot: Helena Patrício, Tetiana Kysla, Minna Rönkä, Osma Suominen, Haris Georgiadis, Agathi Papanoti, and Palko Gabor, as well as Erwin Verbruggen for his coordination. We also would like to acknowledge Adina Ciocoiu from the Europeana Foundation for the analysis of data samples collected during the case study.

This work was partially supported by Portuguese national funds through Fundação para a Ciência e a Tecnologia (FCT) with reference UIDB/50021/2020, the European Commission under contract 30-CE-0885387/00-80, and grant agreement INEA/CEF/ICT/A2018/1633581 and by the NDE-program funded by the Dutch Ministry of Education, Culture and Science.

References

1. Lagoze, C., Van de Sompel, H., Nelson, M.L., Warner, S.: The open archives initiative protocol for metadata harvesting, version 2.0. Open Archives Initiative (2002)
2. Jones, E., Seikel, M. (eds): Linked Data for Cultural Heritage. Facet Publishing, London (2016). ISBN: 9781783301621
3. Szekely, P., et al.: Connecting the Smithsonian american art museum to the linked data cloud. In: Cimiano, P., Corcho, O., Presutti, V., Hollink, L., Rudolph, S. (eds.) ESWC. LNCS, vol. 7882, pp. 593–607. Springer, Heidelberg (2013). https://doi.org/10.1007/978-3-642-38288-8_40
4. Dragoni, M., Tonelli, S., Moretti, G.: A knowledge management architecture for digital cultural heritage. J. Comput. Cult. Herit. (JOCCH) – Spec. Issue Digit. Infrastruct. Cult. Herit. Part 2 **10**(3) (2017). https://doi.org/10.1145/3012289
5. McRoberts, M. (eds): A Guide to the Research & Education Space for Contributors and Developers. BBC (2016). https://bbcarchdev.github.io/inside-acropolis/. Accessed 29 May 2019

6. Vander Sande, M., Verborgh, R., Hochstenbach, P., Van de Sompel, H.: Towards sustainable publishing and querying of distributed linked data archives. J. Doc. **74**(1) (2018). https://doi.org/10.1108/JD-03-2017-0040

7. Freire, N., Robson, G., Howard, J.B., Manguinhas, H., Isaac, A.: Metadata aggregation: assessing the application of IIIF and sitemaps within cultural heritage. In: Kamps, J., Tsakonas, G., Manolopoulos, Y., Iliadis, L., Karydis, I. (eds.) TPDL. LNCS, vol. 10450, pp. 220–232. Springer, Cham (2017). https://doi.org/10.1007/978-3-319-67008-9_18

8. Freire, N., Meijers, E., Voorburg, R., Cornelissen, R., Isaac, A., de Valk, S.: Aggregation of linked data: a case study in the cultural heritage domain. Information **10**(8), 252 (2019). https://doi.org/10.3390/info10080252

9. Meijers, E., de Valk, S., Helmus, W.: A distributed network of heritage information. White paper 2018 (2018). https://zenodo.org/record/1185401. Accessed 15 June 2019

10. Google Inc., Yahoo Inc., Microsoft Corporation and Yandex; "About Schema.org" n.d. https://schema.org/docs/about.html. Accessed 29 May 2019

11. Wallis, R., Isaac, A., Charles, V., Manguinhas, H.: Recommendations for the application of Schema.org to aggregated cultural heritage metadata to increase relevance and visibility to search engines: the case of Europeana. Code4Lib J. (36) (2017). ISSN 1940-5758

12. Freire, N., Charles, V., Isaac, A.: Evaluation of Schema.org for aggregation of cultural heritage metadata. In: Gangemi, A., et al. (eds.) ESWC. LNCS, vol. 10843, pp. 225–239. Springer, Cham (2018). https://doi.org/10.1007/978-3-319-93417-4_15

13. Europeana Foundation: Definition of the Europeana Data Model v5.2.8 (2017). https://pro.europeana.eu/edm-documentation

14. Freire, N.: Specifying a linked data dataset for Europeana and aggregators (Version 0.2). Zenodo (2020). https://doi.org/10.5281/zenodo.3817314

15. Freire, N.: Guidelines for providing and handling Schema.org metadata in compliance with Europeana (Version 0.1). Zenodo (2020). https://doi.org/10.5281/zenodo.3817236

16. Sauermann, L., Cyganiak, R.: Cool URIs for the Semantic Web. W3C Interest Group Note (2008). https://www.w3.org/TR/cooluris/

17. Albertoni, R., Browning, D., Cox, S., Beltran, A.G., Perego, A., Winstanley, P.: Data catalog vocabulary (DCAT) - version 2. W3C Recommendation (2020). https://www.w3.org/TR/vocab-dcat-2/

18. Alexander, K., Cyganiak, R., Hausenblas, M., Zhao, J.: Describing linked datasets with the VoID vocabulary. W3C Interest Group Note (2011). https://www.w3.org/TR/void/

19. Knublauch, H., Kontokostas, D. (eds.): Shapes Constraint Language (SHACL). W3C Recommendation. W3C (2017). https://www.w3.org/TR/shacl/

20. Isele, R., Umbrich, J., Bizer, C., Harth, A.: LDSpider: an open-source crawling framework for the web of linked data. In: Proceedings of 9th International Semantic Web Conference (ISWC 2010) Posters and Demos (2010)

21. Prud'hommeaux, E., Seaborne, A.: SPARQL query language for RDF. W3C Recommendation. W3C (2008). https://www.w3.org/TR/rdf-sparql-query/

Track on Knowledge IT Artifacts (KITA) in Professional Communities and Aggregations (KITA 2020)

The Role of Data Storage in the Design of Wearable Expert Systems

Fabio Sartori[✉], Marco Savi, and Riccardo Melen

Department of Informatics, Systems and Communication, University of Milano-Bicocca, viale Sarca 336/14, 20126 Milan, Italy
{fabio.sartori,marco.savi,riccardo.melen}@unimib.it

Abstract. Wearable technologies are transforming research in software and knowledge engineering research fields. In particular, expert systems have the opportunity to manage knowledge bases varying according to real-time data collected by position sensors, movement sensors, and so on. This opportunity launches a series of challenges, from the role of network technologies to allow reliable connection between applications and sensors to the definition of functions and methods to assess the quality and reliability of gathered data. In this paper, we reflect about the last point, presenting recent reflections on the wearable environment notion. An architecture for the reliable acquisition of data in the IoT context is proposed, together with first experiments conducted to evaluate its effectiveness in improving the quality of data elaborated by applications.

Keywords: Wearable expert systems · Internet of Things · Data storage

1 Introduction

Wearable environments [1] have been introduced as conceptual and computational platforms for the development of wearable expert systems (WES) [2], i.e. expert systems capable to interact with wearable devices and sensors to maximize their performance.

This paper presents recent developments and future challenges for this research field, taking care of the possibilities offered by IoT infrastructures. We focus on data storage, given that IoT applications produce massive data form sensors, that require large storage space [3] and opportune mechanisms to optimize their use by applications [4].

The integration of KAA[1]™ in the wearable environment architecture is a crucial strep to develop new services and functionalities supporting wearable expert systems, thanks to its capability to manage data coming from multiple sensors, storing them in both SQL and NoSQL databases, and delivering interfaces to visualization software.

The content of this paper is an attempt to launch new challenges in the wearable environment definition and is organized as follows: Sect. 2 describes the wearable environment notion from the conceptual point of view, pointing out the data storage role with respect to its components. Section 3 further describes the features of data storage

---

[1] https://www.kaaproject.org/.

© Springer Nature Switzerland AG 2021
E. Garoufallou and M.-A. Ovalle-Perandones (Eds.): MTSR 2020, CCIS 1355, pp. 397–402, 2021.
https://doi.org/10.1007/978-3-030-71903-6_36

in the wearable environment context, introducing its functionalities and components to deliver them. Section 4 illustrates a case study on analysis of data reliability starting form an existing dataset. Finally, Sect. 5 briefly highlight lessons learned and challenges for future research.

2 Wearable Environment Model

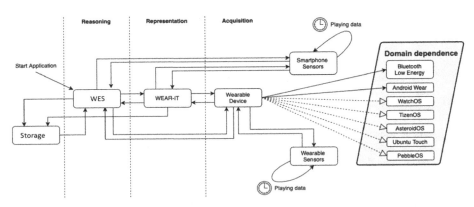

Fig. 1. The wearable environment conceptual model

A wearable environment (WE) is a conceptual and computational framework to allow the development of wearable expert systems in the IoT context.

The main rationale between the WE notion is the following:

- Given that expert systems can profitably exploit wearable technologies to gather (possibly real-time) data to run their decision-making process.
- Given that the expert systems development process is divided into knowledge acquisition, knowledge representation and reasoning steps.
- Given that the reasoning step should be able to work on possibly incomplete data sets coming from heterogeneous sources.

Thus:

- The expert system application should be able to accomplish its algorithm without worrying about data format and availability.
- The expert system should interact with an opportune middleware that, considering application desiderata in terms of sensors/wearable device to use, amount and frequency of data to acquire and format to represent acquired data, provides the application with an opportune API to avoid the overlapping among acquisition, representation and use of knowledge/data in the expert system code.

In other words, the wearable environment concept allows the correct and clear separation of expert systems cycle of life, avoiding that knowledge engineering bottleneck [5] problems arise.

Figure 1 shows the main components of the WE conceptual model:

- **WES**: Wearable expert systems running on the user smartphone are the heart of reasoning level; the execution of a WES is the starting point of the WE cycle of life. From now on, the wearable environment will be responsible for the correct interaction between the application(s) and the other components involved, i.e. Wear-It and wearable devices/sensors (see below).
- **Wear-It** [1]: namely *Wearable Environment Acquisition and Representation-InfrasTructure,* it provides the WES with a complete API for querying sensors on wearable devices and to archive/access data on/from *storage.*
- **Smartphone**: it is both the data collection hub for the Wearable Devices and a data-generating device itself (through its built-in sensors, such as the accelerometer), being also equipped with heterogeneous connectivity capabilities.
- **Wearable Devices**: they connect to the WES (via the Smartphone) through the Wear-It API for the delivery of generated data.
- **Storage**: it is the source of data for WES, managed by Wear-It. Moreover, it provides the user with a set of functions to check the quality of data acquired from sensors, to be sure that the WES will be able to exploit them when necessary. These functions are the subject of the next section.

3   Data Storage

The Wear-It development has enabled wearable expert systems to choose the better device to gather data from. Anyway, this is a limit of the framework, since only one device can be paired with the running application. Although this is not a problem from the expert system execution point of view (an expert system is, theoretically, able to work when needed data are incomplete or partially correct), the main drawbacks of this solution are:

- The impossibility to obtain the best solution from the reasoning strategy.
- The impossibility to verify the reliability and quality of data gathered from sensors.
- The impossibility to select data from multiple sources.

This means that, for example, in case of a wearable expert systems working on environmental data, the decision-making process will answer according to the data detected by a single sensor. What about the possible fault of this sensor? The answer of the system could be wrong or not precise, and the user could be not aware of this mistake.

In order to overcome these problems, we have considered to extend the wearable environment to include data management functionalities. As shown in Fig. 1, we envision data *storage* external to the wearable environment levels, but complementary to them.

Wearable Environment

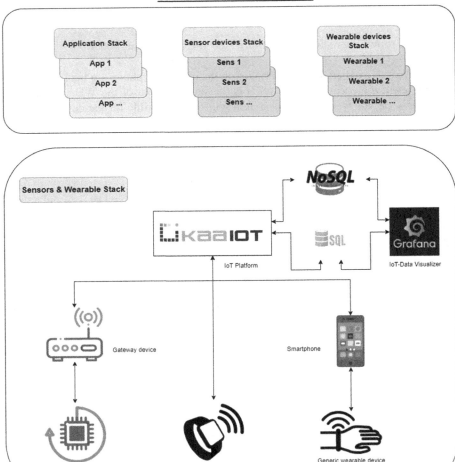

Fig. 2. The IoT framework in a WE: KAA™ provides data storage functionalities.

Data storage is composed of the following parts:

- **Working Station**: it can collect remote data from user's wearable environments and is used to interact with them. It is also equipped with a *Network Module* with advanced *network connectivity* features, being able to autonomously negotiate with multiple fixed, wireless and mobile network providers the creation of *end-to-end (e2e) connections* with the users' Smartphone, relying on the *network slicing* [6, 7] concept.

- **IoT Platform**: it runs on the Working Station and supports Wear-It APIs, used by the user's App for the remote management of the wearable environment (e.g. request for collection of specific data from the Wearable Devices, configuration of a Wearable Device, etc.). It also guarantees users' data persistency.[2]

Figure 2 shows a sketch of the data storage architecture in a wearable environment. The focus here is on the adoption of KAA™ platform to export data management functionalities. Data acquired from many wearable devices can be managed by it, to allow WES at reasoning level to export data correction, completion (thanks to both SQL and NoSQL databases integration), and visualization (thanks to Grafana integration).

4   Case Study

Let us supposed to have an IoT device to measure temperature, *humidity*, *luminosity* and *battery voltage* for a period of 36 days; the dataset [8] simulates this situation and has been historicized in KAA: the resulting table contains 2313682 records. An analysis of anomalies has been conducted on these records, looking for out of bound and null values within them, according to the acceptable values summarized in Table 1, derived from the distribution of values for each variable.

Table 1. Acceptable values for data in the case study

Measurement	Minimum value	Maximum value
Temperature	−15 °C	+50 °C
Humidity	0%h	100%h
Luminosity	0 lx	2500 lx
Voltage	1.5 V	3.5 V

The analysis on the records has allowed to identify 407997 anomalies for the temperature variable, 299084 for the humidity variable, 8 for the voltage variable and 0 for the luminosity variable. Then, a first intervention has been the nullification of outliers. This operation is coherent form the expert system point of view, since null values are generally ignored by rules antecedents, while outliers are considered, with possible mistakes in the right-hand sides execution. This simple intervention has allowed to reduce the standard deviation of each variable, with significant benefits from the reliability of source data perspective, as shown in Table 2.

---

[2] See https://grafana.com/.

Table 2. Outliers nullification results

Measurement	Original std. deviation	Modified std. deviation
Temperature	4.04	2.68
Humidity	6.92	5.73
Luminosity	503.28	503.28
Voltage	0.17	0.12

5 Conclusion and Future Works

This paper indicates how data storage can be exploited to improve the overall performance of wearable environments in supporting wearable expert systems. Thanks to the integration of IoT platforms like KAA, data analysis can be improved, with the possibility to design opportune solutions to increase the quality of data acquired by sensors and, consequently, the quality of suggestions proposed by application at reasoning level of a wearable environment.

Future works are devoted to implement such solutions: in particular, the spatial-temporal algorithm presented in [9] will be exploited as a starting point.

References

1. Sartori, F., Melen, R.: An infrastructure for wearable environments acquisition and representation. In: ACM International Symposium on Mobile Ad Hoc Networking and Computing (2019)
2. Sartori, F., Melen, R.: Wearable expert system development: definitions, models and challenges for the future. Program **51**(3), 235–258 (2017)
3. Cai, H., Xu, B., Jiang, L., Vasilakos, A.: IoT-based big data storage systems in cloud computing: perspectives and challenges. IEEE Internet Things J. **4**(1), 75–87 (2016)
4. Lu, P., Lee, Y.C., Zomaya, A.Y.: Non-intrusive slot layering in Hadoop. In: 2013 13th IEEE/ACM International Symposium on Cluster, Cloud, and Grid Computing, pp. 253–260. IEEE (2013)
5. Aussenac-Gilles, N., Gandon, F.: From the knowledge acquisition bottleneck to the knowledge acquisition overflow: a brief French history of knowledge acquisition. Int. J. Hum. Comput. Stud. **71**(2), 157–165 (2013)
6. Foukas, X., Patounas, G., et al.: Network slicing in 5G: survey and challenges. IEEE Commun. Mag. **55**(5), 94–100 (2017)
7. Savi, M., Sartori, F., Melen, R.: Rethinking the design of wearable expert systems: the role of network infrastructures. In: IEEE International Conference on Wireless and Mobile Computing, Networking and Communications (2020)
8. Madden, S.: Intel lab data. Web page, Intel (2004). https://db.csail.mit.edu/labdata/labdata.html. Accessed 14 Oct 2020
9. Sartori, F., Melen, R., Giudici, F.: IoT data validation using spatial and temporal correlations. In: Garoufallou, E., Fallucchi, F., William De Luca, E. (eds.) MTSR 2019. CCIS, vol. 1057, pp. 77–89. Springer, Cham (2019). https://doi.org/10.1007/978-3-030-36599-8_7

Towards an Innovative Model
in Wearable Expert System for Skiing

Elson Kurian[1]([✉]) [iD], Sherwin Varghese[2]([✉]) [iD], and Stefano Fiorini[1]([✉]) [iD]

[1] University of Milano-Bicocca, Viale Sarca 336, 20136 Milan, Italy
{e.kurian,s.fiorini2}@campus.unimib.it
[2] SAP Labs Rd, EPIP Zone, Whitefield, Bengaluru 560066, Karnataka, India
sherwin.varghese@sap.com

Abstract. Mobile applications and portable devices are being used extensively in the healthcare sector due to their rapid development. Wearable devices having sensors can be used to collect, analyze, and transmit the vital signs of the wearer. In this paper, we have proposed a wearable expert system that supports and monitors the skier during his activity. This research work is motivated by the need to provide rapid assistance to skiers, especially during off-piste skiing, where its more dangerous, and seeking help is difficult with mishaps. Our approach mainly focuses on proposing an expert system that integrates wearable devices (helmet, goggles, digital watch) with the skier's smartphone. We present an architecture model and knowledge artifacts to design a wearable expert system for skiing.

Keywords: Wearable expert system · Skiing · Knowledge engineering · Wearable devices · Internet of Things

1 Introduction

Health services and other organizations often find themselves faced with critical conditions. Collaboration, efficiency, and rapid reaction to changes are what these communities must pursue. Quality becomes a crucial pillar of healthcare and various technologies that allow for the mounting of people's health are in development [16].

In the sports field, various technologies allow athletes to monitor their physical state and prevent possible injuries [9]. Even though the International Ski Federation (FIS) [6] provides guidelines, there are very few applications for the management of ski accidents. Sule Yildirim Yayilgan et al. [18] developed a new architecture for the management and registration of ski injuries effectively after an accident occurs. In this new approach, incident-related communications are made directly between the rescuer and the medical staff at the hospital (with

---

E. Kurian, S. Varghese and S. Fiorini—Equal contribution.

© Springer Nature Switzerland AG 2021
E. Garoufallou and M.-A. Ovalle-Perandones (Eds.): MTSR 2020, CCIS 1355, pp. 403–410, 2021.
https://doi.org/10.1007/978-3-030-71903-6_37

direct access to the patient's condition) using mobile device interfaces and wireless technology.

Current technological innovations are less enhanced for skiing. Our research aims to monitor a skier, especially for off-piste skiing. We designed the **W**earable **E**xpert **S**ystem for **S**kiing (WESS) that simulates the experience of human skiing in reasoning by applying knowledge artifacts [10,12], rules, and inferences. WESS supports ski athletes by providing: i) emergency support, ii) different operating modes, iii) suggestions and recommendations based on the situation iv) real-time analysis of performance.

1.1   Knowledge Engineering

Knowledge Engineering (KE) refers to all the technical and scientific aspects involved in the construction, maintenance, and use of knowledge-based systems (KBS) [4,13]. We define WESS as a hybrid system, as it implements the rule base model, the case-based model, and the non-case based model. The hybrid model helps to organize an interchange of knowledge between the various parts of the expert system knowledge [2].

The three types of Kinds of Knowledge are: i) *Functional Knowledge* consists of descriptions of the functionality of components (or (sub-) systems) and the relationship between them, ii) *Procedural Knowledge* is the understanding of how to apply the concepts learned in any problem solving situations and iii) *Experiential Knowledge* is the knowledge derived from experience [14].

2   Related Work

The most relevant problems in the community concern the field of health care using wearable devices [1,5]. Wearable devices collect and process real-time sensor information measuring the vital health signs of the wearer [17]. A study within the domain of pervasive mobile healthcare, performed by G. Sebestyen et al. [15] depicts protocols and communication models within the IoT healthcare systems.

The goal of using wearables in both medical and sports fields is the ability to continuously monitor the patient or athlete to receive real-time information on their state of health [7,8]. Hermes et al. [3] propose the detection of daily and sports activities with wearable sensors in a controlled and uncontrolled way. S Örücü et al. [11] designed a real-time expert system for athletes comprising of an Expert System. Though skiing guidelines have been provided in the past to avoid possible accidents and relapses, the only existing expert system developed is by Sule Yildirim Yayilgan et al. [19] This project focuses on parallel on the design of interfaces for mobile devices and in presenting an architecture for the digital recording of ski system injuries.

To the best of our knowledge, there is no research or studies to develop an expert system capable of supporting the skier during his activity through continuous monitoring and analysis thanks to a wearable device.

3   Wearable Expert System for Skiing

As defined by Sartori et al. [4, 10, 13, 14], "A wearable expert system (WES) is an expert system designed and implemented to obtain inputs and provide outputs to wearable devices." One of its great distinguishing features is the direct collaboration between domain experts and users and the interaction with a knowledge maintenance system dedicated to the dynamic updating of the knowledge base, as taken care of by the evolution of the scenario [4, 13].

3.1   Components of the Specialised Skiing Gear

The hardware components of the skiing expert system include sensors used for measuring the vitals of the athlete and other parameters like temperature, air pressure, and location. The skiing gear resides on the client's arm or wrist like a smart band. The following sensors are ideal in designing a specialized skiing gear.

- **Display Unit:** The display unit allows the athlete to have a visual interface when placed within the helmet visor. Google Glass acts as an ideal display unit.
- **GPS sensor:** essential for tracking the real-time position of the athlete for an on-piste skiing event.
- **Compass:** to identify the direction in case the athlete gets lost.
- **Accelerometer:** measures the speed of the athlete during skiing. The accelerometer in the wearable device provides precise 'g' forces experienced by the athlete, even in extreme conditions making it better than the accelerometer in the user's smartphone.
- **Gyroscope:** measures the tilt and rotation of the skier.
- **4G/5G mobile network with SIM module:** It is necessary for connecting to the expert system. The skiing hardware can also be connected to the Internet directly from the skier's smartphone.
- **Heat Rate sensor/Pulse Oximeter:** helps to measure the heart rate of the skier. The pulse oximeter would also indicate the blood oxygen levels.
- **Temperature sensor:** measures the temperature of the skier; also measures the atmospheric temperature necessary for warning the athlete about hypothermia.
- **Pressure sensor:** measures the atmospheric pressure.
- **Speakers and mic:** needed in the unlikely event of a disaster when the skier's smartphone is not reachable.
- **SOS Alarm buzzer and lights:** triggers an alarm when the skier has taken a hit and fallen or when the vitals signs are abnormal.
- **Personal Locator Beacon (PLB):** PLB is a passive component of the Wearable expert system. It is triggered only during an SOS emergency, where the network connectivity is absent.

3.2 Architecture

The Skiing Expert system is a wearable expert system that consists of a wearable device worn by the skier that communicates with the expert system through the user's smartphone.

The skiing expert system interfaced with external systems like an emergency, disaster rescue system, or with medical emergency systems, help in the effective rescue of a skiing athlete in the unlikely event of an accident or a natural disaster. Figure 1 depicts the overall architecture of the expert system. The expert system need not be necessarily present within the skiing hardware, but can be deployed as a cloud service consumed by multiple skiing athletes.

3.3 Skiing Expert System Design

The skiing expert system is responsible for collecting real-time data from the wearable sensors of the skiing athlete. It processes the data received based on the rules stored, performs tasks.

The proposed system comprises of various functional knowledge subsystems. A **Knowledge Base** storing the rules and knowledge artifacts [14] form the building blocks of the expert system. The **Database** stores user information, preferences, and the events that occur while the skier uses the expert system. The **Information Retrieval Interface** is responsible for collecting real-time data and for retrieving the user information from the database. The **Rules Processing Engine** loads the procedural knowledge rules and the knowledge artifacts based on the user context and the mode of operation of the system. The **Inference Engine** receives the information from the Information Retrieval Engine and the Rules Processing Engine; checks if the data received matches a rule or a functional knowledge artifact by modeling the causal relationships among the knowledge artifacts using Bayesian Networks (Korb and Nicholson 2010), Influence Nets (Rosen and Smith 1996), Superposed-Automata Nets (de Cindio et al. 1981), Petri Nets or Causal Nets (Van Der Aalst et al. 2011). If the rules match, corresponding tasks get triggered for execution. The **Execution Engine** is responsible for executing tasks received from the Inference Engine. These tasks include monitoring if the skier is within the safe skiing zone, triggering an SOS in case of an accident, measuring and monitoring the vitals of the skier, and also assess the skier's performance; providing recommendations to improve skiing. The **Communication Interface** is responsible for maintaining constant connectivity with the skiing hardware and with other external systems like the medical assistance systems, emergency rescue systems.

3.4 Operation Modes

The skiing expert system is design enables the athlete to operate in 2 modes: Piste Mode and Off-Piste Mode.

The **Piste Mode** (or track mode) allows the user to ski on the slopes indicated by the ski resort and, through the use of the integrated wearable display,

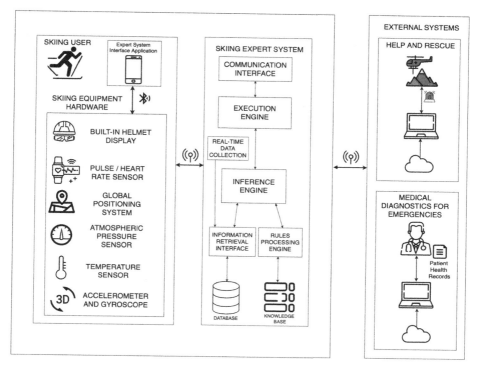

Fig. 1. Architecture of the wearable expert system for skiing (WESS)

is guided from start to finish. If the skier veers off-course, the system navigates the skier back to the piste. This mode also allows the skier to have competitions with other skiers in real-time or based on the lap-time.

The **Off-Piste Mode** is a mode meant for advanced cross country/free-ride skiers. In this mode, the expert system continuously monitors the GPS location of the skier, checks for any weather warnings or avalanches, and ensures that the skier is in the safety zone.

In the event of an accident or a fall with rapid descent of the vital signs indicated by the sensor, the expert system activates the emergency mode. After activation, the expert system communicates with the nearest paramedic and rescue services available, sends the GPS location, and securely retrieves the patient health records for medical diagnostics. The SOS alarm is also triggered, which allows bystanders to locate the skier.

To handle the situation of the skiing gear losing internet connectivity with the Expert System, all the necessary instructions needed to complete the skiing, the map information, and piste rules would be prefetched before the skiing starts. In the unlikely event of the skier being caught in an avalanche or if the skier is out of the network coverage during an SOS, the skiing gear has a mobile network module that triggers SMS messages through the cellular network. The

408 E. Kurian et al.

SMS would contain the last active geo coordinates captured by the GPS module. In case the skiing gear is unable to send out SMS messages during an SOS, the PLB would be immediately activated to call out mountain rescue. The Expert system has the last GPS location of the skier that would help in narrowing the search.

Modeling the knowledge artifacts in the wearable expert system employs expert system languages [14]. The procedural knowledge representation of the expert system uses an extensible markup language (Fig. 2) with Influence Nets representing the Knowledge structure.

```
<MODE_CHOOSE>
  <UserLang name="jess" ext="clp">
    <name> WESS_MODE_CHOOSE </name>
    <discription >Selection of mode </discription>
    <input><element>onClick(CHOOSE_RIDE)</element></input>
    <body> <element>Selected_MODE </element>
    <if> Pre_cond_ckeck </if> <do> update_data </do>
      <subtask> instrction(choosen_mode) </subtask>
    <output> wess_active(choosen_mode)</output> </body>
  </UserLang>
</MODE_CHOOSE>
```

Fig. 2. Sample XML representation of MODE_CHOOSE in WESS

4   Conclusions

To provide proper practice guidelines from skiing beginners to experts and to support the medical emergency, SOS in the skiing grounds, we have proposed a Wearable expert system for skiing. Wearable Expert System for Skiing is a system that comprises of wearable skiing gear and an expert system. The paper describes the various components within the WESS. An outline for modeling the expert system and the different modes of the expert system are also additionally explained. WESS aims to help skiers improve their skills and provides real-time monitoring to save human life in emergency cases, making skiing safer.

4.1   Future Scope

The future scope involves implementing the proposed architecture incorporating smart devices like the Alexa and Google Glass. The system would be enhanced to support skiing race among a group of skiers. A scalable cloud-deployed service would store the skier's data. This data can further be processed using data mining, machine learning algorithms to identify the best skiing strategies for a race. The ability to incorporate the map information from various skiing organizations around the world would allow the skier to have access to a variety of skiing grounds.

References

1. Brugarolas, R., et al.: Wearable heart rate sensor systems for wireless canine health monitoring. IEEE Sens. J. **16**(10), 3454–3464 (2015)
2. Butakov, S., Rubtsov, D.: Synchronization of heterogeneous components within the hybrid expert system. In: Proceedings of the 9th International Scientific and Practical Conference of Students, Post-Graduates Modern Techniques and Technologies, 2003, MTT 2003, pp. 207–210 (April 2003)
3. Ermes, M., Pärkkä, J., Mäntyjärvi, J., Korhonen, I.: Detection of daily activities and sports with wearable sensors in controlled and uncontrolled conditions. IEEE Trans. Inf. Technol. Biomed. **12**(1), 20–26 (2008)
4. De Cindio, F., De Michelis, G., Pomello, L., Simone, C.: Superposed automata nets. In: Girault, C., Reisig, W. (eds.) Application and Theory of Petri Nets. Informatik-Fachberichte, vol. 52. Springer, Heidelberg (1982). https://doi.org/10.1007/978-3-642-68353-4_44
5. Ha, U., et al.: A wearable EEG-HEG-HRV multimodal system with simultaneous monitoring of tES for mental health management. IEEE Trans. Biomed. Circuits Syst. **9**(6), 758–766 (2015)
6. International Ski Federation: FIS medical guide (2013). https://assets.fis-ski.com/image/upload/v1537433174/fis-prod/assets/FISMedicalGuide2013_ConcussionUpdate17CorrectCRTlinks_Neutral.pdf
7. Jones, V., et al.: Mobihealth: mobile services for health professionals. In: Istepanian, R.S.H., Laxminarayan, S., Pattichis, C.S. (eds.) M-Health. Topics in Biomedical Engineering. Springer, Boston (2006). https://doi.org/10.1007/0-387-26559-7_17
8. Li, H.B., Kohno, R.: Body area network and its standardization at IEEE 802.15. BAN. In: Advances in Mobile and Wireless Communications, pp. 223–238. Springer, Heidelberg (2008). https://doi.org/10.1007/978-3-540-79041-9_12
9. Li, R., Kling, S., Salata, M., Cupp, S., Sheehan, J., Voos, J.: Wearable performance devices in sports medicine. Sports Health: Multidiscip. Approach **8**, 74–78 (2015)
10. Mascaro, S., Korb, K.B., Nicholson, A.E.: Learning abnormal vessel behaviour from AIS data with Bayesian networks at two time scales. Tracks J. Artists Writ. 1–34 (2010)
11. Örücü, S., Selek, M.: Design and validation of rule-based expert system by using kinect v2 for real-time athlete support. Appl. Sci. **10**(2), 611 (2020)
12. Pinardi, S., Sartori, F., Melen, R.: Integrating knowledge artifacts and inertial measurement unit sensors for decision support. In: KMIS, pp. 307–313 (2016)
13. Rosen, J.A., Smith, W.L.: Influence net modeling with causal strengths: an evolutionary approach. Program. In: Proceedings of the Command and Control Research and Technology Symposium, pp. 25–28 (1996)
14. Sartori, F., Melen, R.: Wearable expert system development: definitions, models and challenges for the future. Program: electron. Libr. Inf. Syst. **51**(3), 235–258 (2017)
15. Sebestyen, G., Hangan, A., Oniga, S., Gal, Z.: ehealth solutions in the context of Internet of Things. In: 2014 IEEE International Conference on Automation, Quality and Testing, Robotics, pp. 1–6. IEEE (2014)

16. Sweeney, K.T., Ayaz, H., Ward, T.E., Izzetoglu, M., McLoone, S.F., Onaral, B.: A methodology for validating artifact removal techniques for physiological signals. IEEE Trans. Inf. Technol. Biomed. **16**(5), 918–926 (2012)

17. Tahzeeb, M., Tariq, M., Anwar, S., Tahir, N., Niaz, M.: Future Internet of Things architecture to industrial perspective. Int. J. Comput. Appl. **182**, 25–29 (2018)

18. Yayilgan, S.Y., Du, Y., Dalipi, F., Jeppesen, J.C.: A novel system architecture for efficient management of skiing injuries. In: 2015 International Conference on Interactive Mobile Communication Technologies and Learning (IMCL), pp. 73–77. IEEE (2015)

19. Yayilgan, S.Y., Du, Y., Dalipi, F., Jeppesen, J.C.: A novel system architecture for efficient management of skiing injuries. In: 2015 International Conference on Interactive Mobile Communication Technologies and Learning (IMCL), pp. 73–77 (2015)

Author Index